MW01166367

Readings and Cases in Labor Relations and Collective Bargaining

Readings and Cases in Labor Relations and Collective Bargaining

James E. Martin
WAYNE STATE UNIVERSITY

Timothy J. Keaveny
UNIVERSITY OF WYOMING

Robert E. Allen
UNIVERSITY OF WYOMING

ADDISON–WESLEY PUBLISHING COMPANY
Reading, Massachusetts • Menlo Park, California •
Don Mills, Ontario • Wokingham, England • Amsterdam • Sydney •
Singapore • Tokyo • Mexico City • Bogotá • Santiago • San Juan

Library of Congress Cataloging in Publication Data
Main entry under title:

Readings and cases in labor relations and collective
  bargaining.

  1. Collective labor agreements—United States.
2. Trade-unions—Law and legislation—United States.
3. Labor laws and legislation—United States.
4. Collective labor agreements—United States—Cases.
5. Trade-unions—Law and legislation—United States—
Cases.   6. Labor laws and legislation—United States—
Cases.
I. Martin, James, 1943-   II. Keaveny, Timothy J.
III. Allen, Robert E. (Robert Edward), 1946-
KF3408.R43   1985   344.73'0189   84-14484
ISBN 0-201-12353-3   347.304189

ABCDEFGHIJ–DO–8987654

Preface

As teachers of industrial relations, we became aware of the absence of a single book containing the various elements often used in teaching labor relations and collective bargaining. The sponsoring editor of this volume, Janis Jackson Hill, also recognized that void and helped bring the three of us together to develop this book. We hope that other instructors will agree that it is advantageous to have a single volume containing readings and cases relevant to the field.

The book is divided into six sections of readings and two sections of cases. In selecting the readings and cases, our goals were to present labor relations and collective bargaining in an orderly, process-oriented manner and to discuss most of the key topics. Thus we begin with the legal and historical framework of the American labor relations system and move through the organizing process to contract negotiations and the environment in which negotiations take place. We then discuss the subject matter of these negotiations, contract administration, and end the readings with a selection on emerging areas in labor relations. The National Labor Relations Board (NLRB) cases, the arbitration cases, and the two bargaining simulations allow the reader and the instructor to work experientially through the labor relations process just described.

Each group of readings is preceded by an introductory section. These introductions provide an overview of the subject matter under discussion by integrating and placing the material into a coherent framework. The introductions also discuss each reading. They summarize the major points and highlights of the readings that follow and, when appropriate, indicate implications of the section for other labor relations areas. Thus each section opening is designed to prepare students for the readings as well as to introduce the topic areas.

The readings are diverse and are intended to give the student a survey of the entire field. In selecting readings, we have been careful to draw upon a number of types of sources. We have included classical theoretical material, research results applied to specific problems or issues of concern to practitioners, as well as practitioner-oriented materials. In instances where we believed an adequate reading was not available, a selection was written especially for the text.

The cases illustrate what actually happens in the labor relations process, help the student to apply knowledge gained from the readings to real-life situations, and reinforce the material discussed in the text. All cases are based on actual situations; however, the names of the individuals have been changed. The eighteen NLRB cases are preceded by an index, which briefly describes the situation surrounding each case and lists the sections of the National Labor Relations Act (NLRA) that are applicable. The cases follow a relatively standardized format. The parties involved in the case are named and the alleged violations of the NLRA are specified. Next, background facts surrounding each case and the positions of the respective parties are described. At the end of each case, several discussion questions are presented. They are intended to raise broad tactical and decisional issues as well as issues relating strictly to the case. In addition, twenty arbitration cases are included. These cases are preceded by an index of the topics covered in each case. The format of the arbitration cases is similar to that of the NLRB cases, and includes the statement of the grievance as stipulated by the parties.

Both sets of cases were selected to be the basis of classroom discussion rather than to demonstrate appropriate or inappropriate labor relations practices. They were chosen to illustrate principles of law, contract arbitration, different collective bargaining issues, and areas of conflict between the parties. The recommended starting point for a student preparing a case is to read the case discussion questions in order to identify better what may be relevant in the case. The student should then try to determine the real facts of the case, the relevant portions of the NLRA or contract, and the real arguments of the parties. The student will be able to get the most out of these cases by approaching them in this fashion.

The cases can be used in many different ways. They can be used as written assignments

that are not discussed in class. Alternatively, they can be the basis of small-group or classroom discussion. Another approach is to assign student labor and management teams the task of presenting a case to the rest of the class, which acts as the NLRB or as an arbitrator. So that the students may compare their case decisions and rationale to those of the authorities in the field, the Instructor's Manual contains the NLRB decisions and reasoning, and, if the case was appealed, the court decision and reasoning. For arbitration cases, the arbitrators' decisions and opinions are also presented in the Instructor's Manual.

The last section of the book contains two simulations. The first is a short five-issue simulation, which can easily be completed within a class period. Its goal is to give the student a brief introduction to what it feels like to bargain. The second simulation is much longer and may be used in many different ways. The Instructor's Manual offers suggestions on how to incorporate that simulation as part of a course. Many textbooks in labor relations now incorporate a major simulation. Supplementing such a text with this book provides alternative simulations from which an instructor can choose. This approach can be useful when a significant amount of information is exchanged between students from one term to the next.

This book has multiple objectives. We expect the readings to generate an interest in the field and a knowledge of the relevant issues in labor relations. Through application and experiential learning with the cases and bargaining simulations, the student should gain an appreciation for and practice in the actual dynamics of union–management relations and the negotiation process. The NLRB cases and the arbitration cases will also help the reader understand how labor law and contract language are both fluid and subject to more than one interpretation.

Our objectives were selected with many different audiences in mind. *Readings and Cases in Labor Relations and Collective Bargaining* can be used as the major text in an industrial relations course or as a supplement in labor relations, collective bargaining, contract administration, labor economics, or labor law courses. It is aimed at the beginning-level undergraduate courses and graduate-level courses in economics, business administration, public administration, and law. The cases and simulations in the book, as well as the readings that relate to them, also make the text well-suited for union officer and steward training courses and workshops and for management and supervisory development programs in the private and public sectors.

As in any book of readings, we have numerous journals and organizations to thank for granting permission to reprint their publications. The journals and organizations include the following.

Academy of Management Journal

Bulletin of Comparative Labour Relations

Bureau of National Affairs, Inc.

Business Week

Compensation Review

The Conference Board

George Meany Center for Labor Studies, Inc.

Harper & Row

Harvard Business Review

Industrial and Labor Relations Review

Industrial Relations

Industrial Relations Research Association

Journal of Labor Research

McGraw-Hill Publishing Company

Organizational Dynamics

Personnel Administrator

Personnel Journal

The Public Interest

Wisconsin Law Review

We would also like to thank the reviewers who conscientiously examined all or part of the manuscript and made many valuable comments and suggestions: Ben Burdetsky (George Washington University), Paul F. Clark (Pennsylvania State University), James B. Dworkin (Purdue University), Marcus H. Sandver (Ohio State University), and Hoyt N. Wheeler (University of South Carolina).

We would also like to thank Stephen Schiller and Melanie Peterson, graduate students at Wayne State University, for their roles in helping to develop the cases and in assisting in the selection and editing of the readings. We also want to thank those who ably assisted in the typing, including Dawn Havard, Patricia Letherwood, Mary Keaveny, Joan Downham, and the typing pool of the Department of Business Administration at the University of Wyoming. We especially want to thank Fran Palmer Fulton, the project packager retained by Addison-Wesley, who smoothly and ably coordinated the massive amount of editorial and production details involved in this book.

For the others, too numerous to name, who helped and encouraged us throughout this project, please accept our expression of gratitude for your cooperation.

Finally, we want to express our appreciation to our families: Karen, Eric, Kristin, Mary, Molly, Barry, Meghan, Patrick, and Barb. They were very supportive of our undertaking of this project, which we did in addition to everything else we were attempting to do at the same time. Their support and encouragement was extremely useful in completing the project.

Detroit, Michigan   J.E.M.
Laramie, Wyoming   T.J.K.
November 1984   R.E.A.

Contents

PART II

SECTION 7

National Labor Relations Board
and Arbitration Cases   345

SECTION 8
Simulations   473

Readings and Cases
in Labor Relations
and
Collective Bargaining

PART I

SECTION 1
The Framework for American Collective Bargaining

INTRODUCTION

The purpose of this first section of the book is to show how unions, employee-management relations, and the framework for collective bargaining in the United States have evolved over time and where they stand today. Understanding why unions arose and the historical evolution of the framework in which they operate is important so that we may know how we arrived at the point that we are at today. This knowledge also facilitates understanding how changes may occur in our industrial relations system in the future and what those changes might be.

The evolution of the American labor movement has always been closely aligned with public policy toward unions as expressed in both laws and court decisions. One of the first significant court decisions in this area, in 1806, found members of the Philadelphia Journeymen Cordwainers (shoemakers) guilty of a criminal conspiracy for striking for higher wages and attempting to keep others from working at a lower wage. As a result of that decision, unions were viewed as illegal conspiracies and the ''criminal conspiracy

doctrine'' came into existence. That doctrine generally remained in force until the 1842 decision of the Massachusetts Supreme Court in *Commonwealth* v. *Hunt,* which led to the ''illegal purpose doctrine.'' This meant that unions were legal and would only be judged illegal based on their purposes. However, by the late nineteenth century the courts developed a new device to counter unions, an injunction against strikes. Employers could then easily obtain an injunction against a strike — breaking the strike, and then seeking damages from the strikers. This state of affairs, with the government generally on the employers' side, did not essentially change until the 1930s.

At that time, several important laws were passed, including the 1932 Norris-Guardia anti-injunction act, which made it very difficult to obtain an injunction to stop a strike. Also passed in that decade were Section 7a of the National Industrial Recovery Act and the 1935 Wagner Act or National Labor Relations Act (NLRA), which granted employees the right to organize for collective bargaining purposes. However, in 1947, after a wave of postwar strikes and the election of a Republican Congress, the NLRA was amended by the Taft-Hartley Act. Those amendments incorporated business views on public policy toward labor, to help even out the balance of public policy between labor and management.

Also in the 1930s, industrial unionism came about with many of America's factories unionizing. The great depression with its massive unemployment may have suggested to the workers that there was a basic conflict between labor and management. Management's poor treatment of the workers and the lack of civil rights in the work place also made the workers conducive to unionization. Further, the more favorable public policy toward labor that came about with the passage of the laws mentioned above, also helped to set the climate and made it easier to organize unions. However, it took the founding of the Congress of Industrial Organizations (CIO) before labor could be successful in the unionization of America's factories.

A brief understanding of the principal differences between the CIO and the American Federation of Labor (AFL) will demonstrate why the AFL had trouble organizing the mass production factories. Prior to the 1930s, the American labor movement, as embodied in the AFL, consisted primarily of craft unions that organized workers by craft or skill. This AFL structure, which traced its roots back to 1881, was not very well suited for organizing the large factories involved in mass production. There was one AFL union for the carpenters, another for the plumbers and pipefitters, another for the electricians, etc. Factory employees tended to identify more with the industry and many were unskilled. To organize them a new approach was needed and was provided by John L. Lewis of the Mineworkers. In 1935 he formed the CIO within the AFL to unionize workers on a plant-wide industrial basis instead of on a craft basis. Because official AFL policy opposed organizing the fac-

tories on a plant-wide basis, the AFL in 1936 suspended all of the CIO-affiliated unions.

Today, organizing employees into unions, discussed in more detail in Section 2 of this book, is a relatively simple matter governed by National Labor Relations Board elections. However, before the NLRA was implemented, the organization of the mass production industries was very turbulent, with more upheaval occurring between American labor and management than ever before or since. One dramatic confrontation was the 1936–1937 44-day sit-down strike by the United Automobile Workers-CIO (UAW) at the General Motors plants in Flint, Mich. At the end of that strike the UAW was victorious in gaining recognition throughout General Motors. One other dramatic confrontation was the Memorial Day Massacre that took place during the 1937 CIO strike and organizing drive in the steel industry. In that incident, ten people marching in support of the strike were fatally shot and the strike was subsequently broken. The CIO organization of the steel industry was not completed until 1942. In general, however, the CIO was successful in these massive organizing drives. The AFL was only successful in organizing the mass production industries and in gaining more members than the CIO when it too began organizing on a plant-wide basis. The labor movement thus consisted of two rival federations until the AFL-CIO merger in 1955.

In 1959, Congress passed the Landrum-Griffin Act, which sought to correct the imbalance between the union membership and leadership. Thus it cut across the conventional union versus management alignment. One theorist, Jack Barbash, has argued that prior to that public policy change, our industrial relations system was governed by the two major principles: the adversary principle, where the union and management are continually in dispute over the division of the firm's net proceeds between non-wages and wages; and the principle of voluntarism, wherein the parties alone have the maximum freedom to define and implement their own relationship.[1] Thus Barbash argued that defects with the adversarial principle, i.e., in dealing with inflation, disadvantaged ethnic groups, the interests of women, etc., led to voluntarism losing to increased government intervention as reflected by laws such as the Occupational Safety and Health Act and those governing equal employment opportunity.

Do these changes in the environmental framework mean that the adversarial approach to industrial relations is outmoded today? On the one hand, we have a number of programs, such as those dealing with quality of work life, which suggest a mutualistic cooperative view of union-management relations. On the other hand, we have the view that unions have become obsolete and that we are heading for a union-free environment. Finally, there is the view that the old way of carrying out industrial relations is not dead, with unions that made big concessions during the recession threatening to strike now to achieve parity with those unions that did not make concessions. However, it is a fact that the new work force of baby boomers is here, that technological change is increasing again, that the role of the government has changed, and that international competition has increased. How, and even if, our industrial relations system will adapt to these changes is not known at this time. Thus we do not know which view is most likely to characterize industrial relations in this country in the future. When reading the selections in this section, the readers should try to decide this difficult question for themselves.

INTRODUCTION TO THE READINGS

Theories of Labor Unions

The first article, by Philip Taft, presents and discusses several of the more important theories explaining both the origin and the behavior of labor unions, including those of Bretano, the Webbs, the Marxists, Catholic clergy and lay writers, Hoxie, Commons, and Perlman. Those theorists present the reader with several ordered explanations accounting for both the origin and the behavior of labor unions from a variety of perspectives. The theories Taft examines are those that are among the most influential in the labor relations field today. However, the very existence of multiple theories suggests that there is conflict on this subject and that labor unions as a whole may be very complex.

Taft concludes by noting that each theory presented deals with some important aspect of labor activity. However, he notes that American labor, in part tied to a socialist philosophy in the past, appeared to have no doctrinaire philosophy by the 1950s. He argues that American unionism has the simple pragmatism of employee protection from arbitrariness and improvement of the standard of living as its philosophy, and that that philosophy has been very successful. Taft's analysis and presentation should enable the reader to determine whether the varying forces that gave rise to unions in the first place will enable unions to survive future changes in our employee-relations system.

The Legal Public Policy Framework

The legal public policy framework of labor relations is discussed by Jack Barbash in the second article in this section. He shows how the legal climate prior to the 1930s was ''probusiness,'' essentially allowing employers to handle their dealings with employees in any way they wanted. Barbash then discusses the various labor laws that were passed starting in the 1930s and the environment in which that happened. He saw the Norris-LaGuardia Act of 1932 as beginning a pro-union period, in that it began to rectify past inequities so that unions could bargain collectively. He saw that period as lasting through the most important Act, the NLRA of 1935, to the passage of the Taft-Hartley amendments of 1947. He sees these public policy acts as either pro-union or pro-business.

However, the passage of the Landrum-Griffin Act, various manpower acts since 1961, wage-price policies, and the Civil Rights Act of 1964, lead Barbash to suggest that traditional union versus management questions were displaced from the center of the public policy arena. These new laws and policies were aimed at various aspects of the employment relationship. In some cases they were aimed against both management and unions, as with the civil rights law, and resulted in new pressure groups, i.e., civil rights activists. He argues that other policies, such as wage-price policies, appeared to be enforced against unions rather than employers. Thus Barbash concludes that public policy has changed from regulating the *process* of collective bargaining to achieve desired results, to regulating the *results* of that bargaining.

Labor History: A Case Study at Ford

The article by Martin Gannon discusses the evolution of labor relations during most of this century in one large firm, the Ford Motor Company. Gannon divides the history of labor relations into five stages, with four occurring under Henry Ford I and the last one under Henry Ford II. In the first stage, he shows how the company expanded and that labor became extremely routinized, as exemplified by the assembly line. One result was high worker dissatisfaction and a 380 percent turnover rate in 1913.

Gannon suggests that as a result of these problems, Ford turned to a period of benevolence, raising the daily wage from $2.34 to five dollars and instituting various personnel programs. However, beginning around 1921, Ford began the stage of discipline of labor. He notes that while Ford paid the workers well, he treated them very poorly, giving them almost no rights. Thus the workers had many grievances but few rights until the UAW organized Ford in 1941. The last period under Henry Ford I began in

1930, labeled the intolerance of labor. In this period, workers were beaten by the Ford Service Police, union organizers were physically attacked, and many union supporters were fired. When the UAW finally organized Ford, conflict continued and wildcat strikes became common. While the Ford Motor Company may be an exception because it unionized later and somewhat differently than the rest of the automotive industry, the treatment of its employees in the 1930s was typical of that of many employers. Gannon ends his discussion by showing how, when Henry Ford II took over the company in 1945, the old antagonisms between labor and management faded away as mutual confidence took hold.

Where We Are Today

The last two articles in this section discuss the changes taking place in the American industrial relations system today and the conflicting forces affecting where it may go in the future. The article by Milton Derber questions whether or not we are in a new stage of industrial relations. He describes two different views of the new-stage industrial relations: the mutualistic cooperative union-management relations view and the view that we are moving toward a union-free environment. Derber also identifies a third view held by theorists, who believe that once the economy pulls out of the recession of the early 1980s, collective bargaining will again be aggressive and adversarial, the way it was in the past, but still with government intervention.

In an attempt to determine which view or views is correct, he examines the history of the United States industrial relations and the evidence supporting each view. He then discusses the following factors likely to affect the future: demographic trends, technology, the government, and international economics. He concludes that it is very likely that we are in a new stage, and that it will be a cooperative mutualistic stage, but recognizes that his conclusion is guesswork.

The *Business Week* article goes a little further and suggests that the old-stage adversarial approach to industrial relations is outmoded. *Business Week* advocates increases in the number of quality-of-worklife programs, increased worker participation, and other new ways of managing people, all of which should be tied to increased productivity. Thus it would expand upon the current work innovation programs already existing in this country. Additionally, it gives many examples of where such changes have taken place and their positive results. It suggests that the baby-boom generation, with its radically changed work values and greater education will help force such changes on the work place.

Labor Relations Law

The last selection in this section, by James Martin, is an introduction to the NLRA. It includes some of the actual wording of that Act along with much interpretation. Martin's introduction presents examples of violations of the Act that would result in unfair labor practice charges against either or both the union and/or management. He also defines what is a supervisor, what is an appropriate bargaining unit, and what is an

employer. His introduction serves as a guide to help analyze the National Labor Relations Board cases presented in the second half of the book.

NOTES

1. Barbash, Jack, "The American Ideology of Industrial Relations," *Labor Law Journal,* Vol. 30, No. 8, August, 1979, pp. 453–457.

SUGGESTIONS FOR FURTHER READING

In addition to the article cited in this introduction, the following readings may prove useful to the reader.

Aaron, Benjamin, and Paul S. Meyer, "Public Policy and Labor-Management Relations," in *A Review of Industrial Relations Research,* Vol. 2, Madison, Wis.: Industrial Relations Research Association, 1971.

Dunlop, John T., *Industrial Relations Systems,* Carbondale, Ill.: Southern Illinois University Press, 1958.

Galenson, Walter, *The CIO Challenge to the AFL: A History of the Labor Movement,* Cambridge, Mass.: Harvard University Press, 1960.

Lester, Richard A., *As Unions Mature,* Princeton, N.J.: Princeton University Press, 1958.

Mills, D. Quinn, "Flawed Victory in Labor Law Reform," *Harvard Business Review,* Vol. 57, No. 3, May–June, 1979, pp. 92–102.

Theories of the Labor Movement

PHILIP TAFT
Formerly of Brown University

Generalizations to explain the origin and nature of the trade union movement have been developed by a variety of writers. Even a superficial observation of the labor movement reveals a multitude of facts, some of them isolated and some contradictory. A theory is an attempt to give an ordered explanation, to account for the origin and behavior of labor unionism. It may also serve as a basis for predicting the conduct and policies that may be followed by the labor movement in the future. Policies in this connection must be regarded in a broad sense rather than the operations on a day-to-day basis. The first part of the discussion examines the theories which seek to explain the origin of the labor movement. It is followed by an analysis of theories dealing with the behavior of the labor movement, and a section which attempts to discuss the various views in the light of contemporary developments.[1]

THE ORIGIN OF THE LABOR MOVEMENT

Brentano

One of the earliest attempts by a nonsocialist writer to deal with this question was made by the German economist and historian, Lujo Brentano. Writing in the third quarter of the 19th century, Brentano was convinced that "Trade-Unions are the successors of the old Gilds."[2] Brentano, unlike the contemporary critics who see trade unions as a "gild type" of monopoly, was not opposed to organizations of workers. On the contrary, he believed they were both necessary and desirable as offsets to the power of the employer. Unions, in Brentano's opinion, arose under "the breaking up of an old system, and among the men suffering from this disorganization, in order that they may maintain independence and order."[3]

Brentano was a welfarist and reformer and an intellectual opponent of socialism. He therefore emphasized the aspects of trade unionism which harmonize with traditional rather than with revolutionary conduct. What the trade union sought was not class war, but the restoration of the old order which had been upset by innovating businessmen. . . .

Brentano emphasized that the objectives of the trade unions as of the craft gilds "was the maintenance of an entire system of order," or of a standard of life which was being undermined by the growing factory owners. Instead of being a revolutionary mass bent on destroying the system of private property, Brentano emphasized the conservative aspects of trade unionism in its desire to return to an earlier time. In this view, the trade union arose as a result of the breakdown of the customary rights enjoyed by the worker, and it was an attempt to create a new equilibrium by elaborating a system of rules to govern industry. The view that the trade unions were descended from the gilds has been challenged by the Webbs. Nevertheless, the notion that the trade unions arose because of the disturbance of an established custom shows that Brentano well understood one of the essential causes for the origin of trade unionism. An attempt to change a rule or a rate has frequently led to organization. Considering that his essay was written in the 1860s, when most of the English unions were groupings of skilled men, the insistence upon their resemblance to craft gilds is perhaps better understood.

Moreover, the scarcity consciousness which is a characteristic of the skilled unions, in the United States as well as elsewhere, shown in the restrictive rules and the limitation upon admission, is certainly an attitude found in the gilds. Even where no direct connection exists, the spirit is not different. However, Brentano neglected the difference between the "mercantile" attitude of a gildsman and the wage consciousness of a worker. Yet, his emphasis upon the conservative traditional nature of unions, their insistence upon protecting their job territory by restrictions upon free entry and technological change, caught a significant aspect of early trade unionism.

Webbs

The Webbs, who followed Brentano chronologically, refused to accept the latter's interpretation of the origin of the labor movement, although they admired many of his insights. To the Webbs, the origin of trade unionism depended upon the separation of classes. The Webbs defined a trade union as "a continuous association of wage earn-

ers for the purpose of maintaining or improving the conditions of their working lives."[4] They, therefore, dated the beginning of English trade unionism in the latter part of the 17th century with the appearance of a property-less wage earner. The journeymen's revolts of earlier times were interpreted largely as movements against the authority of the gild, and the "bachelors' companies" they find to have been a subordinate branch of the masters' gild. It was only when the skilled journeyman found his prospect for advancement into the ranks of the masters greatly diminished that stable combinations among the handicraftsmen arose. It was only when "the changing conditions of industry had reduced to an infinitesimal chance the journeyman's prospect of himself becoming a master, that we find the passage of ephemeral combinations into permanent trade societies."[5] . . .

Unions arose as soon as "the great bulk of the workers had ceased to be independent producers, themselves controlling the processes and owning the materials and product of their labour, and had passed into the conditions of lifelong wage-earners, possessing neither the instruments of production nor the commodity in its finished state."[6] This separation of classes or the separation of the worker from the means of production preceded, to some extent, the development of the factory system. The reduction of the worker to a mere wage-earner, dependent upon others for employment, may have come about as a result of one or many of several causes. In the tailoring trade, the masters came from a small segment — the journeymen who had acquired the highest level of skills. The great majority of the workers were poor, employed as sewers who prepared the material for their more skilled brethren. Increasing capital requirements accentuated the class divisions within the trade. It was possible

to start a business in a back street as an independent master tailor with no more capital or skill than the average journeyman could command, yet the making of fine clothes worn by the Court and the gentry demanded then, as now, a capital and a skill which put the extensive and lucrative trade altogether out of the reach of the thousands of journeymen whom it employed.[7]

. . .

The universal cause which accounts for the origin of trade unionism is the separation of the worker from the means of production with the consequent rise of a permanent class of workers dependent upon an employer. While other conditions may tend to create a permanent class of wage earners, the rise of the factory system was the most pervasive cause of the separation of the worker from the means of production. For the Webbs, it had

> become a commonplace of modern Trade Unionism that only in those industries in which the worker has ceased to be concerned in the profits of buying and selling — that inseparable characteristic of the ownership and management of the means of production — can effective and stable trade organization be established.[8]

Yet, this explanation raises a problem, for there had always existed in English industry a large class of unskilled and low paid workers virtually debarred from rising to independent craftsmen. The ill-paid farm laborer, and others of low skill, however, had not been the pioneers of trade unionism. On the contrary, it was the highly skilled journeyman who for years had been the object of government protection who was the first to form labor unions. It was not the worker who had the lowest bargaining power but the one with the greatest sense of independence who pioneered the trade union movement. This was inevitable, for only the worker with a great sense of independence was willing to challenge the authority of the employer in the early days of organization, and it required some threat to existing customs and standards to initiate organization. Therefore, it was not the property-less proletariat of Marx but the labor aristocrat who was the pioneer of trade unionism. The Webbs and Brentano agreed that a threat to established relations is likely to stimulate organization of labor in defense of the old conditions or in an effort to

establish a new equilibrium. The Webbs, however, placed emphasis upon the class nature of a union; that it arose when the possibilities of class mobility had been reduced and when the worker felt that he had nothing but his labor to sell. The Webbs' view underlines the special character of the trade union which, despite many attitudes of the old gild, was a new type of organization.

What light does the hypothesis of the Webbs throw upon the origin of the American trade union movement? In the United States, as in England, trade unions were first organized when class differentiation had taken place. This differentiation was evidenced by the exclusion of masters from the union. Unions were pioneered by the printers, cordwainers, and tailors, at the time highly skilled trades, and only much later did the unskilled and the factory workers form organizations of labor. Moreover, the Webbs' emphasis upon the defensive aspects of trade unionism also received confirmation from the American experience. The introduction of the McKay stitcher in the post–Civil War period stimulated organization among the skilled shoemakers who sought to protect their established positions then undermined by an influx of green hands. This is one example of the conditions the Webbs had in mind.

Marxism

Marxist ideas on trade unions are intimately and inextricably related to the general Marxist assumptions and conclusions on social institutions and the directions of their development. In common with the Webbs, Marx and his followers explained the origin of trade unions by the rise of a working class bereft of control over the instruments of production. While the Webbs regarded labor unions as a means used by workers to maintain or improve their traditional standards of life, Marx regarded them as only one — and by no means the most important — weapon in labor's armory for waging the class war. . . . Trade unions were desirable and necessary, but could only conduct what was, in the long run, a losing rearguard action. In the end, labor would be forced to rebel against capitalism and, eventually, to displace it by a socialist economy. Therefore, it was inevitable that all the institutions created by labor, including the trade unions, should be oriented in that direction.

At best, trade unions could only deal with short run, day-to-day problems. They were a response to the need of labor to protect its day-to-day interests. They were spontaneous efforts by workers to restrict the effects of competition in the labor market.[9] Unions were class organizations, which came into existence to protect the worker against the employer. It was the pressure of the employer which drove the worker to revolt. Soon, however, labor established

> permanent associations in order to make provision beforehand for these occasional revolts. . . . Now and then the workers are victorious but only for a time. The real fruit of their battle lies not in the immediate result but in the expanding union of workers. The union is helped on by the improved means of communication that are created by modern industry and that place the workers of different localities in contact with one another. It was just this contact that was needed to centralize the numerous local struggles, all of the same character, into one national struggle between classes. But every class struggle is a political struggle.[10]

This statement, although it was written in 1847, expressed the essentials of the Marxist view of trade unionism, even though Marx continued to write for 35 years and Engels for almost 50 years after these words appeared. . . . The trade unions[11] were more than institutions for the daily struggle with employers. They were a means of mobilizing the strength of labor against the capitalist class. "While, however, the trade unions are absolutely indispensable in the daily struggle between labour and capital, still more important is their other aspect, as instruments *for*

transforming the system of wage labour and for overthrowing the dictatorship of capital.[12]

Selected Catholic Writers on Trade Unionism

The attitude of Catholic clergymen and writers on trade unionism was extremely important in the United States because members of the faith were heavily represented among industrial workers. The question before Catholic students was whether the unions arose to defend the worker against superior economic force or were a section of a movement challenging religion and existing governments. In the United States, the answers given were, in part, influenced by the social and economic background of many of the hierarchy. "Irish priests and theologians rose from the ranks of the people, surrounded by popular influences which inevitably affected their work."[13] The conditions under which the Irish immigrant labored have been graphically described by Professor Handlin.

> An employed laborer could not earn enough to maintain a family of four. And as long as the head of the Irish household obtained nothing but sporadic employment, his dependents lived in jeopardy of exchanging poverty for starvation. Supplementary earnings — no matter how small — became crucial for subsistence. . . . To keep the family fed, clothed, and sheltered, the women were also recruited. In Ireland they had occupied a clearly defined and important position in the cottiers' economy. That place being gone, they went off to serve at the table of strangers and bring home the bitter bread of banishment.[14]
>
> . . .

The view that the trade unions arose as a defense against the exploitation of labor was more explicitly recognized by many members of the Catholic hierarchy in the controversy over the Knights of Labor during the 1880s. In his letter to the Prefect of the Sacred Congregation of Propaganda, James Cardinal Gibbons, then the ranking Catholic prelate of the United States, told

The Origin of the Labor Movement

13

that a "committee of archbishops held a meeting towards the end of last October, at which the association of the Knights of Labor was specially considered. . . . I must add that among all the bishops, we know of but two or three who desire the condemnation of the Knights of Labor."[15]. . .

American prelates explained the formation and existence of trade unions by the workers' need to defend themselves because of their inferior bargaining position. The right of association was a positive right, and an obligation of social justice. This view was reinforced and broadened by the work of Catholic prelates abroad. Catholic laymen and theologians had been watching the evolution of modern industrialism, with its accompanying evils, with growing concern. Not only was modern industry threatening to undermine established institutions, but the excesses of some businessmen and their inordinate lust for gain were encouraging the spread of radical social doctrines. . . .

The writings and works of these reformers culminated in Pope Leo XIII's *Rerum Novarum,* a document which addressed itself to the social problems of the time. At the outset, the Pope attacked the doctrines of materialistic socialism then making considerable headway on the continent. He, however, fully endorsed the trade unions seeking the protection of the worker in industry. Trade unions arose, according to Pope Leo, to redress the advantages held by the employer and to form voluntary associations as was the natural right of man.

Robert Hoxie

Robert Hoxie was impressed by the diversity in the structural arrangements and in the functioning of unions. He found "that unionism has not a single genesis, but that it has made its appearance time after time, independently, wherever in the modern industrial era a group of workers, large or small, developed a strong internal consciousness of common interests."[16] He was convinced, moreover, that unions, over time, responded to changes in conditions, needs and attitudes. He found that unionists "are prone to act and to formulate theories afterward,"[17] and that they attempted to meet whatever problems events had placed before them. Unions arose out of group needs and as they were not uniform, a single theory will not suffice. The

> union program, taking with it all its mutations and contradictions, comprehends nothing less than all the various economic, political, ethical and social viewpoints and modes of action of a vast and heterogeneous complex of working class groups, molded by diverse environments and actuated by diverse motives; it expresses nothing less than ideals, aspirations, hopes, and fears, modes of thinking and action of all these working groups. In short, if we can think of unionism as such, it must be as one of the most complex, heterogeneous and protean of modern social phenomena.[18]

. . .

Hoxie was a shrewd and careful observer, but he overstressed the importance of the differences he noticed between unions. Significant differences in the structure and function of unions existed, but these differences may have reflected the differences in the industrial environment or in the makeup of the membership. If unions are a response to differing group psychology, it is difficult to explain why, despite differences, unions always perform certain basic functions for their members. While one may find Hoxie's explanation of the origin of unions incomplete, his stress on diverse causes did highlight the differences in the structure and the functioning of unions, both with respect to their internal affairs and with respect to collective bargaining. These differences have always existed within American trade unionism, and the attitudes of the workers composing the union have undoubtedly played some role in determining the quality of a particular labor organization. It is difficult to give weight to specific factors, but the makeup of the membership and its response to the problems of industry obviously contribute to determining a union's form and attitudes. Hoxie's emphasis upon variety of origin called attention to a facet in the origin of the labor organizations unstressed by other writers.

John R. Commons

John R. Commons was one of the pioneer investigators of labor. In explaining the origin of labor unions, Commons, similarly to the Webbs in England, based his conclusions upon an examination of records rather than upon an *a priori* theory. Commons attributed the rise of labor organizations to the differentiation of classes, which was in turn due to the expansion of the market. The artisan who embodied within himself the mercantile, manufacturing, and labor functions is, over a period of time, metamorphosed on one side into a capitalist merchant; on the other, into a manufacturer buying labor, and a wage-earner selling his labor power. The differentiation in function was accompanied by increasing competition — both due to the widening of the market. Facing increasingly severe competition, the merchant capitalist attempted to impose the burdens upon labor by depressing wages. Labor responded by forming labor unions, which sought "the practical remedy . . . the elimination of the competitive menace through a protective organization or protective legislation." [19]

Commons maintained that unions arose to overcome the workers' inferior bargaining position. Moreover, he saw in labor organizations the culmination of an age-long process of extending freedom.

> The restraints which laborers place on free competition, in the interests of fair competition, begin to be taken over by employers and administered by their own labor managers. Even organized labor achieves participation with management in the protection of the job, just as the barons and the capitalists achieved participation with the King in the protection of property

and business. A common law of labor is constructed by selecting the reasonable practices and rejecting the bad practices of labor, and by depriving both unions and management of arbitrary power over the job. [20]

THE BEHAVIOR OF THE LABOR MOVEMENT

. . .

The Webbs

The Webbs' theory or theories of union behavior were based upon an exhaustive examination of the practices of labor organization, and they concluded: "For the improvement of the conditions of employment, whether in respect to wages, hours, health, safety, or comfort, the Trade Unionists have, with all their multiplicity of Regulations, really only two expedients, which we term, respectively, the *Device of the Common Rule* and the *Device of the Restrictions of Numbers.*" [21] The principle of the common rule included all terms of employment which uniformly apply to entire groups of workers. Having observed the operation of the principle of the common rule, the Webbs attempted to explain its pervasiveness throughout the trade union movement. The alternative to standardized wage rates and working conditions is free competitive bargaining, by individuals of unequal bargaining power, over the terms of employment. "Such a settlement, it is asserted, inevitably tends, for the mass of workers, towards the worst possible conditions of labor." [22] Consequently, the "Device of the Common Rule is a universal feature of Trade Unionism, and the Assumption on which it is based is held from one end of the Trade Union world to the other." [23] The common rule was a universal principle of trade union policy, which had been devised to equalize the bargaining power of the parties. The enforcement of this policy depended upon conditions in the industry and trade, and the standardizing of wages and hours; the enforcement of sanitary and safety rules and the multitude of other regulations governing the conditions of work were all manifestations of the principle of the common rule. The other principle, restriction of numbers, expressed itself usually through limitation on apprenticeship and entrance into the union. Through these devices the supply of labor in the trade was restricted and the bargaining position of the particular group enhanced.

The Device of the Common Rule, first stated by the Webbs, summarized union policy and practice in the United States as well as in other democratic countries. From the beginning of their existence, the unions in the United States aimed at standardizing wages and working conditions, and the principle enunciated by the Webbs was useful in that it drew attention to a universal policy of trade unionism. On the other hand, the policy of restricting numbers, practiced by both British and American unions of skilled craftsmen, was not as universally practiced as the Device of the Common Rule. Yet they called attention to a policy which the American unions have enforced through apprentice regulations, high initiation fees, and closed books.

While the Webbs believed that unions arose as a result of the separation of classes, they did not emphasize class struggle concepts in the formation of policies by trade unions. Unions in working out their attitudes towards wages and other conditions of employment have been guided by one of several assumptions, described by the Webbs as the "Doctrine of Vested Interests, the Doctrine of Supply and Demand, the Doctrine of the Living Wage." [24] The first principle was used to justify opposition to technological change or other innovations which affected adversely the position of a craft. In addition, the Webbs showed that this principle explained the attitude of unions that established conditions must never be lowered. American unions have often resisted technological changes which diminish jobs of the group, and the difficulty of reducing standards in organized plants is widely recognized. The Webbs' observation that the Doctrine of Vested Interests had been weakened among English trade unionists is also true in the United States. It

is only in the older artisan-type of union that resistance to technological change is very great. Yet, the doctrine still explains much about the attitude of the older craft union and of some present ones.

The Doctrine of Supply and Demand was, for the Webbs, a summation of the policies practiced by the English unions to place themselves in a strategic position in their dealings with their employers. Rules that regulated the ratio of helpers to journeymen were examples of the application of this principle. Emphasis upon this principle led unions to follow a more aggressive wage policy in periods when business was brisk. "Middle-class public opinion, which had accepted as inevitable the starvation wages caused by Supply and Demand in the lean years, was shocked . . . at the nerve of coalminers and iron-workers . . . demanding ten shillings or even a pound a day." [25] But the policy of governing the union's demand for concessions by conditions in the labor market was widespread in the United States as well as England. This principle explains the conduct of the building trades and coal miners' unions in the United States which insist upon wages as high as possible at the moment. The Webbs showed that the pursuit of the supply and demand principle might at times lead to strong organization at both sides of the bargaining table, and eventually to collusive arrangements whereby the public pays a higher price for the product or service than it otherwise would. The collusive bargains in the building trades in American cities whereby the primary interest is in stable prices of labor, as long as the higher costs can be shifted to the consumer, is a good example of the principle.

Supply and demand has not adequately served the unions in all circumstances. Sometimes the unions fell back upon the doctrine of the living wage which manifested itself in the view that the conditions of the labor market should never be allowed to push the standards of living below a given level. In contrast to the supply and demand view, the doctrine of the living wage stressed the rights of the individual to a "civilized" even if indefinite standard. This view was developed later in time both in England and in the United States. It has been especially attractive in both countries to those organized workers who lacked the monopoly position due to special skill and years of training.

In carrying out their policies, unions have not, according to the Webbs, followed a single road. Circumstances have frequently influenced the adoption of one or more of the following methods: the method of mutual insurance, the method of collective bargaining, and the method of legal enactment. One or all methods were used by trade unions everywhere, irrespective of their origin or even official ideologies.

Mutual insurance was widely established in England, the United States and other countries. It provided the worker with protection against wage loss, not then available from the government.

Collective bargaining has been an essential characteristic of trade unionism in all countries with democratic governments.[26] Its purpose has been to prevent either the greater need or the superior skill of particular workers from determining the wage bargain. The Webbs argued that one whose need was great was likely to be more willing to accept a wage even when it was below the level regarded as adequate. Similarly, a superior workman might have been willing to accept a lower piece rate, for he believed that he would be able to offset the lower rate by his superior ability. Collective bargaining was therefore designed to prevent the employer from using such individuals as a means of beating down the earnings of other and more average workers. "The starving man gets his job at the same piecework rate as the workman who could afford to stand out for his usual earnings. The superior craftsman retains all his advantages over his fellows, but without allowing his superiority to be made the means of reducing the weekly wage of the ordinary worker."[27]

The method of legal enactment was the third road which the trade unions, according to the Webbs, followed in seeking adjustment of their grievances. The use of legal enactment for achieving trade union objectives was more popular at certain times than at others. In the United States, it was the policy of many craft unions, and of Gompers, to eschew legal enactment except in behalf of the weaker bargaining groups. This policy has changed in recent years, and even the highest skilled workers favor laws which improve their bargaining position and strengthen their organizations.

Marxism

The view on trade unions initially propounded by Marx has been accepted by his followers. While they must be promoted and encouraged, it was because of the power of the unions to rally and to discipline large masses of workers, and not because of their capacity to win permanent improvements in the position of labor. The unions could resist the oppression of labor by industry, but they could not permanently solve the problem facing the worker in a capitalistic society. Moreover, Marx and his followers emphasized the political character, open or submerged, of every industrial dispute. The essential significance of a strike lay in its sharpening of class differences, and in whetting the worker's appetite for revolt, rather than in the attempts of the trade unions to gain concessions, although that might have been the obvious or efficient cause of the dispute. . . .

It is obvious that the Marxist considers that the trade unions are only capable of achieving limited and transitory gains. The dynamics of the capitalist system always tends to increase competition for jobs, while the capitalist is normally compelled to increase the pressure upon his labor force. Moreover, success by labor organizations in gaining concessions usually begets greater unity and counter action by employers, with the result that it becomes increasingly difficult for labor to defy the will of the employer. With the progress of capitalism, the Marxists also assume a weakening of the ability of the trade unions to gain concessions, because the capitalistic system and its individual components face increasing difficulty in marketing their products profitably. ... The Marxist view on trade unionism sheds considerable light upon the activity of minority groups within the American labor movement. The efforts of the Marxist and Lassallean socialists to impose their views on American unions sprang from the former's convictions that pure trade unionism had only a limited value to the worker, and that permanent relief had to be sought elsewhere, through political action. In the light of the Marxist hypothesis (or of the Lassallean),[28] trade unionism is a weak reed upon which to lean, and the evils of capitalism require other remedies. The refusal of Gompers and his followers to concede this premise, and their refusal to adopt the tactics inherent in this view was regarded as unwisdom bordering on treason. It showed, in the opinion of the Marxists, an obliviousness to historical trends which stamped them as incompetent to lead a workers' movement. . . .

Robert Hoxie

It was noted above that Hoxie rejected a monistic interpretation of unionism. . . . Maintaining that workers exposed to the same industrial conditions are likely to develop similar attitudes, he sought to show that differences in structure and function of unions reflect differences in the psychology of their members. Hoxie's structural distinctions were similar to those of other writers. His functional types represented something original, and showed a high level of ingenuity. They were widely accepted and influenced the thinking of many students of the subject. Hoxie divided labor organizations into four principle types — business unionism, uplift unionism, revolutionary unionism and predatory unionism. The last was divided into two subclasses, hold-up unionism and guerilla unionism.

Each of these groups had differentiating characteristics. Business unionism concentrated upon immediate goals, it concerned itself with the interests of its members rather than with labor as a whole, and its thinking was directed towards higher wages and improved working conditions. The capitalist system was accepted and no concern was shown for distant goals. A business union was likely to emphasize discipline in the organization and frequently develops strong leadership.

Uplift unionism was a trade conscious or even class conscious union which tried to raise the cultural and moral level of its members. Stress was placed upon mutual insurance and this type was likely to be democratic in its internal management. It also "drifts easily into political action and the advocacy of cooperative enterprises, profit sharing, and other idealistic plans for social regeneration."[29]

Revolutionary unionism manifested itself in two forms, socialist unions and revolutionary unions. The former aspired to replace capitalism and depended upon political action to achieve its larger aim. This type of union was likely to be critical of present day institutions, and democratic in its internal affairs. The revolutionary union was described as syndicalistic. It emphasized direct action, repudiated political activity, and looked forward to a society of free industrial (producer) cooperatives.

"Predatory unionism is distinguished by a ruthless pursuit of the thing in hand by whatever means seem most appropriate at the time, regardless of ethical and legal codes or effect upon those outside its own membership."[30] This unionism might have been conservative or radical in philosophy, and its distinguishing mark was its ruthless tactics. Predatory unionism was divided: the subtype, holdup unionism, might have appeared outwardly as a bargaining type of business unionism, but it was monopolistic, boss-ridden, violent, and corrupt, and frequently combined with the employer to achieve its aims; guerilla unionism had all the attributes of holdup unionism, except that it would not enter into deals with the employer.

Hoxie's analysis of union types concentrated upon some special characteristic which was then interpreted as the essence of the particular group. Such a method helped to bring out the diversity in the attitudes and policies of unions, but it obscured the even more basic similarities. Moreover, there is a question whether certain of the types described by Hoxie are unions at all. All unions are business unions, in the sense that they bargain with employers. Their other characteristics are likely to be accidental in the sense that they are not essential for the carrying out of the union's main functions. Nevertheless, Hoxie was a keen observer of unionism who underlined the variety of forms in which unionism expressed itself. His work is a warning against both glib generalizations and the making of hurried distinctions.

John R. Commons

. . .

Commons sought to explain some of the unique features of the American labor movement, and his ideas are still very useful for understanding this subject. He noted a wide difference between European and American political conditions which influenced the shaping of American unionism. An important reason for the difference was related to the establishment of universal suffrage early in American history. Political parties have therefore been forced to contend for the labor vote, which "has tended at all times to break up the solidarity of the labor movement."[31] The American labor movement, according to Commons, was also affected by the variety of racial groups that came to the United States. Many union meetings at the beginning were conducted in English and another language. Commons believed that the differences in race and language "underlie the strenuous demand of American unions for the closed shop, as compared with the relative indifference of English

unionists on this subject."[32] The "advantage of common race and a common class feeling, particularly among British and German wage earners, has made it possible for unions to hold their ground without serious menace from non-unionists."[33] Commons observed that even though employers had used immigrant labor as a club to beat down the standards of the native worker, there was what he regarded a "remarkable" growth of unions made up of many diverse nationalities. Commons linked the demand for the closed shop not only to the absence of class feeling caused by the constant flow of immigration, but to the breakdown of skill caused by the introduction of automatic labor-saving devices. He concluded that

> the American unions have very little industrial or racial protection. Apprenticeship is gone, except as enforced by them, the unions, against the protests of employers. In order to enforce this and other measures needed to keep wages above the market rate, the unions found themselves compelled to enforce the rule that no one should enter the shop except through the union.[34]

Our federal system of government has also, according to Commons, shaped the labor movement. Because of the power of numerous state legislatures over legislation and their varied responsiveness to pressure, uniform standards over a wide area were likely to be lacking. Unions have consequently sought to fill that void and establish uniform conditions through their own rules. Commons studied the working rules of labor unions, and he found that unions through collective action can create rights and liberties for their members not found in the more dictatorial nonunion shop.[35] Commons, who started his working life as a printer in a union shop, "knew from experience that I had more liberty in a union shop and therefore earned more wages steadily, and enjoyed more equality . . . than my brother enjoyed across the street in his nonunion shop."[36] Commons was convinced that the union offered the worker needed protection, that in general it produced equality of treatment in society. . . .

Selig Perlman

Professor Perlman's theory is related to the views developed by Commons. Professor Perlman attempts to devise a general theory of the labor movement, one which will apply to all areas and times, although he notes the specific and peculiar characteristics of the labor movements of different countries. Professor Perlman attempts to deduce a philosophy of labor from the conduct of the worker and from the nature of the institutions labor has created. He contrasts this approach with the one developed by the intellectuals — ''the main characteristic of the intellectual'' is to regard ''labor as an 'abstract' mass in the grip of an abstract 'force.' By the intellectual is meant, of course, the educated nonmanualist, who has established a contact with the labor movement, either through influence acquired over trade union bodies, or else as a leader of labor in his own right. . . .''[37]. . . What is attempted is a distinction between two approaches to the labor movement. Does labor concern itself through its organizations with the day-to-day problems in a pragmatic experimental manner or does it devote itself primarily to building a new type of economy. . . .

Similar to Commons, Professor Perlman stresses the union's parceling out of opportunities and the industrial government in the shop, which demands subordination of individual advantage to the needs of the group. Unions have an idealism, for

> unionism, even ''business unionism,'' shows idealism both in aim and method; only it does so in the thoroughly unsophisticated way of 'Tom, Dick, and Harry idealism.' All unions sooner or later stress 'shop rights,' which to the workingman at the bench are identical with 'liberty' itself, since thanks to them, he has no need to kowtow to foreman or boss as the price of

holding his job. And, after all, is not this sort of liberty the only sort which reaches the workman directly and with certainty and that can never get lost *en route* like the 'broader' liberty promised by socialism. [38]

. . .

CONCLUSION

As one surveys the theories of trade unionism, it is obvious that even when incomplete they usually deal with some significant aspect of labor activity.

. . .

Theories of labor usually are formulated by students rather than by participants in the labor movement. One writer, who is both, has always felt that the lack of philosophy of American labor was one of its fatal defects. According to him, ''the philosophy of no generalizations [is] intended to keep the movement free from doctrinaire shackles. It has achieved little in this direction. It was responsible for a half a century of needless wanderings in the intellectual void, and only now it begins to dawn on some of the leaders of the second generation that the American labor movement is badly in need of an orientation.''[39]

. . .

Let those who are concerned about American labor's lack of philosophy engage in a bit of comparative analysis. Is there any labor movement anywhere which so zealously defends the interests of its members, which hedges its members with as much protection, which seeks to squeeze as many concessions out of the employer as the unions of the United States? What mysterious effect would a philosophy have upon the conduct of the unions? . . . Some unions in the past — the garment workers, machinists, brewery workers, and others — had, at one time, a philosophy: socialism. Without making invidious comparisons, it is only fair to say that those unions were not superior, in most respects, to others which did not have a philosophy. . . .

The American labor movement focuses its

main attention on the shop and upon the interests of its members. It is capable of sacrifice and solidarity in behalf of other groups and issues, but, as the power of each union is derived from the gains it wins for its members, it can never neglect this primary purpose without the risk of undermining its influence. This raises a problem for unions in an age in which government is steadily expanding its economic role. The Webbs believed the role of trade unions, in a society where industry is nationalized or municipalized, would diminish, and each would become "more and more concerned with raising the standard of competency in its occupation, improving the professional equipment of its members . . . and endeavoring by every means to increase its status in public estimation."[40] The Webbs' view has not been borne out by experience, and a recent study by a Fabian Research Group well argues that "in any form of society, and under any form of management, workers will need trade unions to look after their interests not only in relation to their employers but also in relation to government departments and officials and before the courts. . . . At least for the foreseeable future, the trade unions must take as their first objective the maintenance and development of their power to protect their members' interests, and must do nothing that would be liable to undermine their power."[41] This argues that the problems of the plant or industry, of vital concern to unions, are not necessarily eliminated by shifting ownerships. The trade union thinks essentially in terms of individuals and the power exercised over them on the job. To limit that power, or "to constitutionalize" it, is the job of the union, and as long as men are ambitious to advance or have a love of power the union's task will remain unfinished.

Unions, in the main, are concerned with day-to-day problems. Their attitudes are influenced by the economic, political and social conditions in which they operate. Writers who have developed theories of labor have sometimes seized upon certain aspects of union organizations and have tended to overstress particular characteristics.

Unions cannot remain permanently anchored in their views or activities. Their survival depends upon their ability to adjust to changing circumstances. . . . Should they fail to protect the economic position of their members, their outlook and policies would inevitably undergo overhauling — not because their orientation is wrong but because it may not be suitable under all circumstances. American unionism has a philosophy of simple pragmatism. Such a philosophy is not as ostentatious and lacks the architectonic grandeur of philosophical systems such as Marxism. This perhaps makes American trade unionism less attractive to those who enjoy the aesthetic experience of beholding a beautiful intellectual system. However, the absence of these qualities helps to make the American movement more democratic, tolerant, and flexible. Trade unionism in the United States is a means of protecting the individual against arbitrary rule and raising his standard of living. While it may not rank high for philosophy, it deserves high score on the latter count.

NOTES

1. I am greatly indebted to Professors Milton Derber and David McCabe and to my colleague, Professor Caleb Smith, for a number of helpful suggestions.

2. Lujo Brentano, "On the History and Development of Gilds," *English Gilds.* Edited by Toulmin Smith (London: Early English Text Society, 1870), p. clxv.

3. *Ibid.,* p. xlvi.

4. Sidney and Beatrice Webb, *The History of Trade Unionism* (London: Printed by the Authors for the Students of the Workers Educational Association, 1919), p. 1.

5. *Ibid.,* p. 6.

6. *Ibid.,* p. 26.

7. *Ibid.,* p. 31.

8. *Ibid.,* p. 41.

9. A. Lozovsky, *Marx and the Trade Unions* (New York: International Publishers, 1942), p. 16.

10. Karl Marx and Frederick Engels, *Manifesto of the Communist Party* (Chicago: Charles H. Kerr and Company, no date), p. 26.

11. Oscar Testut, *L'Internationale* (Paris: E. Lachaud, 1871), p. 126. Lozovsky, *op. cit.,* p. 16.

12. G. M. Stekloff, *History of the First International* (London: Martin Lawrence, Ltd., 1928), p. 84. Italics in source.

13. Oscar Handlin, *Boston's Immigrants, 1780–1865* (Cambridge: Harvard University Press, 1941), p. 132.

14. *Ibid.,* p. 66.

15. Letter in Allen S. Will, *Life of James Cardinal Gibbons* (Baltimore: John Murphy Co., 1911), p. 153.

16. Robert Hoxie, *Trade Unionism in the United States* (New York: D. Appleton and Co., 1928), p. 34. The first edition was published by D. Appleton & Co., 1919.

17. *Ibid.*

18. *Ibid.,* p. 35.

19. John R. Commons, *Labor and Administration* (New York: The Macmillan Co., 1913), p. 261.

20. John R. Commons, *Legal Foundations of Capitalism* (New York: The Macmillan Co., 1924), pp. 311–312.

21. Sidney and Beatrice Webb, *Industrial Democracy* (London: Longmans Green & Co., 1911), p. 560. Italics supplied.

22. *Ibid.,* p. 561.

23. *Ibid.,* p. 561.

24. *Ibid.,* p. 562.

25. *Ibid.,* p. 575.

26. The term "collective bargaining" was first used by Beatrice Potter, (Mrs. Sidney Webb) in *The Cooperative Movement in Great Britain* (London: 1891), p. 217.

27. *Ibid.,* p. 174.

28. Lassallean socialists merged with the Marxists in the 1870s.

29. Hoxie, *op. cit.,* p. 47.

30. *Ibid.,* p. 50.

31. Commons, *Labor and Administration,* p. 149.

32. *Ibid.,* p. 151.

33. *Ibid.,* p. 152.

34. *Ibid.,* p. 87.

35. John R. Commons, *The Economics of Collective Action* (New York: The Macmillan Company, 1950), pp. 26–27.

36. *Ibid.,* p. 27.

37. Selig Perlman, *A Theory of the Labor Movement* (New York: Augustus Kelley, 1949), pp. 280–283. The first edition was published by Macmillan, in 1928.

38. *Ibid.,* p. 275.

39. J. B. S. Hardman, "The Mind of Labor, Ideas and Leadership," *American Labor Dynamics* (New York: Harcourt, Brace & Co., 1928), Edited by J. B. S. Hardman, p. 284.

40. Webb, *Industrial Democracy,* p. 826.

41. Hugh Clegg, *Labour in Nationalised Industry* (London: Victor Gollancz, 1950), pp. 9–10.

Trade Unionism and the General Interest: A Theory of Positive Public Policy Toward Labor

JACK BARBASH
University of Wisconsin

Historically, public policy toward labor has reflected mainly the legislative and political pressures exerted by employers and unions for the reenforcement of their bargaining positions toward one another. This commentary undertakes to mark a shift in public policy orientation from a pressure group response toward the assertion of a more autonomous interest, neutral as between the claims of business and unions. Positive public policy is the shorthand term employed to designate this new orientation.

I

The Great Depression marks the divide in the direction of public policy toward labor from "probusiness" to "pro-union." In 1932 Edwin E. Witte characterized the prevailing law of labor-management relations as permitting the

> employers for all practical purposes [to] enjoy complete freedom of combination in their dealings with employees. This extends not merely to the organization of corporation and employer associations but to the methods used by them to combat labor combinations. They can deal with unions or not as they see fit. In times of trouble they have a free hand to employ strikebreakers or refuse to employ workmen because of union

membership and, to all practical intents and purposes, can with immunity resort to the blacklist if they so choose.[1]

There were some countertrends during this period. The declaration in section 6 of the Clayton Act (1914), "that the labor of a human being is not a commodity or article of commerce," was initially understood by the labor movement as the "magna charta" which would free it from the bitter affliction of the labor injunction in federal courts. This did not in fact happen until the Norris-LaGuardia Act was passed in 1932. President Wilson's policy for disputes settlement during World War I embodied an unprecedented support for union organization to a degree that the union membership would not be surpassed until after the New Deal era. Although the Railway Labor Act of 1926 established procedures for disputes settlement and protected the railroad workers' right to collective bargaining, it permitted the company union in effect to coexist with the free union. Finally, after years of agitation in union and liberal legal circles, the Norris-LaGuardia anti-injunction act of 1932 ushered in a pro-union period — pro-union in the sense of rectifying procedural inequities weakening the union collective bargaining position.

Norris-LaGuardia was followed in 1933 by section 7a of the National Industrial Recovery Act (NIRA), pressed for by the unions as the

From the *Wisconsin Law Review*, No. 4, 1970, pp. 1134–1144. Copyright © University of Wisconsin, Madison. Used with permission.

price for their support of the NIRA as a whole. The high point of pro-unionism came with the enactment of the Wagner Act (National Labor Relations Act) in 1935 and particularly with its constitutional validation in 1937.[2] The Wagner Act was probably the single most important influence in the ascendance of union power in mass production collective bargaining.

The ebb of union influence and the rise of business influence on public policy toward labor came with the Taft-Hartley Act (the Labor-Management Relations Act of 1947). Taft-Hartley took over most of the pro-union provisions of Wagner but reinstated protections for the employer in the collective bargaining process, thereby reflecting the heavy pressure from business on the first Republican majority in the Congress since 1930. The 8(b) provisions of Taft-Hartley dealing with union unfair labor practices implemented a new legislative finding that "experience has further demonstrated that certain practices by some labor organizations, their officers, and members" can also "impair the interest of the public."

The Labor-Management Reporting and Disclosure Act of 1959 (Landrum-Griffin) represented a mixed bag of interests: on the one hand, the amendments to Taft-Hartley in title VII strengthened employer protections against union secondary boycott practices; on the other, a new order of interests emerged — the protection of individual rights of union members vis-à-vis union officers. For the most part the AFL-CIO supported the principle and much of the detail in this title of the law, as did many members of Congress commonly identified with pro-union voting records. There was, to be sure, support from employers who were perhaps less interested in union democracy as such than they were in what the institution of union democracy would presumably bring about, i.e., the weakening of union power from below. The wave of rank and file discontent of the late 1960s proved to employers, however, that that which weakens the union does not necessarily help management. In

fact, a weakening of union leadership lowers union capacity to come to agreement with the employer, thereby also weakening management. The Landrum-Griffin law in seeking to correct the power imbalance between union leadership and membership cut across the conventional union versus management alignment. This aspect of the law, it is argued here, signals the emergence of a new public policy toward labor.

II

Resolution of manpower, inflation and civil rights issues represent the fuller development of this new bent of public policy which displaces the traditional union versus management questions in the center of the policy arena. Manpower policy as embodied in the series of manpower acts since 1961[3] traverses the traditional union versus management alignment because it enhances the protective interests of both by increasing worker productivity and mobility through education, training, retraining and guidance, and, further, by strengthening the institutions of the labor market to achieve a better fit between the structure of supply and the structure of demand. In its reactive phase manpower policy responded to the immediate urgencies of depressed areas, youth unemployment, technological unemployment and the "competitively disadvantaged unemployed, underemployed, low income earners, youth, older workers, nonwhites, those with low educational levels, etc."[4] . . .

Wage-price policy does not offer as clear cut a case of neutrality between the relative claims of unions and employers. The union view is that the wage-price policy is likely to be more wage repression than price control. There is further, nothing like a consensus as to whether the wage-price program should rely on deflation, "jawboning," "guidelines," or a "freeze," to list the remedies currently in vogue. However, corroborating the thesis that wage-price policy is value free in respect to the relative claims of unions and management are the strong support which wage-price policy has in "pro-union" intellectual circles,[5] and the willingness of the AFL-CIO to accept a wage-price policy in principle, even if the severity of requisite conditions is hardly distinguishable from outright rejection. . . .

Public policy regarding the protection of civil rights in the context of employment situations is embodied in Title VII of the Civil Rights Act of 1964[6] and in the president's authority to prescribe standards for federal procurement. The policy enforced against both management and unions speaks for the existence and ascendancy of a new pressure group, i.e., civil rights activists. It should be noted that although the Civil Rights Law was aimed in part against the unions, nevertheless "without the help and day-to-day work of the [union] legislative representatives . . . no civil rights legislation could have passed in any session of Congress."[7] The AFL-CIO, "keenly and painfully aware of the limitations imposed upon it by its structure" in applying sanctions against unions violating its own civil rights provisions, "turned to federal legislation as its primary instrument for wiping out discrimination. It is now an open secret that the fair employment practices section of the Civil Rights Act of 1964 was written into the law because of the bullheaded insistence of the AFL-CIO."[8]

Civil rights public policy has also undergone a shift from pure reactivism. In the earlier reactive stage, civil rights policy moved to prohibit discrimination in employment. But the reactive policy of no-discrimination has proved not to be sufficient in actually bringing together the black worker and the job. The initiating or positive posture of civil rights policy is demonstrated in the concepts of "outreach" and "affirmative action." These concepts recognize that policy objectives are not fulfilled simply by creating normal market incentives. Incentives alone have, in fact, proved to be inadequate to bring blacks to the job because they have lived so long out of the range of the conventional market incentive system.

In contrast, outreach and affirmative action therefore go beyond the incentive system to

establish, first, the right of black workers as a class to an equitable share in the full range of job opportunities and, second, the obligation of management and unions to implement that right on their own initiative. The Chicago and Philadelphia Plans and their variants amount to a multilateral undertaking among unions, employers, civil rights groups and/or federal government to provide construction jobs to black workers proportionate to their numbers. Sanctions for noncompliance consist of litigation, disruption and loss of federal contracts.

The above summary recital suggests two distinctive aspects of the theory of positive public policy. First, positive public policy seems to unfold in two stages. In the early reactive stage, public policy intervention, although neutral, is nevertheless determined by the frame of reference set by the union management disputants. In the subsequent initiating stage, intervention is based on new ground, relying less on the contentions of the parties and more on a presumed objective or "scientific" interest usually advanced by a government spokesman.

Second, positive public policy appears to assert an unprecedented concern with the *results* of collective bargaining and trade unionism. The expressions of public policy in the Norris-La-Guardia, Wagner, Taft-Hartley and Landrum-Griffin Acts reflect the theory that the regulation of the *processes* of collective bargaining and unionism would be sufficient to achieve the intended effects. In contrast, wage-price policy, civil rights and manpower undertake to define publicly acceptable *results* of collective bargaining and unionism. The underlying assumption of wage-price policy is that to allow even balanced collective bargaining to go its own way is likely to yield economic results incompatible with a stable price level, strong balance of trade and economic growth, and that some kind of external intervention is essential to achieve results compatible with economic policy objectives. Similarly, civil rights policy raises the question whether social peace does not require public intervention to protect the interests of Negro workers from the results negotiated by the white bargaining partners. Manpower policy gets at the results of the union-management relationship at the points of apprenticeship and other training periods which are deemed inconsistent with public policy interests in freer mobility.

The underlying economic theory is that the negotiations between the private parties do not sufficiently take into account the social costs of their bargaining results and that intervention is essential to make adjustments congruent with positive public policy. . . . The AFL-CIO and the National Association of Manufacturers both rejected an asserting and defining role for government with equal firmness.

Positive public policy has by no means displaced the pressure group interests; rather the two coexist. Republican appointees to the National Labor Relations Board are more likely to come down on the side of the employer in their decisions than are Democratic appointments and vice versa. . . . The key public policies toward labor, such as full employment, civil rights, manpower and wages and prices, are, however, now more likely to reflect an autonomous positive line than pressure group demands. Allowing for differences in pace and rhetoric, these key public policies are not likely to vary fundamentally in direction as between Republican and Democratic administrations.

III

The context in which positive public policy emerges may be termed the "post full employment economy" of the 1960s. Full employment[9] has displaced "slack demand, relative overproduction [and] insufficient investment" as the major economic problem because of the "ungovernable tendency of demand to outrun the economy's capacity to meet it without inflation and price rise"[10] — hence, the focus on wage-price policy. In turn, the achievement of around 96% employment has highlighted the

plight of the 4% unemployed, or the uncounted "nonemployed," who have not shared in the general affluence because of ethnic attachment, geographic location, lack of education and training, or some combination of these, and whose condition has been made all the more intolerable by the general affluence — hence, the importance of a manpower policy to alleviate the structural obstructions to full participation by these groups.

The civil rights movement gave force, meaning and organization to the previously inchoate resentment of the blacks. The rising political and social awareness of the Negro masses and the resultant threat of disruption moved the civil rights strategy from the reactive goal of nondiscrimination to the initiating goal of asserting the right to work of blacks as a class — hence, the importance of a civil rights policy.

The full employment condition has moderated class divisiveness which characterized earlier issues. As the mainstream of American business came to accept collective bargaining and to view unionism as a positive force in modern management, it moved from class struggle to problem solving. Management's new comprehension was facilitated by the profitability of enterprise in the era of full employment. Full employment by minority groups also made American business and unionism more amenable to the initiating role of public policy in the area of civil rights.

The evolution of economics from ideology to "science" made a broader consensus possible where before sharp division had prevailed. It was President Kennedy who, in his landmark Yale commencement speech, put his imprimatur on the political legitimacy of economics as science.

> The central problems of our times are more subtle and less simple. They relate not to basic clashes of ideology but to ways and means of reaching common goals — to research for sophisticated solutions to complex and obstinate issues. . . . What is at stake in our economic decisions today is not some grand warfare of rival ideologies which will sweep the country

with passion but the practical management of a modern economy.[11]

The glamor image of economics as a science has tarnished somewhat in more recent times because of the apparent inability of the discipline to grapple with inflation except by the old-fashioned remedies of wholesale deflation and unemployment.

The broader based public policy toward labor has come about because the pressure groups themselves have begun to take a broader and more long range view of their interests. The pressure groups have not, however, abandoned their protectivism but perceive more clearly now the relevance of protection to national policy and the longer run costs of intransigent protectivism. In economic terms the trade unions may be "superimposing upon their traditional, sectional direct bargaining with employers for money wages a new type of indirect bargaining through government for redistribution of real income."[12] In a generation the trade union movement has accordingly moved away from preoccupation with defensive reactions to antiunion measures such as the labor injunction, toward major emphasis on full employment and social welfare. For example, during the 1970 session of Congress, the AFL-CIO put the highest priority on "rising unemployment, occupational safety, environmental pollution, expanded health education, manpower training and antipoverty programs, skyrocketing interest rates and monetary policy reform, true bargaining rights for farm workers and situs picketing rights for the building trades."[13] Only the last item represents a conventional "pure" trade union issue.

Responsibility for the enlargement of trade union policy perspectives can be attributed largely to:

1. the achievement of something like a stable balance of power with business so that the trade union movement is able to perceive its security needs more broadly;

2. the demonstration since the era of the New Deal that public policy can serve as ally as well as adversary;

3. the emerging union awareness that the condition of the nation's economy has much to do with the effectiveness of the trade union performance;

4. the ascendancy of the more expansive industrial union interest;

5. the growing public concern with unionism's power to inflict damage on the economy, a concern understandably less relevant to the underdeveloped unionism of a generation earlier.

Similar factors have been at work in broadening perspectives of modern business enterprise management. Having come to terms, more or less, with unions and collective bargaining, management need no longer view unions as a threat to the free enterprise system. Business has also come to terms with "aggregate demand" as essential for the effective planning of the industrial system.[14] A combination of a sense of social responsibility and the threat of disruption has brought businessmen into the center of the minority employment problem. Here again, business has not abandoned its profit maximizing behavior but has gradually widened its perspectives to take account of the longer run and the urgent need for social as well as economic viability.

Finally, to pull together the diverse strands of this section: The origins of positive public policy stem from the achievement of full employment in the 1960s; full employment gave credibility to economics as science; full employment brought the wage inflation issue to the fore; full employment dramatized, by contrast, the plight of the disadvantaged; the profitability of enterprise which resulted from full employment produced a relaxation of business opposition to the union's economic demands; in turn, full employment brought the unions relief from the insistent pressures of anti-unionism and unemployment and made possible a broadening of union sights. Ultimately, full employment transformed the public image of the union from an underprivileged mass to "big labor."

IV

Some caveats need to be entered against possible misinterpretation of the argument that public policy toward labor is moving from pressure group protectivism toward objective or positive public policy. First, it is no part of the argument that positive public policy necessarily yields results ultimately more genuinely in the public interest. The positive public policy model relates only to the attitudes of policymakers, not to whether, in fact, a better result will necessarily follow. Nor should it be inferred that pressure group public policy is by its nature incapable of yielding results which ultimately prove to be in the "true" public interest. The Wagner Act, for example, a response to a pressure group interest, nevertheless served a "true" public interest by redressing a grave imbalance of power favoring management. Further, the possibility cannot be disregarded that what now purports to be "objective" or "neutral" public policy as between one alignment of classes may over the long run evolve into a class serving ideology and form the basis for a bid for power by a "new class" of economic technocrats.

Finally, I do not intend to imply that conflict over labor problems is obsolete. What has happened, rather, is what might be called the rationalization of the labor problem, *i.e.,* traditional trial by struggle, rigid ideology, and trial and error behavior are giving way to rules, organization and expertise. Divergent interests inherent in labor disputes have not been eliminated — rather the methods of asserting those interests have simply been civilized. Similarly, labor and management are beginning to understand that not only do they have divergent interests, but that they also have interests in common.

Certainly, an assertion is not intended, nor are the above arguments to be construed as asserting the inherent superiority of the positive public policy approach over pressure group public policy. There are indeed many legitimate differences of interest among the pressure groups who have to do with the labor problem. These divergent interests should not be forced into synthetically "positive" molds. The evidence is far from clear that economics is yet sophisticated enough to displace pressure groups in wage determinations, and further, whether such a move would be worth the costs.

The advanced industrial nations of Western Europe came to positive public policy earlier than the United States. The need to repair the war-ravaged economies of Europe, the high priority placed on full employment and the more recent need to correct the inflationary effects of their post full employment era which began earlier than in the United States caused positive public policy to ripen earlier in Europe. . . .

The European experience, nevertheless, does not easily lend itself to adaptation in the United States. This country has not experienced the kind of common ordeal which unifies divergent interests. Moreover, the vastness and complexity of the American economy raise real questions as to the practical manageability of negotiating economic policy. Even if negotiation of national economic policy were feasible, the question remains whether it would be desirable or wise to vest such great power in the hands of pressure groups.

NOTES

1. E. Witte, *The Government in Labor Disputes* 80 (1932).

2. *NLRB* v. *Jones & Laughlin Steel Corp.,* 301 U.S. 1 (1937); *NLRB* v. *Fruehauf Trailer Co.,* 301 U.S. 49 (1937); *NLRB* v. *Friedman-Harry Marks Clothing Co.,* 301 U.S. 58 (1937); *Associated Press* v. *NLRB,* 301 U.S. 103 (1937); *Washington, Virginia, & Maryland Coach Co.* v. *NLRB,* 301 U.S. 142 (1937).

3. U.S. Dept. of Labor, *Manpower Report of the President* 193-97 (March 1970).

4. Studies by the Staff of the Cabinet Committee on Price Stability, Jan. 1969, at 26.

5. For example, the Kennedy "new economist," who in fact initiated in 1962 the first peacetime wage-price policy in the form of the Council of Economic Advisers' guideposts.

6. 78 Stat. 253, 42 U.S.C. § 2000 (e) (1964).

7. Clarence Mitchell, chief lobbyist of the NAACP in Washington, Excerpts from Speech at 14th Annual AFL-CIO National Conference on Community Services, AFL-CIO Release, May 20, 1969, at 1.

8. Tyler, *Contemporary Labor's Attitude Toward the Negro,* in *The Negro and the American Labor Movement* 365 (J. Jacobson, Ed. 1968).

9. Full employment is used as a term of art here because full employment has not been achieved in any literal sense. High level employment is more accurate, but also more cumbersome.

10. M. Postan, *An Economic History of Western Europe 1945–1964,* at 19 (1967).

11. *New York Times,* June 12, 1962, at 20.

12. Forsey, *Trade Union Policy under Full Employment,* in R. Lester, *Insights into Labor Issues* 312 (1948).

13. AFL-CIO, *Labor Looks at Congress,* 1970, at iii (D.C. The Federation, 1970).

14. J. Galbraith, *The New Industrial State* 31 (1968).

Entrepreneurship and Labor Relations at the Ford Motor Company

MARTIN J. GANNON
University of Maryland

RISING LABOR PROBLEMS: 1903-1913

The Ford Motor Company inauspiciously began major operations in 1903 at Strelow's plant, a reconverted wagon shop located on Mack Street in Detroit. Prior to this, Henry Ford had been a partner in some unsuccessful automotive endeavors: The Detroit Automobile Company and the premature Ford Motor Company. It was not until he associated himself with Alexander Malcomson and James Couzens that Henry Ford's operations began to function smoothly. . . .

His relationship with his workers at this time was on a personal basis. Ford's background as a farmer and mechanic led him to identify with his workers. At this time employment in automobile plants was specialized with the result that skilled craftsmen filled most of the positions. Moreover, Henry Ford was able to maintain this personal relationship with his workers until approximately 1909, at which time the Ford Motor Company began to have on their payroll more than 1000 individuals.[1] . . .

During the first few years of its existence the Ford Motor Company manufactured several makes of automobiles. However, it was not until 1909 that actual production began on the Model T. In 1910 the Ford Motor Company moved to the Highland Park Plant. The work force had grown to 2,773. Routinization of the work became the pattern. During the year 1913 Clarence Avery and William Klann introduced the concept of a conveyor belt, which made possible the assembly line. By this time dissatisfaction among the workers had resulted in huge turnovers. There was over 380 percent labor turnover in 1913 alone.[2] Undoubtedly mass production accelerated this trend, for no longer could most workers be accorded the status of skilled employees. Moreover, during the summer of 1913 grievances began to crystallize under the leadership of the International Workers of the World (IWW), a Communist-infiltrated union that appealed to immigrants, a large number of whom worked at Ford. Although small in number, this union served as a focal point for worker hostility. Finally, the country as a whole experienced a minor recession in 1913. For all of these reasons Henry Ford decided to combat the rising labor problems.

BENEVOLENCE: 1914-1920

The major event during the period 1914-1920 was the raising of wages from $2.34 to five dollars a day. On January 14, 1914, the announcement of the five-dollar day electrified the world. Over-

From *Marquette Business Review,* Summer 1972, pp. 63-75. Used with permission of the author.

night Henry Ford became known internationally as a defender of the worker.

As can be easily seen, there were undoubtedly business reasons for the implementation of the five-dollar day. An end to high labor turnover was an overriding consideration. Ford could acquire workers who were not recalcitrant but energetic in the fulfillment of their obligations.[3]

However, even though it is possible to impugn Henry Ford's motives in espousing the five-dollar day, nevertheless the host of other beneficial acts that he undertook during this period quickly dispelled most doubts as to his sincerity. In 1914 a Safety and Health Department was created. The year 1916 witnessed the opening of the Henry Ford Trade School. The popularity of this school was so great that in 1920 it had 15,000 applicants for 1500 positions.[4] Acceptance in the school was largely based on need.

A startling policy initiated during this period was the hiring of partially incapacitated workers, ex-criminals, epileptics, Negroes, and former inmates of mental hospitals. By way of contrast, no other large company had any policy comparable to this one. Moreover, it was not an ephemeral program, as even in 1934 approximately 20 percent of the Ford workmen were in the physically disabled class.[5] Such farsightedness was and is highly unusual, as even today tradition militates against the hiring of less than "normal" workers.

The Ford Sociology Department was an important part of the foundation of Henry Ford's benevolence. This Department acted as investigator of Ford's workmen in order to determine their eligibility for the five-dollar wage. It had, however, more than this function. It gave advice to the Ford workmen as to how they should budget their money. While this Department was to an extent paternalistic, the situation of the workers necessitated such activity. For example, after receiving their first five-dollar-a-day paychecks, Ford workmen were besieged at the gates of the Highland Park Plant by all types of predatory salesmen.[6]

Under the auspices of the Sociology Department the Ford Motor Company conducted a language school for its foreign-born workers. Through this method Henry Ford helped in the acculturation of many individuals who otherwise would have found the American society impersonal and unapproachable.

Another aspect of this period was the profit-sharing system Henry Ford evolved for his workers. In 1919 the Ford Motor Company sold investment certificates to its workers in units of $100. Returns on such investment went as high as 14 percent.

There were also minor indications of Henry Ford's benevolence which are noteworthy. For example, Ford opened grocery stores for his employees which, in 1919, were selling foodstuffs 25 percent below market prices. This action contrasts sharply with the company stores still in existence in some coal towns in the United States. Another point of interest is that the *Dearborn Independent,* the newspaper owned by Henry Ford, supported the union in the steel strike of 1919.[7]

Labor, for its part, reciprocated Henry Ford's good will. In 1918 he decided to run for Senator from the State of Michigan.[8] One of his ardent backers was the American Federation of Labor.

In capsule form, it can be said that Henry Ford was benevolent toward his workers during this period. Prominent historians, in fact, are of the opinion that the only major labor reforms made during the early part of the twentieth century were those carried out by Henry Ford.[9] It is an unfortunate fact that Ford's policies were not imitated by other business enterprises.

DISCIPLINE OF LABOR: 1921–1929

In 1919 Henry Ford bought out the minority stockholders of the Ford Motor Company. This action made him the virtual autocrat of the Ford Motor Company. . . .

Henry Ford in 1920, then, was surrounding himself with sycophantic executives. At the same time, many of the farsighted projects initiated by Henry Ford during the years 1914–1920 had premature funerals. Dean Marquis, the dynamic head of the Ford Sociology Department, tendered his resignation in 1922 when he realized that the interests of the workers were not being supported. Henry Ford then closed down the Sociology Department. The plant foremen were again dictators of the workers; they could fire employees with no fear of reprisal. Even the press was stifled, as William Brownell, the editor of the *Ford News* who was partial to labor, resigned on December 31, 1920, and was replaced by a promanagement spokesman.

At this juncture it is appropriate to discuss the "published" views of Henry Ford concerning consumption and the rights of labor. While it is true that the majority of books published under Henry Ford's name were written by ghostwriters, nevertheless there is a consistency in viewpoint concerning consumption and the rights of labor which is remarkable. Further, this consistency was not only promulgated in written works but actualized in Henry Ford's relations with his employees. An understanding of Henry Ford's views will help in explaining the apparent paradox and seeming illogicality of Ford's treatment of workers.

Henry Ford had an advanced conception of consumption theory which, although expressed in simple language, was almost Keynesian. The more money that management paid the worker, the more industry's products would be consumed. Industry would benefit, consequently, through the payment of high wages.[10]

In his treatment of workers, however, Henry Ford was not so open-minded. While he paid laborers high wages when they did work, he felt little or no responsibility to them if they were laid off.[11] The industrialist's primary service is to the public and not to the workers. To make the workers secure while business is in decline is to harm industry and indirectly the worker. Moreover, workers could always find jobs once industry, after a relapse, began to advance

again.[12] Such specious arguments were the basis of Ford's labor policy.

As indicated above, the workers had many grievances but few if any rights from 1921 until the establishment of the union at Ford Motor Company in 1941. After 1920 the workers were similar to low-grade soldiers in an army. Harsh discipline of workers became the standard practice.[13] . . .

A few words concerning Henry Ford's policies toward labor that were implemented during this period (1921–1929) are appropriate. In 1926, he became one of the first large capitalists to initiate the five-day week. This action, however, was a gift of doubtful validity, for there was an immediate speed-up of work, added insecurity on the job, and a reduction of wages which averaged four dollars a week.[14] In 1929 Henry Ford announced the seven-dollar day. Immediately following this announcement, however, he cut back his labor force by 25,000. On top of this, Henry Ford started to increase his use of suppliers who were paid on a wage scale much lower than his own. In 1929 he had contracts with 2200 outside suppliers; in 1930 the number rose to 3500, and by 1931 it had reached 5500.[15]

As has been emphasized, such actions were not in contradiction to Ford's philosophy of labor. Men have the right to high wages only when employed by the industrialist. Outside of this right Henry Ford believed that workers had prerogatives to little if anything else.

In this section the analysis of Henry Ford's relation with his workers has been pictured as negative in character from 1921 through 1929. However, it is to be noted that many companies treated their workers just as badly or worse than did the Ford Motor Company. Also to be noted is the fact that, when Henry Ford did undertake revolutionary labor policies, he was not emulated but openly scorned by the majority of industrialists. Owing to the environment, it causes little astonishment that Henry Ford bullied his workers and that he had no respect for seniority rights.

Unfortunately the good will that Henry Ford had established from 1914 through 1920 and had maintained, with much difficulty, from 1921 through 1929 was to be eliminated during the 1930s, at which time Henry Ford became actively hostile toward labor.

INTOLERANCE OF LABOR: 1930-1945

The period of intolerance opened in 1930 with nothing more devastating than an edict banning the drinking of alcoholic beverages. The Ford Service Police, however, were soon in full operation. Under Harry Bennett this group was to serve as the oppressor of the workers. By 1938 the number of Ford Service Police was to stand at approximately 3000 regulars. [16] . . .

Ford's entrepreneurial days were over. He was now acting as an anchor on the progress of the company. General Motors continually bested the Ford Motor Company in sales after 1929; in 1933 Chrysler through the Plymouth moved into second place behind General Motors. . . .

The Great Depression was naturally a salient factor during this period. Layoffs were inevitable in every industry. But it is significant that, in Detroit, resentment was crystallized around Henry Ford. In March of 1932 the Ford Hunger March took place. Only a few hundred men were actually participants in it. Their demands were, in terms of present practices, quite conservative: [17]

> In behalf of the Ford worker as such, the hunger marchers demanded jobs, the right to organize, reduction of speed-up, abolition of labor spies, elimination of "graft" in the hiring process, two daily 15 minute rest periods on the Ford line, a six-hour day without reduction in pay, an unemployment bonus of $50 per man and free medical treatment for Ford men and their families.

Instead of meeting a sympathetic group of Ford executives, the hunger marchers were greeted by a barrage of bullets directed at them by the Dearborn policemen, who were naturally under the influence of the Ford Motor Company. Four individuals were killed and over a score were wounded. There was a public outcry concerning this event. Labor conditions at the Ford Motor Company became worse as the nineteen thirties progressed.

In 1933 the Ford Motor Company was again enmeshed in a labor dispute when one of its suppliers, the Briggs Company, stopped production. It is notable that this was the first major strike of the depression. Moreover, the Briggs concern was, through a lease, working in Henry Ford's Highland Park Plant.

Many of the Briggs men had been working a 14 hour day for 10 cents an hour. They now demanded a nine hour day, compensation for dead time, and a daily wage of $3.60 for women and $4 for men. [18] In other terms, they wanted treatment equivalent to that practiced at the River Rouge Plant. This, however, was not forthcoming. Partially through the support of Henry Ford the strike was crushed.

Trouble with labor constantly plagued the Ford Motor Company from 1930 through 1945. On February 26, 1934, there was a strike against speed-ups at the River Rouge Plant. It was quickly ground under foot. The Ford workmen either submitted to conditions then in existence or else they left.

Henry Ford, the former friend of the worker, was gradually becoming the symbol of resistance. Nevins and Hill cite three major reasons for union opposition to Henry Ford during the 1930s. [19] First, the wage policy had collapsed. By 1940 Ford workers were actually being paid less than the employees of the other major groups in the automotive industry. [20] Second, the Ford Service Police terrorized the Ford workers. Beatings of workers were frequent. The Ford Motor Company, consequently, began to be primarily ruled out of fear for the job. [21] Third, the unions were aligned against Henry Ford because of his doctrinaire opposition to any form of labor organization. For these reasons, antagonism to Henry Ford expanded to incredible proportions.

Nineteen thirty-five was an important year for labor in America, as the Wagner Act was passed at this time. It established the first national policy of collective bargaining. Under the protection of this act the United Automobile Workers (UAW) initiated a systematic campaign to organize union shops in the automotive industry. By the end of 1937 the entire automotive industry except for the Ford Motor Company had accepted unions. No violence of major import had been necessary to accomplish this unionization. But the Ford Motor Company proved different and difficult.

On May 26, 1937, the UAW began its program to unionize the Ford Motor Company. Under the direction of Walter Reuther and Ed Frankensteen the union organizers planned to distribute circulars to the Ford workmen on their way home from work. It was on the bridge over the Miller Road, which leads to Gate 4 of the River Rouge Plant, that the well-known Battle of the Overpass occurred. Ford Servicemen were awaiting the advent of the union organizers. When Reuther and Frankensteen arrived they were besieged by press photographers. As their pictures were being taken, Reuther and Frankensteen were ordered to leave the bridge by the Ford Servicemen. Although they started to comply, they were attacked by the Ford Servicemen. Reuther, Frankensteen, and several others ended up in the hospital. Approximately one-half hour later a second group of union organizers arrived. Although it had a large segment of women in its number, the group was also assaulted by the Ford Servicemen.

Time was running out for the Ford Motor Company. However, Henry Ford's tactics of resistance were many and varied. By way of example, Bennett and Ford in 1938 manipulated Homer Martin, the first president of the UAW, into private negotiations. Through such a move they hoped to neutralize the UAW. When the executive members of the UAW became aware of these private talks, they impeached Homer Martin and elected R. J. Thomas as president.

Another tactic was the use of the familiar company union. Four company unions were organized at Ford in 1937 but they proved ineffectual.

A third tactic of significance was employed against workers in Ford plants which were located in St. Louis, Kansas City, Richmond and Long Beach in California. In 1937 Henry Ford appeared to have reversed his position by granting *de facto* recognition to the union at these plants. This stance brought the union out into the open. When the plants reopened for fall production, however, Bennett instituted lockouts and fired key union leaders. [22]

Despite these tactics Henry Ford was using borrowed time. By 1941 the UAW once again felt strong enough to organize the Ford Motor Company. All that was needed was a legitimate excuse for a strike. Such an incident occurred on April 2, 1941, when Harry Bennett discharged the eight Rouge employees who composed the grievance committee of the plant. The workers spontaneously began to walk off their jobs. Under the leadership of the UAW the workers surrounded the River Rouge Plant. They did not dare to stage a sitdown strike in the plant, as they realized that the Ford Servicemen would overpower them. However, the encirclement proved effective. On April 11 the Ford Motor Company capitulated.

The Ford Motor Company signed its first contract with the union on June 21, 1941. In an important sense 1941 was the critical year, as it was at this time that Henry Ford allowed the operation of the UAW in his plants. But the period of intolerance was destined to continue until 1945.

The span from 1941 through 1945 can be viewed from two levels: The intolerance by the Ford Motor Company of labor, and labor's intolerance of the Ford Motor Company. The first level is best illustrated in the case of Willow Run, a Ford plant located 35 miles outside of Detroit. This plant, which was to produce B24 bombers, was built in 1941. It had troubles from the beginning. The major problem was the housing of workers. Henry Ford did not want his workers living at Willow Run because it was a Republican district which enforced tax laws favorable to his interests. He believed that an influx of workers would be detrimental to him, since they would vote democratic and the tax laws would then be altered.[23] Through the efforts of the Federal Housing Administration this problem was eventually alleviated.

From 1941 through 1943, Local 50 of the UAW at the Willow Run Plant had untold difficulties. One man sat in judgment of the complaints of 35,000 workers. Turnover was the highest in the area. Things changed in November of 1943 when August Krech was appointed labor relations director. At this time Willow Run solved most of its labor problems and, under the plan mainly worked out by Charles Sorenson, initiated and sustained large-scale production of B24 bombers.

The second level of the span of time from 1941 through 1945, labor's intolerance of the Ford Motor Company, was best exemplified in the number of work stoppages which numbered 773 from the signing of the contract in 1941 until January 9, 1946.[24] The union regarded the company as an adversary; the workers activated work stoppages in violation of the contract.

In general, the span of time from 1941 through 1945 can be seen as a period of transition. The advent of Henry Ford II in 1945 was destined to even out the irregularities in the relationship between the company and the union.

TOLERANCE OF LABOR: 1945-19--

Henry Ford II was elected President of the Ford Motor Company in 1945. Although Henry Ford lived until 1947, his last few years were passed in relative calm away from the immediate operation of the company. It was at this time that the company was reorganized; Harry Bennett and the Ford Service Police were eliminated. An excellent example of this new outlook is provided by the history of labor relations at Ford Motor Company after 1945.

Immediately after taking office, Henry Ford II notified the union as to his plans concerning the contract negotiations scheduled to start in the near future. He wanted, he stated, two-way bargaining, that is, company security that the union would fulfill its part of the contract and union security that the company would perform in a comparable manner.[25] The Ford workmen were involved in countless unauthorized work stoppages. It was this aspect of the bargaining situation which was crucial.

This contract was negotiated with the usual amount of fanfare that is practiced in such relationships. Generally speaking, the contracts that the Ford Motor Company and the UAW have signed since this 1946 agreement are highlighted by their commonness rather than their uniqueness, since collective bargaining is industry wide. The salient point is that, by 1946, the Ford Motor Company and the UAW established two-way bargaining acceptable to both of them. The old antagonisms lost most of their lustre as mutual confidence gained prominence.

The renewal of confidence in the company through concrete two-way bargaining was strengthened by other projects. John Bugas, director of industrial relations, instituted the use of attitudinal questionnaires in order to discover silent grievances of the workers. Henry Ford II, although he never completed his senior year at Yale, had been a sociology major and had been influenced by the ideas of human relations. The active implementation of such activities as questionnaire distribution, formation of plant sports teams, and the expansion of company recreational facilities promoted an identification of the workers with the Ford Motor Company. The results were promising. Labor turnover dropped from 3.8 percent in 1946 to 2.2 percent in 1947; the national average in manufacturing in 1947 was 2.8 percent. Unauthorized work stoppages dropped from 94 in 1945 to 27 in 1946. Grievances were in decline at the same time: in 1946 there were 14,260 first-stage grievances, but only 11,207 in 1947.[26]

Formal recognition of the Ford Motor Company's excellent relationship with its workers was granted in 1948 when Henry Ford II received the Society for the Advancement of Management's Award for human relations in industry. In 1947 *Fortune* praised the company in the following manner:[27]

> No question about it, Ford is now doing a labor-relations job second to none in the tense Detroit area. How much Henry II's earnest excursions into "human engineering" have helped cannot be assayed, but certainly they haven't harmed.

This tolerance of labor has extended into the present. In 1952 the Ford Motor Company received the Award of Honor from the National Safety Council for its outstanding performance in preventing injuries to employees. Many of the farsighted projects which Henry Ford had espoused received renewed support, for example, the placement of physically handicapped workers, who numbered approximately 4100 at the River Rouge Plant in 1953.[28] . . .

DISCUSSION

The study of the decisions made in the Ford Motor Company in the area of product development and labor relations indicates support for Selznick's viewpoint that organizational decisions are permeated by personal values and that historical events have a strategic influence on performance.[29] Certainly the decisions made at the Ford Motor Company over a period of 50 years reflected the personal values and needs of Henry Ford. For example, we can see that Henry Ford had high ego-strength and, correlatively, a high degree of self-confidence. In fact, his degree of self-confidence can be considered to be excessive, for he was convinced of the correctness of his decisions in spite of the obvious disconfirmation of the

validity of his premises by actual sales figures. This high ego-strength and self-confidence probably resulted from his early success when he proved himself correct and his critics wrong regarding the production of the Model T. Such a high degree of self-confidence led to rigidity and resistance to change to the ultimate detriment of the company.

Henry Ford's labor relations policies also seemed to be the consequence of a distinct set of ideas. Apparently Henry Ford only recognized the right of workers to receive high wages when employed by the industrialist. If the workers were laid off, became sick, or were incapacitated, the industrialist had no obligation to provide for them. Such an outlook explains Henry Ford's antipathy to the unions who, according to Sumner Slichter, have the following goals:[30]

> Collective bargaining, as carried on by labor unions with employers, has two principal aspects. In the first place, it is a method of price-making — making the price of labor. In the second place, it is a method of introducing civil rights into industry, that is, of requiring that management be conducted by rule rather than by arbitrary decision. In this latter aspect, collective bargaining becomes a method of building up a system of "industrial jurisprudence."

In reference to price-making, Henry Ford was definitely ahead of his time, a fact evidenced by his introduction of the five-dollar day. Moreover, he supported workers through such far-sighted practices as the Ford Sociology Department and the hiring of partially incapacitated workers. Henry Ford, however, regarded such practices not as rights but privileges which could be and were withdrawn. In terms of the second aspect that is presented in the above statement — industrial jurisprudence — Henry Ford proved reactionary. Such a thing as industrial jurisprudence would destroy the rights of management whose safeguarding Henry Ford considered essential.

When Henry Ford II was elected President of the Ford Motor Company in the fall of 1945, he engineered many programs beneficial to labor. In a sense, the Ford Motor Company had come full circle from the days of the period of benevolence to those of the period of tolerance. This concept is given full expression in the following statement issued in 1955 prior to the agreement guaranteeing Ford employees the annual wage:[31]

> Years ago, when the elder Henry Ford instituted the $5-a-day wage, he was called everything from a madman to an anarchist by other American industrialists. We wouldn't be surprised to see Henry Ford II, who is fighting to take his company back to the top of the automotive heap, make as bold a move to win the favor of American workers as did his grandfather.

While it is difficult to make final generalizations, it seems that the application of Selznick's model would have benefited the Ford Motor Company. Neither Henry Ford nor his top executives such as Charles Sorenson explicitly outlined a systematic plan consistent with the needs, values, and history of the Ford Motor Company. If such a plan had been outlined, it is probable that the contradictory behavior and self-defeating activity of the Ford Motor Company would have been minimized both in the areas of labor relations and of product development.

NOTES

1. Allen Nevins with Frank Ernest Hill, *Ford: The Times, The Man, The Company*. Vol. I, New York, Charles Scribner's Sons, 1954, 648.

2. Henry Ford with Samuel Crowther, *Today and Tomorrow*. New York, Doubleday, Page, and Company, 1926, 161.

3. Keith Sward espouses this viewpoint, and with some justification. As he shows, in 1916 approximately 30% of Ford workers were making less than $5 per day. The prospect of attaining the five-dollar day and of keeping it fanned worker interest. Henry Ford later admitted that the five-dollar day was one of the finest cost-cutting moves the company ever made. Keith Sward, *The Legend of Henry Ford*. New York, Rinehart, 1948, 57–58; Henry Ford with Samuel Crowther, *My Life and Work*. New York, Doubleday, Page, and Company, 1922, 147.

4. Allen Nevins and Frank Ernest Hill, *Ford: Expansion and Challenge: 1915–1933*. Vol. II, New York, Charles Scribner's Sons, 1957, 341.

5. Federal Trade Commission, *Report on Motor Vehicle Industry*. House Document #168. Washington, U.S. Government Printing Office, 1939, 669.

6. Sward, *The Legend of Henry Ford*, 61.

7. *Ibid.*, 145.

8. *Ibid.*, 119.

9. John R. Commons and Associates, *History of Labor in the United States — 1896–1932*. New York, Macmillan, 1935, 79; and Walter Lippman, *Drift and Mastery*. Englewood Cliffs, Prentice-Hall, 1961, 57.

10. Ford with Crowther, *My Life and Work*, 126; Ford with Crowther, *Today and Tomorrow*. New York, Doubleday, Page, and Company, 1926, 151; and Henry Ford, *Things I've Been Thinking About*. New York, Fleming H. Revell, 1936, 8–9.

11. Sward, *The Legend of Henry Ford*, 226.

12. Ford with Crowther, *My Life and Work*, 47.

13. Nevins and Hill, *Ford: Expansion and Challenge: 1915–1933*, 517–519.

14. Sward, *The Legend of Henry Ford*, 175–176.

15. *Ibid.*, 219–220.

16. *Ibid.*, 371.

17. *Ibid.*, 233.

18. *Ibid.*, 221.

19. Allan Nevins and Frank Ernest Hill, *Ford: Decline and Rebirth, 1933–1962*, Vol. III. New York, Charles Scribner's Sons, 1963, 29.

20. Sward, *The Legend of Henry Ford*, 347–348.

21. *Ibid.*, 311.

22. *Ibid.*, 142 ff.

23. *Ibid.*, 433.

24. Benjamin M. Selekman *et al.*, *Problems in Labor Relations*. New York, McGraw-Hill, 1958, 362.

25. Two-way Bargaining Demand By Ford,'' *Business Week* (November 24, 1945), 93.

26. ''Human Engineering Program Pays Off for Ford,'' *ibid.*, (October 30, 1948), 89.

27. "Rebirth of Ford," *Fortune,* 35 (May 1947), 86.

28. Robert T. Ross, "Ford Plan for Employing the Handicapped," *Monthly Labor Review,* 53 (August 1941), 1299.

29. Philip Selznick, *Leadership in Administration.* White Plains, Row Peterson, and Company, 1957, 31–32.

30. Sumner Slichter, *Union Policies and Industrial Management.* Washington, The Brookings Institution, 1941, 1.

31. "Changing World of Labor," *Christian Century,* 72. (February 1955), 72.

Are We in a New Stage?

MILTON DERBER
University of Illinois

This paper deals with two interrelated questions: Are we in a new stage of industrial relations, and, if so, what should academicians and practitioners do about it?

Supporters of the new-stage theory fall into two opposing camps. One, reviewing developments in labor-management cooperation, quality-of-worklife programs, employee-owned enterprises, and, most recently, recession-based collective bargaining, has concluded that the long-time adversarial system is being significantly modified, if not replaced, by a more integrative, mutualistic approach. The other camp, hostile to the basic ideas of unionism and collective bargaining, argues that unions have been losing ground for over two decades, that unionized industries are declining while industries less susceptible to unionization are growing, and that the dominant trend of industrial relations is union-free.

In opposition to both of these new-stage theories are the supporters of what may be labeled the "rerun theory." These observers assert that

the traditional collective bargaining system is fundamentally as vital as ever, that as in the past it is responding pragmatically to the conditions of the economic environment, and that when the economy regains its health collective bargaining will return to its former aggressive and adversarial self.

Whether any of these positions or some mixture is correct cannot be determined simply by examining the short-run contemporary situation. American society and the entire world by which it is increasingly influenced are so dynamic and volatile that short-run scenarios by themselves are likely to be unreliable bases for long-term prediction.

I therefore turn first to this country's historical experience with labor organization. The primary lesson is that significant growth and advance in union organization have come in short periods (rarely exceeding four to five years), followed by somewhat longer periods of consolidation or retrogression. The rapid growth periods have invariably been the product of abnormal factors — war, economic crisis, or, as in the case of the most recent period involving the expansion of public-sector employee organization, a pervasive sense of inequity and discrimination within a major sector of the labor force. The subsequent longer plateaus or periods of decline appear to be partly a reflection of the need of

From *Proceedings of the Thirty-fifth Annual Meeting of the Industrial Relations Research Association,* Barbara Dennis, Ed., 1983, pp. 1–9. Reprinted with permission of the author and the IRRA.

institutions to digest and absorb the rapid-growth changes and partly a reflection of the counter-vailing forces at work in a pluralist society.

A second historical lesson is that in this vast, intricate, and variegated nation a uniform condition rarely prevails. Different types of industrial relations systems function side by side not only among different regions, but also in the same regions and locations.

A third historical observation is that most American employers and managers have accepted unions and collective bargaining out of necessity rather than conviction, and have generally perceived union participation in decision-making as a burdensome infringement on their functions and rights. As a result, organized labor's status, as Selig Perlman noted 50 years ago, has remained fragile and vulnerable except for short periods.

A fourth proposition is the increased impatience on the part of both organized labor and employers with self-governance and the tendency to turn to public agencies for help. As a result, both parties have often been unwilling to engage in cooperative efforts unless confronted by an external common enemy (that is, competition) or when the enterprise or industry finds itself in economic jeopardy.

Finally, I find in labor relations history continuing struggle over the distribution of industrial power and influence. The struggle has revolved around varied ideas at different times — socialism, producers' cooperation, management rights, employee representation, collective bargaining, etc. Some of the struggle has occurred in the political arena, most in the industrial realm.

That collective bargaining has been the chief institutional survivor to date testifies to its vitality and adaptability in the American environment. That it has been a minority force overall (although not in specific sectors) indicates that it bears limitations and weaknesses. It is a well-known fact that since the mid-fifties the percentage of union members in the labor force has

declined and that only the spectacular growth of unionization in the public sector and the conversion of associations — in education, health care, police, and civil service — to union-like programs have prevented the union decline from being more precipitous.

What do these historical observations suggest about the current evolutionary process of unionism and collective bargaining? The answer is mixed. On the one hand, it is clear that significant changes have occurred over time and further change can be reasonably expected.

On the other hand, the ability of unionism to rebound from setbacks and the resurgent capacity of the collective-bargaining system have been quite remarkable features of the past century. Unions are not institutions fixed in ideological concrete; they are pragmatic, realistic, flexible. They have modified their organizational structure, altered their functions, given ground as needed, and recovered as feasible.

If we turn our attention now to the contemporary scene, what evidence or arguments do we find to support either the ''new-state'' or ''rerun'' thesis?

The proponents of a more mutualistic collective bargaining system often rely on the following facts or propositions: (1) The widespread adoption of labor-management cooperation and quality-of-worklife programs. Autos, steel, communications, and clothing are illustrative, but numerous other less publicized cases can also be cited, ranging in concern from absenteeism, affirmative action, and alcoholism to productivity and protective legislation. (2) The large number of joint agreements freezing or reducing wages and benefits or making workrules more flexible in return for guarantees to stabilize jobs, to refrain from shutting down or relocating departments or plants, and to halt subcontracting. (3) The mounting interest of unions in the investment policies of pension funds and the growing belief that such funds should be used to foster collective bargaining and social objectives, not merely to maximize income. And (4) the growth of worker and union participation in company financial plans, such as profit-sharing, ESOPs, gain sharing, and company ownership combined with self-management.

The proponents of the opposite polar position — that the union-free system is becoming predominant — typically rely on the following facts or arguments: (1) The sharp fall in collective bargaining coverage since the mid-fifties to between 20 and 25 percent of the labor force. (2) The shift of population and industry from the highly unionized Northeast and Midwest to the less unionized South. (3) The drastic job-displacement effects in unionized industries of foreign competition and the new industrial revolution expressed in robotics, microelectronic equipment, and other technological innovations. (4) The rising concern with individual rights in both unionized and unorganized enterprises, as reflected in antidiscrimination legislation, sexual harassment regulations, and proposals to protect individual privacy and to assure due process in disciplinary matters. (5) The rise of a sophisticated body of management practitioners and consultants whose principal objective is to ward off union organization and to keep enterprises union free.

The response of the rerun school to both types of new-state theories is that similar phenomena can be found in the past, that they are either reactions to special conditions affecting particular industries or recurrent phases of familiar cyclical patterns. They assert that pay and fringe-benefit concessions have been a common feature of prior serious recessions and depressions and that strikes have typically declined in such periods. As to the so-called new industrial revolution, they contend that rapid technological change has frequently raised unwarranted fears of massive displacement and unemployment.

Fortified by these data and ideas, the rerun supporters reject the new-stage thesis and predict that when the economy recovers unions will regain members and bargaining power and collective bargaining will return to its traditional ways. Concession bargaining will be succeeded by catch-up bargaining.

Clearly, this is an issue that lends itself to persuasive arguments from a variety of perspectives. Each can turn to history for support. Each can detect in the current scene events and tendencies compatible with its position.

Let us therefore try to peer briefly into the future. In order to do so, we must consider some of the underlying environmental factors that help shape the ideas, values, and behaviors of the parties and, through them, the structure and processes of the system.

I start with demographic trends. We can be reasonably confident that the rate of increase in the labor force will decline in the nineties as the low-birth-rate cohorts of the sixties and seventies enter the market. But even that prediction assumes that the propensity of women to enter the labor force is approaching a saturation level, only a small section of the older work force will prefer employment to retirement, immigration will be controlled, and automation does not displace labor more rapidly than in the past. If the labor force shrinks, stabilizes, or grows more slowly than the demand for it, we can anticipate enhanced bargaining power for labor.

Technological displacement of workers has periodically been a matter of widespread concern, as it was in the late 1950s. The specter of robotics has again arisen, with some predictions that microelectronics will reduce manufacturing employment to a tiny fraction of its current level by the end of the century. The traditional response of economists has been that historically the fear of mass unemployment has been unjustified and that, instead of reducing the demand for labor overall, major technological innovation has led to reduced costs, increased demand for goods and services, and derivatively increased demand for labor. Nonetheless, serious industrial relations problems may arise out of technological advances because of the elimination of occupations or entire industries, necessary adjustments in compensation, and the need for retraining and relocation of displaced employees.

A third issue of potential significance involves the role of government. As long ago as 1948, in the first Presidential Address, to this Association, Edwin E. Witte warned about the excessive growth of "governmental intervention in labor-management relations" and its adverse implications for industrial self-governance. As the chief draftsman of numerous Wisconsin labor laws as well as of the Society Security Act, Witte was by no means opposed to essential protective and regulatory legislation, but he was gravely disturbed by the increasing tendency of the parties to turn to government to achieve their goals.

Self-governance has not only been threatened by the actions of the parties themselves, but has also been challenged by the increasing tendency of individuals and minorities to seek protection of their interests in legislation and the courts. If this trend continues, the collective bargaining system will become increasingly legalized. There is the further likelihood that the unions and companies will divert more and more of their resources and talents from the industrial to the political and judicial arenas.

If increasing legalization poses a major threat to the current industrial relations system, spreading internationalism is a principal economic force for the future. Economic internationalism impacts our industrial relations system in several ways. One is the flow of jobs. So far, at least, it has probably shifted more jobs out of the United States than it has directed to this country. But some reverse flow is occurring, and this is likely to increase. Foreign competition within the American product market has grown substantially, with devastating effects on numerous industries. For the long run, it may stimulate American firms to become more efficient and innovative, although many enterprises and even

entire industries may become permanent victims. Whichever way the economic pendulum swings, the internationalization process bears with it, as my colleague Adolf Sturmthal recognized long ago, a transfer and enrichment of ideas about industrial relations. We are less naive than we used to be about such transfers. In the fifties, many people seriously believed that a simple shift of the principles of the American industrial relations system would resolve the problems of developing countries. Today some believe that American adoption of certain Japanese practices would resolve our problems. More realistically, there promises to be an enlarged sensitivity to ideas from abroad and a willingness to try them out cautiously and piecemeal.

These strategic factors lead me to the belief that although many of the changes resemble past events, the magnitude of the changes affecting so many of our major industries justifies the conclusion that we are, indeed, in a new stage. I am inclined toward a scenario of continued rapid technological advances powered by strong international competition, spot shortages of skilled labor, and little relief in the scale of governmental intervention. Should such a scenario materialize, I would anticipate some significant tilting in the mutualistic direction, partly out of increased trust between employers and union leaders, but mainly because in many industries the parties will continue to be confronted by strong external competitors and conditions which represent threats to their very survival. This development will be reinforced by irresistible pressures toward greater employee participation in decision-making. As in the past, a variety of forms or stages of industrial relations will continue to function at the same time, and unionism and collective bargaining will continue to be firmly entrenched in major segments of American industry.

But this is little more than guesswork. Who can gainsay the possibility of an international economic collapse, the outbreak of more warfare, the emergence of new OPECs, or (more op-

timistically) a new era of scientific and technological advance and economic prosperity?

THE CHALLENGE

I turn now to the second question: If there is, indeed, the possibility that we may be in a new
stage, what can and should academicians and
practitioners do about it?

For academicians, the challenge is twofold.
First, in order to adequately explore the basic
question, given the changing conditions and the
factual uncertainties described earlier, there is
need for more comprehensive and more reliable
data.

However, while facts are essential, they are
not sufficient. To give them analytical meaning
and to develop them as useful predictive tools, effective general conceptual or theoretical frameworks are needed. This is a facet of industrial
relations scholarship that has been neglected in
recent decades in the United States — more so
than in a number of other countries. . . . In such a
time it is essential to subject to critical analysis the
assumptions and values that are the foundation
posts of contemporary thought. . . .

Professor Kochan identifies and briefly
discusses four broad approaches: the orthodox
pluralist built around collective bargaining, the
Marxist, the neoclassical labor market, and the
consensus based behavioral. He suggests the need
for an expanded and revised version of the
prevailing pluralist perspective.

It is not necessary to accept this formulation,
or any one of the four approaches, to appreciate
its utility. Its significance lies in the attention it
focuses on the values and assumptions which
every researcher, interpreter, or participant
bears, consciously or not, and on the choice of
variables and factors for empirical study and
analysis. The validity of the decisions made in
these respects is far more important than the
precision of measurements or the accuracy of
descriptive details. . . .

In brief, I conclude that for the foreseeable
future it will be to the advantage of the industrial
relations field if academicians pursue a variety of
conceptual frameworks and tools, but do not ignore the perspectives of others. Clashes of ideas,
challenges to opposing views, receptivity to possible borrowings are, in my judgment, essential for
the benefit of all.

I turn finally and briefly to the practitioners
(particularly major decision makers and their
aides) who are the principal actors of the field. If
we are indeed in a new stage of industrial relations, how should such practitioners respond?
Like the academicians, they must also respond to
changing conditions; they simply cannot afford to
assume that what worked in the past will continue
to serve their needs. At the same time they must
avoid a reliance on fads which have limited enduring value.

The field can point to a number of experienced practitioners who have contributed importantly to the theory of industrial relations —
Frederick Taylor, Louis Brandeis, Morris
Cooke, Chester Barnard, Clinton Golden, and
Wilfred Brown, among others. Most practitioners, however, lack the time and disposition to
respond in theoretical ways and focus instead on
day-to-day or short run problems of their
organizations. They are more inclined to rely on
professional advisers, either within their
organizations or from outside academic or consultative agencies, for conceptual guidance of a
longer-range nature. Or (more likely) they will
rely on the traditional ways of thinking that they
acquired in their developing years. I would suggest that a rethinking of their own approaches and
a serious consideration of opposing ones are in
order, for from them will flow major critical
organizational and public positions and decisions.

In any discussion of basic perspectives, it is
easy, in a short presentation, to oversimplify.
However, my aim here was not to elaborate on
the numerous alternatives, but rather to stress the

obvious point that different approaches are likely to lead to different behaviors. The manager, union official, or minority group leader who has an explicit awareness of his or her conceptual framework may be better equipped to respond to the problems of fundamental change in the world of practice as the academician is in the spheres of research and teaching.

The New Industrial Relations

With the adversarial approach outmoded, the trend is toward more worker involvement in decisions on the shop floor — and more job satisfaction, tied to productivity.

Quietly, almost without notice, a new industrial relations system with a fundamentally different way of managing people is taking shape in the U.S. Its goal is to end the adversarial relationship that has grown between management and labor and that now threatens the competitiveness of many industries.

The coming of the Industrial Revolution to the U.S. 150 years ago created a profound shock that is still being felt. From the 1830s well into the 20th century, the nation experienced periodic outbreaks of "the labor problem," troubles that accompanied the acculturation of great masses of pre-industrial immigrants and rural migrants into the harsh discipline of the factories and mines. Today's industrial relations system still contains elements that were jerry-built then to deal with work force instability: manual jobs fragmented into simple tasks, foremen with awesome disciplinary powers, and a deeply rooted sense that a wide gap separated those who work from those who manage.

But the changed social values and high educational levels of today's younger labor force, combined with economic strains are putting massive pressure on that obsolete system. Increasing numbers of companies and unions are leading a march away from the old, crude workplace ethos and the adversarial relationship it spawns.

The change will bring current work psychology almost full circle from where it was only 35 years ago, when Elton Mayo, a pioneer work sociologist at Harvard University, accused American management of accepting a "rabble hypothesis" in dealing with workers. Most managers, Mayo wrote, used the wrong incentives to gain labor's cooperation because they viewed employees as a "horde . . . actuated by self-interest" — a money-grubbing rabble with no group loyalty or social goals.

A more enlightened view of worker psychology has taken hold today. It stresses that most people want to be productive and will — given the proper incentives and a climate of labor-management trust — eagerly involve themselves in their jobs. This calls for a participatory process in which workers gain a voice in decision-making on the shop floor. Many companies, some in collaboration with once hostile unions, are creating new mechanisms to gain worker involvement. Among these mechanisms are "self-managed" work teams, labor-management steering commit-

Reprinted from the May 11, 1981, issue of *Business Week* by special permission. © 1981 by McGraw-Hill, Inc.

tees in union shops, problem-solving groups — such as "core groups" or the quality circles that are widely used in Japan — and redesign committees that wed social and technical ideas in designing or rearranging plants.

The concepts behind these innovations are not new; social cooperation at work surely predates recorded history. But organized labor's growth as a deeply adversarial institution in the U.S. coupled with management's retention of obsolete methods of controlling workers — Frederick Taylor's "scientific management" approach, for example — have blinded both sides to their mutual interests. Only a few years ago, work innovations were looked upon as slightly bizarre, if interesting, projects that "couldn't produce any bottom-line results," as Jerome M. Rosow, president of Work in America Institute Inc., puts it.

But evidence is growing that quality-of-work-life (QWL) programs, as some companies and unions call them, can meet their twin goals of increasing job satisfaction and improving quality and productivity. Moreover, the convergence of two major trends is forcing companies and unions to change their ways.

The 'Baby-Boom' Generation

One trend, social and demographic in nature, consists of increasing demands by better educated workers at all levels for more challenge on the job and for participation in decision making. The "baby-boom" generation, which brought radically changed values to the workplace, now just about dominates the labor force. The second trend is economic — the slower growth, declining productivity, and tougher worldwide competition that is shrinking so many basic U.S. industries. These forces must be dealt with, and, increasingly, business and labor are realizing that solving "people problems" is as important as generating capital and introducing new technology. And, as Rosow says, "adversity is a tremendous motivator."

Until recently, the work innovation movement in the U.S. has progressed slowly. The 1950s and 1960s brought increased research and the development of theories on worker psychology. By the early 1970s, corporations such as General Motors, Procter & Gamble, and General Foods had started work improvement programs. Now, the movement has graduated from the experimental phase. Hundreds of companies, profiting from what was learned by forerunners, are trying to redesign jobs and work processes. In the early years, unions feared — and many still do — that these programs would undermine their relevance and position in the workplace. But three of the largest unions — the United Auto Workers, United Steelworkers, and Communications Workers of America — are now involved in what are essentially industrywide projects in their industries.

Richard E. Walton of Harvard, a consultant and an authority on work improvement projects, believes that the last few years have produced a value shift in American industry. In society at large, he says, a return to a "let-the-environment-be-damned" attitude is unlikely. "In the same way, we're not going to treat the psychological and social costs of producing goods and services as if they're the fault of the individuals involved but of the system," he says. "This shift will ebb and flow, but the quality of work will be much more of a concern than it was 10 years ago."

"I'm absolutely convinced that the future of collective bargaining is in quality-of-work-life," says Irving Bluestone, a retired UAW vice-president who is the premier union champion of work innovations. While this is the rhetoric of an advocate, Bluestone's intuition about the growth of the QWL movement has proved correct in the past. In the early 1970s, he was its only supporter on the UAW's 26 member executive board, and he often was criticized for it.

Today, a majority of the board supports worker involvement programs at GM, Ford, Chrysler, and other UAW companies. Labor relations in the entire industry are becoming much more collaborative. But the UAW and the companies have not given up any rights in bargaining contracts. "We can be cooperative on the plant floor and adversarial at the bargaining table," Bluestone says.

Quality Circles

Aside from union-management relations, the workplace is changing in an even more profound way. "It's a real fundamental change in the way we manage people," says Paul W. Chaisson, director of human resources at Malden Mills, a textile manufacturer in Lawrence, Mass. "There's no longer management turf and worker turf," he says. "There's just a sharing of the management of the business, and there's such a thirst among the workers for this process, it's amazing."

The sudden thirst among companies for a quick splash of "consensus management," as practiced successfully in Japan, raises the danger that work redesign will become too faddish. In the 1950s, the Japanese began using an American concept neglected in the U.S. — the quality circle, a committee of workers that analyzes and solves quality problems. Some 200 U.S. companies now have quality circles. Ted Mills, president of the American Center for the Quality of Work Life, warns that a too hasty application of the concept in U.S. companies would smack of the "American 'quick-fix' mentality" and could harm the entire QWL movement.

But the important work innovations in the U.S. are by no means imitations of a Japanese model; they represent an authentic American movement of employee involvement in production related decisions on the plant floor. The movement also differs considerably from the European system of codetermination, in which worker representatives sit on corporate supervisory boards. Although UAW President Douglas A. Fraser is a Chrysler Corp. director, his election to the board was a singular quid pro

quo for UAW wage concessions. "We want participation from the bottom up," says Glenn E. Watts, president of the Communications Workers. "I don't want to sit on the board and be responsible for managing the business. I want to be free as a unionist to criticize management."

There is no longer any question that significant change in the workplace is under way — and not only in heavy industry. Work improvements are being instituted in supermarkets, schools, banks, and government offices, among other places. Whether this will be a lasting change — a continuing process, instead of a "program" with a termination date — depends on whether American management and labor leaders are willing to risk short term profits and political gains to produce long-term change.

THE BUILT-IN OBSOLESCENCE IN TODAY'S SYSTEM

The risks involved in work innovations are worth taking if labor and management hope to respond to the nation's shift in social values and its economic stagnation. The dimensions of the economic problems are well-known: high unemployment and inflation, the decline of basic industries — such as steel, autos, apparel, electrical equipment — because of foreign competition, and a flattening out of a once-high productivity growth.

The social forces that play some part in the productivity slowdown and that call for major changes in the industrial relations system are less well understood. A major factor is the growing influence of the baby-boom generation — people born from 1946 through the early 1960s — on work values. It came to maturity during a period of unparalleled prosperity and social turmoil and therefore brings far different expectations to the job than the generation that grew up during the Depression. Daniel Yankelovich, who heads the research firm of Yankelovich, Skelly & White, describes the younger generation as more concerned with personal growth and enjoyment of work and leisure.

Based on interviews with 3500 families last year, Yankelovich contends that 40% of the labor force is composed of workers who belong to new work-value groups. One new-value group dislikes formal job structures and rejects money as a substitute for fulfillment; the primary objective of the second group is to earn money not for the sake of money but to buy a certain lifestyle. Once that is achieved, this group tends to hold back on the job. Most important, says Richard Balzer, a vice-president of the Yankelovich firm, a large part of the younger generation "can't return to the traditional 'keeping your nose to the grindstone' when hard times come because they've never known hard times."

Older generations tend to bemoan a perceived loss of the work ethic among younger workers and demand a return to a mythical golden era of hard work. But all studies of people's commitment to productive work indicate a "strong affirmation of the value of work," says Michael Maccoby, director of the Washington-based Project on Technology, Work & Character. However, Maccoby and an associate, Katherine A. Terzi, conclude in a recent study that changes in society "have changed the social character so that it is less frightened and submissive, more self-affirmative and critical of inequity." This suggests strongly that U.S. industry must reorganize work and its incentives to appeal to new worker values rather than try to retrofit people to work designs and an industrial relations system of 80 years ago.

'Living in the 1930s'

This old system, with its built-in conflicts, encouraged the perception that "head work" was the responsibility of managers only. "We're still living in the 1930s world, paying for the use of a worker's hands and not what he can offer mentally," says Alfred S. Warren Jr., industrial relations vice-president of General Motors Corp.

Adds Michael Sonduck, corporate manager of work improvement at Digital Equipment Corp.: "One of the most dehumanizing assumptions ever made is that workers work and managers think. When we give shop-floor workers control over their work, they are enormously thoughtful."

The rise of industrial unionism in the 1930s reduced corporate power over workers, ended unfair treatment on the job, and gave workers a voice in wages and working conditions through bargaining. But the unions continued to operate with a 1930s philosophy, demanding rules to spread the work and limit management's flexibility. This only strengthened management's resolve to tighten controls over workers. Moreover, unionism has done little to insert the worker into his work or give him pride in quality, largely because the unions have not demanded a voice in reorganizing the work structure — and undoubtedly would have been rebuffed by management if they had.

What resulted was a sharp adversarial relationship between management and labor. "Workers and management are seen to have diametrically opposed interests," writes University of Michigan sociologist Robert E. Cole in *Work, Mobility & Participation,* a 1979 book comparing Japanese and American labor practices. In Japan, workers view the corporation as "the sustaining force" of their lives and therefore eagerly cooperate with management. But in the U.S., Cole says, "management writes off worker cooperation because it is seen as either irrelevant or impossible to achieve."

Increasing numbers of company, union, and academic authorities are coming to believe that a new industrial relations system must include three basic elements:

○ The development of a nonadversarial relationship on the shop floor, so that workers and bosses can collaborate on means and methods of production by circumventing adversarial procedures, such as grievance mechanisms. This need not violate union contracts or prevent unions from negotiating wages and benefits, but greater cooperation at the production level will involve workers in the business to a much greater extent.

○ A reform of bargaining, based on a mutuality of interests developed on the shop floor. This work-level cooperation might well slip over into the bargaining process, particularly if unions — reflecting the concerns of their members — tie themselves more tightly to the success of the individual company, rather than try to keep up with national wage patterns and outdo other unions.

○ A thoroughgoing change in management style in which the traditional top-to-bottom hierarchical form of decision-making is replaced with a participation process. Decisions should be pushed to ever-lower levels, thereby encouraging employees, by extension, to become involved in the business itself. But this would also mean that management must share information with workers, divide with them the gains resulting from increased participation, and work much harder to provide job security and to prevent the catastrophic blows of unexpected plant shutdowns.

. . .

THE NEW APPROACH IS ALREADY AT WORK

In a cramped, noisy section of a General Motors plant near Dayton, an experiment involving an eight member work crew is testing the effectiveness of a sophisticated form of worker participation. The crew is stationed at the end of a production line in which foam rubber car seats are formed in aluminum molds. Bending over a hot conveyer line, the workers use short hoe-like tools to scrape off excess rubber "buns" that have extruded through bleeder holes in the molds. Then they remove the cushions and toss them on to another conveyor for shipping. All day long they scrape and toss, a job that plant manager Donald W. Birdsall describes as "demeaning."

To relieve the monotony of this job and to reduce costs, GM two months ago implemented a worker suggestion that had been made through a process known as the Socio-Technical System. The STS concept, developed some years ago in Britain, is a method of integrating workers' ideas for improving a job with technical requirements set by engineers. At GM's Inland Div. plant in Dayton, this process meshes the ideas of 30 hourly and salaried workers who serve on social and technical task forces, and often the "human" considerations carry equal or greater weight than the technical.

Improved Morale

In the early years of work innovations, complex projects with twin goals such as those at Inland were rare. Some managers and consultants designed programs with the primary goal of improving the human aspects of work; others insisted on an "economic" goal, such as increasing productivity. And some companies wanted to shower workers with paternal attention to keep the unions at bay. The improvement projects of the past 15 years have helped narrow the focus of the programs and have provided many lessons for today's programs.

The Socio-Technical System, for example, has mostly been used in designing new plants, where planners can start from scratch. It is more difficult to apply it to an existing plant, but Inland's management thought STS would be a useful method of getting worker involvement in redesigning the seat cushion department. General Manager George Johnston believes strongly that "you gain the commitment of people when you involve them in decisions."

Local 87 of the United Rubber Workers,

which represents 5400 workers at Inland, is cooperating with GM in implementing the system. Management pledged that it would not undermine the union's contract or result in job loss. It took two years of exploratory discussions before union and management leaders decided that they could work together in complete trust. But now, says Local 87 President William Hutchins, known as "Red," "there's a less hostile environment than there's ever been."

Hutchins and two assistants, along with several plant superintendents, serve on a Redesign Committee that makes the final decision on task force proposals. Two months ago, it approved a plan by Robert Gibson, an 11-year veteran of the boring job on the so-called demold line, for improving the job and reducing costs — an example of how human and economic goals can coincide.

Gibson suggested that GM expand the work crews from seven to eight members and create the new job of a trouble-shooting monitor who would chart material usage and scrap production. The crew members rotate as the monitor, serving a week at a time before returning to the production line. Gibson contends that a hoped for reduction in absenteeism, along with material and scrap savings, will more than offset the $30,000-per-year cost of adding a member to the crew. If the plan proves out in a current trial run, it will be used on four production lines involving 100 workers.

"Before STS started, it was always us against them [management]," Gibson says. "Now it's only us." His enthusiasm illustrates another benefit of the participation process: For workers who become involved — attending meetings and learning how to analyze problems — there is a significant improvement in job content.

Both union and company officials feel that morale has improved in the seat cushion department, and they note with some surprise that the workers' suggestions more often focus on improving the product than on personal complaints. As for sustaining the current labor-management cooperation, plant manager Birdsall asks: "If it has become a process, how can you stop it?"

The Inland program shows that management and labor can retain their adversarial systems, such as the grievance procedure, and still work cooperatively through "parallel structures," such as the Inland task forces. Many other lessons about instituting work improvements can be cited:

Human and economic goals. If a work improvement aims only at improving productivity, it quickly loses worker support. But a program that has only a vague plan of making workers feel better about themselves is likely to collapse for lack of business perspective. "Improved job satisfaction and improved productivity go hand in hand, and both are as important to workers as they are to managers," says Michael Sonduck of Digital Equipment.

Sidney Harman's Bolivar program, for example, was closely evaluated for a period of 56 months in the mid-1970s by Barry A. Macy, director of the Texas Center for Productivity & Quality of Work Life at Texas Tech University. Macy calculated that, after deducting the costs of implementing the program and providing benefits to workers from savings generated by higher output and other factors, the cost benefit for the company amounted to $3000 per hourly worker. Not all programs will show such a clear benefit. "If a company goes at this merely to ring the cash register, it's going to be disappointed," concludes Inland Div.'s Johnston.

A team concept. In most participation programs, only a relatively few workers' representatives who volunteer for the job are actually involved in the process. But when an entire work force is organized into teams, everybody is a direct participant. Most such programs have taken place in small, non-union plants engaged in light assembly work.

Shaklee Corp. of San Francisco adopted the "self-managed" work team concept when it opened a plant to produce nutritional products, vitamins, and other pills at Norman, Okla., in 1979. Some 190 of the nonunion plant's 230 employees are organized into 13 teams with 3 to 15 members. With a high degree of autonomy, the teams set their own production schedules based on management's volume goals. They decide what hours to work, select new team members from a pool approved by the personnel department, and even initiate discharges if necessary (three people have been fired since the plant opened).

Salaries now average $300 per week, and workers receive increases partly by demonstrating proficiency in a new skill for six months — a provision included in most team approaches that is calculated to make workers adept at many skills and thus interchangeable. William A. Ayers has worked at the Norman plant since it opened. "You aren't just told what to do," he says. "You have a sense of owning the job, and it makes you want to do a better job."

Robert L. Walter, vice-president of operations, claims that the Norman plant produces an average of 88 units (largely pills and powders) per man-hour, compared with only 30 at an older Shaklee plant. "We're producing the same volume at 40% of the labor costs," Walter says, adding that two-thirds of the production increase can be attributed to the management style and one third to better equipment.

Butler Mfg. Co., a Kansas City-based producer of pre-engineered industrial buildings and agricultural equipment, has used work teams at a Story City (Iowa) plant since 1976. The plant, which manufactures grain driers, has 93 employees organized into teams of 5 to 12 workers. These teams set their own production goals. "The whole idea is that people adhere more to the goals they set themselves," says Michael R. Simmons, vice-president of corporate personnel. He says that man-hours required per unit were reduced by 30% to 35% in the first two years, compared with production in two other plants of the company.

Worker receptivity. Most work innovation experts say that the diversity of worker needs must be respected. People should not be pressed into innovative work relationships against their will. Digital Equipment has made similar findings at a Westminster, Mass., computer assembly plant. DEC started a four-member team in 1977 to assemble standup computers. The team is made up of volunteers from four different skill areas. Each taught the others his job, and now they can switch jobs at random.

Joseph B. Daly, a production manager, says to assemble a computer, the team needs only 25% the space an assembly line takes. Cycle time improved by 60%, and output per employee increased "slightly," he says. The team manages its own workplace without close supervision, and its members seem to like the responsibility that comes with directing their own work. "It's better to work under these circumstances because you have a feeling of companionship," says 57-year-old Roy W. Bouley.

But the company has found that only about 65% of other workers are interested in team work. Since it involves defining their own workplace, "some people were complaining that it wasn't clear what their responsibilities were," Daly says. The company plans to extend the concept this summer where it can.

Institutionalizing changes. "You have to allow time for people to adjust to new relationships," says Gene Kofke, director of work relationships at AT&T. "The worst enemy that quality of work life has is the impatience for quick and finite results." AT&T and the Communications Workers agreed last year to create a national committee to help CWA locals and Bell System companies establish problem-solving committees and other innovations. On April 24, after many months of talks, the company and the union agreed on a set of guiding principles. "You measure the success of these things in years," Kofke adds. "Our management is willing to wait."

Even with projects that show results relatively quickly, management must display patience during the early stages of problem-solving meetings as workers test the company's sincerity. At Malden Mills's Lawrence plant, Paul Chaisson, who heads the innovation efforts, says both management and the union must make "a very long-term commitment, or the new process will die." The $200-million-a-year textile manufacturer wants to improve its work relationships because it foresees a shrinking labor pool in Lawrence as more high technology companies move into the area. The International Ladies' Garment Workers Union agreed to cooperate in setting up problem-solving groups, and the company brought in the Northeast Labor-Management Center, a Boston-based organization with experience as a "facilitator" of work innovations.

Malden Mills first established seven core groups with about 15 members each in its Retail Div., where fabric manufactured in the mills is inspected, packed, and shipped. This division had had high turnover and absenteeism and other labor problems, and it was decided to allow the workers to raise issues of importance to them when the core groups started meeting last year. The first six months was a purgative period; the workers focused on long-festering complaints about working conditions, apparently testing management's commitment to solve problems.

But last fall the groups suddenly began addressing problems involving cost reductions and improved quality. "When it gets started, people have an appetite for improving the work that explodes," Chaisson says. "Every place we've started this, it goes like a flash fire."

The workers made suggestions about the use of materials and tools, and by last January the percentage of correct fabric inspections had risen to 94%, up from 88% a year ago. One group of 17 inspectors formed a semi-autonomous team and set their own weekly production goal of inspecting 13,500 lb. of cloth — a target 1500 lb. higher than that management had previously set — and met it. Turnover was cut from an annual rate of 200% two years ago to less than 10% this year.

One of the packers in the Retail Div., 20-year-old Jack O'Keefe, says that "people are getting involved and staying on the job because management is listening to them. They know they can speak up now without worrying about getting fired." Carolyn O'Brien, 24, a department manager, says: "I used to be very autocratic and thought that if people were given a lot of leeway, they'd take advantage of it. Now the people are supervising themselves, and I can be more creative in finding new ways to improve quality."

Union Involvement

The work-innovation movement will continue to grow without organized labor's cooperation although union involvement would help immeasurably. Many union officials, including the AFL-CIO's top leaders, are still reluctant to advocate openly and strongly any concept that tastes of the hated word "collaboration." Within individual unions, small pockets of resistance exist among radical leftists who oppose what they perceive as quality of work life's surrender of shop-floor worker power to management.

But the evidence is growing that rank and file workers for the most part want to be more deeply involved in their work and have an unerring ability to spot exploitative schemes. As Sidney Harman says: "You can't fraudulently create a program without being seen through sooner or later." While it is true that workers do not specifically ask their union leaders to negotiate a provision called "quality-of-work-life" in their contracts, most recent surveys of workers' attitudes confirm that they want something more from their jobs — and of their unions — than wages, benefits, and job security. Most of all, says the UAW's Bluestone, they do not want to go to work merely to be "an adjunct to a tool."

Almost universally, effective work-innovation programs result in a dramatic speed up in management's settling of grievances — and this means quicker justice for workers. And Bluestone cites a striking piece of evidence for the growing rank and file support for quality of work life: In every plant where the UAW is cooperating in a successful program, local UAW leaders who pushed it have been reelected.

In Dayton, the URW's Red Hutchins perceives another important benefit for workers. About 90% of his members, who are not "perennial grievers," see little relevance of the union to their day-to-day lives at work. "This is the guy who wants to do a good job and who will be helped most by quality-of-work-life," Hutchins says. "When we participate on these committees, it's a way of giving service to a guy who's never had service before."

Clearly, a changed social and economic environment in the U.S. demands that labor and management create a new relationship. The lessons provided by the pioneers of work innovations prove that changes in work processes and structures are not only possible, they can be highly successful. Most of all, they show that the U.S. industrial relations system, so long arrested at primitive levels of development, can now evolve into a third stage — a participative stage.

An Introduction to the National Labor Relations Act, as Amended

JAMES E. MARTIN
Wayne State University

This selection serves as an introduction to the National Labor Relations Act (NLRA). It is important that the industrial relations student understand the provisions of the Act so as to be familiar with the basic labor-management relations policy of the United States and the regulatory means adopted by Congress to implement that policy. Section 3 of that act establishes the National Labor Relations Board (NLRB), which in turn interprets and administers the Act. The Office of General Counsel of the NLRB has prepared a booklet, "A Guide to Basic Law and Procedures under the National Labor Relations Act." This section will draw liberally from that "Guide" and from the Act itself. Like the "Guide," it will briefly introduce and discuss the major provisions of the Act.[1]

The Act is administered and enforced principally by the Board and the General Counsel acting through about 50 regional and field offices located throughout the country. The General Counsel and his staff in the regional offices are charged with the duty of investigating and prosecuting unfair labor practice cases and conducting elections to determine employee representatives. The five-member Board decides cases involving charges of unfair labor practices and determines representation election questions that come to it from the regional offices.

The tone of the policy was first set forth in the NLRA of 1935 (the Wagner Act) wherein the promotion of the free flow of goods in commerce was sought by the removal of "certain recognized sources of industrial strife and unrest." Section 8 listed numerous employer unfair labor practices. The NLRA was amended in 1947 by the Labor-Management Relations Act (the Taft-Hartley Act), which added the employee's right to refrain from engaging in concerted union and collective bargaining activities to the employee's existing right to engage in them. In addition, union unfair labor practices were added to Section 8.

Labor relations are constantly changing and thus, the Act is constantly being tested and reevaluated by the NLRB, the courts, and occasionally being amended by Congress. Furthermore, the NLRA does not stand alone as there exists a significant body of rules and regulations, NLRB decisions, and court decisions that make up the body of labor-management relations law.

EXCERPTS FROM AND COMMENTS ON THE TEXT OF THE NATIONAL LABOR RELATIONS ACT, AS AMENDED

Section 1. Findings and Policy

The NLRA recognizes that industrial strife interferes with the normal flow of commerce. The purpose and policy of the Act is to promote the full flow of commerce, by proscribing and protecting the rights of employers and employees, and by providing orderly and peaceful procedures for preventing interference by either with the legitimate rights of the other. This section declares the encouragement of the "practice and procedure of collective bargaining," and protecting of the "exercise by workers of full freedom of association, self-organization, and designation of representatives of their own choosing for the purpose of negotiating the terms and conditions of their employment" with their employers as a means of balancing bargaining power. In summary, this section means that the public policy of the United States is to promote and encourage the principle of free collective bargaining.

Section 2. Definitions

Section 2 defines various terms used in the NLRA.

Section 2(2) defines an employer as including "any person acting as an agent of an employer, directly or indirectly," but excludes all government employers, including government corporations and the Federal Reserve Bank, and any political subdivision such as a state or school district.[2]

Section 2(3) defines employee and excludes from that definition the following classes of individuals to which the Act does not apply:

Agricultural laborers

Domestic servants

Any individual employed by one's parent or spouse

Independent contractors

Individuals subject to the Railway Labor Act

Supervisors

Supervisors were excluded from the definition of employees covered by the NLRA in the Taft-Hartley amendments of 1947. The rationale

was that the interests of supervisors are too closely allied with management. Whether an individual is a supervisor or not is determined by looking at the person's duties, as defined in Section 2(11) below, rather than the title.

In addition to supervisors, the Board applied the same rationale to exclude all "managerial employees" from protection of the Act.[3]

Section 2(5) states:

> The term "labor organization" means any organization of any kind, or any agency or employee representation committee or plan, in which employees participate and which exists for the purpose, in whole or in part, of dealing with employers concerning grievances, labor disputes, wages, rates of pay, hours of employment, or conditions of work.

Section 2(11) of the Act defines "supervisor" as:

> any individual having authority, in the interest of the employer, to hire, transfer, suspend, lay off, recall, promote, discharge, assign, reward, or discipline other employees, or responsibility to direct them, or to adjust their grievances, or effectively to recommend such action, if in connection with the foregoing the exercise of such authority is not of a merely routine or clerical nature, but requires the use of independent judgment.

Section 2(12) defines "professional employees" as those engaged in work predominantly intellectual and varied in character; involving consistent exercise of discretion; where output produced or result accomplished cannot be standardized; or requiring knowledge of an advanced type.

Section 2(14) defines a private health care institution as:

> any hospital, convalescent hospital, health maintenance organization, health clinic, nursing home, extended care facility, or other institution devoted to the care of the sick, infirm, or aged person.

These were brought under the Act in 1974, and include both profit and nonprofit institutions.

Sections 3 through 6.
National Labor Relations Board

Section 3(a) creates the NLRB as a federal agency to administer the Act. The NLRB consists of five members appointed by the President of the United States by and with consent of the Senate.

Section 3(d) authorizes the appointment of a General Counsel of the Board, who investigates cases and brings charges and exercises general supervision over the Board attorneys and officers, and employees in the regional offices of the Board.

Sections 4 and 5 outline compensation and administrative authorities granted to the NLRB by the Congress.

Section 6 gives the Board procedural authority to establish rules and regulations necessary to carry out provisions of the Act. This section has· the effect of empowering the NLRB to administer and interpret the Act in whatever way it thinks is appropriate to the situations encountered, subject to review by the federal courts. In its discretion, the NLRB limits the exercise of its powers to cases involving enterprises whose effect on commerce is "substantial" and meets certain standards.

The Board's requirements for exercising its power or jurisdiction are called "Jurisdictional Standards." These standards are based on the yearly amount of business done by the enterprise, or on the yearly amount of its sales or purchases. They are stated in terms of total dollar volume of business and are different for different kinds of enterprises. Ordinarily if an enterprise, nonprofit, noncommercial, or charitable institution does the volume of business set in the standards, it will necessarily be engaged in activities that "affect" commerce.

The Board must find that the enterprise does in fact "affect" commerce. Where an employer that "affects" commerce refuses to supply the Board with information concerning total annual business, etc., the Board may dispense with this requirement and exert jurisdiction. Finally Section 14(c) (1) authorizes the Board to decline to exercise jurisdiction over any class or category of employers where a labor dispute involving such employees is not sufficiently substantial, subject to certain limitations.

Section 7. Rights of Employees

Section 7 of the Act guarantees certain significant rights of employees and provides as follows:

> Employees shall have the right to self-organization, to form, join, or assist labor organizations, to bargain collectively through representatives of their own choosing, and to engage in other concerted activities for the purpose of collective bargaining or other mutual aid or protection, and shall also have the right to refrain from any or all of such activities . . .

Examples of the rights protected by this section follow:

- Forming or attempting to form a union among the employees of a company.

- Joining a union whether the union is recognized by the employer or not.

- Assisting a union in organizing the employees of an employer.

- Going out on strike to secure better working conditions.

- Refraining from activity on behalf of a union.

Section 8. Unfair Labor Practices

The unfair labor practices of employers are listed in Section 8(a) of the Act and those of labor organizations in Sections 8(b) and 8(g). Section 8(e) lists unfair labor practices that can be committed only by an employer and a labor organization acting together. Other provisions, which provide definitions for and limitations to these sections, will be discussed in Sections 8(c), 8(d), and 8(f) following the presentations of the actual unfair labor practices.

Table 1 identifies the various categories of cases classified by the Board, and illustrates the relationships among the different Section 8 unfair labor practices provisions, as well as the different representation cases relating to Section 9. It should be noted here that the NLRA is a remedial statute, not a criminal statute. It is intended to prevent and remedy unfair labor practices by returning the parties to their previolation state, not to punish the person responsible for them.

Section 8(a). Unfair Labor Practices of Employers

Section 8(a) (1). This section forbids an employer "to interfere with, restrain, or coerce employees in the exercise of the rights guaranteed in Section 7." This is a broad prohibition on employer interference, and an employer violates this section whenever it commits any of the other employer unfair labor practices. Thus a violation of Section (8)(a)(2), (3), (4), or (5) is a violation of Section 8(a)(1).

Employer conduct may also independently violate Section 8(a)(1). Examples of such violations are:

○ Threatening employees with loss of jobs or benefits if they should join or vote for a union.

○ Threatening to close down the plant if a union should be organized in it.

○ Questioning employees about their union activities or membership in such circumstances as will tend to restrain or coerce the employees.

○ Spying on union gatherings, or pretending to spy.

○ Granting wage increases deliberately timed to discourage employees from forming or joining a union.

Section 8(a) (2). This section makes it unlawful for an employer "to dominate or interfere with the formation or administration of any labor organization or contribute financial or other support to it."

A labor organization is considered "dominated" within the meaning of this section if the employer has interfered with its formation and has assisted and supported its operation and activities to such an extent that it must be looked at as the employer's creation instead of the true bargaining representative of the employees. In the case of domination, the Board's remedy will be to order the labor organization dissolved.

Interference that is less than complete domination is found where an employer tries to help a union by various kinds of conduct, such as giving a union improper privileges that are denied to other unions competing to organize its employees, or recognizing a favored union when another union has raised a real representation claim. Financial support of unions violates the noninterference provision of this section whether it is a direct or indirect payment to the union. In the case of interference, the Board's remedy usually is to order the employer to cease such conduct and to withhold recognition of the labor organization as the representative of the employees.

An employer violates Section 8(a)(2) by activities such as:

○ Taking an active part in organizing a union or a committee to represent employees.

○ Bring pressure on employees to join a union, except in the enforcement of a lawful union-security agreement.

○ Allowing some employees, members of one union competing to represent employees, to solicit on company premises during working hours and denying other employees, members of another union, the same privilege.

○ Soliciting and obtaining from employees and applicants for employment during the

TABLE 1
Types of cases

1. CHARGES OF UNFAIR LABOR PRACTICES (C CASES)

Charge against employer		Charge against labor organization			
Section of the Act	**CA**	Section of the Act	**CB**	Section of the Act	**CC**

CA

8(a)(1) To interfere with, restrain, or coerce employees in exercise of their rights under Section 7 (to join or assist a labor organization or to refrain).

(8)(a)(2) To dominate or interfere with the formation or administration of a labor organization or contribute financial or other support to it.

8(a)(3) By discrimination in regard to hire or tenure of employment or any term or condition of employment to encourage or discourage membership in any labor organization.

8(a)(4) To discharge or otherwise discriminate against employees because they have given testimony under the Act.

8(a)(5) To refuse to bargain collectively with representatives of its employees.

CB

8(b)(1)(A) To restrain or coerce employees in exercise of their rights under Section 7 (to join or assist a labor organization or to refrain).

8(b)(1)(B) To restrain or coerce an employer in the selection of its representatives for collective bargaining or adjustment of grievances.

8(b)(2) To cause or attempt to cause an employer to discriminate against an employee.

8(b)(3) To refuse to bargain collectively with employer.

8(b)(5) To require of employees the payment of excessive or discriminatory fees for membership.

8(b)(6) To cause or attempt to cause an employer to pay or agree to pay money or other thing of value for services which are not performed or not to be performed.

CC

8(b)(4)(i) To engage in, or induce or encourage any individual employed by any person engaged in commerce or in an industry affecting commerce, to engage in a strike, work stoppage, or boycott, or *(ii)* to threaten, coerce, or restrain any person engaged in commerce or in an industry affecting commerce, where in either case an object is:

(A) To force or require any employer or self-employed person to join any labor or employer organization or to enter into any agreement prohibited by Sec. 8(e).

(B) To force or require any person to cease using, selling, handling, transporting, or otherwise dealing in the products of any other producer, processor, or manufacturer, or to cease doing business with any other person, or force or require any other employer to recognize or bargain with a labor organization as the representative of its employees unless such labor organization has been so certified.

(C) To force or require any employer to recognize or bargain with a particular labor organization as the representative of its employees if another labor organization has been certified as the representative.

CD

(D) To force or require any employer to assign particular work to employees in a particular labor organization or in a particular trade, craft, or class rather than to employees in another trade, craft, or class, unless such employer is failing to conform to an appropriate Board order or certification.

Section of the Act **CG**

8(g) To strike, picket, or otherwise concertedly refuse to work at any health care institution without notifying the institution and the Federal Mediation and Conciliation Service in writing 10 days prior to such action.

(cont.)

TABLE 1 (cont.)

1. CHARGES OF UNFAIR LABOR PRACTICES (C CASES) (cont.)		2. PETITIONS FOR CERTIFICATION OR DECERTIFICATION OF REPRESENTATIVES (R CASES)			3. OTHER PETITIONS	
Charge against labor organization (cont.)	Charge against labor organization and employer	By or in behalf of employees	By or in behalf of employees	By an employer	By or in behalf of employees	By a labor organization or an employer
Section of the Act **CP**	Section of the Act **CE**	Section of the Act **RC**	Section of the Act **RD**	Section of the Act **RM**	Section of the Act **UD**	Board Rules **UC**
8(b)(7) To picket, cause, or threaten the picketing of any employer where an object is to force or require an employer to recognize or bargain with a labor organization as the representative of its employees, or to force or require the employees of an employer to select such labor organization as their collective bargaining representative, unless such labor organization is currently certified as the representative of such employees: (A) where the employer has lawfully recognized any other labor organization and a question concerning representation may not appropriately be raised under Section 9(c), (B) where within the preceding 12 months a valid election under Section 9(c) has been conducted, or	8(e) To enter into any contract or agreement (any labor organization and any employer) whereby such employer ceases or refrains or agrees to cease or refrain from handling or dealing in any product of any other employer, or to cease doing business with any other person.	9(c)(1)(A)(i) Alleging that a substantial number of employees wish to be represented for collective bargaining and their employer declines to recognize their representative.*	9(c)(1)(A)(ii) Alleging that a substantial number of employees assert that the certified or currently recognized bargaining representative is no longer their representative.*	9(c)(1)(B) Alleging that one or more claims for recognition as exclusive bargaining representative have been received by the employer.*	9(e)(1) Alleging that employees (30 percent or more of an appropriate unit) wish to rescind an existing union-security agreement.	Subpart C Seeking clarification of an existing bargaining unit. Board Rules **AC** Subpart C Seeking amendment of an outstanding certification of bargaining representative.

(C) where picketing has been conducted without a petition under 9(c) being filed within a reasonable period of time not to exceed 30 days from the commencement of the picketing except where the picketing is for the purpose of truthfully advising the public (including consumers) that an employer does not employ members of, or have a contract with, a labor organization, and it does not have an effect of interference with deliveries or services.

Source: A Guide to Basic Law and Procedures Under The National Labor Relations Act, Washington, D.C.: U.S. Government Printing Office, 1976. Charges filed with the National Labor Relations Board are letter-coded and numbered. Unfair labor practice charges are classified as "C" cases and petitions for certification or decertification of representatives as "R" cases. This table indicates the letter codes used for "C" cases and "R" cases, and also presents a summary of each section involved.

* If an 8(b) (7) charge has been filed involving the same employer, these statements in RC, RD, and RM petitions are not required.

hiring procedure, applications for union membership and signed authorizations for the checkoff of union dues.

Section 8(a) (3). This section prohibits discrimination in regard to hiring or tenure of employment, or any term or condition of employment that tends to encourage or discourage membership in any labor organization. Thus "closed shops" wherein only employees with membership in the union may be hired are prohibited. However, the employer and the recognized union may agree to a union shop wherein an employee is required to pay the union initiation fees and periodic dues on or after 30 days following the beginning of employment. However, union membership is not required.[4]

An employer may discharge an employee for failure to tender periodic dues and initiation fees uniformly required of all employees in the bargaining unit. However, no employer can discriminate against an employee for non-membership in a union if the employer has reason to believe that membership in the union was not open to the employee on the same terms and conditions that apply to others, or if the employer reasonably believes that the employee's membership in the union was denied or terminated for reasons other than failure of the employee to tender regular dues and initiation fees.

Examples of illegal discrimination under Section 8(a) (3) include:

○ Discharging employees because they urged other employees to join a union.

○ Refusing to reinstate employees when jobs they are qualified for are open because they took part in a union's lawful strike.

○ Granting of "superseniority" to those hired to replace employees engaged in a lawful strike.

○ Demoting employees because they circulated a union petition among other employees asking the employer for an increase in pay.

○ Discontinuing an operation at one plant and discharging the employees. Then opening the same operation at another plant with new employees because the employees at the first plant joined a union.

○ Refusing to hire qualified applicants for jobs because they belong to a union. It would also be a violation if the qualified applicants were refused employment because they did not belong to a union, or because they belonged to one union rather than another.

Section 8(a) (4). This makes it an unfair labor practice for an employer to discharge or otherwise discriminate against an employee because he has filed charges or given testimony under the Act. Examples of violations of Section 8(a) (4) are:

○ Refusing to reinstate employees when jobs they are otherwise qualified for are open because they filed charges with the NLRB.

○ Demoting employees because they testified at an NLRB hearing.

Section 8(a) (5). This section states that it is an unfair labor practice for an employer to refuse to bargain collectively with the representatives of the employees. The meaning of "bargaining collectively" is more specifically outlined in Section 8(d) of the Act and discussed in that section.

Section 8(a) (5) makes it illegal for an employer to refuse to bargain in good faith about mandatory subjects of bargaining (wages, hours, and other conditions of employment) with the representative selected by a majority of the employees in a unit appropriate for collective bargaining. A union must show that there has been both a demand that the employer bargain and a refusal by the employer to do so.

An employer who purchases or otherwise acquires the operation of another employer may be obligated to recognize and bargain with the union that represented the employees before the business was transferred, especially where there is a substantial continuity in the employing enterprise.

Examples of violations of Section 8(a) (5) are as follows:

- ○ Refusing to meet with the employees' representatives because the employees are out on strike.

- ○ Insisting, until bargaining negotiations finally break down, on a contract provision that all employees will be polled by secret ballot before the union calls a strike.

- ○ Refusing to supply the employees' representative with relevant and necessary information requested for effective bargaining, such as cost and other data concerning a group insurance plan covering the employees.

- ○ Announcing a wage increase without consulting the employees' representative.

- ○ Subcontracting certain work to another employer without notifying the union representing the affected employees and without giving the union an opportunity to bargain concerning the change in working conditions of the employees.

- ○ Negotiating without an intention to reach an agreement.

- ○ Refusing to bargain on a mandatory subject of bargaining.

- ○ Refusing to meet with the opposing side's designated representative.

Section 8(b). Unfair Labor Practices of Labor Organizations

The 1947 and 1959 amendments to the NLRA created categories of labor union unfair labor practices.

Section 8(b) (1) (A). This section states that a labor organization is forbidden "to restrain or coerce employees in the exercise of the rights guaranteed in Section 7." Like Section 8(a)(1), 8(b)(1)(A) is violated by conduct that independently restrains or coerces employees in the exercise of their Section 7 rights, regardless of whether or not the conduct also violates other provisions of Section 8(b). The NLRB has held, based upon its interpretation of the intent of Congress when Section 8(b)(1)(A) was written, that violations of Sections 8(b)(2) through (7) do not also automatically violate Section 8(b)(1)(A). Unlawful coercion may be direct physical acts, threats of violence, and threats that may affect an employee's job status.

A union that is a statutory bargaining agent has the "duty of fair representation" to all the employees in the represented bargaining unit. While it may exercise a wide range of discretion in carrying out that duty, it violates Section 8(b)(1)(A) if it takes or withholds action in connection with an employee's employment because of his or her union activities, or for any irrelevant or arbitrary reason such as race or sex.

Section 8(b)(1)(A) further recognizes the right of unions to establish and enforce rules of membership, and to control their internal affairs. However, this right is limited to union rules and discipline that affect the rights of employees as union members but cannot affect an employee's employment. Also, the union's rules must be of legitimate concern to the union, such as the encouragement of members to support a lawful strike or participate in union meetings. A union may not fine a member for filing a decertification petition, although it may expel that individual from the union for doing so.

Examples of violations of Section 8(b)(1)(A) are:

- ○ Mass picketing in such numbers that nonstriking employees are physically barred from entering the plant.

- ○ Acts of force or violence on the picket line, or in connection with a strike.

- ○ Threats to do bodily injury to nonstriking employees.

○ Threats to employees that they will lose their jobs unless they support the union's activities.

○ Statements to employees who oppose the union that they will lose their jobs if the union wins a majority in the plant.

○ Entering into an agreement with an employer who recognizes the union as the exclusive bargaining representative when it has not been chosen by a majority of the employees.

○ Fining or expelling members for crossing a picket line that is unlawful under the Act or that violates a no-strike agreement.

○ Fining employees for conduct they engage in after resigning from the union.

○ Fining or expelling members for filing unfair labor practice charges with the Board or for participating in an investigation conducted by the Board.

○ Refusing to process a grievance in retaliation against an employee's criticism of union officers.

Section 8(b)(1)(B). This prohibits a labor organization from restraining or coercing an employer in the selection of a bargaining representative. The prohibition applies whether or not the labor organization is the majority representative of the employees in the bargaining unit. Examples of violations of Section 8(b)(1)(B) are:

○ Insisting on meeting only with a company's owners and not with the attorney the company has engaged to represent it in contract negotiations, and threatening to strike to force the company to accept its demands.

○ Striking against members of an employer association that had bargained with the union as the representative of the employers, with resulting individual contracts being signed by the struck employers.

○ Insisting during contract negotiations that the employer agree to accept working conditions that will be established by a bargaining group to which it does not belong.

○ Fining or expelling supervisor members for the way they apply the bargaining contract while carrying out their supervisory functions.

Section 8(b)(2). This section states that it is an unfair labor practice for a labor organization to cause or attempt to cause an employer to discriminate against an employee in violation of Section 8(a)(3). A union's conduct, accompanied by statements advising or suggesting that action is expected of an employer, may be enough to find a violation of this section if the union's action can be shown to be a causal factor in an employer's discrimination. Examples of violations of Section 8(b)(2) are:

○ Causing an employer to discharge employees because they circulated a petition urging a change in the union's method of selecting shop stewards.

○ Causing an employer to discharge employees because they made speeches against a contract proposed by the union.

○ Making a contract that requires an employer to hire only members of the union or employees "satisfactory" to the union.

○ Causing an employer to reduce employees' seniority because they engaged in anti-union acts.

○ Refusing referral or giving preference on the basis of race or union activities in making job referrals to units represented by the union, for example, by operating a discriminatory hiring hall.

○ Seeking the discharge of an employee under

a union-security agreement for failure to pay a fine levied by the union.

○ Forcing an employer to give preferential treatment to its members.

Section 8(b) (3). This makes it illegal for a labor organization to refuse to bargain in good faith with an employer about wages, hours, and other conditions of employment if it is the representative of that employer's employees. This is the same as the duty imposed on the employers by Section 8(a) (5). Section 8(b)(3) has been interpreted not only to require good faith bargaining with the employer, but also to require that the union carry out its bargaining *and* contract administration duties fairly with respect to the employees it represents. Thus this section, along with 8(b)(1)(A), defines the duty of fair representation. Section 8(b)(3) is violated by any of the following:

○ Insisting on the inclusion of illegal provisions in a contract, such as a closed shop or a discriminatory hiring hall.

○ Refusing to negotiate on a proposal for a written contract.

○ Striking against an employer who has bargained, and continues to bargain, on a multi-employer basis in order to compel it to bargain separately.

○ Refusing to meet with the attorney designated by the employer as its representative in negotiations.

○ Terminating an existing contract and striking for a new one without notifying the employer, the Federal Mediation and Conciliation Service, and the state mediation service, if any.

○ Conditioning the execution of an agreement upon inclusion of a nonmandatory provision, such as a performance bond.

○ Refusing to process a grievance for ar-

bitrary or irrelevant reasons, such as the race, sex, or union activities of an employee.

Section 8(b) (4). This section forbids certain types of strikes, boycotts, picketing, and other acts as shown in Table 1. Specifically, clause (i) of this section forbids a union to engage in a strike, or to induce or encourage a strike, work stoppage, or a refusal to perform services by "any individual employed by any person engaged in commerce or in an industry affecting commerce" for one of the purposes or "objects" listed in the Act in subsections (A) through (D). Clause (ii) makes it an unfair labor practice for a union to "threaten, coerce, or restrain any person engaged in commerce or in an industry affecting commerce" for any of those same proscribed objects that are discussed in the following four subsections of the Act.

Section 8(b)(4)(A) prohibits unions from engaging in actions specified in clause (i) or (ii) to force or attempt to force an employer or self-employed person to join any labor or employer organization, or to force or attempt to force an employer to enter a hot cargo agreement prohibited by Section 8(e). Examples of Section 8(b)(4)(A) violations are:

○ In an attempt to compel a beer distributor to join a union, the union prevents the distributor from obtaining beer at a brewery by inducing the brewery's employees to refuse to fill the distributor's orders.

○ In an attempt to secure for its members certain stevedoring work required at an employer's unloading operation, the union pickets to force the employer either to join an employer association with which the union has a contract or to hire a stevedoring firm that is a member of the association.

○ A union pickets an employer (one not in

the construction industry), or threatens to picket it, to compel that employer to enter into an agreement whereby the employer will only do business with persons who have an agreement with a union.

Section 8(b)(4)(B) contains the NLRA's secondary boycott provision. A secondary boycott occurs if a union has a dispute with Company A and in furtherance of that dispute causes the employees of Company B, usually a supplier of or a dealer for A, to stop handling the products of Company A, or otherwise forces Company B to stop doing business with Company A. The dispute is with Company A, "the primary employer," while the union's action is against Company B, "the secondary employer," hence, the term "secondary boycott." Section 8(b)(4)(B) also prohibits secondary action, such as a sympathy strike, to compel an employer to recognize or bargain with a union that is not the certified representative of its employees. Examples of violations of Section 8(b)(4)(B) are:

○ Picketing an employer to force it to stop doing business with another employer who has refused to recognize the union.

○ Urging employees of a building contractor not to install doors that were made by a manufacturer who is nonunion or who employs members of a rival union.

It is important to note that 8(b)(4)(B) does not protect a secondary employer from the incidental effects of union action taken directly against the primary employer. Thus it is lawful for a union to urge employees of a secondary supplier delivering at the primary employer's plant not to cross a picket line there. Also, it does not limit union action to prevent a struck employer from contracting out work customarily performed by its employees, even through an incidental effect of such action might be to force that employer to stop doing business with the subcontractor.

Section 8(b)(4)(C) forbids a labor organization from forcing or attempting to force an

employer to recognize or bargain with a labor organization other than the one that is currently certified as the representative of its employees. Examples of violations of Section 8(b)(4)(C) are:

○ Mere organizational picketing by members of the union when another union had already been certified as the bargaining representative.

○ A trucker's union order not to deliver to a retail store where the sales clerks had voted to be represented by another union.

Section 8(b)(4)(D) forbids a labor organization from forcing or attempting to force any employer to assign certain work to "employees in a particular labor organization or in a particular trade, craft, or class, rather than to employees in another labor organization or in another trade, craft, or class," commonly known as a "jurisdictional dispute." The NLRA sets up a special procedure for handling disputes over work assignments under Section 10(k). An example of a violation of Section 8(b)(4)(D) is:

○ A union urging employees of a building contractor to strike in order to force the contractor to assign to the union the job of installing metal doors when it has already assigned the job to a different union.

The final provision of Section 8(b)(4) states that this section shall not prohibit a union's "informational publicity," which merely advises that a product is produced by an employer with whom the union has a primary dispute. Thus the U.S. Supreme Court has held that a union may distribute handbills at the stores of a neutral food chain, asking the public not to buy certain items distributed by a wholesaler with whom the union has a primary dispute.[5] The Court has also allowed peaceful picketing at the stores of a neutral food chain to persuade customers not to buy a struck employer's product while making purchases in the store.[6] However, such publicity is prohibited if it has "an effect of inducing any individual employed by any person other than the primary employer" to refuse to handle any goods or not to perform services at the site of a "neutral" secondary employer.

Section 8(b) (5). This section states that it is illegal for a union under an authorized 8(a)(3) union-security agreement to charge employees an initiation fee that the Board finds excessive or discriminatory under all circumstances. The Board in making its finding shall consider the practices and customs of labor organizations in the particular industry and the wages currently paid to the employees affected. Examples of violations of Section 8(b)(5) are:

- Charging old employees who do not join the union until after a union-security agreement goes into effect an initiation fee of $15 while charging new employees only $5.

- Increasing the initiation fee from $75 to $250 and thus charging new members an amount equal to about 4 week's wages when other unions in the area charge a fee equal to about one half the employee's first week's pay.

Section 8(b) (6). This section makes it an unfair labor practice for a labor organization to "featherbed," to cause an employer to pay or deliver or agree to pay or deliver any money or other thing of value for services that are not performed or not to be performed. The Supreme Court has reduced the effect of this section by holding that it does not apply as long as employees are performing or willing to perform relevant or productive services, regardless of whether or not the employer needs or wants the work performed.[7] An example of a violation of Section 8(b)(6) is:

- A musician's union demanded compensation for employees who merely "standby" and are to do no work when a radio station plays a record of band music.

Section 8(b) (7). This prohibits a labor organization not currently certified as the employee representative from picketing or threatening to picket with the objective of obtaining recognition by the employer (recognitional picketing) or gaining acceptance by the employees as their representative (organizational picketing). However, this section permits picketing "for the purpose of truthfully advising the public (including consumers)" that the company does not employ union members or have a contract with a union, unless the picketing's effect is to interfere with deliveries or pickups of goods or with other services required by the picketed employer. If a charge is filed against a picketing union under Section 8(b)(7)(C), and a representation petition is filed within a reasonable time after the picketing starts, the Act provides for an election to be held on an expedited basis. It should be noted that generally fewer than one-half of one percent of the representation elections held each year are expedited elections.[8] Examples of violations of Section 8(b)(7) are:

- Picketing by a union for organizational purposes shortly after the employer has entered a lawful contract with another union. (8(b)(7)(A))

- Picketing by a union for organizational purposes within 12 months after a valid NLRB election in which a majority of the employees in the unit voted to have no union. (8(b)(7)(B))

- Picketing for recognition by a union that continues for more than 30 days without the filing of a representation petition where the picketing stops all deliveries by employees of another employer. (8(b)(7)(C))

Section 8(g). Unfair Labor Practices Applying to Health Care Institutions

Section 8(g) was added to the list of union unfair labor practices in 1974, when the NLRA was amended to cover health care institutions. In recognition of the disruptive effect of work stoppages at health care institutions and with the objective of providing continuity of patient care, 8(g) prohibits a labor organization from striking or picketing a health care institution, or engaging in any other concerted refusal to work, without giving written notice to the institution and the Federal Mediation Conciliation Service (FMCS) ten days prior to such action. The section specifies, "The notice shall state the date and time that such action will commence. The notice, once given, may be extended by the written agreement of both parties." An example of a violation of Section 8(g) is:

○ Striking a hospital without giving written notice.

Other relevant differences in the NLRA affecting health care institutions are included in Section 8(d) and are discussed below.

Section 8(e). Unfair Labor Practices Applying to Both Employers and Labor Organizations

Section 8(e), added by the Labor Management Reporting and Disclosure Act of 1959 (the Landrum-Griffin Act), prohibits hot cargo agreements. A hot cargo agreement is one wherein an employer "ceases or refrains, or agrees to cease or refrain from handling, using, selling, transporting, or otherwise dealing in any of the products of another employer" as required or forced by a labor organization. Exceptions are allowed in the construction and garment industries. In the construction industry, the union and an employer may agree to a provision that restricts the contracting or subcontracting of work to be performed at the construction site. In both the construction and garment industries the union and the employer may agree that subcontracted work will go to an employer who has a contract with the union.

A summary overview of the relative importance of the various kinds of unfair labor practices can be seen in Table 2. That table shows the types of unfair labor practices alleged during fiscal year 1981. While the actual numbers of charges vary from year to year, the relative percents do not show as much variation. Typically, many more charges are filed against employers than against unions. The most common charges against employers are of violations of 8(a)(1), 8(a)(3), and 8(a)(5). The most common charges filed against unions concern 8(b)(1), 8(b)(2), and 8(b)(4).

Section 8(c). Employer and Employee Free Speech

Section 8(c) provides that the expressing of any views, arguments, or opinion, or the dissemination thereof during an organizational campaign, shall not be an unfair labor practice "if such expression contains no threat of reprisal or force or promise of benefit." Examples of situations that this section does not protect, and which may be ruled as unfair labor practices, are as follows:

○ Where an employer's communications to employees threatened to close down a plant in the event of a union's winning an election for reasons unrelated to economic necessity.

○ A union statement to employees that if they did not vote for the union, the union would cause the largest customer to boycott their employer, with the result that they would lose their jobs.

○ A statement by management to employees that they will get a wage increase if the union does not win a majority in the plant.

Section 8(d). Collective Bargaining Defined

Section 8(d) defines the requirements of both parties in bargaining collectively and can be considered one of the key parts of the Act. This section imposes a mutual obligation upon the employer and the representative of the employees to do all of the following:

TABLE 2

Types of unfair labor practices alleged, fiscal year 1981

	NUMBER OF CASES SHOWING SPECIFIC ALLEGATIONS	PERCENT OF TOTAL CASES
A. Charges filed against employers under Section 8(a)[1]		
Total	31,273	100.0
Subsections of 8(a)		
8(a)(1)[2]	31,273	100.0
8(a)(2)	869	2.8
8(a)(3)	17,571	56.2
8(a)(4)	1,409	4.5
8(a)(5)	9,815	31.4
B. Charges filed against unions under Section 8(b)[1]		
Total	11,882	100.0
Subsections of 8(b)		
8(b)(1)[3]	8,382	70.5
8(b)(2)	1,513	12.7
8(b)(3)	945	8.0
8(b)(4)	2,392	20.1
8(b)(5)	37	0.3
8(b)(6)	40	0.3
8(b)(7)	454	3.8
C. Charges filed under Section 8(e)		
Total cases 8(e)	131	100.0
Against unions alone	130	99.2
Against employers alone	1	0.8
D. Charges filed under Section 8(g)		
Total cases 8(g)	35	100.0

Source: Forty-Sixth Annual Report of the National Labor Relations Board, Washington, D.C.: U.S. Government Printing Office, 1982, Table 2, p. 176.

[1] A single case may include allegations of violation of more than one subsection of the Act. Therefore the total of the various allegations is greater than the total number of cases.

[2] Section 8(a)(1) is a general provision forbidding any type of employer interference with the rights of employees guaranteed by the Act, and therefore is included in all charges of employer unfair labor practices. There were 6394 cases, or 20.4 percent, of alleged violations of Section 8(a)(1) only.

[3] Alleged violations of Section 8(b)(1) only totaled 6627, or 55 percent.

○ Meet at reasonable times.

○ Confer in good faith with respect to mandatory subjects (wages, hours, and other terms and conditions of employment) or the negotiation of an agreement or any questions arising thereunder.

○ Execute a written contract incorporating any agreement reached if requested by either party.

However, the obligation to bargain does not require "either party to agree to a proposal or require the making of a concession."

Under this section, the Board has recognized three types of subjects of bargaining. Mandatory subjects of bargaining are those that relate to wages, hours, and other terms and conditions of employment, such as pensions for present employees, bonuses, group insurance, grievance procedures, safety practices, seniority, procedures for discharge, layoff, recall, or discipline, and the union shop. Nonmandatory or permissive subjects of bargaining are lawful but not related to "wages, hours, and other terms of employment." The employer and union are free to bargain and to agree on nonmandatory subjects, but neither party may insist upon bargaining on such subjects over the objection of the other party. Examples of nonmandatory subjects include company pricing policies, union label agreements, and pension arrangements for retired employees. Collective bargaining cannot take place on the third category, illegal subjects of bargaining not consistent with the NLRA provisions or other laws, such as "closed shop" agreements, "hot cargo" agreements, and the requiring of employee approval before a contract can be modified.

A provision of Section 8(d) states the steps to be followed in terminating or modifying a collective bargaining agreement. The party wishing to terminate or modify a labor contract must notify the other party to the contract in writing of its desire 60 days before the date on which the contract is scheduled to expire, (90 days in the case of a health care institution), and "offer to meet and confer with the other party for the purpose of negotiating a new contract." That same party must, within 30 days after the notice to the other party, notify the Federal Mediation and Conciliation Service of the existence of a dispute if no agreement has been reached by that time. At the same time it must also notify any state or territorial mediation agency in the state or territory where the dispute is taking place. If the parties so desire, the FMCS will make a mediator available to help them reach agreement.

Two additional subsections of Section 8(d) apply if a dispute arises in a health care institution. When bargaining for an initial contract, a union must give at least 30 days notice to the appropriate mediation agencies. After any notice to the FMCS of any health care contract dispute, mediation is mandatory rather than voluntary.

If the notice requirements are not met, a strike to terminate or change a contract is unlawful and participating strikers lose the protection of the Act.[9] Furthermore, any employee who engages in a strike within a notice period loses his status as an employee of the struck employer. This loss of status ends, however, if and when that individual is re-employed by the same employer.

Section 8(f). Special Provisions for the Building and Construction Industry

Section 8(f) allows an employer in the building and construction industry and a union to enter into an agreement whereby new employees must pay the union dues and initiation fees no less than seven days after the date of hire, rather than the 30 days as provided in Section 8(a)(3) for other employers. It also allows such an employer to enter into such an agreement without the majority status of the union being established prior, under the provisions of Section 9.

Section 9. Representatives and Elections

Section 9 of the NLRA governs the requirements for the designation of bargaining representatives. It provides for three types of representation elections among employees:

1. The *representation election* to determine the employees' choice of a collective bargaining agent. Elections are held upon petition of an individual, employer, employees, or a labor organization. By its rules and regulations, the NLRB will not hold an election unless the petitioner, other than an employer, can show that at least 30 percent of the employees in the proposed unit have indicated their support for the union. (A)(i) and (B))

   The Board also conducts expedited representation elections in connection with Section 8(b)(7)(C).

2. The *decertification election* to determine whether or not the employees wish to continue the bargaining authority of the union. These are held upon the petition of any individual, an employee or group of employees acting on behalf of the employees, or a labor organization acting on behalf of the employees. (9(c)(1)(A)(ii))

3. The *union shop deauthorization referendum* to determine whether or not the employees wish to rescind the authority of their union to enter into a union shop agreement. (9(e)(1))

Section 9(a). This section provides that the union "representatives designated or selected for the purposes of collective bargaining by the majority of the employees in a unit appropriate for such purposes, shall be the exclusive representatives of all the employees in such unit for the purposes of collective bargaining." Once a union has been chosen by the employees, it becomes illegal for an employer to bargain with individual employees, a group of employees, or another union. However, 9(a) further provides that any individual or group of employees has the right to present and settle grievances with their employer without the intervention of the recognized union provided the settlement is consistent with the terms of any labor contract then in effect and that the recognized union is given the opportunity to be present at such settlement.

Section 9(b). This gives the Board the discretion to determine what group of employees constitutes an appropriate unit for collective bargaining, for whom a representation election may take place. The Board shall decide in each representation case "whether, in order to assure employees the fullest freedom in exercising the rights guaranteed by this Act, the unit appropriate for the purposes of collective bargaining shall be the employer unit, craft unit, plant unit, or subdivision thereof."

This broad discretion is limited by other subsections of Section 9. Section 9(b)(1) provides that the Board shall not approve as appropriate a unit that includes both professional and nonprofessional employees, unless a majority of the professional employees involved vote to be included in the mixed unit. Section 9(b)(2) states that the Board shall not hold a proposed craft unit to be inappropriate simply because a different unit was previously approved by the Board, unless a majority of the employees in the proposed craft unit vote against being represented separately. Section 9(b)(3) prohibits the Board from including plant guards in the same unit as other employees. It also prohibits the Board from certifying a labor organization as the representative of a plant guard unit if the labor organization has members who are nonguard employees.

Generally, the appropriateness of a bargaining unit is determined on the basis of the common employment interests, known as the "community of interest" of the employees involved.

Employees who have the same or substantially similar interests concerning wages, hours, and working conditions may be reasonably grouped together in a bargaining unit. The Board also considers the following factors:

1. Any history of collective bargaining.

2. The desires of the employees concerned.

3. The extent to which the employees are organized. (However, Section 9(c)(5) forbids the Board from giving this factor controlling weight.)

Note that a unit may cover the employees in one plant of an employer, or it may cover employees in two or more plants of the same employer. In some industries where employers are grouped together in voluntary associations, a unit may include employees of two or more employers in any number of locations. Bargaining units can include only persons who are ''employees'' as defined by the NLRA, since the Act excludes certain classifications of individuals such as agricultural laborers, independent contractors, and supervisors.

Section 9(c). Section 9(c)(1) provides that if a question of representation exists, the NLRB must make its determination by means of a secret ballot election. In a representation election employees are given a choice of one or more bargaining representatives or no representative at all. To be certified as the bargaining representative, an individual or a labor organization must receive a majority of the valid votes casts.

An election may be held by agreement between the employer and the individual or labor organization claiming to represent the employees. In such an agreement the parties state the time and place agreed upon, the choice appearing on the ballot, and a method to determine who is eligible to vote. The NLRB Regional Director is responsible for the conduct of the election.

If the parties do not reach voluntary agreement on an election, the Act authorizes the NLRB to hold an election after holding a hearing. The Regional Director determines the appropriateness of the bargaining unit, directs an election, and then certifies the voting result. Ordinarily, elections are held within 30 days after they are directed. Seasonal drops in employment or any change in operations that would prevent a normal work force from being present may cause a different election date to be set. Normally, an election will not be conducted when unfair labor practice charges have been filed based upon conduct that would have a tendency to interfere with employee free choice.

To assure an informed electorate, the Board adopted the *Excelsior Underwear* rule, which requires the employer to submit to the NLRB an election eligibility list, containing the names and addresses of all eligible voters. The NLRB, in turn, makes the list available to the union.[10] It also provides that economic strikers who have been replaced by bona fide permanent employees may be entitled to vote in ''any election conducted within 12 months after the commencement of the strike.'' The permanent replacements are also eligible to vote at the same time. A striker is considered to be an economic striker unless found by the NLRB to be on strike over employer unfair labor practices. Whether the economic striker is eligible to vote or not is determined on the facts of each case.

Section 9(c)(3) prohibits the holding of an election in any collective bargaining unit or subdivision thereof in which a valid election has been held during the preceding 12-month period. A new election may be held in a larger unit, but not in the same unit or smaller subunit.

Section 10. Board Powers to Prevent, Remedy, and Enjoin Unfair Labor Practices

Section 10 outlines the procedural requirements for the Board's handling of unfair labor practice cases. The procedure in an unfair labor practice case is begun with the filing of a charge by an employee, employer, labor organization, or any other person. Unfair labor practice charge forms must be signed, sworn to or affirmed under oath, and filed in the NLRB Regional Office in the area where the unfair labor practice occurred. A complaint stating the charges, but not necessarily all pertinent facts, and notifying the charged party of a hearing regarding the charge, will be issued through the NLRB Regional Office once an investigation indicates there is a basis to the allegations. If the Regional Director refuses to issue a complaint in any case, the person who filed the charge may appeal the decision to the General Counsel in Washington, who has the final authority under Section 3(d) to investigate charges and issue complaints.

Once a complaint has been issued, the unfair labor practice hearing is conducted before an NLRB administrative law judge (ALJ) in accordance with the rules of law and procedure that apply in the U.S. District Courts. Based upon the hearing record, the ALJ submits findings and recommendations to the Board in Washington, D.C. If the Board considers that the charged party has engaged in or is engaging in the unfair labor practice charged, the Board is authorized to issue a cease and desist order and to take other appropriate affirmative action. The object of the Board's order in any case is twofold, (1) to eliminate the unfair labor practice and (2) to undo the effects of the violation as much as possible. Ordinarily its order will follow a standard form designed to remedy the unfair labor practice, but the Board can, and often does, change the standard order to meet the needs of the case. Examples of affirmative action required of an employer who has engaged in unfair labor practices may include Board orders to:

○ Disestablish an employer-dominated union.

○ Offer illegally discharged individuals immediate and full reinstatement to their former positions or, if those positions no longer exist, to substantially equivalent positions without prejudice to their senior-

ity and other rights and privileges, and with back pay, including interest.

○ Upon request, bargain collectively with a certain union as the exclusive representative of the employees in a certain described unit and sign a written agreement if an understanding is reached.

Examples of affirmative action required of a union that has engaged in unfair labor practices include orders to:

○ Notify the employer and the employees that it has no objection to reinstatement of certain employees, or employment of certain applicants, whose discriminatory discharge, or denial of employment, was caused by the union.

○ Refund dues or fees illegally collected, plus interest.

○ Cease illegal picketing.

○ Upon request, bargain collectively with a certain employer and sign a written agreement if one is reached.

Section 10(a). This empowers the NLRB to prevent any person from engaging in any unfair labor practice listed in Section 8. On the basis of this section, the NLRB has issued numerous rules and regulations for the processing of unfair labor practice charges. Under what is generally called the *Spielberg* and *Collyer* doctrines, where an alleged unfair labor practice would also be a violation of the contract, the Board will currently defer processing a case and await resolution of the issues through the grievance arbitration procedure. If the process meets the Board's liberal standards, the Board will defer to the arbitrator's decision.[11]

Section 10(b). With this the NLRB is given the power to issue and serve a charge following the filing of a charge. An unfair labor practice charge must be filed within six months of the occurrence of the practice and copies of the charge given to each person against whom it is made.

Section 10(c). This section gives the NLRB authority to not only issue a cease-and-desist order, but also "to take such affirmative action including reinstatement of employees with or without back pay, as will effectuate the policies of this Act."

Section 10(d). In this section it states that until the record in a case has been filed in a court the NLRB may modify or set aside any finding or order made or issued by it.

Sections 10(e) and 10(f). Section 10(e) grants the power to the NLRB to seek court enforcement of its orders, and Section 10(f) allows for appeal to the courts for relief from Board orders by any person aggrieved by a final order of the NLRB. Normally, an appeal from an order of the Regional Office or an ALJ will go to the full NLRB for review in Washington, D.C. The NLRB may seek enforcement of its orders by petitioning a federal district court or court of appeals for appropriate relief or a restraining order. Appeals from a Board or district court order may be made to a federal court, and ultimately an appeal may be sought before the U.S. Supreme Court. In an average year, only about five percent of the unfair labor practice charges originally filed with the Regional Offices are litigated all the way through to a decision of the Board. Only about 350 of those go to the U.S. Courts of Appeals for a decision related to enforcement and/or review. Of these, the courts uphold the Board in whole or in part about 85 percent of the time.[12]

Sections 10(j), (k), (l), and (m).
Special and Priority Relief Provisions

Special proceedings are required by the Act in certain kinds of cases. These include injunction proceedings under Sections 10(j) and (l), the determination of jurisdictional disputes under Section 10(k), and priority proceedings under Sections 10(l) and (m).

Section 10(j) allows the Board to petition the courts for an injunction in connection with any unfair labor practice after a complaint has been issued. It does not require that injunctive relief be sought, but only makes it possible for the Board to do so where it is considered appropriate.

Section 10(k) provides that whenever any person is charged in an unfair labor practice in violation of Section 8(b)(4)(D), the Board must hear and determine the jurisdictional dispute. Section 10(k) further provides an opportunity for the parties to adjust the dispute during a ten-day period after notice of the 8(b)(4)(D) charge has been served. If the parties have not submitted to the Board satisfactory evidence that they have adjusted or agreed on a method of adjusting the dispute, the Board is "empowered and directed" to determine which of the competing employee groups is entitled to be assigned the work.

Section 10(l) provides that whenever a charge is filed alleging a violation of certain sections of the NLRA relating to boycotts, picketing, and work stoppages, the preliminary investigation of the charge must be given priority over all other types of cases in the Regional Office where it is filed in order to avoid irreparable harm to the employer. The unfair labor practices subject to this investigatory priority are those defined in Sections 8(b)(4)(A), (B), or (C), 8(b)(7), and 8(e). If the preliminary investigation shows that there is reasonable cause to believe that the charge is true and that a complaint should issue, Section 10(l) further requires that the U.S. District Court be petitioned to grant an injunction pending the final determination of the Board and authorizes the court to grant "such injunctive relief or temporary restraining order as it deems just and proper."

Section 10(m) requires that second-order priority be given to charges alleging violations of Section 8(a)(3), the prohibition against employer discrimination to encourage or discourage membership in a union, and Section 8(b)(2), which forbids unions to cause or attempt to cause such discrimination. Injunctions are not automatically requested under this section.

Other Provisions

The rest of the NLRA is not as important to collective bargaining as are the provisions presented up to this point. The topics in the most relevant remaining sections will be mentioned only briefly.

Sections 11 and 12 — Investigatory Powers. Section 11 establishes the powers of investigation and hearing by the NLRB. Section 12 provides for penalties under the NLRA for persons interfering with the Board's investigation and duties.

Sections 13 to 18 — Limitations. Section 13 states that except as noted in the Act, the right to strike is not limited by the NLRA.

Section 14(a) — Supervisors. Section 14(a) permits supervisors to be members of a labor organization, but states that employers are not required to treat supervisors as employees for the purposes of collective bargaining.

Section 14(b) — States and Union Shop Provisions. Section 14(b) allows states to ban union shop provisions from labor agreements in their states if they so choose. As of 1984, 20 states had passed such a law, commonly called "right-to-work laws."

Section 19 — Individuals with Religious Convictions. This section was added in 1974 with the health care amendments and amended in 1980 to cover all employees. It allows any employee who adheres to "a bona fide religion, body, or sect which has historically held conscientious objections to joining or financially supporting labor organizations," the right not to have to join or support any union. However, such employee may be required to pay sums equal to union dues and initiation fees to a nonlabor, nonreligious charity. The 1980 amendments further provided that if such employee requests the

union "to use the grievance-arbitration procedure on the employee's behalf, the labor organization is authorized to charge the employee for the reasonable cost of using such procedure."

Sections 201 through 204 — Conciliation of Labor Disputes. These sections define the organization and functions of the FMCS.

Sections 206 through 210 — National Emergencies. These provisions give the President power to intervene in those types of disputes that he or she deems to be national emergencies.

Section 301 — Suits by and Against Labor Organizations. This section provides that suits for violation of contracts between an employer and a union may be brought in the federal district courts. Unions and employers are bound by the acts of their agents. Any money judgments are assessed against a labor organization as an entity and not against any individual members. Suits against unions charging them with failure to carry out their duty of fair representation are filed under this section.

Section 302 — Restriction on Payments to Employee Representatives. This section essentially restricts the payments by employers or their agents to employee representatives, labor organizations, or their agents to regular employee compensation for services. Other exceptions are union dues deducted by the employer and legally established trust funds related to employee health care, insurance, pensions, or other benefits.

Section 303 — Boycotts and Other Unlawful Combinations. This section gives employers the right to sue in the federal courts for damages arising out of Section 8(b)(4) strikes and boycotts in addition to being able to file unfair labor practice charges.

With this overview of the provisions of the NLRA a student of industrial relations should have a sufficient familiarity with the Act to embark upon the analysis of the collective bargaining and unfair labor practice cases that follow. From such case analyses, the student will see how the Act functions to protect the rights of the different parties involved.

NOTES

1. This paper was written especially for this volume. The author would like to thank Roland Hwang, a practicing attorney in Dearborn Michigan, for his assistance on this selection.

2. A number of states have widely varying laws defining the collective bargaining rights and representation election procedures for state and local government employees, including school district employees. Most of the unfair labor practices in those laws are similar to those in the NLRA. Title VII of Civil Service Reform Act (Public Law 95–454, 1978) codified the bargaining rights for most federal government employees. However, the 1970 Postal Reorganization Act extended the NLRB's jurisdiction to the United States Postal Service, effective July 1, 1971. In most states and in the federal government where collective bargaining is permitted, strikes generally are not permitted. Further, wages and fringe benefits for federal government employees are generally determined by Congress.

3. See *NLRB* v. *Bell Aerospace Co.*, 416 U.S. 267 (1974).

4. *Union Starch and Refining Co.* v. *NLRB*, 87 NLRB 779 (1949), enforced, 186 F.2d 1008 (7th Cir. 1951) and *Hershey Food Corp.*, 207 NLRB 897 (1973), enforced 513 F.2d 1083 (9th Cir. 1975). In *NLRB* v. *General Motors*, 373 U.S. 734, 742 (1963) the Supreme Court stated, " 'Membership' as a condition of employment is whittled down to its financial core." Thus the agency shop is really the maximum form of union security.

5. *NLRB* v. *Fruit and Vegetable Packers and Warehousemen, Local 760 and Joint Council No. 28 of I.B.T. (Tree Fruits Labor Relations Committee, Inc).* 377 U.S. 58 (1964).

6. *American Bread Co.* v. *NLRB*, 411 F.2d 147 (6th Cir. 1969). For more about this and the preceding case see Case No. 8, "Picketing a Supermarket to Boycott Paper Bags."

7. See the following Supreme Court decisions: *American Newspaper Publishers Association* v. *NLRB*, 345 U.S. 100 (1953) and *NLRB* v. *Gamble Enterprises, Inc.*, 345 U.S. 117 (1953).

8. See the *Annual Reports of the NLRB.*

9. If the strike was caused by the unfair labor practice of the employer, however, the strikers are classed as unfair labor practice strikers and their protection under the Act is not affected by their failure to follow the required procedure.

10. *Excelsior Underwear Inc.*, 156 NLRB 1236 (1966). The list is known as an *Excelsior* list.

11. See *Spielberg Manufacturing Co.*, 112 NLRB 1080 (1955), as modified by *Collyer Insulated Wire Co.*, 192 NLRB 837 (1971), *Olin Corp.*, 268 NLRB 268 (1984), and *United Technologies Corp.*, 268 NLRB 83 (1984).

12. From the informational pamphlet, "The NLRB . . . What it is, What it Does," Washington, D.C.: U.S. Government Printing Office, 1979.

SECTION 2
Union Organizing

INTRODUCTION

Union organizing is a crucial part of the collective bargaining process in the United States. To become a work group's collective bargaining agent, a majority of the employees must support union representation. As discussed in Section 1, the implementation of a National Labor Relations Board (NLRB) secret ballot election to determine a union's majority status was one of the major developments in the evolution of the nation's labor policy. Prior to the passage of the National Labor Relations Act, union organizing was frequently characterized by labor unrest and violence because many unions were forced to strike in order to convince employers that workers wanted representation. Today organizational strikes are unnecessary because Board-conducted elections have become a basic part of labor-management relations.

Union organizing is currently a topic of great interest because the number of workers in labor organizations is not increasing as rapidly as the expansion of the labor force. After decades of growth, the percentage of nonagricultural employees holding union membership has declined in recent years. While 33.2 percent of the nonagricultural work force was unionized in 1955, only 23.6 percent was unionized in 1980.[1] Two major factors have been identified as contributing to the recent slowdown in union growth. First, an increased number of manufacturing firms have relocated from heavily unionized areas of the north to less unionized states in the Sunbelt. As a result, the rate of unionization has decreased. Secondly, unions have had a difficult time organizing women, a rapidly growing portion of the work force.[2] For unions to slow down or reverse this downward trend in membership, they will have to develop more effective strategies for organizing the growing number of nonunion workers. This subject will be discussed further in Section 6.

Why Workers Organize

A growing body of literature is developing concerning the factors that motivate workers to unionize. While much still needs to be learned about this process, it appears that the urge to organize has two major dimensions to it. First, employees must be dissatisfied with their current working conditions. Secondly, workers must believe that the union is able to bring about desired changes in the workplace. Perhaps this sheds some light on why union growth is not keeping pace with the growth in employment. Union-avoidance programs currently being implemented by an increasing number of firms can be placed into two broad categories. Many organizations are following what are known as "positive personnel policies." This approach focuses on developing employment conditions so attractive to employees that they will see no reason to turn to organized labor. The other major approach involves the use of "hard line" tactics designed to have workers believe that unionizing is futile, that they will not improve their situation by joining a union. This approach may involve the intentional commission of unfair labor practices or the use of tactics intended to delay NLRB election procedures.[3] Despite these practices, over 8000 NLRB representation elections take place each year. In these situations, a union organizing campaign has probably taken place.

Union Organizing Campaigns

A NLRB-conducted union representation election is the most common method for establishing whether a union represents a majority of the employees in a bargaining unit. These elections are preceded by a campaign during which the union attempts to convince employees that they would be better off with union representation. At the same time, the employer is working to establish that union representation is unnecessary or counterproductive. A typical union organizing campaign goes through the following stages:[4]

Identifying the target. It is necessary for the labor organization to establish that employees are interested in being unionized. A dissatisfied employee could contact the union or the labor organization could contact a group of workers to see if they are interested in union representation.

Determining interest. Because of limited resources, most unions will determine whether employee interest is strong enough to warrant initiating an organizing campaign. The union will examine factors such as worker interest in unionization, the pool of good leaders, and company policies and practices likely to influence the union organizing process.

Setting up an organizing committee. An effort is made to develop a group of employees in the plant who will be the nucleus of the organizing effort. This group is responsible for contacting other employees to determine their interest in the union and whether they would be willing to help in the organizing process.

Building interest. At this point, those interested in the union start building majority support. Discussions are held to educate employees about the benefits of unionizing. One-on-one conversations, group meetings, and written literature are commonly used to create interest. An important part of this process is getting workers to sign authorization cards. By signing an authorization card, the employees designate the union as their bargaining representative. While the NLRB requires that at least 30 percent of the employees in the unit sign authorization cards before directing an election, most unions do not proceed to later stages of the union organizing process until a clear majority of the employees has signed cards. If there is majority support for the union, the union can request voluntary recognition from the employer. Typically, employers doubt that the union represents a majority, so the union must petition the NLRB to conduct a representation election.

The NLRB hearing. Prior to most elections, the NLRB conducts a hearing. Basic issues such as whether there is a question of representation and

who should be in the bargaining unit are reviewed. Once these issues are resolved, the
NLRB directs that an election will take place and
sets a date for the election.

The organizing campaign. After the election date
is set, both the union and company are likely
to conduct a campaign to influence the employees' vote in the upcoming election. Arguments in
favor of and in opposition to unionization are
likely to dominate the work place in the days
preceding the election.

The election. On the day of the election, agents
of the NLRB will conduct a secret ballot election. This usually takes place within 30 days of
the election being directed and is held at a location convenient to the involved parties (this usually means polling booths are set up at the workplace).

Election results. If the majority of the employees participating in the election votes in favor
of union representation, the union will be designated by the NLRB as the employees' bargaining representative. If a majority votes against
representation, the company remains nonunion.

The Principle of Exclusive Representation

When a union demonstrates that it has support
from a majority of the employees, the NLRB des-
ignates the union as the exclusive representative
for the purposes of collective bargaining for all the
employees in the bargaining unit. This designation has implications for both the union and the
employer. For the union, exclusive representative
status imposes the obligation to represent fairly all
employees in the unit. From the employer's perspective, exclusive representation means that it is
obligated to bargain in good faith with the union
over wages, hours, and other terms and conditions of employment. Failure to do so would probably be viewed as a violation of Section 8(a)(5) of
the National Labor Relations Act, as amended.

Public Policy Affecting Union Organizing Campaigns

Protecting the employees' free choice is a basic
objective of the nation's labor policy concerning
the representation election procedure. To help insure that workers are not unduly coerced when
deciding whether they want union representation, the NLRB has developed a number of
guidelines limiting the behavior of both organized
labor and management. Section 8(a)(1) and
8(b)(1) of the National Labor Relations Act make
it an unfair labor practice for employers and
unions, respectively, to interfere, restrain, or
coerce employees in the exercise of their rights,
including the workers' right to join a union, as
discussed in Section 1. The Board enunciated its
general view of the representation election procedure in its *General Shoe* decision by stating:

> our only consideration derives from the Act
> which calls for freedom of choice by employees
> as to a collective bargaining representative. Con-
> duct that creates an atmosphere which renders
> improbable a free choice will sometimes warrant
> invalidating an election, even though that con-
> duct does not constitute an unfair labor practice.
> An election can serve its true purpose only if the
> surrounding conditions enable employees to
> register a free and untrammelled choice for or
> against a bargaining representative. . . . In elec-
> tion proceedings, it is the Board's function to
> provide a laboratory in which an experiment
> may be conducted, under conditions as nearly
> ideal as possible to determine the uninhibited de-
> sires of the employees. It is our duty to establish
> those conditions; it is also our duty to determine
> whether they have been fulfilled. When, in a
> rare extreme case, the standard drops too low,
> because of our fault or that of others, the req-
> uisite laboratory conditions are not present and
> the experiment must be conducted over again.[5]

In order to ensure that ''laboratory conditions'' exist, the NLRB has developed election
standards designed to discourage union and
employer behavior that would tend to interfere
with the employees' freedom of choice. These are
discussed in the reading by Martin in Section 1.

INTRODUCTION TO THE READINGS

The Functions of a Union

Before looking at why workers organize, it is useful to have an understanding of the functions served by labor unions. Historically, unions have been viewed as monopolies existing for the sole purpose of increasing wages. Freeman and Medoff, in the first selection in this section, argue that unions have another dimension that also needs to be understood, the "collective voice" that unions provide for their members. They point out that a "voice" is the use of direct communications to bring about change within an organization. Because unions communicate directly with management, they are a "voice" institution that brings about basic changes in the relationships present in the workplace. The power of the individual worker who becomes part of the collective body is enhanced. At the same time, managerial authority is diluted, since the union is able to share decision making on a number of fundamental issues. Freeman and Medoff assert that to understand the role of unions in society, it is necessary to examine the two faces of unionism: the monopolistic "face" and the collective-voice "face."

The authors argue that the predominant view of unionism held by management can influence its response to unions. If management believes unions are monopolistic institutions committed to just raising wages, unions are likely to be viewed as impediments to the social good. However, if unions are viewed as a collective voice that aids labor-management communications, managers are likely to view unions as having some desirable features. The remainder of the Freeman and Medoff article reviews the evidence on the monopoly/collective-voice faces of unionism in an attempt to ascertain the relative importance of each phase. After this review, the authors conclude that unionism is associated with negative monopoly effects as well as some substantial positive effects. In light of these findings, the question becomes: Why do employers so vehe-mently oppose unionism? Freeman and Medoff conclude their article by answering this question.

The Urge to Unionize

Knowing the functions served by unions provides some insights into a worker's motivation to organize. Certainly, the monopoly effects (higher wages) and the collective-voice effects (greater control over the work place) are important objectives for workers. Jeanne M. Brett's article provides some more detailed information about why workers unionize. The Brett article is based on a study of 31 union representation elections. Over 1200 workers participating in these elections were interviewed on two separate occasions. From this information, many useful insights into the union organizing process were obtained.

The results of this study support the view that two conditions must be present for workers to unionize. First, workers supporting unionizing are less satisfied with their working conditions, especially job security and wages. Additionally, dissatisfaction with fringe benefits, treatment by supervisors, and chances for promotion are also correlated with voting for union representation. Satisfaction with the work being done is not significantly related to the decision to unionize. This suggests that unionizing is related more to working conditions than the work itself.

Dissatisfaction with working conditions alone was not found to lead to unionizing. The second factor identified by the research was that dissatisfied workers also had to believe that the union was able to improve working conditions. Brett concludes by saying that employee interest in unionizing is triggered by job frustration and the strong belief that unions can be instrumental in alleviating that frustration through collective action.

The next article, by Heneman and Sandver, identifies additional factors affecting the outcomes of union representation elections. They review a number of empirical studies that were placed into two broad categories, studies looking at how individuals vote in certification elections, such as the Brett study, and those concerned with the characteristics of the elections themselves as predictors of the election outcome. As with the Brett study, other research found that job dissatisfaction and employee perception of union instrumentality were strong predictors of voting behavior. However, the studies reviewed by Heneman and Sandver did not identify any other individual characteristics as useful in predicting voting behavior.

When election level studies were reviewed, each study examining bargaining unit size reported union victories were more likely to occur in relatively smaller bargaining units. Other variables related to election outcomes included the time elapsing between the election petition and the conduct of the election, percentage of the employees signing authorization cards, and voter turnout.

In addition to summarizing the results of the literature, Heneman and Sandver discuss some of the problems associated with research in this area and the direction that should be taken in future research. This is a very useful discussion since it helps the reader become a more informed "consumer" of empirical research in this important area of labor-management relations.

Union Organizing Strategies

As pointed out in the introduction to this section, unions are finding it more difficult to organize nonunion workers. This suggests that traditional approaches to organizing are less effective today than in the past. Traditional approaches emphasize decentralized organizing campaigns that rely heavily on face-to-face communications between the organizer and the worker. The Craft and Extejt article reviews some contemporary approaches to organizing that have been developed to offset the declining proportion of union victories in representation elections. These new approaches can be placed into four major categories:

Corporate power strategy. This approach attempts to force the firm being organized into recognizing the union by applying financial pressures, confronting the employer, and trying to isolate the firm from the business and consumer communities.

Collective bargaining strategy. This is a viable approach when the union already has an established relationship with a company. The objective is to use the leverage of the existing collective bargaining relationship to facilitate the organization of the new or nonunion company facilities. One way to do this is by negotiating a "neutrality clause," wherein the company agrees that it will not oppose organizing drives at its nonunion facilities. An "accretion agreement" could also be negotiated that considers new plants to be extensions of existing facilities, and therefore, only involves the transfer and extension of current operations. With this view, union recognition is automatically granted at the new facilities. A third approach is to negotiate transfer and preferential hiring rights to enhance the union's ability to organize new plant facilities.

Community acceptance and integration strategy. Unions are frequently trying to unionize in areas without a union tradition, where community sentiments may tend to be anti-union. In these situations, it is necessary to build a basis for support in the community. This strategy focuses on the education of people in the community so that the union is considered to be a legitimate member of the community. By so doing, community attitudes toward the labor movement and collective bargaining can be improved so that the union organizing environment in the community is enhanced.

Coordinated-pooled resource strategy. With this approach, two or more unions pool their resources and eliminate rivalries so that they can put on a more effective organizing campaign. Typically, the unions identify a geographic area in which to focus their organizing attention. Then, working together with their shared resources, they concentrate their organizing efforts on that community.

Craft and Extejt point out that these strategies are not used very frequently. For a number of reasons, unions find it difficult to implement these approaches on a widespread basis. As a result, the authors are not optimistic that organized labor will be able to improve on its organizing "track record."

NOTES

1. U.S. Department of Labor, Bureau of Labor Statistics, *Handbook of Labor Statistics 1980,* Bulletin 2070, Washington, D.C.: U.S. Government Printing Office, 1980, p. 412.

2. Krislov, Joseph, and J. Lew Silver, "Union Bargaining Power in the 1980s," *Labor Law Journal,* Vol. 32, No. 8, August 1981, p. 481.

3. Leftwich, Howard M., "Organizing in the Eighties: A Human Resource Perspective," *Labor Law Journal,* Vol. 32, No. 8, August 1981, p. 484.

4. Fulmer, William E., "Step by Step Through a Union Campaign," *Harvard Business Review,* Vol. 59, No. 4, July-August 1981, pp. 94–95.

5. *General Shoe Corp.,* 77 NLRB 124 (1948).

SUGGESTIONS FOR FURTHER READING

In addition to the articles cited in this introduction, the following readings may prove useful to the reader.

Fiorito, Jack, and Charles R. Greer, "Determinants of U.S. Unionism: Past Research and Future Needs," *Industrial Relations,* Vol. 21, No. 1, Winter 1982, pp. 1–32.

Getman, Julius G., Steven B. Goldberg, and Jeanne B. Herman, *Union Representation Elections: Law and Reality,* New York: Russell Sage Foundation, 1976.

Kochan, Thomas A., "How American Workers View Their Unions," *Monthly Labor Review,* Vol. 102, No. 4, April 1979, pp. 23–31.

McGuiness, Kenneth C., *How to Take a Case Before the National Labor Relations Board,* 4th ed. Washington, D.C.: Bureau of National Affairs, 1976.

The Two Faces of Unionism

RICHARD B. FREEMAN

JAMES L. MEDOFF
Both of Harvard University and
National Bureau of Economic Research

Trade unions are the principal institution of workers in modern capitalist societies, as endemic as large firms, oligopolistic organization of industries, and governmental regulation of free enterprise. But for over 200 years, since the days of Adam Smith, there has been widespread disagreement about the effects of unions on the economy. On the one side, such economists as John Stuart Mill, Alfred Marshall, and Richard Ely (one of the founders of the American Economic Association) viewed unions as having major positive effects on the economy. On the other side, such economists as Henry Simons and Fritz Machlup have stressed the adverse effects of unions on productivity. In the 1930s and 1940s, unions were at the center of attention among intellectuals, with most social scientists viewing them as an important positive force in society. In recent years, unionism has become a more peripheral topic and unions have come to be viewed less positively. Less and less space in social science journals and in magazines and newspapers is devoted to unions. For example, the percentage of articles in major economics journals treating trade unionism dropped from 9.2 percent in the 1940s to 5.1 percent in the 1950s to 0.4 percent in the early 1970s. And what is written is increasingly unfavorable. The press often paints unions as organizations which are socially unresponsive, elitist, nondemocratic, or ridden with crime. In the 1950s, 34 percent of the space devoted to unions in *Newsweek* and *Time* was unfavorable; that has risen to 51 percent in the 1970s. Economists today generally treat unions as monopolies whose sole function is to raise wages. Since monopolistic wage increases are socially deleterious — in that they can be expected to induce both inefficiency and inequality — most economic studies implicitly or explicitly judge unions as having a negative impact on the economy.

Our research demonstrates that this view of unions as organizations whose chief function is to raise wages is seriously misleading. For in addition to raising wages, unions have significant nonwage effects which influence diverse aspects of modern industrial life. By providing workers with a voice both at the workplace and in the political arena, unions can and do affect positively the functioning of the economic and social systems. Although our research on the nonwage effects of trade unions is by no means complete and some results will surely change as more evidence becomes available, enough work has been done to

Reprinted with permission of the authors from *The Public Interest,* No. 57 (Fall 1979) pp. 69–93. © 1979 by National Affairs, Inc.

yield the broad outlines of a new view of unionism.

UNIONS AS COLLECTIVE VOICE

One key dimension of the new work on trade
unionism can best be understood by recognizing
that societies have two basic mechanisms for dealing with divergences between desired social conditions and actual conditions. The first is the
classic market mechanism of exit and entry, individual mobility: the dissatisfied consumer
switches products; the diner whose soup is too
salty seeks another restaurant; the unhappy couple divorces. In the labor market, exit is synonymous with quitting, while entry consists of new
hires by the firm. By leaving less desirable jobs for
more desirable jobs, or by refusing bad jobs, individuals penalize the bad employer and reward the
good — leading to an overall improvement in the
efficiency of the social system. The basic theorem
of neoclassical economics is that, under well-
specified conditions, the exit and entry of persons
(the hallmark of free enterprise) produces a
"Pareto-optimum" situation — one in which no
individual can be made better off without making
someone worse off. Economic analysis can be
viewed as a detailed study of the implications of
this kind of adjustment and of the extent to which
it works out in real economies. As long as the exit-
entry market mechanism is viewed as the only efficient adjustment mechanism, institutions such
as unions must necessarily be viewed as impediments to the optimal operation of a capitalist
economy.

There is, however, a second mode of adjustment. This is the political mechanism, which
Albert Hirschman termed "voice" in his important book, *Exit, Voice, and Loyalty.* "Voice" refers
to the use of direct communication to bring actual
and desired conditions closer together. It means
talking about problems: complaining to the store
about a poor product rather than taking business
elsewhere; telling the chef that the soup had too
much salt; discussing marital problems rather

than going directly to the divorce court. In a
political context, "voice" refers to participation
in the democratic process, through voting, discussion, bargaining, and the like.

The distinction between the two mechanisms
is best illustrated by a specific situation — for instance, concern about school quality in a given
locality. The exit solution to poor schools would
be to move to a different community or to enroll
one's children in a private school, thereby "taking one's business elsewhere." The voice solution
would involve political action to improve the
school system, through school-board elections,
Parent Teacher Association meetings, and other
direct activities.

In the job market, voice consists of discussing
with an employer conditions that ought to be
changed, rather than quitting the job. In modern
industrial economies, and particularly in large
enterprises, a trade union is the vehicle for collective voice — that is, for providing workers as a
group with a means of communicating with management.

Collective rather than individual bargaining
with an employer is necessary for effective voice
at the workplace for two reasons. First, many important aspects of an industrial setting are
"public goods," which affect the well-being
(negatively or positively) of every employee. As a
result, the incentive for any single person to express his preferences, and invest time and money
to change conditions (for the good of all), is reduced. Safety conditions, lighting, heating, the
speed of a production line, the firm's policies on
layoffs, work-sharing, cyclical-wage adjustment,
and promotion, its formal grievance procedure
and pension plan — all obviously affect the entire
workforce in the same way that defense, sanitation, and fire protection affect the entire
citizenry. "Externalities" (things done by one individual or firm that also affect the well-being of
another, but for which the individual or firm is
not compensated or penalized) and "public
goods" at the workplace require collective decision-making. Without a collective organization,

the incentive for the individual to take into account the effects of his or her actions on others, or express his or her preferences, or invest time and money in changing conditions, is likely to be too small to spur action. Why not "let Harry do it" and enjoy the benefits at no cost? This classic "free-rider" problem lies at the heart of the so-called "union-security" versus "right-to-work" debate.

A second reason collective action is necessary is that workers who are not prepared to exit will be unlikely to reveal their true preferences to their bosses, for fear of some sort of punishment. The essence of the employment relationship under capitalism — as Karl Marx, Ronald Coase, Herbert Simon, and numerous other analysts have recognized — is the exchange of money between employer and employee in return for the employer's control over a certain amount of the worker's time. The employer seeks to use his employee's time in a way that maximizes the value of the output the employee produces. Even in the case of piece rates, employers monitor employee activity to assure the quality of output. As a result, the way in which the time purchased is utilized must be determined by some interaction between workers and their boss. Since the employer can fire a protester, individual protest is dangerous; so a prerequisite for workers' having effective voice in the employment relationship is the protection of activists from being discharged. In the United States this protection is granted in a section of the National Labor Relations Act which states: "It shall be an unfair labor practice for an employer by discrimination in regard to hire or tenure or employment or any term or condition of employment to encourage or discourage membership in any labor organization." Indeed, court interpretation of U.S. labor law makes a sharp distinction between collective and individual actions at the workplace: Workers acting collectively are protected from managerial retaliation, but an individual acting alone is not.

The collective nature of trade unionism fundamentally alters the operation of a labor market and, hence, the nature of the labor contract. In a nonunion setting, where exit and entry are the predominant forms of adjustment, the signals and incentives to firms depend on the preferences of the "marginal" worker, the one who will leave (or be attracted) by particular conditions or changes in conditions. The firm responds primarily to the needs of this marginal, generally younger and more mobile worker and can within some bounds ignore the preferences of "inframarginal," typically older workers, who — for reasons of skill, knowledge, rights that cannot be readily transferred to other enterprises, as well as because of other costs associated with changing firms — are effectively immobile. In a unionized setting, by contrast, the union takes account of the preferences of *all* workers to form an average preference that typically determines its position at the bargaining table. Because unions are political institutions with elected leaders, they are likely to be responsive to a different set of preferences from those that dominate in a competitive labor market.

In a modern economy, where workers tend to be attached to firms for eight or more years, and where younger and older workers are likely to have different preferences (for instance, regarding pension or health-insurance plans versus take-home pay, or layoffs by inverse seniority versus work-sharing or cuts in wage growth), the change from a marginal to an average calculus is likely to lead to a very different labor contract. When issues involve sizeable fixed costs or "public goods," a calculus based on the average preference can lead to a contract which, ignoring distributional effects, is socially more desirable than one based on the marginal preference — that is, it may even be economically more "efficient."

As a voice institution, unions also fundamentally alter the social relations of the workplace. Perhaps most importantly, a union constitutes a source of worker power in a firm, diluting managerial authority and offering members a measure of due process, in particular through the union innovation of a grievance and arbitration system. While 99 percent of major U.S. collective-bargaining contracts provide for the filing of grievances, and 95 percent provide for arbitration of disputes that are not settled between the parties, relatively few nonunion firms have comparable procedures for settling disagreements between workers and supervisors. More broadly, the entire industrial jurisprudence system — by which many workplace decisions are based on negotiated rules (such as seniority) instead of supervisory judgment (or whim), and are subject to challenge through the grievance/arbitration procedure — represents a major change in the power relations within firms. As a result, in unionized firms workers are more willing and able to express discontent and to object to managerial decisions.

Thus as a collective alternative to individualistic actions in the market, unions are much more than simple monopolies that raise wages and restrict the competitive adjustment process. Given imperfect information and the existence of public goods in industrial settings, and conflicting interests in the workplace and in the political arena, unionism provides an alternative mechanism for bringing about change. This is not to deny that unions have monopolistic power nor that they use this power to raise wages for a select part of the workforce. The point is that unionism has two "faces," each of which leads to a different view of the institution: One, which is at the fore in economic analysis, is that of a monopoly; the other is that of "a voice institution," i.e., a sociopolitical institution. To understand fully what unions do in modern industrial economies, it is necessary to examine both faces.

THE RESPONSE TO UNIONS

Another crucial point about unions is that their effects will depend upon the response of management. This was stressed by Sumner H. Slichter, James J. Healy, and E. Robert Livernash in their classic volume, *The Impact of Collective Bargaining*

on Management. If management uses the collective-bargaining process to learn about and improve the operation of the workplace and the production process, unionism can be a significant plus that improves managerial efficiency. On the other hand, if management reacts negatively to collective bargaining or is prevented by unions from reorganizing the work process, unionism can have a negative effect on the performance of the firm. The important point is that just as there are two sides to the market, demand and supply, there are two forces determining the economic effects of collective bargaining, managements and unions. The economic impact of bargaining and the nature of industrial relations depend on the policies and actions of both. It is for this reason that we use the two terms "collective voice" and "institutional response" to refer to the second view of unionism under consideration.

The monopoly and collective-voice/institutional-response views of the impact of unionism are strikingly different, as the table on page 89 demonstrates. While no sophisticated adherent of the monopoly model would deny the voice aspects of unionism, and no industrial-relations expert would gainsay the monopoly effects, the polar dichotomization usefully highlights the facets of unionism stressed by the two views. The monopoly and collective-voice/institutional-response views of unionism in many instances give completely opposite pictures of the institution. According to the former, unions are by nearly all criteria undesirable impediments to the social good; in the latter view, unions have many valuable features that contribute to the functioning of the economy. In the monopoly view, the current dwindling in the percentage of private-sector wage and salary workers who are unionized (from 37 percent in 1958 to 29 percent in 1974) is a desirable development and should be associated with increased productivity and reduced inequality — and thus ought perhaps to be encouraged. From the collective-voice/institutional-response point of view, the dwindling of private-sector

TABLE 1
Two views of trade unionism

	UNION EFFECTS ON ECONOMIC EFFICIENCY	UNION EFFECTS ON DISTRIBUTION OF INCOME	SOCIAL NATURE OF UNION ORGANIZATION
Monopoly view	Unions raise wages above competitive levels, which leads to too little labor relative to capital in unionized firms. Union work rules decrease productivity. Unions lower society's output through frequent strikes.	Unions increase income inequality by raising the wages of highly skilled workers. Unions create horizontal inequities by creating differentials among comparable workers.	Unions discriminate in rationing positions. Unions (individually or collectively) fight for their own interests in the political arena. Union monopoly power breeds corrupt and nondemocratic elements.
Collective-Voice/ Institutional-Response View	Unions have some positive effects on productivity — by reducing quit rates, by inducing management to alter methods of production and adopt more efficient policies, and by improving morale and cooperation among workers. Unions collect information about the preferences of all workers, which leads the firm to choose a "better" mix of employee compensation and a "better" set of personnel policies. Unions improve the communication between workers and management, leading to better decision making.	Unions' standard-rate policies reduce inequality among organized workers in a given company or a given industry. Union rules limit the scope for arbitrary actions concerning the promotion, layoff, recall, etc., of individuals. Unionism fundamentally alters the distribution of power between marginal (typically junior) and inframarginal (generally senior) employees, causing union firms to select different compensation packages and personnel practices than nonunion firms.	Unions are political institutions that represent the will of their members. Unions represent the political interests of lower-income and disadvantaged persons.

Source: The authors.

unionization has serious negative economic and social consequences and should be an issue of public concern.

Since, in fact, unions have both monopoly and collective-voice/institutional-response components, the key question for understanding unionism in the United States relates to the relative importance of these two faces. Are unions primarily monopolistic institutions, or are they primarily voice institutions that induce socially beneficial responses? What emphasis should be given to these two extreme views for one to obtain a realistic picture of the role trade unionism plays in the United States?

To answer these important questions, we have studied a wide variety of data that distinguish between union and nonunion establishments and between union and nonunion workers, and we have interviewed representatives of management, labor officials, and industrial-relations experts. Although additional work will certainly alter some of the specifics, our research has yielded several important results which suggest that unions do a great deal more than win monopoly wage gains for their members.

EFFECTS ON EFFICIENCY

In the monopoly view, unions reduce society's output in three ways. First, union-won wage increases cause a misallocation of resources by inducing organized firms to hire fewer workers, to use more capital per worker, and to hire higher quality workers than is socially efficient. Second, union contract provisions — such as limits on the loads that can be handled by workers, restrictions on tasks performed, featherbedding, and so forth — reduce the output that should be forthcoming from a given amount of capital and labor. Third, strikes called to force management to accept union demands cause a substantial reduction in gross national product.

By contrast, the collective-voice/institutional-response model directs attention to the important ways in which unionism can raise productivity. First of all, unionism should reduce "quits." As workers' voice increases in an establishment, less reliance need be placed on the exit and entry mechanism to obtain desired working conditions. Since hiring and training costs are lowered and the functioning of work groups is less disrupted when "quit" rates are low, unionism can actually raise efficiency.

The fact that senior workers are likely to be relatively more powerful in enterprises where decisions are based on voice instead of exit and entry points to another way in which unions can raise productivity. Under unionism, promotions and other rewards tend to be less dependent in any precise way on individual performance and more dependent on seniority. As a result, in union plants feelings of rivalry among individuals are likely to be less pronounced than in nonunion plants and the amount of informal training and assistance that workers are willing to provide one another is greater. (The importance of seniority in firms in Japan, together with the permanent employment guaranteed many workers there, have often been cited as factors increasing the productivity of Japanese enterprises.) It is, of course, also important to recognize that seniority can reduce productivity by placing individuals in jobs for which they are not qualified.

Unionism can also raise efficiency by pressuring management into tightening job-production standards and accountability, in an effort to respond to union demands while maintaining profits. Slichter, Healy, and Livernash wrote in 1960, "The challenge that unions presented to management has, if viewed broadly, created superior and better-balanced management, even though some exceptions must be recognized." Their conclusion means that with a unionized workforce management is able to extract more output from a given amount of inputs than is management that is not confronted with a union. This appears to occur largely because modern personnel practices are forced on the firm and traditional paternalism is discarded. Management's ability to make such improvements is a function of the union's cooperation, since the union can perform a helpful role in explaining changes in the day-to-day routine. One recent study supportive of this view reports that while union workers spend more time on formal breaks, they spend *less* time on informal ones and report working harder than nonunion workers.[1]

Finally, under the voice view, the collective bargaining apparatus opens an important communication channel between workers and management, one likely to increase the flow of information between the two, and possibly improve the productivity of the enterprise. As Lloyd G. Reynolds has observed, "Unions can do valuable work by pointing out improvements that perhaps should have been obvious to management but were not, and that, once discovered, can be installed with a net gain to the company as well as the workers."

What does the evidence reveal on these points? Most of the econometric analysis of unions has focused on the question of central concern to the monopoly view: How large is the union wage effect? In his important book, *Unionism and Relative Wages,* H. Gregg Lewis summarized results of this analysis through the early 1960s, concluding that, while differing over time and across settings, the union wage effect averages on the order of 10 to 15 percent. That is, as a result of collective bargaining, a union member makes about 10 to 15 percent more than an otherwise comparable worker who is not a member. Later work, using larger data files which have information permitting more extensive controls and employing more complex statistical techniques, tends to confirm Lewis's generalization. While unions in some environments raise wages by an enormous amount, the average estimated union wage effect is by no means overwhelming.

As predicted by the monopoly wage model, the capital-labor ratio and average "quality" of labor both appear to be somewhat greater than "optimal" in union settings. However, the total loss in output due to this misallocation of resources appears to be miniscule; an analysis done by Albert Rees suggests that the loss is less than 0.3 percent of the gross national product. For 1975, that would have amounted to $21 per person in the U.S. Even this estimate may be too high if one considers the other important and relevant distortions in the economy.

THE EVIDENCE ON PRODUCTIVITY

Our analyses of newly available data on unionism and output per worker in many establishments or sectors suggests that the monopoly view of unions as a major deterrent to productivity is erroneous. In some settings, unionism leads to *higher* productivity, not only because of the greater capital intensity and higher labor quality, but also because of what can best be termed institutional-response factors.

Table 2 summarizes the available estimates of the union productivity effect. The calculations in the table are based on statistical analyses that relate output per worker to unionization, controlling for capital per worker, the skill of workers (in some of the analyses), and other relevant factors. While all of the studies are subject to some

TABLE 2
Estimates of the impact of unionism on productivity

SETTING	ESTIMATED INCREASE OR DECREASE IN OUTPUT PER WORKER DUE TO UNIONISM
All 2-digit Standard Industrial Classification (SIC) manufacturing industries[1]	20 to 25%
Wooden household furniture[2]	15
Cement[3]	6 to 8
Underground bituminous coal, 1965[4]	25 to 30
Underground bituminous coal, 1975[4]	−20 to −25

Sources: All calculations are based on analyses that control for capital-labor ratios and diverse other factors that may influence productivity.

[1] From C. Brown and J. Medoff, "Trade Unions in the Production Process," *Journal of Political Economy,* June 1978, pp. 355–378.

[2] From J. Frantz, "The Impact of Trade Unions on Productivity in the Wood Household Furniture Industry," Senior Honors Thesis, Harvard University, March 1976.

[3] From K. Clark, "Unions and Productivity in the Cement Industry," Doctoral Thesis, Harvard University, September 1978.

[4] From R. B. Freeman, J. L. Medoff, and M. Connerton, "Industrial Relations and Productivity; A Study of the U.S. Bituminous Coal Industry," in progress.

statistical problems and thus must be treated cautiously, a general pattern emerges. In manufacturing, productivity in the organized sector appears to be substantially higher than in the unorganized sector, by an amount that could roughly offset the increase in total costs attributable to higher union wages.

In the typical manufacturing industry, the substantially lower quit rates under collective bargaining can explain about one-fifth of the estimated positive union productivity effect. Kim Clark, in his study of the cement industry, noted that from his discussions with individuals at recently organized plants, it appeared that the entrance of a union was usually followed by major alterations in operations. Interestingly, the enterprise typically changed plant management, suggesting that the union drive was an important signal to top management of ineffective lower level managerial personnel: The drive thus provided valuable information or shock of a distinctive kind. Perhaps most importantly, the discussions with union and management officials in the cement industry indicated that firms often adopted more efficiency oriented and less paternalistic personnel policies in response to unionism in order to raise productivity and meet higher wage demands.

On the other side of the picture, our analysis (with Marguerite Connerton) of productivity in organized and unorganized underground bituminous coal mines indicates that as industrial relations in the union sector deteriorated in the late 1960s and 1970s, unionism became associated with negative productivity effects. As the internal problems of the United Mine Workers have grown and the ability of management to deal effectively with labor issues seems to have deteriorated (most likely because the industry's rapid growth has yielded supervisors who are on average younger and less experienced in labor relations than was typical prior to the late 1960s), the factors that lower productivity have come to dominate underground bituminous coal mining. The striking change in the estimated impact of unionism on productivity in this industry during

the past decade highlights an important fact: The effects of unionism are not universal constants but rather depend on specific industrial-relations settings. An important, and as yet uncompleted task is to determine the differential impact of various industrial-relations practices on productivity and to discover, as far as is possible, the reasons for these differing impacts.

To repeat, unionism may increase productivity in some settings and decrease it in others. If the increase in productivity is greater than the increase in average unit costs due to the union wage effect, then the profit rate will increase; if not, the rate of profit will fall. There is limited tentative evidence that, on average, net profits are reduced somewhat by unionism, particularly in oligopolistic industries, though there are notable exceptions. At present, there is no definitive accounting of what proportion of the union wage effect comes at the expense of capital, other labor, or consumers, and what portion is offset by previously unexploited possibilities for productivity improvements.

Finally, it is important to note that despite what some critics of unions might claim, strikes do not seem to cost society a substantial amount of goods and services. For the economy as a whole, the percentage of total working time lost directly to strikes during the past two decades has never been greater than 0.5 percent and has averaged about 0.2 percent. Even "national emergency" disputes — those that would be expected to have the largest repercussions on the economy — do not have major deleterious impacts. Though highly publicized, the days idle because of the direct and indirect effects of strikes represent only a minuscule fraction of the total days worked in the U.S. economy.

PERSONNEL PRACTICES AND EMPLOYEE BENEFITS

Under the monopoly view, the exit and entry of workers permits each individual to find a firm offering the mix of employee benefits and personnel policies that he or she prefers. As noted earlier, however, the efficiency of this mechanism breaks down when there are public goods at the workplace and when workers are not able to change firms easily. In the voice view, a union provides management with information at the bargaining table concerning policies affecting its entire membership (e.g., the mix of the employee-compensation package or the firm's employment practices during a downturn) which can be expected to be different from that derived from the movements of marginal workers. It is likely, then, that the package of employee benefits and employment-adjustment policies will be different in firms covered by collective bargaining than in those that are not. To what extent does the mix of goods at the workplace differ between union and nonunion firms?

Data on the remuneration of individual workers and on the expenditures for employees by firms show that the proportion of compensation allotted to fringe benefits is markedly higher for organized blue-collar workers than for similar nonunion workers. Within most industries, important fringes such as pensions, and life, accident, and health insurance are much more likely to be found in unionized establishments. While some of the difference is attributable to the higher wages paid to union workers (since higher-wage workers generally "buy" more fringes), Table 3 reveals that much of the difference is in fact due to the effect of unionism. The table also indicates that the greatest increases in fringes induced by unionism are for deferred compensation, which is generally favored by older, more stable employees. This is consistent with the view that unions are more responsive to senior, less-mobile workers.

Studies concerning workers' preferences for fringes, and managers' awareness of these preferences, provide support for the claim that a union can provide management with information that affects the composition of the pay package. For instance, Richard Lester's 1967 review of surveys of managerial perceptions of worker preferences found "limited data . . . that workers value benefits more highly compared to wages than employers believe their workers do." Equally important is the apparent role of unions in evaluating the complex costs and prospective advantages of modern fringe benefits and transmit-

TABLE 3
Estimates of the effect of unions on major fringe benefits with the total compensation of workers held fixed

FRINGE BENEFIT	CENTS PER MANHOUR ON FRINGES, ALL ESTABLISHMENTS	PERCENTAGE OF ALL ESTABLISHMENTS WITH SPECIFIED FRINGES	PERCENTAGE AMOUNT BY WHICH DOLLARS PER MANHOUR SPENT ON FRINGES IS INCREASED OR REDUCED BY UNIONISM
Total fringes	40.9	—	14%
Life, accident, health insurance	10.1	85.0%	48
Pensions	9.4	62.6	21
Vacation pay	8.3	83.6	19
Holiday pay	5.2	77.8	15
Bonuses	1.8	27.1	−49

Source: R. B. Freeman, "The Effect of Trade Unionism on Fringe Benefits," National Bureau of Economic Research Working Paper No. 292, October 1978.

ting these facts to their members. It is unlikely that an individual worker will invest the time required to evaluate alternative compensation packages. Unions, however, can hire the lawyers, actuaries, and other experts necessary to perform these analyses.

The fact that many nonunion firms have imitated several of the provisions of union contracts is indicative of the better information available about workers' preferences in union settings. There is no reason for a nonunion firm to copy what union firms do unless union contracts offer forms of compensation that are also preferred by the average nonunion worker, since the satisfaction of the average (not the marginal) is what matters in a union-representation election. It is also important to note that to the extent that nonunion firms adopt union-initiated practices, estimates of the impact of unionism on the prevalence of such practices will be understated.

Finally, it should be pointed out that knowledgeable representatives of both labor and management agree that one of the major functions performed by American trade unions is determining a division of the compensation package that will be acceptable to workers. They recognize that some of the most important bargaining under unionism goes on *inside* the union, where the desires of workers with disparate interests are weighed in a political process that decides the union's positions at the bargaining table.

One of the most important personnel decisions made by a firm is how to adjust its employment and wages in response to swings in economic demand: by temporary layoffs, cuts in wage growth, reduced hours, or voluntary attrition. The evidence indicates that the layoff mechanism is used to a much greater extent in unionized than in nonunion establishments. It is important to note, however, that the vast majority of these layoffs are temporary, in that the laid-off members await rehire and are recalled after a short spell of unemployment.

By contrast, evidence on the effect on wages of swings in the demand for products shows that the responsiveness of wage rates is smaller in union than in nonunion firms. For example, within the typical manufacturing industry during the very severe economic downturn from May 1973 to May 1975 the fraction of hourly blue-collar union members unemployed due to layoffs grew more than twice the comparable fraction for otherwise similar nonmembers, but the wages of the unionized workers grew by 18.1 percent versus 16.6 percent for nonunion workers. More generally, analysis of monthly data covering the 1958-to-1975 period for manufacturing industries indicates that the hourly wages of production workers vary with shipments in such a way as to reduce the need for layoffs to a greater extent in firms that are nonunion than in those that are unionized, while there is virtually no such linkage in union settings. These findings reflect the fact that since the late 1950s about two-thirds of the major contract manufacturing workforce has come to be covered by agreements of three years or more, and nearly all have provisions for automatic wage increases.

Why do temporary layoffs dominate alternative adjustment mechanisms to a much greater extent in firms that are unionized than in those that are not? The most reasonable explanation is that under the provisions of most union contracts — which specify that junior workers will be laid off before those with more company service — senior workers, who can be expected to have greater power in organized firms, will generally prefer layoffs over the alternatives.

. . .

EXPLAINING MANAGERIAL OPPOSITION

If, in addition to its negative monopoly effects, trade unionism is associated with substantial positive effects on the operation of the economy and on the performance of firms, why do so many U.S. firms oppose unions so vehemently? There are in fact several reasons.

First, the bulk of the economic gains that

spring from unionism accrue to workers and not to owners or managers. Managers are unlikely to see any personal benefits in their subordinates' unionization, but are likely to be quite aware of the costs: a diminution of their power, the need to work harder, the loss of operating flexibility, and the like.

Second, though productivity might typically be higher in union than in otherwise comparable nonunion work settings, so too are wages. It would seem, given the objectives and actions of most unions, that the rate of return on capital would be lower under collective bargaining, although there are important exceptions. Thus there is risk in unionization; the firm may be able to rationalize operations, have good relations with the union, and maintain its profit rate — or it may not. In addition, while the total cost of strikes to society as a whole has been shown to be quite small, the potential cost to a particular firm can be substantial. Since managers — like most other people — dislike taking risks, we would expect opposition to unions even if on average the benefits to firms equal the costs. Moreover, given the wide-ranging differences in the effects of unions on economic performance, at least some managerial opposition surely arises from enterprises in which the expected benefits of collective bargaining are small but the expected costs high. Even the most vocal advocate of the collective-voice/institutional-response view of unionism would admit that, though functional in many industrial settings, unions are not functional in others — and one must expect greater managerial opposition in the latter cases.

Third, management may find unionism expensive, difficult, and very threatening in its initial stages, when modes of operation must be altered if efficiency is to be improved. New and different types of management policies are needed under unionism, and these require either changes in the behavior of current management, or — as appears to be the case in many just organized firms — a new set of managers.

Finally, U.S. management has generally adopted an ideology of top-down enlightened control, under which unions are seen as both a cause and an effect of managerial failure. In this view, unions interfere with management's efforts to carry out its social function of ensuring that goods and services are produced efficiently. In addition, because unions typically come into existence as a result of management's mistakes in dealing with its workforce, managers frequently resent what unionization implies about their own past performances.

We believe that our analysis of unionism has opened up a host of neglected issues regarding the key worker institution in the American capitalist system. While some of our findings will surely be altered by additional research and some may even be proven wrong, we do believe that our findings present a reasonably valid picture of modern unionism in our country. It stands in sharp contrast to the monopoly view of trade unions and to many popular opinions about them. And if, as we have found, the positive effects of unions are in many settings more important than their negative effects, then the on-going decline of private-sector unionism — a development unique to the U.S. among Western developed countries — deserves serious public attention.

NOTES

1. It is important to recognize that productivity gains, from improved methods of management in the face of unionism, run counter to the standard assumption of neoclassical economics that all enterprises operate at peak efficiency. It is, however, consistent with the "satisficing" models of firms developed by the recent Nobel Prize winner Herbert Simon and other analysts and with the model of X-inefficiency put forth by Harvey Leibenstein. In these models, firms strive for maximum efficiency only when they are under severe pressure from competitors, unions, or other external forces.

Why Employees Want Unions

JEANNE M. BRETT
Northwestern University

Twenty-two million American workers, or about 27 percent of the nonagricultural workforce, are represented by unions. What's more, according to a recent survey conducted for the U.S. Department of Labor, 33 percent of American workers who are not represented by unions *would* vote for such representation if given the chance. The findings of this study, which was conducted by the Institute for Social Research and Professor Thomas A. Kochan of Cornell University, support those of the study reported later on in this article.

Why are so many American workers interested in union representation? Although there had been no systematic research until recently on the factors motivating employee interest in unionization or employee reaction to union organizing campaigns, many groups have strong opinions on both matters. These groups include members of the National Labor Relations Board who regulate union organizing in the private sector, employers who wish to avoid it, union organizers who wish to profit by it, and labor lawyers and management consultants who make a business of it. Their individual beliefs often spring from experience with numerous organizing campaigns — experience that, in many cases, has shaped a strong idiosyncratic response in this area. Unfortunately, none of these parties to union organizing has had a systematic means of determining the actual reasons that employees in general are interested in union representation or what campaign tactics influence their votes for and against a union.

To address this need, I recently collaborated with two labor law professors (Stephen B. Goldberg of the Northwestern University Law School and Julius G. Getman of the Yale Law School) in a study, the results of which shed light on why employees want unions and how they react to a union-organizing campaign. The results also indicate that few of the assumptions on which the National Labor Relations Board regulates campaigning can be supported. It's conceivable that many employers, union organizers, labor lawyers, and management consultants are working from a set of assumptions that are also questionable.

Let's look first at a conceptualization of why employees want unions and then see the study results that support this conceptualization.

WHY EMPLOYEES WANT UNIONS — A CONCEPTUALIZATION

There are two main factors behind employee interest in unions. We'll examine them in turn.

1. An employee's initial interest in unionization is based on dissatisfaction with working conditions and a perceived lack of influence to change those conditions. In a nonunion firm, some aspects of employment, like wages and hours, are specified — but most conditions are not. Thus the relationship between the employer and the employee in such firms is based on a psychological contract. Each party to the contract expects the other to behave in a certain way. The employee expects the employer to provide fair wages and fair supervisory treatment, among other satisfactory working conditions, and the employer expects the employee to produce a reasonable amount of work at a particular level of quality.

An employee may violate the employer's expectations in several ways: through excessive absenteeism, for example, or an unwillingness to take directions, or habitually late arrival and early departure. In such instances, the employer can enforce his interpretation of the psychological contract by disciplining the employee. On the other hand, the employer may violate employee expectations in several ways: through unrealistic job previews, for example, that raise expectations so high that they can only be dashed later on, or failure to recognize superior performance, or unequal disciplinary measures meted out to two different employees for the same offense. Employees may also conclude that the employer has defaulted on the psychological contract when they see that their wages and benefits are not keeping up with inflation or with those of other, perhaps unionized, employees doing similar work.

When employee expectations of employer behavior are violated, the employee may complain, hoping to have the situation remedied. Implicit in an employee's acceptance of the employer's authority system is the notion that the employee can influence the system — that his or her complaints will be accepted as legitimate and acted upon. In responding to such a complaint satisfactorily, an employer

both removes the source of dissatisfaction and reinforces the employee's beliefs that he or she has power to influence the employer. Refusal to change the unsatisfactory condition behind the complaint may have one of these consequences: The employee may withdraw from active confrontation or reevaluate the legitimacy of the complaint; if other, desirable employment opportunities are available, the employee may quit; finally, where these employment alternatives are not available, the employee may turn to union representation.

As employees see it, an employer who fails to respond to a complaint has violated the psychological contract twice: first by promulgating the condition that led to the complaint and second by denying the legitimacy of the employee's attempt to exert influence to change the condition. In the face of this outcome, the employee may well conclude that his or her power under the psychological contract is considerably less than the employer's. The issue for the employee then becomes how to increase his or her share of the power — and the answer, frequently, is collective action.

Interest in collective action is naturally heightened when a dissatisfied employee finds that his attitudes are shared by other employees; the fact that they are shared tends to legitimize and reinforce them. Such a situation, in which a group of employees are dissatisfied about conditions, obviously holds potential for the formation of a coalition. But will such a coalition turn to unionization? This brings us to the second conceptualized factor behind employee interest in unions.

2. The likelihood that a coalition of dissatisfied employees will try to organize a union depends on whether they accept the concept of collective action and whether they believe unionization will yield positive rather than negative outcomes for them. The rationale behind collective action is simple enough. Acting alone, an employee who withholds his labor in

an effort to influence the employer is likely to be unsuccessful — either because the loss of his labor has little impact or because he can easily be replaced. A group of employees who withhold their labor will obviously have a much greater impact, considering the large-scale decrease in productivity that would result and the difficulties involved in replacing an entire group. Collective action, then, does give employees a potentially workable means of exerting control over their working conditions.

Even so, some dissatisfied employees may find the concept distasteful. For one thing, collective action implies a loss of individuality; from this point of view, skilled employees may in some instances be less well off under a collective system in which their individual advantages go to serve the collective good. For another, some employees may be so averse to striking that the potential benefits to be derived — improvement in working conditions — lose all appeal.

In the end, a decision to organize a union is instrumental. Do the employees involved believe they will be better off with a union or not? They must ponder the fact that there is no certainty that collective bargaining will improve their wages and working conditions. They must also recognize that some employers cannot increase their labor costs and remain competitive while others, even though enjoying sound fiscal health, will not meet their demands unless compelled to do so by a strike. In sum, then, employees must decide whether they are willing to take the stand required by collective action and whether they believe that such a stand will help or hurt them. The answers to these questions may be the key to their decision on whether to support union representation.

WHY THEY WANT UNIONS — THE EVIDENCE

The evidence on which this conceptualization of why employees want unions is based comes primarily from the research we did concerning the validity of the Board's assumptions about cam-paign tactics. The study measured voting behavior in actual union representation elections and, although the sample involved was somewhat limited geographically, the results are strongly supported by the previously mentioned Department of Labor study conducted by the Institute for Social Research and Professor Thomas A. Kochan of Cornell University. (This study measured employees' intent to vote for or against union representation, if given the chance.) The fact that the Department of Labor's findings support ours is important because the DOL sample is more broadly representative of American working men and women than ours was.

In our study, a significant proportion of employees who were dissatisfied with working conditions — especially job security and wages — voted for union representation. Knowing an employee's initial satisfaction allowed us to predict his or her vote with 75 percent accuracy. This initial satisfaction with working conditions was measured by means of interviews during which employees were asked the eight questions. Satisfaction with wages, job security, fringe benefits, treatment by supervisors, and chances for promotion was significantly related to a vote for union representation. The only aspect of satisfaction queried that did not substantially correlate with a vote for unionization was dissatisfaction with the kind of work being done. In fact, most of the employees interviewed liked the type of work they were doing. Their interest in unionization was triggered by their working conditions, not by the work itself. . . .

Probably the most important factor accounting for employees' interest in unionization lies in their belief in the instrumentality of unions. We found that dissatisfied employees tended not to vote for unionization if they believed the union was unlikely to improve the working conditions that dissatisfied them. On the other hand, even some of the employees who were satisfied with their working conditions voted for union representation because they believed the union was likely to improve conditions. . . .

We measured employee attitudes toward unions. . . . Beliefs that union dues are too high, that unions are too strong, that unions interfere with good relations between companies and workers and that unions cause high prices were all associated with voting against union representation. Instrumental beliefs that unions make sure employees are treated fairly and help employees get better wages and hours were associated with voting for union representation — as was the belief that when a strike is called, it is generally for good reason.

In sum, our study results indicate that employees' interest in unionization is triggered by real frustration in the workplace and strong beliefs that the way to remove that frustration is through collective action.

HOW EMPLOYEES REACT DURING UNION ORGANIZING CAMPAIGNS — A CONCEPTUALIZATION

Our conceptualization of how employees react during union organizing campaigns holds important implications for both employers and unions.

1. *The employer's anti-union campaign that attempts to persuade employees by emphasizing economic power over them and generating fear is unlikely to be successful.* Fear appeals are notoriously ineffective in changing firmly held attitudes and opinions. Employees who are basically fearful of retaliatory moves against them by an employer are not likely to have signed authorization cards in the first place. And in all probability, those who do sign authorization cards have already come to terms with their realization of the employer's hostility toward the union and his ability, albeit illegal, to use economic power against them. If the decision to support unionization is indeed an instrumental one, the pro-union employee has weighed the pros and cons of his or her commitment to the union before making it. In fact, pro-union em-

ployees may view threatening employer behavior simply as confirmation of their poor opinion of him and as support for their previous decision that they need a union to deal with him.

2. *The employer's most effective anti-union campaign emphasizes that he wishes to remain nonunion, that current working conditions are not so bad, and that employees cannot know with certainty what conditions will be like under union representation.* If an employer wishes to remain nonunion but does not campaign, he shows employees no sign of his concern over the extent of their dissatisfaction and frustration. A strong reaction to the union organizing drive will show employees that he does recognize their concerns and that their commitment to union representation holds important consequences for him. Although legally the employer cannot promise to alleviate the conditions that led to dissatisfaction — or actually alleviate them — during the campaign, it is quite simple to convey the impression that he has been enlightened and that conditions can be improved. By reacting strongly to an organizing campaign, the employer may gain the support of some pro-union employees — simply because they see that they can influence him without resorting to unionization.

The employer's campaign is also more likely to be effective if it reinforces the opinions of employees who do not support the union and of those union supporters whose dissatisfaction with working conditions is not strong. Accordingly, the employer may be able to gain support by convincing such employees that conditions are not bad enough to warrant a union and by emphasizing the uncertain benefits of unionization. One way to do the latter is to point out that the union must strive for change through collective bargaining and that the employees cannot be sure the process will alleviate the conditions they find unsatisfactory. He may also inform them that if they strike, they may be permanently replaced. Such appeals to uncertainty should lower the estimated instrumentality of unionization and gain support for the employer.

HOW EMPLOYEES REACT TO A UNION ORGANIZING CAMPAIGN — THE EVIDENCE

We found, as expected, that most employees signed union authorization cards because they wanted union representation. Typically dissatisfied with working conditions and favorable toward unions, most card signers ultimately voted for union representation. Nonsigners, who were significantly more satisfied with working conditions and less favorable toward unions than were the signers, tended to vote against union representation.

The union meeting is the best forum for a unionization appeal by the pro-union coalition. At the meeting, employees learn that others share their opinions both of working conditions and of the employer's unwillingness to change those conditions. Whether formal or informal, discussion during the meeting of problems employees have had with the employer may both create and strengthen employee dissatisfaction with current conditions. The union meeting also appears to be a good forum for conveying information that reduces uncertainty about the union's ability to change conditions through collective bargaining. In conveying this information, union organizers typically emphasize the union's grievance arbitration system and point to union gains made in other firms — not only wage gains, but also gains in such benefits as healthcare, pensions, holidays, and vacations.

The level of attendance at the union meeting is a good barometer of the degree of union support, even if some attendees are as yet uncommitted. If the union can get a good turnout, the anti-employer, pro-union enthusiasm generated at the meeting may create a bandwagon effect that pulls in the uncommitted. Often, however, the union has difficulty getting even pro-union employees to attend union meetings, much less a sizable representation of uncommitted or procompany employees. Typically, then, the meeting serves to reinforce pro-union employees' commitment to the union, although some of those in our sample who originally supported the company did switch and vote for the union after attending union meetings. Contacts with firmly committed union supporters during the meeting — and, possibly, before and after meetings — may have provided information that influenced their beliefs about the instrumentality of union representation. Employees who switched to the union became more positive about unions after the meetings than were company supporters who did not attend union meetings and whose vote preferences did not change. The former were also more familiar with the content of the union campaign than were those who remained company supporters.

The union may also gain supporters through informal social contact between committed union supporters and dissatisfied employees who know little about unions or the changes a union might effect and who fear employer retaliation should they become active in the union. These union supporters may be able to focus uncommitted employees' dissatisfaction against the employer and give the employees enough information about unions to create pro-union attitudes. If other employees reinforce these fledgling pro-union attitudes, the union may have a new convert — but this is a moot eventuality, since pro-union employees have no control over their converts' social environment. Encounters with further information from the employer, the employee's supervisor, or other procompany employees are just as likely — and these may swing the fledgling pro-union convert back to uncertainty. Faced with an ultimate need to decide, the employee who is still uncertain about the benefits of union representation is likely to vote for the status quo: against union representation.

A major criterion in our selection of elections

to study was their potential to be hard fought. And indeed the fight was on in most of the ones we studied — so much so that in 22 out of a total of 31, the employer engaged in unlawful campaigning. Nevertheless, we found no evidence that an employer's unlawful threats and reprisals caused pro-union employees to switch and vote against the union. In fact, the percentage of pro-union employees interviewed who reported employer threats or reprisals for union activity was the same, regardless of whether the employer's behavior could be characterized as lawful, unlawful or, as the Supreme Court says, "egregiously" unlawful. Even more important, the proportion of pro-union employees who switched and voted against the union was approximately the same (nine percent) regardless of the legality of the employer's campaign. . . .

IMPLICATIONS

This research poses a number of implications for the several parties concerned with union organizing.

1. *The factors stimulating employee interest in union representation existed long before the union-organizing campaign was begun.* Union organizers are fond of saying that the best union organizer is the boss. These organizers recognize that it is far easier to interest dissatisfied employees in unions than it is to interest satisfied employees.

2. *Employers wishing to remain nonunion should be concerned with employee satisfaction.* I remember being rather stunned when, as a student, I learned the maxim that although it was nice to provide satisfactory working conditions for employees, employers should not assume that having satisfied workers will necessarily benefit the company. Both our research on union organizing and subsequent studies, all of which corroborated our findings, demonstrate resoundingly that the maxim is false as far as unionization is concerned. Satisfied employees are

seldom interested in unionization; they don't need it.

3. *Employee attitude surveys can provide accurate information about the degree to which employees may be willing to vote for a union if given the chance.* It's not a good idea to include in such attitude surveys any questions about employee intent to vote for or against a union, any questions about their views of labor's image, or any questions concerning their beliefs about the instrumentality of unionization. Even if the survey is conducted in a way that leaves participants anonymous, such questions may open the employer to charges of unfair labor practice. Questions about satisfaction with the working conditions, however, are almost as useful as those concerning unions, and they are not likely to be legally suspect unless the surveys are conducted in the middle of a union organizing campaign. . . .

Obviously, the employer who wishes to remain non-union should be using surveys or some other systematic means of assessing employee attitudes long before organizing efforts begin. He should also be committed to making the changes that are indicated by survey results. . . .

4. *Unions should focus their organizing efforts on units in which employees are dissatisfied.* Unions might also use surveys to determine where to focus organizing efforts. Such surveys could include questions about employees' views of labor's image, unions' instrumentality, and attitudes toward working conditions. One difficulty for the union, of course, is that of identifying the employees of a particular organization and then of obtaining their addresses or telephone numbers. . . .

Our results did show a slight tendency for younger and minority workers, but no other demographic groups, to vote for union representation. It is quite clear that the reason younger workers tend to be in favor of unionization is that they generally hold less desirable jobs and so are typically less satisfied with their working conditions than older workers are. Minority workers' interest in unions, however, represents more than their general tendency to hold less desirable jobs and be dissatisfied with them. Minority workers apparently accept the concept of unionization and collective action more readily than other workers do. Without further analysis of data from the DOL Study, it is difficult to pinpoint the factors that interest white collar women in union representation. Two possible explanations are that they are underemployed relative to their education and competency and that many of them are minority workers who recognize the power of collective action. The reason that other demographic groups of workers are not necessarily interested in unions is that, in each group, some experience satisfactory working conditions and others experience unsatisfactory conditions — so their attitudes cancel each other out. . . .

5. *Union organizers should concentrate on getting employees to attend union meetings.* It's not as easy to attend union meetings as it is to attend employer meetings. Employers typically hold campaign meetings for employees on company time and premises and, although employees are not compelled to attend, most do. In the elections we studied in which company meetings were held, 83 percent of the employees involved reported that they had attended. Unions typically must hold campaign meetings outside of working hours and away from company premises. (There are, however, unusual circumstances — when employees are isolated because they work and live on a ship, an island, or at a resort hotel, for example — in which the Board requires employers to provide access to

company premises by nonemployee union organizers.) Obviously, then, attending a union meeting requires some effort. In our study, only 36 percent of employees attended union meetings in the elections that featured such meetings.

Although familiarity with the themes of employer and union campaigns was not very high among the employees we studied, familiarity was greatest among those who had attended meetings. Furthermore, attending a union meeting and familiarity with the union campaign were related to switching from a pro-company to a pro-union vote. As previously suggested, attending the union meeting may provide emotional support for faltering pro-union sentiments or information that tips the balance of belief about whether unionization can improve wages and working conditions. . . .

CONCLUSION

We know much more about the factors motivating interest in unionization than we did a few years ago. Questions remaining for further research, however, are still numerous. We don't know, for example, what experience or information contributes to a favorable or unfavorable image of "Big Labor" or to beliefs in the instrumentality of unions. Neither do we know with certainty why some initially pro-union employees switched and voted for the company. Thus I cannot really fault employers and management consultants who try to win pro-union employees for the company with campaigns based on idiosyncratic knowledge. Despite all these caveats, however, employers who wish to remain nonunion and union organizers, as well, now have more empirical research evidence on which to base their decisions and actions.

Predicting the Outcome of Union Certification Elections: A Review of the Literature

HERBERT G. HENEMAN III
University of Wisconsin

MARCUS H. SANDVER
Ohio State University

The nature and determinants of union membership growth have long occupied a central position in industrial relations research. The conceptual and intellectual inspiration for this line of research can be traced back to the work of Sidney and Beatrice Webb ([1897]1926) and John R. Commons (1911). Research on union growth has continued unabated since these early writings.

Union membership grows through both non-election sources, such as employment expansion in established units, and election sources; the focus of this review is solely on the latter source. The potential for growth through the election process is great. In the period 1973–78, for example, the National Labor Relations Board (NLRB) supervised over 45,000 single-union elections, in-volving an average unit size of 50 employees and resulting in a union victory rate of 47 percent. Thus unions potentially gained over one million members from elections during those years (Sandver and Heneman, 1981), although a union election victory does not automatically translate into new members.

Research on factors predictive of the certification election outcome has been slow to develop. Even the earliest descriptive work on such elections did not appear in academic journals until the mid-1950s (for example, Spielmans, 1956). Since then, the volume of research on this subject has expanded considerably, especially since the mid-1970s. During the years 1980–82 alone, twelve such studies were published.

With such a proliferation of research on the union election outcome in recent years, it is time to review and appraise this literature, with an eye toward suggesting the improvements needed in future research on this subject. Such is the primary purpose of this paper, although we shall also suggest some policy implications of the research results obtained to date.

Reprinted with permission, from the *Industrial and Labor Relations Review,* Vol. 36, No. 4 (July 1983), pp. 537–559. © 1983 by Cornell University. All rights reserved.

Herbert Heneman is Professor at the Graduate School of Business and at the Industrial Relations Research Institute, University of Wisconsin — Madison, and Marcus Sandver is Associate Professor at the College of Administrative Science of The Ohio State University. Portions of the work on this paper were carried out while Prof. Heneman was on leave at Ohio State University. The authors gratefully acknowledge the contributions of Robert Billings, John A. Fossum, Richard Klimoski, Thomas A. Kochan, David Lewin, and Paula B. Voos.

METHODOLOGY

Selection of Studies

The first methodological consideration of the present review was to determine criteria to be used in selecting the studies to be appraised. Since the overriding objective of this review was to examine factors empirically associated with a union's winning or losing an NLRB election, we decided to include only those studies in which the election outcome was the dependent variable. There were two kinds of such studies. The first, labeled here *individual-level studies,* investigated the voting behavior of individuals and used as the dependent variable whether workers voted for or against union representation. The second, labeled *election-level studies,* used as the dependent variable the outcome of elections, and thus the election, rather than the individual voter, served as their unit of analysis.

Many studies were excluded from this review, on the above, as well as other, grounds. One group of studies was excluded, even though relevant to the issue of union elections, because the researchers did not specifically seek to better understand the election outcome itself. Several of these studies incorporated some data on elections, but they focused primarily on union membership growth (Adams and Krislov 1974; Ashenfelter and Pencavel 1969; Bernstein 1961; Freeman and Medoff 1979; Hirsch 1980; Moore and Newman 1975; Sandver and Heneman 1981). Other studies in this excluded group used as their dependent variable some proxy for the actual vote or election outcome, such as the intention to vote for representation, the perceived need for unionization, or workers' attitudes toward unions (Allen and Keaveny 1981; Bigoness 1978; Feuille and Blandin 1974; Flango 1975; Gordon and Long 1981; Kochan 1979; Sandver 1977; Youngblood, DeNisi, and Mobley 1982).

A second group of studies was excluded because each did little more than repeat an analysis of a data set that had already been analyzed in a previous publication (Brett 1980; DeCotiis and LeLouran 1982; Farber and Saks 1980;[1] Getman, Goldberg, and Herman 1972; Herman 1973). The inclusion of these studies would have consumed valuable space and, more importantly, would have overstated the extent to which some variables were or were not related to the election outcome.

Finally, because of the small number of other studies, we excluded studies of decertification elections (Anderson, Busman, and O'Reilly 1979 and 1982; Chafetz and Fraser 1979; Dworkin and Extejt 1979) and studies of elections outside the United States (Beaumont 1981; Chafetz and Fraser 1979). Nevertheless, future research should examine both kinds of elections, to enable meaningful analysis and generalization about this important topic.

After employing all of the above criteria for selection, we chose a total of 29 studies for inclusion in this review: eight individual-level studies and 21 election-level studies.[2] . . .

RESULTS

Individual-level Studies

It is important to mention two of their methodological characteristics before proceeding to a discussion of their results. First, all of the studies used a self-report measure of voting, rather than the worker's actual vote.[3] Second, in all but two of the studies (Getman, Goldberg, and Herman 1976; Hamner and Smith 1978), data for the independent variables were gathered *after* the election. Workers' responses to attitudinal measures in such studies must therefore be viewed as retrospective.

Individual-level studies examined the voting behavior of diverse employee groups, ranging from production workers to college faculty. The major kinds of independent variables investigated were job satisfaction, attitudes toward unions, individual characteristics, and campaign characteristics.

All eight of the studies contained one or more measures of job satisfaction, and all but one of them (Harrison, Johnson, and Rachel 1981) found significant negative relationships between job satisfaction and pro-union voting behavior.

In those studies using facet measures of satisfaction (such as promotion and the work itself), no specific facet emerged as consistently predictive of voting behavior. This result also held when simply the crude distinction between economic and noneconomic satisfaction was employed as the independent variable. Despite this lack of consistency in results, however, it appears that somewhere between 25 and 50 percent of the variance in voting behavior may be explained by employee satisfaction levels.

Employees' attitudes toward unions also appear fairly predictive of their voting behavior. Both general attitudes toward unions as institutions and more specific attitudes influence voting behavior. Among the more specific attitudes, most impressive are the results for employees' perceptions of the instrumentality of the union as a mechanism for obtaining individually desired outcomes, such as a wage increase or job security (Brotslaw 1967; Getman, Goldberg, and Herman 1976; LeLouran 1979; Schriesheim 1978).

Individual characteristics, either individual-background or current-job variables (such as hours of work or wage rates), so far show little promise as predictors of voting behavior (Brotslaw 1967; Hammer and Berman 1981; Schriesheim 1978). Rarely were significant relationships obtained, and even those relationships that were significant were of very low magnitude. It should be noted, however, that the individual-characteristic variables chosen for investigation were fairly typical ones to include on a questionnaire (such as age) and there appeared to be little if any theoretical basis for their inclusion.

Finally, campaign characteristics were explicitly investigated in two of the studies. Brotslaw (1967) found no significant relationships between voting behavior and the perceived effectiveness of either the union's organizing techniques or the company's resistance techniques. Alternatively, Getman, Goldberg, and Herman (1976) found numerous campaign characteristics to have a significant relationship to voting behavior. Familiarity with the union's campaign and attendance at union meetings correlated most significantly with pro-union behavior.

Election-level Studies

All but four of these studies used the individual election as the unit of analysis (Hyclak 1981; Krislov 1967; Mitchell 1980; Roomkin and Juris 1979); the unit of analysis in these four was an aggregation of quarterly or annual election (and other) data.

Unit size has been the most thoroughly investigated predictor of election outcomes, appearing in 14 of the 21 studies. In each instance, a negative relationship was found between unit size and the union victory rate, for both original elections (Sandver and Latack 1982) and repeat elections (Czarnecki 1969). For example, Rose (1972) found that the union victory rate consistently declined from 66 percent in units of nine or fewer employees to 52 percent in units of 100 or more employees.

The type of unit (such as craft or production), type of employer (by SIC industry code), status as a U.S. or foreign-owned firm, and the union involved in the election all were found to be related to the election outcome. Because of the large number of different units, employers, and unions involved, it is impossible to summarize here the differences in results among the many categories of these variables. The most complete reporting of these differences may be found in Fogel (1964), Greer and Shearer (1981), Rose (1972), and Sandver (1981).

The location of the election unit has also been investigated in a number of studies, with distinctions drawn between metropolitan and nonmetropolitan, southern and nonsouthern, and right-to-work and non-right-to-work locations. The results of these studies indicate that location has little bearing on election outcomes. Moreover, as Sandver (1982) has shown, a seeming location effect may be illusory primarily as the result of locational differences in other variables (such as unit size or type of unit) known to be related to election outcomes.

The time elapsed between the petition for and the conduct of the election was investigated in four studies (Miller and Leaming 1962; Pollitt 1963; Prosten 1979; Roomkin and Block 1981). In all four studies, the length of the time elapsed had a negative, though not large, relationship to the percentage of union election victories. Unfortunately, none of these studies investigated possible reasons for this finding.

The percentage of employees signing authorization cards was used as a predictor in two studies (Drotning 1967; Sandver 1980). Not surprisingly, both studies found that this variable had a positive effect on the percentage of union victories. It should be noted, however, that the relationship was far from perfect.

Voter turnout (the proportion of eligible voters actually voting) was examined in three studies (Becker and Miller 1981; Block and Roomkin 1982; Sandver 1980). It was found to have a significant negative relationship to the percentage of union wins and to the margin of victory in both employer- and union-won elections.

Becker and Miller (1981) and Delaney (1981) confined themselves to predicting election outcomes in a single kind of organization: hospitals. They thereby were able to incorporate specific organizational characteristics of hospitals as potential predictors of the election outcome, but neither study found much support for this hypothesis. Whether this finding is specific to hospitals or holds true for other organizations as well remains to be seen.

Despite the statistical significance of all of the above relationships, their practical significance is open to question. In general, the magnitude of the zero-order correlations was quite small, and even when the variables were used simultaneously as predictors in a regression equation, the percentage of variance explained in election outcomes rarely exceeded 15 percent.

Much higher variance-explained estimates (with R^2 ranging from .71 to .91) were obtained

in the four studies using aggregate data as the unit of analysis (Hyclak 1982; Krislov 1967; Mitchell 1980; and Roomkin and Juris 1979). Another feature of these studies made possible by aggregation is their use of various economic variables as predictors. Unfortunately, a mixed set of results emerged from these four studies. For example, the aggregate (industry or occupation) wage level and the percentage change in the level were related to election outcomes, but not consistently in the same direction. Unemployment and industrial production figures were also not consistently significant predictors. Clearly, these findings must be interpreted cautiously, pending the results of additional research.

Summary

With one exception (Hamner and Smith 1978), the eight individual-level studies that were examined attempted to identify factors to explain employees' voting for or against the union. Employee job satisfaction and attitudes toward unions were consistently strong predictors of voting behavior, whereas demographic characteristics of employees were not. The scant evidence available suggested that various features of the organizing campaign had little effect on the direction of employees' votes.

For the most part, the results of the 21 election-level studies were much less predictive of the election outcome. Most of the researchers confined their samples to election data that were publicly (and conveniently) available from NLRB and other archival records. As such, various bargaining unit and election characteristics were the primary predictors employed. Unit size, the type of unit, the union and type of employer involved, voter turnout, the percentage signing authorization cards, and the petition-to-election time lapse were all predictive of the election outcome. In studies using different (non-NLRB) data sources, pay levels and changes in pay levels were also found to be associated with the election outcome. The significance of all these relationships was typically quite weak, however. Contrary to expectations, certain other variables bore little, if any, relationship to the election outcome. These included locational variables such as southern location, economic variables such as production and unemployment rates, and organizational characteristics of the employer.

ANALYSIS AND DISCUSSION

The results of the studies reviewed here, particularly the individual-level ones, have contributed to our understanding of why elections result in victory or loss for the union. There are numerous limitations of the studies, however, necessitating a rather cautious interpretation of the results to date. We turn now to a discussion of these limitations and their implications for future research.

Kinds of Elections

Elections may be classified in several ways: (1) certification or decertification; (2) single union or multi-union; (3) initial, rerun, or repeat; and (4) consent, stipulated, regional-director-ordered, or Board ordered. These distinctions imply differing conditions surrounding the election and differing attitudes and behavior on the part of labor and management. In turn, these conditions may imply differing causes of election outcomes or a differing relative importance of causes as a function of the kind of election.

While these differences obviously apply in the distinction between certification and decertification elections, they might well extend to the other distinctions as well. Resistance tactics employed by management, for example, might play a more important role in determining the outcome of Board ordered elections than in that of consent elections. As another example, interunion comparisons and rivalry are virtually nonexistent in single-union elections, but they may play a significant role in influencing the results of multiunion elections.

Unfortunately, the studies examined here generally have not maintained these distinctions in data analysis or reported the kinds of elections that were under investigation. In fact, two of the studies (Fogel 1964; Lawler 1982) even combined certification and decertification data into one data set for analysis purposes. Future researchers must be careful to maintain and report distinctions among the various kinds of elections, and they should also investigate the possibility of differing causal models underlying their outcomes.

Definitions of Underlying Constructs

Some of the measures used in the research on union elections appear to have been selected on the basis of their convenience or availability, with little attention to a priori definition of the underlying construct these measures represent. Consider the case of unit size. This measure, readily available from NLRB records, has been the most frequently used independent variable in election-level studies. Yet what does unit size truly represent? A host of post hoc answers to this question has been offered, including the homogeneity of employees' interests and values, employer sophistication in using resistance techniques, and the ease and cost of organizing. Which of these inferences we accept, if any, will obviously influence the interpretation we make of the consistently negative relationship between unit size and the union victory rate.

Another example is the variable measuring the time between petition and election dates. Again, what underlying construct does it represent? Is election delay caused by employer resistance, the legitimate difficulty of specifying the appropriate bargaining unit in many cases, or the administrative inefficiency of the NLRB? Again, the construct we employ will determine, at least in part, how we interpret the variable's consistently negative relationship to the union victory rate. Matters are further clouded by the fact that all but one of the studies (Miller and Leaming 1962) confounded the time-lapse variable with the kind of election involved. Thus, much of the speculation about the underlying meaning of the time-lapse variable may be based on a spurious relationship to the union victory rate.

In short, researchers must pay more attention to defining constructs and developing measures of them before beginning their analyses, rather than simply using readily available measures and providing post hoc explanations of the constructs they represent. Along these lines, we suggest a moratorium on studies using only the independent variables available from NLRB records. It is clear that they serve as poor predictors of the election outcome, and in any event, they are imprecise proxies for numerous underlying constructs. Moreover, construct clarity would be greatly aided by the development of stronger theoretical frameworks.

Theoretical Frameworks

Too much of the research on union elections has not been founded on explicit theoretical frameworks. Rather, the research process has been inductive, with researchers providing post hoc theoretical explanations for the empirical relationships they uncover. In the individual-level studies, notable examples of this are researchers' explanations of the effects of demographic data as independent variables. Many of the election-level studies, particularly those using NLRB data such as unit size, are also primarily inductive.

An inductive research strategy is often useful in initially identifying relationships, but there are limits to its usefulness in explaining why those relationships exist. Consider again the case of unit size and its negative relationship to the union victory rate. If previous studies had defined the constructs underlying unit size, explicitly hypothesized how each was related to the election outcome, and then tested those hypotheses, we would know more about the determinants of the election outcome.

Thus, future research must develop more explicit theoretical frameworks to generate testable hypotheses. Noteworthy in this regard is the work of Fossum (1982) and Brief and Rude (1981) on models of voting behavior in union elections.

Omitted Variables

The use of stronger theoretical frameworks inevitably will suggest additional independent variables that may influence workers' voting behavior. Although the purpose of this review is not to propose new theoretical frameworks, we would like to suggest some variables that might profitably be incorporated in future studies.

For individual level studies, the backgrounds of employees and their previous exposure to unions, either actual or vicarious (such as through family members) should receive more attention than they have to date. It seems highly probable that such experiences influence voting behavior. Second, whether employees vote for or against the union may depend on their belief in the desirability of change in general, their confidence in management, and their intention to use their vote as a means of retaliation against the company. Such attitudes may also be related to whether or not employees choose to even vote in the election (the so-called no-show issue).

Finally, in individual level studies, more attention should be devoted to variables that serve to change employees' intended vote to a different actual vote. As noted earlier, the relationship between workers' actual and intended votes is hardly one-to-one, and we need to know why. Examples of variables that may be important influences here are the behavior of labor and management during the campaign and the role that fellow employees may play in changing voters' intentions. Peer-group pressure, in particular, might well be a powerful determinant of voting behavior.

In election level studies, three major classes of variables deserve investigation.[4] First, both the level of and changes in several economic variables, such as wages, prices, and unemployment, need more extensive examination. Only six election-level studies (Delaney 1981; Hyclak 1982;

Krislov 1967; Lawler 1982; Mitchell 1980; Roomkin and Juris 1979) have used such variables, and four of those used aggregate data. Aggregate data shed little light on how well economic variables can predict the results of *individual* elections. We make this recommendation fully aware of the difficulty of finding economic measures relevant to the elections being studied (such as the unemployment rates for the kinds of employees participating in the elections). Until such studies are done, and on a *nonaggregated* basis, a large empirical void will remain regarding the effects of economic variables on election outcomes.

The second major class of variables needing investigation is the financial (and other) resources used by both labor and management during the organizing campaign. Included here would be the numbers and kinds of people enlisted to influence the election outcome, such as business agents, consultants, and lawyers. It is obvious that both labor and management behave as if both the nature and level of their resource commitments will influence the outcome of elections. The extent to which election results can in fact be so influenced remains an open question. As before, we offer this recommendation knowing full well the difficulties in gathering the necessary data.

Finally, additional research should be carried out to determine the effects of organizational characteristics on election outcomes. Although the results of Becker and Miller (1981) and Delaney (1981) are not particularly promising in this regard, it would be premature to direct future research away from organizational characteristics. In fact, the characteristics of both employers *and unions* should be investigated. We know that union victory rates vary from union to union; it therefore is plausible that organizational characteristics particular to certain unions may help account for this.

Causal Inference

The ultimate objective of research on union elections is to determine what causes unions to win or lose elections. Unfortunately, causal inference has often been hampered by the use of inadequate methodological designs.

The fundamental problem among the individual-level studies has been their reliance on a retrospective research design, in which attitudinal independent variables are gathered after an election and hence after the employees' actual vote. It is thus quite possible that voters responded in such a manner as to be consistent with, or to justify, their vote. Such "decision bolstering" is one plausible explanation for the relationships found between attitudes and voting behavior in these retrospective studies.

Predictive designs, such as that used by Getman, Goldberg, and Herman (1976), are clearly superior to retrospective designs, since they reduce decision bolstering as an explanation of their results. It is nevertheless true that the relationship between attitudes and voting behavior found in this study is quite consistent with the results of the studies using retrospective techniques, which suggests that decision bolstering may not be a major problem in retrospective studies. To make certain of that, however, future studies should use designs, such as predictive ones, that minimize the possibility of decision bolstering.

In many election-level studies, particularly those based on NLRB data, the researchers have established simply concurrent relationships, which needless to say creates problems of causal inference. Future researchers should strive to use more predictive designs, such as those that incorporate the time-lagging of independent variables.

Public Employees

Public employees at any governmental level have been conspicuously absent from the samples analyzed in election outcome studies (the lone exception being Muczyk, Hise, and Gannon 1975). Consequently, it is impossible to determine whether the results of the studies reviewed here are generalizable to the public sector. They may very well not be, given the vast differences between private and public organizations and between their legal, institutional, and economic environments.

Statistical Analysis

The studies reviewed here have uncovered numerous factors that influence election outcomes. All too often, however, these studies have failed to provide any estimate of the combined impact of these factors on the election, such as would be possible through the use of a multivariate analysis. The use of such analysis should routinely become a part of future research on the multiple determinants of election outcomes.

Accompanying such analysis should be a routine calculation and reporting of the statistical significance levels of both univariate and multivariate relationships. In general, previous research has not followed these procedures, or has done so only sporadically, severely hampering the interpretation of results.

Membership Implications

As noted previously, a union victory is no guarantee of additional membership; for many possible reasons, employees may or may not subsequently join the union. These reasons include employees' level of job satisfaction; their attitudes about the union after the election; whether a contract is ever negotiated and agreed upon (Prosten 1979); and the kind of union security clause in the contract.

Unfortunately, we know almost nothing about union joining after a union election victory. Consequently, we do not know what percentage of employees become union members after an election victory or what factors are predictive of employees' postelection membership status. In short, we do not know what proportion of union membership growth is attributable to the election process or why that proportion is what it is.

The research literature would be much improved if union election studies were broadened to investigate the membership implications of election victories for the union. By necessity, this question would require more longitudinal research, with multiple data-collection points. In the meantime, we urge researchers to maintain carefully the distinction between election victories and gains in membership. This distinction is often blurred; the results of union election studies are directly translated into implications for union growth or, worse, they are treated as synonymous with union growth (Block and Premack, n.d.; Fiorito and Greer 1982). In a similarly misguided approach, individual-level studies that use a proxy for workers' actual votes in an election (such as voters' intentions or voters' attitudes toward unions) are often viewed as synonymous with studies of union election outcomes.

POLICY IMPLICATIONS

Although the union election research to date has several limitations, it nonetheless has a number of potential implications for public, union, and management policies. Although we cannot present a full discussion of these implications here, we would like to highlight a few of them.

Public Policy

It is apparent that the size of the election unit is an important influence on the outcome of the election. Although the published research has made little attempt to establish a theoretical relationship between unit size and election outcome — and certainly more needs to be done on this topic (see Sandver and Latack 1982) — the policy implications of the relationship should be emphasized. Anyone formulating or interpreting national public policy that affects the determination of the election unit should realize that any shift in policy favoring larger, more inclusive election units will likely result in fewer certification elections won by unions.

A second policy issue is the relationship between signatures on authorization cards and votes in the representation election. The research results generally show that there is less than a one-to-one relationship between signatures on the authorization cards and votes in the election. Getman, Goldberg, and Herman (1976) found, for example, that only 72 percent of card signers actually voted for the union in the subsequent election. (Also see Drotning 1967; Sandver 1977; and Sandver 1980.) Since these findings suggest that cards are at best an imperfect proxy for workers' desire for union representation, any change in public policy that would substitute card signatures for votes in an election or that would grant "automatic" recognition based on a certain percentage of card signatures (such as the Labor Law Reform Bill of 1977) would be ill advised. Furthermore, the continued interpretation of authorization cards by the courts as a true measure of employee pro-union sentiments should be called into question.[5]

A third public policy issue raised by the research reviewed here is the conduct of the election campaign. Although both the study by Brotslaw (1967) and that by Getman, Goldberg, and Herman (1976) found that the conduct of the campaign does not substantially affect the way workers vote in elections, additional research may be necessary to further substantiate these preliminary findings. Any major change in NLRB policy regulating election campaigns may be empirically premature, but some deregulation of the previous "laboratory conditions" requirement (as the NLRB has done in the Midland National Life Insurance Company case, 263 NLRB 24, 1982) should be possible without altering election outcomes.

Finally, based on the research reviewed here, public policy changes may be recommended with respect to excessive delays between the filing of petitions and actual elections. All of the studies reviewed here suggest that there is a negative relationship between the length of time elapsed in the election procedure and the probability that the union will win the election. Although no one would advocate instant elections, policymakers should recognize that anything serving to prolong the time between the NLRB's receipt of an election petition and the actual election seems to affect negatively the union's ability to win the election. Hearing officers and board members should bear this fact in mind when entertaining motions for delay or continuance in an election hearing.

Union Policy

From the perspective of unions, the major policy issue raised by the research on election outcomes is its potential for helping the union improve its election victory rate. This issue is of particular importance in light of relatively steady decline in that victory rate since the 1940s, as well as the continued decline in the percentage of union representation in the labor force (Prosten 1979; Sandver and Heneman 1981). Several possible inferences can be drawn from the research.

First, employees' job satisfaction and perceptions of union instrumentality do influence how they vote. To enhance their victory rate, unions might therefore carefully target organizing campaigns to work places where dissatisfaction is high and employees have favorable perceptions of the usefulness of unions, or focus organizing campaigns on the specific sources of employee dissatisfaction and the ability of the union to address those sources — effectively and rapidly. These are hardly novel suggestions, but they can now be made from an established empirical base.

The negative relationship between unit size and the union victory rate raises a second policy issue. Between 1973 and 1981, for example, unions won fewer than 25 percent of all elections conducted in units of 1000 or more employees (Sandver and Latack 1982). Unions might therefore exercise more care in choosing larger units as organizing targets. In fact, a recent simulation of potential membership gains from varying unit sizes, as well as from varying victory rates and numbers of elections, demonstrates some of the trade-offs among these variables that unions confront when attempting to increase membership through the election process (Sandver and Heneman 1981).

Finally, although supporting data are limited, it appears that general economic conditions have little bearing on election outcomes; this would suggest that unions' organizing activities should not be unduly influenced by cyclical economic conditions. Moreover, it is likely that organizing activities emphasizing unfavorable economic conditions will have little effect on workers' voting preferences in union elections; instead, the union should appeal directly to employees' specific circumstances and the union's ability to change them.

Management Policy

For employers wishing to remain "union free," the research results also suggest a number of policy implications. First, it is clear that the more satisfied employees are, the less likely they are to vote for the union. Programs to assess and improve employee satisfaction thus could have long term payoffs in defeating the union during an election. Although no relevant data are available, such activities might also lessen the probability of an election ever occurring.

Second, employers seeking to win a certification election must attempt to weaken employees' perceptions of the utility of the union. They therefore must challenge union claims of an ability to deliver successfully those outcomes valued by employees. It would also seem that the employer must attempt to create or strengthen employee beliefs that management will be instrumental in providing valued outcomes — without the presence of a union.

Finally, employers might want to down-play the importance they attached to geographical location when making assessments of their susceptibility to unionization. Union victory rates do not vary substantially as a function of location even though the probability of an election's occurring might. Moreover, much of the alleged locational difference in victory rates is simply a

spurious reflection of other factors that are related to both location and victory rates.

CONCLUSION

The 29 studies reviewed here have been moderately successful in identifying variables that are predictive of the outcome of union representation elections. The numerous limitations of those studies suggest, however, that their results should be interpreted cautiously. It is to be hoped that future research will be theoretically and methodologically improved. In the meantime, the results of the studies to date have many policy implications for those who are willing to act on them.

NOTES

1. Farber and Saks (1980) performed a partial reanalysis of some of the Getman, Goldberg, and Herman (1976) data, cast in a more economic framework. In particular, the treatment of the wage variable as a predictor of voting differed, as Farber and Saks used the individual's relative standing in the company's wage distribution, whereas Getman, Goldberg, and Herman used the individual's absolute wage.

2. We did not have a chance to see three very recent studies (Cooke 1983; Dickens 1983; Seeber n.d.) until well after this paper was completed and accepted for publication; these are therefore not included in this review.

3. Most of these studies reported the actual vote distribution (the percentage for and against the union) and the self-report vote distribution, and in all of these instances the two distributions were very similar. Note, however, that this does not necessarily imply a high correlation between the actual and self-report votes of individuals.

4. These three classes of variables might also be incorporated into individual-level studies. Doing so, however, would require assessing employee perceptions of the variables, rather than using objective indices of them. The reason for this requirement is that the objective indices would have constant values for all employees in a given election, and thus the correlations between the variables and voting behavior would be zero. For example, the actual unemployment rate in a local labor market would be a constant value for all

employees in an election. Employees' perceptions and interpretations of the rate might vary, however, and in turn be related to their voting behavior.

5. See, for example, *United Dairy Farmers Cooperative Assn. v. NLRB,* 633 F.2d 1954 (3d Cir., 1980).

REFERENCES

Adams, Arvil V., and Joseph Krislov
1974 "New Union Organizing: A Test of the Ashenfelter-Pencavel Model of Trade Union Growth." *Quarterly Journal of Economics,* Vol. 88, No. 2, pp. 304–11.

Allen, Robert E., and Timothy J. Keaveny
1981 "Correlates of University Faculty Interest in Unionization: A Replication and Extension." *Journal of Applied Psychology,* Vol. 66, No. 5, pp. 582–88.

Anderson, John C., Gloria Busman,
and Charles A. O'Reilly III
1979 "What Factors Influence the Outcome of De-certification Elections?" *Monthly Labor Review,* Vol. 192, No. 11, pp. 32–36.
1982 "The Decertification Process: Evidence from California." *Industrial Relations,* Vol. 21, No. 2, pp. 178–95.

Ashenfelter, Orley, and John H. Pencavel
1969 "American Trade Union Growth: 1900–1960." *Quarterly Journal of Economics,* Vol. 83, No. 3, pp. 434–48.

Beaumont, Philip B.
1981 "Unionism, Collective Bargaining and Regulation: Statutory Recognition Provisions in Britain, 1976–80." Manuscript, Department of Social and Economic Research, University of Glasgow.

Becker, Brian E., and Richard U. Miller
1981 "Patterns and Determinants of Union Growth in the Hospital Industry." *Journal of Labor Research,* Vol. 2, No. 2, pp. 309–28.

Bernstein, Irving
1961 "The Growth of American Unions, 1945–1960." *Labor History,* Vol. 2, No. 2, pp. 131–57.

Bigoness, William J.
1978 "Correlates of Faculty Attitudes Toward Collective Bargaining." *Journal of Applied Psychology,* Vol. 63, No. 2, pp. 228–33.

Block, Richard, and Steven L. Premack
N.d. "The Unionization Process: A Review of the Literature." *Advances in Industrial and Labor Rela-*
tions; Vol. 1, David B. Lipsky and Joel M. Douglas, eds. Greenwich, Conn.: JAI Press, in press.

Block, Richard N., and Myron Roomkin
1982 "A Preliminary Analysis of the Participation Rate and the Margin of Victory in NLRB Elections." In Industrial Relations Research Association. *Proceedings of the Thirty-Fourth Annual Winter Meeting, December 28-30, 1981, Washington, D.C.* Madison, Wis.: IRRA, pp. 220–26.

Brett, Jeanne M.
1980 "Why Employees Want Unions." *Organizational Dynamics,* Vol. 9, No. 1, pp. 47–59.

Brief, Arthur P., and Dale E. Rude
1981 "Voting in Union Certification Elections: A Conceptual Analysis." *Academy of Management Review,* Vol. 6, No. 2, pp. 261–67.

Brotslaw, Irving
1967 "Attitude of Retail Workers Toward Union Organization." *Labor Law Journal,* Vol. 18, No. 3, pp. 149–71.

Chafetz, I., and C. R. P. Fraser
1979 "Union Decertification: An Exploratory Analysis." *Industrial Relations,* Vol. 18, No. 1, pp. 59–69.

Chaison, Gary N.
1973 "Unit Size and Union Success in Representation Elections." *Monthly Labor Review,* Vol. 96, No. 2, pp. 51–52.

Commons, John R.
1911 *A Documentary History of American Industrial Society.* Cleveland: A. H. Clark.

Cooke, William N.
1983 "Determinants of the Outcomes of Union Certification Elections." *Industrial and Labor Relations Review,* Vol. 36, No. 3, pp. 402–14.

Czarnecki, Edgar R.
1969 "Unions' Record in Repeat Elections." *Labor Law Journal,* Vol. 20, No. 11, pp. 703–15.

DeCotiis, Thomas A., and Jean-Yves LeLouran
1981 "A Predictive Study of Voting Behavior in a Representation Election Using Union Instrumentality and Work Perceptions." *Organizational Behavior and Human Performance,* Vol. 27, No. 1, pp. 103–18.

Delaney, John Thomas
1981 "Union Success in Hospital Representation Elections." *Industrial Relations,* Vol. 20, No. 2, pp. 149–61.

Dickens, William T.
1983   "The Effect of Company Campaigns on Union
       Certification Elections: *Law and Reality* Once
       Again." *Industrial and Labor Relations Review,*
       Vol. 36, No. 4, pp. 560–75.

Drotning, John
1967   "NLRB Remedies for Election Misconduct:
       An Analysis of Election Outcomes and their De-
       terminants." *Journal of Business,* Vol. 40, No. 2,
       pp. 137–48.

Dworkin, James B., and Marian Extejt
1979   "Why Workers Decertify their Unions: A Pre-
       liminary Investigation." Academy of Manage-
       ment. *Proceedings of the Thirty-Ninth Annual
       Meeting, August 7–11, 1979, Atlanta, Georgia,* pp.
       241–45.

Farber, Henry S., and Daniel H. Saks
1980   "Why Workers Want Unions: The Role of
       Relative Wages and Job Characteristics." *Jour-
       nal of Political Economy,* Vol. 88, No. 2, pp. 349–
       69.

Feuille, Peter, and James Blandin
1974   "Faculty Job Satisfaction and Bargaining Sen-
       timents: A Case Study." *Academy of Management
       Journal,* Vol. 17, No. 4, pp. 678–92.

Fiorito, Jack, and Charles S. Greer
1982   "Determinants of U.S. Unionism: Past Re-
       search and Future Needs." *Industrial Relations,*
       Vol. 21, No. 1, pp. 1–32.

Flango, Victor E.
1975   "Faculty Attitudes and the Election of a Bar-
       gaining Agent in the Pennsylvania State College
       System — I." *Journal of Collective Negotiations in
       the Public Sector,* Vol. 4, No. 2, pp. 157–74.

Fogel, Walter
1964   "The Teamsters and NLRB Representation
       Elections, 1962–63." *Labor Law Journal,* Vol.
       15, No. 10, pp. 649–59.

Fossum, John A.
1982   *Labor Relations.* 2d ed. Dallas: Business Publica-
       tions.

Freeman, Richard B., and James L. Medoff
1979   "New Estimates of Private Sector Unionism in
       the United States." *Industrial and Labor Relations
       Review,* Vol. 32, No. 2, pp. 143–74.

Getman, Julius G., Stephen B. Goldberg,
and Jeanne B. Herman
1972   "The National Labor Relations Board Voting
       Study: A Preliminary Report." *Journal of Legal
       Studies,* Vol. 1, No. 2, pp. 233–58.

1976   *Union Representation Elections: Law and Reality.*
       New York: Russell Sage Foundation.

Gordon, Michael E., and Larry N. Long
1981   "Demographic and Attitudinal Correlates of
       Union Joining." *Industrial Relations,* Vol. 20,
       No. 3, pp. 306–11.

Greer, Charles R., and John C. Shearer
1981   "Foreign Ownership Effects on NLRB
       Representation Elections." *Journal of Interna-
       tional Business Studies,* Vol. 3, No. 1, pp. 9–23.

Hammer, Tove H., and Michael Berman
1981   "The Role of Noneconomic Factors in Faculty
       Union Voting." *Journal of Applied Psychology,*
       Vol. 66, No. 4, pp. 415–21.

Hamner, W. Clay, and Frank J. Smith
1978   "Work Attitudes as Predictors of Unionization
       Activity," *Journal of Applied Psychology,* Vol. 63,
       No. 4, pp. 415–21.

Harrison, Edward L., Douglas A. Johnson,
and Frank M. Rachel
1981   "The Role of the Supervisor in Representation
       Elections." *Personnel Administrator,* Vol. 29, No.
       9, pp. 67–71.

Herman, Jeanne B.
1973   "Are Situational Contingencies Limiting Job
       Attitude — Job Performance Relationships?"
       Organizational Behavior and Human Performance,
       Vol. 10, No. 2, pp. 208–24.

Hirsch, Barry T.
1980   "The Determinants of Unionization: An Anal-
       ysis of Interarea Differences." *Industrial and
       Labor Relations Review,* Vol. 33, No. 2, pp.
       147–61.

Hyclak, Thomas
1982   "Union-Nonunion Wage Changes and Voting
       Trends in Union Representation Elections." In
       *Proceedings of the Thirty-Fourth Annual Winter Meet-
       ing, December 28–30, 1981, Washington, D.C.* In-
       dustrial Relations Research Association.
       Madison, Wis. IRRA, pp. 334–350.

Kochan, Thomas A.
1979   "How American Workers View Labor
       Unions." *Monthly Labor Review,* Vol. 102, No.
       4, pp. 23–31.

Krislov, Joseph
1967   "Union Organizing of New Units, 1955–
       1966." *Industrial and Labor Relations Review,* Vol.
       21, No. 1, pp. 31–39.

Lawler, John
1982   "Labor-Management Consultants in Union
       Organizing Campaigns: Do They Make a Dif-

ference?'' Industrial Relations Research Association. *Proceedings of the Thirty-Fourth Annual Winter Meeting, December 28-30, 1981, Washington, D.C.* Madison, Wis. IRRA, pp. 274-80.

LeLouran, Jean-Yves
1980 ''Predicting Union Vote from Worker Attitudes and Perceptions.'' Industrial Relations Research Association. *Proceedings of the Thirty-Second Annual Winter Meeting, December 28-30, 1979, Atlanta, Georgia.* Madison, Wis. IRRA, pp. 72-82.

Miller, Richard U., and George F. Leaming
1962 ''The Extent and Significance of Administrative Delays in the Processing of Union Representation Cases in Arizona.'' *Arizona Review of Business and Public Administration,* Vol. 11, No. 9, pp. 1-11.

Mitchell, Daniel J. B.
1980 *Unions, Wages and Inflation.* Washington, D.C. Brookings Institution.

Moore, William J., and Robert J. Newman
1975 ''On the Prospects for American Trade Union Growth.'' *Review of Economics and Statistics,* Vol. 57, No. 4, pp. 439-45.

Muczyk, Jan P., Richard T. Hise, and Martin J. Gannon
1975 ''Faculty Attitudes and the Election of a Bargaining Agent in the Pennsylvania State College System — II.'' *Journal of Collective Negotiations in the Public Sector,* Vol. 4, No. 2, pp. 175-89.

Pollitt, Daniel H.
1963 ''NLRB Re-run Elections: A Study.'' *North Carolina Law Review,* Vol. 41, No. 2, pp. 209-24.

Prosten, Richard
1979 ''The Longest Season: Union Organizing in the Last Decade.'' Industrial Relations Research Association. *Proceedings of the Thirty-First Annual Meeting, August 29-31, 1978, Chicago.* Madison, Wis. IRRA, pp. 240-49.

Roomkin, Myron, and Richard N. Block
1981 ''Case Processing Time and the Outcome of Representation Elections: Some Empirical Evidence.'' *University of Illinois Law Review,* Vol. 1, No. 1, pp. 75-97.

Roomkin, Myron, and Hervey A. Juris
1979 ''Unions in the Traditional Sectors: The Mid-Life Passage of the Labor Movement.'' Industrial Relations Research Association. *Proceedings of the Thirty-First Annual Meeting, August 29-31, 1978, Chicago.* Madison, Wis. IRRA, pp. 212-22.

Rose, Joseph B.
1972 ''What Factors Influence Union Representation Elections?'' *Monthly Labor Review,* Vol. 95, No. 10, pp. 49-51.

Sandver, Marcus H.
1977 ''The Validity of Union Authorization Cards as a Predictor of Success in NLRB Certification Elections.'' *Labor Law Journal,* Vol. 28, No. 11, pp. 696-702.
1980 ''Predictors of Outcomes in NLRB. Certification Elections.'' Midwest Academy of Management. *Proceedings of the Twenty-Third Annual Meeting, April 10-12, 1980, Cincinnati, Ohio,* pp. 174-81.
1981 ''Inter-Union Differences in NLRB. Election Outcomes: A Cross Sectional and Time Series Analysis,'' paper presented at the Forty-First Annual Meetings of the Academy of Management, San Diego, Calif., August 4, 1981.
1982 ''South-Nonsouth Differentials in NLRB. Certification Election Outcomes.'' *Journal of Labor Research,* Vol. 3, No. 1, pp. 13-30.

Sandver, Marcus H., and Herbert G. Heneman III
1981 ''Union Growth Through the Election Process,'' *Industrial Relations,* Vol. 20, No. 1, pp. 109-16.

Sandver, Marcus H., and Janina C. Latack
1982 ''Unit Size and Outcomes in NLRB Elections: A Group Polarization Effect?'' paper presented at the Forty-Second Annual Meetings of the Academy of Management, New York, August 18, 1982.

Schriesheim, Chester A.
1978 ''Job Satisfaction, Attitudes Toward Unions, and Voting in a Union Representation Election.'' *Journal of Applied Psychology,* Vol. 63, No. 5, pp. 548-52.

Seeber, Ronald L.
N.d. ''Union Organizing in Manufacturing: 1973-1976.'' In *Advances in Industrial and Labor Relations,* Vol. 1, David B. Lipsky and Joel M. Douglas, eds. Greenwich, Conn. JAI Press, in press.

Spielmans, John V.
1956 ''Measuring the Results of Organizational Union Representation Elections.'' *Industrial and Labor Relations Review,* Vol. 9, No. 2, pp. 280-85.

Webb, Sidney, and Beatrice Webb.
[1897] *Industrial Democracy.* London: Longmans,
1926 Green and Co., Ltd., 1926 ed. (Originally published in 1897.)

Youngblood, Stuart A., Angelo S. DeNisi,
and William H. Mobley
1982   "Attitudes, Perceptions, and Intentions to Vote
     in a Union Certification Election: An Empirical
     Investigation." Industrial Relations Research
Association. *Proceedings of the Thirty-Fourth Annual
Winter Meetings, December 28–30, 1981, Washington, D.C.* Madison, Wis. IRRA, pp. 244–53.

New Strategies in Union Organizing

JAMES A. CRAFT

MARIAN M. EXTEJT
Both of University of Pittsburgh

I. INTRODUCTION

Since the 1950s, the proportion of unionized workers in the American labor force has been declining. In addition, knowledgeable analysts forecast that the labor movement will likely experience continued stagnation in the 1980s (BNA 1980), even though recent survey research suggests that a substantial proportion of currently unorganized workers would vote to join a union (Kochan 1979). In response to this secular decline in membership, some union officials have emphasized the need for increased organizing activity and have called for more effective and creative strategies in organizing the sizeable reservoir of nonunion workers. There is, however, little analysis or systematically formulated information available about the activities unions are actually undertaking.

This paper identifies and critically discusses organizing strategies that recently have been developed or re-emphasized and employed by unions. This study is based upon a thorough review of the available scholarly literature regarding union organizing, an extensive examination of union publications, labor reporting service information, newspaper accounts, and other documents describing and identifying union organizing activity, and 18 interviews with national union officials or former unionists who have particular knowledge or experience relating to current organizing strategies and approaches.

Section II presents a perspective on the classical approach to organizing and discusses ways in which this may be changing. Then, a review of emergent organizing strategies being used by some unions is given in Section III. Next, from interviews and other data, a preliminary examination is given of factors which appear to affect the use and success of these approaches to organizing. Finally, concluding comments regarding union organizing in the 1980s are developed in the last section.

II. THE CLASSICAL APPROACH

A review of the available documents, literature and recorded experience regarding union organizing activity over the last 50 years suggests that there is not a standard body of techniques and methods that is uniformly employed in organizing campaigns.[1] The classical organizing process generally consists of various "tactics, expedients, and improvisations" developed by the individual organizers to respond to the immediate situation (Barbash 1956). There appear to be few, if any, broadly coordinated and targeted activities.

From *Journal of Labor Research,* Vol. IV, No. 1 (Winter 1983) pp. 19–32. Reprinted with permission.

Traditionally, most unions conduct highly decentralized organizing programs with the effort directed at individual work units (e.g., offices, plants). The organizer, a person who is generally self-trained in union organizing activity and comes from the rank and file membership, is the key individual who has substantial control over the design and implementation of the organizing campaign. In organizing efforts, the organizer is the embodiment of the union to the prospective union members.

The emphasis in organizing activity appears to be directed heavily toward face-to-face contact with union recruits. The organizer visits homes of employees to discuss the union, develops social contacts and relationships with workers, organizes small informal meetings of prospective members, and occasionally obtains employment in the target company to have direct access to and integration with the employees. Through their contacts and effort, union organizers seek "ways to transform individual dissatisfaction into a collective condition of unrest" and "channel it into the direction of group action through the formation of a union" (Karsh *et al.* 1953, pp. 33, 94). The organizer generally attempts to tailor the organizing approach to the concerns and problems of the prospective members (e.g., the special needs of women workers, skilled workers, racial and ethnic groups, white collar workers). The organizer sells the idea of group action — that through the instrumentality of the union the employees' concerns and dissatisfactions could be addressed effectively.

Traditionally, face-to-face organizing activity is *facilitative* in nature; that is, working with and through employees to convince them of the usefulness of a union. Nevertheless, some organizing activity at the employee level includes coercive tactics as well. Some activities involve the use of group pressure, threats, or violence against union holdouts. Coercive activity has been more common, however, in the less frequent organizing efforts directed at the employer (e.g., owner or plant manager) in a "top-down" organizing program. In such cases, the union gener-

ally demands recognition as bargaining agent for the employees in a proposed unit. To enforce its demand, it directly threatens or conducts a strike, slowdown, boycott, or implements organizational picketing.

This decentralized, personally oriented, and generally reactive approach to organizing appears to have been successful from the 1930s through the 1960s. Since the early 1970s, however, this approach seems to have been less fruitful as witnessed by the declining proportion of union victories in representation elections and the subsequent relative decline of union members in the work force.

III. A NEW EMPHASIS IN ORGANIZING

Leaders of the AFL–CIO have explicitly called for the development of new, more effective, and imaginative strategies and tactics to enhance organizing success (Shevis 1980; Barry 1980). In response to the changing environment and the encouragement of the Federation, some unions have forged new strategic thrusts and approaches to organizing that appear to transcend the classical model. Generally speaking, these approaches are oriented toward the development of coordinated and targeted activities. They seem to be characterized by union institutional planning and control rather than by delegating organizing responsibility basically to the organizer. With some of the newer strategies, increased attention appears to be directed to the employer organization (or group of employers) as a *system* rather than the decentralized orientation with emphasis on the individual plant. A few unions are employing a wider scope of pressure tactics ranging from indirect sophisticated financial pressures to coordinated direct confrontations with the employer. These unions seem increasingly willing to utilize coercive as well as facilitative tactics in organizing. Along with this, face-to-face recruiting and personal organizing activity remain important processes, but are viewed more as integral parts of a *larger program* to induce employees to join or force the employer to recognize the union.

From our review of recent organizing activity and experience, we are able to identify four basic strategic thrusts that seem to represent the "new emphasis in organizing." These include: the corporate power strategy; the collective bargaining strategy; the community acceptance and integration strategy; and the coordinated/pooled resource strategy.

IV. THE CORPORATE POWER STRATEGY

This strategy is designed to coerce a firm targeted for organizing into recognizing the union by applying financial pressures, confronting the employer, and isolating it from the business and consumer communities. Generally, careful analysis of a firm is conducted in terms of its environment and power base. Then, a multifaceted campaign is deployed focusing on the areas in which the firm appears to have the greatest vulnerability. There is a wide array of tactics and actions employed to exert pressure.

Pressure/Harass Business Associates

One significant tactic in this strategy is to prod, harass, and embarrass firms that have directorate ties or are involved in business associations with the target company. In effect, these activities are designed to bring other firms, against their will, into the labor dispute between the company undergoing the organizing drive and the union. The resulting threats of harmful publicity and possible financial loss resulting from the undesired involvement in the dispute constitute the inducement for these business associates to sever relations with the target firm or to exert pressure on it to cease resisting the organizing efforts. Such activity, it is argued, can undercut the object company's financial support and isolate it from the mainstream business community. . . .

Confrontation with Owners/Management

In combination with other tactics, some unions are engaging in direct confrontations with management and stockholders of anti-union companies. The objective is to make the stockholders aware of management's behavior toward employees and unions, to create adverse publicity for the firm, and embarrass management before the owners of the company. The confrontations may take the form of mass demonstrations and picketing at a company's annual meeting. . . . Or, the confrontations may occur in the stockholders meeting itself. For example, the union (as a stockholder attending the meeting) raises questions during the meeting regarding the company's anti-union conduct. . . .

Financial Pressures

One widely advocated tactic, designed to pressure anti-union firms by restricting their flow of investment capital, is for unions to seek increased influence over the investment of pension and welfare funds (Rifkin and Barber 1978; Raskin 1979; Gutchess 1980). With greater voice in policy and decision-making, it is argued that the union can direct investment away from those companies whose behavior is deemed anti-union and which resist organizing efforts. Greater union voice and influence is gained through more assertiveness and focused objectives by labor trustees on jointly administered pension funds (e.g., negotiated multiemployer plans) and by gaining increased control and participation in other plans through collective bargaining (Greenough and King 1976). . . .

Product Market Pressure

As part of a corporate power strategy, unions are also employing more conventional pressure tactics to affect adversely the market position of an anti-union company and create consumer and public support for the union cause. For example, in *conjunction* with other tactics, the boycott has been used in several recent organizing campaigns. . . . The success of a boycott tactic as part of the corporate power strategy is not necessarily in its economic impact on the company as much as it is in its ability to arouse the press, the public, and legislative opinion against the anti-union company. . . .

V. COLLECTIVE BARGAINING STRATEGY

This strategic approach to organizing has been employed by unions which already have an established bargaining relationship with a company. It is an *inside* strategy whereby the union, using its bargaining leverage in the ongoing relationship, attempts to negotiate binding contractual rules that will facilitate the organization of current and planned nonunion company facilities. This strategy has been employed in multiplant firms that traditionally have been well organized but are now closing older unionized plants and opening new plants in nonunion areas. Usually, only one or two key unions represent workers in these firms and the bargaining structure is centralized.

One approach is the negotiation of a "neutrality pledge." Such a pledge, which is part of the negotiated labor agreement, requires that the company remain strictly neutral and not oppose a union organizing drive at any of the company's nonunion facilities. . . . Another approach implementing this strategic thrust is the negotiation of an "accretion agreement." Under such an agreement, the company emphasizes the similarities and functional integration of new facilities with existing plants. When a new plant opens, it is viewed simply as a transfer and extention of current operations — an accretion. In such circumstances, the union is granted automatic recognition as the bargaining agent for employees. . . .

Finally, negotiated transfer and preferential hiring rights have also been used recently to facilitate the organization of new plants. Under the UAW–GM agreement, for example, employees have the right to transfer, with full seniority, to any new GM plant making products like those produced in plants already organized by the union. In the UAW–Budd contract, union workers laid off at the Gary, Indiana, plant are given preferential hiring rights at the new Johnson City, Tennessee, plant. These transfer and hiring rights almost insure experienced unionists in the work force of unorganized plants who may act as inside organizers during an ensuing organizing drive.

VI. COMMUNITY ACCEPTANCE AND INTEGRATION

This strategic approach is increasingly employed by unions attempting to organize workers in communities and areas of the country which have no tradition of unionization. In such communities, the union is often considered to be a "foreign force." The media, educational system, community values, and opinion leaders are frequently anti-union. In such situations, union leaders argue that building a "basis of support in the community itself" to change prevailing perceptions of the labor movement and the role of collective bargaining is a key approach to organizing workers effectively ("Union Community Role . . ." 1978; Shevis 1980). The objectives are to develop an acceptance of the union as a legitimate member of the community and to provide credible and acceptable channels through which the prospective union members may be approached. Implementation of this strategic approach may be direct or indirect in nature.

Using a direct approach, some unions have initiated programs to specifically address social, personal, and health needs of the people in a community. By directly focusing its efforts on meaningful problems and needs, the union develops a positive image, a more credible position, and a community acceptance from which it can begin to concentrate on organizing workers for collective bargaining. . . . An indirect approach involves the union identification with and cooperation of the natural allies in the community that already have legitimacy and acceptance among the workers the union seeks to organize. Such organizations frequently include church groups or civil rights organizations. . . .

VII. COORDINATED/POOLED RESOURCE STRATEGY

Through coordination and/or consolidation of organizing activity, two or more unions can reduce the resources wasted in rivalry and conduct more effective overall organizing campaigns. This strategy is used to increase organizing efficiency, enhance union power and resources, and to improve the image of labor organizations.

One classic approach which is currently being emphasized is the joint union organizing drive. Under such a program, two or more unions (usually within some common sphere of activity such as building and construction trades or the Industrial Union Department) define a particular target locale and agree to pool some resources and cooperate in organizing the employees in the area. This means that the unions would share information, identify employer targets and tactics to effectively deal with them, pool resources to sponsor newspaper and television ads to promote unionization and, to the degree possible, organizers from the various unions will work to assist one another and refer possible members to cooperating unions. In addition, such cooperation and collaboration can be used to reduce administrative costs by renting offices and halls as well as having a support staff which can be used by all cooperating unions. . . .

VIII. CONCLUDING COMMENTS

We have identified, reviewed, and critically evaluated strategies that recently have been developed or re-emphasized by unions to enhance organizing effectiveness. While some of these approaches appear to have possibilities and may even add new dimensions to the organizing process, we remain skeptical as to whether they will have much effect, at least in the short run, in reversing the downward trend in union membership. These methods generally have been rather sparsely used; even then, the results have been mixed. In addition, the prospects are not particularly bright that such strategies will be used more or with greater success in the foreseeable future. Unions have traditionally been rather unclear and imprecise on organizing priorities in terms of long range opportunities or goals. The political realities of union leadership and the general short-term focus of decision making militate against their increased use. It would appear that unions do little hard assessment of organizing activity to better determine how to invest resources for the biggest payoff to the union in terms of its objectives. Subsequently, it is difficult to justify substantial investment in or change toward these "new strategies."

In addition, a number of external environmental factors including declining public approval of union power and union leaders (Lipset and Schneider 1981), a sputtering economic environment with high unemployment and limited growth, and the growing sophistication of management in maintaining a "union-free environment" all work against the prospects for significant union growth over the next several years regardless of strategies employed. While there undoubtedly are other important factors to consider, our analysis of organizing strategies leads us to agree with the pessimistic forecast in the opening paragraph that unions will likely experience continued stagnation in the 1980s.

NOTES

1. Some of the best published research regarding the classical approach to organizing includes: Bambrick and Stieglitz 1959; Barbash 1956; Brooks 1937; Ginzberg 1948; Karsh *et al.* 1953; McKersie and Brown 1953; Perkel 1957; and Strauss 1953.

REFERENCES

Bambrick, James J., Jr., and Stieglitz, Harold. "White Collar Unionization: Case Study: OEIU Organizing Campaign." Reprinted in Jack Barbash ed., *Unions and Leadership.* New York: Harper and Brothers, 1959, 169–175.

Barbash, Jack. *Labor Unions in Action.* New York: Harper & Brothers, 1948.

_____. "The Emergence of Urban Low-Wage Unionism." *Proceedings of the Twenty-Sixth Annual Winter Meeting.* Madison, Wisconsin; Industrial Relations Research Association, 1973, 275–283.

_____. *The Practice of Unionism.* New York: Harper & Brothers, 1956.

_____. *Unions and Union Leadership.* New York: Harper and Brothers, 1959.

Barry, John M. "New Organizing Emphasis Tied to Unity, Cooperation." *AFL–CIO News,* XXV (March 1, 1980), 1, 3.

Bennett, James T. and Johnson, Manuel H. *Pushbutton Unionism.* Fairfax, Virginia: Contemporary Economics and Business Association at George Mason University, 1980.

Berenbeim, Ronald. *Labor Unions: Where are They Heading?* New York: The Conference Board, Information Bulletin #93, 1981.

Berkowitz, Monroe. "The Economics of Trade Union Organizing and Administration." *Industrial and Labor Relations Review.* VII (July 1954), 575–592.

Bilik, Al. "Corrupt, Crusty, or Neither? The Poll-ish View of American Unions." *Labor Law Journal.* XXX (June 1979), 323–333.

Block, Richard N. "Union Organizing and the Allocation of Union Resources." *Industrial and Labor Relations Review.* XXXIV (October 1980), 101–113.

BNA, "Outlook on 1980s Labor Market Changes." *Labor Relations Yearbook, 1979.* Washington, D.C.: Bureau of National Affairs, 1980, p. 25.

Brooks, Robert R. R. *When Labor Organizes.* New Haven: Yale University Press, 1937.

Bok, Derek, C. and Dunlop, John T. *Labor and the American Community.* New York: Simon and Schuster, 1970.

Craft, James A. "The Employer Neutrality Pledge: Issues, Implications and Prospects." *Labor Law Journal.* XXXI (December 1980), 753–763.

Fulmer, William E. "Step by Step Through a Union Campaign." *Harvard Business Review* LIX (July-August 1981), 94–102.

Ginzberg, Eli. *The Labor Leader: An Exploratory Study.* New York: MacMillan Company, 1948.

Gitelman, Morton. *Unionization Attempts in Small Enterprises.* Mundelein, Illinois: Callaghan & Company, 1963.

Gray, Lois S. "Unions Implementing Managerial Techniques." *Monthly Labor Review.* CIV (June 1981), 3–13.

Greenough, William C. and King, Francis P. *Pension Plans and Public Policy.* New York: Columbia University Press, 1976.

Gutchess, Jocelyn. "Pension Investment: The European Model." *The AFL–CIO Federationist.* XXXVII (June 1980), 4–20.

Hurd, Richard W. "Strategies for Union Growth in Food Manufacturing and Agriculture." *Proceedings of the Twenty-Sixth Annual Winter Meeting.* Madison, Wisconsin: Industrial Relations Research Association, 1973, 267–274.

Industrial Union Department. *A Guidebook for Union Organizers,* Industrial Union Department, AFL–CIO; Publication #42, September 1961.

Janus, Charles J. "Union Mergers in the 1970s: A Look at the Reasons and Results." *Monthly Labor Review.* CI (October 1978), 13–33.

Karsh, Bernard; Seidman, Joel, and Lilienthan, Daisy M. "The Union Organizer and His Tactics: A Case Study." *American Journal of Sociology,* LIX (September 1953), 113–122.

Kochan, Thomas A. "How American Workers View Labor Unions." *Monthly Labor Review.* CII (April 1979), 23–31.

Leftwich, Howard M. "Organizing in the Eighties: A Human Resources Perspective." *Labor Law Journal.* XXXII (August 1981), 484–491.

Lipset, Seymour Martin, and Schneider, William. "Organized Labor and the Public: A Troubled Union." *Public Opinion* (August/September 1981), 52–56.

McKersie, Robert B. and Brown, Montague. "Non-professional Hospital Workers and a Union Organizing Drive." *Quarterly Journal of Economics.* LXXVII (August 1963), 372–404.

Mortimer, Wyndham, *Organize,* Boston; Beacon Press, 1971.

Northrup, James P. and Northrup, Herbert R. "Union Divergent Investing of Pensions: A Power Non-Employee Relations Issues." *Journal of Labor Research.* II (Fall 1981), 191–208.

Perkel, George. "The Failure of Communication in an Organizing Campaign." *Monthly Labor Review.* LXXX (October 1956), 1200–1201.

Petzinger, Thomas, Jr. "Union Official in West Wins Over Few Miners in Struggle to Recruit." *Wall Street Journal* (October 8, 1979), 1, 21.

Raskin, A. H. "From Sitdowns to 'Solidarity'." *Across the Board.* XVIII (December 1981), 12–32.

Raskin, A. H. "Pension Funds Could Be the Unions' Secret Weapon," *Fortune*. C (December 31, 1979), 64-67.

Rifkin, Jeremy and Barber, Randy. *The North Will Rise Again*. Boston: Beacon Press, 1978.

Seidman, Joel, *et al*. *The Worker Views His Union*. Chicago: The University of Chicago Press, 1958.

Seidman, Joel; London, Jack; and Karsh, Bernard. "Why Workers Join Unions." *Annals of the American Academy of Political and Social Sciences*. CCLXXIV (March 1951), 75-84.

Shevis, James M. "Organizing Goals Form IUD Convention Theme." *AFL-CIO* News. XXV (September 27, 1980), 1.

Strauss, George. "Factors in the Unionization of a Utility Company: A Case Study." *Human Organization*. XII (Fall 1953), 17-25.

"Union Community Role Seen Key to Organizing." *AFL-CIO News*. (December 2, 1978), 8.

SECTION 3
The Collective Bargaining Process

INTRODUCTION

Section 2 of this book discussed how unions are formed. Once recognized by management, unions attempt to negotiate a contract covering wages, hours, and working conditions. This section includes readings relating to the preparation for and the conduct of collective bargaining. Section 4 will discuss the actual issues dealt with in negotiations.

One way to view the various aspects of the process of bargaining and the behavior surrounding negotiations is found in the model proposed by Walton and McKersie in their book, *A Behavioral Theory of Labor Negotiations.*[1] The Walton and McKersie model is perhaps the most influential model of collective bargaining proposed in recent decades. It recognizes that bargaining is affected by interpersonal and intergroup behavior as well as by economic factors, while earlier theories viewed it in basically economic terms.

Walton and McKersie proposed four processes of behavior surrounding bargaining, each of which has a different goal. The four different processes identified by Walton and McKersie and their respective goals are:

1. *Distributive bargaining,* with a goal to maximize one's share of the fixed benefits, i.e., one side's gain is the other side's loss.

2. *Integrative bargaining,* with a goal of solving problems and increasing mutual benefits, thus instead of splitting a fixed pie, the pie becomes larger.

3. *Attitudinal structuring,* with the goal of obtaining and maintaining a desired working relationship with the other party.

4. *Intraorganizational bargaining,* with a goal of influencing teammates and constituents to accept the compromises necessary for bargaining success, i.e., establishing and re-establishing during negotiations the priorities of each respective side.

Peterson and Tracy empirically tested the Walton and McKersie model.[2] After examining each of the four processes and the tactics that may be involved with each, they developed hypotheses concerning what behaviors and conditions would be most likely to lead to successful attainment of the related goals. Using data collected by questionnaires from union and management negotiators, they then tested those hypotheses.

They found that bargaining power and the estimated cost and probability of a strike have an impact on bargaining behavior. They also found that attitudinal structuring was closely related to integrative bargaining. However, if one side had to lower its expectations when the other side would not budge, they found that intraorganizational bargaining played a large role. They concluded that bargaining behavior and the conditions surrounding negotiations seem to have as much effect on bargaining success as the economic factors do.

Much of the intraorganizational bargaining takes place in the preparations for bargaining and prior to it. Preparation has to be very thorough and in general begins at least six months prior to actual bargaining. In preparation, other contracts, other settlements, financial forecasts and problem areas in the current contract are extremely important. It is difficult to overstress preparation for bargaining.

Intraorganizational bargaining also occurs after bargaining with the other party has begun. Much of this, if done correctly, takes piace in a caucus. The caucus can be defined as a meeting of either the union or management side after bargaining has begun without the presence of the other side. It is used to evaluate any proposal made by the other side and to develop counterproposals. Obviously, this evaluation and development will involve some intraorganizational bargaining that will establish new internal priorities for that party. The caucus is a necessary part of any bargaining and crucial to reaching a settlement.

Often prior to a contract settlement or perhaps a strike, mediation will take place. Mediation is so important to industrial peace in

this nation that Congress established the Federal Mediation and Conciliation Service and incorporated voluntary mediation into the Taft-Hartley amendments to the National Labor Relations Act presented in Section 1. Carl Stevens has defined mediation as

> the intervention (the institution of mediation includes the prospect of, as well as actual, intervention) of a [neutral] third party in collective bargaining negotiation before or after a strike or lockout. The objective of this party is to secure agreement. He does not have the power to make a binding award, although he may be able to bring "pressure" to bear in favor of a recommended settlement. [3]

If mediation is not successful in helping the parties to achieve a new contract, a strike or lockout may take place. The strike or lockout and their associated costs have a potential impact on both the bargaining process and outcomes. The strike and the strike deadline are generally necessary to collective bargaining. A strike is a concerted refusal of employees to perform their jobs. A lockout is management's counter to the strike and consists of preventing employees from working, i.e., locking them out of the work site. Lockouts are seldom used; their most common regular use occurs with multi-employer bargaining associations, such as a trucking association, when a union strikes only one of the members. In such a situation, the other members will lock the union out and will not permit the employees to resume work until the strike is over.

While strikes and lockouts are inconvenient, they play an important role in negotiation strategy. The union strike deadline serves as a goal that forces both parties to try to settle. If a strike occurs, it inflicts costs on both parties; the employer may lose net earnings while the employee loses wage income. Most strikes or lockouts take place because the parties do not agree and thus they are a tactic designed to change the bargaining position of the other side.

Another important factor in the process of

collective bargaining is the structure of bargaining, which affects how the parties bargain, how they settle, and their willingness to strike and/or take a strike. It refers to how centralized or decentralized bargaining is within an industry or employer; i.e., is bargaining on narrow craft basis within a plant, on a plant-wide basis, employer-wide basis, or industry-wide basis. Different organizational needs of both the unions and employers create pressures toward both centralized and decentralized structures. An example is the change in industry toward conglomerates, which has led to a push for coalition bargaining by unions to increase their strike power. In this situation, the unions have put on pressure toward centralized bargaining, while the employer wants bargaining to be decentralized so as to better withstand a strike.

This is quite different from the situation in the automobile industry, where production at several different plants is often interrelated, as parts from one plant go to others. Thus because a strike at one plant would thereby close down others, automobile manufacturers prefer to bargain on a centralized basis in order to have strikes at different plants occurring at the same time. However, the skilled trades within the United Automobile Workers (UAW), who wanted a separate bargaining unit to advance their own interests, have received more power in bargaining. Further, each local automobile plant negotiates a local supplement to the master contract. Yet, the UAW tries to obtain the same basic contract terms at all automobile manufacturers. Thus there are simultaneous forces within the UAW working toward both centralization and decentralization. Hy Kornbluh has summarized this dilemma quite well as follows;[4] "Collective bargaining structures are often a trade-off between increased power, efficiency, and equitable effects of uniformity, on the one hand, and benefits of more localized decision-making on the other." The reader should consider how the resolution of this dilemma, which may not exist in every situation, might affect any particular set of negotiations. However, much bargaining in this country still consists of one union bargaining with one employer for one general location.

INTRODUCTION TO THE READINGS

Bargaining: Practitioners' Views

The first two readings in this section discuss various aspects of bargaining from the standpoint of management and unions. The first selection is a pragmatic and proscriptive set of background principles of bargaining from a partisan management point of view, as given at a seminar by a management labor law firm. It lists a number of points in relation to preparation for bargaining. It begins with a discussion of management rights, what they are, and how management should be prepared to negotiate or not negotiate over them. It also discusses how management can be better prepared for bargaining by knowing about the competition, its union, the industry, and its contract.

That selection offers suggestions for the operation and conduct of the actual negotiations, including note taking, scheduling, and the use of mediation. It lists out the general management goals in bargaining very well, including obtaining a no-strike clause and a good grievance procedure. Thus it links the preparation that must be done in detail to a party's achievement of its bargaining goals.

The first selection also states that the caucus should be used *whenever* anything is needed to be discussed. The second reading in this section, developed by the AFL-CIO Labor Studies Center, is a practical discussion of the use of the caucus from the union point of view. It shows that bargaining is not only a give-and-take across the table but also heavily involves the use of the caucus. It states that the caucus comes into play in the later stages of bargaining. It suggests that while many caucuses are used to evaluate management proposals, much more activity goes on in the caucus, for example, the intraorganizational bargaining among team members.

It also details 15 other reasons why a union caucus may take place. It concludes with a suggested list of ground rules useful to the caucus. In reading that piece, it will become apparent that a union is a political democratic coalition of differing interests that may also be reflected in the union bargaining team and the way it approaches issues at the bargaining table. Therefore while many principles discussed in that selection may be applicable to the management bargaining team, some will not be as relevant because the management side usually has one leader with the delegated authority to bargain.

The Actual Bargaining Process

The third reading, by John Magenau, concentrates on answering a number of questions related to negotiations. He examines in detail how the parties determine their demands, their goals or aspirations, and their limits, i.e., the minimum they are willing to accept. He also examines the interrelationship among these three concepts and shows how they influence both the likelihood of a settlement and the length of time it takes to achieve one. He further discusses various principles that affect how the parties set and change their demands, goals, and limits, and how these also help lead to a contract settlement.

Magenau concludes with a model of the strategies used in bargaining. His model is based on three variables: trust defined as the bargainer's expectation of cooperation from the other party; the motivation to maintain his or her demands; and the motivation to reach agreement. Because a bargainer's trust of the other party and his or her motives change over time, the Magenau model is useful in analyzing the different stages of negotiation and the different strategies that may be used in each stage. His strategies are related to the Walton and McKersie concepts of integrative and distributive bargaining and include breaking off negotiations, concession making, distributive behavior, and coordinative behavior.

Mediation

The selection by Stevens describes the functions of mediation and the tactics that may be employed by a mediator. He discusses a number of specific issues, beginning with the timing of when the mediator enters the collective bargaining dispute. He suggests that the stage at which a mediator enters will affect his or her role in the process. In the early stages, he or she may be involved with the giving and seeking of information and in the later stages, with helping to solve special problems.

He also describes a number of functions a mediator might perform, including helping the parties to see their environment more realistically, allowing the parties to save face, proposing alternative solutions, separating the parties, and determining the real positions of the parties. Because mediation is so involved with the process of bargaining, the Stevens piece also provides additional insights into the process of bargaining, including the stages of bargaining, bluffing, and the role of the strike threat.

Strikes

The final article in this section, by Thomas Kennedy, deals primarily with the strike. It discusses the reasons strikes take place, their role in the free collective bargaining system of our nation, and recent trends in automation and business organization that may affect both the structure of bargaining and strike power. He describes several factors affecting the number of strikes, including the three-year cycle of major contract expirations, employee expectations, strike payments and welfare payments, rebellious rank and file, and a generation gap within unions. Kennedy shows the importance of the strike threat and the role of the strike in helping to pressure the parties to reach an agreement and argues against government intervention to avoid strikes.

He describes in detail how automation affects the union's strike power, with a little automation greatly increasing that power by raising the ratio of fixed costs to labor costs, but a high degree of automation, as in the utility industry and oil refining, decreasing that power as management gains the ability to operate the enterprise during a long strike. He also discusses how changes in the structure of bargaining, such as moves to industry-wide negotiations and the conglomerate form of industry, affect the willingness of the parties to strike and/or take a strike. Kennedy concludes that although the cost of having the freedom to strike may be high, it is a lot lower than using compulsory governmental arbitration to force a settlement in union-management disputes.

NOTES

1. Walton, Richard E., and Robert B. McKersie, *A Behavioral Theory of Labor Negotiations,* New York: McGraw-Hill, 1965.

2. Peterson, Richard B., and Lane Tracy, "Testing a Behavioral Theory Model of Labor Negotiations," *Industrial Relations,* Vol. 16, No. 1, February 1977, pp. 35–50.

3. Stevens, Carl M., *Strategy and Collective Bargaining Negotiations,* New York: McGraw-Hill, 1963, p. 125.

4. Kornbluh, Hy, "Public Schools — Multi-Unit Common Bargaining Agents: A Next Phase in Teacher-School Board Bargaining in Michigan," *Labor Law Journal,* Vol. 27, No. 8, 1976, p. 227.

SUGGESTIONS FOR FURTHER READING

In addition to the readings cited in this introduction, the following readings may prove useful to the reader.

Allen, A. Dale, "A Systems View of Labor Negotiations," *Personnel Journal,* Vol. 50, No. 2, February 1971, pp. 103–114.

Dunlop, John T., "The Function of the Strike," in *Frontiers of Collective Bargaining,* John T. Dunlop and Neil W. Chamberlain, Eds., New York: Harper and Row, 1967.

Karsh, Bernard, *Diary of a Strike,* Urbana, Ill.: University of Illinois Press, 1958.

Weber, Arnold, "Stability and Change in the Structure of Collective Bargaining," in *Challenges to Collective Bargaining,* Lloyd Ulman, Ed., Englewood Cliffs, NJ: Prentice-Hall, 1967.

Fundamentals of Collective Bargaining

I. Management Rights

    A. What are management rights?

        1. Right to determine wages, hours, terms and *conditions of employment* (assuming that there is no union to contend with).

        2. In collective bargaining, some rights should *not* be negotiable (policy-making decisions). These would include layoffs, i.e., "How many people?"

        3. Procedural aspects of implementing operational decisions fall within the phrase "terms and conditions of employment" and thus are negotiable, i.e., *who* gets laid off.

        4. Anything negotiable and not given away is called the "reserved rights of management."

            a. In court cases, the point is made that unless you specifically agree on nonnegotiation of the reserved rights of management during the life of the agreement you face the possibility of having to negotiate them. Reserved rights of management have to be *spelled out*.

II. Preparation of Noneconomic Aspects of Collective Bargaining

    A. Preparation should be extremely thorough and made well in advance (at least 6 months).

    B. Types of preparations

        1. In-depth survey of principal competitors
            a. What unions are involved.
            b. A copy of their latest contract.
            c. Contract sample language.

        2. Obtain collective bargaining agreements from other companies that have the same local as your own.

These "Fundamentals of Collective Bargaining" are based on notes taken at a seminar given by a management labor law firm, in Detroit, Michigan, September 1981.

3. Visit the company person in charge of those negotiations with the local and find out the collective bargaining experience.

4. Be aware of the industry's economic outlook, foreign competition, product substitution, and failures in other businesses.

5. Subscribe to the union newsletter.

III. Read and Know Your Contract

A. Be aware of problem areas — clauses that

1. Interfere with efficient operations.

2. Are costly.

3. Limit management's actions.

4. Result in excessive grievances.

5. Are ambiguous in their meaning.

IV. During the Negotiations (Note-taking)

A. Important to take notes on subjects as they occur for later reference.

B. Use a separate section in a notebook for each topic.

C. Once the topic is settled, use a different color paper to signify such.

D. Proposals and other documents should be initiated by *both* sides.

E. Other data (wage rates, etc.) should be similarly organized in another notebook.

F. Take chronological notes — date, place, time, who was present. Also keep a record of caucuses.

G. Avoid tapes, secretaries, courtroom reporters, joint minutes with the union.

CONDUCTING THE NEGOTIATIONS

I. The First Meeting — Do's and Don'ts

A. Absolutely no bargaining.

B. Should exchange proposals

1. Read their proposals and ask questions as to their clarity.

2. Don't make any comments about their proposals.

3. Make sure that "these" are the subjects to be dealt with (all the cards should be put on the table by the union).

C. Should be a short meeting (one hour).

D. Should be used to get acquainted with each other.

  E. Hold it about 45 days before contract expires.

  F. Establish the ground rules for the negotiations

   1. Do not agree to say nothing about the negotiations to people in the plant.

   2. Avoid language that says ". . . until a contract is settled." In the event of a strike, it would not apply.

   3. Location should *not* be considered in the ground rules. (Don't bargain in the plant if you go on strike).

   4. Time and frequency of meetings — during work, after work — *don't make definite dates* (*do* schedule two meetings in advance, though).

II. The Union Negotiating Committee — Paid or Not?

  A. Do *NOT* put it in your contract.

  B. If paid, pay only for hours lost at *straight time.*

  C. Can be used as a final temptation — contract "plum."

III. Second Meeting

  A. Held one week to ten days after first meeting.

  B. *No* bargaining.

  C. Use it as a forum for the company chief spokesperson to explain what they don't like about the union proposals. Adjourn immediately.

  D. Don't schedule meetings on consecutive days.

  E. Three to four hours should be the longest of these "middle" meetings.

IV. Middle Meetings

  A. Don't expect much to be accomplished.

  B. Usually the time for getting rid of the fluff.

  C. Real bargaining doesn't begin until about ten days before the expiration date.

  D. Hold only two to three meetings per week.

V. Final Meetings

  A. Sessions become longer (not more than eight hours usually).

  B. Avoid marathon sessions (24 hours, etc.).

  C. Caucuses — use them *whenever* you need to discuss something.

  D. Don't make concessions too quickly. Also, never give all the way the first time.

  E. Never make a concession to the union without finding out if *their* stand is still the same.

  F. Wage offers — try to "package" items, i.e., holidays *and* vacations *and* wages.

VI. Mediation and Mediators

    A. Don't call them in unless an impasse has been reached.

    B. Care and feeding of mediators

       1. Save something to give in to him or her.

       2. Don't bring him or her in too early.

       3. Convince him or her of your stance (*nothing* left to give).

       4. Thank him or her — write letters.

       5. Reserve him or her for the next session.

VII. After the Negotiations

    A. Summarize the negotiations

       1. Proposals by both sides.

       2. A short synopsis of what happened to those proposals.

       3. Statement of the final economic settlement and its cost.

       4. Summary of the major problem areas.

       5. Make sure that everything is in order in case someone else needs to use it.

VIII. Summary

    A. What management should get from collective bargaining

       1. A good no-strike clause.

       2. Guaranteed duration of contract.

       3. Detailed management's rights clause.

       4. Good grievance procedure and arbitration clause.
          a. Establish a definition of a grievance.
          b. Clearly define the powers of the arbitrator.

       5. "Entire Agreement Clause" — specifies no later additions or modifications.

       6. Waiver (Zipper) Clause — neither side has to bargain during the life of the contract.

       7. A three-year contract — is cheaper in the long run.

The Caucus — An Important Bargaining Tool

GEORGE MEANY CENTER FOR LABOR STUDIES

To the uninitiated, collective bargaining is a process in which representatives of labor and management sit across the table from each other and work out an agreement. It is thought of as a give-and-take process. Experienced negotiators know this description is far from the truth.

Most of the time, what really takes place at the bargaining table is the announcement of a position by one side accompanied by some words of justification. The other side responds, sometimes with questions, sometimes with a general comment and questions. Often, particularly during the late stages of negotiations, one side will leave the room for a caucus. This is particularly true of the union side. During the caucus, the union reviews its positions and proposals. During the caucus, the union prepares its answer to a management proposal. It is in the caucus that the real give-and-take discussion takes place in bargaining. That's why caucusing is so important to the bargaining process.

The basic reason for many union caucuses is to evaluate a company proposal and decide how to respond. For the local union member on the bargaining committee, that is just what is going on at a caucus. For the experienced bargaining committee, much more is happening. The experienced negotiator is well aware that caucuses give the committee opportunities to do many other things besides deciding to accept or reject a proposal. Experienced bargainers use caucuses for a variety of reasons.

To consider the whys and uses of the caucus in bargaining, let's back up a bit and recall the whole structure of a bargaining committee. Because on a small scale, the bargaining team does not reflect the membership, its diversity of interest and concerns are reflected in their interests and responses to demands the union makes as well as to the company proposals. Examples:

> The long-service employee on the bargaining team is probably more concerned about pensions than improving the amount of vacation for the newer employees.

> The newer employee is less interested in strict seniority than the older employee and is probably more concerned about getting ahead.

> The married employee with a large family is more interested in expanding health and hospitalization benefits than the single worker.

> The members of a bargaining team who are also elected union officers are more interested in

Reprinted by permission of the AFL-CIO George Meany Center for Labor Studies, Inc., Developed in 1976.

changes that will strengthen the union as a whole (i.e., improved grievance procedures, the right to call periodic membership meetings on company property, etc.) than the average member. And the skilled craft workers have less interest in speedup problems than assembly-line workers. And so it goes.

Some members of the union bargaining committee consider themselves as having a constituency among the membership. Their behavior will be governed by what they perceive their constituency wants rather than the desires of the union as a whole. Hence, one of the major functions of the caucus is to keep the members of the bargaining committee together.

There are other uses of and reasons for a union caucus:

1. Make sure everybody understands the company proposal for each group.

2. Find out how each member of the committee "reads" the company's latest proposal or position. Example: Was it a final position? Was it a bargaining position? Are they just playing games? Does it indicate a real change in the company attitude on a given issue? Is it evidence of a split on the company side?

3. Let the members of the committee react (explode) over what's happening at the table. This may be especially true if the committee is operating under a fairly tight one-spokesperson rule.

4. Pull the committee together. This may be especially necessary when everybody has suddenly started talking at the table and they are starting to disagree about the importance of an issue.

5. Cool off some of the committee members, particularly after a heated exchange at the table.

6. Slow down the pace of negotiations when things are moving too fast, i.e., when com-

pany counterproposals are coming too fast to study properly.

7. Change the subject. Decide on the next issue or proposal to be discussed.

8. Add emphasis to a point or proposal the union has just made and pressure the company to respond.

9. Plan strategy and tactics for the rest of that bargaining session as well as those scheduled ahead.

10. Review how the union's basic bargaining game plan is proceeding and how it is working.

11. Deal with unexpected developments away from the bargaining table. Examples: Settlement of a major strike in the industry in a nearby community. Rumor that the company is planning to subcontract part of the work of another union in the plant.

12. Keep the members of the committee mutually apprised of what's going on at the table both in terms of what's being said and what's not being said.

13. Make sure the note-taker on the committee got the last company statement down accurately as it may be useful at the next membership meeting or in the next bulletin to the members.

14. Evaluate the hardness of the company's position on a union proposal and whether or not now is the time to think about modifying the union's proposal.

15. Reassess the members' support on the issue under discussion at the table. This is particularly important toward the end of bargaining when questions like these get raised:

Do you think the members will strike over the difference between what's been offered and what we are asking for?

What do you think we need to settle this issue?

How long would we have to strike to get what we want in this area?

Do you think the members would buy the company's proposal if we do something in this area?

From the above list, it is clear that the union caucus can be an important and useful tool in the bargaining process. For maximum usefulness, a couple of ground rules are useful to the caucus.

○ The caucus should be conducted like any other small group meeting; in an orderly but informal way with one member acting as chairperson.

○ Everybody should be encouraged to present their views but not dominate the discussion.

○ Every effort should be made to arrive at a consensus. Votes should be avoided as voting can be divisive, especially in small groups, and can lead to splits in the committee that will be apparent to the company at the table. Visible splits in the committee weakens the union's position.

○ Caucuses should take place in a comfortable, uncrowded place where everybody can see each other. Avoid the standing-in-a-telephone booth type caucus.

○ Time shouldn't be wasted in a caucus, but take enough time so that everybody on the committee feels satisfied that his or her point of view has been expressed and considered. Skillful use of the caucus can be a great aid to the union bargaining committee in dealing with management at the table.

Behavioral Research in Negotiations: An Application to Collective Bargaining

JOHN M. MAGENAU
Wayne State University

This article will discuss a number of basic questions about negotiations including; (1) how demands, aspirations, and minimum acceptable outcomes are formulated, (2) factors influencing the likelihood of reaching agreement and the time required to do so, (3) conditions where one party does substantially better than the other and, (4) the factors that influence a negotiator's choice of strategy during negotiations. The behavioral research evidence available to answer the questions posed is largely based on the findings of laboratory studies, although many ideas including those behind these studies originate from the observation of collective bargaining between unions and management (e.g., Walton and McKersie 1965; Stevens 1963). Several examples will be used to illustrate how phenomena in the realm of collective bargaining correspond to the principles derived from this research.[1]

DEMANDS, ASPIRATIONS, AND LIMITS

A negotiator's position on an issue can be examined in terms of three reference points—overt demands, aspirations, and limits.

The first of these, called the *demand* (offer, proposal) is the alternative overtly endorsed by a negotiator. For example, the union's current wage increase demand might be 15% and management's offer 0%. At the same time each side normally has a covert target or desired outcome that underlies its publicly stated demand. The values of these targets for each negotiator represent their respective levels of aspiration. Thus although labor is demanding 15% and management is offering 0%, their real underlying objectives may be 9% and 3% respectively. A negotiator's *aspiration* represents an outcome that he or she would *like* to achieve. In many instances, however, negotiators may be willing to accept less than their aspirations in order to reach an agreement. However, both sides normally have a *limit* or *resistance point* beyond which they are unwilling to concede. A bargainer's limit is usually not disclosed and can be defined as the smallest outcome acceptable in the foreseeable future. He or she would rather break off negotiations than accept anything less. For example, the union may strike unless management offers at least a 5% increase while management may take a strike rather than pay more than 7%.

The area between the parties' respective limits is referred to as the *settlement range* or *bargaining zone*. In our example the settlement range is positive since alternatives exist (e.g., 5.5%, 6%, etc.) that allow both sides to satisfy their limits. If the settlement range is positive, agreement can be reached. The settlement range can also be negative. This would occur if management's limit were 5% and the union's limit were 7%. Here there are no alternatives that allow both sides to achieve their minimally acceptable positions.

Usually bargainers are unwilling to disclose their true limits to one another, since such disclosure could be exploited by the other side. Negotiators will therefore often be uncertain about whether or not a positive settlement range exists, as well as its location and size. An important task facing both negotiators then, is to discover the answers to these questions.

The definitions of demand, aspiration, and limit imply that demands will always be greater than or equal to aspirations, and aspirations will always be greater than or equal to limits. In collective bargaining, the practice of demanding more than one hopes to achieve, or is willing to accept, is so customary that Stevens (1963) refers to the "large initial demand" rule. One reason for starting with high demands concerns the norms of good faith bargaining. These may require the parties to make concessions from their initial positions during negotiations and prevent them from withdrawing concessions once made. If these norms apply, negotiators can only realize their aspiration levels if they start with high demands and concede down to their aspirations. A second tactical consideration is that one negotiator's demands can influence the demands and aspirations of the other.

If, for example, union negotiator Smith has a limit at 5% and initially demands a 6% wage increase, management negotiator Jones, expecting concessions from Smith, may believe that Smith will eventually settle below the 5% limit. The underestimating of Smith's limit by Jones would be less likely to occur if Smith's initial demand were higher — say 15%. A bargainer will also usually want to achieve the most advantageous settlement possible within a given settlement range. High demands by Smith may convince Jones that Smith has a high limit and must receive

a generous offer in order to settle. Furthermore the bargainer who starts with very modest proposals will never know if more ambitious proposals would have been eventually accepted by the other side. The danger of making excessively high demands is that they will antagonize the other side or make it so pessimistic about reaching agreement that negotiations will break down.

Location of Demand, Aspiration, and Limit

Research indicates that bargainers make higher demands when they have higher aspirations and limits, suggesting that demands are at least partly based on aspirations and limits. Pruitt (1981) identifies two exceptions to this relationship. First, the effects of limits on demands seem to occur only when demands are relatively close to limits. Perhaps when demands are far from limits bargainers feel little threat to their attainment. However, as the distance between demands and limits decreases, the possibility of failing to reach these objectives increases, making limits more salient. The effects of limits on demands are also less when bargainers have a close relationship with one another as compared to a more distant one. Presumably the trust that characterizes more mature bargaining relationships makes inflated demands less necessary, because negotiators are freer to have frank problem-solving discussions about their true objectives without endangering them.

Aspirations and limits have a variety of sources. Kelley (1966) argues that aspirations are related to a negotiator's estimate of outcomes that can be obtained in the present circumstances (e.g., the ability to pay), and his or her estimate of outcomes that he or she and others have obtained under similar circumstances (e.g., the comparative norm). Limit is partly a function of the perceived value of failing to reach agreement. Limits then will be higher to the extent that relatively favorable outcomes can be achieved in an alternative relationship and the costs associated with failing to reach agreement in the present relationship are low. For instance, management will have higher limits if its capital is easily transportable to other states or countries where wages are lower and unions are unlikely to follow, or if its operations are so automated that supervisory personnel can continue operations during a strike.

Demands, aspirations, and limits are also likely to arise from the particular problems encountered by the parties during the life of the previous agreement. If many workers are laid off, the union may seek restrictions on subcontracting. Or if wildcat strikes have occurred, the management may seek a strong no-strike clause.

Prominent alternatives. Aspirations and limits often will be located around a particualr alternative that has gained prominence in a bargainer's thinking (Schelling 1960). Such alternatives are often intrinsically attractive and they frequently seem fair, and especially defensible, so that conceding to them is less likely to be viewed by others as a sign of weakness.

Magenau and Pruitt (1979) have identified and summarized the research evidence regarding nine principles that can make an alternative prominent. Six of those principles, especially germaine to collective bargaining, are discussed here.

The *equity* principle holds that outcomes should be distributed according to the relative contributions of the parties involved. Thus a craft union representing skilled trades employees will demand that its members receive higher pay than is given to production workers in the same plant. Or if worker output per hour has increased since the last contract, labor may demand that a portion of the productivity increase go to increased wages.

The *equality* principle holds that all parties should receive outcomes of equal value regardless of their contributions. For example, the union and employer may agree to pay equal shares of all ar-

bitration fees. Wage increases that provide equal dollar amounts or equal percentage amounts to everyone are consistent with the equality principle.

The *needs* rule holds that outcomes should be determined on the basis of need. Cost of living (COLA) clauses in collective bargaining agreements recognize this by providing wage increases geared to increases in the cost of living.

The *equal concessions* principle involves splitting the difference between the bargainers' current positions. This principle differs from the previously described equality principle because splitting the difference between current positions does not necessarily yield outcomes of equal value to both parties. Bargainers are often cautious about adopting this principle early in the negotiations since they may feel that the other side is making inflated demands. In the later stages of negotiations however, when demands are in a more realistic range, the principle may be used to clinch a deal.

Historical precedent is another principle often used. For example, if police and firefighters in a given locality have maintained parallel wages for a number of years, a historical precedent may be set so that each group will demand wage increases that maintain the parallel relationship between them.

As long as it falls within a range that seems reasonably fair, a *mediator's suggestion* can serve as a basis for prominence.

Choice among principles of prominence. Many bargaining situations allow for the application of more than one principle of prominence. The choice among competing principles is complexly determined. In general the parties will tend to choose principles that are consistent with their self-interest. For example, managers who are concerned about productivity are likely to advocate the application of the equity principle in the form of merit pay. Union representatives, being concerned with internal harmony and solidarity, may favor the equality principle in the form of equal across-the-board increases.

There are, however, exceptions to the self-interest principle. Where one negotiator feels responsible for the other's welfare, as in mature collective bargaining relationships, a concession may be granted to the other because the other needs a ''win'' to bolster his or her position with a constituency. Research has also found that in a situation where there are two prominent alternatives, low power bargainers tend to pass over the prominent option most in their favor and agree to the prominent option advocated by the high power bargainer.

Principles of prominence have varying degrees of acceptance. The equity, equality, and needs principles for instance are more clearly supported by norms of social justice than are equal concessions or historical precedent. It seems reasonable that options supported by principles of prominence more strongly supported by social norms would be more frequently chosen over options less strongly supported by such norms.

The application of some principles may also require more information than others. Equity and needs rules, for example, cannot be applied unless information is available for calibrating contributions and needs. If the information for a given principle is not available, the parties will be unable to utilize it in bargaining.

An agreement need not be based on a single principle but may incorporate several. For example, one agreement on salary increases in a university divided an 8.5% salary increase among several components derived from different principles of prominence. First, there was an across the board component providing an *equal percentage* increase to all bargaining unit members. A second component provided *equal dollar* amounts to all individuals within the same rank. A third equity component permitted committees within various academic units to award salary increases to individuals on the basis of individual accomplishment.

Another way of handling a situation where

the parties are advocating different prominent solutions involves splitting the difference between them or asking a third party to decide between them.

Effects of Demand, Aspiration, and Limit on Negotiation

Research suggests a number of conclusions regarding the effects of demand, aspiration, and limit on negotiation outcomes. One is that if agreement is reached, a negotiator will achieve greater outcomes to the extent that he or she has maintained higher demands, aspirations, and limits. Another is, the higher one or both bargainer's demands, aspirations, and limits are, the longer it will take to reach agreement and the lower the probability that agreement will be reached. Two exceptions to this generalization have been found. First, when bargainers make very *low* demands, agreement is somewhat less likely than when they make moderate demands. Perhaps the very low demands made by the first party are perceived as an invitation to exploitation by the second party. The other's exploitative responses, being resented by the first party, could then lead to an overcompensative reaction in the direction of toughness. Thus a proposal that is too low may produce a misunderstanding that leads to failure to reach agreement.

Secondly, an intimate relationship between the parties seems to eliminate the effects of high limits on the length of time needed to reach agreement. Presumably, when a close relationship exists, the parties trust one another and exchange information about their limits and priorities. Thus they are able to shortcut the haggling that would otherwise be necessary to locate the subset of options within the contract zone. One would also expect this type of behavior in a mature collective bargaining relationship where trust exists between the parties.

A final conclusion, implied by the first two, is that there is an inverted U-shaped relationship between a bargainer's typical limit, aspiration, or demand and his or her average outcome over a series of negotiations. Bargainers who demand little will usually reach agreement but get little out of it. Those who demand too much will frequently fail to reach agreement and therefore also do poorly. Those who make moderate demands will frequently reach agreement at a good level of benefit.

Effects of Mutual Prominence

A condition of mutual prominence exists when both negotiators find the same option prominent and where both believe the other accepts it as prominent as well. Research shows that agreements are more frequently reached at mutually prominent alternatives than at other options, and that the presence of such alternatives results in more frequent and faster agreements. One possible explanation for these effects of mutual prominence is that both bargainers set their aspirations and limits at the prominent alternative and each assumes the other has done the same. Thus both negotiators have a tacit understanding of where agreement will be reached and then rapidly converge to that point.

Negotiator concession-making behavior is also affected by the existence of a prominent alternative. Specifically, bargainers tend to *match* each others offers in the presence of a mutually prominent alternative. The more one demands initially, the more the other will demand, and the faster one concedes, the faster the other concedes. The matching effect under mutual prominence may be explained as follows; a condition of mutual prominence implies that the aspirations of both parties fall on the same option and that each believes the other accepts the prominent alternative as well. But how can either party be sure that if they concede to the prominent alternative the other will follow suit? Can the other really be trusted? The problem is to coordinate movement toward the prominent alternative. Matching provides the solution. If each step taken by one party is matched in the appropriate proportion by a cor-

responding step by the other, the parties can have confidence that they are moving together to the desired destination. If the other fails to respond to a given step, the process can be halted until the other reciprocates with an appropriate concession.

Matching may be disrupted if a negotiator begins to believe that the other is willing to concede beyond the prominent alternative. This can happen if a bargainer seems overly anxious to reach agreement and concedes immediately to the prominent option or concedes even though the other bargainer fails to reciprocate. Similarly, bargainers with a power advantage fail to match while those at a power disadvantage exhibit matching.

When no mutually prominent alternative exists, bargainers tend to *mismatch* concessions. If one bargainer makes a large initial demand the other will make a small one and if one makes a large concession the other makes a small one. The reason for mismatching is presumably that in the absence of a prominent option, the other's offers often provide the best information available about what the other will eventually accept. A small initial demand and/or large concessions suggest that the other has flexibility and is willing to concede. Thus one becomes hopeful of achieving much in the negotiation and aspirations and demands go up. If the other's initial demands are high and concessions are small, one becomes pessimistic and aspirations and demands go down.

BARGAINING STRATEGIES AND TACTICS

Five strategies that bargainers can adopt at any time can be identified as:

1. *Distributive behavior.* The goal here is to persuade the other party to make a more favorable offer without making a reciprocal concession. Distributive tactics (Walton and McKersie 1965) include threats, deception, persuasive arguments, and positional commitments

in which the negotiator indicates that he or she will not or cannot make further concessions.

2. *Conceding unilaterally.* This is done by making a concession to the other party without expectation of receiving a reciprocal concession.

3. *Problem solving.* This strategy, sometimes referred to as coordination, involves seeking a mutually satisfactory outcome. This might be a compromise in which the parties exchange concessions on a single issue or a package settlement produced by exchanging concessions on different issues. The outcome desired might also be an *integrative agreement.* Such agreements often involve the invention or discovery of nonobvious alternatives that greatly reduce the need for either side to make the large concessions often required to reach a compromise. Thus both negotiators are able to achieve their major objectives resulting in high levels of satisfaction for both parties. Integrative agreements are more likely to occur where the parties honestly exchange information about goals and priorities so that options that satisfy the requirements of both can be found.

Pruitt (1981) distinguishes problem-solving activity in terms of the amount of risk involved. The greater the risk associated with an activity, the more the parties must trust one another before they will engage in that particular type of behavior. High-risk problem-solving behavior would include a large initial concession that seeks a reciprocal concession, making a specific compromise proposal, or providing information about one's aspirations, limits, and priorities. This can be risky because the bargainer may be perceived as being weak, concessions may not be reciprocated, or information may be exploited by the other side.

Moderate-risk problem-solving behavior involves actions that are more reversible, disavowable, and covert than high-risk approaches. The use of ambiguous signals or messages carried by intermediaries are examples.

Signals can be nonverbal such as eye glances or subtle nods of the head. They may also take the form of verbal hints about possible points of agreement or a willingness to modify one's proposal if the other is willing to reciprocate. Low-risk coordinative behavior involves the use of extremely indirect ways of suggesting an interest in problem solving such as signals suggesting an interest in an informal discussion.

4. *Inaction.* Here the negotiation is characterized by inactivity. The parties may engage in "surface bargaining" with meetings taking place and proposals exchanged, but without a genuine effort being made to reconcile differences. Alternatively, negotiations may simply be conducted at a very lethargic pace with infrequent meetings of short duration where little is discussed.

5. *Breaking off negotiations.* This strategy involves terminating meetings with no plans to resume them for the foreseeable future. The parties may resort to a strike or a lockout in connection with this strategy.

Because of the various psychological and practical contradictions among these strategies (Pruitt 1981) it is difficult, although not impossible, to pursue two or more of them simultaneously. This implies that choosing one strategy makes the others less likely to be chosen, and that conditions that increase (decrease) the chances of choosing one strategy will decrease (increase) the chances of choosing the others. A negotiator's choice among strategies can change during the course of negotiations and is likely to be influenced by three main variables; (1) the motivation to reach agreement (MA), (2) the motivation to maintain one's current demand (MD), and (3) trust, defined as the expectation of cooperation from the other bargainer.

Motivation to Reach Agreement (MA)

A bargainer's MA is hypothesized to influence the choice between breaking off negotiations and the four remaining strategies. MA must be positive in order for bargainers to remain actively involved in the negotation process. Furthermore, the greater the strength of MA, the more likely it is that bargainers will choose the unilateral concession-making strategy over problem-solving or distributive behavior. When a bargainer's MA is high, making a unilateral concession may appear to be the surest and least complicated means of securing agreement. Using distributive tactics may run the risk of antagonizing or provoking the other party and jeopardizing agreement. Problem-solving requires the cooperation of the other party and may be viewed as too time consuming or difficult to arrange.

A bargainer's MA is assumed to vary in strength throughout the course of negotiations. At any particular point in time, however, MA is assumed to be a multiplicative function of two components; (1) the bargainer's perception of the value of reaching agreement (VA), and (2) the perceived urgency of reaching agreement (UA). MA can thus be defined in terms of the following equation:

$$MA = VA \times UA \qquad (1)$$

MA is expressed as a multiplicative function of VA and UA because it is assumed that bargainers will only have an incentive to reach agreement when two conditions are met. The first is an expectation that agreement will result in some desired objective. The second is that agreement must be reached within some fairly short period of time. If UA is zero or VA is zero or a negative value, bargainers will not be motivated to reach agreement.

Value of agreement (VA). Following Komorita (1977) (VA) can be defined as follows:

$$VA = EG - L \qquad (2)$$

EG represents the expected gain or the sum value of what a negotiator expects to obtain from all issues currently under negotiation and L represents his or her limit. It follows that a bargainer's EG (and hence VA) will be greater when negotiations involve important issues and when he or she is optimistic about the chances of achieving a favorable settlement. L will be higher the more favorable the negotiator's alternatives to agreement with the other party are, and lower to the extent that the other party seems capable and disposed to imposing penalties for failing to agree or to the extent that the negotiator feels that a valued relationship with the other party could deteriorate.

The definition of limit given earlier implies that bargainers will break off negotiations when EG falls below their limit, (i.e., when VA is negative, resulting in a negative MA). Thus bargainers are found more likely to break off negotiations when they have high limits and more favorable alternatives to agreement. They are also more likely to choose break off negotiations when they expect to gain little from agreement because their opponent makes high demands and concedes slowly or when the payoffs from agreement have little real value.

Urgency of agreement (UA). UA results from a negotiator's perception of time pressure and is usually related to the closeness of a contract expiration date. Anticipated costs of continuing the negotiations in terms of time, money, and resource expenditures can also create urgency of agreement. However, events outside the relationship can also create a sense of urgency. In 1983, an agreement was reached in the steel industry five months before an August 1 contract expiration date, due to pressure exerted by General Motors (GM) and other major customers. Anxious to avoid costly hedge buying in anticipation of a steel strike in August and to assure needed steel supplies, GM threatened to place orders with foreign steel suppliers if domestic suppliers did not reach agreement by March 1.

The importance of time pressure for motivating the parties to reach agreement is illustrated by the negotiations in the auto industry in early 1982. The UAW agreed to a request from

Ford and GM to enter early negotiations because of the weak financial position of the companies at the time. Since the talks began on January 11, nine months before the existing contract expired, there was no pressure of an immediate deadline. As a means of creating such a deadline, Douglas Fraser, then UAW president, scheduled a meeting of the UAW's Ford and GM bargaining councils on January 23rd for the purpose of approving or rejecting any agreement reached. Fraser said (Simison 1982a) that by scheduling the meetings the UAW "gave the companies a target, a deadline." He claimed that without such a deadline "there would be a great tendency to drift" in negotiations (Orr, Bowles, and Risen 1982a). He also commented "I feel comfortable about the timetable we've imposed on ourselves. . . . Normally, you don't do much until the last nine or ten days before the deadline anyway" (Simison 1982b). The UAW subsequently broke off negotiations on January 20th when the talks reached an impasse. At that time Fraser observed "Perhaps it was the absence of the pressure point that we usually have, namely a strike deadline, that was responsible for the failure of the talks" (Orr, Bowles, and Risen 1982b).

Higher time pressure has been shown to produce lower aspirations, demands, and faster concessions resulting in faster agreement. Mismatching of concessions is also accentuated when time pressure is high. Apparently, under those circumstances, if one negotiator concedes slowly the other will concede more rapidly in order to bridge the gap created by the other's failure to concede. This effect is so strong that it appears even when there is a mutually prominent alternative that would normally induce concession-matching under low time pressure.

Motivation to Maintain Demand (MD)

MD refers to the strength of a bargainer's attachment to a proposal he or she is currently advocating. Like MA, MD is viewed as influencing a bargainer's choice among strategies. When MD is weak, a bargainer is more likely to make concessions. When it is strong, he or she is more likely to try to elicit concessions from the other party through the use of distributive tactics.

Proximity to limits and aspirations. As discussed earlier, a demand can be viewed as a tool for achieving one's aspirations and avoiding going below one's limits. MD will therefore be stronger to the extent that one's limits and aspirations are viewed as important objectives and one's current demand is viewed as instrumental to their attainment. It follows that MD will become stronger as bargainers move closer to their aspirations and/or limits because they have less room to concede without sacrificing these goals. In support of this proposition, research has found that bargainers whose demands were closer to their limits conceded more slowly and issued more lies and threats.

The need to project an image of strength. The need to appear strong and competent in the eyes of the other negotiator, ones constituents, and oneself is another source of MD. Sometimes referred to as face-saving, this need is likely to be particularly strong in competitive bargaining situations. A negotiator's image is likely to affect the treatment he receives from his opponent. If an image of strength is projected, the other may lower his or her aspirations and concede. An image of weakness, on the other hand, may encourage the other to raise and strengthen his or her aspirations, become committed to his or her current demand, and employ distributive tactics to defend it. In general, a bargainer's concern with projecting an image of strength is likely to be greater when there appears to be a large divergence of interests, or when an audience is present, especially if its members are viewed as endorsing hard bargaining and future interaction is expected with the same opponent.

Other bargainer's behavior. A negotiator's concern for projecting an image of strength is likely to become activated when the other bargainer employs overt distributive tactics (threats, positional commitments, etc.) or appears to be seeking an unfair advantage. The evidence suggests that threats lead to counterthreats and penalties lead to countercoercion. The other's use of threats slowed the bargainer's concession rate in one study. In another study, bargainers also made fewer concessions and more threats when their opponent was viewed as withholding concessions to achieve an unfair advantage.

The tendency for the parties to reciprocate distributive tactics is illustrated by the comments UAW Vice President Mark Stepp made prior to the UAW-General Dynamics (GD) negotiations in 1982. An internal GD memo intercepted by the union revealed the company's intentions of pursuing a very hard-line bargaining strategy. In a newspaper interview (Robinson 1982) Stepp said, "Right now, the members are pretty damn mad about a secret letter we intercepted from the corporation saying how it is making plans in case of a strike. . . . They are planning to bring in scabs. They are preparing to promote workers to supervisors and have them man the plants. They are hiring extra security, putting up television cameras and microphones — all that Gestapo stuff. . . . If it's a war they want, they damn sure are going to get one. You'll see some old style unionism."

Threats, however, are not always viewed as indicating a competitive intent and consequently do not always elicit face-saving retaliatory action in response. Subtle threats, diplomatically communicated, are less likely to evoke counter reactions than are overt and explicit threats. Some threats may be viewed as legitimate or motivated by such strong underlying needs that they are viewed more as a plea for help than an attempt at intimidation. This seems to have been the case in the 1982 negotiations between Chrysler and the UAW. On December 3, Chrysler Chairman Lee Iacocca issued an ultimatum to striking Canadian employees stating that if they were not back on the job by December 13th, the automaker would break off negotiations until January (Orr and

Risen 1982). Iacocca said, ". . . after December 13, it is inefficient to start up the Canadian plants only to shut them down a few days later for Christmas Holidays." When asked whether he saw Iacocca's ultimatum as a threat, UAW President Douglas Fraser replied, "I'm not upset . . . Sure it adds pressure to the bargaining table. That's not all bad . . . Really it doesn't pay the company to continue negotiations after a [certain date]."

Constituents. In collective bargaining, negotiators usually represent constituents. Representatives are naturally concerned with their image with their constituents since they usually serve at the constituents' pleasure. Constituents often favor a tougher approach than their representatives do for a number of reasons. First, because they are more distant from the negotiations, they are likely to be more optimistic about getting unilateral concessions from the other side. Secondly, they are less likely to have a close relationship with the other side since they have no direct dealings with them. Thus negotiators tend to view their constituents as favoring a strong, aggressive approach.

Negotiator accountability to constituents in the sense of dependency on them for rewards and punishments, is likely to enhance negotiator concerns about looking strong and hence strengthen MD. This hypothesis is supported by research showing that more accountable negotiators tend to make slower concessions and use more distributive tactics. However, accountability alone does not strengthen MD. It is likely to increase a representative's desire to please constituents, which will strengthen MD only if the constituents are believed to favor toughness. If, on the other hand, rank-and-file union members are fearful of job loss unless concessions are made, they may favor a softer approach to negotiation. Research evidence suggests that MD is not strengthened where constituents favor a soft approach. There is also evidence that accountability encourages problem solving when it is coupled with a desire for a positive relationship with the other party (Ben-Yoav-Noble and Pruitt, in press).

When negotiators lack *constituent trust* they may adopt a tough negotiation posture in an effort to earn that trust. A newly-elected union president may, for example, adopt a hard-line bargaining strategy to prove his or her mettle to the rank-and-file. In support of this reasoning, it was found that distrusted representatives made higher initial demands and reached fewer agreements than trusted representatives.

Constituent surveillance also induces distributive behavior. This suggests that "sunshine" laws giving the public the right to observe public sector negotiations would discourage substantive bargaining. In fact Kochan (1979) suggests a fundamental law of sunshine bargaining: "The more people who show up to observe bargaining, the less there will be to see."

Mutual prominence and concern for the image of strength. Studies suggest that a mutually prominent alternative alleviates a bargainer's concern about projecting an image of strength and thus encourages concession-making. In one study a mediator's suggestion facilitated concession-making. Furthermore, bargainers who made concessions in the absence of a mediator's suggestion saw themselves as weak, but those who conceded following a mediator's suggestion did not. In another study, the negative effect of accountability on the concession rate was reduced when there was a solution allowing equal outcomes for both parties. A prominent solution presumably allows a bargainer to justify concessions as the "reasonable thing to do" and avoid having concessions interpreted as a sign of weakness.

Negotiators who are highly accountable to their constituents also have been found to be more receptive to third party (e.g., mediators' or fact-finders') recommendations than those who are less accountable. Highly accountable representatives are probably more responsive to such recommendations because they need a way to make the concessions necessary for agreement

without looking weak. According to one source, this was the case for a union president during the 1982 Detroit Teacher's strike (Macnow 1982), "John ran for president on the promise that our next contract would be a good one . . . Now comes 1982, and the board starts calling for paycuts. John had absolutely no choice but to take us out on strike. After all his tough talk earlier on, he was locked into a 'no concessions' position. In the end, turning things over to the fact-finder was the only way he could extricate himself from the tar pit."

Relative power. In collective bargaining, relative power can be thought of as the capacity to elicit concessions from the other party. It follows then, that bargainers who perceive themselves to have greater power vis-à-vis their opponents will have stronger MDs, will be more likely to employ distributive tactics and will be less likely to concede. Following Komorita (1977) a bargainer's perception of his or her power relative to the other (RP) can be defined as the difference between his or her perception of the motivations to reach agreement for the other party (MAo) and for oneself (MAs).

$$RP = MAo - MAs \qquad (3)$$

Based on the components of Eqs. (1) and (2), this equation implies that bargainers are likely to perceive themselves as having relatively greater power than their opponent to the extent that they have; (1) a lower expected gain, (2) higher limits based on better alternative sources of need satisfaction or a greater ability to impose penalties for failure to reach agreement, and (3) less urgency of reaching agreement.

This formulation is supported by research showing that the party with a greater capacity to penalize the other will make fewer concessions, issue more threats, and impose more punishments. Bargainers have also been found to make fewer concessions the greater the other party's cost of implementing the threats and smaller concessions when there is greater time pressure on the other party.

Model of Strategy Choice

Bargainers will choose the strategy of breaking off negotiations when they have a negative motivation to reach agreement (−MA). This will occur when the perceived value of reaching agreement (VA) is negative. When MA is positive, a bargainer's choice among the remaining strategies depends upon the particular combination of values for the motivation to reach agreement (MA), the motivation to maintain demand (MD), and trust, as shown in Fig. 1.

Distributive behavior is most likely when a bargainer has a low MA and high MD. Under these conditions bargainers will have little interest in making unilateral concessions or in engaging in problem solving. Distributive tactics are also likely since there is little concern about jeopardizing agreement.

Conceding unilaterally is most likely when a bargainer has high MA but low MD. Bargainers are unlikely to engage in distributive behavior since doing so might jeopardize the chance of reaching agreement and there is little incentive to defend one's current demand. Problem-solving is

also unlikely since it is likely to be time consuming and the bargainer wants to settle quickly.

Problem-solving behavior is most likely when bargainers have a high MA and high MD. Under these circumstances, the bargainer is in a dilemma. A high MD makes unilateral concessions undesirable while a high MA makes distributive tactics undesirable because they may jeopardize the chances of reaching agreement.

A compromise agreement, if it can be arranged, provides the way out of this dilemma. Such an agreement can be viewed as an effort to balance the conflicting pressures of MA and MD. The bargainer is able to secure an agreement but the size of the concession (compared to a unilateral one) required to do it is reduced. An integrative agreement, if possible, allows for a more satisfactory resolution of this dilemma, since agreement is reached without sacrificing basic objectives.

Whether high-risk or low-risk problem-solving behavior is attempted depends on the bargainer's trust in the other party. High-risk problem-solving will be attempted only if trust in the other is high. If trust is lower, moderate- or low-risk problem-solving will be attempted.

Finally, when MA and MD are weak the model predicts inaction. Since MA is positive the

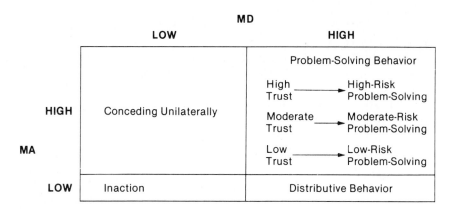

FIGURE 1
Strategy choice as a function of the motivation to reach agreement (MA),
the motivation to maintain one's demand (MD), and trust.

bargainer will not choose to break off negotiations. The bargainer is unlikely to concede unilaterally since MA is weak, and a weak MD makes distributive behavior unlikely. The strong contradictory motives that would engender problem solving are also absent. In short, the negotiations will be characterized by little meaningful activity.

NOTES

1. This article, prepared especially for this volume, draws extensively on a chapter by John M. Magenau and Dean G. Pruitt, "The Social Psychology of Bargaining: A Theoretical Synthesis," Chapter 9, in G. Stephenson and C. Brotherton, Eds., *Industrial Relations: A Social Psychological Approach,* Chichester, England: Wiley, 1979, pp. 191–210. Because of space limitations, most citations to original research studies included in the earlier Magenau and Pruitt article have been deleted here. The interested reader will find a complete list of references to the theoretical literature on negotiations in that article. The author would like to thank Lizabeth Barclay, James Martin, Melanie Peterson, Richard Peterson, Dean Pruitt, Ross Stagner, and George Strauss for their thoughtful comments on an earlier draft of this article.

REFERENCES

Ben-Yoav-Noble, O., and D. G. Pruitt, "Accountability to Constituents: A Two Edged Sword," *Organization Behavior and Human Performance,* in press.

Kelley, H. H., "A Classroom Study of Dilemmas in Interpersonal Negotiations," in K. Archibald, Ed., *Strategic Interaction and Conflict,* Berkeley, Calif.: Institute of International Studies, University of California, 1966.

Kochan, T. A., "Dynamics of Dispute Resolution in the Public Sector," in B. Aaron, J. Grodin, and J. L.

Stern, Eds., *Public Sector Bargaining,* Washington, D.C.: Bureau of National Affairs, 1979, p. 156.

Komorita, S. S., "Negotiation from Strength and the Concept of Bargaining Strength," *Journal for the Theory of Social Behavior,* 7, 1977, pp. 65–79.

Magenau, J. M., and D. G. Pruitt, "The Social Psychology of Bargaining: A Theoretical Synthesis," in G. Stephenson and C. Brotherton, Eds., *Industrial Relations: A Social Psychological Approach,* Chichester, England: Wiley, 1979.

Macnow, G., "Strike Rooted in Politics Nears a Politic End," *Detroit Free Press,* Detroit, Mich., October 3, 1982, pp. 3A, 10A.

Orr, R., B. Bowles, and J. Risen, "GM, Ford Told UAW Expects Equitable Pact," *Detroit Free Press,* Detroit, Mich., January 12, 1982a, pp. 1A, 2A.

Orr, R., B. Bowles, and J. Risen, "UAW Breaks Off Bargaining On Concessions to GM, Ford: Councils to Vote This Weekend on Resumption," *Detroit Free Press,* Detroit, Mich., January 12, 1982b, pp. 1A, 10A.

Orr, R., and J. Risen, "Chrysler gives UAW a deadline in Canada," *Detroit Free Press,* Detroit, Mich., December 4, 1982, pp. 1A, 9A.

Pruitt, D. G., *Negotiation Behavior,* New York: Academic Press, 1981.

Robinson, M. A., "UAW Aim: Regain Tank Plant Losses," *The Detroit News,* June 12, 1982, p. 7B.

Schelling, T. C., *The Strategy of Conflict,* Cambridge, Mass.: Harvard University Press, 1960.

Simison, R. L., "Ford, G.M., Union Open Negotiations On Revising Pacts," *The Wall Street Journal,* New York, January 12, 1982.

Simison, R. L., "UAW Opens Early Contract Talks Today With Ford and GM Due to Layoff Worries," *The Wall Street Journal,* New York, January 11, 1982.

Stevens, C. M., *Strategy and Collective Bargaining,* New York: McGraw-Hill, 1963.

Walton, R. E., and R. B. McKersie, *A Behavioral Theory of Labor Negotiations,* New York: McGraw-Hill, 1965.

Mediation and the Role of the Neutral

CARL M. STEVENS
Reed College

. . .

MEDIATION FUNCTIONS AND TACTICS

Timing of Intervention

Discussions of mediation frequently emphasize the importance of the timing of the mediator's initial intervention in a dispute.[1] Some observers see merit in early intervention. For example, Elmore Jackson remarks:

> In labor conflicts it has proved useful for the mediator to be aware of the dispute at its earliest stages so that his services may be offered before contending positions have become firm. He must enter the dispute at a time when strategic retreat can be gracefully executed.[2]

Other observers are less receptive to early intervention. For example, Northrup contends:

> The early entrance of the mediator upsets the power balance. With the consequences of either intransigence or ignorance — that is, the

strike — still in the distance, early entrance by the mediator usually results in a hardening of positions, instead of a realistic appraisal of the situation.[3]

In analyzing the timing problem, it will prove helpful to recognize a phenomenon that may be termed the "negotiation cycle." While no two instances of collective bargaining negotiation are precisely the same, a number of investigators have suggested that there tends to be a progression of events, a succession of stages common to many contract negotiations.[4]

In this view, the functions discharged by negotiation and the tactics employed by the parties will tend to change as any particular negotiation progresses through its successive stages. This description of the negotiation process implies that the mediator may be expected to serve different functions and may be involved in different tactics depending upon when he enters; his timing may have an important bearing on the appropriateness of his intervention.

I will not attempt here to spell out in detail the negotiation cycle but will briefly suggest the nature of its successive stages.[5]

Two functions may be selected as characteristic of the early stages of negotiation. Some investigators have suggested that these stages are dominated by the negotiators' roles as delegates: that these stages emphasize interparty conflict as

From pp. 274-280, 283-289 ''Mediation and the Role of the Neutral'' by Carl M. Stevens from *Frontiers of Collective Bargaining,* edited by John T. Dunlop and Neil W. Chamberlain. Copyright © 1967 by J. Dunlop and N. Chamberlain. Reprinted by permission of Harper & Row, Publishers, Inc.

contrasted with greater emphasis upon interpersonal (negotiators *qua* negotiators) interaction.[6]

They have also emphasized that it is important, during the early stages, to perform the information-giving-and-seeking job of blocking out the contract zone — that is, the range of outcomes both parties would prefer to a strike.

The middle stages involve the most active tactical play of the negotiation game. Having determined in a general way where his opposite number stands, each party begins to consolidate his own position and to move his opposite number in a direction favorable to himself. The parties may be viewed as "operating" upon each other by means of various tactics — such as persuasion, rationalization, bluffs, threats, promises, and so forth.

The later stages precede an impending strike deadline. As the negotiations have proceeded, it is to be hoped that the information picture has cleared somewhat, and that any contract zone has become outlined at least to some degree. Also as the negotiations proceed, the competitive tactics available to each side are being used and may be "used up" by the later stages. For example, threats have been tried, and the results have been pretty well determined. The approach of the deadline tends to eliminate bluff as a tactic. One may distinguish a number of special-agreement problems which are likely to confront the parties at or just prior to the strike deadline; some of these will be discussed in subsequent sections.

We may conclude roughly that if the mediator enters the early stages of negotiation, he will be involved primarily with "grandstanding" and with the initial giving and seeking of information. If he enters in the middle stages, he will find himself in the most active tactical phase and may well be actively involved with the tactical operations of the parties themselves. If he enters during the later stages, he will confront one or more of the special agreement problems confronted by the parties and his task will be to help to solve them.

A detailed analysis of the timing problem cannot be undertaken here, but some general implications of the foregoing discussion should be pointed out. An adequate analysis of the timing problem must be referred to some general analysis of the negotiation cycle and of the negotiation functions served by various parts of that cycle. Some discussions of the timing problem imply that the mediator should fill more or less the same functions whether he enters early or late — the significant difference being that the discharge of each becomes easier or harder, depending upon early or late intervention. I have implied that the mediator will serve, at least as regards emphasis, very different functions, depending upon when he enters.

It is sometimes suggested that it is useful for the mediator to offer his services before the contending positions have become firm. One could agree that this course of action might make life easier for the mediator without at the same time agreeing that earlier intervention is therefore to be recommended.[7] The parties are in part concerned, during the early stages, to map certain power relations into the outcome of the negotiation. An early attempt to prevent their positions from becoming firm may abort the proper functions of these phases of the negotiations. This raises the important question whether the timing of intervention ought not itself to be guided by the need to be neutral with respect to the substantive (distinguish strike versus no-strike) outcome.

Persuasion I — The Parties' Perception of the Environment

Persuasion is frequently identified as an important mediation tactic. The parties may disagree over the facts — the cost of living, comparative rates, productivity, and so on. The mediator may help them to set the record straight or at least to minimize nonfruitful ways of managing such types of disagreement.

If appeals to the facts in negotiations are usually mere window dressing, serving as rationalizations for the power positions of the parties, then persuasion — in the sense of persuading a party that the facts are other than what he has been contending they are — will not be a potent tactic, in the hands either of the negotiating parties or of the mediator.

Many of the most important "facts" describe the outcome of various courses of action — outcomes that can be known only in terms of probability. Persuasion operating on this front may well modify the parties' appraisal of the power situation. The parties, particularly if they are new to collective bargaining, may underestimate the cost of a strike or a lockout or overestimate the cost of an agreement with their opponent upon the latter's terms; the mediator may assist them to see the realities of the situation. If the parties can be led to agreement in the light of a realistic appraisal of the costs and gains associated with alternative courses of action, the mediator serves a real and important function.[8]

A mediator might attempt to persuade the parties to agree by emphasizing the potential cost to them of a strike. Alternatively, he might undertake to decrease the estimate each makes of the cost of agreement on the other's terms. Both kinds of persuasion tactics may be effective in moving the position of each party toward that of the other. However, the mediator should bear in mind that emphasis upon tactics of the first kind — in contrast to emphasis upon tactics of the second kind — may tend to increase the level of tension and anxiety in the negotiation situation and hence increase the chances of a breakdown.[9]

An awkward problem may arise if the mediator resorts to persuasion. Does he have a direct interest in bringing the parties to a realistic appraisal of the situation? If his objective is to induce them to agree, a realistic appraisal might in some situations be a means to this end. However, in other situations, bringing them to a nonrealistic appraisal might also be a means to this end: that is, a party might be brought to agreement if he were persuaded to overestimate the cost of a strike, to underestimate the gains to be had thereby, and to underestimate the cost of agreement with the opponent upon the latter's terms.

Here the mediator would be abetting the agreement process by deception. (Let me make it clear at this point that, in recognizing this possibility, I in no way intend to advocate that a mediator engage in deception.)

Persuasion II — Mediator Involvement with the Coercive Tactics of the Parties

Frequently tactics of coercion are based upon bluff, and mediation tactics may involve the relationship of the mediator to the bluff tactics of the parties. The mediator's involvement in this situation might be quite deliberate. Suppose, for example, that agreement is impeded because one party believes that his bluff about willingness to take a strike, or to continue a strike indefinitely, will prevail and bring the other party to terms. He would make a concession if he did not believe in the strength of his bluff weapon. The mediator might be able to diagnose the bluffing party's true intentions, so advise the opposing party, and then advise the first party that its bluff is no longer effective. At this juncture an awkward problem arises once more. Presumably the mediator does not have a direct interest in eliminating bluff from negotiations. Presumably his objective is to bring the parties to agreement. Elimination of bluff may be a means to this end. It might be, however, that deliberately neglecting so to do will also be a means to this end. Thus the party might capitulate if he did not suspect that his opponent was bluffing. The mediator, aware that the opponent was bluffing, might neglect to convey this information — or might even undertake to convince the party that this was not the case. (Again, this analysis recognizes a possibility; it does not advocate that the mediator pursue this course of action.)

A different negotiation problem is how to "not-bluff" successfully — that is, how one party can successfully convince his opponent that his stated intentions are his true ones. A party intending to strike in a contingency may state his intentions, but the mere statement does not always convince the other. Why should his opposite number believe him? After all, he may be bluffing.

Failure in dealing with this tactical problem may lead to a certain kind of "unnecessary" strike. Suppose that the opponent refuses to concede and reach agreement because he thinks the other's strike threat is a bluff — but he would have conceded if he had known that the threat was real. Of course, if the strike does eventuate, the opponent will learn the truth; but this kind of strike is unnecessary in that, had some other means for conveying the truth been available, it would not have taken place.

Potentially the mediator has a clear-cut contribution to make to this kind of case. He may be able to determine the party's true intentions and so advise the opponent, who may believe the mediator even though he did not believe the party. In using this tactic, the mediator is once more involved with the parties' negotiation game; that is, he is playing a supporting role to not-bluff tactics. It is an interesting question and pertinent to the concept of neutrality whether a mediator's support of not-bluff tactics should be viewed as more privileged or legitimate than his support of bluff tactics.

Perhaps of more importance is the possibility of inadvertent mediator involvement in the tactics of the parties. A mediator in a bluff situation should guard against becoming an unwitting tool of either or both of the parties. A party may have only partially succeeded in making its bluff convincing to the opposite number. If, however, that party can successfully bluff the mediator, he may enlist the mediator as an unwitting ally in his deception.

. . .

Saving Face and One Function of Rationalization

One of the mediator functions is saving face, which is useful when one or both parties want to dissolve a certain kind of commitment and when its dissolution may open the way to agreement.

This situation may arise under circumstances that we may term the "failure of coercive commitment" — one of the problems characteristic of the later, pre-deadline stages of negotiation. Here the negotiators fail to reach agreement in a tactical situation from which a contract zone, initially inherent in the negotiation situation, has been eliminated by tactical contrivance. An instance of such tactical contrivance is a party's use of a threat with a distinctive characteristic: namely, the party asserts that he will pursue, in a contingency, a course of action that he would — at the time of making this assertion — prefer not to pursue should the contingency arise. For example, the party asserts that he will take a strike unless the position is conceded, although he would actually prefer at that moment not to take a strike in this contingency. This kind of threat depends for its success on the adversary's believing the party to be fully committed to take the strike.

Of particular interest in this context is the possibility that if both parties attempt this tactic, the race to commitment may end in a dead heat: each party becomes committed to taking a strike unless the other concedes, and agreement without strike is impossible.

The mediator has a clear, although difficult, function in this situation. Agreement is possible in terms of the original preferences of the parties — that is, in terms of those prevailing before the commitment tactics altered the situation. Hence, the mediator must somehow assist in the undoing of the commitment. "Saving face" describes the dissolution of this particular kind of commitment.

As Kerr has pointed out, the mere entrance of a mediator into a dispute is in some ways a face-saving device.[10] In an ambiguous situation, the implication that the battle was so hard fought that a mediator had to be brought in may be helpful. More important perhaps, the mediator may share some of the responsibility for the outcome and thereby decrease the responsibility of the parties. He might do this, for example, by making recommendations for a settlement for which he will take responsibility and, if need be, pursuant to this end, public responsibility.

More subtle functions of the mediator in attempting to undo the commitment may be viewed as instances of the negotiation tactic termed "rationalization." For example, if a demand has been wedded to a principle and thereby committed, the mediator might attempt to cut the demand loose by showing that it is not a case in point of the principle. Also, Schelling has suggested that a party attempting to release an opponent from a commitment might confuse the commitment so that party's principals cannot identify compliance with it.[11] The mediator might use the same tactics: he might show that a given standard — cost of living, ability to pay, productivity, comparative rates, etc. — is ambiguous; or that a given package is not really inflationary, thereby providing the party opposing the package on this ground with a set of arguments he can use to show that he miscalculated his commitment.

The foregoing suggestions do not exhaust the possibilities of rationalization. We should note here that to make a useful analysis of the concept of saving face as a mediation tactic, it must be examined in *very particular* terms.

Proposing the Alternate Solution

George W. Taylor stressed the "art of proposing the alternate solution" as a crucial aspect of mediation.[12] We may inquire under what circumstances the proposal of an alternative solution should be expected to help the parties to reach agreements.

This mediation tactic should work only under special circumstances. For example, if the positions of the parties do not overlap — that is, there is no contract zone — then presumably there is no alternative solution that both parties will embrace. If this tactic is to work, the parties must already be in a kind of covert or latent agreement when it is tried. The problem is presumably to keep their agreement latent until they are brought to recognize it by considering the mediator's proposal of an alternate solution.[13]

This situation involves problems of definition; that is, although the parties want approximately the same terms of settlement, they may

have difficulty defining their respective positions in specific institutional terms. It is the function of the mediator to help the parties make their respective definitions, and it requires all a mediator's inventiveness to do this.

Evolution of the maintenance-of-membership provision in collective agreements seems an excellent case of resolution of conflict by definition of a position in equilibrium. Suppose that a management is insisting upon the open shop, while a union is insisting upon the union shop. Each might be willing to compromise his ostensible position, but what kind of shop can be a compromise between the open shop and the union shop? Some shrewdness with respect to the design of institutions may be necessary to come up with an answer to this kind of question — as, for example, by proposing maintenance of membership. Seniority and wage-incentive plans are other areas where institutional complexity may require this particular mediator function.

In other words, a mediator may distinguish between the objectives of the parties and the institutional vehicles that they propose to carry those objectives. The parties may not be inclined to make this distinction in their own thinking. The mediator may be able to free the parties from concentrating upon their particular institutional demands and induce them to think in a more general way about the objectives they are really trying to achieve — via the devices under consideration or in some other way. Once he understands the parties' objectives in more general terms, the mediator may be able to come up with the alternate solution. And once the parties understand their own objectives in more general terms, they may be prepared to accept that alternate.

Separating the Parties — and More About the Alternate Solution

It is frequently pointed out that separating the parties may be at times a useful mediation technique. Separate caucuses provide forums where the mediator may receive confidential and privileged communications from each party.

Also, as Jackson points out in connection with the alternate solution, this technique gives the mediator an opportunity to get each party to adopt the solution as his own, thus avoiding the danger, inherent in making the suggestion to both parties simultaneously, that one party might embrace it and the other feel impelled to oppose it. The control of the communication structure achieved by separating the parties may more generally facilitate attempts at persuasion and also coercion.[14]

In this section I want particularly to draw attention to an aspect of the technique of separating the parties which is less frequently discussed. This aspect relates to the resolution of another of the special agreement problems: how can the parties be brought to agree when their deliberations have become essentially indeterminant?

This is a situation in collective bargaining analogous to the so-called "pure" bargaining game. Suppose there exists a manifest contract zone — that is, a range of outcomes preferred by both parties to no agreement — and both parties know this. This situation is indeterminant in that at least one of the parties would be willing to retreat from each of the potential solutions — those within the contract zone — rather than accept no agreement as the outcome.

Mediation in the face of the manifest contract zone has been recognized as a difficult problem. Kerr remarks:

> A particularly difficult controversy to mediate, strangely enough, is one in which the costs of aggressive conflict to each party are enormous. Then any one of many solutions is better than a strike and the process of narrowing these possible solutions to a single one is an arduous task.[15]

One possible approach to this problem is along lines suggested by T. C. Schelling.[16] First, Schelling has suggested that the solution to a negotiation of this kind is best viewed as the consequence of convergence of the parties' expectations about what will or must be the outcome. Thus a party expects a particular outcome within the contract

zone to be the solution, because he expects — in spite of the circumstances of the pure-bargaining game — his opposite number to yield no more. If the opposite number shares these expectations with respect to that outcome, then their expectations converge, and that outcome is the solution. Schelling suggests that the "prominence" — denoting such properties as simplicity, uniqueness, precedent, and so forth — of a particular outcome may serve to establish such expectations.

In addition, there are consequences of what Schelling terms "tacit bargaining." Tacit bargaining refers generally to negotiations in which there is no explicit communication between the players. Collective bargaining is a "mixed" process; that is, it is neither purely competitive nor purely cooperative but combines both elements. There is the possibility that resort to tacit, rather than explicit, bargaining may force elements of cooperation to the fore. Thus the mediation tactic of converting collective bargaining negotiation into instances of tacit bargaining — for example, by separating the parties — may be helpful in reaching agreement when negotiations have become indeterminant.

Moreover, as I have suggested, in such indeterminant situations it is the prominence of one of the potential outcomes in the contract zone which compels the parties' expectations to converge upon it. This points to another aspect of the mediator's function in this kind of agreement problem. A mediator wishing to use the tacit-bargaining approach may first have to set the situation up by playing an active role — by deliberately contriving to attribute prominence to a particular position.

It should be noted that here we have an analytically distinguishable aspect of "proposing the alternate solution." With the pure-bargaining-game type of agreement problem, there is a range of potential outcomes that the parties prefer to aggressive conflict, but there is no apparent mechanism to compel the selection of one of these over any other. In this context the alternate solution does not work simply because it defines an intersection of areas of reasonable expectation. Indeed, the contract zone already contains too many areas of potential agreement. In this context, the alternate solution works because it ascribes prominence to one of the potentially available outcomes. This, coupled with a separation of the parties, may, as I have suggested, serve to break the deadlock.

Determining the Real Positions of the Parties

It is sometimes suggested that the mediator's ability to determine the real positions of the parties is a valuable adjunct to his management of a dispute. By a party's "real" position, I mean those terms least favorable to himself that he would be willing to accept rather than to take a strike. By a party's "final" position, I mean the last offer he has put on the table prior to the intervention of the mediator. Now let us suppose that the mediator, wittingly or unwittingly, confronts a problem of the following kind. Although the parties have failed to reach agreement on the basis of their final positions, their real positions — that of each unknown to the other — intersect. In this situation the mediator has potentially a clear-cut role to play. If he can determine the real positions of the parties, he can simply inform them that they are in agreement.[17]

Are the parties likely to reach a deadlock on such a basis? This question should be answered at the level of empirical generalization, and perhaps experienced mediators can throw some light upon it. Analysis of collective bargaining negotiations suggests that such agreement problems are unlikely to arise.

Although space will not permit an elaboration of these points, I may suggest some of the reasons that a party may stand on a final position more favorable to himself than is his real position: (1) to announce his real position (a retreat from an ostensible final position) may be prejudicial in that it may be interpreted as a sign of weakness; (2) an advantage may go to the party who waits for his opposite number to make a last pro-

posal — for example, the party may find that it is more favorable to himself than would have been his own last proposal had he been the first to make such; (3) the party may consider either a strike or mediation a possibility and may wish to "save something" for either eventuality.

One would expect that the nature of this aspect of the mediator's relation with the parties would depend in part upon the way, if any, in which they wish to incorporate him into their own negotiation tactics. For example, one or both of the parties may want deliberately to involve him. Thus generally a party will consider that it does not serve his own best interests to inform the mediator of his real position. Indeed, it is more realistic to assume that the parties are typically reluctant to reveal their true positions to the mediator. An experienced negotiator has commented that revealing the position in this way "would be just the same thing as publishing it." Thus if the mediator is to learn the parties' true positions, he will have to infer or deduce them much as if he were himself a party to the negotiations. It is an interesting aspect of the mediation process that the mediator should be expected to play this kind of game.

CONCLUSION

Let me now briefly refer back to the problem of the timing of intervention of mediation with which this discussion opened. A case for late, rather than early, intervention might be constructed on the grounds that the mediator's special professional competence lies precisely in dealing with those special agreement problems that are likely to arise in the later predeadline stages of negotiation. A striking characteristic of these problems is that each is an instance of the technical failure of the parties' unaided direct negotiations. There may be a kind of special legitimacy in bringing the mediator into such situations: given the technical failure, it makes sense to change the structure of the negotiations by adding a third person.

Of course, the parties may fail to reach agreement for other reasons, and the mediator also might hope to make some contribution in these cases.[18] And by involving himself in the tactics of the parties, the mediator might produce earlier agreement or head off disagreement. But these tactics may appear less privileged on neutrality grounds than those designed to cope with the special agreement problems — whose resolution in any event depends upon some change in the format of the negotiations.

The foregoing suggestions regarding the role of the mediator vis-à-vis the eleventh-hour special agreement problems tend to recommend late, rather than early, intervention by the mediator in particular industrial disputes. This does not imply that prenegotiation consultation and concern with the design of bargaining institutions is not important for industrial peace and acceptable substantive outcomes of negotiations. Nor does it imply that persons who are mediators have no role to play in this activity.

Necessity is the mother of social invention, and awareness of necessity on the part of participants in social institutions will prompt them to evolve their own solutions by changing techniques and processes. This is desirable. However — particularly in the case of complex social institutions operating in a rapidly changing environment (such as collective bargaining) — the process of achieving fruitful social innovation might be assisted by the analysis and recommendations of investigators and consultants. Some term other than "mediation" should be applied to such assistance.

. . .

NOTES

1. Although less frequently emphasized, the form of the mediator's initial intervention — whether on his own or at the invitation of the parties; with or without fanfare; etc. — may affect his effectiveness.

2. See Elmore Jackson, *Meeting of Minds — A Way to Peace through Mediation,* (New York: McGraw-Hill Book Company, 1952), pp. 26–27.

3. See Herbert R. Northrup, "Mediation — the Viewpoint of the Mediated," *Labor Law Journal,* (October 1962), p. 837.

4. See, for example, John T. Dunlop and James J. Healy, *Collective Bargaining: Principles and Cases,* revised edition (Homewood, Illinois: Richard D. Irwin, Inc., 1955), pp. 61ff., for a discussion of the stages of typical contract negotiation. See also Carl M. Stevens, *Strategy in Collective Bargaining Negotiation* (New York: McGraw-Hill Book Company, 1963), whose discussion is organized around the concept of "early" and "later" stages in negotiation. My discussion in various places leans upon and borrows from the analysis developed in this book. The reader should consult it for further discussion of some of my points as well as of related points.

5. The concept of a negotiation cycle is analytically useful. Nevertheless, it can be misleading unless one bears in mind that it is an idealization of the actual process. Moreover, use of this idealization should not be taken to imply, for instance, that a tactical function or entity described as characteristic or prominent for one stage may not likewise to some extent be served or appear at other stages.

6. See, for example, Ann Douglas, "What Can Research Tell Us About Mediation," *Labor Law Journal* (August 1955).

The frequent use of the term "grandstanding" with reference to this stage should not obscure the fact that performance during this stage may be functional for the negotiator's role as delegate. For example, Stagner has pointed out that "ritualistic" attacks upon the employer during negotiation may serve the union officials' "role of spokesman for feelings, demands, hostilities, and insecurities among the workers." See Ross Stagner, *Psychology of Industrial Conflict* (New York: John Wiley and Sons, Inc., 1956), pp. 241–242.

7. One could also disagree; see Northrup, *op. cit.*

8. This is a part of what Clark Kerr ("Industrial Conflict and its Mediation," *The American Journal of Sociology* [November 1954] p. 243) terms "removal of nonrationality." Jackson (*op cit.,* pp. 32–33) identifies as important aspects of the mediator's persuasion tactic "factual deflation" and "raising doubt in the minds of the parties about positions already assumed."

9. For a full discussion of this matter, see Stevens (*op. cit.*), particularly Chapter II. The terminology employed here is used by Neil Chamberlain in his definition of bargaining power. See Chamberlain, *Collective Bargaining* (New York: McGraw-Hill Book Company, 1951). Chamberlain's formulation, unlike much discussion of bargaining, does explicitly recognize the two kinds of tactics distinguished in this discussion.

10. Kerr (*op. cit.,* p. 238) discusses the face-saving function of mediation, including the aspect of sharing responsibliity for the outcome.

11. See Thomas C. Schelling, "Bargaining Communication and Limited War," *The Journal of Conflict Resolution* (March 1957).

12. See "The Role of Mediation in Labor Management Relations" (Address at a conference of regional directors of the Federal Mediation and Conciliation Service, Washington, D.C., 1952) cited in Kerr (*op. cit.*).

13. This seems to be the sense of Jackson's discussion of this tactic. See Jackson, *op. cit.,* p. 34. He attributes this point to a paper prepared for the study by Arthur S. Meyer.

14. See Bernard Wilson, "Conciliation Officers' Techniques in Settling Disputes" (paper prepared for discussion at the 18th Annual Conference of the Canadian Association of Administrators of Labor Legislation, Quebec, 1959).

15. See Kerr, *op. cit.,* p. 239. He attributed this point to A. C. Pigou, *The Economics of Welfare* 4th Edition (London: Macmillan and Company Ltd., 1938).

16. See T. C. Schelling, "The Strategy of Conflict Prospectus," *The Journal of Conflict Resolution* (September 1958). See also his *The Strategy of Conflict* (Cambridge: Harvard University Press, 1960).

17. As a way to cope with this agreement problem, the writer has elsewhere suggested the possible utility of a special kind of mediation device: a neutral third party might be continuously informed, during the negotiations, of the true positions of the parties; the sole function of this third party would be to receive this information and to inform the parties of it when they had achieved the necessary conditions for agreement. ("On the Theory of Negotiation," *Quarterly Journal of Economics* [November 1958].)

18. We should not, however, expect that the mediator will have useful functions in every kind of bargaining situation. In some situations, when the parties reach a deadlock — for example, where they know each other very well, have had much experience, and are sophisticated in their approach — it may be a simple, genuine deadlock, reflecting the lack of a contract zone. There may be little the mediator can do about this kind of situation.

Freedom to Strike Is in the Public Interest

THOMAS KENNEDY
Harvard University

FOREWORD

As public frustration grows over strikes, more voices are being raised in favor of some form of compulsory settlement of labor-management disputes. Freedom to strike comes at a price. But when this price is compared with the costs of compulsory settlements, it does not look nearly so high; free collective bargaining is vital to our private enterprise system. The author reaches these conclusions after first examining the reasons for increasing strike activity, the nature of collective bargaining, and the current trends in automation and conglomerate corporations which affect strike power. . . .

Activities on the labor front have confirmed earlier forecasts to the effect that 1970 would be a difficult year. There have been numerous strikes and threats of strikes — and there are more to come.

The year opened with 147,000 General Electric workers already engaged in a stoppage which was to last for more than three months. The GE strike was followed by these events:

○ The threat of a nationwide rail strike or lockout, which ended only after Congress legislated a compulsory settlement.

○ The first major strike of federal employees, when postal workers in New York City and other metropolitan areas refused to work until the government agreed to bargain with their representatives.

○ A second stoppage of federal employees, when a number of the air traffic controllers suddenly became "sick."

○ The refusal of members of the Teamsters Union in a number of the major cities to drive their trucks, in order to protest the terms of a new agreement negotiated by their national leaders.

○ The threat of a strike of the New York City newspapers.

The indications are that 1970 will continue to be a year of heavy activity on the strike front. Major contracts are open or will be open before the end of the year in a variety of major industries, including railroads (more than 500,000 workers not covered in the April 1970 settlement), over-the-road trucking, rubber, automobiles, farm equipment, New York City taxicabs, and New York City newspapers. It may well be that, when the year has ended, the record will show that the percent of working time lost as a result of strikes will have been the greatest since 1959 (the year of the 116-day steel strike), although it is not likely to approach the postwar record of 1946, when the percent of lost time was four times greater than it was in 1969.

IMPELLING FACTORS

Why are so many strikes being waged or threatened? There are at least eight major reasons. Let us review them briefly, limiting ourselves to a few highlights for each.

1. *Numerous negotiations.* Labor contract terminations tend to peak at three-year intervals in the United States. Thus 1967 was a big year for terminations, 1968 was a smaller one, and 1969 was still smaller. But in 1970 we are back again to a big year; contracts covering about 5 million workers have been or will be subject to renegotiation or reopening, in contrast to contracts covering only about 2.7 million workers in 1969.

Considering the great difference in the number of employees affected by contract terminations, it does not follow that labor relations are worse in 1970 simply because the time lost in strikes may have increased over 1969. Even if the batting average on settlements in 1970 should remain the same as in 1969, by the time this year is finished we can expect to have had almost twice as much strike activity.

2. *Great expectations.* The peak in terminations in 1970 comes at a time when the demands and expectations of workers are very high. These high aspirations are due to a number of factors, one of the more basic of which is the continuing high rate of inflation. . . .

The average hourly rate for unskilled workers at Ford, prior to the 1967 contract, was $3.30. The 1967 contract added $.20, plus two 3% increases, bringing the total to $3.71. At the end of the contract in September 1970, un-

skilled workers would have had to receive an additional 16%, or $.59 per hour, in order for their real wages to equal what they would have earned had there been no increase in the cost of living. Instead, they will have received only $.16, leaving a deficit of $.43. For Ford skilled workers, the deficit will be about $.60. . . .

Finally, workers whose last general wage increase occurred in 1967 have watched workers whose contracts terminated in 1968 or 1969 receive increasingly higher settlements than those made in 1967. The 1967 median package increase of wages and benefits, when averaged out over the full term of the contract, was only 5.5%, compared with 6.6% for 1968 and 8.2% for 1969. Living under contract rates negotiated in 1967 has been especially painful for skilled craftsmen, who have seen their counterparts in the building trades receive an average increase of 12.9% in 1969.

3. *Inability to pay.* Unfortunately, the peak in worker expectancy has come at a time when managements feel less able and willing to grant sizable wage and benefit increases. As the various economic indexes show, the trend of the economy has been downward. First-quarter profits in 1970 fell 9% from the first quarter of 1969, for all industries, and 39% in autos and equipment. As a result, managements' bargaining posture has hardened.

When the economy was booming and labor cost increases could be passed on to customers, the "message from above" to the company's men at the bargaining table was "get a reasonable settlement if possible, but in any event avoid a strike." Now the message is more likely to be the reverse: "Avoid a strike if possible, but in any event insist on a reasonable settlement."

4. *Other income sources.* The ability of a union to wage a long strike depends in part on the alternative sources of income which are available to the striking members. The major sources of this type are welfare payments, union

strike benefits, unemployment compensation, and employment elsewhere.

In cases where the union can arrange for only a small fraction of its membership to be on strike at any one time, it may be able to afford sizable strike benefits. This is the case with the International Typographical Union. If it strikes the New York City newspapers again in 1970, its members will receive union strike benefits which will be close to their regular pay. In the steel, coal, aluminum, and automobile industries, however, and in many others as well, the unions have such a large percentage of their membership on strike at any one time that strike benefits can amount to only a very small percentage of the employees' regular pay. . . .

Welfare payments are in many cases more important than union strike benefits. The old management cliché, ''starve them out,'' is no longer applicable in many communities. Instead, when strikers' resources reach the level where they cannot meet certain minimum needs, welfare funds are made available to them. In the 1969–1970 General Electric strike, it was reported that 2500 of the 12,000 strikers in the Lynn, Massachusetts, area received welfare payments of between $65 and $110 per week in addition to $20 per week of union strike benefits. It was reported also that it was very easy to get on the welfare roll in Lynn: ''A family only had to have less than $1000 in savings to qualify.''[1]

In New York and Rhode Island, after a waiting period of six weeks in addition to the regular one week, striking employees are eligible for state unemployment compensation payments. As a result, the pressure on employees to settle, when a strike has lasted more than seven weeks, is greatly diminished.

During a period of relatively full employment, if a strike occurs in a community where there are other plants not on strike, some of the strikers may find temporary jobs. This, too, reduces their willingness to come to terms. During one recent strike it was reported that the vast majority of the strikers who were not on welfare found full-time or part-time jobs or else had wives who worked. Appeals for temporary bus drivers and for men to deliver telephone books went unfilled as many strikers took their choice of jobs.[2]

5. *Revolt of rank-and-file.* Even when management and union representatives at the bargaining table are able to reach an agreement, a strike may occur because the rank-and-file in the union refuse to ratify the settlement and insist on a better package. In 1969, the number of such incidents reached an all-time high, and this trend has continued into 1970.

Unfortunately, management has sometimes been willing to sweeten its offer following a negative vote. Such action makes acceptance of future contracts on the first vote highly unlikely. One group of union employees now has as its motto, ''First vote *no,* then *go.*'' Moreover, such action is very contagious. After all, employees say to themselves, if another group of workers gets more by voting down a contract, why not try it ourselves? Refusals to ratify cause strikes because the vote frequently occurs too close to the contract termination date to allow bargaining officials time to negotiate a change in the agreement. Moreover, if the package finally agreed to by the employees represents a major gain, it not only undermines the influence of the reasonable union leadership, but also causes management in future negotiations to hold back its final offer until after the first vote by the employees. As a result, negotiations become more difficult and strikes more likely.

6. *Vetoes by skilled workers.* Closely related to the revolts of the rank and file as a factor in recent strike activity have been the revolts of the skilled workers. Believing that settlements by the big industrial unions have favored the unskilled majority, the skilled minority has threatened to secede unless it is given more control over the nature of the bargains. For example:

In the automobile industry, a large group of the skilled workers appealed to the National Labor Relations Board to establish it as a separate bargaining unit. The NLRB turned down the appeal, but at the union's convention in 1966 the constitution was changed to provide that all labor agreements henceforth be ratified not only by the majority of all the employees covered, but also by a majority of the skilled employees.

The right of the skilled group to veto a contract settlement makes it harder for negotiators to develop a package which satisfies everyone.

7. *The generation gap.* There is a generation gap today not only between young people and their parents but also between young workers and old workers. This gap is reflected in what workers want their union to insist on at the bargaining table. The young (the group which includes most of the minority workers) want money now plus more income security in case of layoffs; their seniors want better medical care and improved pensions. . . . In a year in which economic conditions require a limited total package, it will be difficult to satisfy both types of demands.

8. *Unrest in public sector.* Public employee unions are the fastest-growing labor organizations in the country. Despite the fact that strikes against government agencies (whether federal, state, or local) are illegal, stoppages in the public sector have been occurring with increasing frequency during the past several years. In many cases these stoppages have been highly successful in securing for the workers sizable wage and benefit increases, and, except in a few instances, penalties have not been invoked. Of special significance in this respect has been the recent postal employees' strike.

Strikes by federal employees probably will continue to be prohibited *de jure,* but since the postal strike everyone understands that *de facto* strikes can occur and succeed without the penalties being enforced.

In the long run, strikes in the public sector will probably decrease as the parties become more skilled and government workers achieve pay parity with private industry employees. But for the next several years a sizable increase of strike activity in this sector can be anticipated.

BARGAINING IN REVIEW

The public has become irritated and frustrated by the strikes and threats of strikes which have caused inconvenience and hardship. It is disturbed by the increases in prices and taxes which have followed many of the settlements. Of particular concern have been the strikes by the postal employees and the air traffic controllers. Until this year, the public had assumed that the federal employment sector, with its vital services, was immune to work stoppage.

Strong pressure may develop for legislation to outlaw strikes in the private sector as well as in the public sector, and to replace collective bargaining with some method whereby wages, hours, and other conditions of employment are determined by compulsory arbitration, labor courts, or government boards. This is an appropriate time, therefore, for a careful review of the free collective bargaining system which we have in the private sector, an essential element of which is the freedom to strike.

How the System Works

While it has always been illegal in this country for public employees to strike,[3] in the private sector of the economy strikes have not been illegal except during wartime. The National Labor Relations Act of 1935 (NLRA) requires a private employer and the union that has been certified as the bargaining agent for a group of the employer's workers to bargain in good faith with respect to "wages, hours and other conditions of employment." Before a contract terminates, the employer and the union must make an honest attempt to reach agreement. However, no union and no company is forced by the government to continue to work under conditions to which it will not agree. Instead, when the labor agreement terminates and an impasse is reached, either party is free to use its economic power in the form of the strike or the lockout to try to force the other party to terms which it considers more reasonable. We refer to this system as *free collective bargaining*. . . .

On three occasions in recent years, strikes have occurred or have appeared imminent on the railroads, and in each case Congress has ordered a compulsory settlement. Aside from these cases, the free collective bargaining system has been maintained during peacetime in the private sector of the economy.

Where the Strike Comes In

The possibility of a strike and the costs which strike action will place on the union, the employees, and the company are inducements to the parties to bargain effectively. To illustrate:

When I used to bargain for a company, there were times when I had made an offer of, say, $.08; but, knowing that the union would indeed strike if I held at that point, I was willing to move up a little more rather than assume the costs of a strike for the company. Likewise, without the threat of the strike, the union might have held at say $.12; but, knowing that I would indeed take a strike if it held at that level, the union was willing to move down rather than face the costs of a strike for it and its membership. Thus the threat of a strike forced both of us to move from an offer and a demand which we would have preferred to a point where agreement was reached.

The threat of the strike was not always successful in forcing us to reach agreement. On a few occasions both parties felt that the other side was so adamant that we had to take a strike. Then the cost of the strike itself began to put pressure on both of us to settle. The loss of production and sales was translated into a loss of profits for the company. Some of our customers who had to turn to our competitors for delivery might be lost for good. The longer the strike lasted, the greater the

pressure within the company to reach a settlement and get back into production.

On the union side, the pressure to settle built up in the same way. The early days of the strike were accepted by the employees with a carnival attitude, but after several paydays without checks, the cost of the strike action to them and their families caused them to put pressure on the union to seek a settlement. Eventually, the pressures forced a retreat from one or both of the previous positions, and with the help of a mediator a settlement was reached.

It is the threat of the strike and, if that is not successful, it is the strike itself which creates the kind of pressures necessary at times to force the parties to reach agreement under our free collective bargaining system. Without the right to strike, our system would not be so effective in bringing about settlements.

IMPACT OF AUTOMATION

In the late 1940s, the United States experienced a series of strikes and threats of strikes in the privately owned utility field which caused great public fear and anxiety. There was good reason for this reaction. A strike by utility employees in those days could paralyze an entire community. Pittsburgh learned this when the employees of the Duquesne Light Company engaged in a stoppage. A blackout of the street lights resulted in a high rate of burglary and other crimes. Hospitals and other institutions, as well as private homes, were without light, heat, and power.

Today, however, the public does not exhibit the same anxiety regarding strikes in public utilities — and for good cause. Strikes in this area no longer result in discontinuance of service. The reason is automation.

True, the early effect of automation is to expand the strike power of a union by increasing the overhead or fixed costs of a company in comparison with labor costs. But the situation changes over time. Thus:

If a company is engaged in manufacturing panama hats by hand and the employees strike, practically all of the company's costs go out the door with the strikers. As a result, the strike power of the union is not very great. However, if the company decides to mechanize, then, as it invests more and more money in hat-making equipment, a smaller and smaller part of its costs go out the door with the strikers. Thus the strike power of the union becomes greater and greater as automation proceeds. This is illustrated in Fig. 1, where the trend line represents strike power at various stages of automation.

The apex of the union's strike power is reached at Point S, where the automation has been very extensive, but not quite enough to enable the nonunion management employees to operate the plant. Once that point is passed, however, and Point M is reached (see Fig. 2), the strike power diminishes quickly. Unable to stop production and sale of the product, the employees and their union have lost the power to cause the company to suffer heavy losses by withdrawing their services. Management personnel are now able to operate the plant.

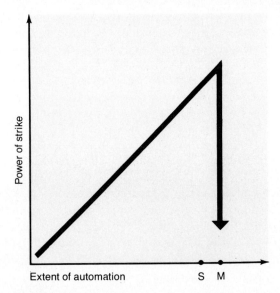

FIGURE 2
When automation is advanced, strike power drops

Reduced Strike Power

Automation has already reached Point M in the electric power, telephone, gas, and oil refining industries, and in some chemical industries. Let us look at some examples. . . .

○ When the installers, repairmen, building maintenance, and construction personnel of the New England Telephone and Telegraph Company struck from April to September in 1968, the company was able to report that "during the strike supervisory people and employees not involved in the strike maintained excellent service."

○ In 1969, when its 1000 unionized employees struck for a period of 11 weeks, the Boston Gas Company was able to report that "gas service was maintained by nonunion employees during the strike."

○ Similar results have been reported following strikes in oil refineries and chemical plants. In 1962, when the Oil, Chemical, and Atomic Workers Union struck the Shell Oil Company's refinery in Houston, Texas, for

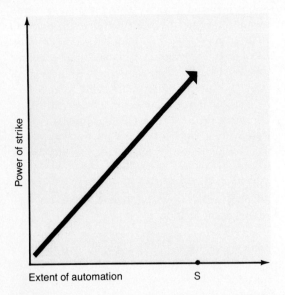

FIGURE 1
Strike power increases during early stages of automation

353 days, the company, by using supervisory, technical, and clerical employees, was able to operate at more than 100% of rated capacity, processing 142,000 barrels per day although the rated capacity was only 130,000 barrels per day.[4]

Although the development of automation in utilities, oil, and chemicals has led the public to lose interest in eliminating free collective bargaining in those areas, the effect on the unions may be quite the opposite. Having lost the power to bring pressure on the companies by means of a strike, the unions may view with favor a move away from collective bargaining to some kind of compulsory settlement. They may prefer to have a neutral arbitrator or a government board rather than have management dictate the terms of employment. For the first time in our history we may see a sizable segment of labor move to support compulsory arbitration of new contract terms.

HOW COSTLY ARE STRIKES?

Despite the fact that peaceful alternatives have replaced most organizational, jurisdictional, and grievance strikes, and despite the fact that strikes in utilities, oil refineries, and some chemical plants no longer create crises, strikes over new contract terms still do occur, and these can be quite costly to companies, employees, unions, suppliers, customers, and the general public. Also, of course, when the strike involves a critical material or service, the effect on the economy as a whole may be disastrous if the stoppage continues beyond a certain point.

Thus while the strike performs a valuable function in our free collective bargaining system, it is legitimate to question whether the costs are too great in relation to the benefits. Might some alternative to the strike, such as compulsory arbitration, serve the interests of the parties and the public better? To answer this question, let us begin by examining the costs of strikes. We can next compare these with the costs of alternative procedures.

Because of the publicity which strikes get, it is easy for their extent and their impact on the economy to be overestimated. When one reads in the headlines that 147,000 GE employees have been on strike for over three months, one is likely to be greatly impressed. But when one realizes that the GE strikers represent only 0.2% of the 71,000,000 nonagricultural employees in the country, one sees it in a different light (although for the company, its dealers, and its employees, the strike is still very significant).

It is estimated that there are approximately 300,000 labor agreements in the United States.[5] On the average, about 120,000 of these agreements terminate each year. Thus, across the country during an average year, 120,000 management bargaining teams sit across the table from 120,000 union bargaining teams and try to work out agreements on new contract terms. The issues which they deal with are wages, benefits, hours, and other important working conditions. These are matters which are extremely vital to the companies, the unions, and the employees. Despite the difficulties of these issues, the parties are successful in 96% or more of the negotiations. Only 4% or less of the negotiations result in strikes, and in most cases these strikes are short-lived. The problem is that a peaceful settlement is seldom front-page news, whereas a strike may be good for a number of headlines.

The Bureau of Labor Statistics estimates that the amount of working time in the total economy which was lost directly as a result of strikes in 1969 was only 0.23%. Moreover, the general trend has been down. As illustrated in Fig. 3, from 1945 to 1949 the average time lost per year was 0.47%, compared with 0.26% from 1950 to 1959, and only 0.17% from 1960 to 1969. We have been losing far more time in coffee breaks than in strikes!

Industrywide Bargaining

The effect of a strike on the economy depends, among other things, on the nature of the product or service and the structure of the bargaining. In the steel industry, where the product is essential

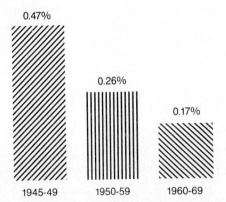

Source: Data in Table 140; "Work Stoppages in the U.S., 1881–1967," in *Handbook of Labor Statistics 1969* (Washington, Bureau of Labor Statistics, 1970), pp. 352–353, plus data for 1968 and 1969 reported currently by the Bureau of Labor Statistics.

FIGURE 3
Working time lost in strikes as a percent of working time in total economy

to many other industries and where the bargaining is practically industrywide, one might expect that a strike of any sizable duration would have drastic effects on the overall economy. Such studies as are available, however, indicate that such is *not* the case.

Following the 116-day steel strike in 1959, E. Robert Livernash of the Harvard Business School made an extensive study for the Department of Labor of the impact of that and earlier steel work stoppages on the economy. Livernash concluded that:

"The actual adverse effects of steel strikes on the economy have not been of serious magnitude. A major reason why steel strikes have had so little measurable impact is that when a strike approaches a critical state, pressure upon the parties to settle becomes substantially irresistible. . . . It is significant that the public interest has not been seriously harmed by strikes in steel, or by steel collective bargaining agreements, despite common public opinion to the contrary."[6]

In January 1970 the Department of Labor

published an extensive study of the effect on the economy of the 1963, 1965, and 1969 longshore strikes.[7] The study concluded that, although the companies and workers involved suffered losses, as did some workers and owners in collateral industries, "the strike had no visible impact on the economy as a whole." Many companies, according to the report, prepared for the strikes by stepping up their business before the stoppages and catching up again afterwards. "There appears to be no evidence," the report stated, "of a permanent loss of export markets because of the strikes." In talking to newsmen when he released the longshore strikes study, Secretary of Labor George P. Shultz stated that "despite warnings of catastrophic economic effects during some major strikes such results are kind of difficult to find afterwards."[8]

Bargaining in Conglomerates

Unions tend to be organized along industry lines. Accordingly, a particular union may find it difficult to bring heavy economic pressure on a conglomerate, since it can close down only a small part of the corporation's total business. . . .

In order to meet the threat of the conglomerate, unions are taking two actions — they are supporting legislation which opposes conglomeration, and they are developing coalition bargaining. Coalition bargaining is a technique whereby a number of unions that have contracts with the same conglomerate cooperate for bargaining with it.[9] The NLRB and the courts have ruled that coalition bargaining is permissible, and union leaders involved in the GE strike of 1969–1970 have expressed the opinion that the new approach is a viable procedure which provides them with much more economic power when dealing with a conglomerate.

Whether the growth of conglomerates and coalition bargaining will result in more or fewer strikes remains to be seen. When such strikes do occur, they are likely to be on a grander scale. Yet they are not so likely to create national emergencies as are strikes which involve industrywide bargaining, such as those in the steel and coal industries.

HIGH PRICE OF COMPULSION

It has often been proposed that strikes in the private sector be made illegal. The managements of the railroads and the maritime industry openly advocate compulsory arbitration as a desirable alternative to free collective bargaining. There is reason to believe, as indicated earlier, that unions in industries where automation has reduced the strike power will also move to that position. Suppliers and customers hurt by a strike are likely to mutter, "It should be outlawed."

Unfortunately, it is not a matter of eliminating strikes by devices which have no costs. The various compulsory settlement methods also are expensive, and it may be that managements, unions, and the public would find such costs more onerous than the costs of strikes. We should be fully aware of these costs before abandoning the present free collective bargaining system in the private sector.

Specter of More Failures

As stated earlier, the costliness of a strike to management and labor is in itself a strong incentive for them to reach agreement. What happens if that incentive is removed? There is reason to believe that the number of failures to reach agreement would increase greatly. This was our experience during World War II, when the strike was replaced with compulsory settlement by a government agency. It was also our experience in the late 1940s, when a number of states replaced free collective bargaining in public utilities with compulsory arbitration.

There are two reasons that the companies and unions find it more difficult to reach agreement when the possibility of the strike has been removed.

1. The parties are not under so much pressure to work out a contract because, while the compulsory settlement may be less desirable than the contract that could have been negotiated, it does not carry a threat of immediate loss of production and wages.

2. If the compulsory settlement authority — whether it be a government board, a court, or an arbitrator — has the right to decide on what it thinks is a fair settlement, then the company and the union may well hesitate to make a move toward a settlement, fearing that the other party will hold at its old position and that the board, court, or arbitrator will split the difference. If, for example, the company is offering a $.10-per-hour increase, and the union is asking for $.16 per hour, why should the company move to $.12 when there can be no strike anyhow, and when the authority might then decide between $.12 and $.16 instead of between $.10 and $.16? For like reasons, the union hesitates to move down from $.16 to $.14. Thus compulsory settlement interferes with the process of voluntary settlement.

In order to avoid the effect just described, the Nixon Administration now proposes that when strikes are threatened in the transportation industries, the President be permitted to order arbitration proceedings in which the arbitrator is required to decide only which of the two final offers of the parties is the more reasonable. It is believed that this method would remove one of the undesirable effects of the usual type of arbitration — that is, the hesitancy of the parties to improve their offers for fear that the arbitrator will split the difference. However, the new proposal has the disadvantage of forcing the arbitrator to choose between two proposals, both of which may seem unfair to him.

While the type of arbitration now proposed by the Administration would probably be less harmful than ordinary compulsory arbitration in terms of hampering efforts to reach a voluntary settlement, it would still have some such effect, for management and labor would not be prodded by fears of strike costs. I believe it is erroneous to expect that the number of disputes which would go to an arbitrator would be the same as the number of strikes which would occur without compulsory settlement. The removal of the strong incentive to settle would result in a great many more failures to reach agreement voluntarily. It would therefore be necessary to establish a sizable government bureaucracy to handle the increased volume of unsettled contract disputes.

More Federal Intervention

The size of the bureaucracy could be lessened by using private arbitrators (with the parties given an opportunity to choose the men they like) instead of a labor board or a labor court. However, the government would have to become involved when the parties were unable to agree on an arbitrator. Moreover, while the Federal Mediation and Conciliation Service has been free from political bias in placing arbitrators' names on its lists for selection by the parties in grievance arbitrations, there can be no guarantee that politics would not play a role in the selection process if the stakes were high enough — as they would be in the compulsory arbitration of new contract terms in the steel, coal, automobile, and other major industries.

If a board or labor court were used to settle disputes, it would have the possible advantage of being able to establish continuing policies. Nevertheless, appointment of at least some of the members would be made by the Administration. (A board could be tripartite, in which case some members would be appointed by labor and some by management.) One of the costs of compulsory settlement, therefore, would be to move management-labor disputes — to some degree at least — from the economic to the political arena.

Will Force Really Work?

Under the free collective bargaining system, the government has no problem of enforcement. For instance, while both the company and the employees suffered serious losses during the 14-week GE strike, once it was over both the management and the workers returned to their jobs voluntarily. This illustrates an important advantage of the present system which is often overlooked — that no use of force by the government is required. Moreover, since the agreement is one which the parties themselves have negotiated, the day-to-day operations under it are likely to be more cooperative. The company representatives sell it to management, and the union representatives sell it to the employees. Since the contract is the negotiators' own handiwork, they make a real effort to get it to work — a greater effort, I believe, than they would make if the agreement were the work of some authority appointed by the government.

This country's experience with legislation that has prohibited strikes on the part of public employees indicates that such legislation does not automatically put an end to the strikes. The Condon-Wadlin Act, which prohibited strikes by state and local government employees in New York State from 1947 to 1967, was violated often, but on only a few occasions were its penalties actually enforced. Since 1967 the Taylor Act, which also prohibits strikes by public employees in New York State, has been subject to numerous violations. Likewise, the illegality of strikes by federal employees has not prevented them from leaving the job.

What would happen, under compulsory settlement, if workers in the coal, steel, automobile, trucking, or some other major industry decided that they did not wish to accept the terms prescribed by the arbitrator or labor court and refused to work? How does a democratic government force 100,000 coal miners, 400,000 steel workers, 700,000 automobile workers, or

450,000 truckers to perform their tasks effectively when they elect not to do so? Perhaps it can be done — but I suggest that this is a question which it is well not to have to answer. It is unwise to run the risk of placing government in a position where the government may reveal its impotence unless it is absolutely necessary to do so.

Threat to Capitalism

Finally, if government becomes involved in the determination of labor contract terms in order to avoid strikes, it may not be able to stop there. With our democratic political structure it would be impossible, I believe, to prevent compulsory settlement of wages for union members from leading to compulsory determination of *all* wages; that, in turn, would lead to government decisions concerning salaries, professional fees, and, finally, prices and profits.

So long as free collective bargaining is per-

mitted, it forms an outer perimeter of defense against government regulation in other areas. If it falls, the possibility of more regulation in the other areas becomes much greater. It is worth noting that George Meany, the president of the AFL-CIO, stated several months ago that he would not be opposed to wage controls if similar controls were placed on salaries, prices, and profits. Meany's view of these relationships is one that many people might share.

In Fig. 4 I have tried to portray the notion just described by showing how government inroads in one area make other areas more vulnerable. In some industries, such as the utilities, the railroads, and the maritime industry, which are already heavily controlled, the threat of inroads may not be an important argument for free collective bargaining; but in the major part of our private economy it is very significant. Businessmen who believe in the effectiveness and desirability of private enterprise should recognize

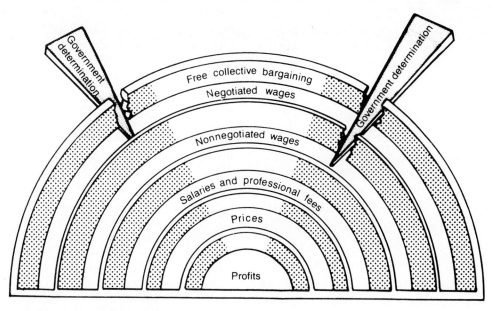

FIGURE 4
Compulsory arbitration threatens the private enterprise system

that free collective bargaining constitutes the outer defense of the entire system. In terms of what they consider of most value in our economic system, the ultimate costs of compulsory settlement would be very high indeed.

CONCLUSION

In 1970 we are in a period of heavy strike activity which is likely to continue for some time. As the public becomes more and more irritated and frustrated by the inconveniences and hardships these strikes cause and by the increases in prices and taxes which follow the settlements, political pressure will probably develop, as it has on similar occasions in the past, to replace free collective bargaining with some method of compulsory settlement. How do the costs of the right to strike compare with the costs of the alternative, compulsory settlement? Taking strike costs first, my analysis indicates that:

○ It is easy to overemphasize the costs of strikes.

○ Much progress has already been made in replacing organizational strikes, jurisdictional strikes, and grievance strikes with peaceful alternatives.

○ Strikes — even the big industrywide ones — have a minimal effect on the economy.

○ Some strikes, such as those in public utilities, which once were very critical, are no longer so because of automation.

○ The number of man-days lost because of strikes is a very small part of the total (only 0.23% in 1969), and the trend has been definitely downward.

On the other hand, my analysis indicates that compulsory settlement involves major costs like these:

○ The elimination from collective bargaining of the strongest incentive to reach agree-

ment which management and labor now have.

○ A great increase in the number of failures to reach agreement.

○ The development of a large government bureaucracy to adjudicate the larger number of unsettled disputes.

○ An increase in political aspects of collective bargaining.

○ The difficulty of enforcement of compulsory orders, with the attendant danger of divulging the impotence of government.

○ The likely development of other wage, salary, price, and profit controls by government.

I conclude that the right to strike is preferable to a compulsory settlement system. It does not follow that the government should never move to protect the public against strikes which create serious hardships, but it does follow that any move to prohibit the use of the strike in the private sector should be made cautiously and only to the extent which is clearly required. Any broad prohibition of strike freedom would prove to be very costly in itself and also lead to major government controls over other parts of the economy. Free collective bargaining, which includes the right to strike and the right to lock out, constitutes the outer defense of the private enterprise system.

NOTES

1. David Gumpert, "Striking the Modern Painless Way," *The Wall Street Journal,* February 5, 1970.

2. *Ibid.*

3. See Executive Order 10988 (1962) and Executive Order 11491 (1969), which provide for collective bargaining for federal employees. In the states, strikes by public employees are prohibited by statute or by common law.

4. *The Wall Street Journal,* August 5, 1963, p. 3.

5. This figure and the ones immediately following are from a forthcoming book by William Simkin, former Director of the Federal Mediation and Conciliation Service.

6. *Collective Bargaining in the Basic Steel Industry* (Washington, U.S. Department of Labor, January 1961), p. 18.

7. *Impact of Longshore Strikes on the National Economy* (Washington, 1970).

8. *The New York Times,* January 11, 1970.

9. For a detailed analysis of coalition bargaining, see George H. Hildebrand. ''Cloudy Future for Coalition Bargaining,'' HBR November–December 1968, p. 114.

SECTION 4
Collective Bargaining Issues

INTRODUCTION

The previous section presents material pertaining to the negotiating process. However, it does not address the subjects of bargaining, the topic of this section. Section 8(d) of the National Labor Relations Act (NLRA) requires ''. . . the employer and the representative of the employees to meet at reasonable times and confer in good faith with respect to wages, hours, and other terms and conditions of employment, . . .'' Over the years since passage of the NLRA, the phrase ''wages, hours, and other terms and conditions of employment'' has been defined and expanded by court decisions. In 1947, the Steelworkers Union was able to convince the Supreme Court to make pensions a required or mandatory subject of bargaining. Today, unions and management bargain over a wide variety of topics, many of which were not conceived of when the NLRA was passed. These include such new issues as job enrichment and quality-of-work-life.

The readings in this section will address selected topics concerning the issues and subjects of bargaining. Evidence concerning the impact of unions on terms and conditions of employment is reviewed. Criteria considered by management in establishing wages and typical employer objectives in bargaining are also reviewed. The recent phenomena of concession bargaining is analyzed. Evidence pertaining to the importance union members attach to job enrichment relative to bread-and-butter issues is presented, a procedure for costing out a contract agreement is described, and finally the implications of the impending round of technological change is analyzed.

INTRODUCTION TO THE READINGS

The Impact of Collective Bargaining

Freeman and Medoff review the research comparing the conditions of employment in union and nonunion settings. Their review suggests that direct wages are ten to 15 percent greater in unionized establishments. The evidence indicates that the union influence on fringe benefits is greater than on direct compensation. The evidence also indicates that by pressing for uniform wage rates across employers and geographic areas, unions appear to reduce the dispersion in the structure of wages.

Their review also indicates that unions influence labor mobility. After controlling for other factors, including wages, quit rates are lower among unionized workers. Also, there is increased reliance on seniority in such decisions as promotion and layoff in union settings, although seniority does play a role in many nonunion settings.

Freeman and Medoff find that union and nonunion workers differ in some dimensions of job attitudes. Interestingly, union members report less job satisfaction than nonunion workers, but also report less willingness to voluntarily quit their current job.

Research pertaining to differences between union and nonunion settings with respect to other factors is also reviewed. Among them are the quality of workers and labor productivity. In summary, the Freeman and Medoff literature review makes clear that unionization has a wide range of effects on the terms and conditions of employment in an organization, as well as on the characteristics of its employees.

Management Objectives in Bargaining

Freedman reports the results of a study investigating employer objectives in contract negotiations and criteria in wage determination. Consistent with the research concerning the structure of wage rates reviewed by Freeman and Medoff, Freedman reports that the primary criteria for wage determination in nonunion settings is local labor market comparisons, but in union settings it is industry wage patterns. This follows from the union objective of taking labor out of competition.

With respect to the nonwage goals of management in contract negotiations, Freedman

found the most frequently mentioned types of issues were; time off with pay, i.e., holidays and vacations; flexibility in making assignments of employees; pensions; and health benefits. The nature of management objectives with respect to each nonwage issue took different forms. In some cases the goal was to secure more favorable contract provisions, e.g., greater flexibility in making work assignments. Another form of management objective with respect to nonwage issues was to hold the line in the face of union pressure to secure increases, i.e., union negotiators seeking more paid holidays. Finally, a management objective with respect to an issue could be to trade an improvement in one area for a union concession in another, e.g., improved health benefits for concessions in the area of cost of living allowances. Freedman reports the incidence of these alternative forms of management objectives with respect to a wide range of nonwage issues.

Concession Bargaining

During the late 1970s and early 1980s, concession bargaining became a relatively common phenomenon in American labor relations. Mills reports the results of a survey of major American corporations concerning the incidence and nature of concession bargaining. He makes clear that concession bargaining is not a one-way street. In return for union negotiators' agreement to actual reduction in wage rates or to foregoing future improvements in wages and benefits, management has had to make concessions. Examples include increases in union access to company financial records and increases in union participation in decisions formerly the exclusive realm of management.

With respect to the incidence of concession bargaining, Mills found that among unionized companies, 56 percent reported concessions were needed and 15 percent reported that concessions in wages and benefits were secured. His data indicates that concessions were limited to union settings. Apparently nonunion employers did not seek to improve their financial situation through reducing wages and benefits of rank-and-file workers.

Mills discusses factors management should consider in deciding if concessions are to be sought from an organization's work force. The principal factor appears to be the potential impact of concessions on the financial well-being of the company and on employee job opportunities. For example, will such concessions enable an employer to more effectively compete in the marketplace with foreign competition or non-union domestic employers?

Job Enrichment

It has been argued by some students of industrial relations that American union leaders are out of touch with the wishes of rank-and-file union members. These critics assert that union members have a greater interest in improving the intrinsic aspects of their jobs than is reflected in the negotiating stance taken by union leaders.

The available research on this issue is not clear. Giles and Holley present the results of a study that seeks to shed light on this question. Their sample of union members were asked, "What percentage of time in contract negotiations do you feel your union representative should spend in negotiating with management on each of these issues?" The alternatives presented were; fringe benefits, pay, working conditions, job enrichment, and job security.

The results suggest that the rank-and-file want their leaders to focus on pay and benefits. This indicates that union leaders have been accurate in assessing the desires of the membership in that the latter do not want their representatives to focus on job enrichment and quality of work issues during contract negotiations.

The Giles and Holley study was published in 1978. Since that year American workers have endured a severe recession and increased competition from foreign companies, and union workers have faced increased competition from domestic

nonunion companies, along with widespread demands for wage concessions from their employers. These forces would seem to lead to increased importance of "bread-and-butter" issues and reduced importance of job enrichment in the minds of union members.

Costing Out a Contract Agreement

Labor costs represent the largest component of operating costs incurred by most American employers. Small changes in wages or benefits can have a major impact on profits. Consequently, both union and management negotiators should be able to accurately estimate the cost of proposed changes in wages and benefits. These estimates are necessary in order to understand the implications of the proposed changes for the financial well-being of the employer.

Allen and Keaveny describe one set of procedures to follow in estimating the cost of proposed changes in a collective bargaining agreement. The procedure they discuss can be described as a static approach. They point out that this approach is subject to several criticisms. For example, it does not take into account possible changes in the composition of the organization's labor force or the level and composition of the organization's business activity during the period covered by the contract being negotiated.

A second problem is that the approach described by Allen and Keaveny focuses on the direct cost of contract changes rather than on the impact of these changes on the financial condition of the firm. However, they assert that these criticisms can be overcome by incorporating into these costing procedures information from human resources forecasting and planning, as well as information from financial managers.

Technological Change

The coming decade is expected to bring widespread technological change proceeding at faster rates than has been true in the past. This will present an especially difficult issue for American labor relations. Wheeler and Weikle present a typology of technological change which is useful for classifying and predicting union responses to new technology.

The authors also describe the range of alternatives unions can select from in responding to technological change. In addition, they discuss variables that influence the alternative response selected. Among these variables are the type of union, nature of the economic environment, number of jobs affected, and stage in the development and implementation of the particular technological innovation.

Wheeler and Weikle note that the typical position regarding technological change taken by American unions has been willing acceptance. And they point out that government has typically encouraged technological change and then sought to regulate it through legislation, as well as mitigate its effects on displaced workers. The authors go on to describe the nature of technological change, its effects, and union responses in the telecommunication, manufacturing, and retailing industries.

They conclude that the changes going on at the present time in these and other industries will almost certainly cause major disruptions in the lives of workers in the short run. Wheeler and Weikle argue that since society in general benefits from these innovations, society in general and not just the displaced workers and their families should share the costs of dislocation.

They expect that during the coming decade implementation of technological change and provisions to accommodate and mitigate the effects of change for displaced workers will be a far more important subject of negotiations than has been true in the past. They also expect that government programs to aid displaced workers will be developed in the near future.

SUGGESTIONS FOR FURTHER READING

Dunlop, John T., *Wage Determination Under Trade Unions,* New York: Macmillan, 1944.

Freedman, Audrey, *Managing Labor Relations,* The Conference Board, Report No. 765, 1980.

Friedman, Marvin, *The Use of Economic Data in Collective Bargaining,* U.S. Department of Labor, Washington, D.C.: U.S. Government Printing Office, 1978.

Gersuny, Carl, "Employment Seniority: Cases From Iago to Weber," *Journal of Labor Research,* Vol. 3, No. 1, Winter 1982, pp. 111–119.

Slichter, Sumner H., James J. Healey, and E. Robert Livernash, *The Impact of Collective Bargaining on Management,* Washington, D.C: The Brookings Institution, 1960.

The Impact of Collective Bargaining: Illusion or Reality?

RICHARD B. FREEMAN

JAMES L. MEDOFF
Both of Harvard University and
National Bureau of Economic Research

In recent years there has been an outpouring of empirical studies on the impact of collective bargaining on the economy. While many of these analyses focus on the traditional question of wage determination under unionism, considerable effort has also been devoted to estimating the effect of the institution on other market outcomes. As a result of this work we have a large body of new evidence regarding differences between union and nonunion workers and union and nonunion enterprises along many dimensions.

Can the observed union/nonunion differences be explained primarily in terms of pre-union characteristics of firms or individuals? Is it that all union/nonunion differences arise only because of the "union wage effect" and are observed only when one or more price-theoretic responses to this effect are being ignored? Or can it be that unions have important effects on the performance of our economic system through routes ignored in standard price theory?

There are a number of different positions on whether union effects are real or illusory. One

belief is that the apparent union/nonunion differences are illusory because of the way trade unions were superimposed on various groupings of establishments or individuals. A second view is that unions have real effects on economic performance, but that all of these effects operate through price-theoretic routes; any effects which appear to be inexplicable in terms of standard price theory are taken as illusory. Finally, there is the perception that unions influence outcomes through institutional channels and, in so doing, have important real nonwage effects on our economy.

The preunion characteristics belief that apparent union/nonunion differences are illusory seems to be held primarily by those who see the world as close enough to satisfying the conditions of perfect competition that, in the short run, unions are more of an epiphenomenon than a substantive force. While it is unlikely that anyone really believes that every apparent union effect is an apparition, the preunion characteristics view lies behind many attempts to explain away particular results suggesting that unions have meaningful economic impacts.

Those whose vision of what unions do comes from standard price theory tend to focus on what we have elsewhere called the "monopoly face" of unionism and believe that every real effect of unions works through price-theoretic channels.[1]

From *U.S. Industrial Relations 1950–1980: A Critical Assessment,* Jack Steiber, Robert B. McKersie, and D. Quinn Mills, Eds., Reprinted with the permission of the authors and the Industrial Relations Research Association.

Thus these individuals tend to limit their focus to the size and ramifications of "the union wage effect," treating any estimated union effect which cannot be rationalized in terms of a price-theoretic response to the wage effect as illusory, that is, as reflecting the poor quality of the experiment at hand.

Those in the industrial relations tradition believe that unionism influences outcomes primarily through what are often labeled "institutional channels" (the "collective voice/institutional response face" in our just-cited work). While this group accepts the existence of important real price-theoretic union effects, it believes in the reality of nonprice-theoretic effects as well. In fact, a primary concern of researchers with an industrial relations world view is with the non-wage effects of collective bargaining.

This paper examines the arguments and empirical evidence concerning whether union/nonunion differences represent illusion or reality, defined in accordance with either the price-theoretic or institutional views. In it we seek to determine the extent to which the union/nonunion differences found in myriad market outcomes are: (1) illusory, explicable in terms of the innately different characteristics of union and nonunion workers or firms; (2) real, working through price-theoretic routes of impact; and (3) real, working through institutional routes of impact.

While we recognize that to some extent we have set up artificial polar cases, and that no sensible researcher would be expected to rely solely on any one of the views for explaining all union/nonunion differences, we believe that the differences noted permeate much of the recent literature on unionism and that the "ideal types" provide a fruitful guide to understanding efforts to determine what unions in fact do. . . .

By way of anticipation, we reach two main conclusions. First, unions and collective bargaining have substantial real effects on diverse economic outcomes; union/nonunion differences appear to reflect much more than the poor quality of our econometric "experiments." Second, many of the real union effects are the result of institutional factors, which many economists have neglected in recent years; the price-theoretic view of reality seems to be much too narrow.

THE EVIDENCE IN QUESTION

It is important at the outset to lay out the union/nonunion differences about which illusion/reality interpretative questions have arisen. Accordingly, this section briefly summarizes the results of recent research concerning the impact of unionism on certain key aspects of the labor exchange. As a guide to the discussion, Table 1 gives the central findings in these studies categorized by the following substantive issues: compensation; internal and external mobility; work rules and environment; and inputs, productivity, and profits. The reader will notice that our set of issues is not exhaustive. We have, in particular, neglected such important topics as the internal operation of unions, strikes, and the survival of the organization itself, in part because these subjects do not lend themselves to the union/nonunion comparisons which motivate the research in the table. In addition, we concentrate exclusively on the private sector. While, as noted, we have no pretense that our set of issues is all-encompassing and while our listing of relevant references is undoubtedly incomplete, we believe that the table provides a reasonably accurate picture of the empirical results in question.

Compensation

The first and probably still the most widely studied issue is the differential between union and nonunion wages. The early literature on this differential was summarized in Lewis's influential 1963 book, *Unionism and Relative Wages in the United States*. Since the publication of Lewis's book, a number of new sources of individual-level data (such as the May Current Population Survey) which permit estimation of the wage ef-

TABLE 1
Recent evidence on union/nonunion differences based on cross-sectional data

VARIABLE	FINDING	PARTIAL LISTING OF RELEVANT REFERENCES
Compensation		
Wage rates	All else (measurable) the same, union/nonunion hourly wage differential is between 10% and 20%.	Ashenfelter (1976), Freeman & Medoff (forthcoming a), Lewis (1980), Mellow (1981a), Oaxaca (1975), Welch (1980).
Fringes[a]	All else the same, union/nonunion hourly fringe differential is between 20% and 30%. The fringe share of compensation is higher at a given level of compensation.	Duncan (1976), Freeman (1981), Goldstein & Pauly (1976), Leigh (1979), Solnick (1978), Viscusi (1980).
Wage dispersion	Wage inequality is much lower among union members than among comparable nonmembers and total wage dispersion appears to be lowered by unionism.	Freeman (1980c), Hyclak (1979, 1980), Plotnick (1981).
Wage structure	Wage differentials between workers who are different in terms of race, age, service, skill level, and education appear to be lower under collective bargaining.	Ashenfelter (1976), Bloch & Kuskin (1978), Johnson & Youmans (1971), Kiefer & Smith (1977), Leigh (1978), Pfeffer & Ross (1980), Schoeplein (1977), Shapiro (1978).
Cyclical responsiveness of wage rates[a]	Union wages are less responsive to labor market conditions than nonunion wages.	Ashenfelter (1976), Hamermesh (1972), Johnson (1981), Lewis (1963), Medoff (1979), Mitchell (1980a, 1980b), Pierson (1968), Raisian (1979).
Determinants of compensation differential	Other things equal, the union compensation advantage is higher the greater the percent of a market's workers who are organized. The effects of market concentration on wage differentials is unclear. The differentials appear to be very large in some regulated markets. They appear to decline as firm size increases.	Dalton & Ford (1977), Donsimoni (1978), Ehrenberg (1979), Freeman & Medoff (forthcoming a), Hayden (1977), Hendricks (1975), Kahn (1978), Kochan (1980), Lee (1978), Mellow (1981b), Weiss (1966).
Internal & external mobility		
Promotions	Seniority independent of productivity is rewarded substantially more in promotion decisions among union members than among otherwise comparable nonunion employees.	Halasz (1980), Medoff & Abraham (1980b, 1981b), Yanker (1980).

(cont.)

TABLE 1 *(cont.)*

VARIABLE	FINDING	PARTIAL LISTING OF RELEVANT REFERENCES
Internal & external mobility (continued)		
Quits[a]	The quit rate is much lower for unionized workers than for similar workers who are nonunion.	Blau & Kahn (1981), Block (1978a), Farber (OLS Results 1979), Freeman (1976, 1980a, 1980b), Kahn (1977), Leigh (1979).
Temporary layoffs[a]	There is much more cyclical labor adjustment through temporary layoffs in unionized manufacturing firms than in otherwise comparable firms that are nonunion.	Blau & Kahn (1981), Medoff (1979).
Terminations[a]	Terminations are more likely to be on a last-in-first-out basis among union employees, ceteris paribus.	Blau & Kahn (1981), Medoff & Abraham (1981a, 1981b).
Work rules and environment		
Rules[a]	There are important differences in the prevalence and nature of various rules in union and nonunion settings, such as those stipulating the role of company service and the way grievances are to be handled. Union work places appear to be run more by rules, with more rigidity in the scheduling of hours and less worker flexibility.	Freeman (1980a), Kochan & Bloch (1977), Kochan & Helfman (1979), Medoff & Abraham (1981b).
Management practices	Management in unionized cement firms appears to be more professional (less paternalistic or authoritarian), more standards oriented, and more in touch with work performance than management in similar nonunion firms.	Clark (1980a).
Management flexibility[a]	Management in unionized manufacturing firms appears less able to substitute nonproduction worker hours for production worker hours, but seems no less able to substitute capital for production labor than similarly situated nonunion management.	Freeman & Medoff (forthcoming b).
Worker assessment of jobs		
Satisfaction with job overall[a]	The stated level of overall job satisfaction is lower, but the wage gain required to induce a job change is higher for union members than for otherwise comparable employees who are not members.	Borjas (1979), Freeman (1976, 1978a), Kochan & Helfman (1979), Mandelbaum (1980).
Evaluation of rules and conditions[a]	Unionized workers state that they are more satisfied with their wages and fringes, less satisfied with their supervision, and less satisfied with their working conditions than nonunion workers. The extent to which stated job security grows with tenure is substantially greater under unionism. While the probability of view-	Duncan & Stafford (1980), Kochan & Helfman (1979), Viscusi (1980).

TABLE 1 (cont.)

VARIABLE	FINDING	PARTIAL LISTING OF RELEVANT REFERENCES
Evaluation of rules and conditions[a] (continued)	ing promotions as fair declines with service among nonunion employees, it increases among union members.	
Inputs, productivity, & profits		
Prefirm quality of workforce	Other things equal, workers in unionized firms tend to have more "human capital."	Allen (1979), Brown & Medoff (1978), Farber (1979), Frantz (1976), Kahn (1979), Kalachek & Raines (1980).
Capital intensity[a]	Unionized firms in manufacturing, construction, and underground bituminous coal appear to have higher capital-labor ratios than similar nonunion enterprises.	Allen (1979), Brown & Medoff (1978), Clark (1980b), Connerton, Freeman & Medoff (1979), Frantz (1976).
Productivity[b]	In manufacturing and construction and in the underground bituminous coal industry in nonturbulent times, unionized enterprises appear to have greater productivity than those that are nonunion, all else equal. In underground coal, productivity appeared to be lower under unionism in the turbulent years around 1975.	Allen (1979), Brown & Medoff (1978), Clark (1980a), Connerton, Freeman & Medoff (1979), Frantz (1976).
Profitability	While profit per unit of sales appears to be the same in similar union and nonunion manufacturing firms, the rate of profit per unit of capital appears to be lower under unionism.	Brown & Medoff (1978), Clark (1980a), Frantz (1976), Freeman & Medoff (forthcoming b).

[a]Wages or total compensation was held constant in generating this finding.

[b]Variables reflecting price-theoretic responses were held constant as well as possible in generating this finding.

fect have become available. With micro-data of this kind, it is possible to compare the wages of union and nonunion workers with similar demographic characteristics who are also in the same detailed industry and/or occupation. As Johnson (1975) has reviewed some of this work, our summary will be brief. The post-Lewis micro-data estimates (derived with Ordinary Least Squares (OLS)) have generally found wage differentials noticeably above the 10 to 15 percent range given in Lewis's book. However, the analyses that have looked within more detailed cells, especially those with industry as a dimension, have tended to yield estimated differentials near the top end of the 10 to 15% range. This makes very good sense given that the studies summarized by Lewis normally examined a very narrowly defined group of workers. A comparison of the union wage effect by groups suggests larger impacts for blue-collar as opposed to white-collar workers, for younger as opposed to older employees, and for the less as opposed to the more educated. In addition, substantial differences have been noted in the size of the differential by industry.

Another form of data which has been used in recent studies pertains to individual establishments. These data (from surveys such as the Employer Expenditures for Employee Compensation Survey (EEC) permit the estimation of wage effects for production or nonproduction workers among firms of the same size within the same three-digit Standard Industrial Classification (SIC) industry. Estimates using these data are quantitatively closer to those of Lewis, yielding union/nonunion differences of 10% or so. All told, with rare exception, recent studies confirm the existence of a sizable union/nonunion wage differential.

While a tremendous amount of effort was devoted in the past to studying union/nonunion differentials in wage rates, very little attention was devoted to analyzing union/nonunion differentials in fringe benefits. With the passage of time, this allocation of resources has become less defensible since the share of total compensation associated with voluntary fringes has been growing rapidly. In contrast to Rice's 1966 cross-industry analysis, which found no union effect on fringes, the recent studies cited in Table 1 have demonstrated that the "union fringe effect" is bigger, in percentage terms, than the "union wage effect." Data from the 1968, 1970, and 1972 EEC indicate, for example, that holding constant the characteristics in employees' establishments, blue-collar workers covered by collective bargaining received fringe benefits that were about 28 to 36% higher than those of blue-collar workers who were not covered (compared to a union wage advantage of 8 to 15%). For workers receiving the same total compensation per hour, the fringe share of labor cost was markedly higher in the union setting (Freeman 1981). Looking at separate fringes, the largest union/nonunion percentage differentials on a per hour basis are for pensions, life, accident and health insurance, and vacation pay.

One key question to ask about the union/nonunion wage differentials is, "How do they vary across settings?" Recent empirical work on this subject has been based on the notion that union wage gains will be high where the elasticity of demand for labor, and hence the cost of increased relative wages in terms of lost members, is low. The evidence that, at least in the

manufacturing and construction sectors of our economy, union wages but not nonunion wages grow with the fraction organized in the relevant product market is consistent with this claim; this is because a high percentage organized is likely to be associated with a low demand elasticity for union products and thus a low demand elasticity for union members. Other work has concentrated on the effect of market regulation on the union wage effect. Ehrenberg (1979) presents evidence consistent with the claim that union wages are raised by the regulation of public utilities. Hayden (1977) argues that the sizable impact of unionism on trucker wages (40% or so) is attributable both to ICC regulation of the sector and to the National Master Freight Agreement, which created industrywide bargaining.

Since their inception, unions in our country have been concerned with the structure as well as the level of wage rates. The practice which most exemplifies unions' efforts on this front is the long-standing policy of pushing for "standard rates"; that is, uniform rates for comparable workers across establishments and for given occupational classes within establishments. Estimates presented in Freeman (1980c) show that, for blue-collar workers, wage inequality is substantially lower among union members than among similar nonmembers. Consistent with this, estimates of separate wage equations for union and nonunion workers have found that virtually all standard wage-determining variables are associated with smaller earnings differentials under unionism. Moreover, union wage policies appear to contribute to the equalization of wages by decreasing the differential between covered blue-collar workers and noncovered white-collar workers. If we add the apparent decrease in inequality due to wage standardization and the apparent decrease due to reduction in the white-collar/blue-collar differential to the apparent increase due to the greater wages of blue-collar union workers, we find that the apparent net effect of unionism is to reduce total wage inequality. Evidence on inequality of net earnings across standard metropolitan statistical areas (SMSAs) and states and over time also shows a negative relationship between unionism and dispersion in pay. In short, it appears that the structure of wages in the United States has been compressed by the wage policies of organized labor.

Finally, with respect to wage adjustments under varying economic conditions, recent analyses of cyclical variation in wage rates have confirmed the earlier finding of Lewis that the union/nonunion wage differential has tended to be greater during economic downturns, which suggests that the reduction in (the growth of) real wage rates in response to a reduction in product demand is smaller under trade unions. Interestingly, the work of Johnson (1981) and Mitchell (1980b) and an analysis of Current Wage Developments establishment-level data suggest that the union wage effect grew substantially during the 1970s to a point where it is roughly comparable to its level in the 1930s.

Internal and External Mobility

The new work on trade unions has, as noted earlier, expanded the set of outcomes under study. One of the most important topics receiving attention has been the impact of unionization on the internal and external mobility of employees.

To evaluate the effects of unionism on firms' employment policies (the awarding of promotions, the ordering of layoffs, etc.), it is necessary to have knowledge of what is actually happening inside both union and nonunion firms. Survey evidence collected by and discussed in Medoff and Abraham (1980b, 1981a, 1981b) and recent case studies have provided relevant information concerning the role of seniority independent of performance in firms' promotion and termination decisions. With respect to promotions, the survey data reveal that whereas 68% of private-sector unionized employees outside of agriculture and construction work in settings where senior employees are favored substantially when promotion decisions are made, only 40% of the non-

union workforce is employed in such settings. When the analysis is restricted to hourly employees, the estimates of concern are 68% for union members and 53% for the nonunion labor force. Regressions with the survey data which include controls for firm size, industrial sector, and geographic region yield differences similar to those just given. Moreover, case studies of a number of U.S. firms tell the same story: company service counts more in promotion decisions in union settings.

One of the essential tenets of the collective voice/institutional response model is that among workers receiving the same pay, unions reduce employee turnover and associated costs by offering ''voice'' as an alternative to ''exit.'' Recent evidence using newly available information on the job changes of thousands of individuals and on industry-level turnover rates shows that with diverse factors (including wages) held constant, unionized workers do have substantially lower quit rates than nonunion workers who are comparable in other respects. The reduction in quits and the accompanying increase in tenure appear to be as substantial for blacks as for whites and greater for older than for younger workers.

With less ability to reduce (the growth of) real wage rates and with lower quit rates, unionized firms can be expected to make greater use of other adjustment mechanisms, such as average hour reductions and layoffs. Both establishment-level and individual-level data sets demonstrate that temporary layoffs and recalls are a more important form of labor adjustment in unionized manufacturing firms than in otherwise comparable firms that are nonunion. Moreover, temporary layoffs tend to be used instead of average hour reductions to a greater extent under unionism. Hence, it appears that the layoff/recall syndrome which has received much recent attention is, for the most part, a unionized manufacturing (in particular, durables) phenomenon.

In union settings, length of service appears to be a much more important determinant of the order of both temporary and permanent layoffs than in comparable nonunion settings. Evidence from the seniority survey just cited reveals that, among those who had witnessed workforce reductions, rules protecting senior workers against being permanently laid off before their junior co-workers are more prevalent and stronger under trade unions. For hourly employees, 95% of the responses pertaining to groups covered by collective bargaining indicated that seniority in and of itself receives substantial weight in termination decisions, compared to 70% of the responses pertaining to noncovered groups. As for "strength," 68% of the survey responses pertaining to unionized hourly employees stated that a senior worker would *never* be involuntarily terminated before a junior worker, whereas only 28% of the responses pertaining to nonunion hourly employees stated that this is so. These survey results could not be explained in terms of company characteristics and are consistent with the findings of Blau and Kahn (1981) who used individual-level data.

Work Rules and Environment

Other personnel practices and procedures also appear to be affected by the presence of unionism. In Clark's (1980a, 1980b) study of six cement firms which were recently unionized, management practices appear to have changed significantly with the coming of a union, in directions which can be labeled "productivity oriented." These observations gain credence from the fact that they are similar to those of Sumner Slichter, James Healy, and E. Robert Livernash, who conducted myriad case studies concerning the relationship between unionism and management behavior for their classic 1960 opus, *The Impact of Collective Bargaining on Management.* It should be noted that, with evidence of the type which has been collected, it is difficult to infer whether managers were moved from noncost-minimizing behavior to cost-minimizing behavior or whether the type of behavior which is cost-minimizing is different in union and in nonunion environments.

It would seem reasonable, given what is believed about the objective function of the typical union, to find less management flexibility in unionized establishments than in otherwise comparable establishments that are nonunion. Consistent with this view, evidence drawn primarily from the *1972 Census of Manufacturers* and the EEC show that within U.S. manufacturing the ease of substitution for production labor, particularly substitution of nonproduction for production labor, is lower under trade unionism. However, it should be mentioned that the limited evidence does *not* indicate that unionism is associated with a lower elasticity of substitution between labor and capital and thus with whatever technological change is embodied in new capital.

Workers' Assessment of Jobs

Several recent studies examining the impact of unionism on the stated job satisfaction of workers have found union workers expressing less satisfaction, or in some instances no more satisfaction, with their jobs than similar nonunion workers, even when compensation is *not* held constant. At the same time, however, union members are also more likely to state that they are "unwilling to change jobs under any circumstance" or "would never consider moving to a new job" than are their "more satisfied" nonunion counterparts, even when the wage is fixed. One interpretation of these results is that the collective voice of unionism provides workers with a channel for expressing their preferences to management and that this increases their willingness to complain about undesirable conditions.

Evidence has also been accumulated concerning workers' stated satisfaction with particular aspects of their jobs. Some of the findings most relevant to the discussion at hand are: (1) union members are much more likely to state that they are happy with their wages and fringes than are otherwise comparable nonunion employees; (2) there appears to be a strong tendency for unionized workers to state they are less happy with their supervisors and have worse relations with them; (3) there is a tendency for unionized workers to report their physical work conditions as less desirable than those reported by nonunion workers; (4) the extent to which stated job security grows with tenure is substantially greater under unionism; and (5) while the probability of viewing promotions as fair is negatively related to seniority in nonunion settings, it is positively related to seniority under unionism.

Inputs, Productivity, and Profits

When unions raise wages or otherwise alter labor costs, enterprises can be expected to change factor inputs and modes of organization in such ways as to raise the marginal revenue product of labor up to the point where it equals the new marginal cost of labor. Two of the most important ways in which firms could potentially do this are to hire "higher quality" workers and to increase their capital/labor ratios. Evidence has been offered showing that blue-collar union workers do in fact have somewhat more "human capital" than similar nonunion workers. With May CPS data for 1973–1975, blue-collar union members are found to be three to four years older than otherwise comparable nonunion blue-collar workers, and to have slightly more education. Separate wage equations for males and females, which differentiate workers by schooling, age, and region, lead to the conclusion that unionized production labor has about 6 percent more "human capital" within 2-digit manufacturing industries (Brown and Medoff 1978). It should be noted, however, that an index of labor quality based on weights from wage regressions is at best only a crude approximation to an index based on "true" productivity weights, as is implied by evidence that a substantial fraction of seniority/earnings differentials cannot be explained by seniority/productivity differentials (Medoff 1977, and Medoff and Abraham 1980a, 1981a). Moreover, it should be recognized that indices of the sort being discussed ignore potentially very important, but not measured, worker characteristics.

There have been a number of recent studies which have attempted to isolate "as well as is possible with existing data" the effect of trade unionism on the productivity of otherwise comparable workers utilizing the same amount of capital. The Brown and Medoff (1978) study, based on 1972 state-by-industry data for U.S. manufacturing, found that unionized enterprises had 24% higher productivity than otherwise comparable nonunion establishments within the same two-digit SIC industries. Studies of particular manufacturing industries — wooden household furniture and cement — have also found a positive productivity differential. Allen reports sizable differences in construction, using a value output measure. His result is supported by the findings of Mandelstamm (1965), who avoided the potential problems of measuring output in dollar terms by having union and nonunion contractors cost out an identical project.

That unionism can be associated with lower as well as higher productivity has been documented for the U.S. underground bituminous coal sector, where unionized mines were estimated to be 25% more productive than comparable nonunion mines in 1965, but 20% less productive a decade later. One potential explanation for the observed change in union/nonunion productivity differentials is that the "quality" of industrial relations in that sector appeared to change over time.

Some effort has been devoted to explaining the routes underlying the apparent union impact on productivity. One relevant finding is that roughly 25% of the union/nonunion productivity differential in the manufacturing sector can be explained by the union/nonunion differential in quit rates. Other evidence suggests that a significant piece of the union productivity effect can be explained by the union/nonunion differential in the quality of management practices.

The association of unionism and profitability has been examined only recently, in part because, like labor quality and capital, profits are an extremely difficult variable to measure. What the available evidence does suggest is that while the gross profit margin (profit as a percentage of the value of output) is no different in unionized firms than in similar nonunion firms, the rate of return on capital is lower in unionized settings. Thus it appears that productivity under unionism is not sufficiently greater than productivity in nonunion settings to offset the higher compensation plus the higher capital intensity, which would be necessary if profits per unit of capital were to be left unaffected.

. . .

NOTES

1. See Freeman and Medoff (1979, 1982).

REFERENCES

Allen, Steven G. "Unionized Construction Workers Are More Productive." (Mimeograph 1979)

Ashenfelter, Orley. "Union Relative Wage Effects: New Evidence and a Survey of Their Implications for Wage Inflation." (Mimeograph 1976)

Blau, Francine D., and Lawrence M. Kahn. "The Exit-Voice Tradeoff in the Labor Market: Some Additional Evidence." (Mimeograph 1981)

Bloch, Farrell E., and Mark S. Kuskin. "Wage Determination in the Union and Nonunion Sectors." *Industrial and Labor Relations Review* 31 (January 1978), pp. 183-92.

Borjas, George J. "Job Satisfaction, Wages, and Unions." *Journal of Human Resources* 14 (Winter 1979), pp. 21-40.

Brown, Charles, and James Medoff. "Trade Unions in the Production Process." *Journal of Political Economy* 86 (June 1978), pp. 355-78.

Clark, Kim B. "The Impact of Unionization on Productivity: A Case Study." *Industrial and Labor Relations Review* 33 (July 1980a), pp. 451-69.

————. "Unionization and Productivity: Micro-Econometric Evidence." *Quarterly Journal of Economics* 95 (December 1980b), pp. 613-39.

Connerton, M., Richard B. Freeman, and James L. Medoff. "Productivity and Industrial Relations: The Case of U.S. Bituminous Coal," (Mimeograph 1979)

Dalton, James A., and E. J. Ford, Jr. "Concentration and Labor Earnings in Manufacturing and Utilities." *Industrial and Labor Relations Review* 31 (October 1977), pp. 45-60.

Donsimoni, Marie-Paule Joseph. "An Analysis of Trade Union Power: Structure and Conduct of the American Labor Movement." PhD thesis, Harvard University, 1978.

Duncan, Greg J. "Earnings Functions and Nonpecuniary Benefits." *Journal of Human Resources* 11 (Fall 1976), pp. 462-83.

Duncan, Greg J., and Frank P. Stafford. "Do Union Members Receive Compensating Wage Differentials?" *American Economic Review* 70 (June 1980), pp. 355-71.

Ehrenberg, Ronald G. *The Regulatory Process and Labor Earnings.* New York: Academic Press, 1979.

Farber, Henry S. "Unionism, Labor Turnover, and Wages of Young Men." (Mimeograph 1979)

Feldman, Roger, Lung-Fei Lee, and Richard Hoffbeck. "Hospital Employees' Wages and Labor Union Organization." (Mimeograph 1980)

Frantz, John. "The Impact of Trade Unions on Productivity in the Wood Household Furniture Industry." Senior Honors Thesis, Harvard College, 1976.

Freeman, Richard B. "Individual Mobility and Union Voice in the Labor Market." *American Economic Review* 66 (May 1976), pp. 361-68.

————. "Job Satisfaction as an Economic Variable." *American Economic Review* 68 (May 1978a), pp. 135-41.

————. "A Fixed Effect Logit Model of the Impact of Unionism on Quits." (Mimeograph 1978b)

————. "The Effect of Unionism on Worker Attachment to Firms." *Journal of Labor Research* 1 (Spring 1980a), pp. 29-61.

————. "The Exit-Voice Tradeoff in the Labor Market: Unionism, Job Tenure, Quits, and Separations." *Quarterly Journal of Economics* 94 (June 1980b), pp. 643-73.

————. "Unionism and the Dispersion of Wages." *Industrial and Labor Relations Review* 34 (October 1980c), pp. 3-23.

————. "The Effect of Trade Unionism on Fringe Benefits." *Industrial and Labor Relations Review* 34 (July 1981), pp. 489-509.

Freeman, Richard B., and James L. Medoff. "The Two Faces of Unionism." *The Public Interest* 57 (Fall 1979), pp. 69-93.

————. "The Percent Organized Wage Relationship for Union and Nonunion Workers." *Review of Economic and Statistics* (forthcoming a).

———. "Substitution Between Production Labor and Other Factors in Unionized and Nonunionized Manufacturing." *Review of Economics and Statistics* (forthcoming b).

———. *What Do Unions Do?* New York: Basic Books, 1982.

Goldstein, Gerald, and Mark Pauly. "Group Health Insurance as a Local Public Good." In *The Role of Health Insurance in the Health Services Sector,* ed. R. Rosett. New York: National Bureau of Economic Research, 1976, pp. 73–110.

Halasz, Peter. "What Lies Behind the Slope of the Age-Earnings Profile." Senior Honors Thesis, Harvard College, 1980.

Hamermesh, Daniel. "Market Power and Wage Inflation." *Southern Economic Journal* 39 (October 1972), pp. 204–12.

Hayden, James F. "Collective Bargaining and Cartelization: An Analysis of Teamster Power in the Regulated Trucking Industry." Senior Honors Thesis, Harvard College, 1977.

Hendricks, Wallace. "Labor Market Structure and Union Wage Levels." *Economic Inquiry* 13 (September 1975), pp. 401–16.

Hyclak, Thomas. "The Effect of Unions on Earnings Inequality in Local Labor Markets." *Industrial and Labor Relations Review* 33 (October 1979), pp. 77–84.

———. "Unions and Income Inequality: Some Cross-State Evidence." *Industrial Relations* 19 (Spring 1980), pp. 212–215.

Johnson, George E. "Changes Over Time in the Union/Nonunion Wage Differential in the United States." (Mimeograph 1981)

Kahn, Lawrence M. "Union Impact: A Reduced Form Approach." *Review of Economics and Statistics* 59 (November 1977), pp. 503–507.

———. "The Effect of Unions on the Earnings of Nonunion Workers." *Industrial and Labor Relations Review* (January 1978), pp. 205–16.

———. "Unionism and Relative Wages: Direct and Indirect Effects." *Industrial and Labor Relations Review* 32 (July 1979), pp. 520–32.

Kalachek, Edward, and Fredric Raines. "Trade Unions and Hiring Standards." *Journal of Labor Research* 1 (Spring 1980), pp. 63–75.

Kochan, Thomas A. *Collective Bargaining and Industrial Relations.* Homewood, IL: Richard D. Irwin, 1980.

Kochan, Thomas A., and Richard N. Block. "An Interindustry Analysis of Bargaining Outcomes: Preliminary Evidence from Two-Digit Industries." *Quarterly Journal of Economics* 91 (August 1977), pp. 431–52.

Kochan, Thomas E., and David E. Helfman. "The Effects of Collective Bargaining on Economic and Behavioral Job Outcomes." In *Research in Labor Economics,* Vol. IV. Greenwich, CT: JAI Press, 1981.

Lee, Lung-Fei. "Unionism and Wage Rates: A Simultaneous Equations Model with Qualitative and Limited Dependent Variables." *International Economic Review* 19 (June 1978), pp. 415–33.

Leigh, Duane E. "Racial Discrimination and Labor Unions: Evidence from the NLS Sample of Middle-Aged Men." *Journal of Human Resources* 13 (Fall 1978), pp. 568–77.

———. "Unions and Nonwage Racial Discrimination." *Industrial and Labor Relations Review* 32 (July 1979), pp. 439–50.

Lewis, H. Gregg. *Unionism and Relative Wages in the United States.* Chicago: University of Chicago Press, 1963.

———. "Interpreting Unionism Coefficients in Wage Equations." (Mimeograph 1980)

Mandelbaum, David. "Responses to Job Satisfaction Questions as Insights into Why Men Change Employers." Senior Honors Thesis, Harvard College, 1980.

Mandelstamm, Allan B. "The Effects of Unions on Efficiency in the Residental Construction Industry: A Case Study." *Industrial and Labor Relations Review* 18 (July 1965), pp. 503–521.

Medoff, James L. "The Earnings Function: A Glimpse Inside the Black Box." (Mimeograph 1977)

———. "Layoffs and Alternatives Under Trade Unionism in U.S. Manufacturing." *American Economic Review* 69 (June 1979), pp. 380–95.

Medoff, James L., and Katharine G. Abraham. "Experience, Performance, and Earnings." *Quarterly Journal of Economics* 95 (December 1980a), pp. 703–36.

———. "Years of Service and Probability of Promotion." (Mimeograph 1980b)

———. "Involuntary Termination Under Explicit and Implicit Employment Contracts." (Mimeograph 1981a)

———. "The Role of Seniority at U.S. Work Places: A Report on Some New Evidence." (Mimeograph 1981b)

Mellow, Wesley. "Unionism and Wages: A Longitudinal Analysis.'' *Review of Economics and Statistics* 63 (February 1981a), pp. 43–52.

————. ''Employer Size and Wages.'' (Mimeograph 1981b)

Mitchell, Daniel J. B. ''Some Empirical Observations of Relevance to the Analysis of Union Wage Determination.'' *Journal of Labor Research* 1 (Fall 1980a), pp. 193–215.

————. *Unions, Wages, and Inflation.* Washington: The Brookings Institution, 1980b.

Oaxaca, Ronald L. ''Estimation of Union/Nonunion Wage Differentials Within Occupational/Regional Subgroups.'' *Journal of Human Resources* 10 (Fall 1975), pp. 529–36.

Pierson, Gail. ''The Effect of Union Strengths on the U.S. 'Phillips Curve.''' *American Economic Review* 58 (June 1968), pp. 456–67.

Plotnick, Robert. ''Trends in Male Earnings Inequality.'' (Mimeograph 1980)

Podgursky, Michael John. ''Trade Unions and Income Inequality.'' PhD Thesis, University of Wisconsin–Madison, 1980.

Raisian, John. ''Cyclic Patterns in Weeks and Wages.'' *Economic Inquiry* 17 (October 1979), pp. 475–95.

Slichter, Sumner, James Healy, and E. Robert Livernash. *The Impact of Collective Bargaining on Management.* Washington: The Brookings Institution, 1960.

Solnick, L. M. ''Unionism and Fringe Benefit Expenditures.'' *Industrial Relations* 17 (February 1978), pp. 102–107.

Viscusi, W. Kip. ''Wealth Effects and Earnings Premiums for Job Hazards,'' *Review of Economics and Statistics* 60 (August 1978), pp. 408–16.

————. ''Unions, Labor Market Structure, and the Welfare Implications of the Quality of Work.'' *Journal of Labor Research* 1 (Spring 1980), pp. 175–92.

Weiss, Leonard. ''Concentration and Labor Earnings.'' *American Economic Review* 56 (March 1966), pp. 96–117.

Welch, Stephen W. ''Union-Nonunion Construction Wage Differentials.'' *Industrial Relations* 19 (Spring 1980), pp. 152–62.

Yanker, Robert H. ''Productivity Versus Seniority: What Is the Determining Factor in Regard to Wages and Promotion?'' Senior Honors Thesis, Harvard College, 1980.

Management Objectives in Bargaining

AUDREY FREEDMAN
The Conference Board

For unionized companies, bargaining — the actual negotiation of a contract — is a crucial event. And while union security, management rights, and other institutional arrangements may once have been major issues, today the wage and benefit package gets the spotlight. Company managements usually negotiate with a specific wage and benefit objective and a set of objectives on nonwage items. Past history and development of the union contract in the individual company is the baseline for analysis of current objectives. The pivot point is where the individual company is, immediately prior to bargaining.

MEANING AND SUBTLETIES OF TARGET SETTING

For unionized companies, wage targets and non-wage goals specify the best deal the company expects to get. Not just a list of what management wants, they are actually an evaluation of what, given the situation, will occur when management's trade-off schedule meets the union's agenda. This interpretation suggests that attaining a target represents a realistic optimum exchange from management's point of view.

From *Managing Labor Relations* by Audrey Freedman. Conference Board Report No. 765, pp. 35-46. Copyright © 1979, The Conference Board. Reprinted with permission.

Thus target setting includes the use of good judgment about the union's ultimate settlement point and trade-offs — and the costs to each party of various strategies and maneuvers, including strikes and lockouts. These judgments temper "what management would ideally prefer" and produce what can be called a realistically planned outcome.

PATTERNS IN MANAGEMENT'S CRITERIA FOR WAGE SETTING

Local labor market comparisons are the primary wage criterion in nonunion companies (see Fig. 1), and also in situations where the employer is the dominant party in collective bargaining (see Table 1). In the absence of unions, or where unions are weak, employers are free to offer wages only in the amount necessary to draw and retain the desired quality and quantity of workers from the local labor market. Companies in this position are also likely to give more weight to criteria specific to the firm, such as financial ability, and to internal comparisons of wages in the firm.

Where unions are present and strong, it becomes necessary for management to add criteria that reflect the union's "demands." The influence of strong unions creates the effect of an industrywide wage level (as opposed to localized

193

wages). One of the ways unions seek to "take wages out of competition" is to induce management to emphasize industry comparisons or "patterns," and to put less weight on differentiated local wage levels. Thus in unionized firms, *industry patterns* are given priority over local wage levels as a wage targeting criterion (see Fig. 1). This priority is even stronger in situations where the union is particularly "powerful" because of high unionization, a multiplant (or even companywide) bargaining structure, or where the costs of a strike are severe. The more powerful the union is relative to the firm, the more weight given to the union-preferred wage criteria and the less weight given to local labor market and firm-specific criteria.

To be more specific, within the unionized group of responding companies, those that gave greater weight to *local labor market conditions* were found to be (1) smaller; (2) in single-plant bargaining structures; (3) less unionized; (4) independent of any "pattern bargaining"; and (5) manufacturing firms in industries with higher labor-to-total-cost ratios. Conversely, firms that assigned greater weight to *industry comparisons* were (1) larger; (2) in more centralized bargaining structures; (3) in pattern bargaining relationships; (4) more likely to be found in the transportation, communications or public utilities industries; and (5) in industries with lower labor-to-total-cost ratios.

Nevertheless, where unionization is present, an overall high priority was accorded to industrywide or bargaining-related criteria as opposed to local or firm-specific factors. This suggests that the majority of the firms have accommodated their wage policies to the "realities" of union agenda in collective bargaining. And, even in union-free companies, as Fig. 1 shows, the industry comparison has secondary importance.

WAGE-TARGETTING CRITERIA IN DETAIL

Among the surveyed companies, as a whole, the wage criteria given priority are: industry patterns and competition; local labor market conditions

TABLE 1

Most important influences on wage and benefit targets, by predominant bargaining structure in the company, multiplant companies[1]

| Factor | PERCENT OF COMPANIES IN EACH BARGAINING STRUCTURE RANKING FACTOR | | | |
	Plant by plant	Multiplant, master contract	Multiplant master, with local supplements	Multi-employer contract
Industry patterns, competition within industry				
ranked first	33	51	63	45
second — third	36	32	27	27
not considered	3	4	1	3
Local labor market conditions and wage rates				
ranked first	36	15	11	27
second — third	32	32	16	18
not considered	4	20	22	30
Expected company profits				
ranked first	16	17	10	6
second — third	24	18	34	18
not considered	10	12	7	18

TABLE 1 (*cont.*)

	PERCENT OF COMPANIES IN EACH BARGAINING STRUCTURE RANKING FACTOR			
Factor	*Plant by plant*	*Multiplant, master contract*	*Multiplant master, with local supplements*	*Multi-employer contract*
Productivity or labor-cost trends in industry				
ranked first	7	10	3	15
second — third	16	23	29	24
not considered	15	6	11	9
Potential losses from a strike				
ranked first	5	8	4	18
second — third	20	19	26	15
not considered	11	19	11	12
Influence of settlement on other settlements and/or nonunion wage level				
ranked first	3	6	1	9
second — third	28	23	14	6
not considered	12	17	18	18
Inflation rate				
ranked first	2	4	3	3
second — third	18	27	11	27
not considered	12	10	21	9
Internal company wage patterns				
ranked first	3	7	—	12
second — third	14	19	7	21
not considered	16	14	29	42
Internal company benefit patterns				
ranked first	2	5	—	6
second — third	12	12	5	15
not considered	15	13	29	42
Major union settlements in other industries				
ranked first	2	5	7	6
second — third	10	17	18	33
not considered	37	32	29	9
National labor market conditions and wage rates				
ranked first	1	1	1	3
second — third	11	16	12	15
not considered	35	30	29	27

[1] Structure of "all or most" bargaining situations.

[2] Percentages in vertical columns add to more than 100 percent because respondents cited more than one factor in a particular rank.

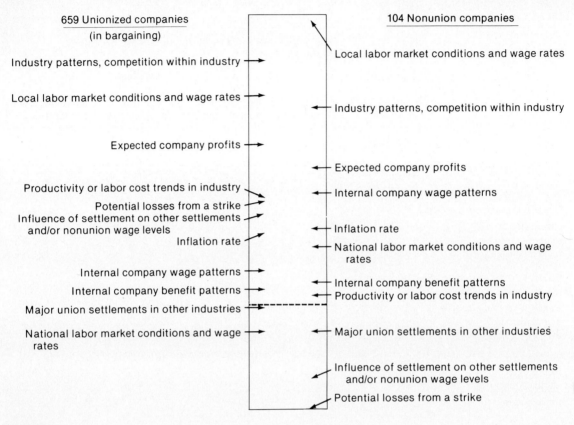

FIGURE 1
Scale of company considerations in setting wage and benefit targets

and wage rates; and expected profits. However, after these top three, a variety of other points were considered. These are all shown on Fig. 1, a ratio scale that depicts their respective importance.

Very few companies gave "national" labor markets first (or even second or third) mention. However, a very small but noticeable group of companies placed high importance on major union settlements in other industries. On closer examination, these companies are not "all of a kind," nor are they all major national companies with companywide bargaining units. Nine, in fact, are companies bargaining plant by plant, and four are single-plant companies.

Companies were also asked to indicate the factors considered in setting wage and benefit targets for their *largest bargaining unit* so that this could be compared with companywide factor rankings. Divergent rankings would suggest a degree of union power in major units (but only in major units) that forces the company to shift considerations. It could also imply that management purposely makes exceptional policy for its biggest unionized group. The two sets of rankings, however, were almost completely parallel. At the major bargaining unit, there is slightly more relative weight given to the productivity or labor-cost factor — perhaps because it is more susceptible of exact quantification in a particular unit such as one plant.

NONUNION COMPANIES RANK THE CONSIDERATIONS

The most noticeable aspect of the nonunion companies' considerations is much more diffusion among the criteria that are taken into account in wage setting. The nonunion respondents cited such items as "internal company wage patterns" more often, and also national labor market conditions and wage rates. The citation of consumer price inflation suggests that, even without union pressure, managements incorporate some concepts of real-wage maintenance into their wage policies.

Without union pressure, nonunion companies more freely stress those comparisons that are particularly important to their individual situations. Withal, nonunion companies are most likely to base their wages on local area wage rates, as already noted.

BARGAINING STRUCTURE AND WAGE TARGET FACTORS

The unionized company's emphasis on industry patterns is even stronger in companies with a centralized, multiplant bargaining structure. Decentralized, plant-by-plant bargainers are somewhat more able to use local wage rates as a primary criterion (see Table 1). In this respect, plant-by-plant bargainers are more like nonunion companies. . . .

The effect of master contract bargaining units is particularly noticeable in the rating of local wage levels as *"not considered"* by one-fifth or more of the multiplant bargainers. These master contract companies are most clearly dealing with an "industry rate." However, there is no commensurately heavy downgrading of in-

dustry patterns by the single-plant bargainers. This is why industry patterns receive the highest rating for the unionized companies taken as an undifferentiated group. . . .

NONWAGE GOALS

Companies often have "policies" — long-standing, companywide positions or traditions with respect to their unionized employee groups. On occasion, these may be specified as *bargaining objectives for a particular contract* negotiation. This could occur, for example, during negotiation of a first contract for a newly organized unit: Management might choose to initiate a policy stance on, for example, union security clauses. Another occasion when "policy" could become an objective or goal in a specific negotiation might occur if the company bargainers expected a union demand on an item that has long been implicit company policy or tradition. Historical examples in actual bargaining are numerous, covering subjects such as union security, cost-of-living clauses, supplemental unemployment benefits, companywide bargaining units, or other structure changes. Thus a union drive to change some contract term that is *also* fundamental company policy, will very likely cause the company to identify the item as an "objective" in negotiations. In this case, the objective would be to maintain the status quo — the company policy — intact.

Bargaining goals or objectives outside the wage area will also include items that, while not part of company policy, complete management's agenda at each bargaining round. Eighty-seven percent of the companies in The Conference Board survey had a set of nonwage goals in their latest negotiation, in their largest bargaining unit. In terms of specific nonwage goals, companies reported objectives in eight to nine subjects per company, with the most frequent mentions: (1) paid time off; (2) flexibility on assignment of employees; (3) pensions; and (4) health benefits (see Fig. 2).

The list derives from two sources: expected union initiatives as well as company goals. Respondents were asked to identify areas where (1) management expected a union initiative and its goal was *to keep the status quo;* (2) management had a goal of making the existing provision *more favorable to the company* by tightening or otherwise improving it; and (3) management was prepared *to give something in exchange* for, or in trade for, something else. Thus a lack of "mentions" in Fig. 2 represents a lack of activity in that subject

area — not necessarily any absence of the subject in the contracts, letters of agreement, or past practices of the employer. Even in the least frequently mentioned subjects — income security bargaining and union security arrangements — over half of the companies had a bargaining objective.

The frequency of mentions suggests relative "heat" in the subject area. The source of the initiative, however, is significant. For example, pension bargaining objectives were specified by more

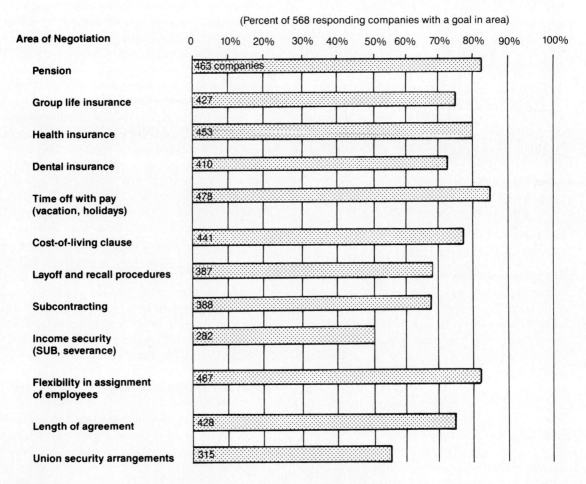

FIGURE 2
Management nonwage goals (percent of companies with a goal in area)

than four out of five companies. But the management plan was to tighten or take back some pension element in less than a tenth of the companies. Figure 3 depicts the company's planned position on each subject for the 568 companies identifying goals and goal achievement. The results show that, in 61% of the 4939 citations, the company expected a union demand and had specified its goal as maintaining the status quo. On average, companies expected to resist about five such union initiatives. On the other hand, companies were prepared to make favorable-to-the-union of-

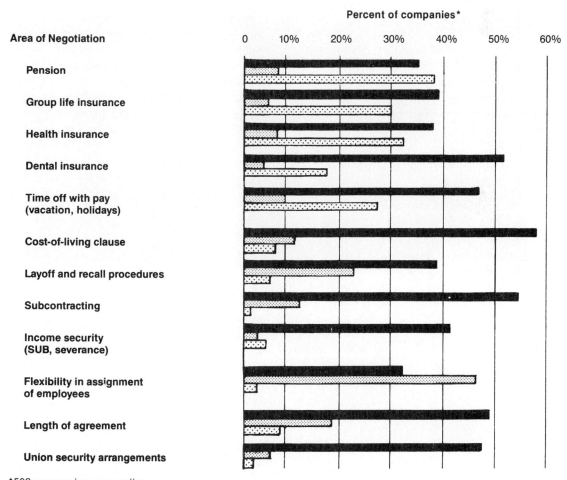

*568 companies responding
■ Goal was to keep the status quo in face of union pressure to add or liberalize
▨ Goal was to tighten existing provision or get a more favorable one
⊡ Goal was to offer a specific element in trade for something else

FIGURE 3
Management nonwage goals (nature of the objective)

fers in over one-fifth (21%) of all goal citations — nearly two per company. Lastly, a little over one-sixth (18 percent) of the goals involved tightening up or obtaining an agreement that would be more favorable to the management.

The overall picture of company bargaining objectives in the mid-1970s is one of status quo or "stand pat" positions on the part of management. Newspaper stories about "take backs" characterizing management's stance in 1978 seem to have overemphasized a few situations. The survey data show management anticipating union demands in many areas, willing to trade on a limited number of subjects (chiefly on funded benefits), and seeking favorable exchanges from the union in one subject area: flexibility in assignment of employees.

COMPANY OBJECTIVES

Management negotiators are guided by company objectives that have been developed in advance. These objectives reflect (1) the reality of the company's current financial position; (2) the union's agenda and power; and (3) a variety of external trends and pressures that — to some extent — "pattern" the anticipations and analyses of both bargaining parties.

When analyzed by a yardstick internal to each company individually, bargaining over *benefit items* contains a substantial potential for exchange: Companies planned to "give" almost as many times as they planned to "hold the line." On the other hand, company positions on those nonwage items that clearly might be called institutional relationships, and/or affect supervision of the work force, ranged from "stand pat" to "take back." There was little room for exchange in this territory. The fairly clear distinction between trading and nontrading territories may bear a very light touch of rationale:

> The nontrading territory is more associated with incalculable (but potentially major) costs; with productivity-altering outcomes; with institu-

tionalizing the union as a participant in work force direction. The trading territory, on the other hand, is simply "money."

The itemized nonwage objectives shown in Fig. 3 are discussed in detail next.

Funded Benefits

A high proportion of all companies had specific bargaining goals in this area, many of them planning to offer benefit liberalization, or entirely new benefit items, in exchange for another goal that management was seeking. This was particularly true in the pension area, where 38% of responding companies planned to liberalize the program. In some cases, where bringing the plan into compliance with the Employee Retirement and Income Security Act (ERISA) may have required changes, the high response for "give" on this item may include some such liberalizations that were treated as bargaining chips for exchange in union negotiations.

Health benefits was a second area of "give." A third of the companies reported plans to use added health benefits in exchange for some other item, and 30 percent planned to use life insurance in this way. The elements for trading may have been wage or other items and union demands in the benefit area. It seems less likely that the trading plan extended outside of the wage-benefit area, into other parts of the list in Fig. 3.

For each of the four benefit areas identified, less than 10% of the companies indicated an objective of tightening, or "getting back" something previously negotiated. Thus within the benefit area the trading may be primarily a company-anticipated union demand for benefit liberalization A; to be resisted by the company, which planned to offer liberalization of Type B (or Type A-1) instead.

Company interviews, and the survey pretest, suggested the great sense of risk felt by management about its benefit programs. To some extent, the price of a health-benefit package, once negotiated, is out of management's control. In the pension area, the risks are seen as even greater — particularly by companies that expect less growth in their work forces in the future. One respondent flatly stated: "We plan and monitor the bargaining on benefits even more than on wages." Another company observed that benefit changes are pattern changes (because of companywide programs) *and* they are long-term commitments that are never rescinded. Therefore even though that company bargains plant-by-plant, its bargaining objectives on benefits are set and reviewed at corporate headquarters.

Time Off with Pay

The most frequently mentioned goals involved paid-time-off practices such as vacations and holidays. Some union leaders have identified the reduction of work time as the major union initiative of the late 1970s, giving as the primary rationale an increase in employment and in membership that was expected to follow.[1] The survey data show that the highest proportion of companies expected to bargain on this subject and had a goal (Fig. 2). About half (46%) planned to hold the line in the face of union pressure; but 28% had an offer they were prepared to make (Fig. 3). Only 10% planned to reduce paid time off in some specific respect.

Cost of Living Clauses

"Escalator clauses" were once considered the concern of only a few industries and unions. But, by the late 1970s, they were the subject of specific bargaining objectives in nearly four out of five (78%) responding companies. Hold-the-line strategy is clearly very strong: Three out of five companies had a firm goal of keeping the status quo; that is, fending it off if they have no cost-of-living clause; and not enriching its formula if they already have COLA. A little over one-third (37%) of the largest bargaining units already had COLA clauses.

Inflation, coupled with increasing duration of union contracts, has been accompanied by growth of COLA to its present level of 43% of *major* bargaining agreements (a Bureau of Labor Statistics grouping of contracts covering 1000 workers or more).[2] However, escalators were present in only 38 percent of the smaller of these agreements (covering 1000–4999 workers), while 78% of the large contracts covering 50,000–99,999 had COLA, and it was present in *all* contracts covering 100,000 or more.[3] The median number of workers in the largest bargaining unit in companies surveyed by The Conference Board was 852, the average was 3045.

Layoff and Recall Procedures

Layoff and recall clauses in union contracts may have been "exercised" in depth during the 1974–1975 recession, the deepest since the 1930s. Bargaining objectives on layoff and recall terms in the contract were specified by 68% of the companies. Two out of five (39%) expected union demands for a more favorable clause, and planned to resist change. Nearly a quarter of all companies (23%) planned to tighten their existing provisions, or obtain one more favorable (to the company.) Thus this subject was the second most likely to have a "take-back" goal. It is closely related to flexibility in assignment of employees — the subject most likely to have a management "take-back" objective.

The role of seniority in layoff and recall procedures is central, and the scope and arrangement of seniority units in the company or plant affect the efficiency with which a work force reduction can be accomplished — and the remaining workers be reassigned for maximum productivity. In a 1972 Bureau of Labor Statistics study analyzing the layoff and recall provisions of 364 contracts, all but one assigned seniority a part in governing the order of layoff.[4] The weight given seniority relative to other factors, the order and timing of successive displacements downward in the job scale ("bumping"), and other aspects of job-placement (and replacement) moves probably represent the bulk of bargaining substance on this subject.

Subcontracting

Layoff insecurities raised by the recession also caused some union demands for more restrictions on subcontracting, "to keep more work for our members." Companies, expecting this, had specific goals of maintaining existing contract clauses in 55 percent of the bargaining cases. This was the second highest "stand pat" position, after that on cost-of-living clauses. Subcontracting restrictions appear in about half (52%) of major contracts (those covering 1000 or more workers).[5] If their incidence is the same or lower among The Conference Board respondents, then a large part of the bargaining goals in this group was avoidance of any *introduction* of restrictions on subcontracting.[6]

Income Security

Half of the responding companies had an agenda on the subjects of severance pay, supplemental unemployment benefits, and similar income-security plans. This was the least often mentioned subject area for planned objectives.

A great majority of companies with objectives on this subject expected union demands for liberalizing benefits, and planned to retain the status quo. Some 5% of companies planned to liberalize — a course that was taken recently in the auto and steel industries.[7]

Flexibility in Assignment of Employees

This was the subject on which management planned to make gains. Eighty-two percent of all companies had a specific goal. In most cases, it was to obtain more favorable contract terms. This was the sole area in which management had a clearly positive stance: In all other subjects, management's position was preservation of the status quo. The nature of the subject area ("flexibility in assignment of employees") is relatively broad and unspecific (as opposed to, e.g., COLA). However, it would cover much of what in bargainers' shorthand would be called "management rights terms." Thus the objective of getting more favorable terms may be interpreted as getting back management latitude and freedom that was eroded in earlier bargains, or by arbitration. It is also possible that, just as the 1974–1975 recession sharpened union awareness of some contract job protections, it also sharpened the pressure on management to adjust and readjust work assignments, schedules, work force arrangements and the like, in ways and at speeds precluded by existing union agreements. . . .

Length of Agreement

Half of the companies (49%) planned to hold the line in the face of a specific union demand on this subject. In the early 1960s, the proportion of major agreements of three years' duration or more was two out of five.[8] It is 70% at present.[9] The long-term trend toward lengthened contract terms may have been encouraged by NLRB rules that prevent replacement of existing union representation during contract terms of up to three years. Cost-of-living clauses have also helped, by making long-term wage contracts responsive to inflation and thus less susceptible to bad guessing. Finally, the cost of bargaining and the attendant risks may have made short-term contracts unappealing to both parties. This mixture of causes and incentives to lengthen contract terms has not recently been interrupted by rapid inflation and the form of wage and price controls instituted in late 1978. In the first quarter of 1979, renegotiated contracts "had an average duration of 31.8 months, compared with 30.5 months when the same parties previously bargained."[10]

Union Security

In addition to recognizing the union as exclusive bargaining agent for the covered employee group, employers have been asked by unions to negotiate various forms of "union security" arrangements in the contract. Essentially, these clauses promote union membership either by requiring it, or by creating strong incentives to join and remain a member. Very generally, "union shop" clauses require all employees to join within a specified time after employment — and to remain members. "Agency shop" clauses require payment of agency fees to the union, by all those who choose to remain nonmembers. "Maintenance of membership" clauses, less stringent, essentially restrict withdrawal from membership to a specified time period.

This subject was a battleground a generation ago, but by now union shop clauses are prevalent except for those 20 "right to work" states where they are prohibited. Some 71% of major contracts have varieties of union shop clauses, and another 7% have "agency" shops. Three percent have maintenance of membership and 18% have no specified union security other than recognition.[11]

Just under half (48%) of the companies had a goal of maintaining the status quo in the face of a union demand on this subject. Given the broad coverage of some kind of union security, it seems most likely that the demands expected were in the nature of a "tighter" security clause — perhaps reducing the time that a new employee can postpone joining to its legal minimum of 30 days.

NOTES

1. "Stimulating new job opportunities while increasing job security and providing workers with more leisure are the aims. We expect that thousands of additional workers will be put on the payroll" from page 1 of a United Auto Workers news release, October 2, 1977. See also "Slowing the Decline in the Auto Work Force." *Business Week,* October 25, 1976, p. 114.

2. See U.S. Bureau of Labor Statistics, *Characteristics of Major Collective Bargaining Contracts,* July 1, 1976, Bulletin No. 2013, Table 1.4; also Victor Sheifer, "Collective Bargaining and the CPI: Escalation vs. Catch-Up," *Proceedings* of the Thirty-first Annual Meeting, Industrial Relations Research Association, August 29–31, 1978, p. 260.

3. Sheifer, p. 259.

4. Bureau of Labor Statistics, *Layoff, Recall, and Worksharing Procedures,* Bulletin No. 1425-13, p. 31.

5. *Characteristics of Major Collective Bargaining Agreements,* July 1, 1976, Table 7.3.

6. An assumption that would best fit the smaller, plant-by-plant bargaining structure in the surveyed group.

7. A fuller discussion of recent bargaining on this subject can be found in Audrey Freedman, *Security Bargains Reconsidered: SUB Severance Pay Guaranteed Work.* The Conference Board, Report No. 736, 1978.

8. Marvin Friedman, "Discussion," *Proceedings* of the Thirty-first Annual Meeting, Industrial Relations Research Association, August, 1978, p. 278.

9. *Characteristics of Major Collective Bargaining Agreements,* July 1, 1976, Table 1.4.

10. U.S. Department of Labor, News Release, April 27, 1979, p. 2.

11. *Characteristics of Major Collective Bargaining Agreements,* July 1, 1976, Table 2.1.

When Employees Make Concessions

D. Quinn Mills
Harvard University

At Eastern Air Lines, employees agree to guarantee profits if necessary by reducing their own paychecks.

In Phoenix, Arizona, construction craftsmen accept a wage reduction from $14.63 an hour to $11.00 an hour.

At Rockwell International, members of the United Auto Workers agree to postpone some pay increases and forgo others entirely.

At General Tire & Rubber, the union agrees to have employees pay part of the cost of health insurance.

To managers and investors struggling to keep companies profitable in today's harsh economic climate, these events may seem to herald a historic shift in favor of business, and much of the business press has hailed them. Managers are asking if such concessions are more than isolated instances, and if their own companies should seek them.

Are employee concessions simply a result of the recession, and will they disappear as the economy recovers? Although to a certain extent concessions are associated with the recession,

other causes affect the picture. Concessions also arise from the pressures of long-term economic decline in certain industries and from new sources of competition, both domestic (due to government deregulation in certain industries) and foreign. Finally, nonunion domestic competition is having a big impact on unionized companies in several major U.S. industries. Each of these influences will extend beyond the current recession and will cause employee concessions to continue to be important even after the business cycle turns upward.

Considering these facts, should companies seek concessions from employees? In many cases, the answer is certainly yes, but some unexpected surprises can follow what seem to be opportunities. So it is important for managers to learn more about this new environment. For example, in the process of negotiating with unions for employee concessions, companies have had to open their books to outside inspection. Sometimes managerial prerogatives have been surrendered, unions have obtained a future financial claim against the company's earnings, and executives have had to face the charge that they traded away the store to the unions to save a few dollars. In some instances where companies have gotten concessions, union members have revolted and sued the unions involved.

Regardless of the employee concessions

achieved, the process of gaining them has such a significant impact on employees that companies must reassess their employee relations strategy. Collective bargaining has never been a one-way street in management's favor, and it is not today.

Concessions are of two different types. In one, employees accept a reduction in a wage rate, benefit, or work rule that they already enjoy. In a second type, they agree to forswear future improvements in pay, benefits, or working conditions that they might have hoped to obtain. In the settlements between the auto companies and the United Auto Workers, for example, most of the concessions reported in the press were of the second type, including postponement of scheduled pay increases from the COLA (cost-of-living allowance) and relinquishment of some part of future pay increases. The auto companies reported a few concessions of the first type, however, including reductions in paid time off for vacations and holidays.

How common are concessions in U.S. companies today? Despite wide press coverage, reliable data on the proportion of companies receiving concessions or on their characteristics by industry, location, or competitive position have not been readily available. Therefore, I undertook a survey to determine the answers to those questions.

CONCESSION PATTERNS

The survey used a two-dimensional research strategy. First, 10 companies and unions that had successfully completed concession bargaining were interviewed in depth. This provided information about the management processes involved. Second, of a random sample of 364 companies drawn from Standard & Poor's, 276 companies (76% of the sample) replied to telephone questions.

Concessions are not the rule but are not isolated events either. Of unionized companies in the survey, 56% reported needing concessions and 12% had tried to reopen a collective bargaining agreement in the preceding two years to get concessions. Fully one-third of the union companies had sought concessions from an agreement when it expired, and virtually all had considered seeking them.

Of the union companies, 15% received concessions in wages and benefits (many in work rules also), and 10% were still seeking concessions in bargaining at the time of the survey. Of durable goods manufacturers, 26% had sought concessions, and of nondurable manufacturers, 32%.

Not only companies that are losing money seek concessions. Of profit-making companies, 31% sought concessions; of the much smaller group of companies with losses, 50% sought concessions.

Union vs. Nonunion Companies

Perhaps the most surprising finding of the survey is that blue-collar concessions in recent years are primarily limited to the union sector of U.S. industry. Of nonunion companies in the sample, only two had extracted concessions from employees. Repeatedly, nonunion companies reported that they would not "do such things" as reduce wages and benefits to employees.

Reports in the press and business periodicals usually show that pay and benefit reductions in nonunion companies have been generally confined to officers and other salaried employees. Only if the recession continues are nonunion companies likely to impose sacrifices on blue-collar workers. In large part, they fear that wage reductions will stimulate union activity among these employees, a well-founded expectation if history is a reliable guide. Ironically, unions are being forced to negotiate give-backs from their own members, while employers' fear of the unions is protecting the pay scale and benefits of many nonunion employees.

At one nonunion company that has greatly reduced the number of its employees to gain a break-even financial position, the top officer reported: "Our executives took cuts, but it was never a consideration for our employees. We're finding more productive ways to run the business. We've eliminated half the departments, and where we used to have 14 managers we now have only 4."

The lower frequency of concessions in the nonunion sector might be considered a result of severe business difficulty experienced by the heavy manufacturing, construction, and transportation industries — all strongly unionized. But nonunion companies in the same industries have been less likely to resort to concessions. Companies in the survey were asked whether compensation increases in the preceding two years had been above, about the same, or below "normal"?

It is surprising that, despite the frequency of concession bargaining in the union sector, the proportion of companies reporting pay increases at above or about the same as normal, even in a recession, is almost the same in the union (84.17%) as in the nonunion sector (80.35%). Companies that are profitable and those showing a loss are also similar — 83.91% and 81.49% respectively, giving the same or above normal increases. (The differences are not statistically significant.)

Many nonunion companies report financial problems, yet virtually none reports employee concessions. Instead, such companies have reduced work schedules and are now turning to layoffs. Union companies, in contrast, have generally had heavy layoffs and are turning to concessions in an effort to avoid further work force reductions and/or plant closings.

Although 54 of the 137 nonunion companies in the sample reported that their economic situation created a need to reduce wages and benefits, only 23 have considered such a move, 3 have done a survey to gauge potential employee reaction, and only 2 actually have cut wages. It is, of course, possible to view reductions in work schedules as an employee concession imposed by nonunion companies, especially since lower take-

home pay results. But reduced work schedules, like layoffs in the union sector, are not ordinarily viewed as employee concessions, since pay rates, benefits, and other conditions of work remain unchanged, and since employees in the United States ordinarily have no contractual right to any given amount of employment. (In the few instances where companies grant employees a specific amount of work by contract or company policy, the survey treats a reduction in work as an employee concession.)

SEEKING CONCESSIONS

Because concessions as defined here are confined mainly to the unionized sector of U.S. business today, for the remainder of this article I will deal with the process of concession bargaining with the unions. Much of the discussion of management tactics and employee responses would apply, however, to nonunion companies should adverse economic and competitive conditions require employee give-backs in the future.

Reducing Wages and Benefits

Lowering a company's labor costs are what concession bargaining is all about, but it is not a simple task for a company to decide the form concessions should take.

Should a company seek concessions in wages, benefits, or work practices? Reductions in wages have the most immediate and direct impact on trimming labor costs, of course, but they are very difficult for today's employees whose paychecks just meet the mortgage payments and car loans. Furthermore, in some instances wage rates are at the market level and reductions can cause a company to lose key people or make it difficult to obtain replacements.

Reductions in benefits can be more attractive because to employees the loss is less readily evident than a cut in pay, but these reductions are less efficient. Benefits are paid with before-tax dollars from the employees' point of view, so that to buy similar benefits on the open market costs the employees far more. Also, a cut in wages affects most workers similarly, while a cut in benefits disproportionately affects those needing the benefits coverage. This may encourage dissension and dissatisfaction in the work force and seems to violate the principle of equal sacrifice that unions and employers often adopt in their negotiations.

Work Rule Changes

Reductions in work rule restrictions appear to offer a favorable alternative. Improving productivity will help employees as well as the company without loss of paychecks or benefits. But altering work rules poses several problems.

First, each restrictive work practice benefits someone who, by virtue of the practice, retains a comfortable job; for example, rules protect senior employees from assignment to tasks that they can no longer perform, either because of physical limitations or because of technical knowledge they lack.

Second, work rules often bear on the relationships between employees and first-line supervisors. They are part of the civil rights of the workplace. Rules are a substitute for good supervisor-employee relations and may be vigorously defended by employees. To abolish the rules puts employees at the mercy of supervisors whom they may fear or distrust and who might, for example, require employees to do certain undesirable jobs.

Third, rules have financial consequences for employees, causing some to make higher earnings than others. As a result, companies often "buy out" work rules for other benefits and for pay raises. But an organization in deep financial trouble may be unable to pay for work rule changes. In industries making autos, rubber, and steel, with industry- or corporation-level bargaining, this is a serious constraint. The economic package — that is, what employees will get in terms of wages and benefits — is determined at the national bargaining table, while work rules are peculiar to each plant and must be determined in plant-level bargaining.

But the companies have usually given away the economic package before they get to local bargaining, so no money is left to buy out adverse work rules. This is a broken link in national bargaining that the companies have somehow failed for decades to mend. This lack is now costing them dearly, as many fail to get adequate rule concessions despite continuing increases in pay and benefits. Nevertheless, in my survey interviews, plant-level people, explaining that they fear misinformed interference from unsympathetic superiors, repeatedly mentioned concessions on rules that they had not reported to the corporate or divisional level.

How Far to Go?

Should a company seek large-scale concessions or simply nibble its way forward? General Motors initially agreed with top UAW officials to seek concessions that would add up to a $1000 per car price reduction. But when the UAW bargaining committee discovered that this would mean a reduction in wages and benefits of almost $5 per hour (about 20% of the then current compensation package), it reacted with hostility. The company's employee relations deteriorated sharply.

This may have been too big a step, but is a little step enough? If concessions leave the work force resentful and feeling entitled to future redress without providing the company enough assistance to recover, the company probably should first try to minimize new costs when an existing contract expires.

Should concessions be temporary? It is difficult for a union to accept the likelihood that if it yields now, workers may have to strike to regain the same level at some later date. It appears far more sensible to grant temporary concessions so that at a future date the previous levels of pay and benefits will be restored (via a step-up clause). Certainly such provisions will help influence members to ratify an agreement involving concessions.

But if the business fails to recover, a clause that returns pay and benefits to the old level at a certain point requires the union and the company to negotiate the concessions all over again. The issue becomes a bargaining quagmire engulfing the attention of union officials and management. Thus unless there is a virtual certainty of a business turnaround, both management and labor have a stake in arranging concessions without step-up clauses. And there are further reasons to avoid imposing future liabilities on a company trying to turn itself around.

WHEN CONCESSIONS MAKE SENSE

Concessions are not a tool to be used whenever a company is in financial difficulty. Their purpose is to improve the company's financial health and to preserve job opportunities. There are circumstances, however, in which compensation reduction will not increase sales or employment. For example, if the company's product is waterproofing applied to concrete used in construction, reducing the price of waterproofing will not increase its use when the construction industry is in a recession.

This point is crucial to how a union views give-backs, and it should affect managers' attitudes as well. Where there is a certain amount of work available and no price elasticity, then the union has no interest in granting concessions, since no jobs will be created or saved. This is true even if a particular company should go under. Competitors will simply pick up the work, and the same union is likely to represent their employees also.

Thus to accept concessions a union has to be convinced that it will create more jobs or that jobs in danger of being lost will be saved. Similarly, employees are much more willing to accept concessions when imminent layoffs are avoided or when people on furlough can be recalled than when the main result will be seen only on the company's books.

A first step in considering whether concessions make sense, therefore, is to determine whether a cut in pay and subsequent reduction in price of the product can boost sales.

Competitive Pressures

When new competition, either from abroad or at home, cuts into sales, an obvious way of regaining volume is by lower costs stemming from employee concessions. From the unions' point of view, compromise in such a situation is almost always wise, if the company has good products and a good sales force to outsell the foreign or nonunion competition.

One company I interviewed manufactures a clothing fabric. The company's foreign competitor has been making a similar fabric for the auto industry, but because of the auto depression in recent years has modified its product for use in clothing. As a result, the U.S. company is losing market share. Employee concessions are helping preserve sales and share by allowing the U.S. company to cut costs.

The survey shows that new competitive pressures are the reason many employers sought concessions and unions granted them. Foreign and nonunion competition, partly owing to deregulation in airlines and trucking, are, in addition to the current recession, principal reasons for the wave of concession bargaining in U.S. industry.

TABLE 1
Percentage of companies seeking concessions who cited nonunion competition as major reason

Construction	100%
Trucking	100
Retail trade	67
Nondurable manufacturing	57
Wholesale trade	50
Durable manufacturing	42

Data derived from interviews with 46 union companies that sought concessions.

TABLE 2
Reasons for asking for concessions

Nonunion competition	43%
Union competition	29
Business conditions	43
Competitors getting concessions	10
An opportunity perceived to cut costs	33

For companies that won concessions from employees. Data derived from interviews with 48 companies.

Were there no recession, however, the competitive pressures might be better disguised and companies slower to seek concessions and unions more reluctant to give them. But in past recessions, unions have been less willing than in the current slow-down, and the reason for the change in the unions' attitudes is the new competition.

When asked to explain why compensation increases in the past two years were lower than "normal" (for the 17% of all companies who so reported), the large majority (60%) attributed this to economic conditions (rather than to domestic or foreign competition). But it is likely, from the importance given to competition in Tables 1 and 2, that the adverse economic conditions referred to during the survey by many managers included the impact of new nonunion or overseas competition. This is important because a recovery in the U.S. economy will not necessarily improve the competitive situation of many companies and is thus less likely to put the high degree of upward (and inflationary) pressure on wages that business recoveries have done in the past.

THE UNION ROLE

The concession question is a difficult one for the unions because of their policy of trying to keep competing companies on the same wage and benefit scales so that labor rates do not become an element of competition between the companies. When the union has most of the competitors organized, this policy permits it to negotiate attractive compensation packages. When some companies begin to depart from the industry pattern, competing companies complain of favoritism and insist on comparable concessions. The pressure for uniformity begins to work in a downward direction against the union.

In some instances, when national unions have refused to permit variations from the master agreements for particular companies, employees of those companies have sued their unions, alleging failure to represent the affected employees in good faith, as required by federal labor laws.

Recently, the national unions have begun to assist locals in working out concession agreements, but the nationals generally insist that members ratify the new agreement that incorporates concessions. Where union leaders at either the national or local level agree to concessions without ratification votes, members have revolted and national union trusteeship has been imposed over the locals, or members have filed lawsuits protesting the concessions as a violation of the duty of fair representation.

The national unions, having had to cope with economic necessity, corporate entreaties, and membership outrage, have now modified policies calling for no variations from industry patterns, and locals are now much freer to make concessions at individual facilities and companies.

A union leader might be forgiven for viewing concession bargaining as a no-win proposition: affected members may sue the union if concessions are not made and the company fails, but if concessions are made and wages or benefits are reduced, members may also take the union to court.

To protect themselves from lawsuits, the unions take little initiative. The locals wait for members to ask that something be done to assist an ailing company; the nationals wait for the locals to suggest action.

PERSUADING EMPLOYEES

Often the rank-and-file have proved far more resistant to concessions than have union leaders. In the automobile industry, Douglas Fraser's membership on the Chrysler board of directors made top UAW leaders conscious of the competitive problems of U.S. companies. But this awareness did not extend fully to local leaders of the UAW or its members.

To acquaint employees with the gravity of the situation, the auto companies have adopted various measures. In 1981, General Motors made a film shown to hundreds of thousands of employees featuring GM President F. James McDonald, who began his message with the grim statement: "Men and women of General Motors, our corporation is in serious trouble."

The film helped make General Motors employees more aware of GM's problems, but it also angered local union officials, who viewed it as an attempt to go over their heads to the employees and to weaken the union's bargaining position in upcoming negotiations. Thus when GM's spokesperson put the case for concessions to the UAW's bargaining council at the outset of negotiations early in 1982, he was met with hostility from local union officials, and the initiative in the auto negotiations passed quickly to Ford.

A corporation seeking to obtain concessions without a test of economic power with the union must walk a thin line between appearing to threaten employees and simply trying to convince them that the alternative to concessions is lost jobs. After the breakdown in the talks between GM and the UAW, the corporation implemented plans for the shutdown of marginal facilities, and this added credibility to the corporation's position without appearing to be a bargaining ploy.

Some companies have developed policies for breaking bad news to employees. One major nonunion company, for example, is careful to inform employees about the business climate that makes a negative action necessary. Furthermore, whenever possible the company tells employees when or under what conditions they will return to their former benefits and sometimes promises a further benefit (such as increased pay or promotion opportunities) to reward employees for the current losses.

My survey indicates that unions that grant concessions do not necessarily reap rank-and-file animosity if the process is handled correctly. In all companies that received concessions the unions ratified the agreements and no work stoppage occurred. In 42% of the companies that received concessions union elections have been held, and in 86% of those elections union officials who supported the agreements were reelected.

BARRIERS TO ACTION

As many U.S. companies are finding themselves in trouble due to recession and foreign competition, unions often wait until these companies are virtually or even actually bankrupt before they offer the relief that could lead to survival.

Why do the unions wait so long to act? Wouldn't they be far wiser to grant concessions sooner to increase the likelihood of the company's survival? It would certainly seem so. But there are powerful constraints to more timely action, not all of the unions' making.

Profitability

Many companies will not admit how difficult their business situation is, hoping for an upturn in the economy that will bail them out. Some unions refuse to consider relief for any company from existing contractual obligations unless the company opens its books, and corporate managers, who ordinarily resent being asked to do this, delay taking this step until it is inevitable and often too late. When a company asks relief and turns over its books, the union's staff does a thorough study of the company's financial situation. Recently, James Smith of the Steelworkers staff prepared a lengthy confidential analysis of many companies' financial positions for review by the union's elected leaders.

But even if the managers come to the union well in advance of possible bankruptcy, the union may be unable or unwilling to respond. After all, how does the rank-and-file know that the company is really in trouble unless there have been extensive layoffs? Any how can a company that reports profits, any profits at all, be considered eligible for concessions by its employees?

When General Motors reported a profit for 1981, it also revealed that a large portion of that profit resulted from reducing the company's funding for its employees' pension programs. But UAW leaders were apparently unwilling to try to convince the members that a profit gleaned in this way did not indicate a recovering company but one still in need of assistance from its employees.

The survey shows that in spite of this credibility problem, concessions are nonetheless being negotiated when the company is profitable. Of the companies that received concessions in the sample, 81% are profitable. (Incidentally, of the two nonunion companies imposing wage reductions on employees, one is profitable and one is not.)

Layoffs

The data underline the importance of reductions in the number of employees as a factor that causes companies to seek concessions and unions to grant them. Employers apparently see compensation as related to employment levels rather than as a production cost that is tied to potential for growth in sales, profit, or market share.

POWER VS. PERSUASION

Persuading employees and the union of the need to grant concessions is sometimes not possible; it may not even be necessary if the company is prepared to use economic power to get its way.

In the late 1970s, a small chemical company acquired a new chief executive officer who was determined to return to financial health a company long only marginally profitable. New management became convinced that practices in the home plant were expensive and inefficient. The company entered negotiations with the union in 1978 seeking substantial work rule changes in

return for a large wage and benefit increase. At the eleventh hour, the union accepted the company's proposals.

The next three years saw an advance in the company's profitability, partly due to new products manufactured elsewhere, but less than expected improvement in operating costs at the home plant. The company made large layoffs in 1980 and 1981. During negotiations in 1981 the company again proposed major work rule changes, with big pay increases.

But this time the union would have none of it. Despite layoffs and the transfer of some production to satellite plants, union leaders expressed mistrust of the company's concerns about efficiency, attributing shortcomings solely to supervisors' incompetence. During many weeks of meetings the union refused to discuss the company's proposals for rule changes.

Finally, the union decided to strike. Using supervisors the company managed to maintain production for several months and was able to ship its products despite the continual picket line. Union discipline held, and no employees returned to work.

Eventually the union accepted, for the most part, the company's proposals and its members returned to work. To the union's credit, work was resumed without retaliation. To the company's credit, efforts to repair personal relationships with the employees began immediately, including reviews of the company's business position at meetings between the president and small groups of employees. This example shows that power bargaining can be successful in extracting concessions.

The costliness of any strike and the example of disastrous failures, such as the confrontation at International Harvester in 1981, have persuaded many companies to approach the question of concessions in a less aggressive fashion.[1] When seeking concessions by consensus, companies must ordinarily deal with both local unions and the national organizations with which they are affiliated.

Naturally a company that tries to achieve concessions by agreement must first determine the position of the national union. If the national is opposed and cannot be persuaded otherwise (33% of the survey cases), there is little possibility that local unions will agree to concessions. If the national supports concessions, the company can work with the national to convince local union officials to go along.

Both successes and failures follow approaches of power and persuasion. If a company seeks concessions via hard bargaining, it must carefully assess its capacity to win a strike and should always remember that striking employees are generally capable of far greater sacrifices than managers believe possible. And if a company seeks concessions via openness and collaboration, it must be prepared to prove to the union the truthfulness of its claims.

As one manager reported: "Every situation is unique. We renegotiated some previous agreements. We did it in a manner that demonstrated to the union that we were hurting. We didn't threaten them. We explained in detail why we were seeking these particular concessions. Our goals were clearly defined. And another said: "On the average, we've gotten great help from the unions we deal with to help us stay in business. We started five years ago. The answer is to anticipate that financial trouble is coming."

IMPACT OF CONCESSIONS

For the past several decades the bargaining strategy of U.S. companies with unions has remained the same regardless of the companies' union relations strategy. That strategy has been to give away money (pay and benefits) to preserve management rights. U.S. companies watched each other to see that they stayed competitive in labor costs. But some industries forgot about foreign competition, and others failed to foresee the rise of competition from nonunion domestic companies.

But now concession bargaining has replaced the old bargaining strategy. U.S. companies trade off managerial prerogatives for cost reductions, and in this new context virtually everything can come up for discussion. Table 3 shows the frequency (reported by surveyed companies) with which unions sought certain types of changes as a part of the process of bargaining about concessions.

TABLE 3
What unions sought in return for concessions

	PERCENTAGE OF SITUATIONS IN WHICH COMPANY SOUGHT CONCESSIONS
More job security	46%
No-layoff policy	17
Guaranteed number of jobs	17
Earnings protection	17
To represent more employees	23
Role in corporate governance	31
Consultation on investment	8
Changes in bargaining structure	8

Data derived from interviews with 35 companies.

Employee Relations

After a company obtains concessions its employee relations will never again be the same. Employees lose faith in the competence of management because of the company's economic difficulties. They wonder if other managers or even they themselves could not run the company better. They lose a sense of security in their jobs and wonder if they should look for more promising opportunities elsewhere. Loyalty to the company suffers. Resentment of management grows because hopes, such as for increasing real wages, are thwarted.

Paradoxically, to keep the company afloat employees are often willing to put aside personal advantages, such as work practices favorable to them, and make stronger efforts in their jobs. Failing confidence in management, increasing insecurity, declining company loyalty, but greater willingness to work are major attitude changes, and they change the culture of a company.

When the company makes a turnaround, employees may expect to have a greater role in how the company is run and a greater share of the rewards from business success. The granting of concessions seems to bring with it a sense of investment, of becoming an owner, in the company.

A company that has no well-defined employee relations strategy may find itself driven willy-nilly into embracing one by the process of concessions. To obtain concessions, management may have accepted the union in a much closer relationship. Top officials may have agreed to periodic meetings with union leaders about the company's business prospects, and the employees may even have become preferred stockholders or creditors of the company. In my survey, 35% of the companies that obtained concessions agreed to require concessions of and to give stock to salaried employees as well. These developments may have foreclosed a long-term strategy of battling with the union. But a company under intense financial pressures may fail to realize that

an old antagonist is suddenly a close partner and that it must now try to make collective bargaining work because the stakes are so much higher.

At Wheeling-Pittsburgh Steel Company, the United Steelworkers obtained voting stock for employees in return for concessions. How will the Steelworkers' union behave now? What responsibility, if any, does the union have to the new stockholders. At a recent meeting of one local at a Wheeling-Pittsburgh plant, a worker asked a visiting national union official if the Steelworkers' research department planned to analyze issues raised at the company's annual meeting and advise the members how to vote their stock. The official was a bit taken aback. "I don't know," he answered the worker, "but if you want us to, we probably will." And so the USWA slowly edges into the new role of investment adviser to its members.

Effect on Productivity

After making concessions, unions are more likely than before to support productivity improvements. Where participative management programs are a quid pro quo for concessions, unions are urging their members to be more cooperative with owners and managers and to think about ways to improve productivity.

The desirability of greater participation of blue-collar workers in management is receiving considerable attention in the basic steel industry. Most of these workers have been hired to do just what they have been told by their supervisors, but managers cannot make people more productive and quality conscious. In 1980, the steel companies and the union executed a Labor-Management Participation Team Experimental Agreement, which today involves 13 plants at 5 companies and some 100 teams. Any topic may be placed on the agenda of an LMPT except a grievance or a change in the basic labor agreement. Samuel Camens, an assistant to the president of the Steelworkers, asserted to a congressional committee that the LMPT teams are serious about their objectives and that each has a strong desire to make its plant number one.

In my survey, 20% of the companies that received concessions reported a change in the quality of union-management relations afterward; of these, four-fifths reported a move toward a more cooperative, less confrontational, relationship, presumably leading to greater productivity.

Effect on Investors

The difficulty a company may have with investors emphasizes the need for moderation in the union's approach to the long process of turning a company around. Right after the company has obtained concessions investors may show renewed confidence in it, because concessions not only promise a reduction in labor costs but also suggest an employee commitment to company success. On reflection, however, investors are likely to become cautious.

After concessions, the employees and their union have in some sense become a privileged claimant against the company's future earnings. The company may have a contract that grants the union the right to return to the preconcession rates and benefits if the company becomes profitable (though in my survey, less than 10% of concession contracts specified a date for return to previous wages or benefits). Sometimes a contract grants the union the right to reopen the agreement to seek improved wages and benefits as the company's financial health improves and to strike if the company refuses to agree to pay and benefit increases. "Use of such language as 'suspend' or 'defer' helps keep the union's claim to benefits alive," one union official told an interviewer.

Even where there is no contractual requirement of management to pay higher rates or to accept a reopening of the contract, the union stands as a claimant for pay increases the moment the company is again profitable. And, on the expiration of a current contract, if the union asks the employees to strike to regain pay and benefits that they once had, who can imagine that a strike would not be called?

Equity investors are understandably reluctant to provide capital to a company that faces such contingent liabilities against its future earnings. As a result, where equity is needed the unions should exercise self-restraint in pursuing improved wages and benefits as the company begins to recover. An overeager union is likely to scare off potential investors and thereby lessen the company's opportunity for survival.

RESTORING FINANCIAL HEALTH

Unions sometimes refuse to grant concessions to failing companies, saying that the companies cannot be saved. This attitude is often legitimate, but when a union agrees to concessions to try to rescue a company, it often finds that it has only begun to deal with the company's problems.

This is because factory labor is not the only factor of production and, to save a company and the jobs it provides, other employees also have to be willing to contribute. When employees are making sacrifices to keep the company in business, they resent the facts that key technical and managerial salaries remain at the market rate, that high interest rates are paid for loans, or that stockholders receive dividends. The company may see these actions as necessary to provide the company with key personnel and capital resources, yet they seem unfair to employees.

A union that supports a company in the rebuilding of its business must try to avert employees' feelings of being mistreated, while permitting the company to take actions necessary for its rejuvenation. There are two ways it can do this.

First, it should not misrepresent the reason for making concessions. The decision should be seen as economic, subject to calculations about the best methods for preserving workers' jobs in the long term, rather than as a moral decision in which sacrifice is equated with the certainty of future reward.

Second, the union should keep abreast of the company's turnaround plans and try to justify them to employees. Modernization expenditures should be pointed out, as well as the role of retained earnings in paying for them.

When managers fully realize that concessions and the participation of unions in corporate decision making have imposed a new employee relations strategy on the company, there is a chance that the loss of managerial prerogatives may be accepted. The new strategy, whether managers initiated it with open eyes or were propelled into it by adverse circumstances, imposes strong demands:

> Lower-level supervisors must be made aware of the new situation.

> Union officials must be acquainted with the significance and meaning of the financial

and market data they will receive, and should be helped to recognize that proprietary information is not shared with competitors.

Union officials must, in short, be made part of a broadened management team, in a way successfully practiced in Japan and Germany. U.S. managers find this idea distasteful and have not, in the past, worked at it. If they realize what is occurring and try to strengthen joint labor-management efforts to build sound businesses, concession bargaining can make a long-term contribution to the U.S. economy.

NOTES

1. Lyn Christiansen, "Corporate Strategy and Labor Relations," DBA Thesis, Harvard Business School, fall 1982.

Job Enrichment versus Traditional Issues at the Bargaining Table: What Union Members Want

WILLIAM F. GILES

WILLIAM H. HOLLEY, JR.
Both of Auburn University

Experiments and projects in job enrichment have been the focus of much interest in recent years. Generally, these efforts have taken place in non-union companies and, in those cases involving unions, management has typically been the initiator of the experiments (Fein 1974). Because of this, it has been claimed that union leaders are either uninterested or antagonistic toward job enrichment and similar motivation programs (Sheppard and Herrick 1972; *Work in America* 1973). A common theme in these charges is that union leaders are not aware that their members desire intrinsic factors in their jobs (Sheppard and Herrick 1972; *Work in America* 1973). Other spokesmen, however, have defended unions against this allegation, their general thesis being that union members are more interested in items traditionally sought by unions (for example, pay, fringe benefits, job security) than in job enrichment or similar programs (Fein 1974; Schrank 1974). Surveying union and management officials, Katzell and Yankelovich (1975) found extrinsic factors were perceived as being much more useful for improving employee attitudes and motivation by union officials than by management, whereas there were relatively small differences between the usefulness ratings of union and management respondents for intrinsic factors.

In view of the reaction of many union leaders to the issue of job enrichment, it would be of interest to determine if rank-and-file union *members* want their union representatives to take a more aggressive stance in regard to the implementation of job enrichment programs. Generally, most of the controversy regarding the role of job enrichment in the union-management relationship has stemmed from statements made by union and management officials. However, Schlesinger and Walton (1977) have noted that their experience with work restructuring projects has emphasized the necessity of conceptualizing three, rather than two, distinct interest groups — management, union, *and* the workers themselves. This is especially true since job design changes affect workers more directly than they do the other two subgroups. In this regard, research conducted by Kochan, Lipsky, and Dyer (1974) indicated that union activists perceived quality of work issues to be less important than traditional bargaining issues. Moreover, their study and another based on the same sample (Dyer, Lipsky, and Kochan 1977) showed that union activists did not view collective bargaining as being a particularly effective way of dealing with quality-of-work issues.

The present research seeks to assess the reac-

Reprinted, with permission, from *Academy of Management Journal,* Vol. 21, No. 4, 1978, pp. 725–730.

tion of union members to job enrichment as a potential collective bargaining issue. This study differs from the work of Kochan *et al.* (1974) and Dyer *et al.* (1977) in a number of ways. First, it asks union members to allocate the percentages of time that their representatives should devote to bargaining for job enrichment and for traditional negotiation issues. This is a different type of measure than was used in the Kochan *et al.* and Dyer *et al.* studies. Second, their sample was composed entirely of persons holding either full-time or part-time union positions, whereas a majority of subjects in the present research did not hold union positions. Third, the studies of Kochan *et al.* and Dyer *et al.* utilized the concept of quality-of-work, while this study deals with job enrichment (which focuses only on intrinsic job factors). For example, "relationships with supervisors" is included as a quality of work factor in their research, whereas it would not be considered a job enrichment factor. Fourth, their subjects came from a variety of plants and were combined for data analysis. In the present research, data were gathered from a plant above average in wages and fringe benefits and one below average in these areas; these data were then analyzed separately to note the possible effect of these plant-specific variables on reaction to job enrichment as a bargaining alternative.

METHOD

The sample consisted of 131 male union members from two plants. Plant A ($n = 55$) is a manufacturing operation, while plant B ($n = 76$) engages in food processing. Both plants are located in small towns (i.e., populations less than 30,000). In both plants, the general level of job enrichment factors could be characterized as average or somewhat below average. Neither plant has ever undertaken or participated in job enrichment or any similar type of program. The average age of respondents was 36, while 69% were white and 31% black. In regard to education, 32% did not graduate from high school, 35% were high school graduates only, and 33% had some college.

In the survey instrument which was utilized, employees were asked the following question: "What *percentage of time* in contract negotiations do you feel your union representatives should spend in negotiating with management on each of these issues?" The employees were asked to allocate 100 percent among five negotiation issues: better pay, better fringe benefits, better working conditions, more job security, and job enrichment. The first four of these issues were used since they are matters on which unions typically bargain (Schrank 1974). Explanations were provided for each of the traditional issues (except for "better pay") in order to define each term more precisely.

The term "job enrichment" was chosen for use in the present study due to its widespread usage; however, other alternatives ("job redesign," "work redesign") would have been equally appropriate. Job enrichment had previously been described in the questionnaire as the process of changing jobs to emphasize five factors: opportunity for independent action, amount of variety, opportunity to do a large part of the job, amount of feedback, and opportunity to use skills and abilities. The first four of these factors are the core dimensions of motivating jobs developed by Hackman and Lawler (1971). The "opportunity to use skills and abilities" factor or a similar construct has frequently been cited in the job design literature (Herzberg 1968; Lawler 1969). Explanations were attached to each of these five factors to insure that respondents understood their meanings.

The questionnaires were distributed at union meetings by union members who were familiar with the concept of job enrichment and available for assistance if needed. The percentage of returned, usable questionnaires out of the number distributed was 71% in plant A (55 out of 77) and 82% in plant B (76 out of 93).

RESULTS

Mean percentages allocated to each of the negotiation issues by the subsample in each plant

TABLE 1
Union members' perceptions of the percentages of time their representatives should devote to negotiation issues

NEGOTIATION ISSUES	PLANT A (n = 55)	PLANT B (n = 76)
Fringe benefits	28%	17%
Pay	24	47
Working conditions	16	13
Job enrichment	13	9
Job security	18	14

are presented in Table 1. In order to assess the relative amount of time that union members in each plant alloted to the negotiation issues appropriate statistical techniques were utilized. . . . In plant A, significant differences existed between fringe benefits and each of the following: job security, working conditions, and job enrichment. There was also a significant difference between pay and job enrichment. In plant B, significant differences existed between pay and each of the other four negotiation issues.

DISCUSSION

The results indicate that union leaders have been fairly accurate in their perceptions of what their members want from the collective bargaining process. The issue of job enrichment received the lowest mean percentage ratings in both plants in the present study, suggesting that in the immediate future there will not be a major demand on the part of union members that unions actively bargain for job enrichment. On the other hand, the fact that job enrichment was not significantly different from the traditional issues of job security and working conditions in each of the two plants indicates that job enrichment may be viewed as a valid, but not crucial, negotiation issue. It may be that union members draw a major distinction between economic (pay and fringe benefits) and noneconomic (job security, working conditions, and job enrichment) issues.

It is of interest to examine the percentage

allocations to the various issues in view of the different nature of the two plants in the present study. Plant A is the wage leader in its geographic area and also has a better than average fringe benefit package for this area. Nevertheless, even though in this plant the economic issues (pay and fringe benefits) may be considered to be "fulfilled," there is no consequent emphasis on bargaining for job enrichment. Although Katzell and Yankelovich (1975) have suggested that job enrichment will be more favorably received in organizations with high "hygiene" levels, the present data did not support such a finding. Rather, both pay and fringe benefits received the highest allocations in plant A. If there was a shift, it may have been toward fringe benefits, since this issue received the highest rating. As for plant B, the high percentage allocated to pay is not surprising since this plant's wage level is somewhat below its area's average.

The results of this study reinforce and extend the findings of Kochan *et al.* (1974) and Dyer *et al.* (1977). Apparently, both rank-and-file union members *and* union activists are not particularly interested in having their representatives actively bargain for either job enrichment *or* quality of work issues. Also, this lack of interest seems to extend to plants with above average pay and fringe benefit levels as well as to those below average in these areas.

Several concluding points need to be made concerning characteristics and limitations of the present study. First, it should be noted that both plants were located in small-town environments. However, this would not appear to be a serious limitation to the generalizability of the findings since research by Susman (1973) indicated that plant location was not a strong enough variable to create opposing responses to job enrichment, as had been implied by previous research (Blood and Hulin 1967; Turner and Lawrence 1965). However, if it is assumed that an urban-rural distinction does exist, it is interesting to note that past research (Blood and Hulin 1967; Turner and Lawrence 1965) suggests that job enrichment would receive *even lower* allocations if the present study was replicated in an urban setting. Second, it is possible that responses to the stimulus question used in this study may have been influenced to some extent by the subjects' views of management resistance to the various negotiation issues. For example, on those issues where management resistance is high, union members may perceive that their representatives have to devote more time to these issues to gain concessions. Third, due to the nature of the question, it was not possible to determine to what extent the low allocations to job enrichment were due to a lack of desire for enriched jobs or to the view that collective bargaining is not the appropriate way to implement job enrichment. However, what the present study definitely does suggest is that there will *not* be widespread demands by union members for their representatives to devote a major part of their negotiating efforts to seeking job enrichment.

REFERENCES

Blood, M. R., and C. L. Hulin. "Alienation, Environmental Characteristics, and Worker Responses," *Journal of Applied Psychology,* Vol. 51 (1967), 284–290.

Dyer, L., D. B. Lipsky, and T. A. Kochan. "Union Attitudes Toward Management Cooperation," *Industrial Relations,* Vol. 16 (1977), 1963–1972.

Fein, M. "Job Enrichment, A Reevaluation," *Sloan Management Review,* Vol. 15 (1974), 69–88.

Hackman, J. R., and E. E. Lawler. "Employee Reac-

tions to Job Characteristics," *Journal of Applied Psychology,* Vol. 55 (1971), 259–286.

Herzberg, F. "One More time: How Do you Motivate Employees?," *Harvard Business Review,* Vol. 46 (1968), 53–62.

Katzell, R. A., and D. Yankelovich. *Work, Productivity, and Job Satisfaction.* (New York: The Psychological Corporation, 1975).

Kochan, T. A., D. B. Lipsky, and L. Dyer. "Collective Bargaining and the Quality of Work: The Views of Local Union Activists," *Proceedings of the 27th Annual Winter Meeting of the Industrial Relations Research Association,* 1974, 150–162.

Lawler, E. E. "Job Design and Employee Motivation," *Personnel Psychology,* Vol. 22 (1969), 426–435.

Schlesinger, L. A., and R. E. Walton. "Work Restructuring in Unionized Organizations: Risks, Opportunities, and Impact on Collective Bargaining," *National Quality of Work Center Special Report,* (1977), 1–8.

Schrank, R. "Work in America: What Do Workers Really Want," *Industrial Relations,* Vol. 13 (1974), 124–129.

Sheppard, H. L., and N. Q. Herrick, *Where Have All the Robots Gone?* (New York: Free Press, 1972).

Susman, G. I. "Job Enlargement: Effects of Culture on Worker Responses," *Industrial Relations,* Vol. 12 (1973), 1–15.

Turner, A. N., and P. L. Lawrence. *Industrial Jobs and the Worker* (Cambridge, Mass.: Harvard University Graduate School of Business Administration, 1965).

Winer, B. J. *Statistical Principles in Experimental Design.* 2nd ed. (New York: McGraw-Hill, 1971).

Work in America (Cambridge, Mass.: MIT Press, 1973).

Costing Out a Wage and Benefit Package

ROBERT E. ALLEN

TIMOTHY J. KEAVENY
Both of University of Wyoming

In this article we describe an approach to estimating an organization's cost for a proposed wage and benefits package. Although we have assumed that a union represents the organization's workers, the steps involved in estimating compensation costs would be the same even if the organization's workers weren't unionized.

IMPORTANCE OF COSTING OUT A LABOR AGREEMENT

The phrase, "costing out a labor agreement," refers to the process of estimating the cost of a particular proposal or component of an agreement, as well as estimating the total cost of a set of proposals. The importance of this process lies in the fact that labor costs make up the largest component of operating costs incurred by most organizations in the United States. U.S. corporations spend over four times as much to compensate their employees as they spend on new equipment and facilities. As a result, relatively small changes in employee compensation can have a

large impact on profits and an organization's ability to invest in new equipment and facilities. Both union and management negotiators should be able to estimate the cost of any proposed change in an agreement and in addition, the effect of that change on an organization's profits. In the unionized company, such estimates should be available before the parties accept or reject any change in their collective bargaining agreement. In the nonunion firm, such estimates should be available before management formalizes a proposed change in the compensation package.

Both management and union negotiators need such estimates so that they can accurately evaluate the organization's ability to pay. Obviously, management recognizes the importance of this factor. It should be noted that most union negotiators realize that it is in the long-run interest of union members to ensure that the organization achieves reasonable profit levels.

In addition, costing out proposals to an agreement can be an integral part of the negotiating process. When "trading" proposals, both parties should know the cost of each item being negotiated. This information is needed to determine how much is being gained or lost by the trade. Another concern is the point in time that proposals take effect. A wage increase or benefit that takes effect in the last year of a multiyear contract, of course, costs an organization less and is of less value to workers than the wage increase or benefit that takes effect in the first year.

Another dimension of costing out proposals is relevant to the negotiating process. Two alternative proposals may have equal utility to union members, but may have different implications for labor costs and organization profits. If management negotiators are able to accomplish a trade in which the less costly proposal is accepted, they have exercised some control over labor costs.

HOW TO COST OUT AN AGREEMENT

Figure 1 describes a sample bargaining unit. This unit and its contract agreement provide examples for costing out different contract provisions to be discussed throughout the rest of this article. Fig. 2 presents the calculations needed to cost out the labor agreement for the sample bargaining unit.

Estimating Increased Costs Attributable to a New Labor Agreement

The following is an example of how to determine the cost of a new contract. The example assumes that Murray and Miller Manufacturing and The International Woodworkers of America negotiated a one-year contract. The new contract included the following changes:

1. *Wages:*   Unskilled laborers
                    $6.50/hour (from $6.00)
            Semiskilled machine tenders
                    $7.75/hour (from $7.25)
            Skilled woodworkers
                    $9.50/hour (from $9.00)

2. *Paid holidays:* Two additional paid holidays.

3. *Pensions:* Employer contribution of $.50 per hour for all hours paid at straight time plus 4 percent of the payroll (this includes straight-time wages, overtime, and shift differentials)

There were no changes in the other provisions of the labor agreement. Figure 3 illustrates a procedure that could be used to cost out the new labor agreement.

Secondary Effects of Wage Changes

As a secondary effect of the wage increases, the cost of several benefits that are not specifically altered in the contract will increase because they are calculated on the basis of wage rates. These costs must be identified and included in determining the cost of a new contract. For example, see step 3 in Fig. 3, which shows how to calculate the cost of pensions under the new contract. In this calculation, because of the new wage rate, the cost of overtime under the new contract obviously is increased, and, thus, the amount of the pension cost also goes up over and above the negotiated increase.

It is also necessary to recalculate the cost of contract provisions that are not changed specifically by the new contract, but whose cost changes as a result of the higher wages. It is necessary, for instance, to determine the secondary effects of the higher wage rates on the cost of vacations, holidays, Social Security taxes, unemployment compensation, and workers' compensation. Thus the calculations in Fig. 2 for these benefits must be repeated substituting the new total for straight-time earnings that were arrived at in Fig. 3. After both the primary and secondary effects of changes in contract provisions have been determined, the cost of the proposed change in compensation can be established.

ESTIMATE THE COST OF CONTRACT PROPOSALS

The above example describes how to estimate the cost of a new contract that has been ratified. Determining the cost of a contract after ratification is analogous to closing the corral's gate after the horses have escaped. Both management and union negotiators, however, should know what a set of proposals will cost before agreeing to them. Failure to do so makes it possible to stumble into an agreement that is beyond an employer's ability

FIGURE 1
Sample bargaining unit

Murray and Miller (M & M) Manufacturing, Inc. is a small manufacturer of wooden kitchen cabinets. The 100 production employees are represented by the International Woodworkers of America. The bargaining unit and the existing collective bargaining agreement have the following characteristics:

Employment Status and Wage Rates.

Job classification	Number of workers	Hourly wage
Unskilled laborers (UL)	20	$6.00
Semiskilled machine tenders (MT)	60	7.25
Skilled woodworkers (SW)	20	9.00
Total	100	

Hours of Work. M & M Manufacturing, Inc. operates two shifts. One-half of each job classification is assigned to each shift. Each shift is eight hours long. A work week consists of five eight-hour shifts (40 hours per week). The day shift runs from 8:00 a.m. to 4:00 p.m. The evening shift begins at 4:00 p.m. and concludes at 12:00 midnight. Workers assigned to the evening shift receive a 20-cents-an-hour shift differential.

Overtime Premium. The labor agreement specifies that any work over eight hours per day will be paid at a rate of one and one-half times the wage rate for the worker's job classification. (In other words, workers are paid time-and-a-half for overtime.) Last year, a total of 2,000 overtime hours were worked. Only employees in the semiskilled machine tenders' category worked overtime.

Vacations. Vacations accrue according to the following schedule:

Service	Vacation	Number of employees in each category		
		UL	MT	SW
0–3 years	1 week	4	12	4
4–7 years	2 weeks	4	12	4
8–12 years	3 weeks	4	12	4
13–20 years	4 weeks	4	12	4
20 + years	5 weeks	4	12	4
		20	60	20

Paid Holidays. Each worker receives 10 paid holidays per year and eight hours' pay for each holiday.

Hospitalization.

Type of coverage	Number of employees	Employer's cost per employee per month
Single Coverage	25	$25.00
Family Coverage	75	$50.00

Pensions. The employer contributes 35 cents per hour for all hours paid at straight time plus 4 percent of the payroll (this includes straight-time wages, overtime, and shift differentials).

Additional Payroll Costs.
1. Social Security taxes (F.I.C.A.) = 6.70 percent of straight-time wages.
2. State and federal unemployment insurance tax = 2.5 percent of total straight-time wages
3. Workers' compensation insurance = 2.5 percent of total straight-time wages

FIGURE 2
Costing out the existing labor agreement

Straight-Time Earnings.

Number of employees in each job class		x	Straight-time hourly wage	x	Number of hours worked at straight time (per year) (2,080 minus vacations and holidays)	=	Total pay for hours worked
UL	20		$6.00		1,880		$ 225,600
MT	60		$7.25		1,880		817,800
SW	20		$9.00		1,880		338,400
							$1,381,800

Night Shift Differential.

Number of employees on evening shift	x	Number of hours worked at straight time/per year	x	Night-shift differential	=	Total night-shift differential
50		1,880		$.20		$18,800

Overtime.

Number of hours of paid overtime	x	Hourly wage	x	Overtime premium	=	Overtime costs
2,000		$7.25		1.5		$21,750

F.I.C.A. Contributions = 6.7% of total earnings*
    .0670 × $1,569,350 = $105,146.45

State and Federal Unemployment Insurance = 2.5% of total earnings
    .025 × $1,569,350 = $39,233.75

Workers Compensation = 2.5% of total earnings
    .025 × $1,569,350 = $39,233.75

Vacations.

Weeks of vacation	x	Number of employees in each category			x	Weekly wage for each category (hourly wage x 40 hrs)			=	Cost of vacations (number of weeks x number of employees x weekly wage)		
		UL	MT	SW		UL	MT	SW		UL	MT	SW
1(40 hrs)		4	12	4		$240	$290	$360		$ 960	$ 3,480	$ 1,440
2(80 hrs)		4	12	4		240	290	360		1,920	6,960†	2,880
3(120 hrs)		4	12	4		240	290	360		2,880	10,440	4,320
4(160 hrs)		4	12	4		240	290	360		3,840	13,920	5,760
5(200 hrs)		4	12	4		240	290	360		4,800	17,400	7,200
										$14,400	$52,200	$21,600

Total Cost of Vacation = UL + MT + SW
                       = $14,400 + $52,200 + $21,600
                       = $88,200

* Total earnings = (Straight-time earnings) + (Night-shift differential) + (Overtime) + (Vacations) + (Paid holidays).

FIGURE 2 *(cont.)*

Paid Holidays.

Number of holidays	X	Number of employees in each category	X	Wage for each category	X	Number of hours paid for a holiday	=	Cost of paid holidays

$$10 \times [(20 \times 6.00) + (60 \times 7.25) + (20 \times 9.00)] \times 8$$
$$10 \times (120 + 435 + 180) \times 8$$
$$10 \times 735 \times 8 = \$58,800$$

Hospitalization.

Number of employees with single coverage	X	Annual cost of single coverage	=	Cost of hospitalization for single coverage

$$25 \times (12 \times \$25.00) = \$7,500$$

Number of employees with family coverage	X	Annual cost of family coverage	=	Cost of hospitalization for family coverage

$$75 \times (12 \times \$50.00) = \$45,000$$

$$\text{Total Annual Cost of Hospitalization} = \$7,500 + \$45,000$$
$$= \$52,500$$

Pensions.

Number of hours paid at straight time (number of employees x 2,080)	X	Per hour employer contribution	+	4% of payroll	=	Total cost of pensions

$$([100 \times 2,080] \times [.35] + (.04 [\$1,381,800 + 18,800 + 21,750 + 88,200 + 58,800])$$
$$(208,000 [.35]) + (.04 [1,569,350])$$
$$72,800 \quad + \quad 62,774 \quad = \$135,574$$

Total Cost of Existing Contract.

Direct Payroll Costs.

Straight-time earnings	$1,381,800.00
Night-shift differential	18,800.00
Overtime	21,750.00
F.I.C.A. contributions	105,146.45
Unemployment compensation	39,233.75
Workers compensation	39,233.75
Direct payroll costs (subtotal)	$1,605,963.95

Employee Benefits Costs.

Vacations	$ 88,200.00
Paid holidays	58,800.00
Hospitalization	52,500.00
Pensions	135,574.00
Cost of employee benefits (subtotal)	334,074.00
Total cost of contract (direct payroll + employee benefits)	$1,941,037.95

† An example of the calculations to generate these numbers:
Number of weeks X Number of employees in MT category X weekly MT wage =
$$(2) \quad X \quad (12) \quad X \quad (290) \quad = \$6,960$$

FIGURE 3
Determining costs attributable to a new labor agreement[1]

Cost of Change in Wages

Number of workers in each job category	X	New hourly salary	X	Numbers of hours paid each year[2]	=	New wages
UL 20		6.50		2,080		270,400
MT 60		7.75		2,080		967,200
SW 20		9.50		2,080		395,200
New total straight-time earnings[3]						$1,632,800
Old total straight-time earnings[3]						1,528,800*
Increase attributable to new contract						$ 104,000

Cost of Change in Paid Holidays.[4]

Number of new holidays	X	(Number of employees in each category x new wage)	X	Number of hours paid for a holiday

2 X [(20 X $6.50) + (60 X $7.75) + (20 X $9.50)] X 8 =
2 X ($130 + $465 + $190) X 8 =
2 X $785 X 8 = $12,560   Cost of new paid holidays

Cost of Change in Pension Provisions.

Number of hours paid at straight time (number of employees x 2,080)	X	Per-hour employer contribution	+	4% of payroll (total straight-time earnings + shift differential + overtime)[5]

[(100 X 2,080) X (.50) + .04 ($1,632,800 + $18,800 + $23,250)]
  (208,000) X .50 + .04 (1,674,850)
    $104,000   + $66,994   = $170,994   new pension cost
                          −135,574   old pension cost*
                          $ 35,420   increase attributable to new contract

[1] There are, of course, alternative ways of costing out subsequent years of a multiyear contract. (See, for example, Figure 6.)

[2] Number of hours worked at straight time (1,880) plus paid vacations and holidays.

[3] Includes pay for hours worked plus pay for paid holidays and vacations.

[4] This cost is included in the $104,000 increase in straight-time earnings attributable to new contract.

[5] The cost of the shift differential is taken directly from Figure 2 because the shift differential rate was not changed and it is assumed that the number of employees working the night shift will not change. To estimate the cost of overtime, we assumed the same number of overtime hours as occurred last year. Overtime calculations must reflect the new wage. The estimated cost is:

      Number of hours of paid overtime X hourly wage X overtime premium
           2,000   X $7.75   X   1.5   = $23,250

*See Figure 2.

to pay — an event that, in turn, has implications for the employment opportunities of union members. It is obviously not in the long-run interest of either union leaders or union members to secure a contract that forces the employer out of business. An AFL-CIO spokesman recently noted that the days when a union bargains for as much as its power can secure have passed. Instead, union leaders recognize the need to base their negotiation decisions on relevant economic data. It is therefore vital that the parties involved in contract negotiations make sure that the costs of proposed contract changes are identified during the negotiation process.

Problems that might be encountered and alternative approaches to determining the cost of contract provisions will be discussed in the following sections.

COMMUNICATING THE COST OF THE CONTRACT

There are no general rules for reporting the cost of a new contract to employees or the public. Negotiators are free, within a broad range, to engage in "creative" arithmetic. Usually the cost of new contract agreements is reported in terms of change in cents-per-hour. Or it is reported in terms of change in compensation as a percentage of payroll. A seldom-used alternative is reporting the total cost of the contract changes — probably because it is difficult for individual workers to ap-

preciate how a new contract will affect their paychecks if this method is used.

To communicate the costs of the agreement in terms of cents-per-hour, one must divide the cost of the changes by some measure of hours. One of the key problems in estimating the cost of proposals during negotiations or the cost of a new agreement is determining which measure of hours should be used. Two possible approaches are basing the calculations on (1) the number of hours of paid employment or (2) the number of hours worked. The former approach calls for including vacations and holidays in your calculation; the latter does not include pay for time not worked — for example, vacations and holidays.

Figure 4 presents sample computations based on the situation at Murray and Miller Manufacturing. Calculations to determine the number of hours of paid employment as well as the number of hours worked are shown. As the example indicates, the two measures of hours are substantially different.

FIGURE 4
Calculating the number of hours of paid employment and the number of hours worked

$$
\begin{aligned}
\text{Number of hours of paid employment} &= \text{Number of employees} \times 2{,}080^{1} + \text{Number of overtime hours} \\
&= (100 \times 2{,}080) + 2{,}000 \\
&= 208{,}000 + 2{,}000 \\
&= 210{,}000 \text{ hours}
\end{aligned}
$$

$$
\begin{aligned}
\text{Number of hours worked} &= \text{Total number of hours paid} + \text{Overtime} - \text{Number of paid holiday hours and paid vacation hours} \\
&= (100 \text{ employees} \times 2{,}080 \text{ hours}) + 2{,}000 - \\
&\quad (12 \text{ holidays} \times 100 \text{ employees} \times 8 \text{ hours}) + \text{paid holiday hours} \\
&\quad \left.\begin{array}{l}
(20 \text{ employees} \times 40 \text{ hours}) \quad + \\
(20 \text{ employees} \times 80 \text{ hours}) \quad + \\
(20 \text{ employees} \times 120 \text{ hours}) \quad + \\
(20 \text{ employees} \times 160 \text{ hours}) \quad + \\
(20 \text{ employees} \times 200 \text{ hours}) \quad +
\end{array}\right\} \begin{array}{l} \text{Distribution of vacation benefits} \\ \text{among employees in hours} \end{array} \\
&= (208{,}000 + 2{,}000) - (9{,}600 + 800 + 1{,}600 + 2{,}400 + \\
&\qquad\qquad 3{,}200 + 4{,}000) \\
&= 210{,}000 - 21{,}600 \\
&= 188{,}400 \text{ hours}
\end{aligned}
$$

[1] Number of hours worked at straight time (1,880) plus hours included in paid vacations and holidays.

FIGURE 5
Computing the cents-per-hour costs of new contract provisions

A. Computing costs on the basis of number of hours of paid employment			B. Computing costs on the basis of number of hours worked		
Change in costs attributable to wages	÷	Number of hours of paid employment	Change in costs attributable to wages	÷	Number of hours worked
$104,000	÷	210,000 = $0.495/hour	$104,000	÷	188,400 = $0.552/hour
Change in costs attributable to new paid holidays	÷	Number of hours of paid employment	Change in costs attributable to paid holidays	÷	Number of hours worked
$12,560	÷	210,000 = $0.060/hour	$12,560	÷	188,400 = $0.067/hour
Change in costs attributable to greater pension contributions	÷	Number of hours of paid employment	Change in costs attributable to greater pension contributions	÷	Number of hours worked
$35,420	÷	210,000 = $.169/hour	$35,420	÷	188,400 = $.188/hour

Figure 5 presents examples of computations of the costs associated with the changes in the Murray and Miller Manufacturing contract. The calculations in part A assume that the measure is the number of hours of paid employment. This choice results in a lower cents-per-hour increase than computations that are based on number of hours worked; the effect of using hours worked to determine the change in cost attributable to wages is reported in part B of Figure 5.

During negotiations when management wants to convince union negotiators that their demands are too costly, they would use the measure shown in part B. On the other hand, when union negotiators want to convince management that the union demands wouldn't prove too costly, they could use the approach depicted in part A.

After the contract is signed, management wants to show that it hasn't conceded too much. Therefore, it would probably use the measure that has the least costly bottom line — that is, the number of paid hours — when reporting to shareholders and the public.

On the other hand, when union negotiators present a new contract to the membership, they want compensation increases to appear as large as possible to win member approval and increase the probability of ratification. And because management negotiators also want the membership to ratify the proposed agreement, they do not dispute the union negotiators' computations. Thus after contract negotiations, there's a reversal of management and union negotiators' preferences for the way in which hours are measured.

PROBLEMS WITH THE TYPICAL APPROACH TO COSTING

The traditional approach to costing the provisions of collective bargaining agreements that is described above runs into several problems. First, the calculations are based on past conditions or, more precisely, a continuation of past practices. In Fig. 3, for example, it was assumed that the number of overtime hours and the category of employees receiving overtime during the coming year would be identical to those items during the previous years. Another assumption was that the composition of the workforce would not change. For example, the number of employees in each job category and the number of single and married employees were assumed to remain the same. In fact, of course, all of these numbers would probably change.

Projections of future business activity and of future workforce characteristics would typically result in more accurate labor cost estimates. Further, the procedures described here could be useful in evaluating alternative staff-planning strategies. For example, organization planners could be considering two approaches to staffing an organization that call for a workforce with different levels of skills and at different levels of compensation. In such a case, the procedures described here could produce information that would be valuable for staff planning, and consequently they could, in part, determine the future composition of the organization's workforce.

A second deficiency with the above approach is that it focuses on the direct cost of contract changes rather than on the changes' effect on the organization's financial condition. Changing contract provisions could have no real effect on profits or they could have a devastating effect, but the above method would not reflect either of these extremes. Changes in sales volume, prices, product mix, and capital investment are often disregarded in estimating the contract costs. Such changes could completely offset the impact of the contract changes, or they could greatly intensify them.

Thomas A. Mahoney has described procedures to assess the impact of labor-cost changes stemming from wages and benefit changes relative to such factors as profits, sales revenue, and productivity. He suggests computations that permit identifying the impact of increased labor costs on net profits, the increase in sales revenue necessary to finance increased labor costs without reducing profits, and the change in productivity necessary to offset the cost of a wage increase

when a portion of the workforce is covered by an incentive compensation plan.

Another problem is that the traditional approach tends to be rigid in its application. In our example, as presented in Fig. 3, two additional paid holidays were assumed. The cost of this change was estimated by multiplying the new wage rate times the number of additional holiday hours. However, the cost of these holidays could be substantially different. They could be floating holidays — that is, days taken at the discretion of each employee, such as one's birthday or the opening of elk-hunting season. In such a case there may be enough slack in the workforce or enough flexibility in work scheduling to cover for the employees taking a holiday without any decline in production even though fewer hours are worked. In effect we are suggesting that, in some cases, increases in labor productivity achieved through scheduling changes and reduced slack time may result in increases in labor productivity that offset the increased labor costs.

On the other hand, the new holidays could fall on days during which the organization must be staffed. If the company must operate on these days, it may be necessary to pay overtime to those who work. If this is the case, the cost estimate for these additional holidays should be based on overtime pay rather than straight-time earnings.

Yet another problem that becomes increasingly significant as the time period covered by a contract increases is the need to consider the time value of money. The value of a dollar to be spent or received one year from now is less than one dollar in today's terms. The difference between the two values is equal to the opportunity cost — that is, the interest rate you could earn on alternative investments. The time value of money is a relevant concern when costing out multi-year contracts because the distribution of benefits during the agreement's term can appreciably influence its cost. Figure 6 presents a simple example involving the cost of three new paid days off. It shows that the cost of the new benefit is much lower when the days are received in the third year

FIGURE 6
The present value of future benefits*

Alternative distribution of days off	Cost in the first year for days off	Cost in the second year	Cost in the third year	Total cost
1. All three days are taken off at the end of the first year	$150,000 × .9091*	0	0	$136,365
2. One day is taken off in each year of the contract.	$50,000 × .9091	$50,000 × .8264†	$50,000 × .7513†	$124,340
3. All three days are taken off at the end of the third year.	0	0	$150,000 × .7513	$112,695

* *Assumption:*
¹ Each day off costs the company $50,000.
² The days off are taken at the end of the year.
³ The interest rate on alternative investments is 10%.

† These numbers are known as the present value interest factors and can be used to determine the costs in today's terms of a benefit to be paid out in the future. For example, to be able to pay a worker $100 in one year, $90.91 ($100 × .9091) would have to be invested at 10 percent today. Similarly, if the $100 had to be paid out at the end of three years, $75.13 ($100 × .7513) would have to be invested today. Tables are available that provide present value interest factors for varying periods and interest rates.

of the contract. Thus a union will typically press to receive the additional day off (or any other benefit) in the first year (front loading). Because of the time value of money, management will try to schedule the days off for the latter years of the agreement. Generally, the longer management is able to delay implementation of a contract provision, the smaller the present value of the provision's cost and, the smaller the present value of the change to workers.

RECOMMENDATION FOR COSTING AN AGREEMENT

Our general recommendation is that management negotiators call on the expertise and information available from organization and human resources planners as well as financial managers in estimating costs of proposed contract provisions. These information sources can address most, if not all, of the criticisms of the traditional approach to costing out agreements that we have presented here.

It should also be kept in mind that, when costing out an agreement, cost estimates are used. Estimates of the composition of an organization's future labor force, estimates of implications of technical change on productivity, and so on must be made. Therefore cost estimates that are made on the basis of information available will certainly result in fewer "bad" wage and benefit programs and will increase the accuracy of the costing-out process.

SUMMARY

Labor costs represent the largest single cost of operation for most organizations. For the unionized employer, the compensation package is determined during contract negotiations. It is important for both union and management negotiators to be able to identify the cost of a proposed agreement. Both parties to a contract should know whether a proposed compensation package is consistent with an organization's ability to pay. In addition, when "trading" demands, both parties should be aware of the cost of the demands being traded.

An approach to costing out a labor agreement has been presented in this article. While it can be described as the standard approach, it is subject to several criticisms. Typically, it is applied in a way that assumes that history will repeat itself. In addition, it focuses on the direct cost of a proposed compensation package. While this is certainly relevant, the impact of the compensation package on organization profits is more important. Finally, the time value of money is not taken into account. This would be important if a multi-year contract is being negotiated. While there are legitimate concerns about the approach presented here, our objective is to provide the reader with a basic approach to costing out a wage and benefit package. Anyone involved in contract negotiations or, in the nonunion firm, anyone responsible for administering a wage and benefit program, should be aware of the problems that we have described and seek out reference materials to provide guidance in addressing them.

Technological Change and Industrial Relations in the United States

HOYT WHEELER

ROGER WEIKLE
Both of University of South Carolina

INTRODUCTION

Technological change lies at the very heart of industrial evolution in the United States. As Robert Heilbronner has said, the 'extraordinary predominance of technology is the decisive characteristic of our times.' (Heilbronner 1962: 7). It has also been an enduring source of turbulence in the American industrial relations system. It is a troublesome phenomenon. By its nature it is intimately involved with conflicting core concerns of both workers and managers, at once offering to managers alluring opportunities for increasing efficiency and to workers threats to job security. Government policy and private pragmatism have driven it inexorably onward as the wheelhorse of economic progress, yet both government and both sides of industry have had difficulty dealing with its consequences.

There are many kinds of technological change. Because of its current importance, both in the American system and elsewhere, this paper focusses chiefly upon one kind of change — mechanisation. This has to do with 'the application of machinery to tasks formerly performed by human . . . labor' (Rezler 1969:5–6). . . .

From *Comparative Labour Relations,* Bulletin 12, 1983, published by Kluwer and Taxation Publisher, The Netherlands. Reprinted with permission.

It appears that mechanisation is occurring at an ever-increasing pace. A recent special report in *Business Week* magazine declared, 'After years of false starts, America's manufacturers are finally in position to make a stunning leap into total automation' (August 3, 1981: 58). Highly sophisticated robots and computers have reached a stage of development and use where they are not only capable of performing a wide range of manufacturing jobs, but are economically feasible. Added to this are developments in word processing and the increased dispersion of existing technology such as automatic scanners.

I. THE INDUSTRIAL RELATIONS SYSTEM AND TECHNOLOGICAL CHANGE

. . .

Our reading of the literature on technological change and industrial relations in the United States reveals no agreed-upon framework for examining particular kinds of change and their consequent problems. We believe that a simple typology, based in part upon some ideas suggested by Barkin, can be useful (1967: 29–38). At the heart of the logic of this typology is the recognition that a crucial aspect of mechanisation is the substitution of capital for labor. This is best understood in terms of a production function, in which a given level of production can be accomplished by various mixes of labor and capital (Fleisher 1970: 120–127; Azevedo 1979: 2). Technological change has different consequences according to the degree to which it causes movement along the production function (i.e., the utilization of more capital and less labor to produce the same goods). The consequences also vary importantly according to whether mechanisation produces increased efficiency and lower production costs, so that the product's price declines, as one would expect this to lead to greater demand for the product and the labor of those that produce it. This would be viewed as a shifting of the production function so that the same, or a greater, amount of labor is required by the firm, even though the proportion of labor is less.

For the purpose of this paper, we will use the following typology of changes at the level of the firm:

Type I.   This involves no change in the mix of labor and capital. The new mechanisation causes no movement along the production function. It has no effect upon either the amount or proportion of labor required, but only upon the kind of work performed.

Type II.   This involves a moderate increase in the ratio of capital to labor. Here mechanisation causes some workers to be redundant, unless the change is accompanied by a favorable shift in the production function.

Type III. This involves a major increase in the ratio of capital to labor. Here, because of significant movement along the production function, a large amount of labor is displaced by capital, unless there is a considerable favorable shift in the production function.

In our view, the type of change would be expected strongly to influence: (1) the seriousness of the problems which are created; and (2) the mechanisms which may serve to solve these problems. The seriousness of the problems increases as one moves from Type I to Type III. As one moves along the scale various mechanisms become more or less adequate. In a Type I change, intrafirm transfers and retraining by the firm are likely to adequately serve the security needs of workers and the cost-containing needs of managers. In a Type II change, when layoffs of moderate size may occur, mechanisms for cushioning the shock of unemployment become necessary. Severance pay, continuation of fringe benefits, assistance in locating new jobs and advance warning of the change are examples of such mechanisms. Here, also, provisions for the avoidance of layoffs, such as guaranteed employment, reduction of the work force by attrition, early retirement, work sharing and shorter work weeks might serve the needs of workers. So long as the number of employees is low, as would be expected in the case of a Type II change, the needs of management to contain costs can be served. In the case of Type III change the mechanisms already considered are less likely to meet the needs of workers and managers. Here, their use to the degree necessary to prevent serious hardships to workers would be destructive of the managerial interest in the profitability of the firm. The magnitude of the problems may be so great as to exceed the ability of a particular industry to cope with them. Under these conditions action by government may become necessary to meet the needs of both workers and managers. Government retraining and relocation programs for workers might serve these needs. This will serve the interests of the public which government serves, if the public benefit provided by encouraging the new technology is sufficiently great to justify the cost of these programs. Of course, such action may not be necessary if either: (1) a shift of the production function occurs, causing greater employment in the firms, or, (2) labor market conditions are such as to furnish a ready supply of new jobs for displaced workers.

II. THE ACTORS AND TECHNOLOGICAL CHANGE

As might be expected, in the U.S. industrial relations system, unions and managers have been the most active actors in instituting technological change and dealing with its consequences. Government action, while important, has tended to be less powerful.

Management

Management has generally served as the prime initiator of such changes. Its right to do so is ordinarily supported by a provision in the omnipresent management rights clause, that says that management retains the right to determine the machinery of manufacture and the methods of work. This places the important decision of whether to institute technological change in the hands of management. Arbitrators have generally interpreted these clauses as giving management broad rights to introduce mechanisation (Elkouri and Elkouri 1973: 412–432). Of course, in nonunion establishments this is also the case.

Unions

The general management right to control the machinery and methods of work has sometimes been limited by unions through collective bargaining agreements. In the Bureau of National Affairs sample of 400 major collective agreements, 17% of them restrict the management's ability to make technological changes. Of these, 50% require discussion with the union prior to institution of the change. Fifteen percent of those containing restrictions, require the employer to make an effort to retain employees displaced by the change. In 20%, retraining of

employees is required. Restrictions on change are particularly common in the printing and maritime industries. They are also found with some frequency in foods, textiles, apparel, communications, and insurance and finance. The Bureau of National Affairs also found that provisions for interplant transfers of workers faced with layoff, for technological or other reasons, were present in a substantial proportion of agreements (Bureau of National Affairs 1979: 64). The U.S. Department of Labor's most recent (1981) analysis of its sample of 1593 major collective agreements shows that 34.7% of agreements covering 49.2% of the workers have some provision for interplant transfer in the event of layoff. Of these, a substantial proportion provides for some maintenance of income for transferred employees (Bureau of Labor Statistics 1981).

Collective agreements include a wide range of provisions dealing with the problems of technical change. A study conducted in the mid-1960s found provisions for: (1) advance notice and consultation; (2) intraplant and interplant transfers; (3) training; (4) pay protection; (5) early retirement; (6) continuation of insurance coverage and other benefits; (7) renegotiation of job classifications and rates; (8) sharing of productivity gains; and, (9) special committees dealing with problems of automation (Perline and Tull 1968). American unions have also attempted to protect their members from job loss by negotiating work rules, broad work jurisdiction, reduction in jobs only by attrition, and protection of long-service workers by seniority (Miller 1979: 17–22). The best known instance of a collective bargaining mechanism for dealing with the problems of technologically displaced workers was the Armour Automation Committee, established in 1959. This was an effort on the part of the company and the union to provide for the needs of displaced workers through the establishment of a special fund, as well as very energetic and innovative actions designed to help workers retrain and relocate (Schultz and Weber 1966). The mechanisms adopted by labor and management are those which would be expected to be adequate to handle Type II changes.

The response of unions to such changes is a subject of obvious importance. It has received extensive study. Most studies have been concerned with predicting what will be the union response. The classic work in this area is by Slichter *et al.* (1960). In this massive study, these writers found five principal types of union response. These were: (1) willing acceptance; (2) opposition; (3) competition — 'attempting to keep the old method in use in competition with the new, perhaps by accepting wage cuts on the old jobs'; (4) encouragement; and (5) adjustment — 'doing what can be done to help the workers immediately affected use it to the best possible advantage and suffer the least possible harm from it' (1960: 344). They concluded that there are four chief determinants of the union response. The first determinant is the nature of the union, principally whether it is a craft or industrial union. They predict more opposition by craft unions. The second is whether the industry, enterprise or occupation is facing stiff competition and whether it is expanding or contracting. Competition makes the union more willing to accept technical change. Expanding employment opportunities usually, but not always, make the union more willing to accept technical change. The third, and most important, determinant is the nature of the change, with respect to which three factors are believed to be important. These are: (1) the number of jobs affected; (2) 'the effect on the degree of skill and responsibility required of workers'; and, (3) 'the effect on the kind of skill or other qualifications required' (1960: 346–47). The fourth determinant is the stage of development of the change and of union policy toward it. When a proposed change is new, and when the union is first presented with it, a policy of opposition is more likely than after the union has had an opportunity to get used to the idea and adjust to it.

A little over a decade after publication of the above study, there was a major study of techno-

logical change in the transportation industry (Levinson *et al.* 1971). This found that the economic environment was the chief variable which determined union responses to technical change. Where jobs are plentiful, resistance to change is low. Where they are scarce, resistance is high. . . . They also found that in some industries the use of incentive payments which gave the worker a stake in increased productivity facilitated union acceptance of technical change.

The latest major study of the response of unions to technological change is by McLaughlin (1979). Her data included the existing empirical literature and 100 interviews with practitioners. Both the literature and the interview data agreed that union acceptance of change was facilitated by a healthy economy and by union leaders' perceptions that: (1) only a small proportion of the jobs in the affected unit would be lost; (2) the change was inevitable; and (3) a quid pro quo for lost jobs could be obtained. . . .

What is the most common response by American unions? Both Slichter *et al.* and McLaughlin agree that it is willing acceptance. According to McLaughlin, adjustment is also quite common. Her study reveals the union response to have been either willing acceptance or adjustment in well over 60% of the cases. McLaughlin finds that the response of opposition is rather rare and, as had been earlier suggested by Slichter *et al.* is often short-lived. Her data do show, however, that the initial union response was opposition in a substantial proportion of the cases (30% of the cases in the literature and 25% of the cases in the interviews). Even after one deducts those cases of opposition which eventually led to another response, the proportion of cases of opposition appears to be quite substantial (24% of literature derived cases and 21% of interview-derived cases). A Conference Board study also found a substantial number of occasions in which major companies had experienced union resistance to such change (Hershfield 1976: 38–41). We conclude that, although American unions have generally accepted technological change, the probability of an unfavorable union response is sufficiently high to warrant concern about it.

Government

Government deals with the problems of technological change by: (1) regulating, through labor laws, the collective bargaining relationship through which labor and management handle change; (2) attempting to encourage such change; (3) instituting mechanisms for mitigating the effects of dislocations caused by change; and, (4) producing studies of change and its effects.

Two areas of labor law are particularly important in their effects upon technological change. The first of these is the set of principles which determines those subjects over which the employer is obligated to bargain. With regard to a subject which is not a 'mandatory' subject of bargaining, but merely 'permissive' the employer may take action without negotiating with the union. While it is clear that American employers have an obligation to bargain over the effects of such change, the law is unclear as to whether they have to bargain over the decision to make the change in the first instance. Several recent cases suggest that there may be an area of management prerogative which includes decisions to adopt technical change (*International Harvester Co.* v. *NLRB; Seafarers Local 777* v. *NLRB; Laredo Packing Co; Fibreboard Paper Products Corp.* v. *NLRB; Brockway Motor Trucks* v. *NLRB*). It has been argued rather persuasively that employers should be required to bargain over whether a change should occur whenever the change has significant effects upon union interests (*Harvard Law Review* 1971: 1822–1855). Although this seems a sensible position, the prevailing political climate in the United States may well mean that the courts uphold unilateral management action.

The second main area of law relates to strikes and boycotts in response to technological change. The courts have approved union action for the purpose of resisting a change which has taken work from union members. This behavior is arguably subject to legal prohibitions against secondary boycotts. However, it has been held to be legitimate where it is for the purpose of preserving work traditionally performed by the workers taking the action (*National Woodwork Manufacturers Association* v. *NLRB*). Even union action which constrained employer hours of operation has been held not to violate anti-trust laws (*Amalgamated Meat Cutters Local 189* v. *Jewel Tea Co.*).

Government has increasingly adopted policies aimed at encouraging change. The latest action is the 1981 legislation which gives new tax advantages to businesses investing in new equipment. Union representatives believe that provisions of this legislation have strong potential for encouraging mechanisation in some already sensitive areas, such as automatic scanners in the retail trade. . . .

The U.S. Department of Labor periodically publishes an excellent series of research reports on the impact of technological change on selected industries. These reports typically explain the nature of the technological development, its labor implications, and its diffusion throughout the industry. Also included is description of the type of adjustments made to deal with displaced workers (Bureau of Labor Statistics (BLS), U.S. Department of Labor, Technological Change Series).

III. ISSUES ASSOCIATED WITH TECHNOLOGICAL CHANGE

In the United States, the fundamental issues are: (1) what changes are adopted; (2) what are the consequences of the changes; and (3) what policies are adopted by the parties to deal with the consequences. In this diverse and fragmented system, it is most convenient to address these questions in three different industries which are currently experiencing dramatic changes. These are: (1) telecommunications; (2) manufacturing; and (3) retailing.

Telecommunications

The field of telecommunications is experiencing rapid technological development at all levels. Modern telecommunications is the combination of two previously existing processes. The first, called switching, is rapidly becoming dominated by electronic switching systems (ESS) which have substantially reduced installation and maintenance manpower requirements. The second process, that of signal transmission, has continuously evolved through the last decade, but the recent introduction of fibre optic cables will have a dramatic impact. These and other scientific innovations, diversification of firms currently dominating the field, and employment of alternative methods such as satellites and computers will contribute to rapidly rising levels of input while decreasing labor content.

The single most significant development in the industry has been the modern silicon-chip microprocessor based ESS. This innovation will soon affect everyone from operators, to service representatives, to test desk technicians. Another development having a substantial impact on the industry has been the more widespread use of satellite micro-wave communication. The next wave of innovation will probably be dominated by changes in transmission capacity through fibre optic cables and computers.

The effects of technological innovation begin with employment in the basic manufacturing of the equipment. At Western Electric, the manufacturing division for the Bell System, employment dropped from 39,000 in 1970 to 17,400 in 1980 (Communications Workers of America (CWA) 1979: 11). Redesign of components has eliminated many manufacturing steps and reduced labor time from 75 to 11 manhours per phone set. One microprocessor replaces 350 parts in the older equipment. It is estimated that all electrical products have only 25% as much labor in them as their predecessors. The employment outlook is also cause for concern for office and operations personnel. Where 10 workers were formerly required to operate a step-by-step switching office, this requirement is reduced to three for an ESS office. Following the same line of technical advancement, there will be a 75% reduction in the need for labor in faultfinding maintenance, repairing, and installation.

There is currently an active debate on the impact of these changes on employment. The Bell System projects a four percent growth in employment between 1980 and 1985. At General Telephone and Electronics, no growth is expected and attrition will not keep pace with the reduced human resource requirement. The biggest decreases in employment, recently reported by Rochester Bell, were blamed on competition, not new technology (CWA 1979: 12).

The changes occurring in telecommunications are of sufficient magnitude to lead to a significant movement along the production function, producing a Type III change. However, the burgeoning international telecommunications market for the products of this new technology may at least partly offset the employment-reducing effects inherent in a Type III change, rendering the usual kind of actions by labor and management adequate to meet the need of workers and managers (*Business Week,* February 11, 1980: 73–76).

In collective bargaining, labor and management have adopted several strategies for dealing with the problems of such changes. One interesting strategy is the development of joint labor-management committees to deal with a variety of problems, including those of technological change. These provide a consultative mechanism which may complement the more adversarial collective bargaining mechanisms. Huge training expenditures over several years have tried to deal with some of the effects of change. The CWA which represents a large majority of telecommunication workers, has strongly urged the establishment of government training programs. Collective bargaining agreement provisions for advance notification, retraining, transfer and other aids to adjustment, have been common in the industry for several years (BLS 1979b: 39). . . .

In the telecommunications industry, change appears to be reaching dramatic proportions. The union response has moved, in our judgment, from willing acceptance toward adjustment, as an extensive framework of mechanisms for dealing with the effects of change has been developed. The growth of joint labor-management committees may signal the growth of avenues of worker influence over the decision to adopt particular changes. If so, at least subtle opposition may develop.

Manufacturing

The most pervasive single technological development in manufacturing is computer assisted manufacturing (CAM) which utilises robots. We now see everything from relatively simple second generation automated machines to 'smart' robots capable of seeing, making their own adjustments and doing detailed assembly jobs. Claims abound that robots may replace thousands of workers. Their use is increasing in the auto industry, in electrical component manufacturing, and in steel and other related machine fabrication.

In 1980, there were approximately 3500 industrial robots in place in the United States. In 1981, 2000 units were sold. Sales are expected to reach 8000 per year by 1985. This represents a capital outlay of over $600 million by manufacturing firms. The core technology for the operation is the computeraided design (CAD) subsystem which provides the software and control components. The physical component, called CAM, that actually performs the task is integrated with the CAD to form a fully operational production unit (*Business Week,* August 3, 1981: 58–67).

Nowhere is the impact of robotics expected to be more important than in the automobile industry. One of the reasons that this industry is in the forefront in considering the use of robotics is the high level of pay and benefits of the American car worker. Robots specifically adapted for automobile plants can easily be taught over 3000 different actions, on seven different planes of movement, with no fatigue or boredom. In addition, the new generation of robots is very flexible, making them compatible with the industry's need for changes related to new models. . . .

Combined with the effects of foreign competition, changes in the types of automobiles manufactured, conditions in the domestic economy, and other factors, these changes bode ill for employment prospects in the automobile industry. Predictions for job losses by 1990 generally run in the neighborhood of 200,000 jobs (Byron *et al.* 1981).

The changes in the American automobile industry appear to be of Type III magnitude. Unlike the situation in telecommunications, there is little prospect of immediate increases in employment resulting from these changes, though this may well happen in the long run. Indeed, unemployment caused by technological change will exacerbate the present situation in this declining industry. Government action to bridge the gap between the short run detrimental effects and the long run positive effects would seem to be a sensible response, but the current political climate may prevent this. . . .

UAW demands concerning technological change in the last round of negotiations at Ford provide some evidence of the expected direction for future talks. The union sought: (1) union access to all information created by computer systems; (2) company assurances that computers would not be used to study, discipline or establish time standards for workers; (3) creation of a 'data committee-man position' in each local to monitor technical change; (4) establishment of a technology committee at the local and national level; (5) right to strike on technology issues with national union approval; (6) company-paid retraining; and (7) guarantees to protect workers against manpower reductions. Most of these demands were not achieved, but the establishment of a joint National Committee on Technological

Progress was a significant development. This committee meets monthly and is charged with the responsibility of decreasing any negative impacts of innovation on workers. The frequency of its meetings seems to indicate a serious attempt to confront the challenge. . . .

The situation in electronic equipment manufacturing is somewhat different. The move toward application of robots has been more gradual, primarily because the technology has just now become sufficiently sophisticated to be of real benefit. The older machines, capable of single functions and movement in only one direction, were not profitable for most small assembly jobs. The newest generation, capable of smooth continuous motion and using servomotors, is of more use to electronic manufacturers.

Because the technology is in a relatively early stage of development and the capital investment required for its adoption is substantial, the unions in the industry have some lead time to determine their policy with respect to it. One of the principal unions in the industry, the International Union of Electrical, Radio and Machine Workers (IUE), has already developed an extensive policy statement which abjures opposition but pledges concern about the adverse effects of technological changes. This union has declared that the use of robots should be restricted so that they are used only on dangerous work, and in such a way that workers are protected from malfunctioning robots. They argue that robots should not be used to check on workers' performance. The union also intends to insist upon advance notice, adjustment of employment levels only through attrition, and company-paid retraining of workers. At the level of public policy, the union argues that tax advantages for investment in the new technology should be limited to those firms which invest in the community affected by declines in employment (IUE 1980: 6–11).

The concern in the steel industry is not so much with the dramatic impact of a single technological innovation but the gradual decrease in work force requirements. So gradual, as a matter of fact, is the change that union leaders believe that creeping technology may actually be going unnoticed in the local plant. The general approach in the steel industry has been to move toward some kind of 'lifetime security guarantee.' This would involve some guarantee of work or pay to all workers. Current collective agreements provide for a worker to choose either a 15 percent decrease in wages or a layoff, compensated at 65 percent of normal pay for one year. Workers selecting a layoff have no right to be recalled to employment. Agreements also provide for earnings protection, work-sharing, supplemental unemployment benefits and joint labor-management committees (Ignatius 1980: 1).

In manufacturing it appears that we see all Types of change. The union responses generally look more like adjustment than willing acceptance. This is perhaps typified by a statement by the International Association of Machinists, that the union knows that new technology has arrived and is necessary, but is unwilling to give employers a 'blank check' where technological change is concerned.

Retailing

After a somewhat stable 20-year period, revolutionary changes have begun to occur in the retail trades. The effects of technology in this industry are more a diffusion of existing innovations than the creation of new devices. More stores are using premarked merchandise, centrally prepackaged specialty items and the 'super-store' concept, all of which are compatible with the newly popularised electronic scanning cash register.

The single most important change is the rapid increase in the use of electronic scanners. The device itself is generally a laser beam which focuses on a small bar code on each item and signals a mini-computer to match that item with its price, which is already stored in a memory. That price is then printed and displayed on a register console.

Although similar technology has been available for approximately 20 years, it's only since about 1976 that widespread application has occurred. . . . A projection prepared for the Food Marketing Institute speculates that by the end of 1982, approximately one-third of the nation's 35,000 supermarkets will be scanner equipped, and near total conversion will be accomplished by the end of the 1980s (Food Marketing Institute 1980).

One of the first advantages to be realised through the scanners is the total elimination of price-marking of each item. Labour requirements per unit of sales are reduced. Both total jobs and total hours will be decreased by the elimination of repricing for sales or promotions, spot checks and periodic inventories. They will also mean shorter training time for checkers (Salmons 1981: 27–28). Inventory control, ordering, and theft detection are also improved by the use of the scanners. . . .

It appears that, in some areas of the retail trade, Type II and Type III changes are occurring. The likely result of this is increased sales in technologically advanced segments of the industry, which may keep employment fairly high in those segments. In addition, because of the large proportions of temporary and part-time employees in this industry, any declines in employment may be managed through attrition.

In the past, when technological change did occur in unionized operations, it was covered only by general seniority layoff provisions and retraining benefits. By the middle of the 1970s about 25% of major agreements contained provisions for advance notification of the change. By 1976, the largest agreement (25,000 workers) of the then Retail Clerks union (now UFCW) contained a guarantee against layoff caused by technological change. This has since been adopted for full-time employees in one region (BLS 1977: 54).

Recently, the UFCW has become much more assertive in dealing with technological change. It has begun to demand more data from employers on employment and hours before and after conversion to electronic scanners. In an October 1980, report, the UFCW indicated that employer refusals to supply it with this informa-

tion had been declared illegal by the National Labor Relations Board (UFCW 1980: 27).

In certain segments of the retail trade large, but manageable, decreases in employment appear to be occurring. The union response, which has been willing acceptance in the past, appears to be moving in the direction of adjustment as it becomes clear that more full-time employees will be affected. . . .

Clerical

Office clerical occupations, which are spread across a number of industries, have been subject to increasing mechanization as word processing systems have grown more sophisticated and more widely used. From the simple paper tape system of the 1950s, word processing has progressed to magnetic tape and disc systems with impressive capacities for flexibility, durability and storage. Ink jet and image printers provide greatly improved speed and clarity. Developments in low cost, efficient, computers have paralleled these improvements in office equipment. The principal changes in office clerical work which flow from these changes in technology appear to be greatly increased productivity, changed skill requirements, and the institution of specialised tasks performed in teams.

The effects on levels of office clerical employment are unclear. . . . Some studies have concluded that the effects on employment are negligible (Vail 1978; Connell 1980). A study by the International Information/Word Processing Association concluded that, after the adoption of modern word-processing equipment, 7% of the companies surveyed showed increases in employment, 42% experienced no change, and 40% reported a reduction (entirely through attrition) (IWP 1981). Although this Association interprets these results as showing little effect on employment, they appear to reflect employment reductions in a substantial proportion of the firms studied. There does appear to be an increasing demand for office work, combined with a shortage of office clerical workers. Therefore even though the changes may reach Type III magnitude, something akin to a production function shift, combined with a shortage of labor, may be sufficient to compensate for what might otherwise be dramatic employment effects.

In the United States, office clerical occupations, at least outside government employment, are largely nonunion. The most important question with respect to the union response is, therefore, the effects of these changes on unionization of these workers. We are not especially sanguine in this respect. For those workers who acquire the new skills, wages should increase and jobs should be plentiful. With high pay, and the ability to leave one organization and enter another, the impetus for unionization would seem to be limited. Of course, as school teachers discovered in the 1960s, these are just the circumstances under which the ability to unionize is greatest. In the long run, because office clerical jobs have become more similar to manufacturing work, and as the close ties between boss and secretary accordingly fade away, these workers may become more susceptible to unionization. Those workers who lack the skill to operate the new equipment may find themselves with a great will to unionize because of threats to their jobs, but without the ability to do so because they are so readily expendible.

One engine of unionization may be the demonstration effect of union gains for those office clerical employees who are unionized. Unions, such as the Newspaper Guild, which have members who operate word processors, have negotiated rest periods, free eye examinations and glasses, and special lighting and furniture (*Wall Street Journal* 1977: 1). Furthermore, the existence of a potential cadre of organizers familiar with this occupation (unionized government office clericals) provides a new element which may facilitate unionization.

IV. CONCLUSIONS

Technological change is advancing rapidly in American industry. The effects of new changes upon workers and the public interest are as yet unclear. Although the long run effects are likely to be beneficial, there may be substantial disruption of employment in the short run. The American industrial relations system has no central mechanism for dealing with the social problems of work. Accordingly, instituting and coping with such change is taking place in a wide variety of ways.

In terms of the framework which we have posited, it appears that many of the current changes are of Type II or Type III. The crucial question is whether the changes themselves, or other factors such as increased general demand for goods, will produce changes in the production functions of firms, so that the numbers of workers employed will not drop dramatically. Even if fewer workers are needed by the economy as a whole, this may not create serious problems if a declining birth rate and the increasing age of the American workforce creates a shortage of labor. If change does create massive dislocations of workers and unemployment, government action to mitigate the short run adverse effects will be a compelling need. Even if this problem does not reach great magnitude, it seems to us that it is sound to argue, as the unions do, that society in general, and not just affected workers, should pay the price for the social benefit of increased productivity and wealth.

Union response to technological change is likely to continue to be pragmatic. American unions have generally accepted the need for new technology. Where changes reach the magnitude that appears likely in a number of industries, unions may move from willing acceptance, to adjustment, to opposition. Even a policy of adjustment may impose substantial costs upon firms wishing to institute technical change. Union officials are concerned about this, not wishing unionized firms to become uncompetitive with nonunion firms. Although the AFL-CIO has not recently issued a major policy pronouncement on this subject, its preferred solution (expressed to one of the authors by an AFL-CIO official) appears to be that society should assume the reasonable costs of adjustment, rather than leaving this burden upon the shoulders of labor or management.

As the performance of work has become more predominantly performed by machines, we have seen some shifting of the relative power of labor and management in collective bargaining. A fully automated plant, such as exists in the chemical industry, can be run by supervisors. It has long been argued that, for workers, this may lead to the strike declining in utility. On the other hand, if the plant can be shutdown, the automated operation's savings in wages during a strike are less than in one which is labor intensive. The machinery may also become more vulnerable to sabotage by disgruntled workers. The skilled workers who maintain the machines may become more powerful, while operatives lose power proportionately. Most importantly, the ability of the American labor movement to deal with technological change may determine whether it is able to maintain even the degree of power in society which it now has. In order to survive as an effective force it must find ways to facilitate needed technical change, while at the same time protecting the interests of workers. This is a truly Herculean challenge, but one that a strong movement rooted in the rank-and-file should be able to meet successfully.

REFERENCES

Azevedo, R. E. 1979 "Productivity bargaining: A 'promising challenge to the public sector," in Victor V. Veysey and Giles S. Hall (eds.) *The new world of managing human resources,* Pasedena, Calif.: Industrial Relations Center, California Institute of Technology.

Amalgamated Meat Cutters Local 189 v. *Jewel Tea Co.,* 227 NLRB 1189 (1977).

Barkin, S. 1967. "A systems approach to technological change." *Labor Law Journal.* (January): 29–38.

Brockway Motor Trucks v. *NLRB* 84 LC 10,758 (3rd Cir., 1978).

Bureau of Labor Statistics (BLS). United States Department of Labor, Technological Change Series.
1973   Bulletin 1774. *Outlook for technology and manpower in printing and publishing.*

1974   Bulletin 1817. *Technological change and manpower trends in six industries.* (textiles, lumber, tires, aluminum, health services).

1975   Bulletin 1856. *Technological change and manpower trends in five industries.* (pulp and paper, hydraulic cement, steel, aircraft and missles, wholesale trades).

1977   Bulletin 1961. *Technological change and its impact in five industries.* (apparel, footwear, motor vehicles, railroads, retail trade).

1979a   Bulletin 2005. *Technological change and its impact in five energy industries.* (coal, oil and gas, petroleum refining, petroleum pipeline, electric and gas utilities).

1979b   Bulletin 2033. *Technology and labor in five industries,* (bakery products, concrete, air transportation, telephone communications, insurance).

Bureau of National Affairs. 1979. *Basic patterns in union contracts,* 9th Edition. Washington: BNA, 64.

Business Week. 1980. "A market where the U.S. Lags." (11 February): 73–76.

Business Week. 1981. "The speedup in automation." (3 August): 58–67.

Byron, G., O'Donnell, J. and Kouetch, G. 1981. *"Facilities planning and regional employment assessment."* Cambridge, Massachusetts: U.S. Department of Transportation. Transportation Systems Center.

Communications Workers of America (CWA). 1979. *Technology-its impact on the communication workers of America.* The 1979 Conference: A Final Report. Washington. 1980. *The 'Settlement' Guide-1980.*

Connell, J. J. 1980. "Office of the 80s: 'productivity impact.'" *Business Week.* (18 February): 22.

Elkouri, F. and Elkouri, E. A. 1973. *How arbitration works.* Washington, D.C.: Bureau of National Affairs.

Fiberboard Paper Products Corp. v. *NLRB,* 379 U.S. 204 (1964).

Fleisher, B. M. 1970. *Labor economics.* Englewood Cliffs, N.J.: Prentice-Hall.

Food Marketing Institute. 1980. *The food industry speaks.*

Harvard Law Review. 1971. "Automation and collective bargaining" 84: 1822–55.

Heilbronner, R. L. 1962. "The impact of technology: The historic debate." *In:* Dunlop, J. T. (ed.) *Automation and technological change.* Englewood Cliffs, N.J.: Prentice-Hall.

Hershfield, D. C. 1976. "Barriers to increased labor productivity." *The Conference Board Record.* (July): 38–41.

Ignatius, P. 1980. "Steel industry talks on lifetime security." *The Wall Street Journal.* (4 April): 1.

International Harvester Co. v. *NLRB.* 88 LC 12, 042 (9th Cir., 1980).

International Information/Word Processing Association. 1981. ''The video display terminal controversy.'' *Words.* Vol. 10, No. 1 (June-July): 34-38.

International Union of Electrical, Radio, and Machine Workers. 1980. *Constitutional convention paper on robotisation.* (15 September).

Levinson, H. M., Rehmus, C. M., Goldberg, J. P. and Kahn, M. L. 1971. *Collective bargaining and technological change in American transportation.* Evanston, Illinois: Northwestern University.

Laredo Packing Co., 254 NLRB n 1, 106 LRRM 1350 (1981).

McLaughlin, D. B. 1979. *The impact of labor unions on the rate and direction of technological innovation.* National Technical Information Service, PB-295 084.

Miller, B. A. 1979. ''Providing assistance to displaced workers.'' *Monthly Labor Review.* (May): 17-22.

National Woodwork Mfrs. Assn. v. *NLRB,* 386 U.S. 612 (1967).

Perline, M. M. and Tull, K. S. 1968. ''The impact of automation on collective bargaining agreements.'' *Labor Law Journal.* (February): 693-698.

Rezler, J. 1969. *Automation and industrial labor.* New York: Random House.

Salmons, S. 1981. ''Impact of checkout scanners.'' *New York Times.* (5 October): B1-27-28.

Seafarers, Local 777 v. *NLRB,* 84 LC n 10,865 (DC Cir., 1978).

Schultz, G. R. and Weber, A. R. 1966. *Strategies for the displaced worker.* New York: Harper & Row.

Slichter, S. H., Healy, J. J. and Livernash, R. 1960. *The impact of collective bargaining on management.* Washington: The Brookings Institution.

United Food and Commercial Workers (UFCW). 1980. The retail food industry — How the union sees it (29 September).

Vail, H. 1978. ''The automated office.'' *In:* Cornish, E. (ed.) *1999 — the world of tomorrow.* Washington: World Future Society.

Wall Street Journal. 1977. ''Computer terminals in the office.'' (11 November): 1:5.

SECTION 5
Contract Administration

INTRODUCTION

The collective bargaining process does not end when the union and management sign the labor agreement. Collective bargaining continues on a day-to-day basis as the parties operate under the new agreement. Disagreements inevitably arise as the parties apply and interpret their contract. To handle these disputes over the administration of the agreement, most labor contracts include a grievance procedure with binding arbitration. Grievance handling mechanisms have been described as the heart of union-management contracts because their effectiveness largely determines how well the parties adhere to the labor agreement.[1]

A grievance procedure is a multi-step process that is usually initiated when an employee believes managerial actions violate some provision of the labor agreement. Initially, the employee and the union steward attempt to resolve the disagreement with the first level supervisor. If this effort leads to an agreement, the grievance process ends. However, if attempts to resolve the issue at the first step fail, then higher levels of management and the union will become involved. Through grievance meetings, the parties attempt to resolve the dispute. Most commonly, grievance procedures have four steps with each successive step involving higher levels of the union and management hierarchies. The objective is to identify mutually acceptable solutions to the problem, thereby resolving the grievance. However, if the parties are not able to handle the dispute through the grievance procedure, the disagreement is then submitted to a neutral, third party for final and binding resolution.

Submitting a dispute arising during the life of the contract to a third party for resolution is known as grievance arbitration and is the final step in approximately 94% of the contracts with grievance procedures.

Functions of Grievance Procedures

Grievance procedures serve a number of useful functions for both the union and management.

These functions have been placed into five major categories.[2]

Conflict management. Before the development of grievance procedures with arbitration, strikes and slow downs were commonly used to resolve disputes arising during the life of the contract. The grievance procedure provides a means for resolving contract interpretation and administration problems without having to resort to tests of economic strength. Additionally, as noted in Section 4, a review of the parties' experiences under the grievance procedure can help identify problem areas in the existing labor agreement. This is especially useful as the parties prepare for upcoming negotiations. Problem contract language and unmet needs can be identified by looking at the types of grievances filed. These problems can then be addressed in the next round of negotiations.

Contract clarification. No matter how hard the parties attempt to eliminate ambiguous contract language, some ambiguity is likely to exist in any contract. These ambiguities can lead to interpretation problems after the contract is implemented. In addition to unintentional ambiguity, the parties occasionally include deliberately vague language in the agreement. Rather than bargaining to impasse on the wording of a provision, the parties can intentionally select ambiguous wording in order not to extend negotiations or risk a strike. Then the parties can address the specific meaning of the language during the life of the agreement through the grievance process and arbitration if necessary.

Communication. The grievance procedure offers a well-defined, dignified way for employees to express themselves and process complaints that might otherwise not come to light. In addition to providing employees with a mechanism for expressing their discontent, managers are provided a formal mechanism for communicating with the union. This is especially useful when day-to-day communications between the parties are not particularly good.

Due process. By allowing for third party intervention (arbitration) when the parties cannot resolve a disagreement through the grievance procedure, impartiality is brought into the process. This ensures that most disputes arising during the life of the contract are not resolved unilaterally by management. Similarly, unions are provided the opportunity to challenge management action but they are not given the right to unilaterally reverse it. The possibility of having a case reviewed by an arbitrator pressures the parties to go beyond the emotionalism enshrouding many grievances and focus on the more rational, contract-based issues and evidence.

Strength enhancement. Workers employed under collective bargaining agreements are protected from arbitrary and capricious discipline decisions. While management has a right to discipline and discharge employees, the grievance process insures that an individual employee will be able to have the disciplinary action reviewed and set aside if found to be unfair. Being able to protect employees' rights through the grievance procedure helps unions encourage loyalty by its members. It also serves as a regular reminder of the union's presence in the bargaining unit during the life of the labor agreement.

As can be seen, the grievance procedure has the potential to serve a number of functions useful to the union, management, and individual employees. Well-designed, effectively implemented and operated grievance procedures contribute greatly to sound labor-management relations. The readings in this section of the book introduce you to the grievance process and types of issues commonly discussed as part of the grievance handling procedure.

Grievance Arbitration

The arbitration of grievances is the other major topic covered in this section. The term arbitration is used to describe situations in which a neutral, third party resolves problems by issuing decisions that are binding on both parties. Arbitration of disputes arising while the parties are negotiating a new contract is known as interest arbitration. With interest arbitration, the parties submit issues unresolved at the bargaining table to an arbitrator instead of striking over them. This is used extensively in the public sector and is discussed in detail in Section 6. However, in private sector situations where the parties prefer not to or cannot endure the costs or disruptions of strikes, interest arbitration is also used. Such is the case in the steel industry where the parties, in 1973, agreed to submit unresolved contract issues to arbitration. The second major form of arbitration is known as grievance or rights arbitration, and is discussed in this section of the book. It involves the use of neutral, third parties to resolve disputes arising during the life of an existing contract. This is the type of arbitration found as a final step in most grievance procedures.

Arbitration has been part of the industrial relations scene since the late 1800s, but emerged as a major dispute-resolution device in labor-management relations only since World War II. The War Labor Board's experiences during World War II clearly indicated that arbitration could be used to resolve labor-management disputes. It was demonstrated that arbitration was an effective way to resolve disagreements arising during the life of a contract over the proper application or interpretation of the agreement. Grievance arbitration proved to be such an effective approach to conflict resolution that the U.S. Congress, the National Labor Relations Board (NLRB) and the courts have supported its use for resolving private sector rights disputes.

When the parties are unable to resolve a dispute through the grievance procedure, either party can request that it be settled through arbitration. In most cases going to arbitration, a hearing is conducted at which both the union and management have the opportunity to present the facts and arguments making up the case.

Such cases can be placed into two broad categories, discipline and contract-interpretation cases. When you examine the arbitration cases presented at the end of this book, you will find a number of each type of situation.

In discipline cases, the arbitrator usually must decide whether or not there was "just cause" for the company's disciplinary action. While many labor agreements require that discipline or discharge of employees must be for just cause, a definition of "just cause" is not provided. It then becomes the arbitrator's job to review the facts of the case to determine whether or not the company had just or proper cause for its disciplinary decisions. No universal standard exists for determining whether just cause is present. However, Arbitrator Carroll Daugherty posed seven questions to be used when deciding whether or not the company has sufficient grounds for its disciplinary actions. If the answer to any of the questions is "no," just cause probably does not exist. The seven questions are:

1. Did the company give the employee fore-warning or foreknowledge of the possible or probable disciplinary consequences of the employee's conduct?

2. Was the company's rule or managerial order reasonably related to (a) the orderly, efficient, and safe operation of the company's business and (b) the performance that the company might properly expect of the employee?

3. Did the company, before administering discipline to an employee, make an effort to discover whether the employee did, in fact, violate or disobey a rule or order of management?

4. Was the company's investigation conducted fairly and objectively?

5. At the investigation, did the "judge" obtain substantial evidence or proof that the employee was guilty as charged?

6. Has the company applied its rules, orders, and penalties evenhandedly and without discrimination to all employees?

7. Was the degree of discipline administered by the company in a particular case reasonably related to (a) the seriousness of the employee's proven offense and (b) the record of the employee's service with the company?[3]

In contract interpretation cases, the parties disagree over the meaning of a provision in their labor agreement. The arbitrator's task in such cases is to ascertain the intent of the parties when they negotiated the language in question. To do so, the arbitrator looks first to the contract itself. It is necessary to try to resolve the dispute in terms of the contract language and the general interpretation of the agreement when read as a whole. In situations where the parties may disagree on the meaning of a specific provision, the arbitrator will look to see if other parts of the agreement provide an interpretation to the language in dispute. If the arbitrator cannot determine the meaning of the ambiguous language by examining the entire agreement, it is then possible to go outside the contract and look at other factors when determining the intent of the parties when they negotiated the language.

Past practice and bargaining history are two commonly used approaches for providing meaning to ambiguous contract language. When basing a decision on past practice, the arbitrator is attempting to provide the contract with the same meaning the parties did when they applied it in the past. In their classic book on the arbitration process, Elkouri and Elkouri state that for a past practice to be binding, it must be unequivocal, clearly stated and acted upon, and readily ascertainable over a reasonable period of time.[4] If a practice has these attributes, it is appropriate to conclude that the parties have, at least implicitly, agreed on the practice. In these situations, the arbitrator interprets the contract language in question in line with the parties' past behavior. Some-

times, the arbitrator will rely on bargaining history to provide meaning to ambiguous contract language. While oral statements made during negotiations cannot be used to modify unambiguous contract language, the parties' discussions during negotiations can be used to interpret ambiguous contract language. Arbitrators will give weight to testimony about what was said during negotiations and to notes taken while the parties were bargaining. Such information may shed light on the intent of the parties when the language in question was being negotiated.

INTRODUCTION TO THE READINGS

An Overview of the Grievance Process

James Kuhn's article provides the reader with a general overview of the grievance process. He argues that the grievance process allows the parties to solve their mutual problems and share the administration of the plant. Through this process, collective bargaining becomes a continuous, i.e., daily process. Kuhn points out that when there is a grievance procedure for handling disputes arising under the labor agreement, a new function requiring staffing and a commitment of resources is created. The first level supervisors, the shop steward, and the workers become directly involved in the collective bargaining process as they attempt to handle contract administration problems. As they do so, Kuhn asserts that both employees and managers benefit. Employees are afforded, through the grievance process, a means to protect the rights they received as a result of the labor agreement. At the same time, first level supervisors have a mechanism for seeking changes and work rules needed to respond to unforeseen production problems. Because of the grievance process, workers have greater independence and managers have greater autonomy in the work place.

In addition to the basic function served by the grievance process Kuhn also identifies two secondary functions. First, the grievance process is a means of communication, since information is transmitted between the parties as complaints are processed. Secondly, it provides training for the people involved in its operation. As grievances are handled, first level supervisors learn the value of persuasion, political compromise, and bargaining. Union officials learn the same lessons. Through this process, both groups obtain greater insights into labor-management relations.

The Grievance Process in Practice

From Kuhn's overview of the grievance process, attention turns to a detailed discussion of the grievance process in practice. Dalton and Todor's article reviews the grievance experience of one West Coast local union. Their study provides some very interesting insights into the nature of the grievance process and its implications for the involved parties. The information they present concerning the time involved in processing grievances suggests how expensive and disruptive that procedure can be.

Dalton and Todor also examine the types of grievances handled. They found that suspensions and seniority issues were the most common categories of grievance issues. They further found that unions were least successful in the categories in which most grievances were filed and were more likely to experience a favorable outcome to grievances in categories in which relatively few grievances were filed. The authors conclude by pointing out that while the grievance process is expensive and disruptive, it is essential to labor-management relations in many organizations. Further, despite the problems associated with having a grievance procedure, probably no better alternative is available to the parties.

Grievance Arbitration and the Legal Environment

The legal environment is a major reason that arbitration became the primary mechanism for resolving disputes arising during the life of a labor agreement. The National Labor Relations Act

(NLRA) encouraged the use of arbitration. Later, the courts and the NLRB supported the use of arbitration. Consequently, when the parties agree in the labor contract to utilize a private system of dispute settlement (arbitration), they will have to live with that arrangement. Because of the way public policy regarding arbitration has evolved, the final and binding nature of grievance arbitration is now firmly established. As a result, it is very difficult to get the courts to vacate an arbitration award or to not direct the parties to arbitration if their contract calls for it.

C. Ray Gullett provides a concise description of the current public policy as it affects grievance arbitration. He points out that the 1957 *Lincoln Mills* decision ruled that arbitration clauses could be enforced through law suits filed under Section 301(a) of the NLRA. Then, the Steelworkers Trilogy, three Supreme Court decisions handed down in 1960, strengthened and established the legitimacy of the arbitration process. As a result of these decisions, the primary responsibility for the arbitration process rests with the arbitrator, with little possibility for legal intervention. The thrust of these decisions was to make the arbitration decision final and binding.

In situations where an action violates both the contract and is an unfair labor practice under the NLRA, there was a possibility that the arbitrator's decision would not be final and binding. After going to arbitration, it could be possible for the losing party to then file charges with the NLRB. As a matter of law, the NLRB is not obligated to honor the arbitrator's decisions. Gullett points out that the NLRB could hear unfair labor practice cases that were also contract violations. However, the Board has chosen not to do so. Gullett describes the development of Board policy that established criteria that, if met, will allow it to defer to an arbitrator's decision. It is also possible for an action to violate both the labor agreement and the Civil Rights Act. For example, the termination of a woman because of her sex could violate the nondiscrimination clause in the labor contract as well as the Civil Rights Act.

In such cases, the EEOC (Equal Employment Opportunity Commission) will not defer to arbitration. In its *Alexander* v. *Gardner-Denver* decision, the Supreme Court ruled that an employee is entitled to file charges with the EEOC even if the matter has already been arbitrated. As a result, persons whose discrimination claims have been rejected by an arbitrator can still file charges with the EEOC and ultimately have the case reviewed by the courts.

Gullett concludes his article by talking about the implications of the legal environment for the arbitration process. He suggests that arbitration is not truly a private process. Whenever statutory law such as the Civil Rights Act butts up against the arbitration process, the law must be given more weight than the labor agreement. As a result, arbitrators are put into a difficult position of having to rule on grievances that involve statutory issues. Not only will arbitrators have to have a firm understanding of the labor relations and personnel policies, they will also have to be well versed on the laws relevant to the case under review. This development may exacerbate the current shortage of acceptable arbitrators.

Improving the Arbitration Process

The next three articles look at different ways to improve the effectiveness of the arbitration process. Arbitration evolved as the preferred way to handle contract disputes because it was relatively quick, inexpensive, and understandable to the parties. Over the years, arbitration has become more expensive, time consuming, and legalistic. As a result, the arbitration process is not as responsive to the parties' needs as it has been in the past. Because of the importance of the need to maintain the viability of the arbitration process, three articles are presented that discuss different approaches to making arbitration work more effectively.

Goldberg and Brett argue that one way to avoid the costs, time delays, and other problems associated with arbitration is to avoid going to ar-

bitration. As an alternative, they discuss the mediation of grievances, a system that would allow the parties a choice after the final step of the internal grievance procedure. They could opt for mediation rather than arbitration. Mediation is a less formal process where the mediator tries to help the parties reach a mutually acceptable solution to the problem. If the mediation process fails to yield an agreement, the mediator tells the parties how the dispute would probably be resolved if it went to arbitration. This advisory opinion from the mediator is then used as a basis for further discussion by the parties. If the parties are unable to reach agreement, they are then free to arbitrate the matter.

In an effort to determine whether grievance mediation could be effective, Goldberg and Brett reviewed 153 grievances that were taken to mediation. Of these, 89 percent were settled at the mediation stage. The authors report that mediation of grievances proved to be a quicker and less expensive approach than arbitration. They conclude that the mediation of grievances is a viable alternative to submitting them to arbitration.

Peter A. Veglahn's article is also concerned with the time and cost problems associated with grievance arbitration. His article examines a number of different approaches the parties can take to make the arbitration process more efficient. Some of his suggestions relate to better preparation for arbitration. Pre-arbitration conferences and the joint stipulation of facts and the issues to be arbitrated make the hearing go more quickly. Veglahn also looks at some of the practices becoming popular in arbitration that take more time and are expensive. He suggests that the parties use transcripts judiciously, eliminating them whenever possible. He also encourages the parties to be cognizant of the problems associated with the use of prehearing and posthearing briefs. Veglahn strongly argues that the cost and time problems plaguing arbitration are, to a degree, within the control of the parties. Therefore it is up to the parties to develop approaches to the arbitration process that will improve its effectiveness and efficiency.

The final article in this section discusses a different approach to improving the arbitration process. After discussing some of the factors decreasing the effectiveness of arbitration, Stessin describes an approach known as expedited arbitration. This is a form of arbitration designed to decrease the time needed to get an arbitration decision and to decrease the costs of arbitration. With this approach, attorneys are not used and the arbitration hearing is conducted at the job site. The arbitrator must usually render a decision the day after the hearing. This approach can be quite useful in situations involving routine grievances not likely to have precedential value. However, Stessin emphasizes that expedited arbitration is not intended to replace traditional arbitration. It is a parallel procedure available to the parties when they believe it would be useful.

NOTES

1. Slichter, Sumner H., James J. Healy, and E. Robert Livernash, *The Impact of Collective Bargaining on Management,* Washington, D.C.: The Brookings Institution, 1960, p. 692.

2. Briggs, Steven, "The Grievance Procedure and Organizational Health," *Personnel Journal,* Vol. 60, No. 6, June 1981, pp. 471–473.

3. *Enterprise Wire Co.* 46 LA359 at 363–364, Daugherty 1966.

4. Elkouri, Frank, and Edna Aspen Elkouri, *How Arbitration Works,* Washington, D.C.: Bureau of National Affairs, 1973, p. 391.

SUGGESTIONS FOR FURTHER READING

In addition to the readings cited in this introduction, the following readings may prove useful to the reader.

Fairweather, Owen, *Practice and Procedure of Labor Arbitration,* Washington, D.C.: Bureau of National Affairs, 1973.

Hays, Paul R., *Labor Arbitration: A Dissenting View,* New Haven, Conn.: Yale University Press, 1966.

Kagel, Sam, *The Anatomy of Labor Arbitration,* Washington, D.C.: Bureau of National Affairs, 1961.

Trotta, Maurice, *Handling Grievances,* Washington, D.C.: Bureau of National Affairs, 1976.

The Grievance Process

Columbia University

The grievance process allows managements and unions to carry on a sort of continuous collective bargaining daily to solve mutual problems of work and production, and jointly to administer a wide array of plant or shop affairs. Such activities seem to encompass many of the recent suggestions for creative collective bargaining, which some observers, including Secretary of Labor Willard Wirtz, declare is needed to meet the challenges of scientific advance and technological invention. The long and varied experiences of workers, union leaders, and managers in grievance work would seem to be able to provide some promising lessons for those who advocate new forms of high-level bargaining and novel negotiating procedures.

Unfortunately neither industrial relations staff officers, union officials, arbitrators, or students of labor seem to learn much from the grievance process. The author of the Brookings Institution study of collective bargaining present a common point of view when they entitle a chapter "The Problem of Grievances."[1] While

From pp. 252–263, "The Grievance Process" by James W. Kuhn. From *Frontiers of Collective Bargaining,* edited by John T. Dunlop and Neil W. Chamberlain. Copyright © 1967 by J. Dunlop and N. Chamberlain. Reprinted by permission of Harper & Row, Publishers, Inc.

grievance work may occasionally involve serious matters, for the most part it is merely bothersome, workaday activity seldom raising vital issues or providing opportunities for more propitious collective bargaining. Professor George Taylor has recently deplored the " 'traditional wisdom' in grievance settling" which asserts that "grievance handling was merely a matter of strictly administering the terms of the agreement . . . [that] can become a game in which advantages and disadvantages are sought on technical grounds."[2] David Cole sadly notes that all too often "procedures for handling grievances are customary. The trouble is that they have been surrounded with so many safeguards that they have become almost self-defeating."[3] The Rosens reported in 1957, after studying some 50 shops, that grievance work provided little prestige or authority for stewards. Business agents showed only slight concern for handling grievances because it had become "fairly routine business; well within the scope of established policy."[4]

If grievance work generally is routine and if the parties in most situations have bound themselves to inflexible procedures so that they face the same old problems again and again rather than resolve them through new approaches, the grievance process certainly can contribute little to the improvement of collective bargaining. The real problem may be not that grievance work is dull and routine, but rather that union leaders and managers have assumed it to be so. This assumption could lead them to ignore a number of activities vital to sound industrial relations and thus to disappoint the workers on the job and to neglect the needs of foremen and supervisors in the plant. Confusion about the function and purpose of the grievance process may have hindered full and effective use of it. Certainly it is not easy to understand; for most of its work is informal, and many of its varied activities are carried on under the cover of conventional procedures.

ADMINISTRATION AND PROBLEM SOLVING — A NEW POWER BASE AT THE PLACE OF WORK

Workers able to organize informal groups at the place of work often are able to penalize and to aid their supervisors. This ability gives them a bargaining power which they use, when and if they can, to protect "the rate," even without a union's support. The entrance of the union, the availability of a grievance procedure, the rise of shop stewards and committeemen, and the development of an industrial relations staff, all tend to make more explicit than before the bargaining relations among the parties involved in the production process. New opportunities for bargains now appear, and new bargaining techniques become available to both union leaders and managers. Unions are able to unite and organize the workers on the job into stronger groups and to furnish militant protection of work groups; shop officers can provide open, regular leadership of the groups. They were recognized by union and management alike and enjoy special rights and privileges not accorded other workers. Industrial relations staffs introduce a new influence within management that alters and not infrequently weakens the authority of foremen and supervisors.

Union officers handling grievances can, and sometimes do, become important officials at the place of work. They are often able to help as well

as to hinder production; adept stewards help solve problems of both workers and managers by informally adjusting and flexibly interpreting, or even overlooking, union rules and provisions of the agreement. Both shop stewards and shop managers become involved in a complex relation, at once beneficial and threatening to the purposes of the two parties. A withdrawal of cooperation by the union grievance handlers or managers at the place of work can snarl daily adjustment and administration of the agreement, piling up small annoying problems to exacerbate work problems.

Besides the informal work of applying shop rules and interpreting customs and traditions, union grievance handlers have formal administrative activities. Agreements purposely allow variation of application and interpretation to fit special local conditions. Collective agreements often spell out the parties' rights and duties in general, and not uncommonly in ambiguous terms. Compliance, thus, may be not so much an issue as is the sensible application of a general rule to a changing and changeable work situation. Shop or local union officials frequently help work out the complex bumping maneuvers under the provisions for layoffs by seniority. They also typically sit on such administrative committees as safety, apprenticeship, absenteeism, and community drives. Less commonly they join managers to administer more substantial matters such as inequities, job classification, job evaluations, and worker training.

Work Groups, Shop Stewards, and Foremen

Despite management's initial and reluctant acceptance of the grievance process as merely a means of adjudicating disputes under an agreement, the dynamics of the system create an additional function of administrative work and problem solving. This new function then allows the grievance handlers to expand their activities, to probe the boundaries and ambiguities of an agreement and to seek modifications of and adjustments in its terms and provisions. The grievance procedure itself — with the flow of written grievances; requirements of meetings, hearings, and review; time limits for decisions; and appeals to higher offices — affords shop stewards the means for penalizing managers. Flooding a foreman or an industrial relations office with grievances, each of which requires answers or discussions, can be bothersome and costly; numerous hearings that require workers from the shop as witnesses and testimony of shop supervisors can interfere with production; and written grievances that detail every error or mistake of a lower-level supervisor may paint an unflattering picture to higher-level managers.

Foremen and managers are by no means helpless; they can make life miserable for stewards and local union officers by refusing to settle grievances, clogging the procedure, forcing cases to costly arbitration, making grievance handlers stick strictly to the rules, and limiting their time for investigation and hearings. They can refuse to deal informally with stewards, refusing them the chance to win favors for their electorate or to save face when they have to drop grievances.

In bargaining, stewards and committeemen offer inducements at least as often as they try to use force, and perhaps more often. Moreover, the union men by no means initiate all the bargained adjustments in work rules and changes in the agreement. Foremen and lower-level supervisors seek changes in their attempts to meet new, unforeseen production requirements through flexible use of workers and working time. The bargaining is usually a *quid pro quo* arrangement, with both parties gaining, though managers tend to forget the benefits they receive and note only the continuing cost of work rules once established as precedents. A managerial demand unilaterally to change work rules established through shop negotiations, with its *quid pro quo* bargaining, almost always leads to trouble. The demand typically provokes a strong reaction from workers and their grievance representatives.

A major problem of industrial relations arises

if either union or management tries to resolve issues arising out of negotiations at the place of work between foremen and stewards with no regard for the complexity of the activities that brought them about. Production managers pressed to speed up schedules, to increase the pace of work, or to adjust production to meet unexpected sales and variations in raw material, find fractional bargaining an advantageous method of getting help from workers to meet the special conditions. To meet production changes, they need greater effort from workers, lifting of work limits, or freedom to use workers without being hindered by job, occupation, or classification restrictions. The parties reach agreement usually through informal shop negotiations: the workers agree to increase their effort or to lift customary or agreed-upon work restraints in exchange for such benefits as longer lunch hours, extra washup time at the end of a shift, looser rates, less strict discipline, and the assignment of certain unpleasant or low-paying tasks to helpers.

Once immediate production needs have been met and other managerial objectives, such as cutting costs, reassert themselves, management may be tempted to undo the "agreements" made by foremen and stewards, either unilaterally or through high-level negotiations with national union officers. The attempt meets resistance and resentment and is considered by the men at the place of work as an attack upon their good faith in bargaining and their hard-won job gains. The remedy must be appropriate to the issue. Shop rules can best be changed and work-group or shop agreements can best be renegotiated by the same parties who worked them out in the first place. Rather than try to handle the complex bargaining themselves, higher-level authorities would do well to facilitate shop negotiations at the place of work, by maintaining or increasing the relative bargaining power of the parties involved in line with the desired outcome.

The availability of bargaining tactics to work groups and the ability of their representatives — usually shop stewards — to bargain with foremen and lower managers do not necessarily mean that the grievance process will be used for bargaining purposes, extending its functions beyond those of adjudication and administration. Shop stewards, local union officers, and workers must also be *willing* to bargain and to try to enforce their demands. If judicial hearings under the agreement were able to fill workers' needs and satisfy their expectancies at the place of work, the grievance process would not have expanded as it has.

In the worker's view, the judicial aspect of grievance proceedings may not provide appropriate or adequate solutions to problems. Usually workers are expected to grieve some action of supervision; if upheld, they receive recompense for the wrong done them or their rights. A worker may be restored to a hiring list, reassigned to a rightful position, or receive back pay to make up his loss. In some situations, however, recompense after the fact is hardly satisfactory. Workers are reluctant to obey management directives if they believe they will thereby endanger health and safety; recompense after possible injury does not recommend itself. They want either immediate, on-the-spot adjudication of such a grievance or — what probably in practice amounts to the same thing — negotiations over how the directive will be followed, if at all.

Many other grievances do not involve matters appropriate to adjudication, not because there are no standards by which to judge them, but rather because they do not involve questions of standards at all. An examination of lower-stage grievances or of oral grievances shows that many, if not most of them, have no standing under the agreement. Workers still want answers to their grievances and hearings even though they know what the formal answer will be. Grievance hearings appear to be as important as impartial grievance judgments.

A quick hearing and reply can be more important than back pay in some grievances. If through tardy recognition of his complaint a worker suffers a loss of dignity and self-respect, management cannot easily recompense him. Workers are, perhaps, as interested in assurance of justice *before* the act as in justice through the grievance procedure *after* the act. They want a manager to hear and explicitly to consider their interests before he acts, as well as afterward. How better can a foreman or a superintendent show his consideration than by giving the workers or their steward a hearing, listening to their gripes, views, or proposals? He may still proceed exactly as he intended originally, but the workers have had a kind of accounting and a recognition of their concern.

Since the formal grievance procedure usually does not allow for discussions and hearings before managers act, workers and stewards must seek such consideration informally or under the guise of a grievance about a past action. When workers want to discuss approaches to industrial problems before decisions are taken or to examine managerial decisions before action is taken, they are not always willing to accept the answers provided by foremen, time-study men, or the industrial relations staff. They may then go beyond demanding a hearing and insist upon answers or solutions. If work groups enjoy any bargaining power, they may well be tempted to exercise it through one or a number of the available tactics. Possessing both the ability and the willingness to use bargaining tactics, they may be expected to employ them to serve their interests as they understand them.

Bargaining at the place of work will not necessarily be guided by the collective agreement or limited to the objectives of the local or the national union. If, on the one hand, a work group enjoys an especially favorable bargaining position, it may be able to display more bargaining power in pursuing its parochial interests than can the local union in bargaining for its objectives. If, on the other hand, a work group is weak and disorganized, it may be unable to bring enough pressure even to enforce the agreement and secure the full rights supposedly assured by local and national negotiations. Members of such work groups can be easy marks for foremen who wish to escape the restraints of the agreement, for foremen also bargain with their work groups whenever possible to serve their own interests.

Grievance bargaining is by no means merely a worker's or a shop steward's device, as already noted; foremen and plant managers use it to gain advantages. Through the grievance process, both members of work groups and managers at the place of work develop expectations that their larger organizations do not ordinarily fulfill. Workers come to expect democratic participation in decisions that affect their jobs. They become used to setting the pace of work, determining the earning level, or working out for themselves the rules of job bidding and work assignment; they may look with little favor upon the provisions of the agreement that regulate these activities and standards. Further, they may resist strongly when higher-level managers attempt to change them unilaterally or through the local union rather than bargain for changes through the foremen and shop managers. Likewise, foremen who have been able to run their departments with few restraints from the workers, may have no intention of abiding by the agreement or may approach it casually. In the same way that powerful work groups may consider themselves independent from the local union in dealing with shop issues, foremen in a strong bargaining position vis-à-vis their workers may consider themselves autonomous within their departments. The local union is often unable to challenge such foremen, regardless of its members' rights under the agreement; for without a militant work group for support, it seldom possesses the constant check and surveillance needed at the place of work to protect the agreement.

Those who encouraged the development of acceptance of the grievance procedure as a contribution to industrial democracy built more than they recognized. This instrument, devised only to protect and apply the limited job rights of workers secured through a union's collective bargaining, has tended to promote independence among workers and autonomy of managers at the place of work. The grievance process, thus, may promise either more or less than the guarantees of the collective agreement. Depending upon the relative bargaining strength of the parties, work groups may participate in a far wider or a much narrower range of decisions and activities than those mentioned in the written agreement.

Other Functions of the Grievance Process

Besides the dramatic function of the grievance process, there are two secondary functions, which can be very useful to union, management, and industrial relations. The first is that of communications. The use of the grievance process as a means of receiving and transmitting information requires some care and sophistication. Written grievances and answers may be purely formal, describing problems in conventional terms that hide or distort more than they reveal. Much about the mood of men at the place of work and the sources and causes of problems in the shop can be inferred from the kinds and number of complaints. There is no simple correlation, though, between the quantity of grievances and the quality of industrial relations. It requires subtle and skillful discrimination to interpret grievances properly. An increase in the number of grievances may indicate an approaching union election, the replacement of several old, experienced grievance representatives with new ones, an intraunion factional fight, a crackdown by a plant superintendent upon long-standing lax enforcement of production standards, the appearance of a new, young foreman, or a failure of managers to abide by the agreement. If few grievances are being processed in a firm, the management cannot safely conclude that union relations are good; they may also indicate that the foremen are giving the company away to the union.

Grievance meetings, informal discussions, bargaining sessions, arbitration hearings, political campaigns, joint consultations, and collaborative efforts can all furnish information to managers, union leaders, and workers about each others' needs, desires, hopes, and understandings. Misunderstandings can often be avoided if shop stewards and committeemen learn early and at first hand about changes in piece rates, adjustments in job standards, methods of time study, layoffs, and new machinery. As the initiator of most action, management usually has primary responsibility for communications; it is the source of the most important information relevant to the work place. All too often managers have no regular policy of supplying information about company policies or activities to union grievance representatives. Where they do keep in close communication with stewards and committeemen, the exchange of information is usually dependent upon personal relations; changes in personnel can disrupt this exchange at critical times.

A second subsidiary function of the grievance process is that of training those who participate in grievance work in the opportunities and requirements of industrial relations. Both unions and firms commonly sponsor training programs, instructing stewards and foremen in the complexities of the agreement's provisions, the intricacies of arbitration, and the rules of processing grievances. Formal grievance instruction is probably the lesser part of the training, however; the daily grievance work itself teaches the most important lessons. From the confrontation with work groups and their leaders, foremen learn the value of persuasion, political compromise, and unsentimental bargaining: the hard realities of gaining cooperation among men of different interests.

Shop stewards, too, learn the same lessons; though owing to their high turnover, managers sometimes feel that they always deal with uninitiated, inexperienced grievance representatives. The continual training of new stewards and grievance representatives is not entirely wasted, though; for those who were trained earlier and have served the more or less thankless

role of grievance handler, usually possess a lively appreciation for the limits as well as the possibilities of grievance work and collective bargaining. Workers who serve a term as stewards return to their regular work better educated than before they left. When a foreman insists he is only carrying out orders, they may not always be impressed, suspecting correctly that he may be acting on his own; but they may also be more ready to help foremen in times of real emergency. Experienced in the ways of give-and-take bargaining and familiar with the real pressure on managers, they are likely to be reasonable, though tough, men to deal with.

Workers also learn much from the grievance process about industrial democracy, as they participate in local and shop decisions that affect their work lives. In dealing with stewards, meeting at work to discuss grievances on work rules and rate changes, and helping to devise or execute the tactics of grievance bargaining, workers voice their opinions and exert more effective control than is possible in the larger local union. Dissenters have a better opportunity to air their views and to recruit support among their fellow workers on the job than in the union meeting.

Thus the grievance process has evolved from a policing procedure for worker protection into a means for on-the-job joint determination of work conditions. There is no reason to believe that its evolution has stopped now: union and management may well be developing other functions within and around this flexible process to accommodate it to new and unforeseen demands.

Special Procedures

A study of the grievance procedure shows that both parties commonly recognize its different provisions for handling different problems. Because issues of discipline and discharge must be adjudicated by higher authorities, who are removed from the immediate scene and less involved than shop stewards and foremen, they are commonly appealed directly to a higher or a final step of the procedure. Not only do the parties act swiftly because discipline is a matter of urgency, but they also take the issue directly to the level where the judicial function begins to operate. Further, the shortened procedure acknowledges that a disciplinary penalty is a serious matter to a worker; he is usually satisfied with nothing less than resort to the highest possible judicial authority. Even though the discipline imposed by a manager may be upheld and the penalty merited, he insists upon the right to appeal to the top — the right of due process.

Workers also wish to remove consideration of their disciplinary penalties from the shop and even the local level because they distrust their own union representatives. It is not unknown for stewards or local union officers to collude with managers to dismiss, to transfer, or otherwise to discriminate against workers without justification. Particularly where workers from minority groups are employed, the shortened appeals procedure may be most appropriate, as it allows them to take disciplinary cases directly to the company-wide level and to a third-party judge.

Under some agreements, grievances of a general nature — those affecting a large number of employees or more than one plant, or those involving interpretation and application of general provisions of the agreement — may be initiated at an intermediate or a top level where the parties obviously have the authority to deal with the issue.

Disputes involving difficult issues — such as job evaluation, time studies, job classification, and apprentices — may be submitted to special committees, individuals, or impartial agencies for review and settlement. The issues may be too complicated for the regular procedures and the ordinary grievance handler. The special pro-

cedures may also result from the failure of the negotiators of the overall agreement to agree upon standards for settling the disputed issues and their decision to provide the means for local bargainers to hammer out settlements case by case. For such issues it is wise to separate the judicial and the bargaining processes.

A few agreements have provided for separate procedures and personnel to deal with such technical matters as supplemental unemployment benefits, pension plan details, and health and welfare arrangements. Settlement of grievances arising out of these fringe benefits usually requires an expert's knowledge of the programs. Answers can seldom be tailored to fit relative bargaining power, nor can adjustments be made on the basis of give-and-take; actuarial tables and precise rules must be carefully administered by people with technical competence.

Thus the grievance process has developed to meet the felt needs of workers, the requirements of union leaders and managers, and the constraints of union and company organizations. . . .

NOTES

1. Sumner H. Slichter, James J. Healy, and E. Robert Livernash, *The Impact of Collective Bargaining on Management* (Washington, D.C.: The Brookings Institution, 1960), chap. xxiii.

2. George W. Taylor, "The Public Interest — Variations on an Old Theme" (Speech given before the National Academy of Arbitration, January 29, 1965), pp. 10, 11, 13.

3. David L. Cole, *The Quest for Industrial Peace* (New York: McGraw-Hill Book Co., 1963), p. 81.

4. Hjalmar Rosen and R. A. Hudson Rosen, "The Union Business Agent's Perspective of His Job," *Journal of Personnel Administration and Industrial Relations,* III (July 1957), pp. 50–51.

Win, Lose, Draw: The Grievance Process in Practice

DAN R. DALTON
Indiana University

WILLIAM D. TODOR
Ohio State University

The grievance process plays a significant role in American industrial relations. Justice William O. Douglas in *United Steelworkers of America* v. *Warrior Gulf Navigation Company* (363 U.S. 574) underscored the ubiquity of the process:

> "apart from matters that the parties specifically exclude, all of the questions on which the parties disagree must therefore come within the scope of the grievance . . . provisions of the collective agreement. The grievance procedure is, in other words, a part of the continuous collective bargaining process."

To suggest that the grievance procedure properly addresses *all* issues (except those specifically excluded) upon which labor and management disagree is indeed a wide charter. Despite the demonstrated importance of the grievance in labor relations, surprisingly little is known of the process. There have, for example, been repeated attempts to determine what kind of employees file grievances and, of course, to determine those that do not file. These investigations have, unfortunately, not been very enlightening.

Naturally, management is very interested in such questions, as well they should be. The grievance process is expensive. Many hours are dedicated to the resolution of grievances. To illustrate the typical expenses involved, a recent investigation established that to process 500 grievances (the actual number filed in a *single* West coast union local during 1979), a total of 4580.2 workhours were used. This means that, on the average, 9.1 workhours were needed to dispose of each grievance. This time, as impressive as it seems, is probably very much understated.

TIME INCREASES COSTS

This is only the time used for formal meetings on the grievances which could be resolved at one of three steps in the process: 1) the first level where 52% were settled; 2) the second level where 30.9% were resolved; or 3) the third level where 17.1% were resolved. Clearly, the cost and time required increases with the level of resolution. Importantly, the meetings require management's time which is presumably quite expensive. Even so, this is only an estimation of the *direct* time involved in meetings. It does not include preparation time, informal meetings, lost time wages for the grievant, clerical time and administrative overhead for management and the union.

Not only is the grievance process expensive, but it is disruptive as well. Obviously, during the process, grievants are taken off their job to testify and managers must abandon their normal assignments, among a host of other disturbances.

Under the circumstances, it is little wonder that the grievance process is a cause of concern for both management and labor. Given the costs and disruptiveness allegedly associated with the grievance process, it remains, as we noted earlier, something of a mystery. We do not, for example, know the subject matter on which grievances are ordinarily filed. Moreover, we don't know their final resolution: Are they won? Is a compromise reached? Are grievances withdrawn? Are they abandoned? The remainder of this article is committed essentially to a discussion of these factors. The information within may serve as a guide by which other organizations and union managements may compare their experience.

WHAT GRIEVANCES ARE FILED?

As we said earlier, grievances can be filed over virtually anything. And, indeed, they are filed over a spectrum of incidents and conditions ranging from relatively minor disagreements concerning the exact date of a vacation to more serious matters: suspension, termination and so forth.

CATEGORIES OF GRIEVANCES

The following is a brief explanation of typical grievance categories. Included are the issues that ordinarily would be contained in such grievances:

Suspension — Here an employee has been ordered not to work for a period of time usually ranging from one day to two weeks. Almost all these suspensions are the result of absenteeism, avoidable accidents, insubordination, or job performance.

Seniority — Here an employee is grieving because of "seniority bypass." Almost all such grievances are filed because an employee has been overlooked for overtime, transfers, promotions, training, or scheduling.

Transfer — Most grievances in this category are filed because an employee has been refused a transfer for which they have applied. This may be because of low supervisory ratings, excessive absenteeism, medical transfers receiving priority and so forth.

Termination — Simply, the employee has been fired. Almost all actions in this category are because of excessive absenteeism, a history of avoidable accidents, insubordination, or job performance.

Disciplinary memoranda — This is essentially a warning to an employee which presumably will be followed by more serious consequences should the employee continue or repeat the incident. Ordinarily, these are a reaction to absenteeism, accidents, insubordination, tardiness and job performance.

Vacation — This occurs because employees do not receive the vacation dates they prefer. This may be because junior employees have been given the dates of preference, or because the organization has limited the number of employees which may be on vacation at any given time.

Grievance process — Here, the union ordinarily charges that the company has not met in good faith on a grievance. Also, a case is occasionally found when the company is alleged not to have met the conditions of a grievance settlement.

| | Management performing productive work | This is self-explanatory. The union alleges that management employees are doing work which is (or should be) restricted to *per diem* personnel. |

Management performing productive work — This is self-explanatory. The union alleges that management employees are doing work which is (or should be) restricted to *per diem* personnel.

Safety — Here, the union alleges that a procedure or a condition involving employees is unsafe. The union, in this case, is usually asking that this procedure or condition be modified.

Discrimination — This may be a forum for Title VII disagreements. However, this is not ordinarily the case. Grievances in this category are "catch-alls." Discrimination here means that an employee charges that he or she is not being treated the same as other employees. These grievances do not necessarily, indeed, rarely, have race, sex, or national origin overtones.

Performance evaluations — Here an employee charges that his or her annual performance evaluation is not a fair representation of his or her job performance over that period.

Union representation — The union filed a grievance in this case because an employee, facing a disciplinary hearing, has requested union representation and has had this request denied.

Sick benefits denial — An employee has not come to work for some period. This employee claims to have been ill and requests sick pay compensation. For whatever reasons, the company has refused to pay this sick leave.

Pay (differentials, travel, etc.) — These grievances usually occur over the nonpayment of special pay provisions (not ordinarily hourly wages). Meal allowances, night shift differentials, travel reimbursements are most common.

Excused or complimentary time — An employee has requested time off without pay. The company has denied the request.

Work out of classification — Here an employee is asked to do a job which is allegedly not in his or her job description. It is argued that this particular job should be done by someone in a different job classification.

Training — An employee has requested training for some aspect of his or her job. The company has denied the request.

Table 1 illustrates the experience over a

TABLE 1
Percentage of grievances filed by category

	PERCENTAGE
Suspension	20.8
Seniority	10.4
Miscellaneous	8.6
Transfer	7.4
Termination	6.6
Disciplinary memoranda	6.6
Scheduling	6.4
Vacation	5.8
Grievance process	4.4
Management performing productive work	4.0
Safety	3.4
Discrimination	3.4
Performance evaluations	3.0
Union representation	2.0
Sick benefits denial	2.0
Pay (differentials, travel, etc.)	1.8
Excused and complimentary time	1.6
Work out of classification	1.2
Training	0.6

single year of a large West Coast union local representing some 4600 rank-and-file members. The constituency of this local are nonmanagerial/nonprofessional employees: Male, female, blue and white collar personnel of various ages and seniority involved in a range of technical and nontechnical occupations are represented.

COMMON GRIEVANCES

Some of the more interesting categories may be worthy of comment. Foremost, it has often been suggested that unions often engage in filing "trivial" grievances. Perhaps. In this case, however, there may be some evidence to the contrary. We, of course, do not know if the grievances filed were viable, *i.e.,* whether there was a realistic possibility that they could have been decided in favor of the union. The subject matter of the grievances most often filed, however, certainly seems to be meaningful: employee suspension, seniority, transfer, terminations, and disciplinary memoranda.

On reflection, most of these categories should not be surprising. Notice, for instance, that the majority of these are concerned with employee discipline. In fact, the entire range of managerial reaction to employee discipline is covered from the introductory disciplinary memorandum, through suspensions, and, finally, to termination. We would expect that employees might be dissatisfied and reactive in these areas: Evidently, they are.

Seniority has been referred to as the *sine qua non* of organized labor. The very substance of many individual work rights for union employees is based on the concept of seniority. Shift assignments, vacation preferences, transfers, promotions, trainings, among others are based on the amount of time that an individual has with a company. It is, therefore, not especially surprising that incidents or conditions which threaten this "security" are often grieved.

The remainder of the categories illustrated in Table 1 are self-explanatory with no single category accounting for a great deal of the grievances filed.

WHAT ARE THE RESOLUTIONS OF THESE GRIEVANCES?

It is one thing to know the categories in which grievances are filed. It is quite another to know if they are won, or lost, or whatever other outcomes there may have been. Table 2 represents the outcomes by category of the grievances filed. However, the possible outcomes of the grievance process can be quickly reviewed. There are five such outcomes:

○ The union can *win* the grievance. Simply, in this case the union has received whatever it demanded in the grievance.

○ The union can *lose* the grievance. Here, obviously, the union has not received what it demanded.

○ A *compromise* can be reached in the grievance. For example, suppose an employee has been suspended for five days without pay. The union has filed a grievance arguing that the suspension was unjust. If, for instance, the company agrees to reduce the suspension to three days and pay the employee for the remainder, a compromise has been reached.

○ The union may *withdraw* the grievance without prejudice. This means that after the grievance has been formally filed, the union decided not to pursue the matter. The grievance, of course, is dropped. "Without prejudice" means that no precedent has been set. In other words, the union does not admit that such a grievance could not have been won. They merely withdraw this particular action. No inference can be made about subsequent incidents of the same or similar nature in the future.

TABLE 2

	WON	COMPROMISE	WITHDRAWN	ABANDONED	LOST
Suspension	9.7	20.4	3.9	38.8	27.2
Seniority	39.6	17.0	11.3	28.3	17.0
Miscellaneous	17.5	12.5	35.0	25.0	10.0
Transfer	18.9	10.8	5.4	45.9	10.8
Termination	5.9	17.6	5.9	41.2	29.4
Disciplinary memoranda	12.1	27.3	3.0	45.5	12.1
Scheduling	50.0	18.8	6.3	25.0	0.0
Vacation	37.9	6.9	17.2	27.8	10.3
Grievance process	36.4	18.2	13.6	31.8	0.0
Management performing productive work	65.0	10.0	10.0	10.0	5.0
Safety	35.3	17.6	17.6	29.4	0.0
Discrimination	18.8	18.8	31.3	31.3	0.0
Performance evaluations	73.0	13.3	13.3	0.0	0.0
Union representation	70.0	0.0	20.0	10.0	0.0
Sick benefits denial	20.0	0.0	10.0	50.0	20.0
Pay (differentials, travel, etc.)	44.4	22.2	11.1	22.2	0.0
Excused and complimentary time	37.5	25.0	12.5	12.5	12.5
Work out of classification	16.7	16.7	0.0	66.7	0.0
Training	33.3	0.0	0.0	66.7	0.0

○ The union may *abandon* the grievance. This is similar to a withdrawn grievance except that it occurs after the first step in the grievance process. At the first level the company may not agree to the union's demands. Ordinarily, such a matter would now go to the second step. If the union does not follow-up and request a second level hearing, the grievance is considered to have been abandoned.

Table 2, then, illustrates the specific outcomes of these grievances by category. We have little comment on Table 2 as such, but there is a fascinating trend somewhat concealed in the information that it contains. It is not easy to interpret outcomes of the grievances by all five categories. It is, for example, difficult to differentiate in a meaningful way the difference between occasions when grievances are withdrawn and abandoned. We can certainly appreciate that there is a technical difference, but pragmatically the "bottom line" would appear to be the same; i.e., the union did not, for whatever reason, receive its demands.

Bearing this in mind, we have simplified the outcomes of the grievances into two intuitively appealing groups: those which are positive outcomes for the union and those which are positive outcomes for the company. For instance, it is arguable that both winning and reaching a compromise represents a certain victory for the union. We, therefore, combine winning and compromise and refer to these outcomes as positive for the union. Correspondingly, for the union to lose, withdraw, or abandon the grievance would seem to represent positive outcomes for the company.

Table 3 illustrates the outcome of grievances

TABLE 3

	POSITIVE OUTCOMES FOR UNION	POSITIVE OUTCOMES FOR COMPANY
Sick benefits denial	20.0	80.0
Termination	23.5	76.5
Transfer	29.7	70.3
Miscellaneous	30.0	70.0
Suspension	30.1	69.9
Training	33.3	66.7
Work out of classification	33.3	66.7
Discrimination	37.6	62.4
Disciplinary memoranda	39.4	60.6
Vacation	44.8	55.2
Safety	52.9	47.1
Grievance process	54.6	45.4
Seniority	56.6	43.4
Excused and complimentary time	62.5	37.5
Pay (differentials, travel, etc.)	66.6	33.4
Scheduling	68.6	31.4
Union representation	70.0	30.0
Management performing productive work	75.0	25.0
Performance evaluations	86.3	13.7

according to whether the outcome was positive for the union or positive for the company.

Table 3 points to something of an intriguing paradox. It seems that the very categories over which grievances are most often filed (disciplinary memoranda, suspension, transfer, termination) are among the ones which the union most infrequently receives a positive outcome. Conversely, those categories in which relatively fewer grievances are filed, are accompanied by much higher "winning percentages."

OBSERVATIONS

We do not know why grievances which are most often filed also most often have positive outcomes for the company. We can, of course, speculate and make some, we hope, reasonable observa-

tions which may account for some of these tendencies.

First, it may be that the grievances which are most often filed are more contentious. There is a good deal more at stake both for the union and the company. As a result, the company may take such matters somewhat more seriously. They may dedicate more of their time and energies to obtain positive outcomes in such cases.

Another possible conclusion which may be drawn from the union view is based on the very fact that these are very important issues. If, for example, an individual is terminated, the union may have an obligation to file a grievance even when, on its face, the grievance has very little viability, such that the union cannot reasonably expect a positive outcome.

Conversely, grievances which are filed less

frequently appear to include those which are relatively less consequential. On these occasions, the company may be less involved and much more likely to compromise or even capitulate.

There is still another aspect which may be an important indicator of whether grievances are ultimately won or lost: the language of the collective bargaining agreement. Areas in which the union enjoys an edge with respect to positive outcomes include seniority, scheduling, union representation and management performing productive work, among others. These categories are ordinarily very well explicated in the contract. It may be that there is less ambiguity with accordingly fewer issues of interpretation involved. If so, behavior by management which may be outside these boundaries may be more easily identified.

On the other hand, terminations, suspensions, and disciplinary memoranda, for example, may be alleged to be "unjust." Needless to say, unjust is subject to various interpretations and is certainly less than concrete with respect to contract language. Perhaps it is not surprising that positive outcomes for the union are more difficult to obtain under these circumstances. It should be remembered that the burden of proof in a grievance proceeding is ordinarily on the union.

SUMMARY

As we have noted, the grievance process plays a significant role in American industrial relations.

The grievance process may be thought of as a procedure whereby the necessity of management and labor marshalling all their respective resources to resolve what may otherwise be relatively minor disputes for an employee can be curtailed. This procedure is absolutely central to the employee-organization relations in many organizations. Virtually any dispute is subject to the grievance procedure. While this procedure may be expensive and disruptive, it is probably better than its alternative. What, for example, would be the cost of organized labor and organization having to go to the mat over every dispute?

It may well be the more we know about the grievance process, the matters over which grievances are filed and their subsequent resolutions, the better for management and labor alike.

Certainly, the dynamics involved in determining which incidents are more likely to result in grievances and those forces which may affect the positive outcomes for organizations and organized labor are areas worthy of examination. If both parties were able to use this information responsibly, a more effective grievance process, less onerous to both management and labor, might evolve. We also should note that the dissatisfied employee is likely to benefit from such a process as well. Arguably, it is for the benefit of such individuals that the process was presumably developed.

Legal Intervention in Labor Arbitration

C. RAY GULLETT
Texas Eastern University

Labor arbitration has historically been a private process, agreed to by unions and management, designed to settle disputes arising during the life of a labor agreement. Traditionally, the courts have affirmed the private nature of this system, regarding it as a contractual arrangement which the parties create and with which they must live.

EARLY COURT DECISIONS

The binding nature of labor arbitration agreements was upheld by the Supreme Court in its famous Lincoln Mills decision of 1957.[1] In that case the Court ruled that arbitration clauses can be enforced through suits under Section 301(a) of the Taft-Hartley Act. Thus neither a union nor management can avoid arbitration on an issue falling within the jurisdiction of an arbitration clause if the other party seeks to have the issue arbitrated.

The legitimacy and strength of the arbitration process was further clarified by three Supreme Court decisions occurring on June 20, 1960. Called the Steelworkers' trilogy (since each

case involved appeal by the United Steelworkers' union), these cases reinforced the Court's Lincoln Mills decision by placing additional reliance on the wisdom and ability of the arbitrator and by deemphasizing the role of outside legal intervention in the arbitration process.

The first of these cases proclaimed that the merits of a grievance are for the arbitrator to decide. The Court denied the right of either party to refuse to arbitrate a grievance based on a claim that the complaint is frivolous and without merit. They further barred the courts from ruling on the merits of a grievance based on such claims. Such decisions are reserved for the arbitrator and not for "outsiders" (meaning the courts), who presumably have less knowledge concerning labor agreements and the "common law of the shop."[2]

In the second Steelworkers' case, the Court ruled that arbitration clauses should be interpreted broadly so that when there is doubt whether a dispute should be covered by arbitration, "doubts should be resolved in favor of coverage."[3] This ruling means that if either party wishes to remove a contractual issue from possible resolution through arbitration, the labor arrangement must specifically exclude it. Otherwise, the issue is presumed to be within the authority of the arbitrator, and the courts must enforce the former's right to decide a dispute if either party presses for arbitration.

Arbitrators' powers were further broadened in the third case. The issue here dealt with the right of the courts to overturn an arbitrator's decision. In brief, the Court stated that a decision can not be overturned by the courts simply because it is a poor one. The Court reasoned that since management and the union are responsible for the creation of the arbitration clause and for the selection of the arbitrator, they must accept the arbitrator's decision as binding, no matter how poor it may be.[4] Only on very narrow grounds may the courts review an arbitrator's ruling. Chief among these is if the arbitrator exceeds his or her authority. If the arbitrator makes a decision which goes beyond the authority granted by the submission agreement and the contract, such a decision may be overturned by the courts.[5]

The net effect of these four Supreme Court rulings was to put great weight on the private nature of the arbitration process and to give the arbitrator a broad area of exclusive authority not subject to legal intervention. But both before and after these decisions, another series of cases was placing constraints on the arbitrator's freedom of decision making.

THE NLRB AND DEFERRAL TO ARBITRATION

Many of the disputes that arise between labor and management involve both contractual rights and legal rights under the Taft-Hartley Act. For example, if a company chooses to subcontract some of the work traditionally performed by members of the firm's bargaining unit without first conferring with the union, what potential violations are involved? First, the firm may be in violation of the labor contract's general recognition clause. This clause typically states that the company recognizes the union as the sole bargaining agent for the covered employees and agrees to meet and bargain with union representatives over wages, hours and other conditions of employment. The same action may also be a violation of Section 8(a)(5) of the Taft-Hartley Act, which states that

it is an unfair labor practice for an employer to refuse to bargain collectively with the employees' chosen representatives.

If the subcontracting dispute is regarded as a contractual one, the appropriate vehicle for settlement is the grievance process and, ultimately, arbitration. But if it is viewed as an unfair labor practice, the proper means for resolution is the National Labor Relations Board. Of course, the circumstances of the case will determine whether the employer has violated either the contract or the law. But the point of this example is that there is likely to be overlapping jurisdiction between the arbitrator and the NLRB in many labor disputes.

How are issues in which both contractual and Taft-Hartley questions play a part ultimately resolved? Conceivably either an arbitrator or the Board has the right to decide the case. But as a matter of law the NLRB is not required to honor an arbitrator's decision or to defer to the arbitration process. Thus it could choose to hear all cases that involve unfair labor practice charges even if they also involve contract violations.[6] But in actuality the Board has chosen to defer some types of cases, such as the following, to the private arbitration process.

The Spielberg Doctrine

In 1955 the NLRB issued a series of criteria for deferring to arbitration which has come to be called the Spielberg doctrine.[7] In essence the Board stated that it would defer to an arbitrator's ruling when the proceedings are fair and regular, the parties agree to be bound by the arbitrator's ruling, and the arbitrator's decision is not clearly repugnant to the purposes and policies of the Taft-Hartley Act. In a later decision[8] it added the further requirement that the statutory issue(s) be presented to the arbitrator and that the arbitrator rule on them. Failure to meet these standards would result in the NLRB's rehearing the case and making its own decision. It should also be noted that these standards were intended to be applied to cases on which an arbitrator had already ruled.

The Collyer Doctrine

In 1971 the Board clarified its position regarding deferral to arbitration. Its ruling stated that whenever potential contract violations occur which also involve Section 8(a)(5) or 8(b)(3) unfair labor practices, the Board will defer these cases to arbitration.[9] The cases are not, however, dismissed until the arbitrator's ruling is made and the Board has reviewed it. If the ruling is thought to resolve the unfair labor practice issues as well, the NLRB will at that time dismiss the case. If the issues are not adequately resolved by the arbitrator, the Board may then decide to hear the case.[10]

Implications of Deferral

At first glance it may appear that the arbitrator's position is strengthened by the Board's willingness to defer some cases to arbitration. From this point of view, one might argue that deferral is consistent with the earlier line of Supreme Court cases which added to the arbitrator's autonomy. The deferral process does, however, differ markedly from the earlier cases in its effects. First of all, it should be remembered that the Board has *not* surrendered its authority to the arbitrator. It has merely held the case in abeyance until the arbitration ruling is made. If the arbitrator's decision does not meet Collyer standards, the Board will then reassert its jurisdiction and retry the case.

The net effect of this approach is to pressure the arbitrator to resolve unfair labor practice issues, as well as any contractual violation. Failure to do so may result in the decisions being overturned. Further, the management and union representatives are also to require that the arbitrator investigate and resolve unfair labor prac-

tice issues, since they face relitigation before the NLRB if this is not done.[11]

In effect the arbitrator has been made a subdivision of the Board, hearing and trying some unfair labor practice cases for it. Whether or not arbitrators are qualified to rule on unfair labor practice issues is, of course, a question that can be answered only in terms of the individual arbitrator. Some are qualified and some are not. Arbitrators are selected for their knowledge of labor agreements and for the "common law of the shop." Many, if not most, lack expertise in Board interpretation of the Taft-Hartley Act.

In essence, Board deferral has added a significant constraint to the arbitration process and placed added pressure on the arbitrator to decide issues which are outside the scope of the contract and thus outside traditional jurisdiction. The effect may also be to narrow the range of arbitrators acceptable to those who are knowledgeable of Board interpretations of the Taft-Hartley Act.

CIVIL RIGHTS CASES AND ARBITRATION

Title VII of the Civil Rights Act protects persons from employment discrimination on the basis of race, religion, sex, or national origin. When a person believes that he or she has been treated unfairly because of one of these reasons, a complaint may be filed with the Equal Employment Opportunity Commission. If attempts at conciliation fail, the EEOC or the aggrieved party may then press the case in federal court.

Alternatively, an employee of a unionized company might choose to file a grievance to settle the dispute. Since many negotiated agreements now contain a nondiscrimination clause, a case involving discrimination would have contractual implications. And even without such a clause, some discrimination complaints might be pursued on other contractual grounds.[12]

As with unfair labor practice cases, we can again see the potential problem of overlapping jurisdiction between the arbitrator on one side and the EEOC and the courts on the other. Not surprisingly, the Supreme Court has ruled that the Civil Rights Act is superior to any contractual agreement or arbitration ruling regarding discrimination cases. In a landmark case in 1974, *Alexander* v. *Gardner-Denver*, [13] the Court stated that an employee does not give up any of his or her Title VII rights by choosing to process a complaint through the grievance and arbitration procedure. Thus a person whose claim is rejected by an arbitrator may still file a complaint with the EEOC and, ultimately, the courts.

An interesting distinction can, however, be made between unfair labor practice and Title VII cases. Whereas standards for deferral of unfair labor practice cases have been created by the NLRB, no such standards exist for discrimination cases. In fact the Court in its *Alexander* v. *Gardner-Denver* ruling was careful to set no deferral criteria. It did, however, note that an arbitrator's ruling should be admitted as evidence and given such weight as the Court thinks appropriate. And although the Court did not specifically deal with the question, it has been inferred from the ruling that a party may simultaneously file a complaint with the EEOC while pursuing the case through the grievance procedure. [14] In a later decision, [15] the Court ruled that the 180-day maximum filing period with the EEOC is not protected from expiration by the filing of a contractual grievance over the same issue. Thus for self-protection an employee might be pressured to file an EEOC complaint before the grievance is fully resolved under the contract. [16]

From the arbitrator's viewpoint, grievances with Title VII implications present even thornier problems than do unfair labor practice cases. Not only are there no agreed-upon standards for deferral to an arbitrator's ruling, EEOC and court proceedings may be going on while the arbitrator is hearing the grievance. Thus an arbitrator has a great incentive to consider statutory as well as contractual issues in deciding such a case. Failure to develop a ruling that is consistent

with EEOC and court interpretations of Title VII will almost certainly result in an overturning of the decision. Yet most arbitrators are not, and do not pretend to be, experts in interpretation of the Civil Rights Act.

IMPLICATIONS FOR ARBITRATION

. . .

What are the implications of this intervention? First, it is clear that today arbitration is *not* a strictly private process dealing only with contractual issues. Whenever there is statutory law which touches a grievance, it must be given greater weight than contractual agreements. If the arbitrator chooses to ignore these statutes, the decision is likely to be overturned. Thus the arbitrator is placed under pressure to consider not only such factors as the labor contract, the "common law of the shop," and past practices of the parties, but also applicable statutes.

Since legislative regulation of business appears to be accelerating, it is logical to assume that there will be increasing areas of overlap between contractual agreements and federal and state law. Examples of such growing overlaps include the Occupational Health and Safety Act and the Employee Retirement Income Security Act. In both instances, arbitral rulings may be influenced by statutory requirements. There is no reason to suspect that such regulation will do anything but continue to grow in future years.

So arbitrators may be placed upon the horns of a dilemma in the near future: either qualify themselves to rule on grievances that involve statutory issues or watch an increasing number of cases bypass the grievance and arbitration procedure altogether. If the parties to a dispute perceive arbitration to be less than a court of last resort, they will be encouraged to turn directly to government regulatory agencies or the courts to resolve the issues.

Given a choice, it is believed that a majority of employers and probably the majority of union representatives would prefer the use of a private arbitrator, mutually agreed upon, to settle a dispute. This means that arbitrators who are well-versed in those laws that influence the personnel process will be in greater demand in coming years. These opportunities seem especially great in the near future, since those arbitrators who process the majority of cases today are nearing retirement. In 1975 it was reported that 41.9% of available arbitrators were 60 years of age or older, while only 1.8% were under 40.[17] Another study found that 80% of arbitrators responding to a survey questionnaire were age 50 or older.[18] Younger persons who aspire to be "main-line" arbitrators may fill this upcoming void by becoming adept not only at contract interpretation but statutory interpretation as well.

Clearly, the view taken here of the future of arbitration envisions a change in its traditional position. In essence, it appears that labor arbitration is becoming increasingly "public," with fewer issues capable of resolution based purely on private agreement between the parties. Such a change necessitates an evolving role for arbitrators if the profession is to remain viable in future years.

NOTES

1. *Textile Workers of America* v. *Lincoln Mills of Alabama,* 1957, 353 U.S. 448.

2. *United Steelworkers of America* v. *American Manufacturing Company,* June 20, 1960, 363 U.S. 564.

3. *United Steelworkers of America* v. *Warrior and Gulf Navigation Company,* June 20, 1960, 363 U.S. 574.

4. *United Steelworkers of America* v. *Enterprise Wheel and Car Corporation,* June 20, 1960, 363 U.S. 593.

5. Additional grounds for overturning an arbitrator's decision include the failure to hear relevant evidence and fraudulent actions of the arbitrator.

6. Section 10(a) of the Taft-Hartley Act states in part that the Board's power to prevent unfair labor practices "shall not be affected by any other means of adjustment or prevention that has been or may be established by agreement, law, or otherwise."

7. *Spielberg Manufacturing Company,* 112 NLRB 1080 (1955).

8. *Raytheon Company,* 140 NLRB 883 (1963).

9. *Collyer Insulated Wire,* 192 NLRB No. 150 (1971). Section 8(a)(5) cases are those in which the employer is charged with refusal to bargain in good faith with a union. Section 8(b)(3) cases involve similar charges against a union.

10. For a time the Board was also deferring other types of unfair labor practice cases to arbitration. See, for examples, *National Radio,* 198 NLRB No. 1 (1972); Kenneth J. Simon-Rose, "Deferral Under Collyer by the NLRB of Section 8(a)(3) Cases," *Labor Law Journal,* April 1976, pp. 201–216. The Board has, however, essentially returned to its original *Collyer* position of deferring only 8(a)(5) and 8(b)(3) cases. See *General American Transportation Corporation,* 228, NLRB No. 102 (1977) and *Roy Robinson Chevrolet,* 228 NLRB No. 103 (1977).

11. In one recent case in which an arbitrator did not consider any unfair labor practice issues that were raised, an appeals court ruled that NLRB deferral to arbitration was improper. See *Stephenson* v. *NLRB,* CA9, 1977, 94 LRRM, 3224.

12. For example, labor agreements typically state that employees can only be dismissed for "just cause." Presumably, discrimination would not be included as a just basis for discharge.

13. *Alexander* v. *Gardner-Denver,* 1974, 415 U.S. 36.

14. Marvin Hill, Jr., "The Effects of Non-Deference on the Arbitral Institution: An Alternative Theory," *Labor Law Journal,* April 1977, pp. 230–239.

15. *International Union of Electrical, Radio, and Machine Workers, AFL-CIO, Local 790* v. *Robins and Meyers,* 1976, 97 U.S. 441.

16. For a further discussion of this issue, see Marvin Hill, Jr., "Grievance Procedure and Title VII Limitations," *Labor Law Journal,* June 1977, pp. 339–343.

17. Walter J. Primeaux, Jr., and Dalton E. Brannen, "Why Few Arbitrators Are Deemed Acceptable," *Monthly Labor Review,* September 1975, pp. 27–30.

18. A. Dale Allen, Jr., "Labor Arbitration: A View From the Horse's Mouth," *Proceedings,* (Southern Management Association; Atlanta, Georgia), November 1976.

Grievance Mediation:
An Alternative to Arbitration

STEPHEN B. GOLDBERG

JEANNE M. BRETT
Both of Northwestern University

Labor arbitration was developed as a means by which employees could challenge an employer's actions other than through a strike or a lawsuit. The advantages of arbitration over the strike are obvious; its advantages over litigation were thought to be that it would be faster, less expensive, less formal, and more attuned to the realities of the industrial world.

In some respects, arbitration has been quite successful. Strikes during the term of a collective bargaining contract are rare and, with the exception of the bituminous coal industry, do not constitute a major national problem. Arbitration is also faster, less expensive, and less formal than most civil litigation.

Still, there is a sense, and has been for some years, that arbitration has not lived up to the expectations of an earlier time. The average cost of arbitration is in excess of $1000; the average time from request for arbitration to receipt of the arbitrator's decision is around six months, and complaints about excess formalism are commonplace. Another criticism of arbitration has been that its adjudicatory mode encourages an

adversarial approach, in which each side is tempted to do all it can to "win" the grievance, often without regard for the effect of such tactics on the long-term relationship of the parties.

In response to the criticisms of arbitration, we have proposed that, to a substantial extent, the resolution of grievances through arbitration be replaced by the resolution of grievances through mediation — more precisely, through a particular type of mediation system. The essence of this system is as follows: After the final step of the internal grievance procedure, the parties will have the option of going to mediation rather than directly to arbitration. This option can be triggered by one party or by mutual consent, as the parties prefer. In either event, the mediation procedure is wholly informal in nature. The relevant facts are elicited in a narrative fashion rather than through examination and cross-examination of witnesses. The rules of evidence do not apply, and no record of the proceedings is made. The grievant is encouraged to participate fully in the proceedings, both by stating his or her views and by asking questions of the other participants in the hearing.

The primary effort of the mediator is to assist the parties to settle the grievance in a mutually satisfactory fashion. If no settlement is possible, the mediator provides the parties with an immediate opinion, based on their collective

---

From *Proceedings of the Thirty-Fifth Annual Meeting* of the Industrial Relations Research Association, Barbara D. Dennis, Ed., 1983, pp. 256–259. Reprinted with permission of the authors and the IRRA.

bargaining agreement, as to how the grievance would be decided if it went to arbitration. That opinion is not final and binding, but is advisory in nature. It is delivered orally, and is accompanied by a statement of the reasons for the mediator's opinion. The advisory opinion can be used as the basis for further settlement discussions, for withdrawal, or for granting of the grievance. If the grievance is neither settled, withdrawn, nor granted, the parties are free to arbitrate. If they do, the mediator cannot serve as arbitrator, and nothing said or done by the parties or the mediator during mediation can be used against a party in arbitration.

The theoretical advantages of this system of grievance resolution are substantial. The absence of a written decision should make it both faster and less expensive than arbitration. The lack of formalities and the increased opportunity to discuss whatever seems relevant to the participants should increase their sense of getting at the problem as they see it. Because success in mediation is defined as a mutually satisfactory resolution, mediation should be easier on the parties' relationship than is arbitration, in which success is defined as defeating the other party. If the parties learn settlement skills at mediation, and utilize those skills at the earlier steps of the grievance procedure, they should be able to settle more cases without the need for mediation or arbitration.

The central risks of this procedure are two-fold. The first is that mediation will lead to few, if any, settlements. This would increase, rather than decrease, the time and cost of dispute resolution. Second, the availability of mediation may lessen the pressure to settle in the internal grievance procedure. If the internal settlement rate goes down significantly, the overall cost of dispute resolution will go up.

In an effort to determine whether mediation can successfully resolve grievances faster, less expensively, and more satisfactorily than arbitration, we conducted a series of experiments with mediation in the bituminous coal mining in-

dustry. These experiments took place over two six-month periods in four states — Illinois, Indiana, Virginia, and Kentucky.

Three different procedures for triggering mediation were used in these experiments: (1) *mutual-consent* (no grievance was mediated without the consent of both parties); (2) *single-party trigger* (either the employer or the union could submit a grievance to mediation); (3) *everything-goes* (all unresolved grievances were submitted to mediation, with exceptions only by mutual agreement).

RESULTS

One hundred and fifty-three grievances were taken to mediation during the experimental period. Of these, 135 were finally resolved without resort to arbitration — a final-resolution rate of 89%.

The final-resolution rate appeared to vary according to the trigger mechanism. Under mutual-consent, the final-resolution rate was 90%, under single-party trigger it was 95%, and under everything-goes it was 78%. Analysis disclosed, however, that these differences were not a function of the trigger mechanism, but of the comparatively low settlement rate in one state which changed trigger mechanisms in the course of the experiment. In that state, the settlement rate was 81% under the mutual-consent trigger and 78% under everything-goes. In the other three states, the final-resolution rate was in excess of 95% regardless of trigger mechanism. The conclusion that we draw from this is that how the parties get to mediation is less important than their attitude once there. If they make a serious and good-faith effort to settle all grievances at mediation, they will settle a very high proportion of those grievances without regard to the nature of the trigger mechanism.

Slightly more than half (51%) of the mediation conferences resulted in a compromise settlement, 22% in a noncompromise settlement (grievance sustained in full or withdrawn), and

20% in an advisory decision. Approximately half of the advisory decisions were accepted, and the remaining half were taken to arbitration. Of the 12 cases that went to arbitration after an advisory opinion, nine were decided as the mediator had predicted.

The mediator's success in resolving grievances was due to a number of factors. At times the mediator found that the parties were not listening seriously to each other's proposals. In such a situation, the presence of the mediator frequently resulted in better communications between the parties, leading to a prompt settlement. Settlements in other cases were achieved by such devices as narrowing the scope of the dispute, expanding its scope, or proposing an experimental solution. Frequently, the mediator's opinion as to the likely outcome if the grievance was arbitrated was sufficient to persuade the representatives and, sometimes more importantly, their constituents that one party or the other was so likely to prevail that arbitration would be a waste of time and money. Finally, the mere opportunity to be heard by a mediator was sometimes sufficient to put a dispute to rest, as the parties' main concern was to have their grievance considered by a neutral. Once this had been accomplished, they had little interest in being heard by another neutral, the arbitrator, particularly in view of the time and cost associated with arbitration.

The time and cost savings of mediation over arbitration were great. The average grievance was resolved in 15 days from the date on which mediation was requested, some three months faster than resolution through arbitration. The cost of mediation averaged $295, less than one-third of the cost of arbitration. The total financial savings to the parties in the experimental period was approximately $100,000.

The internal settlement rate did not diminish with the advent of mediation, except in the state that changed its trigger mechanism from mutual-consent to everything-goes, a change that was associated with a 12% decrease in the internal settlement rate. That decrease took place at the same time that a union election was pending, however, so we are not certain of the extent to which the availability of mediation was responsible for the decrease. Furthermore, because of the low cost of mediation compared to arbitration, the overall costs of grievance resolution remained well below such costs prior to the availability of mediation.

User satisfaction with mediation was tested among five groups — company labor relations representatives, union representatives, operating personnel, local union officers, and grievants. A substantial majority of all groups was satisfied with all aspects of the mediation procedure. When asked which procedure they preferred — mediation or arbitration — all groups preferred mediation, particularly at the local level where company operating personnel preferred mediation 6–1 and union officers did so 7–1. The reason for the preference was primarily the lack of formality at mediation, which was said to lead to a more relaxed atmosphere, better communications, more satisfactory outcomes, and an absence of the hard feelings that frequently accompany arbitration.

In sum, the results of this experiment show that mediation is capable of resolving a high proportion of grievances promptly and inexpensively, through a procedure that the parties prefer to arbitration.

Arbitration Costs/Time:
Labor and Management Views

PETER A. VEGLAHN
Clarkson College

The cost and time required to complete an arbitration case have been increasing. The average cost of an arbitration case requiring a one-day hearing has been reported to be over $2000 per side.[1] This figure does not include any costs encountered in complying with the arbitrator's award. The average time from grievance date to receipt of arbitration award is over 220 days.[2]

The cost of the typical arbitration case and the time required to complete the procedure have been the subject of much discussion among neutrals and academicians.[3] The numerous articles dealing with expedited forms of arbitration also seem to lead to the conclusion that arbitration costs/time are subjects of concern. The suggestion has been made that the parties are not concerned with the costs or time delays of the arbitration process.[4] The views of the labor and management, who pay the costs and are most affected by time delays are, however, largely unknown.

Are the time required to complete an arbitration case and the cost of the procedure concerns of labor and management? Is there a different degree of concern in the private and public sectors? What methods are being used to reduce the time and cost? How effective are these methods? The results reported below seek to answer these questions.

Individuals responsible for overseeing the processing of grievances through arbitration in unions and companies were sent questionnaires. One hundred and fifty-four union organizations and 161 companies were surveyed. Mailing lists were generated by a random sample of the *Directory of Labor Organizations in New York State* and the 1976 *New York State Industrial Directory*. Some of the union organizations had either changed their offices or ceased to exist and five companies had gone out of business or changed their locations. In addition, twelve companies replied that the survey was inapplicable since they were non-union.

The questionnaire produced 72 usable returns from management and 33 usable returns from unions. The usable return rates were 50% of the management sample and 23% of the union sample. The low return rate for the union sample may have been caused by the date of the sampling frame (1971). Of the management responses, 66 were from the private sector and six from the public sector. Private sector union organizations accounted for 24 of the 33 union responses, with public sector organizations making up the remainder. Company size ranged from less than

From *Labor Law Journal*, January 1979, pp. 49–57. Reprinted by permission of the author.

100 unionized employees to over 2000 unionized employees. Union size ranged from less than 100 members to over 4000 members.[5]

Neither the time involved in arbitration nor the costs of the process were viewed as a problem by a majority of the respondents. Of the unions responding, 42% (14) considered time a serious or potential problem and 33% (11) viewed costs as a problem or potential problem. The percentages for management were slightly lower with 40% (29) of the management respondents feeling time was a problem and 30% (22) feeling cost was a problem. The majority feeling seems to be that costs/time are not serious concerns. Neither the size of the organization nor the number of grievances taken to arbitration per year was significantly related to the consideration of time or cost as a problem for both unions and management.

Many organizations, whether concerned with time and cost or not, used time and cost saving steps in their arbitration procedures. . . . Some of the time and/or cost saving methods are directed at reducing the arbitration hearing time while others seek to reduce the time/cost required to receive an award. Still other methods seek to make the entire process more efficient and effective. A brief discussion of some of the methods, the intent of the method, and management and union utilization of the method follows.[6]

JOINT STIPULATION OF THE ISSUE AND FACTS

The use of joint stipulation can reduce both time and cost. The hearing time needed can be substantially reduced if the parties can stipulate the issue to be heard by the arbitrator. A mutually agreed upon issue allows the arbitrator to more easily focus attention on crucial points. A joint stipulation of facts eliminates the time required to establish basic foundation points through testimony.

Companies utilized joint stipulations of fact and issue as time saving methods more than any other technique. When one of these methods is used, the other tends to be used. The joint stipulation of issues was the second most popular cost saving technique among companies, with joint stipulation of facts being the third most heavily used method.

Unions utilized the joint stipulation of issue as a time saving method fairly often, the technique being the fourth most heavily used method. As a cost saving device, joint stipulation of issue was the third most popular method. Joint stipulation of facts was not as popular with unions as with management. As a time saving device, the joint stipulation of facts was the ninth most heavily used method. As a cost saving technique stipulation of facts was the eighth ranked method.

PRE-ARBITRATION CONFERENCE

The object of a pre-arbitration conference (after the appointment of an arbitrator and scheduling of a hearing but prior to hearing date) is to give management and labor one final opportunity to resolve the dispute without intervention. Such a result would obviously eliminate both time and cost. In the absence of resolution of the dispute, time/cost can be reduced through the establishment of ground rules, procedures, and facts.

For both managements and unions, a pre-arbitration conference was a frequently used time saving device. Unions utilized the method more than any others and management utilized only joint stipulations more frequently. As a cost saving technique, a pre-arbitration conference was not heavily utilized by management (ranking tenth). Unions, however, frequently used this method as a cost saver.

If the arbitrator is present at a pre-arbitration conference, the opportunity for mediation exists. Even if no pre-arbitration conference is held, an arbitrator will occasionally attempt to mediate a dispute. Mediation could potentially save both time and costs. Neither unions or management utilize mediation efforts by neutrals in the grievance procedure to any great extent.

ELIMINATION OF TRANSCRIPTS

This technique reduces both time and cost. The hearing can proceed more quickly without a court reporter. Advocates do not have to wait to receive the transcript before preparing and filing post-hearing briefs. The arbitrator tends to reduce his study time since a voluminous transcript does not have to be analyzed. These points, in addition to the substantial costs associated with transcript preparation, have led several authorities to recommend elimination of transcripts in all but the most important and complicated cases. [7]

As both a time and cost saving procedure, the elimination of transcripts was frequently used by management. The method was the third most heavily used time saving procedure (tied with a pre-arbitration conference) and the third most heavily used cost saving procedure (tied with the joint stipulation of facts). Among unions the method was frequently used as a time saving technique (fourth most heavily used procedure along with several others). As a cost saving device, the elimination of transcripts was not utilized to any great extent by unions (tied for eleventh most heavily used method). One union indicated that the existence of a transcript is invaluable in establishing the positions of the parties to the arbitrator and, as such, should not be eliminated as a way of saving time or money.

BRIEFS AND EVIDENCE

The use of briefs can be viewed as either adding to costs and time or reducing costs and time. A well written pre- or post-hearing brief can concisely summarize the positions of the parties and eliminate the need for lengthy opening and closing statements. Others would contend that briefs add to the neutral's study time, increase advocate's costs, and add little to the material presented in the hearing. As a time saving method among companies, the use of pre- or post-hearing briefs was the fifth most heavily used method. The elimination of briefs was the sixth

ranked method. Unions rarely utilized pre- or post-hearing briefs as time savers with the method ranking fourteenth. The elimination of briefs, however, was the most popular time saver.

As a cost reducing technique, the use of pre- or post-hearing briefs was the fifth most utilized technique by management and the eighth most utilized technique by unions. The elimination of briefs was the eighth most utilized method by both unions and management. A related time saving technique, the reduced use of cites, was not utilized to any extent by either unions or management.

The use of expert witnesses normally adds to the cost of the procedures. Less reliance on such witnesses was the sixth most popular cost saving method with management and the third most popular with unions. The extensive use of affidavits and exhibits can reduce time and cost. However, the method was not popular as a cost saving device although unions utilized the technique somewhat frequently as a time saving device.

The use of precedent was more popular with unions than with management, being the sixth most utilized time saving method by management and the third most utilized by unions. As a cost saving device, the use of precedent ranked tenth with management and third with unions.

ARBITRATOR DECISIONS

Several methods seek to reduce time and cost by reducing the time/cost associated with an award. Among these methods are the issuance of bench awards, reducing the time between the hearing date and the award date, the appointment of a permanent umpire, and the repeated use of the same *ad hoc* arbitrator. None of these methods were heavily utilized by either unions or management as time or cost saving methods. The expedited labor arbitration procedure of the American Arbitration Association was, however, the most heavily used time and cost saving method by unions. Managements ranked expedited arbitration tenth as a cost saving device and eighth as a time saver. The expedited procedure calls for, among other things, the elimination of briefs, an award in summary written form, and the elimination of a stenographic record.

USE OF NONLAWYERS AS ADVOCATES

Reducing the costs of advocacy was the most popular method of cost reduction by management and the third most popular by unions. Both groups feel that, in a majority of cases, a well-trained nonlawyer can adequately represent their interests in the arbitration procedure.

Some major differences in usage of methods between unions and management existed. The differences in time saving techniques were over the methods of using a pre- or post-hearing brief, joint stipulation of facts, AAA expedited arbitration, and reducing the time between arbitration and the previous step in the grievance procedure. Major differences in the utilization of cost saving techniques were over the methods of AAA expedited arbitration, pre-arbitration conferences, elimination of transcripts, use of precedent, and extensive use of affidavits and exhibits existing between management and unions. Neither group engaged to any extent in the use of inexperienced neutrals or bench awards to reduce costs.

Companies and unions feeling that either cost or time was a problem were asked to rate the success of their overall attempts to solve the cost and time problem. Unions rated their attempts at cost reduction as less successful than management. Neither group rated their cost saving attempts as more than moderately successful. Unions also rated their time reduction attempts as less successful than management. Management rated their attempts at time reduction as moderately successful.

Those respondents among both management and unions who specified some other method of either cost or time reduction (e.g., those who utilized a method which did not fall into the types of methods specified in the questionnaire) felt that

their method was effective in reducing time and/or cost. The most frequent comment about methods made by both companies and unions concerned the overall management-union climate. A good relationship, the parties indicated, is the best method for reducing the time and cost of arbitration. A good relationship allows grievances to be settled at lower steps and, if the issue goes to arbitration, reduces the hearing time required.

One company indicated that no arbitration cases had occurred in the past ten years. This was attributed to allowing additional union-management meetings beyond those established in the grievance procedure. If the time limits set up in the procedure were violated, the company felt that a past practice defense would make the issue arbitrable. This company also attempted to research the issue, examining published awards in similar cases. The company was aware of the difficulty of finding established patterns and of the nonbinding aspects of precedent in arbitration cases. However, the company indicated that such investigations were useful in shifting both management and union positions on issues.

Companies also indicated that the use of participative management and labor-management grievance review committees is useful in reducing the time and cost of arbitration. One company which felt that cost and time were not problems attributed the absence of these problems to its initial investment of time and money in the grievance procedure and arbitration. This effort had, according to the company, resulted in a "winning" record which led to a significant reduction in the number of cases going to arbitration. Another company indicated that, while the use of nonlawyers could significantly reduce both the cost and time of arbitration, the union was unwilling to follow such a procedure. This company was apparently unwilling to follow such a procedure unless the union also used nonlawyers.

A large company felt that the cost and time problems of arbitration occur due to the increasing numbers of cases being processed through the arbitration step. This company felt the reason for the increase in arbitration activity was a desire by the unions to avoid lawsuits by their members charging them with unfair representation.

Several union organizations in both the public and private sectors indicated that the costs of arbitration were not a problem due to cost-sharing arrangements with the parent body. One private sector union indicated that the international union pays the entire cost, but that the excessive time delays of the typical arbitration procedure had led them to agree to an expedited procedure. This procedure was too new to evaluate. Several companies felt that costs were much more of a problem for unions than managements.

CONCLUSION

Labor and management in both the private and public sectors are not greatly concerned with the time and cost of arbitration. Those organizations which do express concern tend to disagree over the causes of time delays and cost increases. The methods frequently followed by unions and managements to reduce the time problem are joint stipulation of the issue, the elimination of transcripts, and a pre-arbitration conference seeking to resolve both substantive and procedural issues. The parties do not frequently use methods of reducing time such as reducing their use of cites or the amount of time between the hearing and the award, relying on a bench (verbal) award instead of a written award, improving the method of selecting an arbitrator, or allowing the arbitrator to mediate.

Cost reduction methods which are used by both union and management are the joint stipulation of the issue and the use of nonlawyers as ad-vocates. Those methods which are used infrequently by both sides include the use of inexperienced neutrals, mediation by the arbitrator, using the same arbitrator over a period of time, and relying on a bench award.

NOTES

1. Zalusky, "Arbitration: Updating a Vital Process," *AFL-CIO American Federationist,* Vol. 83, No. 11 (November 1976), p. 108.

2. These FMCS averages are reported in the article cited above.

3. Both the National Academy of Arbitrators and the Society of Professionals in Dispute Resolution have shown concern over the costs/time of arbitration. See Prasow, "The Arbitrator's Role," *The Public Interest and the Role of the Neutral in Dispute Settlement* (Society of Professionals in Dispute Resolution: Washington, D.C., 1973), pp. 85–92; Luskin, "The Presidential Address," *Developments in American and Foreign Arbitration.* Proceedings of the 21st Annual Meeting. National Academy of Arbitrators (BNA: Washington, D.C., 1968), pp. 126–135: Nash, "The NLRB and Arbitration," *Arbitration — 1974,* Proceedings of the 27th Annual Meeting, National Academy of Arbitrators (BNA: Washington, D.C., 1974), pp. 133.

4. Kane, "Current Developments in Expedited Arbitration," *Labor Law Journal,* Vol. 24, No. 5 (May 1973), pp. 282–287.

5. Company size was determined by ascertaining the number of unionized employees. Union size was ascertained by determining the number of members over which the union official assumed the responsibility for processing grievances through arbitration.

6. In the following discussion, 18 time saving methods and 17 cost saving techniques are discussed.

7. Among those discussing this issue are F. and E. Elkouri, *How Arbitration Works.* 3d Edition (Washington, D.C.: BNA, 1973); and Smith, Merrifield, and Rothschild, *Collective Bargaining and Labor Arbitration,* (Indianapolis: Bobbs-Merrill, 1970).

Expedited Arbitration: Less Grief over Grievances

LAWRENCE STESSIN
Hofstra University

Labor arbitration is the final act in a real-life industrial drama that usually opens with the line, "I've got a grievance." No one knows how many times a day any one of the close to 20 million unionized workers utters this snippet of verbal eloquence. But one thing is certain: the settlement of the complaint, if it goes to arbitration, as thousands do every year, becomes a waiting game of frustration for both labor and management.

For more than half a century, arbitration as a road to industrial peace resolved countless on-the-job disputes under the banner of "speed, justice, and efficiency." In 1940, Walter Reuther expressed the prevalent view: "You cannot strike General Motors plants on individual grievances. You have to work out something. I don't want to tie up 90,000 workers because one worker was laid off for two months. This is a case for arbitration."

Today, this implicit confidence has a hollow ring. Grievance arbitration as it is structured in over 100,000 union contracts has lost many of its virtues, being neither economical nor quick, neither flexible nor informal. Evidence abounds that the system has succumbed to the vice of rigidity and is often ill-designed to serve as a quick means for settling disputes between workers and the boss.

Any random group of arbitration decisions tells a dismal story of how long it takes, how costly it has become, and how tempers of employees and supervisors flare when dealing with even the most prosaic complaints. In a typical case, a worker is suspended for two days over some alleged violation of company rules, so he sets forth his complaint on a grievance form. Before he receives an arbitrator's essay, which is often both lofty and obscure, 100 to 250 days might pass.

One case took four years of intermittent hearings before an award was finally handed down. Then there is the still unsettled grievance that is going into its tenth year before the Railway Arbitration Board in Chicago. The grievant has long since died, and any monetary balm that might be due him will go to his meager estate.

The spiraling cost of labor arbitration is also a problem. It costs each party between $500 and $1000 a day if one includes the whole panoply of stenographic records, witnesses, lawyers, hearing rooms, arbitrators' fees, and "think time" (a charge that most industrial referees add for deliberation preliminary to the writing of an award.

But there are more deep-rooted causes for the declining state of the art:

1. *The changing nature of the work force has added to the work load of standard grievance machinery.* Today's rank-and-file, brought up in a counterculture of permissiveness, have a low boiling point. They are more easily provoked by job frustrations once accepted as the price of working for a living, and these vexations spill over into formal grievances. A supervisor "loses his cool," raises his voice to a worker, and in no time there is a demand for the dismissal of the supervisor.

Since it is now the law that every employee must receive a copy of the union agreement, every unionized company has its share of shop lawyers dedicated to finding loopholes in the contract. A worker phones his foreman and says he will be out for three days. "Why?" asks the supervisor. Replies the shop legalist: "The union contract doesn't say I have to give a reason."

2. *Arbitration has lost its cracker-barrel ambiance.* Every discipline has its hot-stove league that likes to talk about the "good old days." When arbitration is mentioned, someone is sure to bring up the name of Harry Shulman, the dean of industrial peacemakers. Named in 1943 as impartial chairman to preside over the none-too-happy relationship between the Ford Motor Company and the United Auto Workers, Shulman (of Yale Law School) stamped arbitration with the credentials of speed and informality in settling day-to-day disputes. He set very few ground rules. Transcripts were generally forbidden. Formal rules of evidence were rarely invoked. One contemporary described Shulman's freewheeling comportment as uncontrolled sessions in group therapy.

Over the years, advocates of the Shulman style of handling labor-management rifts have not prevailed. As issues became more complex, contracts became longer and arbitration began to take on the trappings of a court procedure — including the gavel. In one case the parties produced 29 witnesses, 1936 pages of transcribed testimony, 145 exhibits, 15 pages of briefs, and 82 pages of rebuttal. The arbitrator, with a sense of whimsy unappreciated by the parties handed down an award in 27 words.

3. *New legislation motivates unions and management to arbitrate the application of statutes.* Three laws of relatively recent vintage (antidiscrimination guidelines, OSHA, and the pension reform act) account for more than a 15% rise in the number of disputes that go to arbitration.

In this era of raised consciousness, workers covered by the Equal Employment Opportunity Act and other antidiscrimination laws (women, blacks, hispanics, 40- to 65-year-olds, religious minorities) are sensitive to any managerial signs of token compliance with the law. With complaints being filed at state and federal antibias agencies at the rate of 300,000 a year, labor and management are resorting to arbitration more and more for a resolution of such disputes.

Few women take chauvinism lightly, no matter how "well intentioned," as in the case of the gallant supervisor who refused to promote a woman into a department where the men used language from the salty to the obscene. It took arbitration to force the employer to forsake his genteel attitude. Some time later, when she was asked whether the grimy language disturbed her, the woman reported: "It's not the swearing that bugs me; it's the constant apologies!"

The Occupational Safety & Health Act (whose administration polices and penalizes employers for safety hazards) has clogged the arbitration calendars because management has become hard-nosed toward workers who do not obey safety rules. In this area, the days of progressive discipline are over — when workers were warned two or three times before being given the gate. Outright discharge at the first serious safety offense is becoming the common rule. This comes as a shocking reality to many employees, who then insist that their unions go to arbitration to lessen the penalty.

It has been said that the Employee Retirement Income Security Act (ERISA), which deals with employee pensions and profit sharing, is the most complex piece of legislation ever passed by Congress. Just reading the act is an exercise in endurance. Controversies over the meaning of specific provisions are already in the datebooks of every professional arbitrator. And this is only the beginning.

CHANGING THE PATTERN

The streamlining of arbitration to manageable dimensions has not been without its advocates. At the extremes, they range from the philosophy of Lemuel Boulware, one-time labor relations head at General Electric, to Dennis McCarthy, a New York bus driver. Boulware's solution was to do away with arbitration. He had little faith in the notion that an outsider — an arbitrator — had better judgment than the parties to a dispute. Arbitration, he once observed, was a lazy substitute for eyeball-to-eyeball bargaining.

Dennis McCarthy found an even simpler solution. The classic silver-tongued Irishman, McCarthy was in the second hour of the hearing where he charged the New York Transit Authority with short-changing him $2.60 on one of his paychecks. Finally, Theodore Kheel, the famous arbitrator, asked him gently whether he felt there was some way in which the arbitration hearing could be speeded up. McCarthy thought for a moment, drew a long breath and replied: "Yessir. Let everyone talk faster."

Whether Boulware and McCarthy were the inspirations for draining arbitration of its tired blood, it is hard to say. But the traditional arbitration procedures have been undergoing some dramatic pruning. Although it has not yet taken on the characteristics of a crusade, a speedier process is attracting attention from executives and union leaders.

It began in earnest in 1971, when ten of the nation's largest steel companies and the United Steelworkers Union decided that the time for breast-beating and rhetoric was over. They entered into a three-year supplementary agreement and called it "expedited arbitration" — "mini-arb" in shop-talk. The objective was to go back in time to resurrect the old virtue of the arbitration process — speed in resolving internal disputes. After the experimental period, the parties were convinced that what they had wrought was good, and they incorporated the innovation into the collective bargaining agreements between the "Big Ten" in steel and the Steelworkers Union.

The expedited arbitration system in no way replaces regular arbitration for settling certain types of cases. The expedited version is a parallel track on the grievance route, and it helps to ease the backlog of cases awaiting an arbitrator's yea or nay. The decision to assign a case to regular arbitration or to the expedited setup is usually made by a labor-management committee at the second or third step in the grievance procedure.

PRESENT STATUS

As steel goes, can others be far behind? Today, more than 500 companies and unions use expedited arbitration as a mutually adopted policy including dozens of Teamsters locals, the Long Island Railroad, a consortium of aluminum companies, and General Electric, and none of these are known for veering from beaten paths.

The first question that inevitably confronts executives who may be rethinking their company's dispute-settlement policies is whether the adoption of expedited arbitration is worth the candle in terms of time saved. The answer is no longer academic.

Several task forces made up of union-management teams in the steel industry have monitored the time tables, and the results are dramatic. It is rare for a case channeled through the expedited route to stay on the books for more than 60 days. Indeed, the arbitration part of a typical dispute has shrunk to a day or two of hearings. As for the decision or the award, in most expedited agreements the arbitrator is formally charged with the duty to render his opinion by the next day.

If he pleads for an extension, a 24-hour "reprieve" may be granted by the parties. It is not unknown in "mini-arb" for an arbitrator to render a bench decision, verbally, minutes after the last of the arguments has been heard. Usually, most of the 60-day period is consumed by the preliminary grievance procedure, where the parties attempt to settle the disputes between themselves.

Union contracts ordinarily call for a three- or four-step grievance procedure, where the controversy grinds through a hierarchical mill until it reaches the upper ranks of labor and management. If the parties find themselves still at odds, the unresolved issue is bucked up to the arbitrator to finally close the case. But there is some movement to cut down on the step-by-step procedure.

One union (Philadelphia Marine Trades) recently took the plunge in its contracts with several employers and agreed to a one-step grievance setup. If a dispute is not settled between worker, supervisor, and union agent at the worksite, the issue proceeds to arbitration the following day. However, such a shortcut draws little praise from brass on either side of the collective bargaining table, because it denies them the opportunity to use their own negotiating skill to try to settle a dispute.

Limits to Expediency

In some cases, however, such as in the interpretation of a clause in an agreement, speed may not be an all-important criterion for settling confrontations between labor and management. Collective bargaining is a delicate and complex process. And a union contract, because it is drawn while the clock ticks toward a strike deadline, has many

vague areas. It is through the grievance machinery that disputes can be clarified without all the trauma of slowdowns and stoppages. There are always controversies that neither side would want to subject to the frailties of a one- or two-day expedited arbitration that produces a decision under the rule of the clock.

For example, the question whether a company can subcontract work while some of its employees are on layoff can become a delicate issue that seriously affects long-range planning. Most union contracts allow outside companies to perform certain work if the company can justify the action for economic reasons, or if there are no regular workers with the required skills for the particular project. Any arbitrator assigned to a subcontracting dispute cannot, if he's doing his homework, race through a hearing. He needs detailed briefings — the history of the issue in previous collective bargainings, the industry practice, the economic data on cost savings to the company, an analysis of the skills of the employees on layoff, and so on.

For this reason, some union-management agreements confine the use of expedited arbitration to discipline cases on the theory that the awards are not likely to have any serious impact on the economic fortunes of the company or on the power base of the union. Whether a five-day suspension for horseplay is a punishment that fits the crime is a value judgment that need not engage the time and talent of a whole array of specialists in the shop law of industrial relations. This rationale has led General Electric to restrict "mini-arb" to discipline situations and to provide that other issues go the straight and narrow of the formal arbitration route. . . .

ADDITIONAL BENEFITS

One of the big advantages of expedited arbitration is that it has brought many new faces into the dispute-settlement orbit. As arbitration is now formally practiced, 10% of the professional arbitrators handle about 90% of the cases. For one reason or another, labor and management have become attached to a small coterie of long-time practitioners. This creates a serious problem, because the chosen few have big backlogs of cases. It is not unusual for a case to be delayed as much as three months because the mutually agreed-upon referee is so solidly booked. The innovators of expedited arbitration (principally the steel industry and its union) quickly realized that if the "favorite son" syndrome were maintained, then all the advantages of the new procedure would be dissipated.

From the beginning, company and union representatives selected arbitrators for the expedited system who were newcomers to the art. The law schools, their faculties and deans, and in some instances regional bar associations, became the recruiting grounds for the new breed of industrial peacemakers. In the steel setup, for example, each plant facility selects its own panel of arbitrators, and persons are chosen from this listing to hear cases as they come up. Since the choice is simply alphabetical, there is no wrangling over who should hear and decide a case — and neither side can turn down the next available arbitrator. This is a radical departure from formal arbitration, where either side has the right to reject suggested panelists until agreement is achieved.

A criticism often expressed by old-timers is that the parties to the expedited process leave delicate issues to the fumblings of new and inexperienced hands. This does not appear to have curtailed the growth of expedited arbitration. In steel, in aluminum, and in other industries, new arbitrators are given background tours and periodic seminars to acquaint them with the issues that may give rise to disputes. Not to be overlooked is the fact that panelists usually live in the region and are not unfamiliar with the industrial mores of the area, as well as the cultural makeup of the work force.

Another innovation is that minorities and women are being selected as arbitrators in a profession that until now has been male and lily-white. In steel alone there are more than 60 minority arbitrators on the expedited panels.

One of the myths of arbitration is that the hearings should be held at some "neutral spot," away from the origins of the dispute. The logic is that distance makes for greater objectivity. The expedited system has completely abandoned this concept; in fact the hearings are usually held in the very plant where the controversy arose. This localized peacemaking has many advantages:

1. No travel is required for the principals in the dispute, which saves time and money.

2. The arbitrator can quickly visit the site of the dispute if necessary and even conduct on-the-job interviews with those involved.

3. Lawyers are rarely used to represent the parties, so the arbitrator can elicit the facts and clarifications needed, and more and more unions and managements are permitting supervisors and workers to present their own versions with a minimum of direction or coaching from headquarters.

4. The mystique goes out of arbitration. What happens in a hearing room becomes part of shop gossip and the communication mill. Neither management nor labor officials see this as a handicap.

The length of the award or decision in expedited arbitration is perhaps its most appealing feature. The rules caution arbitrators not to write for posterity. A page or two is the average — although some arbitrators unaccustomed to such brevity use narrower margins and legal-size paper.

One would think that men and women with such talent for condensing weighty labor-management issues into brief decisions should be paid their weight in gold. Maybe so, but their checks don't show it. In expedited arbitration, the compensation of the panel members is cosmetic. The highest pay for arbitrators is only about $100 per day. With arbitrator costs so low, the average case runs about $60 per party. It can be even cheaper, for in many expedited cases the parties bunch several disputes into one package and reap decisions at bargain prices.

Is expedited arbitration an idea whose time has come? No easy assessment can be made. The procedure does have its many influential and highly articulate detractors. For example, there are professional arbitrators, most of whom are lawyers trained in the toilsome ways of the judicial process, who have not rallied around "instant arbitration." Cynics might say that their opposition is self-serving. In expedited arbitration the pay is small, the cases are short, and the opportunity for massaging one's literary ego through writing of elaborate awards is negligible.

Expedited arbitration will prevail and grow primarily if there is energetic prodding from the top. Once a chief executive officer begins to ask questions about the impact of delayed grievances on employee morale and production, expedited arbitration will inevitably emerge as an attractive alternative to the status quo.

SECTION 6
Emerging Areas of Collective Bargaining

INTRODUCTION

At the present time the American labor movement faces a major challenge. Changing patterns of industrial employment, technological change, nonunion employers, and foreign competition are combining to reduce union membership. This trend has been underway for many years. As mentioned in Section 2, union membership as a percent of nonagricultural employment peaked at 35 percent in 1954, and has been declining since. In 1980 less than 24 percent of the nonagricultural work force was unionized.

While the general trend has been unfavorable from the labor movement's point of view, there are areas in which progress has been made. Union membership in the public sector and in the health care industry has increased dramatically in the last two decades. Progress is also being made in the organization of agricultural workers, and while their numbers are small, the organization of professional sports is largely complete.

Even with these advances, the proportion of the work force that is organized continues to decline. The labor movement has as yet been largely ineffective in responding to the two challenges posed by the unionization of women and the threats to the job security of American workers posed by multinational corporations. The readings in this section address emerging sectors of collective bargaining. Included are the public sector, health care industry, organization of women workers, and multinational unionism.

INTRODUCTION TO THE READINGS

Multilateral Bargaining

Michael Marmo presents a new perspective on multilateral bargaining in the public sector. In contrast to the bilateral bargaining relationship between the certified bargaining agent and the employer in the private sector, public-sector bargaining involves various groups with vested interests concerning the outcome of negotiations and other labor relations processes. This stems largely from the diffuse nature of management in the public sector. For example, within city government, possible decision-making centers include the mayor, city council, and personnel director.

Marmo notes that the original multilateral bargaining concept assumed that government decision-makers reacted to interest groups. For example, public-sector unions, groups activated by public-sector unions, and other groups concerned about the outcome of labor relations processes were assumed to bring pressure on government officials in order to influence their decisions. It was assumed that government decision-makers weighed the political clout of the various interest groups and made decisions to maximize their own political well-being, i.e., "formulate policy to win elections."

The article by Marmo asserts that government officials can play a far more active role in this process. Through news releases, news conferences, and interviews covered by the media, government officials can activate particular interest groups. Further, by controlling the information presented through these channels, government officials can influence the position taken by interest groups. Marmo makes it clear that the government decision makers' role in labor relations processes can be proactive rather than reactive as implied by the original concept of multilateral bargaining.

Dispute Resolution in the Public Sector

Thomas Kochan discusses the dynamics of dispute resolution in the public sector. Because of prohibition and limitation of the right to strike in the public sector, alternative impasse procedures have been developed that are designed to avoid strikes. Along with the objective of avoiding strikes in the public sector, American labor relations has placed major emphasis on free collective bargaining, i.e., minimization of third party involvement. The latter represents a competing objective, in that without the right to strike, some form of third party intervention is typically necessary when negotiations reach an impasse.

The potential narcotic effect and chilling effect of impasse procedures are described by Kochan. He describes the major procedural mechanisms used to resolve bargaining impasses in the public sector; mediation, fact-finding, and arbitration. With reference to mediation, Kochan discusses factors which appear to be associated with successful and unsuccessful efforts at mediation. He notes that the weight of the evidence suggests that mediation is more likely to lead to settlement when the next step is arbitration than when the next step is fact-finding.

Kochan points out that fact-finding is more than the name implies. Typically, fact finders also try to identify an acceptable compromise recommendation that will serve as a basis for settlement. He notes that comparability is a primary factor influencing fact-finding recommendations. The evidence reviewed by Kochan suggests that the effectiveness of fact-finding is decreasing. This may explain the increased incidence of state legislation providing for arbitration of bargaining impasses in the public sector.

The third impasse procedure is arbitration. Kochan observes that tripartite arbitration enables the parties to retain more control of the outcome of arbitration than does the single arbitrator system. This is relevant because mediation and negotiation continue during the arbitration process.

Kochan concludes by reviewing the multiple objectives that must be considered in designing public-sector dispute resolution procedures. He then discusses the impasse procedure most consistent with attainment of particular objectives.

Health Care Industry

Collective bargaining in the health care industry has grown rapidly in recent years, reflecting the 1974 health care amendments to the NLRA. In the 1960s approximately 9% of hospital employees were represented by labor unions. By 1978 the proportion of organized hospital employees exceeded 20%. Since health care expenditures represent just under 10% of total gross national product, it is important to understand labor-management relations in this industry.

Miller describes labor-management relations in hospitals. He contrasts the types of contract provisions typically found in hospital collective bargaining agreements with those observed in other industries. While there are major similarities, he notes that hospital collective agreements have relatively few provisions pertaining to job security. He also points out that the available evidence indicates that unionization appears to have a smaller impact on wages and salaries than that found in other industries.

Miller also discusses trends in labor-management conflict in hospitals. It was hypothesized by some that the health care amendments to the NLRA would lead to increases in the incidence of strikes in hospitals. Miller reports that even though there were large increases in the number of collective bargaining agreements following 1974 when the amendments became law, the number of work stoppages remained at approximately the same level. He discusses possible explanations for the absence of an increase in strikes following 1974 as well as reasons for the lower level of conflict in the hospital industry relative to other industries.

Organization of Women

Koziara and Insley report data that make it clear that women represent a major portion of the labor force who are as yet largely unorganized. They note that two-thirds of all women employed full-time work in white-collar occupations. However, only about 13 percent of women employed in white-collar jobs are union members. This suggests that unions modeled along traditional lines are not successful in organizing women employed in such jobs.

Koziara and Insley describe new organizations that have developed outside the traditional labor movement that focus on improving the employment conditions of women, particularly women in low income jobs. These organizations seek to improve "bread-and-butter" conditions of employment, but in addition they try to ensure that women are treated with dignity. For example, efforts are made to eliminate sexual harassment and demeaning treatment by supervisors.

These organizations do not rely on traditional union tactics to bring about change. Rather, they rely on information gathering, conciliation, and pressure through adverse publicity. Further, Koziara and Insley point out that these organizations typically seek to remain independent of traditional unions. The authors also suggest that the motivation of women to join these organizations is different from the reasons that motivate workers to join traditional unions. They indicate that women joining the nontraditional organizations, in addition to seeking increased earnings, also express a concern about their limited advancement opportunities. Possibly in the years to come we will see a new breed of union that will be more effective in representing the interests of women, and consequently more effective in organizing women.

Multinational Unionism

Lloyd Ulman discusses incentives, barriers, and alternatives to development of international unionism and collective bargaining. Among the incentives for national unions in high wage nations to promote international unions is the fear of probable loss of their jobs to developing nations. Therefore it is in the interest of unionists in high wage nations to facilitate wage increases in developing nations. On the other hand, Ulman notes that workers in developing nations do not have to fear loss of jobs as a consequence of such wage increases. Finally, the multiplant nature of multinational corporations, coupled with limited product differentiation, would enable such employers to temporarily switch production from those closed by labor disputes to plants in other countries.

However, we have observed little effort and

progress in the development of international unionism and collective bargaining. This suggests that the barriers discussed by Ulman may be too formidable. Among them are the reluctance of national union leaders to give up a portion of their autonomy to some international union body. Other barriers discussed are the possible inconsistency of international unionism with the economic goals and labor laws of individual nations and the extreme differences in ideologies of union leaders and structures of union movements across national boundries.

Another factor contributing to limited development of international unionism may be the availability of alternative, short-term solutions to problems posed by the growth of multinational corporations. For example, Ulman points out that national unions may bargain for assurances that plants will not be closed or that advance notice will be provided in the event of mass layoffs. Other alternatives involve increased involvement of national governments, i.e., protectionist legislation limiting imports.

Ulman's paper was written about ten years ago when the problems of international competition faced by unionists in North America and Western Europe were pale in comparison to those faced in the 1980s. As of this writing, efforts to protect these workers largely involve variations of the alternatives described by Ulman. However,

these are short-term solutions. Perhaps the coming decade will see the emergence of an effective international union movement.

SUGGESTIONS FOR FURTHER READING

For those interested in additional material related to the topics addressed in this section, the following readings are suggested.

Aaron, Benjamin, Joseph R. Grodin, and James L. Stern, Eds., *Public Sector Bargaining,* Washington, D.C.: Bureau of National Affairs, Inc., 1979.

Chelius, James R. and James B. Dworkin, "Free Agency and Salary Determination in Baseball," *Labor Law Journal,* Vol. 33, No. 8, August 1982, pp. 538-45.

Flanagan, Robert J. and Arnold R. Weber, Eds., *Bargaining Without Boundaries: The Multinational Corporation and International Labor Relations,* Chicago, Ill.: University of Chicago Press, 1974.

Koziara, Karen S., "Agriculture," in *Collective Bargaining: Contemporary American Experience,* Gerald G. Somers, Ed., Madison, Wis.: Industrial Relations Research Association, 1980, pp. 263-314.

Reed, Keith A., "The National Labor Relations Act and Health Care Institutions: The Persistent Paradox," *Employee Relations Law Journal,* 1979, pp. 357-76.

Stieber, Jack, Robert B. McKersie, and D. Quinn Mills, Eds., *U.S. Industrial Relations 1950-1980: A Critical Assessment,* Madison, Wis.: Industrial Relations Research Association, 1981.

Multilateral Bargaining in the Public Sector: A New Perspective

MICHAEL MARMO
Xavier University

Some 14 years ago, McLennan and Moskow coined the term multilateral collective bargaining to distinguish public-sector negotiations from the essentially bilateral process that prevails in the private sector.[1] They reasoned that because various interest groups have a vested concern in the outcome of public-sector negotiations, they would seek to exert an influence on the bargaining process. In subsequent formulations, the term multilateralism was also used to refer to the diffuse nature of public management.[2] Although at present the term refers to both the multiplicity of groups applying pressure on public decision-makers and the fact that there are many decision-making centers (mayor, city council, personnel director, etc.) to be pressured, this paper will deal only with the former concern. It begins by presenting a "traditional" multilateral model and then refines this construct by viewing government as a more active participant in determining which groups become interested in the bargaining process and which aspects of the process are viewed as most significant. Of particular concern is the manner in which the media are used by government officials to activate interest groups, to structure the expectations of these groups, to determine which are the significant issues in bargaining, and to resolve the competing claims of various groups.

EXISTING MULTILATERAL MODELS

The central assumption of virtually all treatments that explicitly or implicitly utilize a multilateral approach to public-sector negotiations is that government decision-makers weigh the political "clout" of each of the interest groups seeking to influence the bargaining process, then make a decision to maximize their political well-being. This approach is well supported in the political science literature and is perhaps epitomized by Anthony Downs who observed that politicians "formulate policies in order to win elections, rather than win elections in order to formulate policies."[3] Following this tradition, Fogel and Lewin explain the behavior of politicians in the collective bargaining process by indicating that "they view the electorate as a number of interest groups, and then seek to determine and respond to the relative importance of such groups."[4]

These multilateral models of bargaining, then, owe their intellectual debt to interest group explanations of political behavior. This approach views politicians as approaching their jobs in tabula rasa fashion, simply adding up the votes of

From *Proceedings of the Thirty-Fifth Annual Meeting,* Industrial Relations Research Association, Barbara D. Dennis, Ed., 1983, pp. 49–59. Reprinted by permission of the author and the IRRA.

295

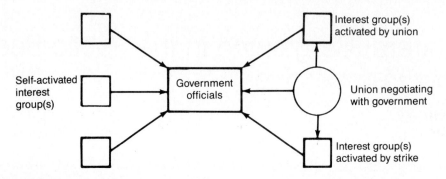

FIGURE 1

the various interest groups and then implementing into policy the predominant direction of their pressures. Diagrammatically, the government official is a centrally located blank box upon which interest groups, including the union with which they are negotiating, exert pressure (See Fig. 1).

The various interest groups presumed to be putting pressure on government officials in the bargaining process are entities such as the PTA, welfare rights organizations, and other groups that, without prodding, realize they have a vested interest in the collective bargaining process and attempt to exert pressure. In addition, more sophisticated multilateral models recognize that it is possible for a union that is engaged in bargaining to activate other interest groups to put pressure on government officials. For example, a union negotiating with city officials may prevail on other unions or the local Central Labor Council to pressure city government on their behalf. Finally, much has been written of the ability of unions to activate interest groups by virtue of their power to call a strike. When interest groups are activated by the deprivation of critical services, their sole concern is typically that the strike be ended.

ACTIVATING INTEREST GROUPS — THEORY

Perhaps the major shortcoming of existing models of multilateral bargaining is that they do

not recognize the ability of government officials to "create" support for their policies. Regardless of how it is achieved, a government official will enjoy political support so long as congruity exists between the views of the electorate and the response of the official with regard to those issues that are considered salient by voters. Of course, as existing models indicate, government officials can maintain their support by responding to the felt needs of various interest groups. However, a considerable body of recent political science literature indicates that it is also possible for a public official to achieve congruity between constituent views and government actions by influencing which issues become salient and by helping determine the position assumed by the various pressure groups regarding these issues. As perhaps the leading exponent of this view, Murray Edelman, observes, "Political actions chiefly arouse or satisfy people not by granting or withholding their stable substantive demands, but rather by changing the demands and the expectations."[5]

It should not be too surprising that in a complex society, with hundreds of issues clamoring for public attention, individuals and groups must depend on external cues regarding which issues are worthy of their consideration. Priorities for discussion of public issues seldom relate directly to the amount of money or manpower to be expended, nor are individuals or groups automatically activated because their own interests will be affected. Instead, matters that experts consider to have a very high priority may arouse only apathy unless they can somehow be elevated to a position of social importance. "The mass public does not study and analyze detailed data [about complex issues]," asserts Edelman, but instead "ignores these things until political actions and speeches make them symbolically threatening or reassuring. . . ."[6]

Although the ability of government officials to determine which issues become salient and their ability to influence "what" individuals and groups think about those issues are conceptually distinct, frequently both of these functions can be achieved by a single act. For example, a news conference by a mayor in which he or she denounces a welfare union's demands as benefiting welfare "cheaters" at the expense of middle-class taxpayers would both make this issue salient for particular interest groups and set the parameters for "how" the issue will subsequently be discussed.

Because government officials are typically unable to directly activate either the mass public or specific interest groups to become part of the collective bargaining process, it is critical that the media be used to achieve such activation. To return to the schematic representation, we now have an "interactive" system in which government officials are both acted on and initiate action (see Fig. 2). When government officials do activate interest groups, it is by using or, to employ the pejorative connotation, manipulating the media.

ROLE OF THE MEDIA

Because of the significance of the media for this analysis, a brief overview of how the media operate is necessary. Contrary to their frequent self-characterization as "mirrors of society," the news media, in fact, exercise an enormous degree of discretion in reporting the news. The media "are not a passive conduit of political activity," one media analyst has written, but rather "a 'filter' or 'gatekeeper,' whose institutional interests, definitions and prejudices influence what is reported and what is not. . . ."[7] Such institutional requisites of the news media determine both "what" is reported and "how" it is reported.

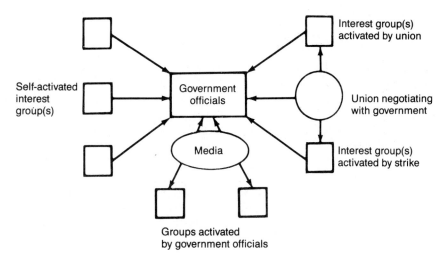

FIGURE 2

Although the media now include both print and electronic journalism, the old newspaper standard of "good copy" still applies as the primary determinant of whether a story will be covered. More specifically, the media generally use the following criteria to decide if a story has sufficient news interest to be reported. Most importantly, stories are considered newsworthy if they involve conflict, such as wars or strikes. Second, events should be close to home and should be perceived as having a high impact on readers or viewers. Next, stories should be "familiar" in the sense that they should involve familiar situations or well known individuals. And a final criterion for television news, the event should have "film value"; that is, it should be visually suitable for presentation on TV.

In addition to these criteria which relate to audience appeal, many stories are covered simply because they are guaranteed to materialize. Assignment editors will send reporters to cover news conferences or follow up on news releases because they are able to predict in advance that a newsworthy story is present. Thus a news conference by a mayor to discuss an impending strike is eminently newsworthy: it is local, involves a well-known politician, presents conflict, and is guaranteed to take place in time to be reported on the news that evening.

The requirements of a "good story" also dictate "how" the article or report will be presented — the "angle" of the story. Walter Lippmann's observation some 60 years ago that newspaper reporting is, in large part, a process of filling out an established "repertory of stereotypes" with current news is still valid.[8] In fact, the advent of television news has exacerbated the problem of the news media dealing with problems stereotypically. Because a TV news report lasts only a few minutes, it is impossible to deal accurately with complex issues or long-term trends. As television news executive Reuven Frank has observed, news programs should contain the same elements as fiction or drama; they should have structure and conflict, a problem and its resolution, rising and falling action, and a beginning, a middle, and an end.[9]

Since conflict is presumed to be of greatest interest to the news audience, it is always stressed. If the conflict involves confusing elements, it will typically be reconstructed in the form of a two-sided conflict because confrontations between clearly defined sides are considered most dramatic.[10] Ideally, for maximum dramatic impact, the conflict should pit the forces of good against the forces of evil.

ACTIVATING INTEREST GROUPS — IN PRACTICE

The attempt by government officials to "sell" their policies is hardly a cottage industry. In recent years the expenditures by government to influence perceptions of their activities had equalled the outlays of commercial advertisers. As pervasive as such activity is, however, it is not typically regarded as being manipulative because it almost always has the trappings of "objective" fact. The historian, Daniel Boorstin, has dubbed the staging of events by government officials so that they simulate reality "pseudo-events."[11] Because such "pseudo-events" are created specifically for the purpose of achieving media coverage, they are potent forces in defining issues as being worthy of societal attention. "Pseudo-events" typically used by government officials to stimulate one or more groups' interest in what is happening in collective bargaining include press conferences, briefings, interviews, press releases, and news leaks. The success of "pseudo-events" in garnering media attention is illustrated by a recent study which indicated that 75% of the news stories on local television stations originate from press releases.[12] Thus a mayor bargaining with a firefighters' union over how a reduction in force should be accomplished might activate black and women's organizations by stating in a press release that the union's proposal to use strict seniority would disproportionately create layoffs among black and women firefighters.

Because our concern is with activating interest groups, it must be emphasized that efforts at manipulating public attitudes are typically directed at "opinion leaders" rather than the mass public. As one analyst has recently written, "Mass media impact on a handful of political decision makers usually is vastly more significant than similar impact on thousands of ordinary individuals.[13] A newspaper story indicating that a police union is pushing very hard in negotiations to end the city's residency requirement for police officers may be of little interest to the general public. However, the story would likely be of considerable interest to leaders of black organizations who would readily see the implications of such a change on the racial composition of the police department.

GOVERNMENT INFLUENCE ON "WHAT" THE PUBLIC THINKS

Government officials enjoy a uniquely privileged status in being able to influence the way in which public issues are perceived, for three reasons: they have control over the flow of information, they have the ability to act in an official capacity, and they have access to the media.

Government officials have access to certain information that is not generally available, and they also have the ability to control the dissemination of such relevant facts. By controlling much of the information that is available concerning public-sector negotiations, they have tremendous control over the public's perception of what is taking place. As a recent study of government agencies concluded, "bureaucratic propaganda uses truth for organization goals" by "presenting managed and often contrived reports as though they were done 'scientifically' and therefore depict 'objective' truth."[14] For example, a local school board negotiating with a teachers' union might issue a press release indicating that because of the state reimbursement formula and the presence of categorical federal grant monies, the school board's proposal has a *net* cost to the school district that is lower than the union's proposal,

even though the total cost of the board's proposal is considerably greater. Lacking such information themselves, interest groups such as the PTA would be hard pressed to disagree with the school board's assessment.

Public officials can also mold opinion regarding public-sector negotiations by simply exercising official powers. A mayor may prevail upon the city's health commissioner to declare a health emergency during a strike by municipal sanitation workers, thereby putting the onus on the union for endangering public health. Or, in those situations where public-sector strikes are enjoinable, government officials may initiate legal actions in order to brand the striking union as having no respect for the law.

Finally, government officials can disproportionately influence perceptions of public-sector negotiations because their position accords them ready access to the media. If a mayor has a statement concerning negotiations with a municipal union, it will be covered by the media simply because the opinions of well-known officials concerning conflict situations are considered news.

Astute politicians are well aware that the issues involved in public-sector negotiations are far too complex to be accurately reflected by the media. They therefore seek to focus attention on a particular aspect of the bargaining process that satisfies media requirements for a "good story" and presents the government officials involved in a favorable light. "Power," writes political sociologist Peter Hall, "is achieved by controlling, influencing, and sustaining your definition of the situation since, if you can get others to share your reality, you can get them to act in the manner you prescribe."[15]

Perhaps the most effective way that government officials define problems to insure their own success is by the use of condensation symbols. Condensation symbols are names, phrases, maxims, etc., that evoke highly valued societal or group goals, but which are not subject to empirical verification. The basic function of condensation symbols is to provide instant categorization and evaluation — things that are essential for media presentation.

By using a condensation symbol, a complex set of issues that precipitated a teachers' strike may be reduced to the issue of "whether teachers who were hired to be role models for our children should be allowed to break the law." Or, a set of firefighter negotiations, which might involve such issues as pay parity with police officers, scheduling practices, and a voluntary affirmative action program, might symbolically become a question of "whether employees who have control over life and death situations ought to be allowed to hold a city hostage." In addition to being directed at the general public, condensation symbols can also be directed at specific interest groups as, for example, the characterization of a police union's proposal to carry shotguns in the front of their police cars as constituting racial genocide. Each of these examples of the use of condensation symbols contain the same basic elements: they are made for the media, they are stereotypic confrontations of good versus evil, and the government official is depicted as acting from the best of motives.

RESOLVING CONFLICTING EXPECTATIONS

Regardless of how various interest groups are activated or how they come to hold particular expectations of the appropriate course of government action to deal with labor relations questions, a final question remains: How are these conflicting expectations resolved? Wellington and Winter argue that these differences are resolved by performing a political calculus involving the distribution of fixed economic resources. "What he gives to the union," they observe, "must be taken from some other interest group or from taxpayers."[16] While correct in observing that differing expectations will be resolved on the basis of political considerations, Wellington and Winter exhibit considerable naivete in viewing government decision-making as involving only the distribution of "material" rewards. In fact, competing claims on government can be met through

the allocation of both material and "symbolic" rewards. As political scientist Dan Nimmo reminds us, ". . . politicians win popular acceptance and support as much because of emotional leadership as their ability to allocate material rewards. The tangible gains that citizens actually accrue are less critical in affirming popular loyalties to regimes than what people think they get."[17]

A wide range of symbolic gestures are available to politicians as a means of gaining acceptability for their actions. Again, it must be recognized that the granting of symbolic rewards is accomplished through the media, so politicians must frame such gestures with the media in mind.

Members of particular interest groups may be reassured through the device of well-publicized consultations with individuals who are perceived as "representing" their interests.[18] Even more reassuring is the establishment of a "blue-ribbon" committee to dramatize government concern and to delay decision-making until such time that the issue will no longer be salient for the interest group in question.[19] Thus an ad hoc parents group and various black organizations which have different opinions on the assignment of teachers to particular schools may all be pacified by the establishment of a high level commission to study the question.

In addition to symbolic acts, symbolic rhetorical devices are also available to government officials. Perhaps the most effective rhetorical device, because it meets all media requirements for a "good story," is to personify an enemy so that a dramatic encounter can take place between the forces of good and evil. The enemy may be a labor "boss" who is more interested in maintaining his own job than the fact that citizens simply cannot afford higher taxes, or a state legislature that requires local school boards to provide certain programs without providing commensurate financial support. By acting confident and self-assured in attacking a personified enemy, politicians will likely succeed because most individuals "want to believe that their leaders know what they are doing and so will accept a dramaturgical presentation of such ability on its own terms."[20] However, even if it is clear that a government official does not completely succeed in a dramatic confrontation, he will likely be perceived as having acted heroically, thus remaining worthy of support.[21]

SUMMARY

Of those interest groups participating in multilateral bargaining, some are self-activated, others are convinced by unions to become active, while additional groups may become activated by a strike. In addition, through the use of the media, government officials themselves have the power to activate interest groups. Regardless of how these various interest groups are activated, their competing claims will be resolved by government officials dispensing either material or symbolic rewards in a manner which maximizes the official's political well-being. Finally, symbolic rewards are typically disseminated through the media.

NOTES

1. Kenneth McLennan and Michael Moskow, "Multilateral Bargaining in the Public Sector," *Proceedings of the 21st Annual Winter Meeting,* Industrial Relations Research Association, 1968 (Madison, Wis.: IRRA, 1969), p. 31.

2. See, for example, Peter Feuille, "Police Labor Relations and Multilateralism," *Proceedings of the 26th Annual Winter Meeting,* Industrial Relations Research Association, 1973 (Madison, Wis.: IRRA, 1974), p. 170.

3. Anthony Downs, *An Economic Theory of Democracy* (New York: Harper & Bros., 1957), p. 28.

4. Walter Fogel and David Lewin, "Wage Determination in the Public Sector," *Industrial and Labor Relations Review* (April 1974), p. 414.

5. Murray Edelman, *Politics as Symbolic Action* (Chicago: Markham, 1974), p. 7.

6. Murray Edelman, *The Symbolic Uses of Politics* (Urbana: University of Illinois Press, 1964), p. 172.

7. James E. Combs, *Dimensions of Political Drama* (Santa Monica, Calif.: Goodyear, 1980), p. 123.

8. Cited in Edward Jay Epstein, *News from Nowhere: Television and the News* (New York: Random House, 1973), p. 164.

9. Epstein, p. 4.

10. Epstein, p. 262.

11. Daniel J. Boorstin, *The Image: A Guide to Pseudo-Events in America* (New York: Harper & Row, 1964).

12. David L. Altheide and John M. Johnson, *Bureaucratic Propaganda* (Boston: Allyn and Bacon, 1980), p. 62.

13. Doris Graber, *Mass Media and American Politics* (Washington: Congressional Quarterly Press, 1970), p. 15.

14. Altheide and Johnson, p. 23.

15. Peter Hall, "A Symbolic Interactionist Analysis of Politics," *Sociological Inquiry* 42 (1972), p. 51.

16. Harry H. Wellington and Ralph E. Winter, Jr., "The Limits of Collective Bargaining in Public Employment," *Yale Law Journal* 78 (June 1962), p. 63.

17. Dan Nimmo, *Political Communication and Public Opinion in America* (Santa Monica, Calif.: Goodyear, 1978), p. 87.

18. Edelman, *Politics as Symbolic Action,* p. 37.

19. Combs, p. 60.

20. Edelman, *Politics as Symbolic Action,* p. 38.

21. Orrin Klapp, *Symbolic Leaders: Public Dramas and Public Men* (New York: Minerva Press, 1968), p. 126.

Dynamics of Dispute Resolution in the Public Sector

THOMAS A. KOCHAN
Cornell University

INTRODUCTION

The central theme running throughout this paper's analysis of the dynamics of dispute resolution in the public sector is that the challenges became greater as the majority of states moved through their first decade of experience under collective bargaining statutes. Thus the transition to the second decade is characterized by (1) political and economic environments that produce disputes of greater intensity and complexity, (2) highly sophisticated bargaining representatives who are able to pursue aggressively the interests of their organizations through the various stages of dispute resolution, and (3) more assertive union members, management negotiators, politicians, and public interest groups. These developments follow the decade of experimentation with numerous dispute-resolution procedures designed to substitute for the right to strike — procedures so varied and so often changed that by now we have had some experience with most of the commonly discussed alternative systems.

Two important assumptions underlie the analysis: (1) the factors causing collective bargaining impasses are diverse; and (2) there is no "one best way" for resolving all types of disputes. Thus after reviewing the record of the

strike and its alternatives during this first decade of bargaining, the paper will conclude with a description of the options available to policy-makers holding different normative premises or assumptions regarding the appropriateness of alternative processes — fact-finding, arbitration, and the strike. . . .

PERFORMANCE OF DISPUTE-RESOLUTION PROCEDURES

Since impasse procedures are designed to avoid strikes, the central criterion for evaluating their effectiveness revolves around their relative effectiveness in deterring strike activity. In addition, however, the collective bargaining system in the United States has historically placed a premium on the process of "free" collective bargaining. That is, there is a deeply shared ethos among scholars, policy-makers, and practitioners that values the ability of the parties to settle their own disputes without the intervention of an outside third party. Thus one of the central objectives of any dispute-resolution procedure is to minimize the dependence of the parties on impasse procedures.[1] But some observers fear that the absence of an effective strike threat reduces the motivation to bargain and ultimately results in a process in which the parties become overdependent on the alternative procedures. This has been discussed in the literature as the "chilling" or the ''narcotic'' effects.[2] To the extent that these two problems occur in the bargaining system, we would expect over time to find (1) an increase in reliance on the procedures, and (2) less meaningful bargaining taking place prior to the intervention of third parties.

The same problems exist in evaluating the impact of impasse procedures on the bargaining process as were present in attempting to make aggregate comparisons of strike activity across different types of laws and procedures. The absence of adequate controls for other factors affecting the use of impasse procedures limits the conclusiveness of most analyses. A number of studies of experiences in specific jurisdictions or states can be used, however, to reach a number of tentative conclusions regarding the performance of these alternatives over the first decade of bargaining.

Dependence on Procedures: A Narcotic Effect?

There are at least two points in the sequence of impasse-resolution efforts that are often used for comparing the degree of dependence on the procedures. The first point is the rate of initial impasses filed. Most impasse procedures start with an effort at mediation. This point of the procedure is analogous to the rate of reliance on mediation in the private sector. The second point is the percentage of negotiations that require issuance of either a fact-finding report or an arbitration award.

Since the majority of jurisdictions outlaw the right to strike, it is not surprising that the rate of impasses is higher than the rate of reliance on mediation in the private sector. Similarly, the rates of going to either fact-finding or arbitration appear to be higher than the average rate of strikes in private-sector bargaining. For example, the Federal Mediation and Conciliation Service (FMCS) annual reports for the years 1967 through 1976 show that between 8 and 10% of all 30-day notifications of a contract expiration require a formal meeting with a mediator. Approx-

imately 15 to 20% of the contracts in the private-sector covered by FMCS require either a formal mediation meeting or informal discussions with the parties over the telephone.[3] Of the 30-day notifications, only between 2 and 3% of the negotiations end up in a strike.[4]

Although the rates of initial impasses and the use of fact-finding and arbitration in the public sector vary widely, every study examined for this paper shows a higher rate of intervention than do private-sector data. Consequently, the relevant question becomes not *whether* the absence of the right to strike will lead to greater intervention by third parties, but rather the *magnitude* of the difference that is associated with alternative forms of dispute-resolution procedures. . . .

The Chilling Effect

Most theories of the bargaining process suggest that hard bargaining or movement will occur when the costs of continuing the dispute exceed the costs of making a compromise or a concession to settle the dispute.[5] In short, the parties are expected to make significant compromises toward an agreement only when under pressure to do so. This explains why most intensive bargaining appears to occur in the final days or hours prior to a strike deadline. In the public sector where the strike is constrained, we should expect it to be even more difficult to get hard bargaining in negotiations prior to an initial impasse. To the extent that multiple steps are built into the impasse procedures that proceed from milder to stronger forms of intervention (e.g., mediation followed by fact-finding and/or arbitration), the ''final hour'' or moment of truth is even farther removed from the initial bargaining process. Thus while policy makers hope that the existence of impasse procedures will not ''chill''' bargaining, our theories of bargaining suggest that this is exactly what should happen.

A number of studies have attempted to assess the amount of hard bargaining or movement that takes place prior to impasses. Some of the early

studies of this issue provided reasonably optimistic findings.[6] More recently, studies of the
actual movement or compromising behavior have
reported greater evidence of a chilling effect in
negotiations. For example, a comparison of fact-
finding in Wisconsin and New York in 1972
revealed that 80% of the parties rated bargaining
prior to fact-finding as either slight or nonexistent,[7] and a multivariate study of fire fighter
bargaining found a number of cases in which no
movement off the initial positions took place prior
to an impasse.[8] Similar results were obtained in
an analysis of police and fire fighter bargaining in
New York State: unions and employers held back
concessions from their resistance points or
bottom-line positions, and the parties reported
that no or very little movement occurred prior to
impasse under both fact-finding and arbitration
statutes.[9] Even more disconcerting was the
disclosure that less movement (and a higher probability of impasse) occurred in negotiations involving more experienced negotiators.

Thus there is at least some direct evidence
that as the parties gained more experience with
bargaining, they became *less* willing to engage in
meaningful negotiations prior to impasse. While
these findings may not be generalizable to all of
the public sector, they do suggest that the chilling
phenomenon has become a significant problem in
these jurisdictions. Furthermore, the studies
reviewed above suggest that the chilling effect
may have become more serious in the latter half of
the first decade of bargaining, after the parties
became more experienced with negotiating under
dispute-resolution procedures.

DYNAMICS OF MEDIATION,
FACT-FINDING, AND ARBITRATION

In this section some of the dynamics of the three
major procedural mechanisms used to resolve
public-sector impasses — mediation, fact-finding, and compulsory arbitration — will be described. The theories underlying each procedure
will first be outlined in order to identify the expec-

tations that scholars and policy-makers had for
each technique when they were first proposed,
debated, and implemented. Then the performance of each technique in the public sector will
be reviewed in order to illustrate the extent to
which these a priori expectations were fulfilled in
practice. Emphasis will be placed on the ways in
which these procedures were modified and
adapted over time to fit different situations and
jurisdictions.

The Mediation Process

Mediation is perhaps the most widely used and
least understood dispute-resolution procedure in
collective bargaining. It is the first form of intervention in most disputes in both the private
and public sectors. Yet there are few empirical
studies of the mediation process. The few
theoretical statements that can be drawn from
studies of the private-sector mediation process
suggest that mediation can be most successful
when (1) the negotiations cycle has progressed to
the point where the parties are under the greatest
pressure to settle; (2) the mediator is acceptable to
and trusted by the parties; (3) the real bottom-line
positions of the parties either overlap or are not
far apart; and (4) the obstacles to a settlement
reflect a breakdown in the communication process more than a real substantive difference on the
economic or political issues involved.[10] The application of mediation as the initial step in impasse procedures in the public sector raises an additional important policy question: How effective
is mediation when followed by fact-finding, conventional arbitration, final-offer arbitration, the
right to strike, or some other form of dispute
resolution?

The above hypotheses were formalized into a
model of the mediation process and tested using
the New York police and fire fighter sample.[11]
Specifically, the effectiveness of mediation under
fact-finding and conventional arbitration was
compared, controlling for the effects of (1) different sources of impasse, (2) characteristics of the

mediator, and (3) the strategies employed by the mediator. The sample was drawn from the last round of negotiations by police and fire fighters under New York State's fact-finding statute and the first round of bargaining under conventional arbitration. Approximately 30% of the impasses that went to mediation were resolved at this stage prior to passing the dispute on to the next stage of the procedure. After controlling for the other factors outlined above, it was estimated that the change in the law from fact-finding to arbitration increased the effectiveness of mediation, or the probability of settlement, between 13 and 18%. That is, there was a marginal increase in the number of settlements achieved under the arbitration statute as compared to what would have been expected had fact-finding remained in effect. This marginal increase, however, was limited to small jurisdictions that were experiencing a catch-up effect in their wage settlements. Management negotiators in these jurisdictions, because they recognized that arbitration would very likely impose a relatively high wage settlement, were under pressure to avoid it, and the mediators recognized that they could use the threat of arbitration to induce the management negotiators to make significant movement. Thus the estimates of the effect of the change in the law probably suggest more about the impact of the threat of going to a procedure in which one party will be at a severe disadvantage than they imply about the inherent differences between mediation under fact-finding and under conventional arbitration.

The net effects of the change in the law were less important than the effects of some of the control variables examined. Specifically, the mediation process at this initial stage of the impasse procedure was *most* effective in resolving impasses where (1) the negotiators — especially the union negotiators — lacked experience; (2) the negotiations process broke down because one of the parties was overcommitted to a particular position; (3) a dispute was below average in intensity or difficulty, that is, the magnitude and number of

sources of impasse were relatively small; (4) the parties were motivated to reach a settlement; and (5) an aggressive, experienced, and high-quality (as perceived by the parties) mediator was involved. On the other hand, mediation was *least* successful in situations (1) where the underlying dispute arose because of an employer's inability to pay; (2) where the parties had a history of going to impasse and to the later stages of the dispute-resolution procedure; and (3) where the jurisdiction was among the largest. Some of the larger jurisdictions chose to skip the mediation process entirely since it was clear that any effort to resolve the dispute through mediation at the early stage of the impasse procedure was futile.

Other studies of the mediation process in the public sector have shown higher rates of settlement through mediation in the earlier stages of bargaining. For example, the early experience in Wisconsin under fact-finding was that more than 50% of the disputes were resolved through mediation. Under Wisconsin's final-offer statute, 70% of the cases going to mediation between 1973 and 1976 were settled at this step. [12] According to statistics published by the New York State Public Employment Relations Board, from 30 to 42% of all mediation cases involving teachers were settled at this initial stage of the procedure between 1968 and 1972. Furthermore, the same source reports that from 42 to 57% of all PERB cases were settled at the mediation stage over these five years. The data show a small drop in the percentage of cases settled by mediation in the later years and again reflect the tendency for the parties to go further into the procedures in this more recent time period. [13]

A group of mediators discussing the relative effectiveness of mediation under fact-finding, conventional arbitration, and final-offer arbitration indicated that, in general, mediation appears to be more meaningful under final-offer arbitration than under either of the other alternatives. This perception is consistent with the finding noted above that the percentage of cases going on to an award under final-offer arbitration in

Massachusetts, Wisconsin, and Michigan were all less than the percentage of cases going to conventional arbitration in New York State. Thus there does appear to be a stronger incentive effect associated with mediation under final-offer than under conventional arbitration. This effect is weakened, however, the farther the mediation process is removed from the arbitration step of the procedure (e.g., compare mediation in Wisconsin where arbitration follows immediately with mediation in Massachusetts where fact-finding follows mediation before final-offer arbitration).[14] It is further weakened when mediation is an expected part of the arbitration process (e.g., compare Wisconsin and Massachusetts where few disputes are mediated at the arbitration stage with Michigan where mediation in arbitration settled 64% of arbitration cases in 1973 and 1974).[15]

It was reported that the conferees also felt that mediation was more effective under conventional arbitration than under fact-finding. This was contrary to the view of the Michigan mediators interviewed as part of that study. There it was reported that the parties felt that some of the life had gone out of mediation under arbitration that had been present in earlier years under fact-finding.[16]

As noted above, it would be a mistake to assume that mediation in the public sector takes place only at the initial stages of the impasse-resolution procedure. On the contrary, over time the distinctions between mediation, fact-finding, and arbitration have become blurred in the sense that mediation is often employed during, and sometimes even after, the fact-finding and arbitration processes have become initiated. A number of people have debated the wisdom and appropriateness of mixing the fact-finding and mediation processes or the mediation and arbitration processes.[17] Some have argued that if we want to preserve the integrity of fact-finding and arbitration and provide a greater incentive to settle in mediation prior to going to these procedures, mediation should be discouraged or prohibited once these more formal impasse pro-

cedures are invoked. This position was adopted as the official policy of the Michigan Employment Relations Commission in the early years of bargaining in that state. Studies in Michigan, however, have shown that despite the official policy, fact-finders mediated in the majority of disputes.[18] In New York, the distinction between mediation and fact-finding not only has become blurred in practice, but has become institutionalized by a change in the way in which neutrals are assigned to cases. New York State's PERB no longer assigns a mediator at the first stage of the impasse procedure; instead a fact-finder is assigned under the assumption that he or she will attempt to mediate the dispute prior to conducting a formal hearing. Thus one additional step at which mediation traditionally occurs is eliminated, thereby not only saving time and money but also reducing the parties' incentive to delay and hold back concessions. The disadvantage of combining the two procedures is that the parties may hold back information from the mediator because they fear it will jeopardize their positions if the dispute goes to fact-finding. The more the parties hold back information and fail to put their strongest effort forward in mediation, the less likely the dispute will be settled prior to the fact-finding hearing. Although there has been considerable debate over whether mediation is more effective under this type of an arrangement or where the mediator will not be the fact-finder, there is little systematic evidence one way or the other.

In some cases mediation occurs after fact-finding. Again, in the State of New York it has become common for the parties to request and require post-fact-finding mediation, or what has been labeled "superconciliation." The term itself illustrates the difference between mediation at the initial stage of impasse and at the later stage of the negotiations where the process involves a much more aggressive intervention strategy by the neutral. In superconciliation the parties are at the final stage of bargaining and are faced with the threat of arbitration, a legislative hearing, a strike, or simply continued impasse. There is less room for delaying or holding back concessions because there is no next step in the procedure. Thus the mediator can exert pressure on the parties to face reality, make concessions, or change their expectations.

Finally, there is "med-arb," a term that has been popularized as the public-sector bargaining process has evolved.[19] As the term implies, mediation occurs in the arbitration process itself — especially in tripartite arbitration. Some neutrals have argued for procedures in which the mediator serves as the arbitrator if the parties fail to reach an agreement through his mediation efforts. While we have few examples of this option built into the statutory impasse procedures (Wisconsin's new law provides for it), the strategy is widely used by arbitrators on an *ad hoc* basis. The dynamics of this process will be discussed in a later section.

The Fact-Finding Process

Every discussion of fact-finding in the public sector has noted that the term is a misnomer. The fact-finding process involves more than the searching-out of the factual basis of the parties' positions; it also involves an effort to identify an acceptable compromise settlement. Most studies have found that fact-finders tend to give the greatest weight to some variant of comparability. The criteria of ability to pay, cost of living, interest and welfare of the public, and "good" labor relations practice tend to follow in mixed order as secondary factors.[20] Underlying the application of these criteria, however, is a search for an acceptable compromise. Thus, the effort to frame a recommendation that the parties will accept or use as the basis for negotiating an agreement captures the heart of the fact-finding process in the public sector. In a sense, when applied in this fashion, fact-finding is little more than mediation with written recommendations.

In a review of the early experience of bargaining under fact-finding, McKelvey found

that most initial assessments of this process were quite favorable. She questioned, however, whether these early successes would prove illusory as the parties became more experienced and accustomed to bargaining under this procedure. In short, she feared that the fact-finding process would become less effective over time.[21]

Although the majority of states that have enacted bargaining legislation still have fact-finding as an important part of their impasse procedures for nonuniformed services, the bulk of the evidence suggests that its effectiveness, both in avoiding strikes and in achieving settlements, has atrophied over time. For example, Gatewood's study of fact-finding in teacher disputes in Wisconsin found that of the 44 teachers' strikes between 1968 and 1974, only 11 were preceded by fact-finding, and in only two of 18 teachers' strikes in 1974 was fact-finding used before the teachers turned to the strike as a tactic for reaching an agreement.[22] The data in the Gatewood study also documented an increased rate of rejection of fact-finding reports over time. The deterioration of the efficacy of the process was part of the motivation underlying Wisconsin's adoption of final-offer arbitration for fire fighters and police in 1972 and, more recently, of the final-offer/strike option for other state employees.[23] The move to arbitration in Wisconsin along with the adoption of arbitration for police and fire fighters in other states that had fact-finding procedures in the early years of bargaining provides perhaps the strongest evidence that the half-life of the fact-finding procedure in the public sector has been rather short.

Yet approximately half of the states with arbitration statutes covering police and fire fighters have kept fact-finding as an intermediate stage in their procedures. The question arises, therefore, what role does fact-finding play in an arbitration statute? Does it serve as an effective intermediate step with a unique function, or does arbitration simply become an instant replay of the fact-finding process? In New York State between 1974 and 1976, approximately 20% of the police and fire fighter cases that went to fact-finding were resolved at that stage. [24] For those cases that were not resolved, however, the arbitration awards tended to follow the fact-finders' recommendations very closely. In 70% of the cases examined, the salary award was identical to the fact-finder's recommendation; where there were differences, the magnitude was relatively small. The major reasons indicated by arbitrators for deviating from a fact-finder's recommendation were that economic conditions had changed since the recommendation was issued, new information on comparable settlements was available to the arbitrator, or the parties found the fact-finder's recommendation to be unacceptable and therefore some modifications were necessary in order to increase the acceptability of the arbitration award.

The New York State PERB attempted to have the arbitrators use a "show cause" approach to the arbitration hearing, that is, they wanted the parties to identify what was wrong with the fact-finder's report. However, the parties objected to this approach and demanded the right to present their cases *de novo*. Yet in the executive sessions of tripartite arbitration panels, most of the arbitrators adopted a show-cause approach as a means of trying to either negotiate a settlement or resolve the disputed issues around the fact-finder's recommendations. Many of them were somewhat uncomfortable with having to second-guess the recommendations of another neutral, recognizing that in some future case *they* might be the fact-finder and someone else serving as an arbitrator might be second-guessing their opinions.

Thus in New York State arbitration did look very much like an instant replay of fact-finding. Presumably, if the show-cause approach to arbitration following fact-finding could be effectively implemented, the role of fact-finding under an arbitration statute could be strengthened and improved. Fact-finding followed by final-offer arbitration might be still another way to strengthen its role in an interest-arbitration system. While the disadvantages of fact-finding in the New York procedure were found to outweigh its contributions to the dispute-resolution system, there may be ways of designing an important role for this procedure under alternative arbitration schemes.

The Arbitration Process

One of the major questions facing designers of arbitration procedures centers on the pros and cons of tripartite vs. single-arbitrator systems. Advocates of tripartite arbitration argue that it allows the parties greater control over the outcomes of the award, reduces the risk of obtaining an unworkable award, facilitates mediation in arbitration, and increases the commitment of the parties to the award. Opponents argue, on the other hand, that the public interest may be compromised by the involvement of the parties, bargaining and mediation in the earlier stages of the procedures will be less vigorous because mediation is available again, and the procedure is more time-consuming and cumbersome.

There is clear evidence that tripartite arbitration does become an extension of bargaining and mediation. Approximately 60% of all arbitration awards issued in the first two years under the New York statute were unanimous. [25] Furthermore, interviews with the parties to these arbitration panels clearly documented the heavy emphasis on negotiation and mediation in the executive sessions. The same has been true in tripartite arbitration under the Michigan final-offer statute since a high proportion of cases are settled in arbitration prior to an award. Thus the med-arb process is a prominent component of tripartite arbitration structures in the public sector.

The pressure for negotiation in mediation and arbitration sessions is most evident in the larger jurisdictions when the economic and political stakes in the outcomes of the awards are the greatest and where the parties are militant enough to pose a threat to the "finality" of an award through strikes, refusals to implement the award, or court appeals. The 1976–1977 dispute between New York City and its police officers is a case in point. There the central issues were wages and a management proposal to change the number of hours worked and the deployment of personnel in patrol cars. The dispute went through several job actions, strike threats, mediation efforts, written mediation recommendations, court appeals, and an impasse-panel recommendation; ultimately it was placed before an arbitrator. After the arbitration award was written but before it was made public, the arbitrator gave the parties one more opportunity to negotiate a settlement. At this final stage, the parties were successful in reaching a negotiated accommodation. This case is instructive for a number of reasons. First, it shows that where the issues are complex, the stakes high, and the parties militant, negotiations continue through every stage of the impasse-resolution process. Second, it suggests that when the dispute involves a major change in operating procedures, arbitrators are reluctant to impose their own solutions. Third, it also illustrates the need to fashion an acceptable award when one (or both) of the parties is militant enough to seriously threaten to overturn or ignore the award. Fourth, it suggests the difficulty of adopting a "judicial" approach to complex interest disputes. There simply is no one best answer to these types of complex problems, nor is it very easy to identify what the "public interest" would dictate as the outcome of this type of dispute. [26]

A number of studies have examined how arbitrators use statutory criteria in framing an award. The most common finding is that comparability is used rather extensively, with cost of living or ability to pay taking top priority only in unusual circumstances. [27] As in fact-finding, however, the criteria are not applied in any consistent fashion. Instead of serving as uniform standards, these and other criteria, such as general labor relations practices, interests and welfare of the public, etc., appear to be used as general guides that are considered and applied on a case-by-case basis and used by the parties to ra-

tionalize their positions in arbitration. These findings again illustrate the premium that neutrals and partisans place on shaping an award that is acceptable to the parties.

Some commentators have expressed the fear that the arbitrators' stress on comparability as a decision criterion will make it difficult for either party to achieve a major innovation in arbitration. If this is true, arbitration may also have a limited half-life as the parties find that there are few gains left to achieve without breaking new ground. There is some evidence that this problem has emerged in the Canadian federal sector where a union has the option of arbitration or the right to strike. [28] In that system, the preference for arbitration declined among unions once they had achieved comparable contract provisions. The point of diminishing returns may have contributed to the decision of more units to shift to the strike route. As yet, there is little evidence of this problem arising in the U.S. systems. It is, however, an issue that merits attention in future studies.

BEYOND THE PROCEDURAL DEBATE

The design of a dispute-resolution system requires balancing the multiple objectives of avoiding strikes, minimizing third-party dependence and maximizing good-faith bargaining, protecting the public interest and the accountability of elected officials, and, in the long run, building the commitment of the parties and the public to a bargaining system that forces the parties to confront their problems effectively.

The record of various forms of dispute resolution that have been tried over the first decade of public-sector bargaining suggests that no "one best way" or optimal procedure for achieving all of these objectives has yet been identified. Thus in this final section a number of comments will be made to interpret the results discussed earlier in this paper in order to identify the tradeoffs that are associated with alternative systems.

Those wishing to provide as iron-clad a no-strike system as possible will probably need to embrace some form of compulsory arbitration. While no system can guarantee the complete absence of strikes, the record of strike avoidance, at least for police and fire fighters, so far has been better under arbitration than under fact-finding or in the absence of legislation. Whether this same experience will generalize to other occupational groups will be known only if more states extend these rights to a broader array of employee groups. There also is no way to determine at this point whether final-offer and conventional arbitration differ in their strike-avoidance potential.

For those concerned about the chilling effect of arbitration, the evidence from Massachusetts and Wisconsin suggests that the best choice is a system providing mediation followed closely by final-offer arbitration with a single arbitrator who is constrained from mediating at the arbitration stage. Under this type of system, a relatively high proportion of disputes will likely go to mediation; however, the mediation process should be relatively successful in reducing the number of cases that are passed on to arbitration. The mediation process, therefore, is the focal point of this system for resolving impasses.

A variant of this system — a tripartite arbitration structure — can be designed for those who wish to increase the parties' control over the final outcome. Even greater control can be imposed by using the issue-by-issue method of final-offer selection in a tripartite structure. This system builds the potential for further mediation into the arbitration stage of the procedure and would likely result in a similarly high percentage of negotiations reaching impasse, a lower settlement rate in mediation prior to arbitration, and a higher settlement rate in arbitration without an award. Another variant on this system for those who are opposed to final-offer arbitration — conventional arbitration with a tripartite structure — would be expected to have relatively similar effects, except that we might observe a higher rate

of unanimous awards rather than mediated settlements without an award.

All of the above options assume that a high priority is placed on avoiding strikes. Relaxing this priority a bit relative to other objectives opens a wide array of additional options. For example, if one wishes to deal with the fear that arbitration stifles innovation or the ability to make major breakthroughs in collective bargaining, the dual impasse routes of arbitration or the right to strike can be built into the law. If the Canadian experience under this system generalizes to other jurisdictions, then we would expect that over time (1) the weak bargaining units lacking an effective strike threat will stay within the arbitration route as long as they can benefit from a "catch-up" argument, (2) the strong bargaining units with an ability and willingness to strike will prefer the strike option, (3) the rate of impasse will be relatively high in order to get to the critical pressure point in the procedure, and (4) the parties may switch from one option to the other over time as they grow dissatisfied with the outcomes from one route. A variant on this option, which makes it more difficult for the stronger party to dominate the choice of the routes, is found in the Wisconsin statute, where both parties must agree on the strike route or else the arbitration route becomes automatic.

A more liberal strike-based system might adopt the approach of Hawaii and several other states by allowing strikes after mediation and/or fact-finding have been exhausted, subject to a limitation in cases affecting public health and safety. Although experience under these statutes has not been very thoroughly analyzed, some evidence from Hawaii and Pennsylvania suggests that a reasonably high rate of impasses can be expected.[29] The number of strikes is likely to vary considerably depending on the nature of the economic and political environments and the characteristics of the relationships between the parties. For example, a higher strike rate might be expected in relationships involving strong, militant unions in complex political environments under a system of this type than under one where there was no statutory right to strike. Strikes that do occur might also tend to be of longer duration here than in jurisdictions where the strike is illegal.

Finally, those who are philosophically opposed both to the right to strike and to any form of compulsory arbitration can still rely on the most commonly used system — mediation followed by fact-finding. While it might be difficult, if not impossible, to return to this system once arbitration or the right to strike has been provided, this approach still may be useful as a first step in establishing bargaining rights in jurisdictions where the parties are unfamiliar with collective bargaining and dispute resolution. Since the states that have yet to establish bargaining rights are largely located in environments where there is less reason to expect a rapid rise of militant unionism, the process of fact-finding with recommendations may have a longer half-life than it had in some of the states that adopted and then abandoned this system in the first decade of public-sector bargaining.

In summary, a variety of options are available to public policy-makers, depending on the weights they assign to different policy objectives. Although each alternative offers a slightly different approach, in practice their similarities may outweigh their differences. As Rehmus recently noted, the parties have adapted the various dispute-settlement procedures in ways that suggest that the dispute-resolution process has come full circle.[30] Instead of the distinct steps envisioned by most states that start with negotiations, proceed to mediation, and then go to fact-finding and/or arbitration, the parties and neutrals have found ways to mix each of these processes together in combinations that fit the needs of their particular dispute. Thus we have fact-finding followed by mediation, med-arb, arbitration followed by negotiations, strikes followed by fact-finding, mediation and/or arbitration, etc. Over time, as more experience is gained with these strategies and better data become

available on their performance, we can understand more fully the potentials and limitations of all of the options. The more we learn, the more we are likely to be convinced of the futility of searching for the "one best way" or the "optimal" system for resolving all collective bargaining disputes. Instead, we should become better equipped to design alternative systems to meet different policy objectives or to adapt to changing circumstances.

NOTES

1. See, for example, the statement of the Taylor committee on this issue in Governor's Committee on Public Employee Relations: Final Report (Albany: State of New York, at 33.

2. For a discussion, see Hoyt N. Wheeler, *Compulsory Arbitration: A Narcotic Effect.* 14 Ind. Rels. 117 (February 1975); Peter Feuille, *Final Offer Arbitration and the Chilling Effect,* 14 Ind. Rels. 302 (October 1975); John C. Anderson and Thomas A. Kochan, *Impasse Resolution in the Canadian Federal Service: Effects of the Bargaining Process,* 30 Ind. & Lab. Rels. Rev. 283 (April 1977), at 283–301; or Thomas A. Kochan, Mordehai Mironi, Ronald G. Ehrenberg, Jean Baderschneider, and Todd Jick, Dispute Resolution Under Factfinding and Arbitration: An Empirical Analysis (New York: American Arbitration Association, 1978).

3. Annual Reports of the Federal Mediation and Conciliation Service, 1967–1976.

4. *Ibid.*

5. See, for example, Neil W. Chamberlain and James W. Kuhn, Collective Bargaining, 3d ed. (New York: McGraw-Hill Book Co., 1965), 171–73.

6. See, for example, James L. Stern, Edward B. Krinsky, and Jeffrey B. Tener, Factfinding Under Wisconsin Law, 1966 (Madison: University of Wisconsin Extension, 1966); or Byron Yaffe and Howard Goldblatt, Factfinding in New York State Public Employment: More Promise Than Illusion (Ithaca: New York State School of Industrial and Labor Relations, Cornell University, 1971).

7. William Word, *Factfinding in Public Employee Negotiations,* 95 Monthly Lab. Rev. 6 (February 1972).

8. Hoyt N. Wheeler, *How Compulsory Arbitration Affects Compromise Activity,* 17 Ind. Rels. 80 (February 1978).

9. Kochan *et al., supra* note 44.

10. See Carl M. Stevens, *Mediation and the Role of the Neutral,* in Frontiers of Collective Bargaining, eds. John T. Dunlop and Neil W. Chamberlain (New York: Harper & Row, 1967), 271-90. See also Carl M. Stevens, Strategy and Collective Bargaining Negotiations (New York: McGraw-Hill Book Co., 1963), 122-46; and Kenneth Kressel, Labor Mediation: Exploratory Survey (Albany, N.Y.: Association of Labor Mediation Agencies, 1972).

11. Kochan *et al., supra* note 2, at ch. 5.

12. *Id.,* at ch. 3.

13. Annual Reports of the New York State Public Employment Relations Board, 1975.

14. James L. Stern *et al.,* Final-Offer Arbitration (Lexington, Mass.: D.C. Heath and Co., 1975), 124.

15. *Id.,* at 54.

16. *Id.,* at 62-63.

17. For a review of these debates, see Ralph T. Jones, Public Sector Labor Relations: An Evaluation of Policy Related Research (Belmont, Mass.: Contract Research Corp., 1975), 162-67.

18. Jack Stieber and Benjamin Wolkinson, *Fact-Finding Viewed by Factfinders: The Michigan Experience,* paper presented to the 1975 meetings of the Society of Professionals in Dispute Resolutions, 4.

19. Sam Kagel and John Kagel, *Using Two New Arbitration Techniques,* 95 Monthly Lab. Rev. 11 (November 1972).

20. Howard S. Block, *Criteria in Public Sector Interest Disputes,* in Arbitration and the Public Interest, Proceedings of the 24th Annual Meeting, National Academy of Arbitrators (Washington: BNA Books, 1971), 165; or Richard Pegnetter, *Fact-Finding and the Teacher Salary Disputes: The 1969 Experience in New York State,* 24 Ind. & Lab. Rels. Rev. 165 (January 1971).

21. Jean T. McKelvey, *Factfinding: Promise or Illusion,* 22 Ind. & Lab. Rels. Rev. 543 (July 1969).

22. Lucian Gatewood, *Factfinding in Teacher Disputes: The Wisconsin Experience,* 97 Monthly Lab. Rev. 47 (October 1974).

23. See Report of the Wisconsin Study Commission on Public Employee Labor Relations (Madison, Wis.: Legislative Reference Bureau, 1976).

24. Kochan *et al., supra* note 2, at ch. 3.

25. *Id.,* at ch. 8.

26. For an argument supporting a more judicial approach to arbitration, see Raymond D. Horton, *Arbitration, Arbitrators, and the Public Interest,* 27 Ind. & Lab. Rels. Rev. 497 (July 1975).

27. See, for example: Kochan *et al., supra* note 2, at ch. 8; or Jones, *supra* note 17.

28. Anderson and Kochan, *supra* note 2, at 292-93.

29. See Peter Feuille, *Symposium Introduction: Public Sector Impasses,* 16 Ind. Rels. 265 (October 1977).

30. Charles Rehmus, *A Circular View of Government Intervention,* in Symposium on Police and Firefighter Arbitration in New York State (Albany, N.Y.: Public Employment Relations Board, 1977), 165-78.

Hospitals

RICHARD U. MILLER
University of Wisconsin

. . .

COLLECTIVE BARGAINING PATTERNS AND ISSUES

In 1976 an estimated 2500 collective bargaining agreements were in effect at hospitals across the United States.[1] As such, these contracts reflect the personal and institutional objectives of all the parties who participate in the negotiations. Since more often than not objectives sought by one party may be in conflict with those of other parties, contracts also are a concrete measure of bargaining power. Although precise measures of hospitals' bargaining outcomes are not available, sufficient descriptive evidence has been gathered to provide a basis for reaching tentative generalizations.

The most extensive examination of hospital contracts to date is that carried out by Juris and associates.[2] After analyzing more than 800 collective agreements, Juris concluded ''the contracts in [the hospital] industry are developing in a way indistinguishable from steel, auto, meatpacking, police, and fire.'' This finding is surprising in

From *Collective Bargaining: Contemporary American Experience,* Gerard G. Somers, Ed., 1980, pp. 417–431. Reprinted with permission of the author and the Industrial Relations Research Association.

view of the uniqueness often ascribed to the industry. In specific instances, however, hospital contracts are in fact quite different from those in other industries, pointing not to the assumed uniqueness but rather to the inability of hospital unions to generate the bargaining power of their counterparts in other industries.

Union Security, Job Control, and Income Protection

In the first place, a major objective of health-care organizations would be to obtain contract provisions that strengthen the union institutionally. By most measures, hospital contracts have a way to go to provide the institutional security achieved by other unions. Not only has the union shop been achieved half as frequently as in other industries (30% v. 63%), but hospital contracts are twice as likely to be without any form of union security (34% v. 18%).[3]

A second concern for hospital labor organizations in their bargaining would be contractually provided job and income security for their members. Unions customarily seek restrictions on subcontracting, crew size, and supervisors performing work in bargaining units; stipulations that length of service will govern layoff, recall, transfer, and promotion; and provisions for severance pay and supplemental unemployment benefits. Table 1 gives a picture of the frequency of occur-

TABLE 1
Contractual restraints on management rights, selected provisions 1974–1975

| | PERCENT OF TOTAL CONTRACTS WITH PROVISION | |
CONTRACT PROVISION	Hospitals[a] N = 817	All industries[b] N = 400
Seniority		
Layoff	75.0	85.0
Recall	66.0	75.0
Transfer	44.0	48.0
Promotion	66.0	69.0
Supplemental unemployment benefits	*	17.0
Severance pay	9.0	39.0
Subcontracting	9.0	40.0
Crew size	5.0	NA
Work by supervisors	NA	57.0

* Less than 1 percent.

NA — not available

[a] Hervey Juris, "Labor Agreements in the Hospital Industry: A Study of Collective Bargaining Outputs," *Labor Law Journal* (August 1977), pp. 504–11.

[b] Bureau of National Affairs, *Basic Patterns in Union Contracts* (Washington, 1975).

rence of job- and income-related contract clauses, using data from Juris and the Bureau of National Affairs. Here again hospital agreements not only provide less union security but also less job security to individual members. From the hospital's standpoint, however, the relative absence of traditional work rules means that management retains a good deal of discretion in the utilization of its employees. These hospital contracts generally do not seem to pose the impediments to productivity that have been historically true of other industries.[4]

Wage Levels and Fringe Benefits

Through their attention to salaries and fringe benefits, labor-management agreements also directly affect the employee's income and standard of living. One author observes, for example, that as a consequence of the bargaining activities of 1199 in New York City the wages of nonprofessional hospital workers tripled between 1959 and 1969.[5] Wage bargaining results for hospital unions generally, however, have been far less spectacular. Thus Fottler, using data from the BLS Area Wage Surveys, found that unions had an impact on hospital wage levels of between 4.5 and 8.2%.[6] When compared with effects estimated at upwards of 15% for unions in other industries, the contrasts are striking.[7] Table 2 presents additional data on collective bargaining provisions relating to wages and fringes which are consistent with those for wages generally. Only in the area of sick leave do hospital agreements exceed the standards of other industries. Thus for example, in the case of holidays, hospital contracts not only provide fewer holidays but at considerably lesser rates of pay.

It could be argued that with employment expanding rapidly in the 1960s and early 1970s, hospital employees would feel few pressures to protect either their job or income security. Moreover, with ample financial resources and cost-pass-through, management would have little in-

TABLE 2
Frequency of contract provisions containing selected wage and fringe benefit items 1973–1974

PERCENT OF CONTRACTS MENTIONING PROVISION	HOSPITALS	ALL INDUSTRIES
Cost-of-living adjustment	6.0	36.0
Shift differential	58.0	82.0
Reporting pay	29.0	71.0
Call back pay	48.0	62.0
Premium pay for		
Saturday	11.0	52.0
Sunday	14.0	68.0

Source: Bureau of National Affairs, *Daily Labor Report,* No. 116, June 15, 1976, p. A4.

centive for cost-cutting efficiency measures. Hence the absence of work rules, severance pay, SUB, and the like may not reflect a lack of union bargaining power. If this were true, however, we should also see higher wages, better fringe benefits, and stronger union security.

An alternative explanation which could be postulated is that since the contract data discussed above were largely obtained from agreements negotiated before the health-care amendments, they are no longer representative of labor relations in the industry. Unfortunately, more recent information has not been published to support or refute this conclusion. Inferentially, we can speculate that given the change to prospective reimbursement systems, the strong political pressure to control hospital costs, and the lack of organizing success by hospital unions, the picture portrayed by the 1973–74 contract data is still applicable. It is small consolation for hospital labor unions to say that at least they are not responsible for the rapid rise in health-care costs.

Patient-Care Issues in Bargaining

From the hospital administrator's standpoint, few issues seem to have less of a place at the bargaining table than those concerned directly with the substance, form, and control of decisions affecting patient care. Hospital management's views in

this regard are represented by the position taken by the Executive Committee of the American Hospital Association:[8] ''The staffing of a hospital must be an objective process and should not be controlled by a group with special interests. . . . Nurses as an organized group are not legally responsible for patient care. Only management has the responsibility to determine the number of employees, their qualifications, and their assignment within the institution so as to be consistent with the best patient care and the most effective utilization of personnel.''

The AHA's policy statement is directed at what has often constituted a major source of conflict between registered nurses and hospitals: the minimum number of RNs assigned by a hospital to a ward, department, or specialized task. Such staffing issues have arisen also in disputes between hospitals and their housestaff when the latter have sought through bargaining to increase the employment not only of RNs, but also LPNs and nurses aides.

Related to staffing is the question of out-of-title work. Nurses, in demanding the right to refuse specialized work assignments when training was felt to be inadequate, have cited the ANA's *Code for Nurses* which reads in part:

Provision 3 — The nurse maintains individual competence in nursing practice, recognizing and accepting responsibility for individual actions and judgments.

Provision 5 — The nurse uses individual competence as a criteria in accepting delegated responsibilities and assigning nursing activities to others.

Attempts to incorporate the Nursing Code in contracts have been staunchly resisted by hospitals, resulting, as in the case of Youngstown, Ohio, in long and bitter strikes.[9]

The Youngstown strike of registered nurses as an example of conflict over out-of-title work has been duplicated in such cities as Chicago, Seattle, San Francisco, and St. Louis. In addition, it has also been a focal point for collective bargaining between hospitals and their committees of interns and residents when housestaff organizations have sought to limit such assignments as drawing blood, clerical tasks, and setting up I.V. systems. At times demands have also been made that nurses and paramedics be trained to handle work formerly assigned to interns and residents.

Although out-of-title work and staffing have been the primary collective bargaining issues, union demands have included other subjects related to patient care: length of workday and week, scheduling of hours and weekends, number of allied workers employed, guarantees of laboratory equipment improvement, the purchase of emergency medical supplies, and reactivation of previously closed patient-care units. In a dispute involving Cook County Hospital of Chicago, for example, interns and residents presented more than 100 patient-care demands.[10]

Beyond the substantive decisions concerning patient care, hospital labor organizations have also attempted to negotiate the procedures by which employees would participate formally in such decisions. Thus health-care advisory committees have been sought by interns and residents, and registered nurses have proposed a variety of joint committees carrying such titles as professional staffing, professional performance, or joint study, to name a few.

Whether it be procedural or substantive issues related to patient care, hospitals have resisted such efforts as, at best, attempts "by unions to mask economic demands in the form of patient-care and quality of care issues,"[11] and at worst, as evidence of a desire by employees and their organizations to take control of the hospitals.

Analysis of hospital labor contracts reveals little in the way of provisions relating to patient care. Agreements seem to be silent on staffing, out-of-title assignments, and related working-condition issues.[12] Although joint-participation committees are prevalent for both professional and technical employees (73 and 52%, respectively),[13] the authority and scope of the committees in dealing with patient-care questions are unclear. Moreover, if we note that joint committees occur in only 16% of nonprofessional employees' contracts according to Juris, the fear that participation in hospital management decision-making by professional employees will lead inevitably to demands for similar participation by nonprofessional unions seems unsupported.

The absence of patient-care-related clauses from hospital labor contracts may be explained by several factors. First, channels for resolving patient-care issues may continue to be informal and individual in orientation, or formal mechanisms may exist under extra-contractual conditions. Particularly in the nurse's mind, the role conflict of professional vs. union member may be a deterrent to mixing patient-care questions with collective bargaining.

Second, the attitudes of hospital administrators are also important in limiting the scope of collective bargaining to "traditional issues." The willingness of administrators to "buy-off" patient-care demands with economic counterproposals places health-care professionals in an obvious quandary. With salaries and fringe benefits comparatively low and the likelihood also low that patient-care demands will be conceded without strikes, the bargaining outcomes are predictable.

Finally, the general weakness of the bargaining position coupled with the professional hesitancy to engage in work stoppages reinforces the logic of the situation. Thus hospital professionals' collective agreements in fact may, as Juris contends, be nearly indistinguishable in principle from those of union contracts in other industries both by design and by circumstance.

LABOR-MANAGEMENT CONFLICT IN HOSPITALS

A major point of controversy surrounding the passage of the health-care amendments of 1974 was the effect such legislation would have on strikes and other forms of labor-management conflict. Proponents of the amendments argued that coverage of hospitals and related institutions under Taft-Hartley would reduce the incidence of conflict, citing statistics that showed that of 248 strikes in the private health-care sector between 1962 and 1972, nearly half were caused by disputes over union recognition.[14] Fewer recognition strikes occurred in those states in which representational machinery was present and union organizing was regulated. Thus it was expected that the availability of the NLRB together with such devices as secret-ballot representation elections and majority rule in all state jurisdictions would remove a significant issue from resolution by force.

Those against the amendments saw legislative efforts to encourage collective bargaining as an open invitation to further strikes in the industry, which the public would not tolerate. In the words of one management representative:

> [An] extremely high price will be exacted if strikes occur in the hospital setting. Not an economic cost, but a human cost. The human cost of suffering or loss of life. The human cost resulting from an inability to restore vital life functions because of delay in bringing appropriate [sic] skills to bear. A second, a minute, an hour, a day — each of these can be the critical time span which determines success or failure in treatment of a sick or injured person.[15]

While the advocates of expanding Taft-Hartley to include all private health-care employees prevailed, the amendments ultimately reflected congressional misgivings over granting full rights to strike and to engage in related concerted activity. Hence came the 10-day notice of intent to strike or picket, the stipulation of compulsory mediation, the extended periods allowed for mediation and negotiation, and the provision for Boards of Inquiry. The strike was not forbidden, but it also was not to be a weapon used capriciously or punitively.

The Incidence of Hospital Strikes

The number of work stoppages registered for private health-service employees generally and hospitals in particular was almost identical in 1977 to the figures for 1973 and 1969. Thus despite a significant increase in collective bargaining contracts in the industry, the number of work stoppages has not increased proportionately.

Other measures of strike activity also support the conclusion that the incidence and severity of labor disputes in health care are less than in other industries. For example, in 1977 the average number of workers involved in strikes in all industries was 411 compared with 259 for all private health care and 367 for private hospitals. The same BLS figures also show that the mean duration of health-care strikes was approximately half that of industry generally — 15 days as opposed to 28 days.[16]

Explanations for the patterns of health-care work stoppages are not difficult to find. In the first place, the shift from state to federal coverage for the private sector of the industry removed the necessity for strikes as a mechanism to achieve recognition and made the employment of work stoppages in contract disputes more difficult. Secondly, major credit has also been given for a "relatively strike-free environment" in hospitals to the 10-day strike notice requirement.[17] According to one observer, this "provides a sizeable period of time for emotions to cool off and for a mediator to do his job.''[18]

In addition, the availability of the Boards of Inquiry has also played a role. The picture with regard to the effect of the BOIs, however, is not entirely clear. They have been criticized by the parties on a number of issues, most particularly on timing, and their use has declined over the years. For example, 24 boards were appointed during the first four months following passage of the amendments and an additional 31 were named in the subsequent six-month period. In 1975–76, 50 boards were created; in 1976–77, only 37 boards were named. From August 1977 through August 1978, there were only 34.[19]

The attitudes of the parties also have an effect on the number of work stoppages. Neither labor nor management supports use of the strike except as a last resort, and they have used interest arbitration for the resolution of disputes to a much greater degree than have other industries. Formal provisions for third-party resolution of disputes often have been incorporated directly into contracts. Illustrative are the so-called ''pre-election'' agreements negotiated by labor and management in Chicago and the stipulations to arbitrate new contract terms which have long been a part of the hospital agreements in Minneapolis-St. Paul. It should also be noted that provisions for arbitrating grievance disputes are also widespread, appearing in approximately 88% of all hospital contracts.[20]

Professional health-care employees such as nurses have a particularly strong aversion to walking off en masse. The American Nurses Association carried a prohibition against strikes in its constitution for 20 years after the Economic Security Program had been launched, and even though the national association was to discard the ban in 1968, many state associations including New York continued such provisions for nearly a decade thereafter. The ANA also followed closely a policy of neutrality in the labor disputes of other health-care unions, most notably declining to honor others' picket lines.

Given the lower perceived utility of strikes for health-care workers, other weapons of concerted activity often have been substituted. Thus at times, job actions have taken the form of mass resignation, sickouts, work-to-rule, and noon-hour and off-time demonstrations. One of the more creative approaches employed on occasion by interns and residents has been to refuse to bill patients.

Conflict also may be individualized in the sense that workers may have excessive rates of absenteeism and turnover, file large numbers of grievances, and constitute a continuing series of disciplinary problems for theft, drug and alcohol abuse, and poor work performance. The nature of the work force and its working conditions are such, however, that behavior described above gives a very mixed picture of conflict, particularly as a substitute for strikes. While turnover and absenteeism often are high, research suggests this is less a problem for unionized hospitals.[21] Further, the usage of grievance machinery and resort to arbitration also seem to be low by the standards of other industries.[22]

In general, labor-management relations in health care at the present time give little evidence of the conflict which was feared would accompany the unionization of the industry. While there are exceptions, strikes tend to be fewer, smaller, and shorter than in other industries. Compared to the situation in other newly organized industries, ''the lack of intense, violent conflict in hospitals is perplexing.''[23]

However few hospital strikes occur or however short their duration, those that do may have severe repercussions on the delivery of health-care services in a community and on a hospital's patients in particular. Therefore it would be useful to examine, to the extent possible, the impact of hospital strikes. A first point to consider is that it appears to be an exceptional case when a hospital is forced to cease operations completely when a work stoppage occurs. In the first 12 months following the enactment of the amendments, for example, 20 strikes occurred, only three of which caused the hospital to close down.[24] Rather, elective surgery is curtailed, outpatient services reduced, and all but the acutely ill discharged or transferred. Although picket lines may be set up, supplies usually continue to be delivered and nonstriking employees work. In the case of a strike by nurses, supervisory nursing personnel, licensed practical nurses, and nurses aides may be available to provide patient care.

Not all outcomes associated with strikes may in fact be negative from the hospital's standpoint. At the conclusion of a lengthy work stoppage of RNs in Seattle hospitals, benefits perceived by administrators from taking the strike were reassessment of staffing patterns and more economical use of personnel, intense press coverage which was a means of informing the public of the hospital's services as well as generating support for their position in the strike, and "most importantly," according to a management representative, "the firmness with which the hospitals resisted the nurses' demands will be noted by other bargaining units."[25]

Thus hospital work stoppages do not appear to threaten the health and safety of patients and in this respect are no longer categorized by any of the parties involved in hospital bargaining as unthinkable. On the contrary, it appears that at times they can be considered as not an unwelcome outcome in bargaining. Even from the standpoint of public authorities, such action may be one means of forced economizing and cost control in an industry reluctant or unable to deal with its surplus beds and redundant personnel.

COLLECTIVE BARGAINING IN HOSPITALS: CONCLUDING THOUGHTS

It is clear from the foregoing that as a late arrival to the health-care industry, collective bargaining is still in its formative stages. Unlike the majority of industries discussed in this book, labor market structures are fluid, unionization uneven, and bargaining outcomes often uncertain. Amidst this turbulence the outlines of a structure for the in-

dustry's system of labor relations now seems to be discernable and with it, the basis for a forecast of things to come. In this concluding section of the chapter we shall sum up collective bargaining in hospitals, paying particular attention to current issues and problems. In this way perhaps we shall be better able to see what lies ahead for labor relations in the industry.

Growth and Change of Hospital Bargaining

Taken from the vantage point of two decades, the level of unionization in hospitals has increased significantly. The momentum of the early years was not maintained in the 1970s, however, even with the enactment of the 1974 Taft-Hartley amendments. Although individual unions, such as District 1199, have achieved important numerical gains in members, overall the rate of growth has been slow and quite limited geographically.

In many respects consolidation seems to characterize the organizing of labor organizations in health care. More often than not unionization is directed at hospitals already possessing bargaining units and comes as a consequence of initiatives arising within the employer's work force. In the face of frequent strong and bitter opposition from management, this is a rational policy calculated to economize on scarce union resources. It is also a policy of gradualism which forecloses any great breakthroughs or profound changes in the incidence of hospital bargaining in the coming years.

Hospital Bargaining Structures

The current patterns of collective bargaining reveal strong tendencies of centralization for both labor and management. The latter, working through urban or regional councils, is well structured both to counter organizing drives and to present unified or coordinated strategies for bargaining. The unions in the hospital field, on the other hand, tend to subsume their hospital members in large, so-called "dispersed" locals or state associations in which hospital negotiating policy is made with an eye to other kinds of workers within the local or to other health-care bargaining units administered by the local.

The structural problems of bargaining in health care are intensified by the occupationally fragmented nature of the hospital workforce and by the multitude of potential union rivals seeking hospital members. In the former situation, the possibility for competition and conflict is great between negotiating units within hospitals; and in the latter case the likelihood of raiding or organizational battles also exists.

At the present moment the amount of within-hospital unit proliferation is low. As pointed out above, the average hospital has only one labor contract. Moreover, the NLRB has, for the most part, followed the dictates of Congress in this regard. If for no other reason, however, than union organizing strategies of consolidation, the average number of bargaining units will gradually increase. Whether this will have negative consequences for bargaining is dependent on several factors including the extent to which different unions have title to the hospital's units or all are held by the same union. If the latter situation prevails, one would predict less interunit conflict. On the other hand, multiple union presence within the hospital may lead to an initial increase in conflict which later subsides. As has occurred in other industries, coalition bargaining may arise as unions seek to coordinate their efforts and to avoid being "whipsawed."

On the employer side, the gradual increase in union bargaining power will reinforce the existing tendencies already working to expand the scope of units. Thus in addition to the labor activity of the hospital councils, the economics of health-care delivery which are compelling coordination and sharing of technology and services provide a strong rationale for multi-employer negotiating units and pattern bargaining. As a consequence, bargaining may become increasingly remote from the individual hospital worker as units expand and administration is centralized.

The Impact of Hospital Bargaining

In terms of increased labor cost, the effects of collective bargaining on hospitals remain to be felt. Wages and fringes have tended to rise slowly, offset at times by decreased employee turnover. Moreover, as compared to unions in other industries, hospital labor organizations have yet to seek contractual restraints on management discretion in its utilization of certain groups of registered nurses and housestaff physicians. But even here the successes in achieving demands related to such issues as out-of-title work, staffing, or joint control have been outweighed by the failures. In either case, win or lose, efforts to obtain so-called patient-care demands have been accompanied by long and bitter conflict.

A related aspect of bargaining impact is the role of the strike and the availability of substitutes. Traditional in the context of private-sector labor relations, the work stoppage in hospitals was long held to be untenable. Experience has proven, however, and especially since 1974 that strikes have not grown concomitantly with unionization. By comparison with other industries, hospitals have enjoyed a relatively strike-free environment. The impediments posed by the legal framework have reduced the utility of the strike, but as much as anything the parties' own willingness to substitute such devices as interest arbitration have played an important role.

It would be unwise, however, to assume that in the future labor-management harmony will prevail. On the contrary, the ingredients for significantly increased levels of conflict in hospitals appear at hand. In the first place, the urgencies of cost control confront directly the goals of employees and their unions. Management efforts to raise productivity and restrain expenditures bring it on a collision course with worker needs for income security, job control, and a constantly improving standard of living. As has already happened in the public hospitals of many urban areas, both professional and nonprofessional employees have engaged in militant job actions in protest against layoffs, "low" staffing levels, and poor working conditions.

Other factors which are likely to be a source of future conflict are the attitudes of management and workers. Hospital administrators in the 1970s, perhaps reflecting more conservative trends in the general society, have adopted strong anti-union stances, apparently contesting unions at every turn and on every issue. Such a policy, while holding unions at bay for a time, is productive of both short-term and long-term conflict. The end results may be a climate of hostility and mistrust which may not be undone for many years into the future.

The Third-Party Payer Once Again

How much conflict and with what consequences are questions whose answers lie in good part with the so-called third-party payers. Those who control the financial condition of health-care delivery also are in a position to influence the structure and behavior of hospital labor and management. Although the actual intervention of third parties is still quite limited geographically, the potential is increasing rapidly. Further, where the intervention has occurred, its effects have been profound. Bargaining has been chilled, settlements left to arbitrators or public authorities, and the process itself increasingly politicized. As private hospitals more and more have taken on the characteristics of a regulated utility, the distinction between private and public-sector institutions has become blurred. Given the role of the third-party payers, the fact that often the same unions operate in both sectors, and the commonality of technology and labor markets to private and public-sector hospitals alike, the significant distinctions may disappear altogether.

In sum, one has a vision of the future in which the large urban hospitals contain a complex of interrelated bargaining units, some professional and some not, in which much of the negotiation is carried on by councils of unions acting as a coalition. The hospital in turn will be but one unit in a network of other health-care institutions encompassed by a master contract. Much of the bargaining may consist of joint labor-management presentations to public authorities and their arbitrators.

Strikes will be few but potentially devastating as the hospitals of large geographical areas are shut down. Moreover, more often than not, while the objectives of the work stoppage may be economic, the actual thrust may be political — to force the public authorities to accept the agreements already reached by labor and management.

While the scenario presented above is imaginary, the foundation by which the events prophesied can occur is already in place. What implications these effects have for the future quality and accessibility of health-care in the United States can only be guessed. It does not seem unreasonable to conclude that in any case the results will not be positive.

NOTES

1. BNA, *Daily Labor Report,* June 15, 1976, pp. A3–A4.

2. Juris and others, "Nationwide Survey . . . ," pp. 122–30, 192; Juris and others, Employee Discipline . . . ," pp. 67–69, 70–72, 74; and Juris, pp. 504–11.

3. Juris and others, "Nationwide Survey Shows Growth in Union Contracts," p. 192, and BNA, *Basic Patterns in Union Contracts,* 8th Edition, May 1975.

4. See also Richard U. Miller and others, "Union Effects on Hospital Administration: Preliminary Results of a Three State Study," pp. 517–18.

5. Raskin, p. 24.

6. Fottler, p. 54. See also Richard U. Miller and others, "Union Effects on Hospital Administration: Preliminary Results of a Three State Study," p. 649.

7. A useful review of studies on the impact of unions on wages is contained in Johnson, pp. 23–28.

8. *Health Labor-Management Report,* July 1974, p. 3.

9. Lewis, p. 49.

10. *Health Labor-Management Report,* November 28, 1975, p. 1.

11. *Ibid.,* July 1974, p. 3.

12. Richard U. Miller and others, "Union Effects on Hospital Administration: Preliminary Results of a Three State Study," p. 518.

13. Juris, p. 511.

14. *Coverage of Nonprofit Hospitals Under the National Labor Relations Act, 1973,* pp. 158-285.

15. *Ibid.,* p. 165.

16. FMCS, *Minutes,* of the Third Meeting, Health Care Labor Management Advisory Committee, December 6, 1976, p. 3.

17. BNA, *Daily Labor Report,* September 25, 1978, p. A10.

18. *Ibid.*

19. Department of Research, Federal Mediation and Conciliation Service, personal communication, September 26, 1978.

20. Juris, p. 508.

21. Richard U. Miller and others, *The Impact of Collective Bargaining on Hospitals: A Three State Study,* pp. 182-183.

22. See Nash on this point, pp. 98-105; and R. U. Miller and others, *The Impact of Collective Bargaining on Hospitals: A Three State Study.*

23. Nash, p. 7.

24. Rosmann, "One Year Under Taft-Hartley," p. 67.

25. See a description of a ten-week strike of 1200 RNs at 15 Seattle hospitals in Roach and others, pp. 49-51.

REFERENCES

Bureau of National Affairs. *Basic Patterns in Union Contracts,* 8th Edition. Washington: BNA, May 1975.

Coverage of Nonprofit Hospitals Under National Labor Relations Act. Hearings before the Subcommittee on Labor and Public Welfare, United States Senate, 93rd Congress, 1st Session, on S. 794 and S. 2292, July 31, August 1, 2, and October 4, 1973.

Fottler, Myron D. "The Union Impact on Hospital Wages." *Industrial and Labor Relations Review* 30 (April 1977).

Johnson, George E. "Economic Analysis of Trade Unionism." *American Economic Review* 65 (May 1975).

Juris, Hervey. "Labor Agreements in the Hospital Industry: A Study of Collective Bargaining Outputs." *Labor Law Journal* 28 (August 1977).

Juris, Hervey, Joseph Rosmann, Charles Maxey, and Gail Bentivegna. "Employee Discipline No Longer Management Prerogative Only." *Hospitals, JAHA* 51 (May 1, 1977).

———. "Nation-wide Survey Shows Growth in Union Contracts." *Hospitals, JAHA* 51 (March 16, 1977).

Lewis, Howard L. "Nurse: How Much Like Doctors?" *Modern Health Care* (June 1975).

Miller, Richard U., Brian E. Becker, and Edward B. Krinsky. "Union Effects on Hospital Administration: Preliminary Results from a Three State Study." *Labor Law Journal* 28 (August 1977).

Miller, Richard U., Brian E. Becker, Edward B. Krinsky, and Glen Cain. *The Impact of Collective Bargaining on Hospitals: A Three State Study.* Madison: Industrial Relations Research Institute, University of Wisconsin-Madison, 1977.

Nash, Abraham. "Labor Management Conflict in a Voluntary Hospital." Ph.D. dissertation, New York University, 1972.

Raskin, A. H. "Union with a Soul." *New York Times Sunday Magazine,* March 22, 1970.

Roach, David L. "Hospitals Stand Firm, Ensure Care in Lengthy Areawide Nurses Strike." *Hospitals, JAHA* 51 (August 1977).

Rosmann, Joseph. "One Year Under Taft-Hartley." *Hospitals, JAHA* 49 (December 16, 1975).

Organizing Low-Income Women in New Ways: Who, Where, and Why

KAREN S. KOZIARA

PATRICE J. INSLEY
Both of Temple University

Almost two-thirds of all women employed full-time work in white-collar occupations. Relatively few of these women belong to unions. About 13% of the women working in white-collar occupations are union members, leaving most white-collar women unrepresented.[1] During the last few years, however, a number of new organizations have formed outside the traditional labor movement to address working women's problems.

This paper has two purposes. The first is to provide a general description of these new organizations of working women. This description includes their goals, tactics, organizational structure, and relationship with the labor movement. Second, the paper provides more detailed information about the women who joined one of these organizations. This information includes why they joined their organization, as well as what they expect from that organization and the role they play in it.

There are a number of efforts being made within the labor movement to increase the number of women belonging to unions. These efforts are not discussed here. The focus of this paper is

specifically new organizations of working women external to the American labor movement.

GENERAL BACKGROUND

Between 15 and 20 major organizations of working women formed in urban areas during the last decade. About 12 of them are linked nationally; the others are local and autonomous. All are still relatively small given the size of their potential constituencies. Few have more than a thousand members. Those members work for a number of employers in a given area, and any one firm may employ only a few members.[2]

These organizations have a number of commonalities. First, they are all organizations for working women. Most of the members and virtually all of the officers are female. Most of them began in the mid-1970s and are outgrowths of the feminist movement. Many of the founders were active feminists who became convinced of the importance to women of collective action aimed at employment-related problems.

Second, these organizations do not consider themselves to be unions. In fact, although they share some of organized labor's goals, they operate, with few exceptions, independent of the labor movement. Additionally, their tactics are quite different than those of most unions. The relationship between working women's organiza-

From *Proceedings of the Thirty-Fourth Annual Meeting* of the Industrial Relations Research Association, Barbara D. Dennis, Ed., 1982, pp. 381–389. Reprinted with permission of the authors and the IRRA.

tions and the labor movement will be discussed more fully in a later section.

GOALS

The general overarching goal of these organizations is improving employment conditions faced by working women, particularly low-income white-collar women. This overall goal has two related dimensions. The first dimension involves economic or "bread and butter" issues. The problems in this dimension include low wages, employment discrimination, and lack of promotional opportunities. The second dimension involves the right to be treated with dignity and to have one's work be seen as meaningful and serious. This dimension includes problems such as sexual harassment and arbitrary and demeaning treatment by supervisors.

A related goal is building a firm organizational base. This involves continuing organizing efforts designed to introduce working women to the idea of working together to solve shared problems.

TACTICS

These organizations generally focus on resolving immediate problems as a way of achieving their goals. The tactics used vary enormously and are tailored to the specific problem being addressed. These tactics can be classified into four general categories: Information Gathering, Conciliation, Direct Action, and Education.

Information Gathering

Information gathering is both an important first step in becoming established and also an important ongoing activity for these organizations. Initially, surveys conducted among selected populations of working women help identify particular employment problems and problem employers. This information serves as a basis for program planning and as a way of letting people know of

the organization's existence. Employment problems are handled on a case-by-case basis. Examples of the issues handled are failure of a firm to live up to an affirmative action plan, specific incidents of sexual harassment, low wages, and employer failure to post promotional opportunities.

Before programs are implemented, much more detailed information is gathered about the specific problem being addressed. Having good background information is considered extremely important when dealing either with government agencies or employers. Inaccurate or incomplete information lessens the credibility of spokespersons and can significantly undermine efforts to change employment policies.

Conciliation

Once information about a specific problem has been gathered, the involved employer or governmental agency is approached in an effort to resolve the identified problem. In some instances the identified problem can be resolved through discussion sessions. In other instances the employer or concerned agency is unwilling to meet with representatives of the organization, or, if willing to meet with them, unwilling to make any concessions. If efforts at conciliation through discussion are unsuccessful, then direct action can be used.

Direct Action

Because not enough members work for any one employer to make effective use of strikes and strike threats, other forms of direct action are used. There are many forms of direct action, but most of them are designed to bring the involved employer unfavorable publicity. Examples of such activities include public awards, such as a Christmas "Scrooge of the Year" award and a "Pettiest Office Procedure" award. These have the combined impact of making the organization visible, while at the same time putting pressure on the involved employer. Other forms of direct action include presentation of signed petitions, picketing, and even sit-ins.

Another form of direct action involves using government agencies to pressure employers to live up to their legal obligations. This is most frequently used when the issue is affirmative action, equal employment opportunity, or age discrimination. Banks have been a major focus due to the large numbers of low-income women employed in banking. Efforts have been made to have the U.S. Department of Labor's Office of Federal Contract Compliance Programs monitor affirmative action programs in the banking industry, and a number of administrative complaints have resulted. These tactics have had a reasonable amount of success. A number of banks have made back-pay settlements, four banks in Baltimore raised the wages of low-level bank employees, several banks and insurance companies have agreed to job-posting programs, and at least one bank has instituted a major training program for clerical employees.[3]

Education

Education and outreach are extremely important activities for working women's organizations. They are accomplished through programs, seminars, and publications. They serve two major functions. First, they are a way to get visibility and to reach potential members. Getting people involved in educational programs is also an important way of increasing member commitment. It is also a service that encourages people to maintain their membership, perhaps even after a specific employer-based problem has been resolved.

The second major function performed by these educational activities is to help women understand and develop ways of handling problems facing them at work. As such they serve both personal enrichment and job counseling needs. Examples of typical subjects include skills assessment, conflict management in an office setting,

equal employment opportunity law, retirement planning, assertiveness training, and career planning. Additionally, some educational programs are more general and aim at developing an understanding of common problems and solutions.

ORGANIZATIONAL STRUCTURE

One of these organizations, Working Women, is national in scope. It has three national offices and 12 affiliates in major cities. Locals get support, both informational and financial, from the national offices, but most of their decision-making is autonomous. Additionally, there are several organizations, such as Women Employed (WE) in Chicago and The Interfaith Women's Alliance for Job Equity (WAJE) in Philadelphia which do not have national affiliates. There is communication and information sharing among all these organizations.

Typically local offices are staffed by a director and a small staff. They administer programs on a day-to-day basis, but major decisions are made at executive board meetings. Dues are kept low to encourage membership and they supply only partial funding for operational costs.

PROBLEMS

The two major problems faced by these organizations are closely intertwined: building both a strong membership and a firm financial base. These problems are not unusual for new organizations, but a particular problem they face is keeping members committed to broad goals when the operational focus is on solving narrow problems that affect only a few members at a time.

Another problem they face is the historical difficulty in organizing white-collar workers. Many reasons can be given for this including the masculine image of the labor movement and the unwillingness of women to confront their employers. One reason that is often stressed, however, is the reluctance to join expressed by many office workers due to fear of employer reprisal.[4]

Office automation and its impact on the number and type of future jobs is a future problem for these organizations. Currently they function by reacting to existing problems. Affecting employer decisions with respect to office automation will be extremely difficult, particularly without ongoing employer relationships.

RELATIONSHIP WITH THE LABOR MOVEMENT

One question to ask about these organizations is how their relationship with the labor movement will evolve. Currently they do not perform the functions performed by unions. They do not press for certified bargaining rights, they negotiate with employers only over limited issues, and they do not sign collective bargaining contracts. Additionally, they have relatively little contact with the labor movement.

A major reason for their independence from the labor movement is the belief that the organizing model used by organized labor is ineffective in organizing women in clerical occupations. There are several explanations for the labor movement's inability to effectively organize these workers. One explanation is that the labor movement has not been willing to expend the resources or develop the tactics necessary to organize successfully in these areas. A second explanation is that women clericals and service workers have not been ready to join unions.[5]

Both explanations are consistent with the emergence of working women's organizations. They do provide a new model for organizing clerical women. Some observers have described this model as "pre-organizing," or creating the conditions that make union organizing viable.

In theory the potential exists for innovative and cooperative arrangements between working women's organizations and the labor movement. There are mutual interests. Many unions are interested in organizing in new areas, and working women's organizations do not provide as broad

employment protections as do collective bargaining contracts. In fact, members of one Working Women affiliate, Nine to Five in Boston, formed a local union, which joined the Service Employees International Union (SEIU) as Local 925.

This indicates that innovative arrangements can be developed. However, the essence of innovation is doing things differently than before, and that type of organizational change is often difficult to achieve because of institutional barriers facing it. As evidence of these institutional barriers, Local 925 approached ten other unions before SEIU agreed to work with it.[6]

One of the factors important in the future relationship of working women's organization and the labor movement are the members themselves. The following section describes demographically the members of one working women's organization, WAJE. It also discusses their reasons for joining WAJE, how they perceive it spends its time, and how satisfied they are with it.

SURVEY OF WAJE MEMBERS

An anonymous mailed questionnaire focusing on participation was sent to 302 members of Philadelphia's Interfaith Women's Alliance for Job Equity. A total of 129 members returned the questionnaire, yielding a response rate of 43 percent. Of the respondents, 93% are female, and 74% are white. A majority are 25 to 39 years old with the concentration in the 25 to 29 age group. Most members are Protestant, and Baptist is the single largest denomination.

Seventy percent of the respondents work in white-collar occupations. No one salary level reflects an overwhelming response. The greatest frequency of responses for gross weekly salary is in the $200 to $299 category. Twenty-three percent receive $300 to $399 weekly gross salary.

WAJE respondents' job tenure ranges from a few months to over ten years. Working for less than one year is the most frequently noted category with 21% of the respondents checking it. A majority of the employed respondents do not have a regular grievance procedure at their place of employment.

Motivation to Join

WAJE members were asked to rank the reasons why they joined WAJE. To change the employment situation for women (73%) and to educate themselves (73%) were the most frequent responses. The third most frequent response was job-related problems (50%). Although job problems and change the employment situation for women were most frequently given as the number one reason for joining, more members noted change the employment situation for women as their second and third reasons, giving it the highest overall response rate.

These responses suggest that although specific job problems were the major reasons for about one-fourth of members joining WAJE, other motivations were also important. The concern for improving the employment situation for women is particularly interesting. It suggests that members join working women's organizations for somewhat different reasons than people join unions given the labor movement's focus on wages and job problems. It is consistent with the notion that working women's organizations not only have a different organizing model than the labor movement but appeal to members for different reasons.

About two-thirds of the respondents (67 percent) reported they were satisfied with their current job. However, many reported facing problems at work. The most commonly cited problem was lack of opportunity for advancement, a problem shared by 47% of the respondents. Low wages were noted by 31% and 28% gave frustrating situations as a job problem.

The concern over promotional opportunities was also evident when members responded to a question asking them their career goals. Changing careers was cited as frequently as increased wages as an objective (34%). Additionally, 31% sought increased status as an objective, and 21%

wanted more responsibility. Only 7% responded that their goal was to leave the labor force.

Changing careers, increased status, and more responsibility are closely related objectives, and all are related to increasing wages. However, they also indicate a different type of job objective than increased wages alone suggests. They indicate that personal growth and self actualization are very real career objectives for the respondents. These are goals consistent with joining WAJE to improve the employment situation for women and to educate themselves. They are also issues that are not emphasized by the labor movement.

Participation

Participation at WAJE meetings and activities was reviewed. About 70% of the respondents note their attendance to be 25% or less of the time. A majority (54%) would like to attend more while 44% are satisfied with their participation.

For those who would like to participate more in committee meetings, seminars, public actions, and fund-raising events, the impediment to participation noted with the most frequency is no time. Of the respondents, 57% indicate they have no time to participate more. Other impediments in order of frequency are distance, no interest, home pressures, and no opportunity.

To analyze participation, a regression was completed with participation and the demographic factors of age, marital status, residence, number of children, and education. Although the entire model was significant (s = .044), it accounts for only 12% of the variation in participation. Marital status proved to be the most influential factor, with nonmarried persons participating more than married persons. Participation decreases as persons reside further from WAJE headquarters. Education has a negative coefficient indicating that as education increases participation decreases. Age, education, and number of children together account for less than 2% of the variation.

Role of WAJE

The respondents reiterate their reasons for joining WAJE when they describe the role of WAJE. They chose from the following list items describing how they perceive WAJE's functions: improve pay, solve members' problems, organize educational activities, conduct demonstrations, organize social activities, improve WAJE, combat sexual harassment, obtain publicity, conduct fund-raising events, improve safety and health at work, keep members informed, and organize nonmembers. When asked how WAJE should spend its time, 57 percent of the respondents felt WAJE should help solve members' problems, 47% felt WAJE should combat sexual harassment, and 47% thought WAJE should organize educational activities. These expected objectives are similar to the reasons noted for joining WAJE.

The respondents were also asked to indicate how they perceive WAJE's use of time with the same items. The same three items appeared in a different frequency. Fifty-eight percent believed WAJE spends time combating sexual harassment, 53% note helping solve members problems, and 33 percent feel WAJE spends its time organizing educational activities. Regarding their own perceptions, the responding members want WAJE to attend to solving members' problems somewhat more than to combating sexual harassment.

A majority of respondents believe that what WAJE does and what WAJE should do are about the same thing. A correlation of the perceived "should do" and "does do" responses produces significant results in all items except organize new members.

SUMMARY

This paper provides a description of the working women's organizations currently organizing clerical workers. It discusses their functions and structure and points out differences between these organizations and unions. It also presents findings of a survey of the members of one of these organizations. The results of this survey also point out differences between the role these organizations play and the role many unions play in our society. However, although they currently have a somewhat different focus, it is not clear what the future relationship will be between working women's organizations and the American labor movement.

NOTES

1. Linda H. Legrande, "Women in Labor Organizations: Their Ranks Are Increasing," *Monthly Labor Review* 101 (August 1978), p. 9.

2. Information in the following section comes primarily from interviews with officers and directors of Working Women, Women Employed, and Interfaith Women's Alliance for Working Women conducted by the authors during 1980 and 1981.

3. Working Women, *Report from Working Women,* April 1980.

4. Roberta Lynch, "Women in the Workforce," *The Progressive* (October 1979). p. 29.

5. Lynch, p. 29.

6. Nancy Seifer and Barbara Wertheimer, "New Approaches to Collective Power," in *Women Organizing: An Anthology,* eds. Bernice Cummings and Victoria Schuck (1979), p. 180.

Multinational Unionism:
Incentives, Barriers, and Alternatives

LLOYD ULMAN
University of California, Berkeley

Both advocacy and forecasts of international unionism and collective bargaining — as responses to the extraordinary growth of multinational enterprise — have been compounded out of two principal ingredients. The first is the element of novelty which is found in the extension of the area of corporate decision-making beyond national boundaries on such a large scale. Such extension should, it seems, somehow generate some countervailing power of comparable range, and in the absence of effective international public authority, this countervailing power would have to be wielded by private organizations. The second ingredient is the element of precedent which can be found in the formation of national trade unions and in the establishment of companywide and industrywide bargaining, phenomena which have been associated with the development of interregional markets and of multiplant firms within national borders.

Despite the appeal of these arguments, the growth of international collective bargaining has not matched advocated or predicted rates. While there have been instances of mutual assistance involving unions in plants of multinational firms, systematic efforts to coordinate and institu-

tionalize union bargaining strategy and tactics on an international scale have been slow to develop. Clearly, forces making for the development of international unionism and bargaining do exist and, under certain conditions, could conceivably prevail. However, after attempting to assess the implications of some of the incentives, this paper reaches the view that, on balance, the prospects for such developments are not favorable at this time.[1] To anticipate the subsequent discussion, it is concluded that strong incentives to engage in coordinated union activity do exist; that barriers are in some instances strong, in other cases not as formidable or enduring as is sometimes assumed, and that alternatives to international unions and collective bargaining are frequently more conveniently available. Moreover, these alternative approaches and mechanisms appear to tackle the problem of job security more directly than international collective bargaining.

INCENTIVES FOR MULTINATIONAL UNIONISM

Incentives to engage in multinational union activity emerge from (a) certain *problems* which unions might experience as a result of the operation of multinational enterprise and (b) certain *inducements* or factors which facilitate unionists' attempts to cope with those problems. Both the problems and inducements which are viewed as

Reprinted, with permission, from *Industrial Relations,* Vol. 14, No. 1, February 1975, pp. 1–31.

emerging on the contemporary international scene will be considered in this part of the paper in the light of problems and inducements which were associated with the emergence (before World War II) of national unions within their respective countries.

In the first section, it will be argued that (1) unionists in high-wage parent countries face the problem of loss of jobs as a result of foreign direct investment and would therefore welcome a relative rise in the wages in potential host countries. It will further be argued (2) that special conditions tend to minimize any potential job loss which could result in host countries from such relative wage increases, and this would tend to increase the net inducement to unionists in those countries to cooperate in international wage-raising ventures. In the second section, it is maintained that (1) the multiplant character of a certain type of multinational enterprise confronts national unions with "whipsaw" problems in raising or protecting their respective wage levels, (2) the ability and willingness of large-scale international firms to pay high wages constitutes both a problem for national unionists and an inducement to form companywide unions, and that (3) the existence of certain international labor institutions can facilitate union attempts to narrow international wage differences.

Avoiding Job Loss

The first question it is useful for us to address is whether problems of the same nature as those which national unions have faced now exist on an international scale. National unions have, in the past, attempted to secure coordination of wage determination in different regions for any or all of three reasons:

1. To resist downward pressure on the entire level of the industry's wages, brought about by competition among employing units (established or potential) in different sub-

markets or by cost-minimizing efforts of large multiplant firms.

2. To induce or resist changes in geographic patterns of employment — and therefore investment — by attempting to alter the geographic structure of wages. This attempt takes the form of pressing for an increase in wages in the area of actual or prospective job gain relative to wages in the area of actual or threatened job loss. Unionists in both areas stand to gain from this policy. Those in the job-loss area gain by virtue of increased job security and wage stability. Those in the job-gain area, especially if it is a relatively low-wage area to begin with, benefit from increased wage "equity" or "parity." Nor would incumbent job-holders in the job-gain region suffer from reduced job security as long as their increase in relative wages merely reduced or eliminated a potential increase in jobs which would have occurred in its absence.

3. To eliminate or to create a "whipsaw" advantage by striking (or refusing to handle struck work in) other plants when a particular plant is shut down in the course of a labor dispute. This activity can be engaged in either to implement the strategies above or for its own sake, in the absence of other strategies. In the latter case, however, the selfish interest served by coming to the aid of another group is less likely to be regarded as commensurate with the sacrifice required, and, therefore, the effective authority of the national union over the locals is likely to be weaker.

Market- or Cost-Oriented Investment?

To what extent do the above reasons for coordinated wage determination now exist on the cross-national scene? The fact that world exports have grown more rapidly than GNP in industrial countries reflects international expansion and interpenetration of markets. Moreover, the fact that U.S. foreign direct investment in the 1960s grew more rapidly than direct investment from other countries in the U.S.[2] indicates that important flows of job-creating capital from higher-wage areas to lower-wage regions took place — in addition to heavy direct investment flows from advanced industrial nations to the industrially underdeveloped areas. Finally, the importance of the activity of multinational enterprise is reflected in the fact that, throughout the fifties, direct foreign investment increased more rapidly than world trade — it has been estimated that in the subsequent decade direct foreign investment accounted for 5 to 10% of the increase in aggregate GNP of the group of industrialized countries.[3]

Why has the tendency been for companies to invest in foreign countries rather than merely to export to them? Trade unionists, especially American unionists, tend to regard multinational manufacturers as ''runaway'' firms in ceaseless quest of cheaper labor. Economists and managers, however, stress market enlargement as a dominant incentive to so-called ''horizontal'' overseas investment (whereby the same types of goods are produced abroad as at home) and risk avoidance and exclusion of rivals by control over raw materials inputs as the primary reasons motivating ''vertical'' investments. Johnson and Caves[4] suggest that product differentiation and oligopolistic exploitation of a domestic market endow firms with stores of ''free'' knowledge as well as excesses of both specialized managerial capacity and liquid funds. Caves argues that product differentiation may be necessary to enable foreign firms to compete on an equal footing with native enterprises. However, such reasoning does not completely account for preference by firms for direct foreign investment over exports — except possibly in the case where further product differentiation is regarded as necessary to conform to particular characteristics of the host country market. Managers themselves stress another

point: the importance of various public restraints and incentives — e.g., tariffs and import quotas, ''local content'' requirements, subsidies, and tax concessions — deployed by host country governments in an effort to condition market availability on the foreigner's active contributions to domestic industrial development, import restraint, and export growth.[5]

Two estimates by the U.S. Tariff Commission support the view that direct investment by at least U.S.-based international firms has been aimed primarily at exploiting additional markets rather than at producing more cheaply for old ones. The first is that, in the aggregate, multinational activity generated a net increase of about four billions in exports during the period 1966–1970. The second is that direct foreign investment by U.S.-based multinational companies actually might have generated small net increases in employment in most manufacturing categories (and in the aggregate), if it is assumed that such direct foreign investment did not displace domestic investment, either in the U.S. or abroad.[6]

Nevertheless, the apprehensions of unionists, not only in the United States but increasingly in other industrialized countries, may prove well founded. Despite the above arguments, a considerable volume of direct foreign investment is cost-oriented rather than market-oriented. It is concentrated in less developed countries and is often of the ''vertical'' variety, directed to the extraction of raw materials or to the production of components which are exported from the host country. Such investment, according to Reuber, is motivated ''almost invariably (by) low wage costs (and) the ready availability of skilled and semiskilled labor'' as well as by public incentives.[7]

In the second place, even market-oriented investment may be carried out in host countries where wages are lower than in the home country of the parent corporation; this is certainly true of investments by U.S.-based concerns. Where this is true, a basis is created for export from the host country to the home country; such substitution of imports for home production is discussed by Vernon as the last phase of the "product cycle."[8] Another basis for displacement (which can reinforce a wage differential) can be found in insistence by the host country that "inward" direct investment be on a scale sufficient to generate exports as well as to supply its domestic market. Thus supplies of managerial skills and, possibly, of internally generated funds, which before foreign investment were in excess of the requirements of oligopolistic profit maximization in the firm's home market, could be transformed through imports from host country plants into excess plant and equipment in the home market.

Buffers Against Induced Job Loss

It was implied in the beginning of the previous section that minimizing job loss in one area by raising relative wages in another can be an effective incentive to national or international unionism only if it does not entail appreciable job loss to union members in the area where relative wages are to be raised. In fact, two potential buffers against such induced job loss can be found, one on the demand side in some underdeveloped economies and the other on the supply side in some European countries.

With respect to the first type of buffer, it has been noted that where a product has been developed in the high-wage market of an industrially advanced economy, the technology exported to a lower-wage, and often less developed economy, might be more appropriate — more capital-intensive and less labor-intensive — to the factor price ratio in the home economy than to that in the host economy.[9] Under these conditions, wages can be raised in the host country (which, since capital costs to the multinational firms are not subject to significant interregional variation, implies raising the costs of labor relative to capital) without inducing management to make the process more capital-intensive than it

already is. Substitution away from labor inputs in the host country would thus be minimized and, to this extent, so would actual job loss.

In industrialized continental countries of Western Europe, a potential buffer exists on the supply side in the form of temporary foreign labor. Foreign nationals from lower-wage countries have comprised between 8 and 15% of the work force in some of the larger industrial countries, and while their migration has been in response to economic demand in many sectors, it has entailed heavy social costs and has given rise to serious social problems. The loss of jobs held by foreign workers would not be regarded by nationals as a serious offset to their own wage increases — nor by the unions which they naturally dominate. This buffer, however, is only partial and tends to become progressively thinner. It is only partial because the foreign workers are primarily unskilled and semiskilled, and any reduction in demand would presumably include complementary bundles of more highly skilled native workers. The buffer would tend to shrink, because after each succeeding increase in relative wages, fewer foreign workers would remain to buffer subsequent raises. However, the greater the progress made in the direction of international parity, the less is the need for a foreign buffer. On the other hand, the social tensions referred to above have been generating significant political pressure to reduce the intake of foreign labor, and such a development could well outpace the progress of international unionism in narrowing intraindustrial wage differences.

Raising or Protecting Wages

Employer whipsaw capabilities. Unionists in different national sectors of an international corporate domain could face a tradeoff: to the extent that the company's investment behavior spares them from problems of job loss, it confronts them with whipsaw problems. For the weaker the tendency of market oriented investment to displace output and employment in the parent market, the more that investment results in expansion of the firm's overall capacity in the form of additional producing units. The latter increases the firm's ability temporarily to switch production from plants shut down by labor disputes to other plants in other countries or simply to generate cash flow during partial shutdowns. The capability of switching production to plants in other countries — which are not represented by the same national unions — is, however, limited to the extent that what has been referred to above as further product differentiation has occurred. Thus proliferation of very similar production facilities gives a firm what might be called industrial relations economies of scale, which can exist in the absence of conventional scale economies.

Conventional scale economies can also endow a multinational employer with a bargaining advantage. Where international firms operate specialized plants in different countries, their subsidiaries tend to be less vertically integrated than their smaller domestic competitors.[10] Hence, where the domestic firm might be shut down by a "bottleneck" strike in a key operation, the subsidiary might normally import the component from abroad and thus remain in operation. Thus both "horizontal" investment and "vertical" investment (or "multiple sourcing") can endow international firms with whipsaw advantages, and in either case international union activity could neutralize the employer's advantage and approximate the power possessed by the national unions vis-à-vis domestic multiplant employers.

Economic conditions and the employer's ability and willingness to pay. Although two of the three problems which once helped to account for the rise of national unionism now exist, at least potentially, on an international scale, the problem which we listed first, i.e., general wage deflation, has not existed on a significant scale since the Second World War. Before then, hard times had intermittently made interregional unionism a necessary condition (although definitely not a suf-

ficient condition) of viable unionism in many markets; afterwards, the prevalence of high levels of employment and of locally generated "drifting" of wages above industrywide rates in Western Europe have contributed to a weakening of the authority of national unions. Thus an important cause of interregional unionism has been absent during the period characterized by the growth of international enterprise.

In depriving unionists of a powerful defensive incentive to internationalize their activities, might not good times have held out the promise of payoff to offensive operations? Prosperity and growth have combined with strong market positions and generally lower unit labor costs[11] to endow multinational subsidiaries with relatively high "ability to pay" levels of compensation. At the same time, the high fixed costs of these generally more capital-intensive firms make for lower resistance to strikes — once their international whipsaw advantage is removed. But ability to pay can serve as an incentive to prospective international unionists only to the extent that it awaits exploitation through international bargaining. Translated before-hand into generous wages and benefits, it can serve as an obvious disincentive to international unionism, if that is the intention of the employer. Now, multinational subsidiaries can be inhibited in the operation of high-wage policies by fear of incurring the displeasure of domestic firms — especially firms with more labor-intensive production functions which, intentionally or not, could be placed at a competitive disadvantage by such multinational generosity — unions, and public authorities, and according to the FTC study,[12] European subsidiaries of American multinationals, on the average, conform fairly closely to national wage averages. On the other hand, many multinational subsidiaries do have the reputation of being high-wage firms. Steuer and Gennard found that this was the case in Britain where, moreover, multinational subsidiaries helped to pioneer in the introduction of productivity bargaining and other industrial relations reforms.[13] Furthermore, it might be noted, as a corollary to the partial exploitation of their discretionary wage-setting capability, that some multinational firms have refrained from taking full advantage of their whipsaw advantage in strike situations. Of course, the mere existence of that capability constitutes an incentive to the formation of international unionism, but restraint in its exercise tends to weaken that incentive. Thus thanks to its superior ability to pay, multinational management faces a low-profile tradeoff. It must try to keep pay at levels sufficiently low to avoid unfavorable notice by public authorities and private groups in host countries and sufficiently high to prevent companywide unionism from appearing highly desirable and achievable to employees and their various national representatives.

International labor institutions. Transformation of the old international trade union secretariats — located in the chemical, metal, food, transport, and printing sectors — and the postwar establishment of industrial committees relating to the European Economic Community could facilitate the development of international unionism. Some of the secretaries do not aspire to international bargaining over wages and hours,[14] while others (notably Charles Levinson[15]) have claimed for these organizations a role in organizing ad hoc activities, such as simultaneous strikes or threats of strikes in different plants of multinational companies, refusal to handle "blacked" work, and consumer boycotts. The final outcome of such activities is seldom reported in great detail. In fact, it is doubtful whether they could stand as an efficient and viable alternative to systematic and coordinated bargaining on a companywide level. Each potential national participant must be able to regard such activity as serving its own immediate or ultimate self-interest, and to that end, some form of "continuous association," as the Webbs put it, is necessary. The Metalworkers and the Chemical Workers' Federations have made a beginning in this direction by establishing companywide committees of national unions corresponding to a number of firms in the electronic and petrochemical industries, and the European Metalworkers' Federation has conducted top-level discussions with some international firms. But nothing like companywide bargaining has occurred.

On the other hand, in performing the more mundane task of collecting and disseminating information about the often widely differing terms and conditions of employment which prevail in various countries in plants owned by the same parent companies, the secretariat or committee performs a function of historic importance to interplant and interregional unionism. A request by a union to the management of a particular subsidiary for information about specific conditions negotiated or prevailing in subsidiaries in other countries is frequently rejected on the grounds that each subsidiary is possessed of its own corporate identity and enjoys managerial autonomy. However, it so happens that monopoly of information is one of the most important bases of monopoly power, and the power to discriminate among markets, if that is an objective of corporate policy, can be served by restraining the flow of information across national market boundaries. But to the extent that unionists in different countries are knowledgeable about conditions within their respective jurisdictions, they need not depend on managers of subsidiaries to provide it to one another. They can computerize and exchange information among themselves, and through the medium of the international secretariat or committee they have begun to do so. Naturally, this process should be of particular benefit to unionists in the low-paid areas and should potentially serve the interregional union objective of narrowing geographic wage differences.

BARRIERS

In the discussion of incentives for multinational unionism, we have suggested some reasons why unionists in relatively low-wage host countries may not be deterred by the prospect of job loss from pressing for a greater measure of "parity" in pay with unionists in the higher-wage regions in which an international industry (and company) are located. We have also pointed to the informational role played by international labor bodies as conducive to the compression of international wage structures. Nevertheless, unionists might feel that the game is not worth the candle, in view of the costs involved in securing relative pay increases — which could include costs to their national union leaders in terms of abridgement of institutional and bargaining autonomy and even to the members themselves in the form of strike costs. Such costs constitute barriers or obstacles to the development of international unionism. These and other types of barriers . . . reflect the influence of (a) national and international wage structures, (b) public policies, (c) labor institutions, including the goals and structure of national labor movements and bargaining systems. Under the first heading the stability of and similarity among industrial wage structures are regarded as constituting a barrier insofar as they weaken the "pull" of international wage differences on wage earners in different national branches of the same industry or, indeed, multinational company. This centripetal influence has been reinforced in the short run by international differences in cyclical timing, but it is subject to erosion by longer-run forces, which make for reduction in international differences in pay, and by better knowledge by workers of the existence of such differentials. Moreover, the centripetal influence exerted by "national orbits of comparison" in some less developed countries might prove to be weaker than is commonly assumed.

Public policies which could have the effect of inhibiting the growth of international unionism include general economic policies in such major areas as the promotion of growth, balance of payments stability, price stability with high levels of employment, and income redistribution. Their implications are . . . potentially formidable obsta-

cles. The magnitude and diversity of national systems of employment-related transfer payments and certain characteristics of national labor legislation also create serious problems, but these are less formidable than might be supposed. Finally, in the category of institutionally induced obstacles, [are] the interrelated influences of radical ideology and trade union structure and the significance of established bargaining relationships and bargaining structures. In the former case, we observe that the waning of older ideological resistance stemming from the commitment to public ownership for its own sake might be compensated for by the emergence of a new tide of egalitarianism within the national setting. With respect to the latter category, it is argued that national systems of industrywide bargaining might lie athwart the path of international bargaining but they would not be inherently capable of offering decisive resistance to the development of multinational bargaining. . . .

ALTERNATIVES: JOB BARGAINING

The failure thus far of international unionism to develop in response to the incentives, which were discussed in the first part of this paper, cannot be ascribed wholly to the obstacles discussed in the second part — especially since some of the latter are probably less formidable than commonly supposed. The failure must also be ascribed to the existence of certain national alternatives to international unionism and bargaining which, from the union viewpoint, hold promise of restraining both management's investment and locational decisions and management's capacity to divert production from struck plants. The possibility that the economic power of international firms might be countered through national institutions contravenes the generally accepted premise, stated at the outset, that the source of countervailing power be comparable in geographic range to the domain of international enterprise. Moreover, some of the national alternatives which we shall discuss in this section involve the deployment of governmental authority and influence; this contravenes the second popular premise, i.e., that, in the absence of effective international public authority, the countervailing power would have to be generated through private institutional arrangements.

To a certain extent, it is true this alternative approach can be implemented through existing channels of collective bargaining. Unions in some countries, especially in Italy, have begun to bargain for guarantees from employers that particular plants will not be shut down or that employers commit themselves to future investments which will assure jobs to particular groups of union members. This amounts to direct bargaining over the nature of the firm's production function and, as such, bears a family resemblance to the common practice of bargaining over work rules in the interest of job security — a practice, incidentally, in which unions had engaged in the U.S. even before they were in a position to bargain effectively over wages on an industrywide basis. Moreover, demands for the retention of particular facilities have sometimes been backed up by strike action — in the case of multiplant firms by striking unaffected plants as well as the disputed ones. Thus if a multinational enterprise has a number of subsidiary facilities in a particular country in addition to one (or more) which it may wish to close down, a multiplant strike within that country may deflect the multinational from its objective and not require sympathetic responses from unionists in plants in other countries.

For antiwhipsaw purposes (especially the "blacking" of struck work by workers in other establishments), on the other hand, this tactic might not be very effective, since an international firm would be able to expand production in other countries. Moreover, because the costs to management potentially involved in bargaining over a new plant location can greatly exceed costs resulting from negotiations over work rules affecting only a portion of the work force, management resistance to union demands would be greater in the former case. And, if, as a result of the pecuniary value placed on such an extended demand for guaranteed employment there remained little "room" for a general increase in pay and other benefits, unionists in other plants would have little selfish incentive to engage in protracted strike action in support of the locational demand. The fact that in some well publicized cases concerted employee action took the form of "work-ins," or plant occupation and seizure of inventory, suggests the limited capacity of conventional strike activity to cope directly with problems of this variety.

Hence, it is probable that an effective measure of restraint by national unionism on locational policies of international companies would require (a) deterrents or inducements to the employer, originating outside the direct union-management relationship and (b) some possible structural changes in decision-making centers within the firms. In either case the national government would have to be a party to job bargaining. It is certainly true that the existence of sovereign authority within the several regions of an international market affords some options to unionists within those regions which have not been available to unionists in regions within national markets. The potential availability of restrictions on foreign trade and even of exchange rate adjustment, which could reduce incentives for a multinational to close down an existing plant and invest in additional export-oriented facilities in other countries, is an obvious case in point. It helps to account for the new demands for more protectionist legislation made by the AFL-CIO and by some individual American unions, to the detriment of prior attempts to encourage international coordination of bargaining activities. But the prospects for success in moving official policy in this direction are rather limited, if only because the competing claims of different narrow economic interests make passage of general measures required for this purpose very difficult.

Exchange rate flexibility is also a very general instrument and, therefore, of limited helpfulness in such highly specific circumstances as are created by threatened closing of a particular plant in a particular firm or industry.

However, the increased acceptance in Europe and elsewhere of two guiding principles might yield instruments of greater specific efficiency. These principles call for (a) increased worker involvement and authority (ranging from "participation" to "autogestion," or worker control) in industrial management and (b) increased security of job tenure. Statutory provision for worker representation on boards of "supervisory" directors can be regarded as an expression of the first principle, and it is interesting that such "codetermination" has been frequently associated with proposals for compulsory advance disclosure of management's investment and employment plans. By having representatives of the employees seated on both sides of the bargaining table, with detailed investment plans spread out before them, union leaders would hope to deprive management negotiators of an important bargaining tactic: the threat to shut down the plant and "run away" to another country. More importantly, employee representatives on boards of supervisors which appoint managing directors might be in a good position to alter the nature of the plans themselves so as to prevent or minimize job loss.

National unions have also attempted to prevent layoffs in specific situations by exerting political influence on host-country governments. Hence any strike or strike threat would be directed at the government as well as at the company, but the government might be responsive to appeals to intervene even in the absence of such pressure. Public policy towards mass layoffs is often colored by experience under strong legal restrictions on employers' freedom to dismiss individual workers (under the "principle of justification"). Moreover, in some countries (notably France and West Germany) mass layoffs may be conditioned on advance notification to an authorization by public authority; while in many others, as the International Labour Office gingerly puts it:

> . . . the absence of formal regulations regarding reduction of the work force for economic reasons does not necessarily preclude that questions related to the reduction may be the subject of mediation, conciliation, arbitration and other established procedures to deal with disputes. [16]

In addition, procedures which are not "established" tend to be brought into play, for governments can and are often motivated to play the role of an interested party when multinational companies are involved. A government might offer an employer subsidies or tax concessions, or it might threaten to withdraw concessions which had been originally made to induce entry and which the company might have expected to continue in its other plants in the country in question. Especially important in cases where multinational investment is market-oriented rather than export-oriented would be a governmental threat to extend local-content policy to cover conditions of exit as well as entry: if you don't manufacture and employ here, you can't expect to sell here. Since governments are large-scale customers, such a threat could be virtually self-enforcing in some cases. Finally, government could nationalize the plant and run it, if necessary, on a subsidized basis.

The more effective national job bargaining in one form or another promises to be, the more it will commend itself to unionists, but the more attractive an alternative international bargaining would be to employers. (That the impetus to international bargaining could come from the employer side — possibly through the medium of works councils or shop committees — is less paradoxical than might appear; some large-scale American firms were not adverse to national unionism as an alternative to competitive wage-and-price cutting in the Great Depression.)

On balance, it is unlikely that job bargaining would prove effective enough to throw multinational employers into the arms of international unionism. Blocking or forced utilization of fixed assets would be a disincentive to new direct investment, so that governments, often competing with one another for foreign investment, would be reluctant to exploit job bargaining to the extent desired by unionists. But even if national job bargaining proves to be of only limited effectiveness, it could hold out at least as much promise to unionists threatened by the loss of employment as more indirect international alternatives. Further, it would not entail the conscious alteration of familiar parochial arrangements.

CONCLUSION

In view of certain historically familiar incentives to the development of interregional unionism and bargaining, which the growth of multinational enterprise has projected on an international scale, the failure of international bargaining institutions thus far to develop to an appreciable extent (notwithstanding certain efforts emanating from some of the trade secretariats and related bodies) has frequently been attributed to national institutions which inherently constitute obstacles to such developments. Some of the obstacles examined in this paper, notably various governmental economic policies and ideological influences on national labor movements, are indeed strong. But others, like some legal restraints on union activities, are less formidable than might appear. Still others would be subject to erosion by equilibrating economic and political forces and by the spread of knowledge about international differences in pay and benefits. These include the centripetal influence of national wage structures, national differences in social security benefits and other statutory pay supplements, and established national systems of industrywide bargaining.

The foregoing suggests that in the long run

international unionism might not be dead; it could be very much in the cards, especially if the employees concerned and their own plant leadership decide to break out of their "national orbits." But is also suggests that what has thus far been a nonevent cannot be explained solely or even primarily by obstacles. This paper seeks enlightenment in two other areas: incentives and alternatives. In the first area it finds that while two of the three historic economic incentives to national unionism — avoidance of regional job loss and countering the whipsaw capability of multiplant firms — also exist on an international scale, the third and possibly most important — the need to resist competitive reductions in industrywide wage levels — has not been experienced for over a generation. Moreover, the whipsaw power of some large international firms has been subject to self-restraint by the need to differentiate product lines to meet local market requirements and also, although within limits, as part of a constrained "low-profile" policy. Thus while some characteristics of the international economic climate operate to lower barriers to the development of international unionism, other environmental characteristics have prevented the emergence of an historically proven incentive.

Finally, where incentive is strong — where it is prompted by fear of job loss in relatively high-wage countries — an alternative to international unionism is also relatively strong. Job bargaining, as we have characterized this group of alternatives, is designed to restrain investment patterns directly to avoid job loss rather than indirectly through international coordination of wage determination on the union side. The job-bargaining alternative relies heavily for its effectiveness on governmental authority and the political process. Hence national authority, which underlies many of the obstacles to international unionism, also underlies a powerfully attractive alternative in jurisdictions of potential job loss. Thus at least in the short run, any countervailing union power to the international corporation is likely to be neither so wide in geographic scope nor so private in origin as might have been contemplated in the past decade.

NOTES

1. The author was a Visiting Fellow at All Souls College, Oxford, during the academic year 1973-1974 when this was written.

2. The U.S. Congress, Senate Committee on Finance, *Implications of Multinational Firms for World Trade and Investment and for U.S. Trade and Labor* (report submitted by the U.S. Tariff Commission), 93rd Cong., 1st sess., 1973, pp. 94-95. (Hereinafter cited as *Tariff Commission Report.*)

3. *Ibid.,* p. 95.

4. H. G. Johnson, "The Efficiency and Welfare Implications of the International Corporation," in C. P. Kindleberger, ed., *The New International Corporation* (Cambridge, Mass.: MIT Press, 1970), pp. 35-56; and R. E. Caves, "International Corporations: The Industrial Economics of Foreign Investment," *Economica,* XXXVIII (February 1971), 1-27. Both are reprinted in J. H. Dunning, ed., *International Investment* (Middlesex: Penguin Books Ltd., 1972).

5. J. N. Behrman, "Industrial Integration and the Multinational Enterprise," `Annals of the American Academy of Political and Social Science,* September 1972, pp. 34-45.

6. *Tariff Commission Report,* pp. 351-352, 645-672.

7. Reuber refers to this as "export-oriented" investment. G. L. Reuber, *et al., Private Foreign Investment in Development* (Paris: Development Centre of the Organization for Economic Cooperation and Development, Clarendon Press, Oxford, 1973), pp. 73-74.

8. R. Vernon, "International Investment and International Trade in the Product Cycle," *Quarterly Journal of Economics,* LXXX (May 1966), 190-207.

9. Johnson, *op. cit* (in Dunning), p. 461.

10. Caves, *op. cit.*

11. *Tariff Commission Report,* pp. 414-418, 634-642; J. Gennard and M. D. Steuer, "The Industrial Relations of Foreign Owned Subsidiaries in the United Kingdom," *British Journal of Industrial Relations,* IX (July 1971), 151.

12. *Tariff Commission Report,* pp. 620-628.

13. M. D. Steuer and J. Gennard, "Industrial Relations, Labour Disputes and Labour Utilization of Foreign Owned Firms in the United Kingdom," in J. N. Dunning, ed., *The Multinational Enterprise* (New York: Praeger, 1971), pp. 89-144.

14. E. Jacobs, *European Trade Unionism* (London: Croom Hehn, 1973), p. 119.

15. C. Levinson, *International Trade Unionism* (London: George Allen & Unwin Ltd., 1972), pp. 8-21, 96-123.

16. International Labour Conference, Forty-Sixth Session, 1962, *Termination of Employment (Dismissal and Lay-Off)* (Geneva: International Labour Office, 1961), p. 43.

PART II

SECTION 7
National Labor Relations Board and Arbitration Cases

HOW TO DETERMINE THE FACTS OF A CASE

The cases in this book all have the background facts at the beginning of the case. However, one of the reasons these cases arise may be that the parties do not always agree on the facts. Thus to determine the facts of a case, first find out if the parties agree on them. If one party makes a statement as a fact, i.e., a certain event happened, and the other party does not disagree, either by not saying anything or by tacitly agreeing, then you have to assume that the first party is correct. If the two parties disagree on a particular fact, then there is a problem of credibility. If there is a problem of credibility, you may have to decide if it is really relevant to the issue at hand and if so, which side is more credible. Persons who have little interest in the outcome of a case may be considered more credible. Persons who have a more direct interest in the outcome of a case may have more to gain by lying. You may have some difficulty in determining the credibility of the parties where there is a conflict.

INDEX TO NATIONAL LABOR RELATIONS BOARD CASES

CASE NUMBER AND TITLE	SITUATION	PRINCIPAL NLRA SECTIONS INVOLVED
1. Company Domination of a "Labor Organization"	Charges filed when an in-plant committee was established to increase worker participation in the organization.	2(5), 8(a)(1), 8(a)(2)
2. Discharge of a Union Supporter	Company termination of a drunk and insubordinate employee who was involved in the union organizing campaign.	7, 8(a)(1), 8(a)(3)
3. Union Organizing on Company Property	Company refused to allow non-employee union organizers to talk to workers in company owned public cafeteria.	7, 8(a)(1)
4. Who Is in the Bargaining Unit?	Parties disagreed concerning composition of bargaining unit.	2(3), 2(11)
5. Union Threats During an Organizing Campaign	Union threat to discipline members not supporting union's organizing efforts.	7, 8(b)(1)(A)
6. The Right to Conduct a Vigorous Campaign	Company misrepresentation of union effectiveness and financial position during an organizing campaign.	7, 8(a)(1)
7. Opposition to the Union Steward	Discharge of an employee who was disruptive in opposing the union steward.	7, 8(a)(1), 8(a)(3)
8. Picketing a Supermarket to Boycott Paper Bags	Union picketing urging a consumer boycott of paper bags while striking the bag manufacturer.	8(b)(4)(ii)(B)
9. Which Union Should Represent the Employees?	Management recognition of one union when two were seeking recognition; locking employees out of the plant until they ratified the contract.	2(2), 8(a)(1), 8(a)(2)
10. Did the Union Deny Privileges to Nonmembers in a Discriminatory Fashion?	Privileges for union members not granted to employees who did not join the union.	7, 8(b)(1)(A)
11. Was the Superseniority Clause Overbroad?	Allowing union stewards to have preferential job bidding rights.	8(a)(1), 8(a)(3), 8(b)(1)(A), 8(b)(2)

INDEX TO NATIONAL LABOR RELATIONS BOARD CASES (*cont.*)

CASE NUMBER AND TITLE	SITUATION	PRINCIPAL NLRA SECTIONS INVOLVED
12. Did Technological Change Lead to a Jurisdictional Dispute?	Disputed work claimed by two unions as part of the jurisdiction of each.	8(b)(4)(D), 10(k)
13. Must a Company Honor a Union's Request for Equal Employment Data?	Refusal of company to supply the union with information relating to employee equal employment opportunity.	8(a)(1), 8(a)(5)
14. The Protracted Negotiations	Company behavior in bargaining for an initial contract.	8(a)(1), 8(a)(5)
15. Did the End of Subcontracting and the Establishment of a New Workplace Lead to a Successor Employer?	A company that hired most of the employees doing its subcontracted work refused to honor the collective bargaining agreement.	8(a)(1), 8(a)(5)
16. Is the Health Center Covered by the Act?	The employer asserted that it was not covered by the Act and consequently did not engage in collective bargaining with the union.	2(2), 2(6), 8(a)(1), 8(a)(5)
17. Can the Work be Subcontracted?	The employer terminated its contract for housekeeping and maintenance services with a subcontractor and discharged its employees.	8(a)(1), 8(a)(5)
18. Can Doctors Strike?	Two doctors took part in sympathy picketing at a health care-facility. They asserted that the employer discriminated against them as a result.	8(a)(1), 8(a)(4), 8(g)

1. Company Domination of a "Labor Organization"

PARTIES: Streamway Division of Scott and Fetzer Company and Susan Smith,* an individual.

ISSUES: 8(a)(1) and 8(a)(2) charges, company domination of a labor organization, nonunion labor-management committee communications, handling complaints.

BACKGROUND

The Streamway Division of Scott and Fetzer Company produces water faucets and valves at its Westlake, Ohio plant. Two attempts by the United Auto Workers, in October 1976 and again in November 1977, failed to obtain majority support for its efforts to be certified as the collective bargaining agent for the company's production and maintenance employees. The union filed no objections to the conduct of either election and no unfair labor practice charges emerged either before or after these elections.

In March 1977 the Streamway Division established an in-plant committee of employees. The committee was created by the company's president, Michael Tenorio. Quoting Tenorio, the purpose of the committee at the company's plant was:

to satisfy a number of specific issues. The first issue was to allow a number of employees in the hourly unit to come in contact with the management on a regular basis. The third was intended to provide this experience for a number of people so the program was designed to have a unit of membership, yet a lot of different participants. The third was intended to provide a sampling of the ideas and thoughts of the employees of the group. It also was to allow them to raise certain issues, submit suggestions, and allow us to communicate and convey information forward and backward.

Tenorio acknowledged that a major purpose of the committee was for employees to develop a mechanism through which they could complain about conditions of employment. After establishing the committee, Tenorio met with the employees to explain how the committee would work. He posted a memorandum to all hourly employees after meeting with them. The memorandum established the number of representatives chosen from the company's four production departments, the schedule of one general and one departmental meeting each month at designated hours (during working time), the maximum term allowable for each representative to serve, the procedure for nominating employee representatives, a method of counting votes "with the assistance of senior employees," and rules governing what happens

---

*All names in the cases of this section are fictitious.

in the case of ties. Subsequent to the issuance of this memorandum, the elections of representatives to the in-plant committee were conducted on working time, on ballots prepared, distributed, and counted by supervision (presumably with the assistance of some senior employees).

One complaint voiced by employees during the 1978 in-plant committee meetings was over a 1977 change in the company's vacation policy. Prior to 1977 the company used the employee's date of hire as the seniority date used for computing vacation eligibility. At some time in 1977 the policy was changed so that seniority credit would not begin to accrue until the beginning of the fiscal year following the employee's date of hire. Some representatives on the in-plant committee complained about the change in policy at a regularly scheduled committee meeting held in October or November 1978. As a result of this complaint, the policy was changed so that all seniority dates were advanced to the first of the fiscal year preceding rather than following the employee's date of hire for the purpose of computing vacation eligibility. This solution was satisfactory to the employees. Other complaints discussed in these meetings were answered with the company's justifications, but there was no evidence that any other grievances were adjusted because of the complaints presented during meetings of the in-plant committee.

Susan Smith who had been terminated for poor job performance, charged that the in-plant committee was a labor organization within the meaning of Section 2(5) of the Act. It was further charged that the employer was dominating this labor organization in violation of Section 8(a)(2) of the Act. Section 8(a)(2) of the Act makes it an unfair labor practice for an employer:

> To dominate or interfere with the formation or administration of any labor organization or contribute financial or other support to it.

Section 2(5) of the Act provides that:

> The term "labor organization" means any organization of any kind, or any agency or employee representation committee or plan, in which employees participate and which exists for the purpose, in whole or in part, of dealing with employers concerning grievances, labor disputes, wages, rates of pay, hours of employment, or conditions of work.

ARGUMENTS SUPPORTING THE SECTION 8(a)(2) CHARGE

Section 2(5) defines a "labor organization" as any organization "dealing with" an employer over grievances, wages, hours, etc. The term "dealing with" is broader than the term "collective bargaining." When the facts of this case are reviewed, the in-plant committee was "dealing with" Streamway division management. Tenorio established that a basic purpose of the in-plant committee was to discuss working conditions. The committee was designed to be a representative body of the entire work force. It was also argued that this committee went way beyond the simple discussion of problems. As a result of the committee's actions, terms and conditions of employment were actually changed. For example, the change in vacation policy sought by the in-plant committee was secured.

It was also pointed out that the in-plant committee was clearly dominated by the company. It was a creature of management that was dominated and supported financially by the company. Because of management's prominent role in the formation and operation of the in-plant committee, it was argued that the company dominated and interfered with the operation of a labor organization in violation of Section 8(a)(2) of the Act.

POSITION OF THE COMPANY

The company denied that the in-plant committee was a labor organization within the meaning of the Act. The purpose of the committee was to develop readily accessible channels of communication within the manufacturing operations and to provide better coordination between plant workers and management. The company pointed out that the organization of the committee supported its view that improved communications was the objective when creating the in-plant committee.

The committee included eight employee representatives and management personnel who were present at both general and departmental meetings. To insure that the committee would provide as many employees as possible the opportunity for direct input, a rotating schedule for committee membership was established. Initial terms varied from three to six months. All later terms on the in-plant committee were three months in duration. To maximize employee participation in the program, no employee could serve for more than three months of the calendar year except for those initially serving six month terms. Broad-based participation was obtained by having management representatives solicit comments from employee representatives on the committee who were hesitant to speak on their own. The company emphasized that the broad-based, rotating membership was intended to develop better communications.

Mr. Tenorio emphasized that the in-plant committee was designed to improve communications between employees and the management of the firm. He claimed that the committee did not exist for the purpose of engaging in collective bargaining, and in fact, had not engaged in any activity that could be characterized as collective bargaining. Nor, as a realistic matter, could it be said that the committee dealt with employees on subjects involving working conditions. Therefore the company denied that the in-plant committee was a labor organization within the meaning of the Act and that employees were denied their Section 7 rights because of the employer's involvement with the committee.

DISCUSSION QUESTIONS

1. Is the in-plant committee a labor organization within the meaning of the Act?

2. Does the existence of the in-plant committee that was created and influenced by the company management constitute a violation of Section 8(a)(2) of the Act?

3. A number of companies with progressive personnel policies have developed advisory committees composed of employees designed to facilitate communications between employees and company management. Does Section 8(a)(2) of the Act impinge upon the ability of employees and their employers to work together through such committees to enhance the welfare of both employees and the company?

2. Discharge of a Union Supporter

PARTIES: Alumina Ceramics, Inc. and the United Steel Workers of America.

ISSUES: 8(a)(1) and 8(a)(3) charges, discharge of union supporter for being drunk and insubordinate, union organizing drive, management reaction.

BACKGROUND

Alumina Ceramics, Inc., manufactures and sells aluminum oxide sealing rings. It employed approximately 59 employees at its Benton, Arkansas facility. On March 17, 1980, the union filed a petition for a representation election. According to Frank Izzo, the company president and highest ranking supervisor at the facility, the company's approach to the election campaign was to just tell the facts. For example, the company advised the employees that just because they had signed a union authorization card it did not mean they had to join the union. The company also counseled employees that they could vote "no" in the election even if they had signed authorization cards. Another tactic that the company used during the campaign was to put together a computer list of all its employees. Then during a supervisors' meeting, each name was reviewed. Based on the experience of the supervisors present, they would indicate whether the individual was a union sup-

porter. One of the employees identified as being a union supporter was Ted Novak. Novak, an employee for four years, was considered by his supervisor, Lyle Storch, to be a fair employee who needed medium supervision. Novak was then employed in the highest job classification in his department. He was also known to be a union partisan because he wore a blue and white button bearing the words "AFL/CIO, Steelworkers Union." Novak actively participated in the union campaign to organize the company. He had told his immediate supervisor that he favored the union. It was apparent that the company's management was fully aware of Novak's sympathies toward the union.

On April 3, 1980, a short time before the union representation election, Novak reported to work badly hungover as a result of an all-night drinking bout. He had been drinking much of the previous day but had stopped about 2:00 A.M. He then slept in his truck at the Tull Bottoms, an area of woods, creeks, and swamps located a short distance from the plant. When he awoke, he drove to work and reported at approximately 7:00 A.M., his normal starting time. He proceeded to the break room where other employees were waiting for the shift to begin. Storch appeared and announced it was time to start work. Novak responded with the following: ". . . . We'll go to work when we get ready." Storch replied, "I'll overlook that this time.'' According to Storch, Novak responded "Who . . . do you think you are? . . .'' He then made an obscene gesture at Storch. During this dialogue, the employees in the break room laughed at Novak's remarks. Novak claimed that he had been "funning." As the employees left the break room for their jobs, Storch asked if anyone had a "smoke." Novak replied, "Someone give the man a cigarette or he'll fire you." One of the employees did give Storch a cigarette.

As a result of his heavy drinking, Novak did not look or feel very well. Storch talked to Novak about his condition as Novak was leaving the break room. Storch told Novak to go home and to return to work when he felt better. Instead, Novak went to the ball mill area where he worked and began his job for the day. Together with another employee, Novak got involved in a process that requires three or four 500-pound barrels to be hoisted to the top of a platform located about 15 to 20 feet off the ground.

Before a break at 8:30 A.M., Storch ran into Novak in the ball mill area. They again discussed Novak's going home. At this point Novak agreed with Storch that he was not feeling well enough to work and said that he would go home. Novak then went to the break room. Storch subsequently met Jack Paintin, the company's director of manufacturing. Storch provided Paintin with an account of what had transpired that morning with Novak. Storch told Paintin that Novak was drunk and insubordinate to him, that Novak had been instructed to leave the plant twice, and that Novak had given him "the finger." Paintin then suggested that they check to see whether Novak had left the plant. Upon entering the break room, they found Novak sitting there eating a sandwich. Paintin asked Novak whether he had been asked to leave. Novak responded that he had and then left the plant.

Paintin called the police shortly after Novak left reporting that he had sent a drunk employee home and that this employee was driving a truck. Novak was then stopped by the police on his way home. The police officer administered a breathalyzer test to determine whether Novak was driving under the influence of alcohol. When the results indicated that Novak was not legally intoxicated, he was released.

At approximately 9:00 A.M., Paintin requested that Storch meet with Company President Izzo, to discuss the events involving Novak. Storch described the morning's events to Izzo. The subject of disciplinary action was raised. Paintin recommended that Novak be fired. Izzo agreed. After Paintin and Izzo suggested that Novak be terminated, Storch indicated he also supported the decision. Izzo decided to think about the matter for awhile longer. Later, Izzo decided to fire Novak. Izzo notified Novak by telephone at lunch time that he was being terminated. He told Novak that he was discharged because of his insubordination and because he had been drunk on company property. Novak was the first employee ever disciplined or discharged for reporting to work hungover or for being insubordinate. The union filed a Section 8(a)(3) charge alleging that Mr. Novak's termination in the context of a union organizing campaign interfered with the employees' Section 7 rights.

THE POSITION OF THE UNION

The union argued that Novak's conduct was seized upon as pretext for his discharge. It was known that the company was unsympathetic toward the union and had committed several unfair labor practices during the course of the certification election campaign. The company knew that Novak was a union partisan. Novak was a fair employee who required minimum supervision. No evidence was provided by the company indicating Novak had been a problem employee. Prior to the entry of Izzo and Paintin into the affair, Storch had overlooked Novak's intemperate remarks. Indeed, Novak's conduct did not take on the character of a "federal case" until it reached the Izzo-Paintin level. Additionally, the inference is strong that Paintin attempted to cause the arrest of Novak for driving under the influence of alcohol for the purpose of strengthening the reasons for firing Novak. In this regard, it is significant that Paintin sent Novak from the plant in what he believed to be a drunken condition although such a condition would obviously have constituted a danger for Novak and others on the highway.

The union also pointed out that Novak's case was the first in which an employee had been discharged or disciplined for being drunk on the job or for being insubordinate. He was the only person ever reported to the police by management personnel after leaving the plant in an allegedly drunken condition. The union argued that this "special treatment" indicated that Novak was the subject of discrimination for his activities on behalf of the union.

THE POSITION OF THE COMPANY

The company argued that it had good reason to discharge Novak. He disobeyed a clear order to go home. Instead, he went into the plant and attempted to do his regular work; work that was potentially dangerous not only to himself but to his fellow employees. Reporting to work intoxicated or hungover and then talking back to a foreman alone might not be grounds for discharge in view of the fact that such practices had been condoned by the company in the past. However, Novak's insubordination was especially serious. The company argued that Novak would have been discharged for insubordination even if he had not been a union member. His conduct was simply too flagrant to ignore. The company knew Novak was a union member but pointed out that he was not particularly active in the union. Furthermore, the company emphasized that it had promoted union adherents and it had given wage increases to other such individuals.

DISCUSSION QUESTIONS

1. With regard to Novak's discharge, who has the burden of proof, the union to establish the discharge was discriminatory or the company to establish that it had legitimate business reasons for terminating Novak?

2. Did the company have just cause for terminating Novak? If you decide it did not, what is the appropriate remedy?

3. Union Organizing on Company Property

PARTIES: Montgomery Ward Company, Inc. and Warehouse, Mailorder, Office, Technical, and Professional Employees, Local 743, affiliated with the International Brotherhood of Teamsters.

ISSUES: 8(a)(1) charges, union organizing drive, no solicitation rule, right of union representatives to contact employees on company property.

BACKGROUND

Montgomery Ward operates a department store in the Yorktown Shopping Center, a large enclosed shopping mall located in Lombard, Illinois. The facility included a retail sales area, a cafeteria known as the Buffeteria, two credit service centers, and a credit operating center. The credit service centers are not open to the public as are the retail sales facilities. There is, however, a conference area adjacent to the credit service centers where the customers can discuss their credit accounts with service center employees. In early November 1977, an unidentified employee in the credit operating facility telephoned the union to obtain information about union organizing. A few days later, Linda Cummings an organizer, began an organizational campaign at the company's credit operating center. The union was not interested in organizing retail employees. The organizing drive was limited to the

company's credit operating center employees. In a letter dated November 12, 1977, the union informed Al Simpson, manager of the credit center, of the organization drive. Several days later, union organizers Linda Cummings and Joe Perez met with a number of employees of the credit center after work in a restaurant adjacent to the Yorktown Shopping Center. In response to a request by the employees, Cummings and Perez agreed to have lunch with another group of credit center employees at noon on December 2, 1977, in the Montgomery Ward Buffeteria while the employees were on their half hour lunch breaks. On the morning of December 2, 1977, Cummings and Perez stood on the sidewalk (owned by Montgomery Ward) in front of the store and distributed union literature. Jack Green and Eric Stein, the personnel and operating managers respectively at the credit center, observed Cummings and Perez distributing union literature. Hearing "through the grape vine" that the union organizers would meet several credit center employees in the Buffeteria for lunch, Green and Stein also arranged to eat their lunch in the Buffeteria so that they could monitor the organizers' actions.

The Buffeteria where the organizers and employees planned to meet is a cafeteria style restaurant operated by Montgomery Ward as part of a separate food service department.

Customers select food and beverages from a self-service display area, place the items on a tray, and pay for their purchases at a cash register station. There are no waiters, waitresses, or table service, and there is no counter where customers can sit while eating. Moveable tables, seating two persons each are arranged in groups of two to four and are available for use by customers wanting to eat in the Buffeteria. Aisles three to three and a half feet wide separate the groups of tables from each other. Customers may enter the Buffeteria either directly from the mall or from the Montgomery Ward parking lot. There is no access to the Buffeteria directly from the Montgomery Ward retail store area. While there is an aisleway connecting the retail sales area and the Buffeteria, it was cordoned off. When employees of Montgomery Ward ate in the Buffeteria they were treated the same way as other customers and received no special benefits. In fact, ten to twenty percent of the sales in the Buffeteria was attributable to Montgomery Ward employees.

Union organizers Cummings and Perez entered the Buffeteria at noon on December 2, 1977, and upon seeing that the credit center employees they had planned to meet were already seated at tables eating their lunches, they went directly to a table adjacent to the employees. The Buffeteria was about half full at this time. Buffeteria patrons closest to the organizer-employee group were seated about 15 feet away. The organizers chatted briefly with the employees, and upon the request of one of the employees, distributed union authorization cards. Green and Stein, who had been standing in the self-service line, observed Cummings and Perez sit down with the credit center employees. Green and Stein immediately approached the organizer-employee group and asked to speak to the organizers.

Green, Stein, and the union organizers then left the Buffeteria and went into the aisleway between the Buffeteria and the store area. They were, however, still within sight of the credit center employees who remained seated at their tables. After exchanging introductions, Green

told the union organizers that they were trespassing on Montgomery Ward property and violating company policy by soliciting company employees. He told the union organizers that if they did not leave, he would have the police remove them. Cummings and Perez said they would not leave because they thought Green's request violated the employees' rights. They then returned to the table where they had been sitting. After discussing the incident with Cummings and Perez, the credit center employees left. The union organizers purchased some food in the self-service line and returned to the table they had been occupying. In the meantime, Green called the police.

After two uniformed police officers arrived, Green and Stein accompanied by the police officers, sat down at the union organizers' table. Green told the organizers that they could finish eating their lunches, but if they spoke to any employees or refused to leave after eating, he would sign a complaint against them and have them removed. The police officers took the organizers' names and addresses and then left. Green and Stein remained seated at the table located next to Cummings and Perez. About ten minutes later, the union organizers left the Buffeteria accompanied by Green, Stein, and a plain clothes security guard.

The union's efforts at contacting the employees after the Buffeteria incident were not very successful. When the organizers distributed union literature on the sidewalks next to the store, the company called the police to remove them. The union was also unsuccessful in gathering information about the credit center work force. Employees sympathetic to the union were unable to secure a complete list of credit center employees. Further, the union was unable to accurately identify (by license number) cars belonging to credit center employees after Montgomery Ward told the credit center employees to park in a new area where their cars were interspersed with automobiles belonging to other shopping mall employees and customers. On December 7, 1977, the union filed unfair labor practice charges alleging that the company violated Section 8(a)(1) by discriminatorily enforcing its no solicitation rule against nonemployee union organizers in the Buffeteria. By so doing, the company prevented nonemployee union organizers from meeting with off-duty credit center employees in the company's restaurant.

POSITION OF THE COMPANY

The company maintained a no-solicitation rule. The rule read as follows:

> Employees may not distribute union literature or solicit memberships in unions or fraternal, religious, social, or political organizations on company time, or while employees to whom literature is being distributed, or whose membership is being solicited, are on company time. Company time is that time which the employee is scheduled to be on duty and for which the employee is being paid, excluding rest periods, lunch periods, and time before and after the employees working day.

> Solicitation by employees is permitted on company property so long as the employees, those soliciting and those being solicited, are on their own time and the solicitation is being conducted in a quiet and orderly manner and does not interfere with the operation of the company's business. Meetings or speeches are not to be permitted; solicitation which results in disturbing or interfering with the work or function of any of the employees or department is forbidden; solicitation which is detrimental to maintaining the premises in a clean and attractive condition is forbidden.

> Solicitation by nonemployees of the company is prohibited at all times in the store and store operated buildings.

> It is a violation of the company's no-solicitation rule either to solicit or be solicited in a manner prohibited by this rule.

> Solicitations for charity drive and fund raising campaigns are to follow the guidelines for solicitation as outlined above. The company

generally supports one all out community charity drive. Prior approval is required for any additional charity drive held on company property. There are times when expressions of goodwill for co-workers are permissible, but in order to protect employees from too frequent collection for such purposes written permission for such solicitation must be obtained from the store manager or personnel manager.

> Any violations of the company no-solicitation rule should be reported at once to your immediate supervisor or a store manager.

The company acknowledged that a copy of the rule was not given to the employees when they were hired. Evidence also indicated that the rule was probably never posted at the store. There was no indication that this rule had ever been made public prior to the meeting between the union organizers and credit center employees in the Buffeteria on December 2, 1977. Subsequent to this meeting, however, the rule was posted in the store.

The company held that it had the right to post its property against the distribution of union literature by nonemployees as part of an effort to maintain productivity and discipline in the workplace. The company held that it was legal for it to prohibit the distribution of union literature by nonemployees on company premises as long as the union was able through reasonable efforts to develop other channels of communication, thereby enabling it to reach employees with the union's message. This is the case as long as the no-solicitation rule does not discriminate against the union by allowing others to distribute literature on the company's premises. Personnel manager Green emphasized that the purpose of the rule was to prevent any type of activities disruptive to the company's normal business operations. Green also emphasized that this same rule would lead him to prohibit a representative of the American Cancer Society from soliciting contributions from persons in the Buffeteria, either orally or by displaying a sign at his or her lunch table. Green pointed out that the rule would also lead him to prohibit representatives from any charity group from discussing a charity drive with employees in the Buffeteria. Green admitted, however, that he had never enforced the rule against any other group. He emphasized that the purpose of enforcing the no-solicitation rule in the store, including the Buffeteria, was that the company just did not want employees or customers to be inconvenienced. Green also pointed out that the company needed customer turnover in the Buffeteria. Therefore it could not afford to have people filling chairs in the Buffeteria when they had not purchased food there.

POSITION OF THE UNION

The union contended that the company's application of the no-solicitation rule to nonemployees was intended to discriminate against union organizing efforts. It was argued that the purpose of a no-solicitation rule was to prevent any disruptions to the company's selling function and avoid any customer confusion and interference caused by solicitations within the company's facility. However, since the discussions between credit center employees and the union organizers were in no way disruptive, the no-solicitation rule was only a pretext to interfere with the union's organizing efforts. In other words, the company administered the no-solicitation rule in the Buffeteria for the purpose of preventing the union from discussing unionization with employees. The record of this case indicated that the company would not attempt to bar nonemployee solicitation of employees as it did in the situation involving Cummings and Perez had the topic of discussion not been unionization.

The union contended that the company administered the ban discriminatorily for an antiunion purpose. To support this position, the union argued that Green was in the Buffeteria at the time the nonemployee organizers were meeting with employees because he had heard that they were there for the purpose of union solicitation. The union contended that it would be

highly unlikely for Green to go up to any other group eating in the Buffeteria and ask them what they were talking about as he did when he approached Cummings and Perez. The union argued that this unusual behavior was an indication of discriminatory intent on the part of Green. The union rejected the company's argument that the purpose of enforcing the rule was to bring about turnover in the Buffeteria. It was pointed out that the Buffeteria was half empty at the time of the meeting between the union organizers and the credit center employees. It was also pointed out that at no time have employees been informed that they had to get out of the Buffeteria so that other people could come in. The company could cite no rule forbidding employees from eating "brown bag" lunches in the Buffeteria without buying anything there. These facts indicated that the company was not particularly concerned about problems relating to Buffeteria turnover and the use of Buffeteria chairs and tables by persons who had not bought food there until union organizing took place in the Buffeteria.

In summary, the union argued that the rule was enforced against the union organizers only because they solicited for union membership. It was emphasized that the union organizers and the employees were involved in essentially private conversations in a restaurant opened to the public. The employees were off duty. The organizers had come to the restaurant at the request of the employees. The union argued that it was difficult, if not impossible, to envision how a no-solicitation rule as broad as the company's could be applied to such a situation in a nondiscriminatory manner. The only way the rule could be enforced on a broader basis would be for Montgomery Ward to monitor the conversations of patrons of the Buffeteria to establish whether the conversations concerned a solicitation that was limited by the company's no-solicitation rule. Monitoring appears to be the only way Montgomery Ward could effectively and nondiscriminatorily enforce the rule in the Buffeteria. If a solicitation not involving a labor organization took place discretely during the course of a luncheon conversation, it is doubtful that the company would have risked the sort of customer disruption that took place in this case when the police were called in to enforce the no-solicitation rule.

DISCUSSION QUESTIONS

1. What is the purpose of a no-solicitation rule?

2. Under what conditions can nonemployee union organizers be denied access to company facilities for the purpose of distributing union literature or soliciting support for the union?

3. What are the conflicting rights operating in this case? Why is the resolution of the problem faced in this case so difficult?

4. Did the company violate the act by enforcing its no-solicitation rule in the Buffeteria?

4. Who Is in the Bargaining Unit?

PARTIES: Maidsville Coal Company and the United Mine Workers of America, District 31.

ISSUES: Job duties, supervisors and coworkers, bargaining unit composition.

BACKGROUND

Maidsville Coal Company operates a tipple (a facility for loading coal) in Maidsville, West Virginia. Coal is obtained from area coal mines and then shipped to industrial customers by either railcar or barge. The president of the company is Jack Little. The company's vice-president is Jack Little's brother, Henry Little. Vern Landrum, Jack Little's brother-in-law had been employed by the company since 1970 as the tipple superintendent. Coal is brought to the company's facility by truck. The trucks are weighed and then the incoming coal is stockpiled. A river tipple with barge access is used to load barges. There is also a railroad tipple used to load railcars. Coal is purchased from mines owned by the Little family or from independent mine operators. Independent truckers deliver the coal to the company's Maidsville facility. When the coal is received at the facility, it is weighed by a scaleman who records the amount of coal received and then the coal is dumped either for further preparation or raw processing prior to being loaded and shipped.

On April 19, 1979, the United Mine Workers demanded to bargain with the company. The union believed it had attained collective bargaining representative status as a result of having secured signed authorization cards from a majority of the employees in the bargaining unit. The union had signed authorization cards from five of the nine hourly employees at Maidsville Coal Co. During the course of the union's organizing drive, a number of issues requiring NLRB review and unfair labor practice charges arose. This case focuses only on the issue concerning the composition of the bargaining unit.

THE BARGAINING UNIT COMPOSITION ISSUE

The company refused to recognize the union as the employees' bargaining agent because it did not believe that the union had valid authorization cards from a majority of the employees in the bargaining unit.

The company argued that Lyndon Heater, an employee who did not designate the union as his bargaining agent, should be considered as an employee within the meaning of Section 2(3) of the National Labor Relations Act and should be counted as part of the bargaining unit. The union claimed that Heater was a supervisor under section 2(12) of the Act and should not be part of the

359

bargaining unit. The parties also disagreed concerning the bargaining unit status of Nick Rawson. Rawson had signed an authorization card designating the union as his bargaining agent. The company argued that Mr. Rawson was part of the management team, and therefore, his signed authorization card should not be considered as part of the union's majority. The union, on the other hand, argued that Mr. Rawson was an employee under section 2(3) of the Act and that his authorization card should be counted as part of its majority status.

THE POSITION OF THE PARTIES CONCERNING MR. HEATER

Lyndon Heater worked the second shift at the company's facility. He was a jack-of-all trades. He could operate every piece of equipment at the plant and had a variety of skills including welding and a knowledge of electricity. The union contended that in addition to his operating responsibilities, Heater also served as a supervisor on the afternoon shift. In support of this contention, the union pointed out that no other supervisor was present throughout that shift. It was also pointed out that other employees considered Heater to be their boss and foreman. When an employee asked Heater for a raise, Heater came back two or three hours later and told the employee that he had a raise of a dollar per hour effective immediately. On another occasion, Heater told employees that if they did not work overtime, they might just as well not come back to work because they would be fired. Employees testified that Heater had assigned work to them, i.e., had taken them off of a job and put them on another one.

The company's position concerning Heater's status was basically different. It was claimed that Heater was not a supervisor. This position was taken because he was never granted authority to hire or fire, discipline employees, grant wage increases, or recommend the granting of wage increases. The company contended that the after-

noon crew was a closely knit, experienced work group that knew what had to be done. Therefore it was not necessary to have a supervisor on that shift. Heater was characterized as a skilled employee and a hard worker; a go-getter with nerve. He kept the plant running on the afternoon shift mainly because of his wide range of skills. Because of his personal attributes and characteristics, he became a self-appointed lead man in the eyes of the company and a spokesman for the employees on the afternoon shift.

The union pointed out that Heater was able to tell people what to do on the second shift. It was emphasized that Heater did more than just mechanical work at the plant. He was responsible for overseeing everything on the second shift and checking that the second shift was operating as planned. Heater regularly told second shift employees what they were to do and was responsible for ensuring that they had the needed equipment. While Heater was an hourly employee like the other second shift employees, his wage was higher than that received by anyone else. Additionally, Heater lived rent-free in a house owned by the company. The union also indicated that Heater would be the person to whom employees would report if they wanted time off or to leave their shift early. Occasionally, Heater made the decision to have the afternoon crew work overtime. The union asserted that Heater spent most of his time moving around the plant ensuring that its operations were kept running.

THE POSITION OF THE PARTIES CONCERNING NICK RAWSON

Nick Rawson held the position of scaleman or weighmaster with the company. As a scaleman, his duties were to weigh the incoming coal and record all coal tonnages coming into the company's facility by dump truck from the various coal suppliers. Rawson was also responsible for the daily recording of coal tonnages that were shipped to the company's industrial customers by barges or railcars. He was responsible for keeping track of the barges that arrived at the company's facility, which were loaded and hauled away by tugboat. He also identified the railcars that were received at the plant, loaded, and shipped. As part of his job, Rawson was responsible for notifying a tugboat dispatcher in Pittsburgh, Pennsylvania that barges were ready to depart from the company's river tipple. Then the dispatcher would arrange to have barges pulled away by tugboats. Similarly, Rawson scheduled railcars for departure. While other bargaining unit employees worked outside in a yard area where coal was stored and readied for shipment, Rawson conducted most of his duties in the scale house, working at a desk or standing behind the scales.

Rawson had several additional responsibilities. He had to total up the hours worked by the day shift and forward a record of them to the company's office. Employees would turn in written excuses for their absences to Rawson, which he would forward to the company's office. This constituted an administrative task, since he had no authority to approve or disapprove any absences or to reprimand or discipline any employee for being absent. Rawson occasionally contacted independent truckers to move coal within the company's tipple facility. He was also responsible for taking periodic samples of the coal. This required that someone go into the yard and obtain a sample from the coal stocks. Rawson would bring the sample back to the scale house and then notify a testing laboratory to pick up the samples. Test results would be phoned back to Rawson, who would pass them on to higher company officials. It must be noted that Rawson had no control over what coal was to be sent out for testing purposes. He would be directed by other company officials concerning the coal to be sampled.

The company considered Nick Rawson to be a supervisor or part of management under section 2(11) of the Act because he served as a weighmaster. The company argued that as weighmaster Rawson had access to certain daily purchase and sales tonnage information that Little regarded important to management and confidential. The company argued further that the confidential business information that Rawson regularly gathered would be invaluable to the union in the event of a strike. It was pointed out that his function as weighmaster was closely related to the management of the firm. As a result, he would have a conflict-of-interest in any dispute between the company and its employees. Finally, the company argued that if Rawson was not found to be a supervisory/managerial employee, he should still be excluded from the bargaining unit because he was an office/clerical employee.

The union's position in this matter was quite simple. It argued that the company's claim that Rawson was a supervisory employee was self-serving and that the claim was made only after the union demanded recognition. The union held that the weighmaster position should be in the bargaining unit given the nature of the task. There was nothing about the weighmaster's job that would justify its exclusion from the bargaining unit.

DISCUSSION QUESTIONS

1. Why is the composition of the bargaining unit such an important issue to the parties?

2. Should Lyndon Heater be included in the bargaining unit?

3. Should Nick Rawson be included in the bargaining unit?

5. Union Threats During an Organizing Campaign

PARTIES: S & M Grocers, Inc. and Amalgamated Meat Cutters and Allied Workers of North America, Local 593.

ISSUES: 8(b)(1)(A) charges, union organizing drive, union activities, rights of employees.

BACKGROUND

In March 1976, the union began an organizing drive at three supermarkets owned by S & M Grocers, Inc. The stores were located in Silver Spring, Beltsville, and Hyattsville, Maryland. On May 12, 1976, the union held an organizing meeting with the employees of the company's stores. At this meeting, a number of employees claimed that some union members working for S & M Grocers were not participating in the organizing effort. The complaint focused on company employees who held part-time or full-time jobs with other grocery stores that had contracts with the union. As a result of employment in grocery stores with contracts containing union security clauses, a number of S & M Grocers' employees were already members of Local 593. In response to this problem, on June 21, 1976, the union mailed a letter to its members employed by S & M Grocers that stated in part that:

> All members are hereby requested to assist and cooperate with the organizing committee of this

Union and be it further resolved that any member of this Union that does not support when so requested or actively opposes the organizing activities of this Union will be called before the Executive Board and will suffer such disciplinary action as the Board deems necessary including but not limited to expulsion from this Union.

On July 12, 1976, the company filed unfair labor practice charges against the union, charging a violation of section 8(b)(1)(A). The charge alleged that the union's letter threatening to discipline S & M Grocers' employees who did not support the organizing effort restrained and coerced the employees in the exercise of their Section 7 rights.

THE POSITION OF THE UNION

The union did not disagree with the facts but argued that the disciplining of its membership would not violate the Act unless the disciplinary action either affects an employee's employment status or infringes upon certain federal labor policies. The union raised several points in support of its major argument. First, it noted that a proviso to Section 8(b)(1)(A) preserves the union's "right . . . to prescribe its own rules with respect to the acquisition or retention of membership therein." Thus it argued that its rule disciplining its membership fell under this proviso.

It further noted that while the rule restricts its members' exercise of free speech during an organizing drive, the rule requires them to act only in a manner consistent with their voluntary membership status in the union. As members, they participate in the election of officers and in the other internal affairs of the union that lead to the decision to organize particular employees. They are free to resign any time the union sets out on a course they do not agree with, as long as they continue to meet their financial obligations to the union. Having resigned, they would be totally free to campaign against the union. However, as long as they remain members, the union has a right to expect their support, including actual participation in the union's organizing drive. Moreover, although the members are subject to discipline if they do not support the union's campaign and have not resigned, they are still free to make their own determination on how to vote on the issue of union representation. Thus the union argued that the threat of discipline was a valid enforcement of a legitimate internal regulation that did not contravene an overriding policy of labor law.

Further, the union asserted that the Executive Board issuing the letter did not have the power to take any action against S & M Grocers' employees who were not supporting the organizing drive. Since disciplinary action would not be taken, no threat impinging on Section 7 rights could have been made. Therefore the union held that the unfair labor practice charge against it should be dismissed.

ARGUMENTS IN FAVOR OF THE COMPANY

It was argued that the letter threatening to discipline union members who did not support or participate in the organizing drive was a violation of Section 8(b)(1)(A) of the Act. The proviso in Section 8(b)(1)(A) referred to by the union does not legalize a union's enforcement of its internal regulations if such enforcement conflicts with public policy. The free and uncoerced selection of a bargaining representative is an overriding public policy concern that should not be compromised when a union enforces its internal rules and regulations. It was argued that employee rights to freely select a bargaining representative override the union's interest in getting membership support in its organizing drives.

It was also argued that the union claims that its members could quit the union or vote against it in a representation election were not valid. Although the employees appear to be free to resign from the union if they do not wish to be subject to the union's discipline, at least some of these employees were members as a result of their simultaneous employment by another employer. Such employees should not be forced to resign their membership in the union. By resigning, they would give up their right to influence the union's relations with that other employer. This should not be necessary to ensure their Section 7 rights to choose a bargaining agent at S & M Grocers without fear of union discipline. The union's action, if not stopped, would force the members to choose between having an effective voice in the affairs of the union with respect to the already represented unit and having a right to fully exercise their rights in the campaign being conducted at S & M Grocers. It was argued that the union's legitimate interest in solidarity was not so great that the employees should be forced to choose between these alternatives.

It was further argued that upholding the union's position would interfere with the holding of a fair election. While the employees may be free to vote against the union in an election, that freedom is substantially inhibited by the effects of the union's coercion of employee-members' pre-election activities. It was noted that, because of differing circumstances in the employment relationships the employee has with his or her respective employers, it would be quite understandable and reasonable for an employee to vote for union

representation at one employer and decide to reject union representation at another.

Finally, it was argued that the union's last
point that its Executive Board lacked the authority to discipline its members was not valid. A
union cannot avoid the consequences of its unfair
labor practices on the grounds that it was acting
contrary to internal laws.

The union should be found in violation of
Section 8(b)(1)(A) of the Act and be ordered to
cease and desist from its coercive activities.

DISCUSSION QUESTIONS

1. What are the conflicting rights operating in this
   case?

2. Did the union infringe upon the employees'
   Section 7 rights by threatening to discipline
   them for not supporting the union organizing efforts at S & M Grocers?

3. Why is the issue addressed in this case an important one?

6. The Right to Conduct a Vigorous Campaign

PARTIES: Midland National Life Insurance Company and United Food and Commercial Workers, Local 304A.

ISSUES: 8(a)(1) charges, union financial reports, campaigning, NLRB review of campaign misrepresentations.

BACKGROUND

On April 28, 1978, a representation election was held at the Midland National Life Insurance Company located in Sioux Falls, South Dakota. The vote was 127 to 75 against the union, United Food and Commercial Workers, Local 304A. The union filed objections to the election and unfair labor practice charges against the company. The NLRB found that the employer had committed unfair labor practices and had interfered with the employees' free choice in the election. As a result, a second election was ordered. The second election was held on October 16, 1980. The vote was 107 in favor of the union and 107 against it, with one void ballot and 20 challenged ballots. Again, the union filed objections to the election. On January 26, 1981, the NLRB hearing officer recommended that the election objections be sustained and that a third election be held because the employer had engaged in objectionable conduct.

The situation that led the hearing officer to recommend a third election arose on the afternoon of October 15, 1980, the day before the second election. On that day, the employer distributed campaign literature to its employees with their pay checks. One of the pieces of literature was a six-page document that included photographs and text describing the experiences of three local employers who had contracts with Local 304A. The document also contained a reproduction of a portion of a union financial report that was submitted to the U.S. Department of Labor as required by the Labor Management Reporting and Disclosure Act of 1959. The union learned about the document the next morning, approximately three to three and a half hours before the polls were to open for the second certification election.

The first company described in Midland National's campaign literature was Meilman Food, Inc. A picture portrayed this company's facility as being deserted. The accompanying text read as follows: "They too employed between 200 and 300 employees. This Local 304A struck this plant — violence ensued. Now all the workers are gone! What did the Local 304A do for them? Where is the 304A union job security?" Vern Jacobs, the union's business representative, testified that Local 304A had been the representative of Meilman's employees, but that the union had not been on strike against the company when the plant closed. Jacobs added that the employees had been working for at least one and a half years following the strike and prior to the closure of the Mcilman facility.

The second and third employers pictured and discussed in the campaign literature were Luther Manor Nursing Home and Blue Cross/Blue Shield. The text accompanying the pictures of Luther Manor explained that:

> Almost a year ago this same union that tells you they will "make job security" (we believe you are the only ones that can do that) and will get you more pay, told the employees of Luther Manor (here in Sioux Falls) that the union would get them a contract with job security and more money. Unfortunately, Local 304A did not tell the Luther Manor employees what year or what century they were talking about. Today the employees have no contract. Most of the union leaders left to work elsewhere. Their job security is the same (depends upon the individual as it always has). There has been no change or increase in wages or hours. The union has sent in three different sets of negotiators. Again, promises and performance are two different things. All wages, fringes, working conditions are remaining the same while negotiations continue.

The text accompanying the pictures of Blue Cross states that:

> The same local union won an election at Blue Cross/Blue Shield after promising less restrictive policies, better pay, and more job security. Since the election, a good percentage of its former employees are no longer working there. Ask them! The employees have been offered a wage increase — *next year* of 5% . . . .

Jacobs testified that the union took over negotiations at Luther Manor and at Blue Cross/Blue Shield on or about July 1, 1980, after the union had merged with the Retail Clerks, Local 1665. He also claimed that the Retail Clerks, Local 1665, not Local 304A, had conducted the prior negotiations and won the election at Blue Cross/Blue Shield.

The handout distributed by Midland National on October 15, 1980, also included a portion of Local 304A's 1979 financial report that listed information concerning the union's assets, liabilities, and cash receipts and disbursements. Three entries on the page reproduced by Midland National were underlined: Total receipts, reported at $508,996; disbursements "on behalf of individual members" reported at $0; and total disbursements, reported at $492,701. Other entries on the reproduced page showed disbursements of $93,185 to officers, and $22,662 to employees of the union. The accompanying text stated that $141,000 of the union's funds went to "union officers and officials and those who work for them" and that "nothing — according to the report they filed with the U.S. government — was spent on behalf of individual members." A review of the report actually showed that the union dispersed only $115,847 dollars to its officers and employees ($25,000 less than stated in the company handout). The handout prepared by Midland National also attributed 19 percent more income to the officials and employees than they had actually received. A review of the union's report revealed that no money had been spent "on behalf of individual members" as was claimed by the company. However, the instructions for the report required this entry to reflect dispersments for "other than normal operating purposes." The company failed to include this fact in its election-eve handout.

THE ISSUE BEFORE THE NLRB

The effect of the hearing officer's decision was to order a new election because of the misrepresentations contained in the anti-union literature distributed by Midland National Life Insurance Company on the afternoon before a certification election. The Board had to decide whether campaign misrepresentations should provide grounds for setting the results of an election aside and for ordering another election to be conducted.

ARGUMENTS IN FAVOR OF A NEW ELECTION

The objective of the nation's labor policy pertaining to certification election campaigns is to provide laboratory conditions in which employees are able to exercise a free and untrammelled choice when selecting a bargaining agent. An election can serve its true purpose only if the circumstances surrounding the election enable employees to register a choice for or against a bargaining representative in a free and informed manner. Campaign misrepresentations involving very significant issues make it impossible for employees to exercise free choice. This is especially the case when these misrepresentations take place at such a late point in the campaign that the other side does not have a chance to correct them.

The union argued that the document distributed by the Midland National on the day before the election contained numerous misrepresentations of important facts. It was held that the document was designed to portray the union as an organization staffed by highly paid officials and employees who were ineffectual as bargaining representatives. Therefore the employees would suffer with respect to job security and compensation if this union was elected as their bargaining agent. It was pointed out that the document was distributed on the afternoon before the election and that the union did not become aware of it until approximately three and a half hours before the polls were to open. The union believed it did not have sufficient time to respond effectively to the serious misrepresentations by the company. For these reasons, the union objected to the election that had taken place on October 16, 1980, and argued that a third election should be directed.

ARGUMENTS AGAINST A NEW ELECTION

The company argued that the Board should not examine the truth or falsity of campaign statements. This is because the effects of misrepresentations on voters is difficult to determine.

The company maintained that any misrepresentation that may have occurred would not interfere with employee free choice. It was held that when the Board attempts to regulate the content of campaign rhetoric, it restricts free speech. Maintaining the free flow of information is another important objective of the Board. It was pointed out that the parties should have the opportunity to conduct a free, unrestricted, and vigorous campaign. Doing so helps ensure that employees will have an opportunity to express their free choice. The company argued that any attempt to determine what is a "substantial" departure from the truth is very subjective. Similarly, it is difficult to determine whether there has been enough time for an "effective reply" after a misrepresentation has occurred. It is also difficult to determine what may reasonably be expected to have a "significant impact" on the employees' perception of the campaign. The company held that employees are capable of identifying campaign propaganda for what it is. They do not need to be protected by the Board. It was emphasized that it is necessary to view employees as mature individuals who are capable of recognizing inaccurate campaign propaganda and discounting it when it is not correct. The company pointed out that while the Board still should get involved in evaluating campaign statements that are misleading because of fraud or forgery, it should not be involved in the review of campaign rhetoric in other cases.

DISCUSSION QUESTIONS

1. Should the Board review the truth or falsity of campaign statements made by the parties during a union organizing campaign?

2. Did the company's misrepresentations on the day before the election impinge upon the employees' free choice?

3. Why is it so difficult for the Board to formulate a policy governing campaign propaganda?

7. Opposition to the Union Steward

PARTIES: General Indicator Corporation, Redco Division and Jimmy Hunt, an individual.

ISSUES: 8(a)(1) and 8(a)(3) charges, discipline and discharge, union activities, solicitation.

BACKGROUND

The company manufactures electrical switchgear and controls in Peoria, Illinois, and in 1980 employed 43 employees in the bargaining unit as represented by Local 34 of the International Brotherhood of Electrical Workers. Jimmy Hunt was hired by the company in 1965 and became a "lead man" in 1973 in the wiring department. In 1976 Hunt was removed from this position after fellow employees complained that he was arguing with them over work assignments. Howie Chapman, who worked in the department while Hunt was lead man, testified that he was instrumental in having Hunt removed. Chapman stated he drafted a petition to remove Hunt, which listed complaints from other employees, and then gave it to the former production manager. Hunt acknowledged that he blamed Chapman for the loss of his lead man's position. He also stated that the reasons given to him for his removal and subsequent transfer were that other employees were complaining about him and his giving orders. Chapman subsequently became the lead man and also was appointed union steward for the unit by Local 34 on May 17, 1977.

After Hunt's disciplinary transfer, he continued to argue with other employees about work assignments and to order them to do certain jobs although he had no authority to do so. He also kept the wiring department in turmoil by repeatedly voicing his desire to replace Chapman. He stated his concern that Chapman was the nephew of foreman Mark Cornog, and thus should not be union steward. Both Cornog and Hunt admitted disliking each other.

Several incidents took place in the month prior to Hunt's discharge. On March 13, 1980, Hunt refused to follow Chapman's "lead" on the assigned tasks as required by the company's "lead man" policy that ensures that each assignment is wired correctly. After Chapman complained to Cornog, Cornog told Hunt that he was to take his directions from the lead man, Chapman. No warning was given to Hunt on that occasion. However, on March 24, 1980, Hunt again refused to accept a wiring assignment from Chapman and began swearing at him when Chapman directed him to resume his assigned task. This time Cornog took both Chapman and Hunt to Joe Chapin, the production manager, to settle the dispute. After discussing the problem with the three men, Chapin determined that Hunt was not wiring the assigned task according to Chapman's direction. Cornog at this time suggested firing Hunt but Chapin refused and reassigned him to work on his own, independent and away from any other employees, with the warning that this was Hunt's last chance. However, no written warning was given. In the next few days, Hunt estimated he talked to about 25 of the employees about removing Chapman as steward.

Several events happened on April 3, 1980, Hunt's last day of work. At about 10:30 A.M., employee Roger Smith went to see employee Gary Combs on company time to discuss Hunt's plans to replace Chapman. At approximately 11:15 A.M., Hunt approached Smith and one other employee at their work station and said he wished to talk with them about union steward Chapman and asked them to step away from their work station. Both employees refused, stating that they wished to continue their work assignment, but Hunt insisted they stop work. The employees repeatedly told Hunt to leave, and after about five minutes suggested that he could talk to them during the lunch break at 11:30. At this point, Hunt relented and the men returned to their work.

During the lunch break, Smith told Chapman that Hunt had tried to enlist his support in replacing Chapman as shop steward and had interfered with his work schedule. Combs and three other employees subsequently came to Chapman on company time to tell him the same thing. Afterward, Smith also approached Cornog and repeated his complaint that Hunt had kept him from working. Later that afternoon, Chapman met with the company controller and two union business agents to discuss the pension plan. At the end of that discussion, Chapman called in Cornog, Combs, and Smith to tell the group what the latter two had told him, and the events of the day were discussed. The controller felt that this subject was important enough to relate to the company president. Thus everyone but Smith and Combs met with and informed the president about Hunt's disruptive behavior that day. His inability to get along with other employees was also discussed. Cornog recommended that Hunt be discharged because his erratic conduct was keeping the shop in constant turmoil. The president agreed and had a letter authorizing Hunt's termination drafted for Cornog's signature. On April 4, 1980, Cornog informed Hunt that his services were no longer necessary and presented him with the following letter of termination:

> I am sure you are aware of the concern for the unsettling relations with other employees resulting from your actions on numerous occasions. Your supervisor and representatives of the Union have brought these matters to your attention in the form of warnings, without result. Since the unsettling effect has recently become very serious, it is my responsibility to inform you that your employment is being discontinued effective immediately.

On September 3, 1980, Hunt filed an unfair labor practice charge against the company.

ARGUMENTS IN FAVOR OF HUNT

It was argued that when Hunt disrupted the productivity of his fellow workers in order to seek changes regarding the union representation of employees in his bargaining unit, he was engaged in activity protected by Section 7 of the Act. It is to be noted that the company did not have or uniformly enforce a rule prohibiting employees from entering into discussions on working time and that the reason given Hunt for his termination was "unsettling relations with other employees." Thus the company's justification for discharging Hunt, i.e., that he had a long history of creating dissension among the other employees, was nothing more than a mere pretext to conceal the real discriminatory reason for his discharge — that he opposed shop steward Chapman. Other employees, such as Smith and Combs, had engaged in similar conduct and had not been admonished or disciplined.

Thus the company should be found guilty of

violating Sections 8(a)(1) and 8(a)(3) of the Act. It should offer to reinstate Hunt in his former job or a substantially equivalent job, without prejudice to his seniority and other rights and privileges and make him whole financially.

ARGUMENTS OF THE COMPANY

The company argued that Hunt disrupted the work of others by talking to them about changing the union steward. He had opposed the steward for years and it was common knowledge throughout the plant. Had the company wished to discharge him because he wanted to replace the union steward, it would have acted much earlier. Further, the company's managers were not concerned about, or in some cases even aware of the content of the conversation between Hunt and his fellow workers, but rather were disturbed that he was away from his work station and was disrupting the efforts of others. Since the company had repeatedly warned him and even demoted him, it bent over backwards and went beyond any legal obligation to protect him and accommodate his disruptive personality. The company's interest in maintaining productivity and order should outweigh the employees' unprotected interest in disrupting production schedules.

The company requested that the charges be dismissed.

DISCUSSION QUESTIONS

1. Does the fact that the company kept Hunt employed for as long as they did support their case or work against their case? Why?

2. What is the possibility that Chapman and the union could be found in violation of Section 8(b)(2) of the Act for causing the employer to discharge Hunt?

3. Was the stated reason for discharging Hunt only a pretext? Was Hunt engaging in activity protected by the Act?

4. How does a conflict among the employees within the union put a company in a bind?

5. Why did Hunt not file a grievance over his discharge? Why did the NLRB not defer this case to the company and union negotiated grievance procedure?

8. Picketing a Supermarket to Boycott Paper Bags

PARTIES: Duro Paper Bag Manufacturing Company and United Paperworkers International Union, AFL-CIO, Local 832.

ISSUES: 8(b)(4)(ii)(B) charges, strikes, boycotts, consumer picketing.

BACKGROUND

Duro is a Kentucky corporation engaged in the manufacture and sale of paper bags. The union is the exclusive collective bargaining representative for the production and maintenance employees of Duro at its Ludlow, Kentucky and Covington, Kentucky plants.

Beginning about February 10, 1977, and continuing into June 1977, the union engaged in a lawful economic strike against Duro. On May 19 and 20, 1977, the union established a picket line at the entrance to a retail supermarket operated by the Kroger Company store in Covington, Kentucky. On May 20 and 23, 1977, the union established a picket line at the Kroger store in Ludlow. The picket signs carried read as follows:

Consumer Boycott
of
Duro Paper Bag
Manufacturing Co. Products
B.Y.O.B.
(Bring Your Own Bag)

Duro Paper Bag Mfg. Co.
UNFAIR
Local 832, United Paperworkers International
Union, AFL-CIO

The picketers also distributed handbills to customers at the two stores. The handbills read as follows:

BOYCOTT LEAFLET

Consumer Boycott
Please bring your own bag when you shop at this store, or ask for a box. Please do not use bags manufactured or supplied by THE DURO PAPER BAG MANUFACTURING CO.

The DURO PAPER BAG MANUFACTURING CO. is unfair to members of Local 832, United Paperworkers International Union, AFL-CIO, who have been on strike for fair benefits since February 10. We have no dispute with any other Employer.

This handbill is directed at CONSUMERS ONLY.

It is not an appeal to cease performing work for, or to cease deliveries to, any other employer.

This organization has no dispute with any other employer.

BRING YOUR OWN BAGS!

Local 832, United Paperworkers International
Union, AFL-CIO

During the period when the picketing occurred, the Covington store supplied 70 customers with boxes in lieu of grocery bags and
several customers utilized their own containers.
Approximately 15 other customers were refused
boxes after they were requested because the store
had run out of them. During the picketing at the
Ludlow store, approximately 30 customers were
supplied with boxes in lieu of grocery bags upon
request, but approximately 35 other customers
were refused boxes because the store had run out
of its supply. The Covington store normally furnishes boxes to an average of 12 customers per
week, while the Ludlow store normally furnishes
only one box per week.

While the picketing took place, approximately 2800 customers shopped at the Covington
store and about 1500 patronized the Ludlow
store. On May 20 at the Ludlow Store, after a
customer's groceries were tallied and placed in
grocery bags, she stated that she did not want any
"scab bags." She then left the store without paying for or taking the groceries.

On May 23, 1977, Duro charged Local 832
with engaging in unfair labor practices.

ARGUMENTS OF THE COMPANY

Duro argued; (1) that the paper bags have lost
their identity and have become an integral part
of Kroger's operation — thereby equating the
union's picketing with an effort to encourage
cessation of business with Kroger; (2) that the furnishing of paper bags is actually a service so that
picketing Kroger to force cessation of the service
could be translated as an effort to force Kroger, a
secondary employer, to cease doing business with
Duro, the primary employer, as a result of the
force of the injury created by the picketing; and
(3) that shoppers, having no viable alternative to
the use of the paper bag, will shop elsewhere. It
argued that the union's picketing violated Section
8(b)(4)(ii)(B) of the Act.

In *American Bread,** the union had a dispute
with a bread company and, in furtherance of that
dispute, picketed certain restaurants that used the
bread as part of their meals. In that case the
NLRB stated that a customer in those restaurants
was "hardly in a position to choose the brand of
bread he will consume, as a customer in a retail
store is able to do" that the bread had lost its
identity when served, becoming part of the restaurant's product; and accordingly, that the
picketing was in violation of the Act since the
bread had become an integral part of the secondary employer's business.

The company argued that the situation was
similar to that found in *American Bread.* Thus it requested that the union be found guilty of unfair
labor practices violating Section 8(b)(4)(ii)(B) of
the Act.

ARGUMENTS OF THE UNION

The union argued that the picketing activity was
not in violation of Section 8(b)(4)(ii)(B) of the
Act. It noted that the Supreme Court, in its *Tree
Fruits†* decision, held that Section 8(b)(4)(B) does
not proscribe consumer picketing of a neutral
secondary employer when the picketing is
employed only to persuade customers not to buy a
struck product as opposed to picketing to persuade customers not to trade at all with the secondary employer.

Further, unlike the *American Bread* situation,
the facts do not disclose a loss of product identity.
The consumer picketing was, as stated, directed
solely at the paper bags used by Kroger to bag
groceries. Kroger's customers could purchase all
the products they desired without necessarily us-

---

* *Teamsters, Chauffeurs, Helpers and Taxicab Drivers Local 327,
(American Bread Company),* 170 NLRB 91 (1968), affirmed 411
F.2d 146 (6th Cir. 1969).

† *NLRB* v. *Fruit and Vegetable Packers and Warehousemen, Local
760 and Joint Council No. 28 of I.B.T. (Tree Fruits Labor Relations
Committee, Inc.),* 377 U.S. 58 (1964).

ing paper bags to carry the groceries. Cartons were provided when available and some people brought their own containers with them. The fact that cartons were not available for all who requested them demonstrates only their present unavailability, not that they were never available. Thus unlike the bread served as part of a meal, the paper bag did not lose its identity in the overall operation of the supermarket.

The paper bag supplied by Kroger to its customers does not lose its identity as a product simply because it is offered as a service. The union did not agree that (1) without the use of this service Kroger could not, as a practical matter, sell its groceries; and (2) the picketing must of necessity be viewed as having as an objective the cessation of patronizing Kroger. The record is clear that Kroger continued its business and shoppers found other means of carrying groceries from the store. The "service" therefore cannot be said to have been so integrated into the supermarket's operation that the loss of it would equal a cessation of business for Kroger. It is thus clear that the picketing cannot be said to have had such cessation as its intended result.

The union requested that the unfair labor practice charges against it be dismissed.

DISCUSSION QUESTIONS

1. Does the fact that many more Kroger customers used boxes during the picketing than before, establish that the Duro paper bags had a separate identity from the Kroger business? How relevant is it that about 50 customers were refused boxes because the stores had run out of them?

2. Does real damage appear to have been done to Kroger's operations? Is it relevant that one customer, who brought her groceries to the checkout counter, left the store without them, saying she did not want any "scab bags"?

3. Based on the facts of this case, which has more relevancy, the Supreme Court decision in the *Tree Fruits* case or the decision in the *American Bread* case? Why?

4. The union struck Duro on February 10. Why would it wait until May 19 to picket the two Kroger stores?

5. Why, since both the picketing and the strike were over, would Duro pursue this case rather than dropping the charges against the union?

9. Which Union Should Represent the Employees?

PARTIES: Mountaineer Shaft and Tunnel Construction Company, and United Mine Workers of America, and Southern Labor Union.

ISSUES: 8(a)(1) and 8(a)(2) charges, authorization cards, voluntary recognition, competing unions, lockout.

BACKGROUND

In June 1976 Mountaineer Shaft and Tunnel Construction Company entered into an agreement with the Blue Diamond Coal Company for the construction of shafts and underexcavation at a site in Leatherwood, Kentucky. During August 1976, several employees at Mountaineer became dissatisfied with their wages and other working conditions and held discussions about the possibility of joining the Southern Labor Union (SLU). On September 6 Martin Edmunds, a Mountaineer employee, contacted an SLU representative, who began a campaign to get Mountaineer employees to sign SLU authorization cards. On September 14 Dennis Chace, a project manager for Mountaineer, was visited by three SLU representatives who presented him with 17 SLU authorization cards signed by employees of Mountaineer, requesting recogni-

tion.* At that time, Mountaineer had between 22 and 24 employees on its payroll.

On September 15, 1976, employee Edmunds met with two representatives of the United Mine Workers of America (UMW), at Short's Tavern and signed a UMW union card. Edmunds indicated to the UMW representatives that other employees apparently dissatisfied with SLU representation would also be interested in UMW representation. On Friday evening approximately eight Mountaineer employees met with those UMW representatives at Short's Tavern to discuss UMW representation. Copies of the UMW contract with other employers were distributed and some employees signed UMW authorization cards. During the meeting, Ray Baker, a new employee of Mountaineer, passed through the backroom of the tavern and was able to observe the meeting and the employees, many of whom he had already met. After the employees' meeting at the tavern, Baker, who had identified himself as a new foreman for Mountaineer, engaged in a heated discussion with the UMW representatives concerning the merits of unions in general and the UMW in particular.

Mountaineer's exclusive negotiations with

---

* Employers may voluntarily recognize a union without going through an NLRB certification election.

SLU appeared to begin that same weekend. On Sunday, September 19 a meeting took place between Larry Long from SLU, Jim Jay, Blue Diamond's representative, and two Mountaineer representatives, Chace and Paul Kennedy. Long submitted an agreement that, after discussion, was changed in several respects. According to his testimony, Kennedy had signed the agreement but could not recall any discussion about ratification procedures. On Sunday afternoon Long visited Edmunds to ask him and two other employees to come to the union hall in Cumberland to sign the SLU contract. Edmunds refused and immediately notified the UMW that an SLU representative had approached him about signing a contract.

On Monday morning, September 20 when the employees arrived for work, they found the entrance to the job site blocked by parked cars and the gate locked. Abe Jones, president of SLU, and two other SLU representatives were in front of the gate, as were Jay, and Paul Pierce, a supervisor at Mountaineer. Pierce told the employees, as they assembled for the 7 A.M. shift before the locked gate, that the company was anxious to settle the matter, that they should vote the SLU in, and that if they did not they could not go to work. Jay similarly told the employees, "You can't vote no union. But if you vote UMW in, we will put the lid on." Jones then proceeded to read a contract aloud that purported to contain the same provisions as those included in the existing agreement between SLU and Blue Diamond. The assembled employees indicated their approval by voice vote. Jones then told the men to hold an election for officers. As a result, the employees chose Edmunds as president, and also a vice-president and secretary-treasurer. The newly elected officers signed the contract in front of the roadblock before 7:30 A.M. and then the employees went to work. In accordance with the relevant provision in the contract, Mountaineer began checking off dues and initiation fees for SLU in October 1976.

The UMW subsequently filed unfair labor practice charges against the company, claiming that Mountaineer had violated Sections 8(a)(1) and 8(a)(2) of the Act and requested appropriate remedies.

ARGUMENTS OF THE UNION

The employer knew that the UMW was mounting an organizational campaign at its premises as early as September 17, 1976. While Baker may not have been an employee or even a supervisor on that date, he had been introduced to the employees at the work site as a new "boss" during the prior week by supervisor Pierce. Baker appeared to consider himself to be a supervisor and so stated to Edmunds and the UMW representatives at their meeting on September 17 in the tavern.

Jim Jay, while he was Blue Diamond's representative, had the status of an agent of Mountaineer since he was intimately involved in the day-to-day affairs of Mountaineer. He and supervisor Pierce further violated 8(a)(1) when they threatened to close the plant on September 20. The lockout on September 20 was an attempt to violate the rights of the employees under Sections 8(a)(1) and 8(a)(2) of the Act and coerce them to support the SLU.

Finally, by executing a contract requiring union membership pursuant to a union-security clause and by checking off union dues and initiation fees, Mountaineer gave full support to the SLU in violation of Section 8(a)(2) of the Act.

The UMW requested that the company be required to withdraw its recognition of the SLU as the representative of the employees and that its contract with the SLU be declared illegal. The UMW further requested that the company be ordered to cease its discriminatory activities in favor of the SLU and that it be required to return all dues and initiation fees collected on behalf of the SLU to the employees. The UMW also requested that the NLRB conduct a representation election for Mountaineer employees in order to determine their true preference.

ARGUMENTS OF THE COMPANY

When Chace met the three SLU representatives on September 14, he did not recognize the SLU as the bargaining representative, nor did he make any arrangement for contract negotiations. Instead he contacted the main office and informed Paul Kennedy, the Mountaineer construction manager, of what had transpired. Because of the possible economic ramifications of SLU representation, Kennedy decided to contact the Blue Diamond Coal Company, with whom Mountaineer had the "fixed fee cost pass through" contract, which permitted it to pass any wage increase on to Blue Diamond. It was only after discussions with Blue Diamond, and its site representative, Jay, that contract negotiations began. Jay determined that it was all right to bargain with the SLU since it had a contract with Blue Diamond.

Mountaineer management argued that it did not know of a concurrent UMW organizing drive until after the contract had been ratified. It had only heard rumors of a UMW organizing drive until that time. In support of that contention, the company pointed out that Baker was not even an employee at the time he observed the UMW organizational meeting. Also, he did not become a supervisor until September 30.

In regard to the contract ratification meeting, Jay was not an employee of the company. Therefore his remarks could not lead to an 8(a)(1) violation of the Act by Mountaineer. Since an overwhelming majority of the employees had signed authorization cards for the SLU, the company's cooperation with the union in getting the contract ratified was not coercive under the Act, but actually facilitated the obtaining of contractual rights for the employees. Because the signed authorization cards contained a provision allowing for the checkoff of union dues and initiation fees, even without a contract such a checkoff would not be an 8(a)(2) violation.

The company requested that the agreement with the SLU be recognized as valid and that the unfair labor practice charges against it be dismissed.

DISCUSSION QUESTIONS

1. Since the UMW goal was to disestablish the SLU, why did it not file charges against the SLU instead of Mountaineer? Did the SLU violate any sections of the Act?

2. Why did Mountaineer care which union represented its employees?

3. Does it make any difference that Jay was neither an employee of nor in the pay of Mountaineer?

4. Was the "lockout" a violation of the Act?

5. What is your decision as an NLRB agent? If the company were guilty of unfair labor practices, what remedy would you order?

10. Did the Union Deny Privileges to Nonmembers in a Discriminatory Fashion?

PARTIES: International Association of Machinists and Aerospace Workers, Lodge 720 (McDonnell Douglas Corporation) and Gloria C. Beatty and Dale Luther, supported by the National Right to Work Legal Defense Foundation.

ISSUES: 8(b)(1)(A) charges, union membership rights and privileges, union security.

BACKGROUND

The collective bargaining agreement between the employer, Douglas Aircraft Company Division of McDonnell Douglas Corp., of Los Angeles, California, and the union contains a union security provision. All employees must either join the union or pay the equivalent of union dues and fees. If an employee's dues are not paid for two months, the employee must pay a reinstatement fee or its equivalent, equal to three months' dues. In 1977 dues were $15.70 per month; in 1978 they were $17.20. Pursuant to the parties' agreement, before an employee is terminated for failure to pay dues and fees or their equivalence, the union is to notify the employer of the delinquency in writing. The employer then notifies the employee of the delinquency, giving the employee 48 hours to tender the dues or reinstatement fee before actual termination. A member

who is off the payroll because of layoff, sickness, or disability, can obtain monthly unemployment stamps for 50 cents to be used in lieu of regular dues, according to Article G of the union's constitution, which states in part, "Unemployment stamps are issued for the purpose of aiding members to maintain their good standing."

Gloria Beatty has been employed by the company since February 1966. She was a member of the union from that time until February 21, 1975, when she resigned during a strike. She was fined $2,075 by the union for strike-breaking activities, but the fine was later withdrawn. Since her resignation from the union in 1975, Beatty has been a dues and fees equivalence payer, i.e., she was no longer a union member but was still represented by the union, remained in the bargaining unit, and paid the union a fee equal to the dues. From October 3, 1977, to May 1, 1978, Beatty was on leave for an occupational disability. Because she was not on the payroll, no deductions could be made from her paycheck pursuant to her checkoff authorization. In December 1977 she received a "Courtesy Notice of Arrearage" from the union. Such notices are regularly sent to members and nonmembers to enable them to avoid the reinstatement fee. Upon receiving the notice, Beatty went to the union office and tendered $1.00 to cover her November and December obligation. The clerk refused to accept the dollar, stating that only members could receive unemployment stamps. Beatty paid the full dues while she investigated the matter.

In February 1978 Beatty received another notice. She responded by letter to Union Secretary-Treasurer Dave Aiello, indicating that she was eligible for unemployment stamps and enclosed $1.00. Aiello wrote her that "Nonmembers are not entitled to the privileges specified under the union constitution" and returned her check for $1.00 but not her payments for November and December. Beatty made no further payments until she returned to work and began paying the full equivalence of dues. The union took no action against her for dues not paid while she was disabled.

Dale Luther began working for the employer in 1966. He also resigned from the union during the 1975 strike and has been an equivalence fee payer since that time. He went on leave-of-absence for illness in February 1978 and received a courtesy notice of arrearage in April. He called the union financial office, requested to pay the 50 cents, and was told that he was not eligible. He then sent a letter and a check for $1.00 to cover two months' dues. Aiello returned the check stating that Luther was not qualified for the unemployment stamps. Luther paid no further dues. He had not returned to work as of late 1979 and had not been discharged or suffered any adverse action by the union.

Beatty initially filed unfair labor practice charges against the union on March 22, 1978. Luther filed similar charges on May 3. The charges were consolidated for hearing by the NLRB on May 25.

ARGUMENTS OF THE UNION

The union had three major arguments. First, Beatty and Luther did not meet the eligibility requirements for unemployment stamps because they did not subject themselves to internal union disciplinary procedures as provided in Section 4 of the unemployment stamp article in the union's constitution. This means that they failed to agree to subject themselves to internal union discipline, as provided in Article L of the union's constitution, should they attempt to defraud the union in obtaining the stamps.

The second argument was that unemployment stamps are a privilege of union membership that is permitted under the Act. The union argued their practice fell within the following exception provided by Section 8(b)(1)(A): "That this paragraph shall not impair the right of a labor organization to prescribe its own rules with respect to the acquisition or retention of membership therein." The union argued that this use of the unemployment stamps is a legitimate means to insure the eligibility of its members for active participation in union activities, such as attending union meetings, voting, and running for and holding union office, and therefore the issuance of the stamps is a privilege of membership permitted under the Act. In support of its argument, the union noted that the NLRB decision in *Local No. 717, Association of Western Pulp and Paper Workers (Boise Cascade Corp.)*, 165 NLRB 971 (1967), upheld a union rule that refunded a portion of one's dues for attendance at membership meetings. Thus a finding against the union would be an unwarranted intrusion into its internal affairs in a manner proscribed in the exception to Section 8(b)(1)(A).

The union's third argument was that Beatty and Luther had adequate notice that they had to subject themselves to union disciplinary provisions in order to receive unemployment stamps. The union pointed to the employees' strikebreaking activities in 1975 and their subsequent disciplinary hearings as proof of their familiarity with the disciplinary procedures.

The union argued that the charges filed against it should be dismissed.

ARGUMENTS IN FAVOR OF THE EMPLOYEES

The counsel for Beatty and Luther contended that by refusing to grant their applications for unemployment stamps, and by requiring them to pay the full equivalency of regular monthly dues while they were on medical disability leave, the union impermissibly discriminated between union and nonunion members in a manner affecting their tenure of employment. Their counsel further argued that the NLRB decision in *Boise Cascade* was not relevant, as it dealt only with the union members; it did not address the comparative rights of members and nonmembers.

Their counsel argued that the other union arguments were not relevant. Neither employee was ever told that she or he could obtain stamps upon submission to union discipline; they were repeatedly told that they were ineligible because they were nonmembers. Further, the constitutional provision referred to by the union was applicable only to individuals obtaining the stamps fraudulently. However, even if submission to union discipline were a proper eligibility requirement, the union would still be in violation of Section 8(b)(1)(A) because it failed to inform Beatty and Luther of that requirement, thus violating its duty to notify employees of their obligations.

In summary, the employees' counsel argued that the union allowed substantially lower dues when employees' earnings were reduced, but that employees Beatty and Luther were denied the reduced dues because they were not union members. The union operated this discriminatory dues structure in the context of a union security clause requiring payment of union dues as a condition of continued employment. Thus the union, by conditioning employment upon the payment of nonuniform dues, unlawfully encouraged employees to join the union, in violation of the Act.

Counsel for Beatty and Luther urged that the union be found guilty of violating the two employees' rights as guaranteed by Section 7 of the Act. It urged that the union be ordered to cease and desist and to make Beatty whole for any monetary loss she may have suffered. Further, that the union should allow both employees to fulfill their dues obligations while unemployed through the purchase of unemployment stamps at the same monthly rate at which members can purchase them.

DISCUSSION QUESTIONS

1. Should union membership place both privileges and obligations on members? How far can those privileges go, beyond holding union office, before they become discriminatory to the rights of nonmembers? Discuss.

2. Why would a union want the right to discipline its members?

3. Why would the parties want to contest this case when the union took no further action against the employees? What principles are involved?

4. What decision and/or remedy would you suggest?

5. What is the role of management in this situation?

11. Was the Superseniority Clause Overbroad?

PARTIES: John Gordon and Preston Trucking Company, and International Brotherhood of Teamsters, Chauffeurs, Warehousemen and Helpers of America, and its Local 20.

ISSUES: 8(a)(1), 8(a)(3), 8(b)(1)(A), and 8(b)(2) charges, superseniority, job bidding, union activity, steward system and grievance handling.

BACKGROUND

This case focused on unfair labor practice charges filed by an individual employee against the Preston Trucking Company, the International Brotherhood of Teamsters, and its Local 20. Specifically, the NLRB had to determine if the negotiation and enforcement of a superseniority clause for union stewards that went beyond layoff and recall violated the NLRA.

All the parties to the case and the Board agreed that the Board decision in *Dairylea Cooperative Inc.* was applicable.* *Dairylea* established that a superseniority clause covering union stewards for layoff and recall purposes was lawful. The *Dairylea* rationale was that superseniority for layoff and recall has the proper aim of furthering the effective administration of bargaining

agreements on the plant level by keeping the steward on the job and that any "discrimination as it may create is simply an incidental side effect of a more general benefit accorded all employees."† Under the principle established in *Dairylea,* a superseniority clause not limited to layoff and recall was presumptively unlawful. However, such a clause might not be unlawful if it could be justified.

Preston Trucking Company, an interstate shipper, was one of approximately 9800 companies engaged in multi-employer bargaining with the International Brotherhood of Teamsters and its various locals, including Local 20. At the time of the case, it employed approximately 31 drivers who worked out of its Toledo, Ohio terminal, including both the steward involved, Chester Wells, and the complainant, John Gordon. The company and Local 20 were parties to a contract, effective April 1, 1976, to March 31, 1979, and known as the National Master Freight Agreement and Central States Area Over-The-Road Local Cartage Supplemental Agreement.

This three-year agreement contained a new superseniority clause in the Central States Supplement that provided in part:

> Stewards shall be granted super-seniority for all purposes, including layoff, rehire, bidding and

---

* 219 NLRB 656 (1975), enforced by the Second Circuit Court of Appeals, 531 F.2d 1162 (1976).

† *Ibid.,* at p. 658.

job preference, if requested by the Local Union within sixty (60) days after the effective date of this Agreement; but only one (1) steward shall have super-seniority for such purposes.

Wells had been an employee for approximately five years and was, at the time he exercised superseniority, tenth in natural seniority. He had been road steward for the company since his election in November 1975 by fellow members of the bargaining unit. In February 1977 and again in April, Wells exercised his superseniority and was assigned to a route in preference to other more naturally senior employees. Employee Gordon would have secured that route assignment if Local 20 had not requested superseniority for Steward Wells. The route selected returned Wells to Toledo three times each week, whereas his previous schedule had returned him to Toledo only once a week.

Gordon asserted that Wells's run paid him $5,000 more per year than the other runs. However, Wells testified that there was little difference in earnings among the drivers working out of the company's Toledo terminal.

Gordon filed unfair labor practice charges against the company, the International Union, and Local 20; charging them with violating Sections 8(a)(1) and 8(b)(1)(A) of the Act by negotiating the superseniority clause and with violations of 8(a)(3) and 8(b)(2) for enforcing that clause.

ARGUMENTS IN FAVOR OF GORDON

The counsel for Gordon argued that maintaining a clause granting superseniority to stewards for "all purposes" unlawfully encouraged union adherence. He further argued that even if the company and the union could justify superseniority in job bidding, maintaining such a broad superseniority clause was not justified as necessary to allow steward Wells to carry out his representational responsibilities. He argued that Wells had performed his steward's duties suc-

cessfully while working his previous route. Thus by being assigned to the particular run to which he bid, Wells received significant on-the-job benefits, both in terms of the desirability of the actual run and in increased earnings.

Finally, Gordon's counsel argued that the clear language of the superseniority clause necessarily had the effect of encouraging and promoting union membership or activism. The language clearly gave the impression that the benefits accompanying superseniority could be obtained only by becoming a union steward. Thus enforcement of the clause was discriminatory against the rights of those employees who were unable and/or uninterested in becoming a steward. Gordon's counsel requested that the company and the union be found guilty of violating Sections 8(a)(1), 8(a)(3), 8(b)(1)(A), and 8(b)(2) of the Act. He requested that the company and the union be ordered to cease giving effect to the superseniority clause, that Gordon be permitted to bid for his old route, and that he be made whole for any loss of earnings he might have suffered as a result of having a less desirable route.

ARGUMENTS IN FAVOR OF LOCAL 20

Local 20 argued that the granting of superseniority for "all purposes" was not overly broad since the collective bargaining agreement afforded no benefits based on seniority other than those mentioned in the disputed clause, thus qualifying "all purposes." Regarding the express benefits of "bidding and job preference," it explained that those "benefits" were one and the same, as all of the employees were drivers and that the only "preferences" involved route assignments that are bid for. It contended that enforcing the clause with respect to job bidding was justified because the route assigned to the steward best enabled him to perform his duties by being present to process grievances. It also argued that Wells could have chosen an assignment permitting his return to Toledo five times each week instead of three, but that he had not chosen it because it would have left him with insufficient time in which to transact union business after allowing for commuting and sleeping time.

Local 20 has approximately 12,000 members, of which about 5000 are in the over-the-road division, covering approximately 163 truck terminals. Only three full-time business agents service those 5000 employees. Thus Local 20 argued that the steward was the first-line union representative and was needed to police the collective bargaining agreement. It further argued that Wells had some difficulty functioning as the road steward while on his prior route. Since he was in town only on weekends he had little opportunity to meet face-to-face with company representatives and to attend to necessary business at the union hall. The union further argued that Wells did not earn more as a result of his new route. Therefore Local 20 requested that the unfair labor practice charges against it be dismissed.

ARGUMENTS IN FAVOR OF THE INTERNATIONAL UNION

The International Union, in addition to supporting Local 20's contentions, claimed it was not properly a party to the proceeding because it was not a signatory to the contract and the disputed clause specifically makes superseniority a local union option. It also requested that the charges against it be dismissed.

ARGUMENTS IN FAVOR OF THE COMPANY

The company also argued that at the initial stages of a grievance, it was the steward and not a business agent who was involved and who was the front-line representative for the employees in discussions with the company. When Wells was on his previous route, Johnson, the company labor relations director for its western division, noted that many times Wells would call from another terminal and they would try to discuss matters. However, the company stated that it was very difficult to hold such discussions over the phone and argued that Wells's general unavailability limited the ability of the parties to discuss grievances effectively. The company requested that the unfair labor practice charges filed against it be dismissed.

DISCUSSION QUESTIONS

1. Was the company an innocent bystander in a fight among employees? Did the company benefit from enforcement of the clause?

2. How can the rights that a steward has be balanced against the objectives of the NLRA? Will some other union member lose rights?

3. How would you handle the dispute about the amount of money that Gordon could have earned on the route that Wells took?

4. If an unfair labor practice is found, did the local union option protect the International Union?

12. Did Technological Change Lead to a Jurisdictional Dispute?

PARTIES: International Printing and Graphic Communications Union, AFL-CIO, Local 51, and Format Printing Company, Inc., and New York Typographical Union No. 6.

ISSUES: 8(b)(4)(D) charges, jurisdictional disputes, technological change, strike threats, factors considered in awarding jurisdiction.

BACKGROUND

Format Printing Company is engaged in the business of manufacture, sale, and distribution of business forms at its Totowa, New Jersey, facility. In the early 1960s the employer utilized flexographic and letterpress printing processes and a "hot-type" composing room. Its composing room employees were represented by the New York Typographical Union No. 6, the Typographers. Its printers were, and continue to be, represented by the International Printing and Graphic Communications Union, Local 51, the Printers. Around 1967 the employer began to convert to a web-offset printing process, which used lithographic plates, and the hot-type composing work was phased out. As their work decreased, the two composers, Hays and Berg, were assigned plate filing, supply ordering, and other noncomposing duties.

In the early 1970s, the employer purchased a camera and related equipment in order to make its own negatives for platemaking. It reassigned Hays and Berg to operate the camera and "strip" the negatives, that is, prepare them for the platemaking process. Berg quit in 1973 and, upon the employer's request, the Typographers referred a member, Nagle, as a replacement. In 1975 Nagle was discharged and the employer again requested a replacement. The Typographers, however, did not refer anyone. The employer then assigned employee Smith, a member of the Printers, to assist Hays. At no time did the Typographers complain to the employer about Smith's assignment to assist Hays. Hays notified the employer in 1979 or 1980 that he intended to retire at the end of 1981. The employer thereafter provided Smith with intensive training so that he could assume Hays's full duties upon the latter's retirement. Smith replaced Hays as planned, in January 1982.

In February 1982 the Typographers complained that the employer had not hired one of its members to replace Hays. When the employer continued to refuse to do so, the Typographers filed an arbitration request pursuant to its contract with the multi-employer Printers League Section for the New York City metropolitan area. The employer appeared at the arbitration hearing under protest and argued that it did not have a contract with the Typographers and that, even if it did, the contract did not cover the work in

383

dispute. The Printers did not appear at the hearing. The arbitrator found that the employer was bound to the Typographers/Printers League Section collective bargaining agreement and ordered that the cameraman/stripper work be assigned to a member of the Typographers. When the employer received a copy of the arbitrator's award, it notified Smith and the Printers' steward. The next day, the Printers' president, Felix, in a telephone conversation with the employer's president, stated that if Smith were replaced, he, Felix, would "pull the whole damn shop," i.e., strike the employer.

The employer then filed an unfair practice charge against the Printers, charging them with violating Section 8(b)(4)(D) of the Act. Based on the record, the Board found that there was reasonable cause that the "object of the Printers action was to force the employer to continue to assign the disputed work to an employee represented by the Printers and that therefore a violation of Section 8(b)(4)(D) has occurred." Thus under Section 10(k) of the Act, the Board was required to make an affirmative award of the disputed work. The Board had to use its judgment based on common sense and experience and had to weigh several factors. These factors, commonly used in most jurisdictional disputes, were; (1) certifications and collective bargaining agreements, (2) arbitration awards, (3) employer past practice, (4) employer present assignment and preference, (5) industry practice, (6) relative skills, and (7) economy and efficiency of operations.*

ARGUMENTS IN FAVOR OF THE TYPOGRAPHERS

The Typographers asserted that the employer is bound by the Typographers/Printers League Section contract as the employer executed an agreement in late 1966 or early 1967 in which it

recognized the Typographers as the exclusive representative of its composing room employees. Thus it agreed to be bound by the Typographers contract enforced in the New York City Metropolitan area. The Typographers also argued that by continuing to apply the terms and conditions of its current contract to Hays, the employer manifested an intent to be bound by the agreement. Further, under the contract the Typographers won the arbitration that awarded them the work.

The employer's past practices further favored an award of the work to the Typographers, they argued, as the Printers would not have the work at the current time if the employer had not replaced a Typographer with a Printer. They noted that they represented employees in other companies engaged in cameraman/stripper work. In conclusion, they argued that they be awarded the work.

ARGUMENTS IN FAVOR OF THE PRINTERS

The employer has a collective bargaining contract with the Printers recognizing them as the exclusive representative of "all employees in the pressrooms of the [Employer], engaged as printing pressmen as listed in the wage scales contained in this Contract." The job classifications of cameraman and stripper were included among those listed in the wage scales of the agreement. Because of this valid agreement with the employer, the Printers did not participate in the arbitration hearing and were not bound by the arbitrator's decision. The Printers noted that their members have been doing the work for some time as the technology has changed. Further, employees represented by the Printers do this type of work at other employers. They argued that they should be awarded the work in dispute.

ARGUMENTS IN FAVOR OF THE EMPLOYER

The employer noted that neither union had been certified by the Board as a collective bargaining representative for any of its employees. However,

* See the Supreme Court decision in *NLRB* v. *Radio and Television Broadcast Engineers Union, Local 1212, International Brotherhood of Electrical Workers, AFL-CIO (Columbia Broadcasting System),* 364 U.S. 573 (1961).

it argued that only the Printers had a valid collective bargaining agreement with the company. Because the employer did not have a valid contract with the Typographers, it attended the arbitration hearing under protest and felt that it should not be bound by its results.

In terms of its past practice, it argued that as the technology changed, and as the Typographers did not supply a replacement for Nagle, the work in dispute gradually fell to the Printers. It also argued that it preferred that the disputed work be performed by employees represented by the Printers.

The employer presented evidence that its negative stripping operation was more sophisticated and more complex than the similar operations of other printer employers. The employer estimated that a new employee represented by the Typographers, who had experience as a cameraman/stripper, would require a year of training to perform the work properly. In such a case, the employer would lose its investment in the current employee and its entire printing operation would be hampered during the training period. In addition, if the work were awarded to employees represented by the Printers, the employer would be able to train another of its Printers-represented employees to cover for the current employee's absences. On the other hand, if the work is awarded to employees represented by the Typographers, temporary replacements, presumably unfamiliar with the employer's operations and untrained in the work in dispute, would have to be obtained through the Typographers. The employer urged that the disputed work be awarded to employees represented by the Printers and not to those represented by the Typographers.

DISCUSSION QUESTIONS

1. Did the change in technology lead to a loss of the Typographers' jurisdiction over the disputed work? Did the Typographers waive their right to the work in 1975 when they did not supply a replacement for Nagle?

2. Given the low number of employees involved, why did the unions fight this case?

3. What are the seven primary criteria that the Board uses when making a decision in a jurisdictional dispute? For each of the seven, which do you think favors the Typographers, the Printers, or neither union? Which are most relevant? Discuss.

4. Does the fact that the Printers threatened an illegal action have any impact on the Board's decision?

5. How should the disputed work be assigned?

13. Must a Company Honor a Union's Request for Equal Employment Data?

PARTIES: Safeway Stores, Inc. and Retail Clerks Union, Local 73, United Food and Commercial Workers International Union, AFL-CIO.

ISSUES: 8(a)(1) and 8(a)(5) charges, equal employment opportunity, bargaining information, confidentiality, contract administration.

BACKGROUND

The company and union had maintained a collective bargaining relationship over a substantial period of time and were parties to a multistore collective bargaining agreement extending from April 16, 1978, through April 18, 1981, covering some 1500 employees in the retail food industry in the Tulsa, Oklahoma area.

On November 10, 1978, the president of the union Robert A. Cooper sent the following letter to the company:

> In order that we may insure that the "No Discrimination" article of the present agreement is being administered fairly and equitably, I am requesting the following information:
>
> 1. The number of male, female, black, handicapped, Indian, and Spanish-surnamed employees in each classification for all units covered by contract between Safeway Stores, Inc. and this local union.
>
> 2. The hourly wage rate for each employee.
>
> 3. The number of employees by race, sex, handicap, and Spanish surname, by seniority grouping.
>
> 4. The number of persons hired in each classification during the 12-month period immediately preceding the effective date of the information covered in items 1 through 3, with a breakdown as to sex, race, handicap, and Spanish surname, showing the sex of all black and Spanish-surnamed persons.
>
> 5. The number of promotions or upgrades for the same 12-month period, broken down by race, sex, handicap, and Spanish surname, by job level.
>
> 6. A list of all EEO-type complaints and charges filed against Safeway Stores, Inc., Tulsa Division, under the applicable laws and orders. Also, copies of each complaint or charge relating to employees in bargaining units covered by this local union, with any related documents pertaining to the status of such charges, provided that the names of the charging parties were deleted.
>
> 7. Copies of the most recent work force analyses filed under Executive Order 11246 and Revised Order 4 of the Office of Federal Contract Compliance Programs for or covering each store or location covered by the local union.

The information requested by the union was virtually identical to and patterned after the request for information made in *Westinghouse Electric Corporation,* 239 NLRB 106 (1978).*

The company replied by letter dated November 13, 1978, stating:

> Due to the quantity of information requested, and as all of your request may not be possible to comply with, I request the specific nature of the grievance involved.

In a letter dated November 15, 1978, Cooper reiterated that the information was necessary to insure that the company was complying with the "no discrimination" provision of the contract, which provided that the company "shall not discriminate against any employee on account of race, sex, creed, nationality, color, religion, age, or on account of union affiliation or on account of any legitimate union activity." In addition, Cooper's letter noted that the information requested in the sixth paragraph of the November 10 letter involved several charges of union members pending under Title VII of the Civil Rights Act of 1964 and other statutes.

The company continued in its refusal to furnish the requested information and on March 16, 1979, the union filed an unfair labor practice charge against the company.

ARGUMENTS OF THE COMPANY

Safeway argued that, because the union has no duty under the Act to uncover undetected discrimination, the information was not relevant to collective bargaining. The company also noted that in several NLRB cases upheld by the courts,† even when the information requested is objectively relevant, a union's request may be denied if its compilation would be unduly burdensome or if the employer's interest in its confidentiality outweighs the union's interest. The company argued that neither of the two tests of cost and confidentiality could be met in this instance. It testified that it would take approximately 38 days of clerical time and would cost about $6,378 to search out, accumulate, and copy the requested information. It argued that it should not be required to make such expenditures, particularly as the union could obtain the information through research and the personal observation of its stewards. In support of the latter argument, it noted that the union has a contractual right to have a steward at each of the company's stores.

It also cited the Supreme Court decision in *Detroit Edison Co.* v. *NLRB,* 440 U.S. 301 (1979), in support of its contention that the requested information need not be furnished. *Detroit Edison* involved a request for psychological tests administered to employees and the resultant employees' scores. The confidentiality of such information was deemed by the court to outweigh the union's need for it, particularly in the absence of appropriate safeguards to prevent inadvertent leaks. The company also argued that the purpose of the union's request was vague. The statement of its purpose in the union's November 15, 1978, letter was so general that it failed to satisfy the requirement set forth in the Board's decision in *Westinghouse.* Further, in the past, the company had frequently and routinely furnished the union with an abundance of requested information when its purpose was clear.

The company requested that the unfair labor practice charges against it be dismissed.

---

* In *Westinghouse,* the Board upheld the union's right to most of the requested information. It found that the union had demonstrated that most of the information was relevant to the administration of the collective bargaining agreement.

† *NLRB* v. *Truitt Manufacturing Co.,* 351 U.S. 149 (1956), *Shell Oil Co.* v. *NLRB,* 457 F.2d 615 (9th Cir. 1972), and *Emeryville Research Center, Shell Development Co.* v. *NLRB,* 441 F.2d 880 (9th Cir. 1971).

ARGUMENTS OF THE UNION

The union disagreed with the company on all points. It argued that the union had agreed to pay the costs of retrieving and furnishing the information. It further argued that the cost of furnishing such information may have been exaggerated by the company. The union noted that much of the information was easily obtainable from computerized records or other readily available sources. Thus the union argued that the expense and inconvenience involved in furnishing the information was not great enough to justify the company's avoidance of its bargaining obligation.

In relation to the confidentiality issue, the union noted that the parties had resolved similar matters by giving the company a statement to the effect that the information would not be released by the union. The union would give the company a similar statement in this instance. The union argued that the Supreme Court decision in *Detroit Edison* was not applicable here. Unlike psychological test scores, the information requested was not of the type that would have the potential of compromising the privacy rights of individual employees. Moreover, the company argument that the Court would find the information requested to be confidential, was negated by the fact that the company acknowledged that it is readily available to the union stewards on an *ad hoc* basis at each store.

The union argued that the Board decision in *Westinghouse* did apply, that its justification in the letter of November 15 was not vague, and that it needed the information in order to ascertain whether the applicable discrimination provision of the parties' contract was being complied with in a number of pending matters involving the statutes and orders described in the request.

In conclusion, the union maintained that the company's obligation to furnish the requested information was so clear, that its refusal was so blatant, and that its defenses and positions were so patently frivolous, as to warrant an extraordinary remedy, namely the assessment of reasonable legal fees and expenses incurred by the union in pursuing the matter. In support of this position, the union presented evidence at the hearing to show the company's prior history of similar violations.* The union urged that the company be found guilty of violating Sections 8(a)(1) and 8(a)(5) of the Act, that it be ordered to furnish the requested information, and that it pay the union's reasonable legal expenses.

DISCUSSION QUESTIONS

1. Is the information requested really necessary to the union's obligation to administer the collective bargaining agreement?

2. Can this information really be kept confidential by the union? If the union routinely got EEO complaints with the names of the individuals deleted, would that deter employees from filing complaints?

3. Is cost an important factor in this case? Does the fact that the union would pay for the photocopying make any difference?

4. What decision would you make? Does the fact that Safeway had settled five 8(a)(5) charges with this union in the previous ten years make a difference? Does it matter that they were settled voluntarily rather than through orders of the NLRB or an Administrative Law Judge?

---

* The record showed that from 1970 until the time of this case, the union filed five 8(a)(5) charges against the company for failure to furnish information. In all five cases, the charges were settled prior to a formal decision by an Administrative Law Judge or the Board, with the company furnishing the requested information.

14. The Protracted Negotiations

PARTIES: Wright Motors, Inc. and International Brotherhood of Teamsters, Chauffeurs, Warehousemen and Helpers of America, Local 215.

ISSUES: 8(a)(1) and 8(a)(5) charges, company delaying meeting with union, delaying furnishing of wage information, surface bargaining.

BACKGROUND

On June 5, 1973, an NLRB representation election was held among the mechanics, bodymen, painters, general laborers, partsmen, and service writers employed by the company, an Evansville, Indiana, automobile dealer. The vote was 14 to 12 in favor of the union, with three ballots contested.

On October 19, 1973, over the company's objections, the union was certified by the Board. The company refused to accept the validity of the certification or to meet with the union for any purpose. As a result, on October 2, 1974, the union filed charges against the company, alleging violations of Sections 8(a)(1) and 8(a)(5) of the National Labor Relations Act. On January 23, 1975, the Board found that the company refusal to meet and bargain with the union violated Section 8(a)(5) and ordered bargaining (261 NLRB 279). The Board's Order was enforced by the courts (529 F.2d 529, 7th Circuit, unpublished),

on January 20, 1976. The company's petition for a review was denied by the Supreme Court on October 4, 1976 (429 U.S. 826).

On November 15, 1976, the union president formally requested the company to meet and bargain. In reply, the sales manager advised him to contact its attorney, Donald Salkowski. On January 3, 1977,* the union president wrote to Salkowski, requesting a meeting for the purpose of negotiating a contract. Salkowski responded on January 17, suggesting a meeting date of February 14. In separate letters dated January 20 and January 25 respectively, the union's president and staff counsel protested the delay in meeting. Salkowski remained firm and the union yielded.

At the first bargaining session on February 14, the union representative, Tom Jones, presented several proposals, and requested information on the employees' wages and fringe benefits. Salkowski indicated he would go over the union's proposals with the company and would have counterproposals to make. He also promised to mail the wage and benefit information within a week.

On February 21 Salkowski sent Jones a letter that listed the wage or commission rate paid

---

*All dates are 1977 unless otherwise noted.

389

various categories of employees and the health, welfare, and vacation benefits in general terms. Jones responded on March 1 that he needed the actual dollar amounts of pay and benefits paid each employee prior to the next meeting, scheduled for March 9. On March 4 Salkowski replied that the union could obtain the information from the employees' W–2 earnings statements to which it had access, and that a good part of the unit was on a 50/50 commission basis. He also stated that the company did not have any of its benefits broken down in actual dollar amounts for each employee.

At the meeting on March 9 the company presented 36 written counterproposals, providing in part for; (1) an open shop in which the union would not interfere with the employees' choice concerning union activities or pressure any employee to join the union or to sign a checkoff for union dues and initiation fees; (2) a management-rights clause, not subject to the grievance procedure, giving the company exclusive control over hours, work rules, and production and authorizing it to subcontract, curtail, or shut down its business completely without regard to the effect on employment; (3) a no-strike no-lockout clause requiring the union to fine "any employee" who engaged in a prohibited work interruption and granting the company the right to seek an injunction and damages against the union without arbitrating the claim; and (4) an article on arbitration that provided for only limited and permissive arbitration. Hourly wage rates and promotions would be set at the company's sole discretion.

Jones reviewed the company's proposals briefly and asked Salkowski to explain some. He insisted that they needed to know the amounts of wages and benefits paid each individual. Salkowski replied that he did not know if the company had those figures and whether or not the union was entitled to such information. Salkowski promised to provide the union with whatever information the company had relating to the benefits and agreed to check if the dollar figures paid to

each individual were available and if the union was entitled to them. On March 29 Jones wrote to Salkowski asking that the requested information be forwarded to Jones prior to the next meeting. On March 31 Salkowski acknowledged receipt of Jones's letter and confirmed the meeting date of April 15, but did not refer to Jones's request for information. On April 4 Jones again wrote to Salkowski, renewing his request. On April 8 Salkowski forwarded the information to Jones.

No agreement was reached on any issues during the first two meetings. On April 15 the parties agreed, with minor changes, to the company's proposals relating to recognition, plant visitation, a 30-day leave-of-absence to be granted at the company's sole discretion, and language forbidding union stewards to solicit grievances.

On May 9 Local 215 filed unfair labor practice charges against the company, alleging violations of Sections 8(a)(1) and 8(a)(5) of the Act for delaying meeting with the union, delaying furnishing relevant bargaining information to the union, and engaging in surface bargaining without a sincere intention to reach agreement.

The fourth bargaining session of May 24 was very brief. At the fifth session on June 14 the parties agreed, with minor changes, to the articles relating to certain general provisions; a bulletin board; reporting pay; call-in pay; examinations; and the intent, purpose, and scope of the agreement. Jones indicated that real movement had been made. He suggested that they finish the non-economic items at the next meeting on June 28 and then move on to monetary items.

The June 28 meeting was cancelled by the union due to an emergency in Jones's family. No other summer or early fall meetings were held due to schedule conflicts. The parties met on October 18 and 21. On October 21 there was basic agreement on holidays, seniority, union representation, the grievance procedure, arbitration, and no-strike no-lockout provisions. The company dropped its proposals that wage rates and promotions be determined at its sole discretion and that there be a specific article guaranteeing an open shop.

Discussed, but unresolved, were articles on management rights, the union's proposals on maintenance of standards, probationary employees, nondiscrimination (relating to employees' right to refrain from union activity), work by nonbargaining unit employees in the unit, and the union's article on discharge and suspension. Not discussed during any of the meetings were wages, hours, fringe benefits (except holiday eligibility), overtime and premium pay, union security and checkoff, union pensions (except for their legal status), duration of the contract, temporary transfers, separability and savings, and classifying employees.

ARGUMENTS IN FAVOR OF THE UNION

In relation to the delay, the union pointed to several facts. When the union wrote Salkowski on January 3, 1977, requesting a meeting for bargaining, it took another month, until February 14, before Salkowski was willing to meet. Ordinarily, a delay of a month or so in scheduling an initial meeting would not in and of itself be evidence of bad faith. But these employees had been denied their bargaining rights for the preceding three years while the company litigated its obligation to bargain. In such circumstances, good faith required that the company respond promptly to the union's first request rather than merely provide it with the name of its attorney, who then insisted upon further delay.

It was further argued that the company delayed furnishing the union with current wage and fringe benefits information, to which it was clearly entitled. The company vacillated, providing the information in general rather than specific dollar amounts, then asserting that the union could get the wage information itself, later stating that the company did not have the dollar amounts of fringe benefits, and finally Salkowski saying that he was not sure that the union was entitled to the information. Almost two months following

the union request, after further, urgent correspondence, Salkowski forwarded the requested information to the union.

It was also argued that the company was only engaged in surface bargaining with no real intent to reach agreement. Some of the company's 36 counterproposals would have put the employees in a far worse position with the union than without it. Others would have so damaged the union's ability to function as the employees' bargaining representative that Salkowski, a skillful and experienced practitioner, could not possibly have expected that they would result in serious and meaningful collective bargaining. Further, at the March 9 meeting, when the union asked whether the company was refusing to negotiate on wages, Salkowski responded that the company was willing to negotiate the question as to whether or not it would negotiate on wages! Considering his competence and long experience, Salkowski must have known better. Wages are a mandatory subject of bargaining. They *must* be negotiated.

Not until May 24, after the charge in this case was filed, did the company agree to mandatory arbitration, remove its limitation on the arbitrator's authority under the no-strike no-lockout provision, agree that management rights would be subject to the grievance procedure, and eliminate lesser, but equally unacceptable, language. Not until October 21, after the complaint in this case was issued and it was four days before the hearing, did the company withdraw other extreme proposals under its no-strike no-lockout article, the article on arbitration, the specific requirement for an open shop, and the provision that wage rates and promotions be set at its sole discretion.

In summary, the company's proposals were so outrageous that they could not have been made in good faith. The company did not attempt to defend its extreme proposals, clinging to them for six months. There were not even any bona fide concessions on substantial issues to indicate that the employer was not merely being stubborn. Any concessions that did occur coincided with the filing of the union's charges. Thus examining the totality of the company's conduct, it should be found guilty of violating Section 8(a)(5) of the Act.

ARGUMENTS IN FAVOR OF THE COMPANY

The company argued that it did not unduly delay the meetings. The courts have not allowed a company to be penalized for a decision to litigate a union's certification.* Even the union agreed that a one-month delay, by itself, would not be evidence of bad faith. Further, the company was not evasive when contacted on November 15, 1976, but referred the union to its attorney. The union then waited six weeks to contact Salkowski, a delay that was longer than the one caused by Salkowski. The company also argued that it did not delay in furnishing relevant bargaining information, that information with regard to wages was not easily available since most of the employees were paid on a commission basis and the company did provide it within a reasonable time.

In relation to that part of the charge concerning "surface bargaining," the company argued that it was engaged in "hard bargaining." It noted that Salkowski never took an adamant position on any of the company's 36 initial bargaining articles. Those proposals that presented the greatest obstacles to agreement on language were withdrawn. Salkowski made it clear from the very beginning that he was not wedded to every comma in the proposals. He was willing to negotiate, depending on the entire agreement.

---

* *Jones Steel Workers* v *A.O. Jones Corporation*, 420 F.2d 1, 9 (7th Cir. 1969).

The company also argued that the charges filed against it were premature, since they were filed after only three bargaining sessions had been held. At that time, the union had only become aware that the company was not going to be a pushover in bargaining, even though Salkowski had stated at the second session that he was willing to negotiate on everything.

Thus while the company was engaged in hard bargaining, it also made concessions that indicated its good faith attempts. At their negotiating session on June 14 the union even stated that the company had made some real movement. The company also pointed to the fact that in October it had relinquished its extreme positions on the management rights and no-strike issues as evidence of its good faith, and suggested that it was illogical and counterproductive to find from the later concessions that the earlier positions were unreasonable. The company requested that the charges against it be dismissed.

DISCUSSION QUESTIONS

1. Could the company properly delay bargaining until the first litigation was terminated?

2. Was the delay of the company in providing the wage and benefit information an unfair labor practice in and of itself?

3. What is the difference between "hard bargaining" and "bad faith" bargaining? In which was the company engaged?

4. What motives might explain the company's actions?

5. If the company is guilty, what remedy would you order?

15. Did the End of Subcontracting and the Establishment of a New Workplace Lead to a Successor Employer?

PARTIES: Saks and Company d/b/a Saks Fifth Avenue and Amalgamated Clothing and Textile Workers Union, AFL–CIO–CLC, Local 86.

ISSUES: 8(a)(1) and 8(a)(5) charges, subcontracting, past practice, multi-employer bargaining units, successor employers.

BACKGROUND

For many years, Saks operated a "Saks Fifth Avenue" store in Pittsburgh, Pennsylvania, located on the sixth floor of the building that houses the Gimbels department store. All of the capital stock of Saks has been owned by Gimbels since 1924. Gimbels files consolidated income tax returns that include the operations of Saks. However, both stores operate independently and the two companies have separate officers and separate labor relations policies.

Until August 10, 1977, Saks operated its Pittsburgh store in the Gimbels building pursuant to a written lease. Saks subcontracted its alterations work on women's garments to Gimbels. Until about August 12, Gimbels maintained separate work areas for the alterations employees; one for alterations work on garments sold by Gimbels, and the other for work on garments sold by Saks. The two areas occupied a large room that was divided in half by a partition. Gimbels

employed 18 employees in the Saks area and ten in the Gimbels area. While Gimbels's manager of alterations supervised both work areas, Joseph Blondi, Saks's manager of alterations, was responsible for the quality of work performed in the Saks area.

The union was voluntarily recognized by Gimbels in 1937 as the exclusive bargaining representative of its alterations employees.* The collective bargaining agreement recognized the union as the exclusive bargaining representative of its alterations employees. The agreement, which contains union security and checkoff provisions, was negotiated between the union and the Labor Standards Association, a multi-employer association of which Gimbels is a member. The bargaining unit had 110 employees, 35 at Gimbels (including 7 at another location) and 75 at Kaufman's Department Store.

On June 15, 1977, Saks signed a lease for a retail store facility, located one block from the Gimbels store. In a letter dated July 7, 1977, Saks notified Gimbels that it would be establishing its own alterations workroom in its new Pittsburgh store and therefore would no longer require the services of Gimbels's alterations workroom. Subsequently, Robert Evola, the labor relations

---

* Employers may voluntarily recognize a union without going through an NLRB certification election.

director at Gimbels, contacted Ray Evans, a senior vice-president at Saks, expressing concern about Gimbels's liability for severance pay under the union contract and requested Evans to consider hiring the displaced Gimbels alterations employees. Evans replied that Saks would arrange such interviews and noted that both the Saks personnel director and the Saks manager of alterations would be interviewing applicants in late July. Evola informed the union's business representative of Gimbels's intention to close the Saks alteration work area. Evola then informed the employees in the Saks area that it was closing and that they could apply for jobs at Saks's new store.

Following interviews, Saks hired 16 of the 18 Gimbels employees who had worked in the Saks area. Saks ended alteration work at the Gimbels location on August 12, 1977, and on August 15 the 16 former Gimbels employees began working at Saks's store under the supervision of Blondi. The weekly wage of the former Gimbels employees hired by Saks remained unchanged at first. However, changes were made in both working conditions and fringe benefits, which included a shortening of the workweek and an alteration in the paid vacation policy. The pension plan was also changed, with the Gimbels-Saks pension plan extended by Saks to the affected alterations employees. They did not lose their starting date at Gimbels because of a long-standing informal agreement governing transfers between the two companies. These changes meant that their fringe benefits were now consistent with those applied to Saks employees nationwide.

On or about July 29, 1977, the manager of the union's Pittsburgh Joint Board, an International vice-president of the union, asked Evans, the Saks vice-president, whether Saks would honor the collective bargaining agreement between the Labor Standards Association and the union and whether Saks would recognize the union as the bargaining representative of its alterations employees at the new store. Evans stated that Saks would not recognize the collective bargaining agreement as applying to the alterations employees in its new store and did not recognize the union as their bargaining representative.

On August 24, 1977, the union filed unfair labor practice charges against Saks.

ARGUMENTS OF THE UNION

The union contended that Saks is a successor to Gimbels with respect to those alterations employees previously employed by Gimbels and represented by the union who were hired by Saks at its new Pittsburgh store. It noted that the Supreme Court decision in *NLRB* v. *Burns International Security Services,* 406 U.S. 272 (1972), found that Burns's retention of a majority of its predecessor's work force bound Burns to bargain with the former Wackenhut employees' union. In that situation, one security guard company, Burns, displaced another, Wackenhut, by winning the contract to provide security services at a Lockheed plant. Burns retained 27 of Wackenhut's 42 guards and brought in 15 of its own. The union argued that Saks has a duty to bargain with the union as a successor to Gimbels, that the unit in which the union sought recognition is appropriate, and that Saks violated Section 8(a)(1) and 8(a)(5) of the Act by refusing to recognize and bargain with the union on and after July 29, 1977. Finally, the union contended that Saks violated Sections 8(a)(1) and 8(a)(5) of the Act by unilaterally setting the initial terms and conditions of employment of the alterations employees at its new Pittsburgh store, as 16 of the 18 employees previously employed by Gimbels constituted a majority of Saks's alterations work force.

The union requested that Saks be found guilty of violations of the Act, that it be forced to recognize the union as the representative of its employees, and that the terms of the contract the union had with multi-employer Labor Standards Association be applied as of August 15, 1977.

ARGUMENTS OF THE COMPANY

Saks contended that it did not succeed to Gimbels's obligation to bargain with the union because there was no continuity in the business enterprises of Gimbels and Saks. It argued that the Supreme Court decision in *Burns* did not apply here because Gimbels did not discontinue, nor did Saks succeed to, any of Gimbels's business operations. It further argued that there was no continuity in the work force of Gimbels and Saks and that the bargaining relationship between the Labor Standards Association and the union remained unchanged. It also argued that, unlike the situation in the *Burns* case, it was not a successor to Gimbels because it did not hire a majority of the 110 employees in the "relevant" bargaining unit at Gimbels, which also included the alterations employees of another Pittsburgh store, Kaufman's Department Store. Finally, Saks contended that since it did not succeed to Gimbels's obligations to bargain with the union, it was free to set the terms and conditions of employment for all its alterations employees to match those of its employees nationwide. In addition, Saks contended that even if it were a successor employer under *Burns,* a successor is still free to set terms and conditions of employment if it did not definitely intend to retain all the employees from the predecessor bargaining unit.

In light of the above arguments, Saks requested that the NLRB dismiss the unfair labor practice charges filed against it.

DISCUSSION QUESTIONS

1. How relevant is it in this case that the two stores are commonly owned? What about the separate corporate identities? Does the geographic distance between the new Saks store and Gimbels in downtown Pittsburgh have any relevance?

2. What is the relevant bargaining unit? Is it confounded by either the voluntary recognition of the union in 1937 (non-NLRB certified) and/or the multi-employer group?

3. What do you think was the intention of Saks in hiring the former Gimbels's employees?

4. What would be your recommended decision and/or remedy in this case?

16. Is the Health Center Covered by the Act?

PARTIES: St. Louis Comprehensive Neighborhood Health Center, Inc. and Service Employees International Union, Local 50.

ISSUES: 8(a)(1), and 8(a)(5) charges, government funding, employers covered by the Act, refusal to bargain.

BACKGROUND

The St. Louis Comprehensive Neighborhood Health Center is a nonprofit corporation that provides health services for residents in St. Louis, Missouri. From the time of its incorporation in 1969 until 1977, government funds for its operation were given to the center by the Human Development Center (HDC), a nonprofit corporation operating an antipoverty program in St. Louis. After 1977 and until the hearing involving the center in 1980, its funding came directly from the U.S. Department of Health, Education, and Welfare.

Local 50 sought to organize the employees of the center. The center denied that it came under the jurisdiction of the National Labor Relations Act because it was not a health care institution as defined in Section 2(14) of the Act and that it was not an employer engaged in commerce as defined in Section 2(2) of the Act. On May 18, 1977, the Regional Director of the NLRB ordered an election and on June 13, 1977, the Board denied the center's request for review of the decision.

Shortly thereafter separate elections were conducted for clerical employees and technical employees of the center. Local 50 won both elections and was certified as the exclusive bargaining representative of both the center's clerical and technical employees.

Beginning in July 1977, Local 50 requested meetings with representatives of the center to discuss contract proposals. On August 5, 1977, Mann, a field representative for the union wrote to Andrews, the director of the center, requesting a meeting to negotiate a labor agreement covering wages, hours, and working conditions for the employees represented by Local 50. Andrews responded by letter, agreeing to a meeting but stating, "we don't have the authority to make agreements in these areas, however if you will present your proposals in writing we will forward them to appropriate authorities for their consideration." On August 22 Mann sent a letter to Andrews requesting information needed to prepare for the meeting agreed to by Andrews. The information requested included a list of employee wage rates and seniority dates, a copy of the center's personnel manual, current health insurance policies and their cost, and descriptions of any pension programs and guidelines from the Department of Health, Education and Welfare.

After receiving Andrews's letter, Mann called him five or six times, but never reached him and never had his calls returned. This being the case, Mann went to the center on September 1. About five minutes after the receptionist announced his visit to Andrews, Mann saw him leaving the center by another exit. Mann caught up with Andrews in the parking lot and said that he wanted to set up a meeting date for contract negotiations and that the union needed the information requested in the letter of August 22. Andrews replied that the contract negotiations were in the hands of the center's board of directors and that he would get back to Mann.

Having been so advised, on September 8 Mann attended the board's regularly scheduled meeting. Before the meeting Mann approached the board chairman, Clarice John, and stated that he wished to introduce himself to the board and explain the union's position since the board was handling contract negotiations. John asked Mann to sit down and about 15 minutes into the meeting told the board that a union representative was present. The board voted to go into executive session and John told Mann to leave the meeting.

In a letter dated September 9, 1977, John wrote to Mann that the center had recently become directly funded by HEW and that the board had voted to "formulate an official policy for dealing with your organization," and that in two weeks the policy would be drafted and sent to the union. John's letter concluded that after the union had reviewed the policy statement, the board would meet with Mann concerning it.

In a letter dated September 30, Andrews sent HEW a copy of the policy statement and asked for HEW's reaction before submitting it to Local 50. It stated that the center did not oppose the principle of collective bargaining. However, government regulations and restrictions could be impediments to collective bargaining and the center would seek advance clearance from appropriate agencies on all matters that might affect the center's funding. A copy of the policy statement was never submitted to the union.

Richard Hill became a leader of Local 50 on October 17. A few days later he sent a letter to Andrews requesting a meeting at any convenient time or place for the purpose of discussing wages, hours, and conditions of employment for the center's workers represented by Local 50. Hill threatened that unfair labor practice charges would be filed unless a response was received by October 31. In a letter dated October 28, Andrews stated that the center's policy statement concerning its position with respect to any meetings pertaining to collective bargaining had been forwarded to HEW for review.

Hill sent another letter to Andrews on November 8, 1977, with a copy to David Kennedy the current chairman of the center's board of directors. The letter again requested a meeting for the purpose of discussing wages, hours, and other conditions of employment. The letter also stated that unless the center replied by November 11, unfair labor practice charges would be filed. Andrews responded in a letter dated November 10. He stated that a meeting with the board could be held but that it would not discuss substantive issues until after hearing from HEW.

A meeting involving a Local 50 business agent, Andrews, Kennedy, and other members of the board took place on December 7. The meeting began with the business agent passing out copies of the union's contract proposals and requesting point-by-point discussion. Kennedy replied that the board needed time to study the proposals, and that discussions concerning them would have to wait until after HEW's review of the board's policy statement. Spear requested a firm date for the next negotiating meeting but Kennedy refused. The meeting ended with Spear threatening to file unfair labor practice charges.

In a letter dated December 13, 1977, HEW responded to the board's policy statement. The letter stated that HEW had very limited experience in collective bargaining, that only rarely do supplemental funds become available, and that in the event that a collective bargaining agreement would require an increase in funding, it might be necessary to develop an additional source of funds. This is the only existing information concerning HEW's position on the center's collective bargaining obligations. During the first three weeks of January 1978, another Local 50 business agent, attempted to contact Andrews by telephone. She was unable to reach him and none of her calls were returned.

ARGUMENTS OF ST. LOUIS COMPREHENSIVE NEIGHBORHOOD HEALTH CENTER

The center argued that it was not an employer under the Act because of its relationship with HEW. It was pointed out that HEW requires it to submit its budgets and contracts to HEW for approval, and that HEW exercises some control over the use of other revenues generated by operations of the center. Consequently, the center was not a health care institution covered by the Act, but was exempt from the Act because of its relationship with HEW. As a result the center was not obligated to bargain with Local 50.

ARGUMENTS OF LOCAL 50

The center had the direct funding relation with HEW when the NLRB Regional Director ordered a certification election. At that time the center presented its arguments concerning exemption from the Act because of the degree of control *exercised* over its operations by HEW. The Regional Director had determined that the center was covered by the Act and the Board had denied the center's request for review of the decision. Consequently the center is covered by the Act and because it refused and failed to bargain collectively with Local 50, the center violated Section 8(a)(1) and 8(a)(5) of the Act.

DISCUSSION QUESTIONS

1. Is the center an employer under the Act or is it exempt from the Act because of its relationship with HEW?

2. Did the management of the center engage in behavior that violated Section 8(a)(1) and 8(a)(5) of the Act?

17. Can the Work be Subcontracted?

PARTIES: Hillside Manor Health Related Facility and Service Employees International Union, Local 144.

ISSUES: 8(a)(1) and 8(a)(5) charges, refusal to bargain, appropriate remedy, subcontracting.

BACKGROUND

Hillside Manor provides nursing and other health related services. Beginning on August 1, 1975, Environmental Consultants, Inc. had a contract to perform housekeeping and maintenance services at Hillside's facility in Jamaica, New York. On July 1, 1979, Local 144 of the Service Employees International Union was recognized as the exclusive collective bargaining representative of all housekeeping and maintenance employees at the Hillside facility. On October 2, 1979, Judith Benson co-owner and administrator of Hillside, notified Environmental that its housekeeping and maintenance contract with Environmental would be terminated on October 31, 1979. Hillside terminated the contract with Environmental on that day and discharged the 26 bargaining unit employees. There were no collective bargaining negotiations among Hillside, Environmental, and Local 144 over Hillside's decision to terminate its contract with Environmental and to discharge the workers.

On November 1, 1979, Hillside retained Baine Service Systems, Inc. to perform the housekeeping and maintenance services at its Jamaica facility. Also on that date, Baine and Local 917, International Brotherhood of Teamsters, Chauffeurs, Warehousemen and Helpers of America signed a collective bargaining agreement covering the employees in the housekeeping and maintenance unit formerly represented by Local 144, Service Employees International Union. Inspection of the names of the 35 persons employed by Baine on January 24, 1980, indicates that 21 had been on Environmental's payroll on October 31, 1979.

On November 2, 1979, Local 144 filed a complaint with the NLRB alleging that Hillside Manor and Environmental Consultants, Inc., as joint employers, unilaterally and unlawfully discharged the employees represented by Local 144 and subcontracted the work to another employer without giving the union an opportunity to negotiate and bargain about the decision. The complaint alleged that these actions were in violation of Section 8(a)(1) and 8(a)(5) of the Act.

The Administrative Law Judge (ALJ) concluded that Hillside and Environmental, at the time in question, were joint employers of the employees represented by Local 144. The ALJ also concluded that Hillside's failure to meet and bargain with the union concerning its decision to ter-

minate the contract with Environmental constituted a refusal to bargain in violation of Section
8(a)(1) and 8(a)(5) of the Act. It was ordered that
Hillside cease and desist from such conduct in the
future and take action to dissipate the effects of its
unfair labor practice. The remedy called for: (1)
the return of the terminated employees to their
former or substantially equivalent positions of
employment with Environmental and Hillside or
if Environmental is unwilling to undertake the
contract to provide housekeeping and maintenance services, with Hillside alone; (2) Hillside to
make whole the terminated employees; (3)
Hillside to recognize and bargain with Local 144
as the collective bargaining representative of the
bargaining unit workers; and (4) Hillside to cease
and desist from refusing to bargain with Local
144 and to stop recognizing any other labor
organization as the collective bargaining representative.

POSITION OF HILLSIDE MANOR

Hillside did not dispute that it had a joint
employer relationship with Environmental at the
period in question, i.e., they were integrated enterprises with a common labor policy and Hillside
administrators exercised substantial control over
the housekeeping and maintenance employees.
Consequently Hillside did not take the position
that Environmental, rather than Hillside Manor,
was obligated to bargain with Local 144.

Hillside's contention was that the remedy
was too broad, in that Hillside should not be required to reestablish its former relationship with
Environmental. Hillside's position was that
severing its contractual arrangement with Baine
and directly employing the discharged workers
would not necessarily effect a satisfactory
remedy. Hillside offered several arguments to
support this position. First, 21 of the 26 workers
discharged when the contract with Environmental was terminated were employed by Baines
within a few weeks and the remaining workers
would be given the opportunity to return to Hill-

side. Thus each worker had been or would be
given the opportunity to be reinstated to his or her
former or substantially equivalent employment
position. Secondly, undue hardship could result
from the proposed remedy because a third-party
employer (Baine) had contracted to deliver the
housekeeping and maintenance work for almost
two years. (The decision reviewing the ALJ's decision by the NLRB is dated August 25, 1981, almost two years after termination of the contract
with Environmental and initiation of the contract
with Baine). Hillside claimed that the remedy un-
necessarily encroached upon a two-year-long
business relationship with Baine and that the
workers might risk possible loss of employment if
they were again employed by Environmental.
This could occur if Environmental and Hillside
were ordered to reestablish a joint-employer relationship, because Hillside would have the right to
again terminate the contract on 30-days notice. It
was implied that such a decision by Hillside
would be likely because of hostility between top
administrators of Hillside and Environmental.

ARGUMENTS OF LOCAL 144

The union argued that restoration of employment
conditions to their status of October 31, 1979,
could only be achieved by ordering Hillside to
rescind its subcontract with Baine and directly
employ the maintenance and housekeeping workers.

DISCUSSION QUESTIONS

1. Which, if any, sections of the Act were violated
   by Hillside Manor?

2. Is the proposed remedy too broad as argued by
   Hillside Manor? Evaluate the arguments put
   forth by Hillside Manor.

3. Did those discharged workers employed by
   Baine return to work under equivalent or substantially equivalent conditions of employment?

18. Can Doctors Strike?

PARTIES: Montefiore Hospital and Medical Center and Molly Brown and John Patrick, individuals.

ISSUES: 8(a)(1), 8(a)(4) and 8(g) charges, discrimination because of union activities, notice of intent to strike, sympathy picketing and striking, professional privileges, and professional ethics.

BACKGROUND

Montefiore Hospital and Medical Center is a health care facility in the Bronx, New York City. The health center operates two clinics, the Martin Luther King Health Center and the Bathgate Clinic, which provide out-patient care. Both clinics serve a lower income, minority population residing within walking distance. The clinics are the principal sources of out-patient health care in their geographic areas.

Molly Brown and John Patrick are licensed physicians specializing in family practice medicine. Beginning July 1, 1976, they were preceptors in family practice medicine at the Bathgate Clinic on a regular part-time basis. As preceptors they acted in a teaching and consultative capacity to the residents at Bathgate. The residents are graduates of medical schools who serve on the staff of the clinic, either as interns or postgraduate students. The preceptors participate in the treatment of patients by reviewing medical charts and assisting residents in diagnosis and treatment.

The case stemmed from a lawful economic strike, with ten-days notice, of unionized employees at the Bathgate Clinic. The striking workers were service, maintenance, technical, and some professional workers represented by District 1199 of the National Union of Health and Hospital Employees. Drs. Brown and Patrick were not union members.

On July 14, 15, and 16, 1976, District 1199 picketed the Bathgate Clinic. During the strike, of the 34 to 39 employees normally working at Bathgate, only four to five reported for work. They were one physician, three nurses, and one receptionist. Drs. Brown and Patrick were in sympathy with the striking workers. During the strike they refused to perform labor services at the clinic and at times participated in the picketing. They gave no advance notice to their employer of their intention to participate in the strike.

While Drs. Brown and Patrick participated in the picketing they tried to discourage prospective patients from entering the Bathgate Clinic for treatment. There were no physical interferences or threats. The procedure Brown and Patrick followed was to identify themselves as doctors to

401

the prospective patients. They informed the patients there was a strike involving most employees of the clinic and that normal services and facilities were not available. They advised the prospective patients that better medical care would be available at some nonstruck medical facility. Brown and Patrick did not inquire as to the nature of the medical condition of the prospective patients.

On July 22, 1976, Dr. Kind, the hospital director and Dr. Cherk, president of the Montefiore Hospital and Medical Center reviewed the actions of Drs. Brown and Patrick. Because of their refusal to carry out assignments during the strike, failure to give notice of their intent to withhold their services, and obstructing patients seeking care, the decision was reached to terminate them.

The residents at the Bathgate Clinic did not approve of the termination of Brown and Patrick. As a result a panel of staff physicians was established to review their discharge. The panel considered the charges in late August 1976. The panel concluded that the charges were well-founded but felt that the separation without pay since July 22 was sufficient discipline and recommended reinstatement. On September 8, 1976, Dr. Cherk interviewed Drs. Brown and Patrick separately. Dr. Cherk told them he was going to make a recommendation to the Board of Trustees concerning their reinstatement the following day, but before doing so he wanted to understand their views of their responsibilities as doctors. He told them that they had the right to engage in legal strike action, but that during the strike they had gone on strike without notice, refused to perform their work assignments during the strike, and interfered with patients' entry to the clinic, all of which were inappropriate. Both Drs. Brown and Patrick indicated that in retrospect they felt that their actions may not have been appropriate in all respects and that they would not repeat them in the future. As a result, on the following day Dr. Cherk recommended that Drs. Brown and

Patrick be reinstated to their part-time positions on October 1, 1976, and that their discharges be converted to suspensions without pay.

About November or December 1976, the Montefiore Hospital and Medical Center decided to expand its family practice program effective February 1, 1977. This resulted in the creation of two full-time faculty positions in family practice medicine. Dr. Brown applied for one of the positions, an in-house committee recommended that her application be accepted and Dr. Ford, Director of the residency program, approved the recommendation and on January 14, 1977, sent a change of status request to Dr. Lincoln, Deputy Director of Professional Affairs. The request was to change Dr. Brown's status from part-time to full-time, effective January 31, 1977.

In the meantime, on November 17, 1976, a complaint was issued by the NLRB charging Montefiore Hospital and Medical Center with unfair labor practices in the discharge of Drs. Brown and Patrick. Dr. Cherk interpreted the charges as evidence that Drs. Brown and Patrick now viewed their actions during the strike as appropriate, a view inconsistent with his understanding of those expressed during the meetings of September 8.

When Dr. Ford's recommendation concerning the full-time employment of Dr. Brown was received, Dr. Cherk and Dr. Kind met to discuss the matter. It was decided that Brown's application would not be considered until the NLRB proceeding had been completed.

On February 2, 1977, Dr. Patrick applied to Dr. Ford for the second new full-time position. At that time Dr. Ford informed him that his situation would be the same as Dr. Brown's and that no action would be taken pending the NLRB decision on the case. On June 2, 1977, the selection committee, including Dr. Ford, responsible for screening applications for the full-time positions met and unanimously approved Patrick for the second full-time position.

For a physician to practice at, or to have patients admitted to, Montefiore Hosptial, the physician must have admitting privileges. Such privileges require approval of the hospital's Board of Trustees, after review by various departmental heads and staff committees, including the executive committee of the Medical Board. Employee physicians such as Drs. Brown and Patrick are granted temporary privileges when hired.

Prior to becoming preceptors, Brown and Patrick had been residents at Montefiore Hospital. They completed their residencies in June 1976 and made application for permanent privileges at that time. Normally such requests are approved within 90 days. In February 1977, having received no response to their applications, Drs. Brown and Patrick inquired about their applications. Dr. Hammer, head of the Department of Medicine told them the decision was basically Dr. Cherk's. They inquired again in April 1977 and were told that their applications were in process. Although the executive committee of the Medical Board meets monthly, the applications of Brown and Patrick for admitting privileges were not included on the agenda of this committee until shortly before the NLRB hearing on charges of unfair labor practices in November 1977.

POSITION OF DRS. BROWN AND PATRICK

Drs. Brown and Patrick maintained that the Section 8(a)(1) violations affecting them included their discharges, the withholding of admitting privileges, and the interrogations of them by Dr. Cherk on September 8, 1976. They also argued that Section 8(a)(4) was violated by the failure to grant them full-time employment.

POSITION OF THE EMPLOYER

The employer alleged that Drs. Brown and Patrick engaged in practices that violate professional ethics and that are not protected by the Act. Specifically it is argued that they; (1) struck without notice, (2) ceased and refused to perform their assigned duties, and (3) while on the picket line disparaged the Bathgate clinic and advised prospective patients against and obstructed them from entering the clinic.

The employer presented evidence that the conduct of Drs. Brown and Patrick violated medical codes of ethics and was therefore not protected by the National Labor Relations Act. The employers also argued that Section 8(g) requires that notice of intent to strike be given by Drs. Brown and Patrick, in addition to the notice given by Local 1199.

Dr. Cherk declined to approve Dr. Brown's and Dr. Patrick's applications for full-time employment pending the outcome of the NLRB proceedings. His explanation was that their complaint to the NLRB constituted a retraction of the assurances he thought they gave him in the meetings of September 8. Regarding these meetings, the employer contends that Dr. Cherk interviewed Brown and Patrick concerning their strike activities in order to determine their views on the propriety of their actions. With respect to the failure to grant admitting privileges, the employer alleged that the review process of their applications had not been completed and that nothing had been done to expedite or retard that process. He stated that he needed to gain further information before making a recommendation concerning their reinstatement.

DISCUSSION QUESTIONS

1. Which, if any, sections of the Act were violated by the employer?

2. Which, if any, actions on the part of Drs. Brown and Patrick are not protected by the Act?

3. Were the doctors required to give ten-days notice of their intent to strike?

4. What behavior by physicians engaged in picketing a health care facility is protected and what is not protected?

5. What is the importance of the fact that the doctors were supporting a union of which they were not members and which did not represent them?

6. What is the significance of a professional code of ethics in determining what is protected behavior under the Act?

INDEX TO ARBITRATION CASES

INDEX TO ARBITRATION CASES

19. Did Administrators Follow the Performance Appraisal Procedures?

PARTIES: Board of Education of Cincinnati (Ohio) School District and Cincinnati Federation of Teachers.

ISSUE: The issue before the arbitrator was to determine if the procedures for performance appraisal were specified in the collective bargaining agreement.

BACKGROUND

The grievant had been employed by the Cincinnati School District for nearly 16 years. In the course of his employment, he attained a continuing contract as a tenured teacher and a limited contract as a counselor. On June 9, 1978, the grievant received a memorandum from the Board of Education that stated the following with respect to his employment duties as a counselor:

> Inasmuch as we have serious concerns about your performance and professional conduct, we plan to reinitiate the appraisal process again for the 1978–1979 school year, and all appraisal guidelines will be followed to the letter. Specific concerns include the following:
>
> (a) ineffective staff interpersonal relations.
>
> (b) weak planning and organizational skills.
>
> (c) ineffective group guidance skills.
>
> (d) ineffective communication of the guidance program and guidance procedures to staff.
>
> (e) unkept personal appearance and professional image.
>
> (f) negligible community involvement in the Sawyer School District.
>
> (g) lack of follow through on agreed upon plans and procedures.
>
> (h) negligible participation in extracurricular activities and functions.
>
> We would also like to see you participate in more staff development activities in order to improve your professional skills.

In accordance with the above memorandum, the grievant's performance as a counselor during the 1978–1979 school year was appraised and evaluated by his school principal and the Board's Associate Director of Guidance Services. From late October 1978 to early March 1979 these evaluators worked closely with the grievant in order to appraise his performance as a counselor and to achieve an improvement in his professional skills. On at least five occasions, they met with the grievant to review his performance and work product as a counselor, identify his deficiencies, make constructive criticisms and suggestions as to how his counseling skills could be improved, and develop written job targets for him. These meetings took place on November 15, 1978; December 21, 1978; January 18, 1979; February 1, 1979; and February 15, 1979.

On March 8, 1979, this period of formal evaluation was concluded and the grievant's appraisers issued a Performance Evaluation Summary. This evaluation concluded that the grievant's professional performance as a counselor was "unsatisfactory." The summary stated that "in compliance with provision T202.021 of the collective bargaining contract you are hereby advised that, on the basis of this appraisal report, your limited contract as a counselor may not be renewed for the 1979–1980 school year."

As a result, on March 12, 1979, Paul Adams filed the following grievance:

> On March 8, 1979, (my) 1978–1979 performance as a counselor at Sawyer Junior High School was appraised as less than satisfactory. This unsatisfactory rating was made in the absence of any observations and Observation Report Forms. The evaluators also failed to list the date, time, place and subject of the nonexistent observations which served as the basis of the evaluation. As such, the (collective bargaining contract) has been violated.

The Board and the union are parties to a collective bargaining contract in which the union is recognized as the exclusive bargaining agent for all teachers and counselors in the bargaining unit. This contract contains the following appraisal provision (Section T203.01–T203.0123):

.01 APPRAISAL

.011 Before teachers are appraised they shall receive an orientation to the appraisal process. The appraiser shall prior to conducting an initial observation, introduce himself/herself to the teacher and explain his/her purpose for being there.

.012 Teachers shall be evaluated as outstanding, very good, satisfactory, marginal or unsatisfactory.

.013 There shall be one (1) standard evaluation form used for evaluation of classroom teachers which shall be provided to teachers in the orientation.

.014 The principal or assistant principal shall be responsible for administering the appraisal process. Supervisory instructional consultants may assist in the evaluation process at the request of the principal or the teacher. The individual who performs or assists in the evaluation of a teacher shall be competent to do so.

.015 The evaluator shall demonstrate or have demonstrated teaching techniques in the teacher's class or in a classroom situation with comparable instructional needs upon the request of the teacher.

.016 The evaluator shall, as part of the evaluation process, list the date, time, place and subject of observations made with the teacher which are used as the basis of the evaluation.

.0170 Before a teacher may be given an unsatisfactory rating, the evaluator must:

.0171 have made at least four (4) observations of the teachers performance sufficient in length to justify the conclusions;

.0172 have consulted with the teacher being observed;

.0173 have provided the teacher with written suggestions for improvement which are reasonable; and

.0174 provide written reasons for such decision after a final consultation with the teacher.

.0180 Teachers may be evaluated annually.

.0190 Principals shall conduct an appraisal upon receipt of a written request from a teacher.

.0120 The observation and evaluation process shall be carried out with the full knowledge of the teacher and shall not be used in a manner inconsistent with the purpose of evaluation.

.0121 Special assistance shall be given to newly assigned teachers using such resources as can be provided by the principal and other personnel.

.0122 Teachers shall be given a copy of all report forms and supportive documents forthwith, following each observation.

.0123 The final written appraisal reports for teachers rated unsatisfactory shall be completed and submitted to the Certified Personnel Branch no later than the second (2nd) Friday in March. All other appraisal reports shall be completed and submitted by May 15. Copies of all appraisal materials shall be furnished to the teacher evaluated prior to placement in the teacher's personnel file. The teacher shall have the right to attach a written comment to the report. In the event the teacher is to be terminated, the Board shall advise the person in compliance with the Ohio Revised Code.

The collective bargaining agreement includes the Teacher Appraisal Manual. This manual establishes specific minimum guaranties that the Board must satisfy before it may issue and act upon an "unsatisfactory" evaluation of a certificated employee, such as a counselor. These minimum guaranties may be summarized as follows:

1. The evaluator must list the date, time, place, and subject of the observations made of the teacher that form the basis of the evaluator's findings and conclusions.

2. The evaluator must make at least four observations of the teacher's performance sufficient in length to warrant the findings and conclusions in the evaluation.

3. The teacher being evaluated must be provided with a copy of all report forms and supporting documents following each observation.

POSITION OF THE UNION

The union challenges the "unsatisfactory" Performance Evaluation Summary on procedural grounds. It is contended that the evaluators failed to follow the procedures specified in the collective bargaining agreement. Specifically, the union argues that the two evaluators failed to conduct four formal observations of the grievant's performance as required in Section T203.0171 of the collective bargaining agreement.

POSITION OF THE BOARD

The Board argued that the duties of a classroom teacher and a counselor are substantially different. Because of these differences the formal observations called for by the collective bargaining agreement are not appropriate for a counselor, although they are appropriate for a classroom teacher.

A classroom teacher, whose interaction and relationships with pupils are most often within a classroom context of group dynamics, can be easily and unobtrusively "observed" by an evaluator who takes a seat in the classroom. On the other hand a counselor and his or her students come together in a highly intimate relationship that often depends upon privacy for its success. This highly personal relationship would be shattered if an evaluator were to seat himself or herself at the table and "listen in" in order to "observe" the counselor in action. Under these circumstances when evaluating counselors, the "four observations" requirement must be based on something other than the physical presence of the evaluator during the counselor's working sessions with a student, parent, or staff member.

The Board noted that the grievant's duties as a counselor consisted of two primary functions. First, he was responsible for the organization, compilation, and utilization of materials such as student records, report cards, room assignments, scheduling and enrollment data, surveys and tests. Secondly, the grievant was responsible for maintaining personal communications with students, parents, and staff who required interaction with the school administration in order to deal with problems. Although this latter function occasionally may take place in a group counseling session, it is more common for a counselor to establish his or her communications on a personal level.

The union's principal objection to how the Board's evaluation process was applied to the grievant, centers upon the failure of the Board's evaluators to make any ''observations'' of the grievant's performance in either private or group counseling sessions. However, it must be noted that his evaluators had complete access to those aspects of the grievant's duties that involved the organization, compilation, and utilization of written materials.

The Board contended that the four-observations requirement specified in the collective bargaining agreement is satisfied in the appraisal of a counselor where his or her evaluators have on at least four occasions met with the counselor in order to review his or her progress, analyze his or her deficiencies, study and critique his or her work product, and otherwise make a good faith and empirically sound effort to evaluate his or her performance as a counselor.

DISCUSSION QUESTIONS

1. Compare and contrast authoritarian and progressive discipline, and evaluate the Board's approach to the situation described in this case.

2. Did the Board meet the procedural requirements specified in the collective bargaining agreement for performance evaluation where the person's performance evaluation is rated unsatisfactory?

3. Should the grievance be sustained or denied?

20. Can Summer Employees be Paid Wage Rates Less than Specified in the Contract?

PARTIES: Cherokee Electric Cooperative and United Steelworkers of America, Local 14530.

ISSUE: Did the employer violate the collective bargaining agreement by establishing wage rates and fringe benefits for summer employees that were different than those specified in the collective bargaining agreement?

BACKGROUND

This case involves the status and rates of pay of so-called summer employees of the Cherokee Electric Cooperative. Since 1980, the cooperative has employed several college-age students under its summer employment program to perform general labor work during the summer months.

The cooperative paid these summer employees the prevailing minimum wage required by the Fair Labor Standards Act and did not make them regular employees after completion of 30-days service. Consequently, the cooperative did not provide them with the contractual benefits to which regular employees are entitled.

Mary Meghan and Barry Warbonnet filed grievances protesting these actions of the cooperative. They were summer employees hired in June 1984. They were paid $3.35 an hour and

agreed that their jobs would terminate on August 31, 1984, so that they could return to college.

Meghan and Warbonnet filed these grievances on August 28, 1984. They contended that the cooperative violated the collective bargaining agreement by not paying them the utility laborer rate of pay and by not giving them other benefits provided to regular employees covered by the collective bargaining agreement.

The cooperative denied the violations. The collective bargaining agreement contains no provision for part-time summer help. The utility laborer starting rate of pay is $5.20 per hour. Article 7 (Seniority), Section 3, of the agreement provides:

> All new employees shall be considered as probationary employees for a period of thirty (30) days actually worked. During the probationary period, the Cooperative retains the right to layoff, terminate, transfer or discipline such employee without recourse by them to the Grievance Procedure. Upon completion of the probationary period, the employee shall be given seniority credit as a regular employee and immediately credited with the time which has accumulated during the probationary period.

Section 8 of Article 7 provides that an employee on layoff shall accumulate seniority and have recall rights for all purposes for a period of two years. Section 10(1) of Article 7 provides that an employee's seniority is lost if the employee voluntarily terminates his or her employment.

Article 1, the recognition clause of the collective bargaining agreement covers "all employees including store keepers and janitors employed by the Employer at Centre, Alabama, and working out of its Centre, Alabama, operation, but excluding all accountants, cashiers, and all other office clerical employees, professional employees, guards and supervisors."

The parties agreed in Section 1 of Article 2 of their agreement, ". . . that this written Contract reflects the entire agreement between the Union and the Cooperative. Amendments or clarifications of this Agreement mutually agreed upon by the Union and the Cooperative, shall be reduced to writing, attached to, and shall become a part of this Contract."

POSITION OF THE UNION

The union contends that the grievants were not paid the required contractual rate of pay and that they became regular employees after completion of a 30-day probationary period.

The union also contends that it informed the cooperative in 1983 that in the future the union would consider all employees hired to do bargaining unit work to be covered by the agreement. The union argues that as the exclusive representative of all employees in the bargaining unit, side agreements between the cooperative and individual employees, such as those with Meghan and Warbonnet, violate the collective bargaining agreement. It denies that any binding past practice allows employment of summer employees at less than contractual rates of pay or deprives them of regular status and other rights under the agreement.

POSITION OF THE COMPANY

The cooperative contends that two factors justify its denial of the grievances filed by Meghan and Warbonnet. First, the cooperative asserts that the management-rights clause protects its right to employ temporary summer employees and to pay them less than the rates of pay specified in the contract. Secondly, apart from the protection afforded by the management-rights clause, the well-established past practice acquiesced to by the union enabled the employer to hire and compensate summer employees by the terms under which Meghan and Warbonnet were employed.

The cooperative also contends that the discussions between the parties in 1983 concerning summer employees did not end their right to exercise their managerial discretion and apply past practice in the employment of summer employees.

DISCUSSION QUESTIONS

1. Does the principle of exclusive representation prohibit the employer from entering into side agreements with individual employees, which provide for rates of compensation and benefits less than provided by the collective bargaining agreement?

2. Does a management-rights clause or past practice provide the Cherokee Cooperative with the right to employ Meghan and Warbonnet under the conditions described in the case?

3. Should the grievances be denied or sustained? If they are sustained what should be the remedy?

21. Who Is to be Laid Off?

PARTIES: Monroeville Dodge, Inc. and International Association of Machinists, Local 63.

ISSUE: Did the employer violate the provisions of the contract agreement pertaining to work force reductions when it retained Donald Olsen and Joseph Baker and laid off the grievants, Block, Hunter, Kelly, and Daniels?

BACKGROUND

On September 24, 1982, Monroeville Dodge, Inc. employed Donald Olsen as a Journeyman Body and Fender Man. He was immediately designated a working foreman. On December 12, 1982, Joseph Baker, a Journeyman Mechanic whose seniority date was October 23, 1981, was also named a working foreman. On December 12, grievants Block (Journeyman Body and Fender Man), Hunter (Journeyman Mechanic), Kelly (Journeyman Mechanic), and Daniels (Journeyman Mechanic), all with more seniority than the two working foremen, were laid off while Olsen and Baker were retained. This management action resulted in grievances that allege that the company failed to follow the seniority rules governing work force reductions that are specified in the collective bargaining agreement.

The relevant portions of the collective bargaining agreement are:

ARTICLE III — Job Classifications and Wage Rates

Section 1 — The following are the job classifications of employees in the bargaining unit covered by this Agreement and the basic hourly rate of compensation to be paid to the employees in their respective classifications. . . .

B. Flat-Rated Employees
(1) All Journeymen Mechanics and Journeymen Body and Fender Men shall be guaranteed the following rate. . . .

Section 2 — The Working Shop Foreman shall receive a premium of ten percent (10%) over the basic hourly rate paid to Journeymen Mechanics. . . .

ARTICLE VII — Seniority

. . . . *Section 2* — Seniority is based on length of service regular employees have with the Employer and seniority shall prevail at all times. . . . When it becomes necessary to reduce the working force, seniority rights shall prevail . . . .

Section 3 — It is further agreed that in addition to his seniority with the Employer or Company seniority, each employee shall have classification seniority based on length of service such regular employee has with the Employer within the classification. When it becomes necessary to increase or reduce the working force in any classification,

classification seniority shall prevail. In case of layoff in any classification, the employee so laid off in accordance with his classification may bump any employee with less Company seniority in an equal or lower classification rather than to accept a layoff, provided, however, that such employee is qualified to perform such work. However an employee in the lower classification may not bump an employee in a higher classification regardless of his Company seniority. . . .

. . . . *Section 6* — In filling any position of a supervisory nature including that of a working foreman, it shall be recognized that the selection of the individual to fill such position shall be determined by management without regard to seniority. . . .

POSITION OF THE UNION

The union argued that Article VII requires that when it becomes necessary to reduce the working force, seniority rights shall prevail. Further, Section 3 specifies that when it becomes necessary to increase or reduce the work force in any job classification, classification seniority shall prevail.

The union also contended that the position of working foreman is not a separate job classification. Consequently, Olsen was in the job classification Journeyman Body and Fender Man, and Baker was a Journeyman Mechanic, and the layoffs should have been made on the basis of their classification seniority dates relative to other workers in these classifications.

The union also noted that during the previous year the company sought to retain a work-ing foreman when a more senior worker in the job classification was laid off. When this action was grieved, the company conceded the grievance.

POSITION OF THE COMPANY

The company argued that Article VII (Section 6) applies in this situation. This provision gives management the right to designate as working foreman any employee it chooses, without regard to seniority. The company also asserts that in the event of a force reduction this provision entitles it to retain the employees designated as working foremen without regard to seniority.

DISCUSSION QUESTIONS

1. Distinguish between competitive status and benefit seniority. What significance does the seniority unit have when measuring competitive status seniority.

2. Why do union members prefer to have such decisions as layoffs based on seniority rather than some other criteria?

3. What risks or inconveniences does basing decisions such as layoffs on seniority present to employers?

4. What is the relevance of superseniority when applying seniority in layoff decisions?

5. Should the grievances be sustained or denied? Why?

22. Is the Janitor Entitled to Overtime Each Day?

PARTIES: Hilliard Corporation and The International Union of Electrical, Radio and Machine Workers, Local 311.

ISSUE: The issue before the arbitrator is whether or not the company has the right to reduce the working hours for Lloyd Carter, the janitor, from 8.5 to 8 hours per day.

BACKGROUND

For many years the janitor-watchman at the plant began his shift at 6:30 A.M. and worked until 3:30 P.M. for a total of 8.5 hours per day. The regular eight-hour shift began at 7:00 A.M. and ended at 3:30 P.M. During the one-half hour between 6:30 and 7:00, the janitor started the compressor and heaters on the assembly fixtures so that they were ready for use at 7:00. As a result the janitor received one-half hour of daily overtime.

William Herman, who held that position, bid out to another position, creating a vacancy. When the company initially posted the vacancy, the working hours were listed as 6:30 A.M. to 3:30 P.M. However, this posting was withdrawn and a new posting was made listing the hours as 6:30 A.M. to 3:00 P.M.

The grievant, Lloyd Carter, bid on the revised posting and was awarded the position. He has since worked at the posted hours, 6:30 A.M. to 3:00 P.M., which is eight hours, after a one-half hour lunch period. He claims that he should be paid for an extra one-half hour at overtime rates from the time he started working in the position.

POSITION OF THE UNION

The union contended that the change in job hours for the janitor-watchman at the plant was "unjust and uncalled for without agreement from both management and the union as agreed" upon in the collective bargaining agreement. In support of this position the union refers to Article I(A)(1), which provides that:

> The Company recognizes the Union as the sole and exclusive bargaining agent for all its production and maintenance employees with respect to rates of pay, wages, hours of employment and all other conditions of employment.

and Article XII(2), which provides that:

> The Company shall not make any changes in its practices or policies which will have the effect of depriving the employees of any rights or privileges previously enjoyed.

The union pointed out that for some eight or ten years the practice was to have the janitor-watchman work for eight hours at regular pay and one-half hour at time and one-half overtime pay. When the position became vacant the company posted a notice of the opening on January 5, which called for work from 6:30 A.M. to 3:30 P.M. Then on February 12, 1980, the company posted a new notice that called for work from 6:30 A.M. to 3:00 P.M. This change in the hours of work was done without negotiation with the union. As a result, the position lost a half-hour overtime by a unilateral action of the company. Unilateral changes in hours and rates of pay are violations of the terms of the agreement.

The union also asserted that there is enough work for the janitor to do during the extra half-hour. Formerly, the janitor would shut off the machines at 3:30. Now this is done by someone else. The union requested that the old schedule be reinstituted and that the janitor be awarded the overtime pay retroactively.

POSITION OF THE COMPANY

The company position was that the management rights clause enabled it to take this action (change the workday for the janitor-watchman position from 8.5 to 8 hours). The management-rights clause in the agreement, Article XII(4), provides that:

> Except as herein provided, the management of the plant and the direction of the working forces, including the right to hire, suspend or discharge for proper cause or transfer or promote, and the right to relieve employees from duty because of lack of work, or for other legitimate reasons, is vested exclusively in the company, provided that this will not be used for purposes of discrimination against any member of the Union.

The company also called attention to Article II(2) of the agreement, which deals with hours and overtime and provides as follows:

2. For Janitors and Watchmen:

A. Each individual employee shall have a schedule of five (5) consecutive working days of eight (8) hours per day. However, the employer may stagger the working schedule of each

employee in order to obtain continuous seven (7) days operations.

B. The work performed in excess of eight (8) hours in any single day or in excess of forty (40) hours in any given week . . . shall be paid at time and one-half.

The company had decided that it did not need the extra half-hour of work by the janitor after 3:00 P.M. Anyone could shut off the machines and the other janitorial work completed between 3:00 and 3:30 was not essential. The company also noted that the job description for janitor does not call for him to shut off the machines. This duty came within the scope of the provision that the janitor "performs all other work that may be required to carry out the primary function," and the primary function of the janitor was to maintain cleanliness in all departments.

The company argued that cutting down the janitor's workday was well within the management-rights clause that recognizes the right of the company to manage the plant and direct the working forces. The company contended that under this clause management has a right to schedule work except as restricted by agreement, and in this case there was no relevant restriction. The company has the right to curtail or eliminate overtime work in the interest of economy and efficiency. There was nothing in the collective bargaining agreement that deprived management of these rights. It therefore had the right to change the janitor's stopping time and was under no obligation to provide the janitor with overtime work.

DISCUSSION QUESTIONS

1. What is a management-rights clause and what purpose is it intended to serve?

2. What is the significance of the fact that for many years the incumbent of the janitor-watchman position worked 8.5 hours per day and was paid one-half hour overtime each day

even though the contract provided for eight hours per day?

3. Does the provision in which the company recognizes the union as the exclusive bargaining agent for all production and maintenance employees with respect to rates of pay, wages, and hours of employment require the employer to negotiate with the union before changing the hours of work for the janitor-watchman position?

23. How can it be Proven that an Employee Is Sleeping on the Job?

PARTIES: Chevron, U.S.A. Inc. (Salt Lake City Refinery) and Oil, Chemical and Atomic Workers (OCAWIU), Local 2–931.

ISSUE: Did the company violate the Articles of Agreement of OCAWIU and Chevron U.S.A., Inc. by not having just cause when it suspended Sarah Parrish for sleeping on the job on October 29, 1980? If the answer is affirmative, what is the proper remedy under the provisions of the Articles of Agreement?

BACKGROUND

Chevron U.S.A., Inc. operates an oil refinery in Salt Lake City, Utah. On October 29, 1980, Sarah Parrish, an hourly employee at the refinery, was suspended for four days. Later, this suspension was reduced by the company to two days and she received two days back pay. Parrish had been suspended for sleeping on the job. At approximately 4:30 A.M., her supervisor, Harry Bradford, noticed her sitting in a warming booth with her head down. A warming booth looks like a large telephone booth and is used to allow employees to observe refinery operations while protected from inclement weather. The bottom half is made of wood. The top half has windows on all four sides.

Shortly after Bradford's initial observation,

he walked by the warming booth and noticed that Parrish's position had not changed. She was sitting on a chair in the booth with her head and arms resting on a shelf below one of the windows. At this point, Bradford decided that Parrish was sleeping on the job and that discipline was warranted in light of her past work record. Bradford discussed his decision to send Parrish home with his supervisor. When his supervisor concurred with the decision, Bradford returned to the warming booth to find that Parrish was still sitting with her head down. As he entered the booth, Parrish raised her head. Bradford asked her to meet him in his office. During that meeting, Bradford notified Parrish that she was being sent home for that morning's incident of sleeping on the job as well as for previous warnings concerning the same offense. After a review of the matter later that day, the area supervisor made the decision to suspend Parrish for four days. Later on that day, October 29, 1980, Bradford notified Parrish that she was suspended for October 30, and 31 and November 5, and 6, 1980.

Parrish denied that she was sleeping on the job. While acknowledging that she was sitting with her head down, she stated that her eyes were open and that she was watching the refinery equipment located in the area near the warming booth. She disagreed with a number of points raised by the company in conjunction with the

October 29, 1980 incident. Bradford said that her shoes were off and that she was drowsy when he entered the warming booth. Parrish denied both allegations, testifying that she was not drowsy and that while her shoes were unlaced they were still on her feet.

When reaching the decision to suspend Parrish, the company also considered four incidents during the preceding two months in which it was believed she was sleeping on the job. The parties disagreed sharply on their characterizations of three of the four incidents.

On August 27, 1980, at approximately 4:00 A.M., Bradford found Parrish sleeping in the refinery's control laboratory. He woke her up. She stated that she had attended a funeral that day and had not slept. Later on during that shift, Bradford counseled her about sleeping on the job. There was no disagreement between the parties about this incident.

On September 27, 1980, at about 4:00 A.M., Bradford entered the central control room. He noticed that Parrish had her head down on a table. As he came in, another employee nudged Parrish and she raised her head from the table. Nothing was said about sleeping on the job at that time. However, later in the shift, Bradford again counseled her about sleeping on the job. He also told her that stronger discipline could be expected for repeated offenses.

On October 17, 1980, Bradford noticed that the light in the warming booth was out. Upon looking into the booth, he found Parrish sitting on a small, low rack along one wall of the warming booth with her head down on the seat of a chair. As Bradford entered the booth, she raised her head and said, ''I'm not asleep.'' The next evening a similar incident took place. Parrish was down out of sight, sitting on the low rack with her shoes off. She said her shoes hurt so she took them off. At the arbitration hearing, Parrish testified that she had books on the seat of the chair and was studying while sitting on the small, low rack. Since Parrish was in a company training program, studying while on duty was permissible. Bradford testified that he did not see any books.

Based on the incident of October 29, 1980, as well as the previous incidents, Parrish was suspended for four days. After the suspension, the supervisor of the area in which Parrish worked uncovered additional information indicating that a two-day suspension would have been more appropriate. Parrish received two days back pay. Since Parrish held that she was not asleep and that no discipline was warranted, she grieved her two-day suspension.

POSITION OF THE COMPANY

The company held that sleeping on the job is a serious offense warranting discipline. This was particularly true in Parrish's case since she was responsible for the operation of a refinery unit involving high temperatures, high pressures, and hazardous gasses. It was noted that failure to alertly and attentively attend to her responsibilities could bring about serious injuries to herself and fellow employees and severe damage to company facilities.

The company argued that a four-day suspension, later reduced to a two-day suspension, was warranted because of Parrish's unacceptable performance. She had repeatedly been found asleep on the job. It maintained that Bradford had been tolerant and had exercised restraint when dealing with her. He had counseled her about the problem and warned her that more severe actions would be taken in the event of repeated offenses. Given the nature of the offense, the company held that its actions constituted modest and just discipline.

In conclusion, the company held that it had just cause to suspend Parrish and did not violate the labor agreement. It requested that the grievance be denied.

POSITION OF THE UNION

Based on the facts of the case, the union held that Parrish's discipline was unjust. This position was taken for two major reasons. First, the company did not establish that Parrish was sleeping on October 29, 1980. Parrish stated that she was in the control room at 4:10 A.M. only minutes before Bradford claimed that she was sleeping. Also, Parrish looked up and promptly responded as Bradford entered the warming booth. It was also noted that it would be very difficult to sleep in the warming booth because of its shape and size. The union argued that it is improper to discipline workers for *appearing* to be asleep. It is necessary to prove that the employee is sleeping.

Secondly, with the exception of the incident on August 27, 1980, when Parrish acknowledged she was sleeping, the other events did not constitute discipline. Parrish denied that she was sleeping on those occasions. While she was counseled, she was not disciplined. In the absence of disciplinary action, there was no basis for her to protest these events even though she disagreed with Bradford's contentions.

In light of these circumstances, the union requested the Board of Arbitration to sustain the grievance. As a remedy, the union asked the Board of Arbitration to make whole Parrish for the two days' pay lost due to the suspension and that the letter in her personnel file referencing the suspension be expunged.

DISCUSSION QUESTIONS

1. Who has the burden of proof in this case? Must Parrish prove that she was not sleeping or must the company establish that she was? What is the appropriate standard of proof used in this type of case?

2. Based on the information provided by the parties, did the company act reasonably when it concluded that Parrish was sleeping?

3. Did Parrish's suspension violate the tenets of progressive discipline?

4. Was the company's decision to suspend Parrish reasonable? Were there grounds for the Board of Arbitration to set aside the company's decision?

24. Who Unloads the Trucks at Away Football Games?

PARTIES: The University of Pittsburgh and Service Employees International Union, Local 29.

ISSUE: The question before the arbitrator was whether Local 29 personnel were entitled to accompany equipment to away games when such equipment is shipped by truck?

BACKGROUND

The University of Pittsburgh commonly utilized its own truck to transport equipment to away football games when those games were relatively close to Pittsburgh. For example, when away games were played in places such as Annapolis, Maryland; State College, Pennsylvania; Morgantown, West Virginia; or South Bend, Indiana, the university trucked its own equipment to the games. When travel to games was by airplane, the truck was loaded at the Pittsburgh campus and transported to the airport where it was unloaded by employees covered by the labor agreement with Local 29.

During the 1978 football season, equipment was transported by truck to two away games. Local 29 employees loaded the truck but when the truck reached its destination, the equipment was unloaded and then reloaded after the game by nonbargaining unit personnel.

THE POSITION OF THE UNION

The union contended that Article 2 of the labor agreement preserved the work of loading and unloading university trucks for Local 29. The labor agreement referred to "various classifications," one of which is groundkeeper. The university acknowledged that workers in the groundkeeper classification were responsible for loading and unloading trucks. The union pointed out that Local 29 personnel have traveled to away games in the past to handle the unloading and loading of the football team's equipment. However, there was no clearly established practice concerning the use of university personnel in away game situations.

The union maintained that the university's argument that it is not economical to send Local 29 personnel with the trucks is not valid. It was argued that economic problems do not give the university the right to have work performed by nonbargaining unit personnel.

As a remedy, Local 29 requested that the university be directed to have bargaining unit personnel accompany the university truck to away games and that one person be paid the wages that he or she would have earned had bargaining unit personnel accompanied the truck to away games for the 1978 season.

POSITION OF THE UNIVERSITY

According to the university, Local 29 employees accompanied the truck to away games on only three occasions in the preceding 29 years. It was the position of the university that three occasions do not constitute a practice that is binding upon the university. The university also pointed out that no such trips had been made during the terms of the last two agreements with the union, but that no grievances had been filed and the union had never brought the matter up during negotiations. The university held that sending an employee along with the truck would be too expensive and that it is clearly the right of the university to have the work done in the most efficient manner possible.

RELEVANT CONTRACT LANGUAGE

The following provisions found in the labor agreement between the parties are relevant to this case:

Section 2.1 — The University hereby recognizes and acknowledges the union as the sole and exclusive bargaining representative of all employees working the various classifications in the operation and maintenance of all school and administration buildings, student housing facilities, athletic facilities, plants and adjacent grounds owned and operated by the University and the city of Pittsburgh. This provision shall apply to all present and subsequently acquired

building facilities and grounds by the University that are used for school purposes. It shall not apply to building and/or grounds acquired for investment purposes.

Section 13.10 — The job duties to be performed by the employees in the various job classifications shall be substantially the same as in the past. If substantial changes are made in the regular job duties and requirements of any job, either the union or University may propose a revision of the wage rates for that job. If the parties are unable to mutually agree, such matters shall be handled in accordance with the grievance procedures as set forth in this agreement.

Section 13.13 — No benefits, prerogatives or other substantial rights to which any employee shall be legally entitled at the time of the execution of this agreement, shall be abridged, or otherwise effected except by the terms hereof, and the same shall remain intact and in full force and in effect.

Section 23.1 — Subject only to the limitations stated in this agreement, the University shall have the exclusive right to manage and operate its business and operations in such a manner as it sees fit including (but not limited to) the right to determine the methods and means by which its operations are to be carried on, to direct the work force, and to conduct its operation in an efficient manner.

DISCUSSION QUESTIONS

1. What constitutes a binding past practice?

2. Evaluate the position of the union.

3. Evaluate the position of the university.

4. How would you decide this case?

25. When can an Arbitrator Set Aside Company Disciplinary Actions?

PARTIES: Safeway Stores, Inc. and United Food and Commercial Workers, Local 7.

ISSUE: Was the grievant, Sharon Oman, discharged for good and sufficient cause? If not, what is the appropriate remedy?

BACKGROUND

Sharon Oman worked as an all-purpose clerk at one of Safeway Stores, Inc.'s retail grocery stores located in Sterling, Colorado. On July 17, 1981, she was working as a checker. At approximately 8:20 P.M., Oman sold a six-pack of beer to Tito Valenzuela. Valenzuela was only 16 years old at the time. In Colorado, it is illegal to sell beer to anyone under the age of 18. Later that evening, Valenzuela was picked up by the Sterling police, who found the beer in his possession.

When Oman reported to work on Sunday, July 19, she was informed about the Friday evening incident and was instructed to go to the police station at 2:00 P.M. that day. After discussing the matter with the police, Oman was issued a summons for selling beer to a minor.

After work on Monday, July 20, 1981, at approximately midnight, Oman was terminated by the store manager, Bruce Garnett. Earlier that day, Garnett discussed the matter with Frank Andrews, the district manager. In turn, Andrews discussed the situation with Steve Stilpen, employee relations manager for the company's Denver district. It was decided that the sale of beer to a minor was a serious violation of company rules and that termination was warranted. Stilpen reported that other employees had been terminated (but not in the Denver region) for selling beer to minors and those terminations were not grieved.

Subsequent to her discharge, Oman was found guilty of violating Colorado state liquor laws and was given six months probation. The company pled guilty to the illegal sale of beer to minors and had its liquor license suspended for three days. The suspension was for a weekend, when beer sales are greatest. Also, the incident received local newspaper coverage.

Oman's termination was grieved on the grounds that there was not sufficient cause for the action as required by the labor agreement.

POSITION OF THE COMPANY

The company pointed out that the Colorado state liquor laws forbid the sale of beer to minors (those under the age of 18). Further, the company has a rule concerning this subject. The policy states in part:

> . . . there will be a possibility of termination for any employee knowingly or unknowingly selling beer to a minor.

Oman signed a statement at the time she was hired acknowledging that she had read and was familiar with the policy concerning the sale of beer to minors. The practical effect of the company's policy was to require employees to request picture identification if they had any doubt concerning the age of the customer attempting to purchase beer. If the customer did not have the required identification, the manager on duty was to be called to handle the matter. Because of the seriousness of the policy for the minor involved, the public, and the company, employees violating the rule are terminated.

In the case at hand, it was established that Oman sold beer to a minor. By not asking Valenzuela for identification, Oman violated Colorado law and store policy. She was found guilty of the violation, as was the company. Given that the company has the rule, had informed the employees about the rule, periodically reminded the workers of the rule, and consistently enforced the rule, the decision to terminate was warranted.

The company emphasized that Andrew's decision to terminate Oman was proper. The decision was consistent with other discharges attributable to the sale of beer to minors. Also, these other incidents had not been grieved. Despite the fact that Oman was an extremely good employee, the consistent application of the rule required that she be terminated. For these reasons, the company requested the arbitrator to deny the grievance.

POSITION OF THE UNION

The union argued that the termination of Oman was not warranted in light of the facts of this case. Oman was an excellent employee who inadvertently sold beer to a minor. On two earlier occasions on July 17, 1981, Oman requested the assistance of the manager on duty to handle cases in which the customer could not provide adequate proof of age. In the incident leading to her discharge, Oman did not ask for identification because Valenzuela looked more than 18 years old. Even the judge who found Oman guilty of the li-

quor law violation commented that he could understand how she could think Valenzuela was older than he really was. The union argued that the company's policy allows the employee to exercise discretion when requesting identification. A memo dated January 20, 1981, from the company to all employees concerning the sale of alcohol to minors established a new rule and stated in part:

> Identification should be checked on all individuals where there is a possibility of being under age. Although the employee is responsible for making the transaction, the company also has the responsibility to see that the law is obeyed.

> Effective immediately, there will be a possibility of termination for an employee knowingly or unknowingly selling beer to a minor.

This rule was distributed to all stores. Employees were asked to sign it. The union noted that the memo stated that "identification should be checked on all individuals where there is a possibility of being under age." It was argued that this language means that identification is requested if there is doubt concerning the customer's age. In this case, Oman did not doubt Valenzuela's age.

The union emphasized that Oman did not know Valenzuela, had not seen him before July 17, 1981, did not remember selling beer to him, and pled not guilty to the charge of selling beer to a minor. This indicated that Oman believed Valenzuela was of age and that identification was not needed.

The union also argued that termination was not the only penalty available under the company's policy. Prior to the distribution of the memo quoted above, another rule was publicized. This earlier version stated, in effect, that employees would be terminated for selling beer to minors. When employees refused to sign a statement acknowledging their understanding of the rule, the company revised the policy. This revised version became the memo cited above. Based on this change in the policy statement, the union urged the arbitrator to reject the company's claim that termination was the only appropriate penalty in this case. The union also argued that the company did not show that other employees had been terminated for violating the policy regarding the sale of beer to minors. The union pointed out that the issue had not previously arisen within its jurisdiction, the state of Colorado. Therefore any claim by the company that other terminations were not grieved is irrelevant.

As a remedy, the union requested the arbitrator to reinstate Oman to her former position as an all-purpose clerk. The union also requested that the reinstatement be made with back pay, interest, and no loss of seniority and benefits. Finally, Oman's personnel record should be purged of any mention of this matter.

DISCUSSION QUESTIONS

1. Did Oman commit an offense warranting discipline?

2. Was the rule under which Oman was terminated worded specifically enough so that it could be enforceable?

3. How would you decide this case? If you decide that the termination was not for good and sufficient cause, how can you defend your decision to set aside the company's action in this matter?

4. If you decide that the discharge was not for good and sufficient cause, what is the appropriate remedy?

26. Seniority versus Merit When Making Promotions

PARTIES: Decker Coal Company and the Progressive Mine Workers of America.

ISSUE: Did the company act properly and within the terms of the labor agreement by promoting two employees (Bob Temple and Tom Gray) with less seniority than the grievant as a result of a job posting on August 23, 1978?

BACKGROUND

Decker Coal Company operates two open pit coal mines in southeast Montana. On August 23, 1978, the company posted a notice to solicit bids for two plant oiler positions. Plant oilers are responsible for lubricating all the equipment in a coal loading facility. The posting elicited bids from five employees. On August 30, 1978, the plant oiler positions were awarded to Tom Gray and Bob Temple. Sutton, the grievant in this case, did not receive the plant oiler position for which he had bid. Rather, he was awarded an oil spray serviceman position, another job for which he bid on August 23, 1978. Oil spray servicemen maintain the oil spray system in the coal loading facility. It pays a lower wage than the plant oiler position. When Sutton asked why two less senior employees received the plant oiler jobs, he was told that Gray and Temple had more skill and

ability for the job. Since Section VI(A) of the labor agreement between the parties specifies that seniority will determine promotions only when qualifications and requisite skill and ability are the same between candidates for the job, the work histories of Sutton, Gray, and Temple must be reviewed.

Sutton was hired as a laborer on August 4, 1976. He worked in that capacity until he was laid-off on December 3, 1976. He was subsequently recalled from layoff on February 28, 1977. From February 28, 1977, to November 28, 1977, he worked in several capacities as a laborer. Initially, he worked on the crew installing the plant's oil spray system. Subsequent to completion of the system in mid-August 1977, he worked as a plant laborer and extra laborer. On November 28, 1977, Sutton was reassigned as a rotary drill helper, a position for which he had successfully bid. He worked as a rotary drill helper until August 30, 1978. On August 23, 1978, he bid for two positions. His first choice was a plant oiler position and his second choice was a job as an oil spray serviceman. On August 30, 1978, he was awarded the oil spray serviceman position.

The work histories of Gray and Temple were quite similar. In anticipation of the opening of a second coal loading facility due to mine expansion, the company embarked on a training program to ensure that an adequate number of employees would be prepared to staff the new facility. Gray and Temple were part of this program. Gray was hired as a plant laborer on April 10, 1978, and was promoted to oil spray serviceman on June 12, 1978. Like Sutton, he bid on the plant oiler position on August 23, 1978. On August 30, 1978, he was awarded the plant oiler position. Temple was hired April 5, 1978, became an oil spray serviceman on June 12, 1978, and then advanced to a plant oiler position on August 30, 1978, as a result of successfully bidding on the job on August 23, 1978.

Sutton grieved the promotion of Temple and Gray, both less senior employees than himself, to the plant oiler positions on August 30, 1978. Sutton considered himself qualified for the plant oiler position, and therefore, believed he should have been awarded the position based on his greater seniority. The company disagreed, contending Temple and Gray were more skilled for the plant oiler position.

RELEVANT CONTRACT LANGUAGE

The following provision contained in the labor agreement is relevant to this decision:

SECTION VI

Seniority

(A) Promotions shall be made by the company on the basis of seniority, qualifications and requisite skill and ability to perform the job assigned. In the event the company determines that the qualifications and requisite skill and ability are the same as between two candidates for the promotion, seniority shall be the determinative factor.

The company agrees to post a notice of a job vacancy five (5) days on the bulletin board provided for employee notices, before it is filled. Those employees interested in applying for the job must complete a qualification form and turn the form into the personnel manager in the Decker Mine office. An employee must be in classification thirty (30) days before bidding on a new job. The company will make a selection to fill such vacancy based on experience, ability, and seniority from the interested employees if qualified, and they will be given a reasonable trial period of not to exceed ten (10) days. If such employee does not qualify in the vacancy or new position within the reasonable time, the employee shall be returned to his original position. The company may fill a vacancy on a temporary basis not to exceed ten (10) days with an employee of its choice before posting a notice of a job vacancy.

POSITION OF THE UNION

Sutton acknowledged that oil spray servicemen have a better opportunity to learn the plant oiler job than individuals working in other positions outside the coal loading facility and that the custom was to progress from plant laborer, to oil spray serviceman, to plant oiler. Sutton contended, however, that although he had not worked as an oil spray serviceman, he had the ability to work as a plant oiler as a result of other experiences. He maintained that he was already familiar with the oil spray system as a result of working as a laborer on the system's installation. He also testified that when employed as an extra laborer, he was exposed to all parts of the coal loading facility and had the opportunity to work with plant oilers.

In addition to Sutton's testimony, other union witnesses testified concerning Sutton's character. One employee testified he was impressed by Sutton's willingness to learn, his interest in his job, and that Sutton was as intelligent and ambitious as other workers. Another employee testified that Sutton was eager to learn and that he was a real handyman. The thrust of this line of testimony was that Sutton was willing and able to learn a job even though he may not have been formally exposed to it.

Shortly after Sutton became an oil spray serviceman, he had the opportunity to work as a plant oiler. Between September 5, 1978, and September 15, 1978, Sutton worked as a plant oiler. Sutton testified that he had no problems fulfilling the plant oiler's responsibilities during this period. Kercher, the plant operator who was responsible for running the coal loading facility, stated that during this time period Sutton did a good job as a plant oiler. The union argued that this favorable experience as a plant oiler supported Sutton's claim that he was able to perform the job.

In conclusion, it was the position of the union that Sutton had the ability to do the job as a plant oiler, and therefore, should have been promoted to plant oiler being that he had more seniority than Gray and Temple. Based on the company's failure to comply with Section VI(A), the union requested that Sutton be made a plant oiler and that a back-pay award be granted representing the difference in pay between a plant oiler and oil spray serviceman.

POSITION OF THE COMPANY

The company argued that Section VI(A) established that seniority is a factor in granting promotions only when the company decides that the qualifications and requisite skills and abilities of the employees bidding on the job are equal. The company maintained it did not violate the labor agreement by promoting Temple and Gray since they were more qualified to work as plant oilers. This position was taken for two related reasons.

First, the normal progression for an employee in a plant is to go from laborer to oil spray serviceman to plant oiler. While Gray and Temple went through this progression of jobs, Sutton did not. This sequence of jobs is designed so that employees in one category work closely with and periodically substitute for workers in the next higher job classification. Through this procedure, employees can acquire the skills needed to perform the next higher job in the hierarchy of coal loading facility positions.

The second reason for the company to conclude that Temple and Gray should get the promotion was that they had participated in an accel-

erated training program designed to ensure an adequate supply of new personnel when the new coal handling facility became operational. Sutton had not participated in the program. Since November 28, 1977, Sutton had been working as a rotary drill helper, a position that did not provide training opportunities for the plant oiler position. The rotary drill helper works in the mine itself drilling holes as part of the blasting operation. The company noted that while Sutton had probably worked, on occasion, as an oil spray serviceman while employed as a laborer, this experience was almost one year old. Temple's and Gray's experience and training occurred immediately before their bidding on the plant oiler positions.

Finally, the company argued that little weight should be given to the fact that Sutton adequately served as a plant oiler subsequent to his assumption of oil spray serviceman responsibilities on August 30, 1978. This position was taken for two reasons. First, Sutton's 11 days of work as a plant oiler are not comparable to Temple's and Gray's months of exposure to plant oiler responsibilities. Secondly, the company maintained that the work experience was irrelevant being that it was not available to the company when it was deciding who would fill the plant oiler positions. The company held that it can consider only the facts available at the time of the decision when evaluating employees for promotion.

In conclusion, the company argued that it acted within its rights under the labor agreement in awarding the plant oiler positions to Temple and Gray rather than to Sutton.

DISCUSSION QUESTIONS

1. What factors must be given consideration under Section VI(A) when making promotion decisions? What is the relative weight given to these factors?

2. How should the term "skill and ability are the same between two candidates" be inter-

preted? Does it mean exactly the same or is there some variance?

3. Who has the burden of proof in this case? Must management justify its actions or must Sutton prove that his qualifications are the same as those of Gray and Temple?

4. Evaluate the company's reasons for by-passing Sutton and promoting less senior em-

ployees to the vacant plant oiler positions. Do these arguments justify the company's decisions in this matter?

5. What weight, if any, should be given to the fact that Sutton successfully filled the plant oiler's position shortly after he was denied the position through the bidding procedure?

6. How would you decide this case?

27. Is This a Layoff?

PARTIES: Decker Coal Company and the Progressive Mine Workers of America.

ISSUE: Was the company required to use the layoff procedure contained in the labor agreement in order to handle the short-term production shutdowns?

BACKGROUND

This case involves 19 grievances filed on January 18 and 19, 1978. The grievances arose out of a procedure implemented by the Decker Coal Company to scale down the work force during periods when coal could not be shipped from its Decker, Montana mine.

During the winter of 1977–78, a shortage of trains provided the company by the Burlington Northern Railroad precluded the shipping of all the coal that could be mined for which purchase commitments existed. Reasons cited for not receiving an adequate supply of trains included a shortage of engines and coal cars, weather problems, and the upgrading of railroad track.

Because of the shortage of coal trains, the company was unable to maintain a level of operations that would require the services of its complete work force on certain days. Once the storage areas and coal silos were full, the company had to curtail coal mining and hauling operations. The mine would then operate at less than full capacity until coal trains could be obtained from Burlington Northern. Production slowdowns could be for a half shift or a full shift, but typically not longer.

The effects of the curtailed production were most strongly felt by the coal production crews (i.e., the job classifications responsible for mining, hauling, and shipping the coal). During the typical idle period, there was enough work available to keep the maintenance and overburden removal crews fully employed.

When it became apparent to the company that there would not be trains available to ship coal on a particular day, a decision was made by mine management to either add to the stockpile or curtail production. If the decision was to cut back on production, the coal production crew would either be sent home before completion of their regularly scheduled shift and/or told not to report to work on their next scheduled shift. As previously mentioned, the effect of this procedure was to limit the workweek of the coal production crews while leaving other groups, such as maintenance and overburden crews, relatively unaffected. This was the problem. While higher seniority employees on coal production crews were having their workweek shortened with a resulting decrease in pay, lower seniority workers on the maintenance and overburden crews were not experiencing any cutbacks.

Nineteen coal production crew employees grieved this situation, arguing that Section VI(B) of the labor agreement concerned with the application of seniority to layoff situations should be applied. In general, this meant that more senior production crew employees could bump less senior employees on crews unaffected by the production slowdown. The company maintained that the production cutbacks and the ensuing shortening of the workweek were not layoffs as envisioned by the labor agreement, and therefore, seniority did not have to be used.

RELEVANT CONTRACT LANGUAGE

The following provisions in the labor agreement are relevant to this case:

SECTION III

General
(C) The union and the company recognize that subject to the specific provisions of this agreement, and the employee's right to adjust grievances as provided herein, the management of the company and its property including but not limited to improvement in method, business practices, technological changes, as well as direction of the work force, and the right to employ, assign, promote, discipline, discharge, and lay off employees are vested in and reserved by the company.

SECTION VI

Seniority
(B) Layoffs because of lack of work shall be made by the company on the basis of seniority and qualifications and requisite skill and ability of employees. In the event the qualifications and skill and ability are equal, seniority shall be the determining factor in the layoff. The determination of requisite qualifications, skills and ability shall be the sole prerogative of the employer, subject to the grievance procedure in the Agreement.

When laid-off employees are to be recalled, those employees most recently laid-off on account of curtailment of work shall be the first to be re-employed provided they are physically qualified to return to work.

(H) When an employee returns to work after a layoff, the company will give the employee and the local union five (5) working days written notice to be sent to his last known address informing him of the company's need for such employee to return to work. Upon failure to return to work after the above requirements have been carried out by the company, all seniority rights shall be forfeited.

POSITION OF THE UNION

The grievants in this case believed that Section VI(B) was violated when less senior workers performing jobs, for which the grievants were qualified, were allowed to work while the grievants were losing time due to production shutdowns. Testimony at the arbitration hearing indicated that workers lost between approximately 40 and 140 hours of work due to the production cutbacks. The union argued that whenever workers are sent home before the scheduled end of the shift or told not to report to work, they have been laid-off, and consequently, Section VI(B) would be applicable. Since the company failed to implement a procedure that would allow more senior coal production crew employees to bump less senior workers on crews unaffected by the production cutback, the union argued the company violated Section VI(B).

POSITION OF THE COMPANY

The company argued that the temporary production shutdowns experienced as a result of the unavailability of coal trains are not subject to Sections VI(B) and VI(H) of the labor agreement. The company indicated that the production shutdowns were beyond the control of the company. The company was notified daily by Burlington

Northern concerning the number of trains to be expected that day. Sometimes an adequate number of trains would arrive at the plant. On other days, however, too few or no trains would arrive. Also, the daily number of train arrivals was an independent event, that is, the number of trains arriving on one day did not appear to influence the number of trains arriving on subsequent days.

The company also argued that the short duration of the production shutdowns (one day or less for a given crew) precluded the application of Section VI(B) and VI(H) of the labor agreement. Section VI(B) requires that layoffs be made on the basis of qualifications and requisite skill and ability as well as seniority. The company maintained that it could take days to evaluate the affected employees' qualifications. Also, under Section VI(H), recalled employees would have up to five days to report back to work. Since it is quite likely that the mine would be operating at full capacity the day after a shutdown, the company argued that it did not have the luxury of waiting as many as five days for employees to return to work.

Finally, the company contended that Section VI(B) and VI(H) did not apply to coal crew shutdowns that were the subject of this arbitration. The company maintained that Section VI(B) and VI(H) clearly comtemplated a layoff situation where the company is able to plan and control the amount of work to be performed.

Despite this position, the company attempted to implement a union-proposed bumping system that allowed more senior employees to bump less senior employees within the same job classification. This procedure did not prove workable because there was, typically, very little time to determine who was going to be bumped and then notify them not to report to work.

Even if the bumping procedure could be made operational, the company held that other problems existed that argued against its implementation. The company maintained that the reassignment of workers during temporary shutdowns would lead to a decline in efficiency, impair plant safety, and would be plagued by logistic problems as workers were moved around the mine site.

In lieu of the union-proposed in-class bumping system, the company attempted to implement a bumping system under which more senior coal production crew employees could bump less senior laborers. The company concluded that this procedure was also too complex given the limited amount of time available to implement it once the need for a temporary shutdown became apparent.

In conclusion, the company held that it made a good faith effort to implement a bumping procedure allowing seniority to be reflected in temporary shutdown decisions. More important, however, was the argument that the company was not contractually bound by Section VI(B) and VI(H) of the labor agreement given the temporary and unplanned nature of the coal production crew shutdowns.

DISCUSSION QUESTIONS

1. Do the short-term cutbacks constitute a layoff within the meaning of the labor agreement between the parties?

2. What are the implications for the union and the company of applying bumping language to short-term layoff situations as found in this case?

3. If the contract is silent with respect to the bumping of junior employees by senior employees during short-term cutbacks, is the company obligated to allow bumping since it is used in long-term layoffs? In other words, how does the reserved rights theory apply to this case?

4. How would you decide this case?

28. Can a Company Tell its Employees to be Clean Shaven?

PARTIES: Allied Chemical Corporation, Industrial Chemical Division, Syracuse Works and United Steel Workers of America, Local 12457.

ISSUE: Did the company have just and proper cause to suspend and terminate Roscoe Harding, Grady Masters, and Benny Shanahan, effective October 22, 1979, for failure to shave their beards? If not, what shall be the remedy?

BACKGROUND

The three grievants in this case, all employees of the Allied Chemical Corp., Industrial Chemical Div., Syracuse Works, were first suspended for ten days and then terminated for failure to comply with a company directive to shave their full-face beards by October 22, 1979. The company held that the absolute prohibition of beards announced on October 12, 1979, was mandated by safety considerations, and therefore, was a reasonable exercise of managerial authority. The company maintained that no exceptions to this rule would be made for the three bearded employees involved in this case. The union insisted that the blanket prohibition against all beards was unreasonably broad on the surface. The union argued further that the rule was particularly unreasonable when applied against the three grievants.

The company's motivation for limiting facial hair was based on safety-related concerns and not on the matters of personal appearance or grooming that are frequently raised in other cases involving no-beard rules. From its inception, the policy banning beards was derived directly from the company's rules and policies concerning the use of respirators and other breathing apparatus. Prior to 1979, limitations on beards because of respirator use were restricted to certain areas of the Syracuse Works known as "respirator areas." Employees working in the designated respirator areas were not to wear facial hair, which interfered with the seal around the respirator's face mask. The employees working in locations not designated as respirator areas were not prohibited from wearing facial hair, including beards.

Roscoe Harding, who began working at the company in 1966, wore a full beard during the last eight years of his employment. Since 1976, he worked as a utility man in the Stores Section. Most of his time was spent in an area known as the oil house. The oil house was not designated as a respirator area. Harding claimed that in the past he declined promotion opportunities in order to avoid working in respirator areas because he did not want to cut off his beard. Grady Masters, the second grievant in this case, sported a full beard when he began working for the Syracuse

Works in 1973 and continued to wear it while working at various positions at the company. At the time the grievance arose, Masters was working in the Calcium Chloride (CC) area. As with the Stores Section, the CC section had not been designated as a respirator area at the time of the grievance. Neither Masters nor Harding had been required to carry or wear a respirator in the course of their regular duties. Harding apparently was issued a respirator nearly two years before his termination and Masters was issued one in January 1979. However, neither grievant received instructions on when to use the respirator or the techniques for using it. With respect to the third grievant, Benny Shanahan, the record did not establish his employment history. However, it did indicate that he worked on the coal gang in the Power House section at the time that the grievance arose.

During the period between June 1977 through February 1978, the Syracuse Works was the subject of an intensive on-site inspection by OSHA. Following that inspection, OSHA notified the company in April 1978 that it was liable for a number of safety and health violations. Included among those citations were several related to inadequate maintenance, selection, and placement of equipment in several respirator areas. In addition, OSHA found that the training of personnel in the use of respirators had been inadequate. The company was ordered to correct these cited deficiencies.

Immediately after receiving the citation, the company notified the union that progressive discipline would be used against employees who violated safety regulations. The part of the memo pertinent to this case read as follows:

> Gentlemen:
> The Syracuse Works has been cited and fined by the Occupational Safety and Health Administration for specific violations related to contaminant overexposures such as noise, dust, coal tar pitch volatiles, and ammonia. These citations are the result of the recent six month, wall-to-wall,

OSHA investigation. These citations mandate immediate compliance. Failure to comply with this mandate will result in more severe penalties to the company up to and including the potential closing of the plant.

Effective immediately all employees affected by the respirator and hearing protection requirements listed on the attached sheet *will* use the personal protection equipment provided them (including ear plugs/muffs and/or respirators while working in designated areas).

This letter is to advise you that employees who fail to comply, thereby jeopardizing not only their own health but the integrity of the plant, will be subject to progressive disciplinary action, including discharge. The following procedure will be followed:

First offense — written warning

Second offense — one day suspension

Third offense — three day suspension

Fourth offense — discharge

Because of the serious consequences of noncompliance to the company an employee will be entered into the program with the first violation and there will be no provision for regressing to an earlier step of the program over a period of time.

These citations have been issued by OSHA with the employees' welfare in mind. Compliance not only assures the stability for the Works but protects employees from possible long-term effects to their health. The Union's cooperation in encouraging compliance with these new requirements regarding use of respirators and hearing protection is essential to the success of these industrial hygiene programs.

Employees in all designated respirator areas were ordered to use the protective equipment provided them. This policy of more stringent enforcement of existing respirator requirements constituted no change in the existing beard policy and employees outside designated respirator areas continued to wear their beards without limitation by the company. While the union did not necessarily agree with the progressive discipline system, it did not dispute the fact that beards should not be worn in respirator areas. After further study, the company expanded its list of designated respirator areas in June 1979. The Power House section where Benny Shanahan was employed was so designated, but the Stores Section employing Harding and the CC section where Masters worked were not designated as respirator areas. Over time, additional areas were designated as needing respirator equipment. Individualized respirator standard operating procedures were developed for each new respirator area in the plant. At the time of the arbitration not all areas of the Syracuse Works had had respirator standard operating procedures developed for them. Work on this project was ongoing.

In January 1979 the General Manager of the Syracuse Works posted the following notice:

FACIAL HAIR AND THE SYRACUSE WORKS RESPIRATOR PROGRAM

A revised respirator program has been written and approved for the Syracuse Works concerning the use of all respiratory protective equipment including disposable dust masks, half masks, cartridge respirators, full-face gas masks, or self-contained breathing apparatus. On the basis of this program, requirements for the use of respirators throughout the plant are being reevaluated and it is anticipated that most Works personnel will be required to be able to use respirators from time to time, at least in emergencies.

For this reason I am restating the Syracuse Works policy regarding facial hair: Hair lying between the sealing surface of a respirator face piece and the wearer's skin prevents a good seal. This results in leakage of contaminated air into the respirator as the user inhales. As a result, the respirator is rendered less effective. This can cause over-exposure which in some cases could be extremely hazardous. For this reason, facial hair which interferes with the proper sealing of

breathing equipment is not permitted. Specifically, beards and goatees must be shaved off and mustaches and sideburns must be trimmed so as not to extend into the sealing surface area.

This requirement applies to all Syracuse Works employees.

After the notice of January 1979 was posted, Harding and Masters were encouraged by their foremen to shave their beards. Both declined to do so. From January to October 1979, the company did not enforce a blanket prohibition on beards but rather continued the former policy of permitting employees to have beards in areas other than those in which respirators were required. The record of this case showed that at least one employee in the Stores Section where Mr. Harding worked shaved his beard when the January 1979 policy first was announced. However, he grew it back after a grievance was filed in the machine shop. In January 1979 two employees in the machine shop filed grievances protesting an order to shave their beards. Those grievances were denied by their foremen but were settled at the next level when the company responded as follows:

> With current guidelines in regard to the respirator program and since your job does not require you to use a respirator, facial hair will be allowed.

Over the next several months, respirator standard operating procedures were developed for each area within the plant. Additionally, individualized fitting of respirators and training of employees was undertaken. For approximately the first week of training, the company followed a policy of gradual enforcement of the no-beard rule through education about the rule banning facial hair. If employees in the training program designed to implement the respirator standard operating procedure for their work area were found to have a beard, the employees were sent back to their foremen without being fitted for a respirator. The foremen were ordered not to let the employees work in respirator areas. Employees would be sent back for respirator fitting and training only after the beards were shaved. The record for this case established that under this procedure approximately 20 employees shaved their beards and then were fitted for respirators. The record did not indicate that any of these employees grieved this process of enforcement of the beard policy as specified in January 1979.

Someone in management apparently decided that sending employees with beards back to their foremen and not allowing them to be trained until their beards were shaved was unwieldy and inconvenient. It was decided that the policy of selective prohibition followed since the grievance of January 1979 was administratively unwieldy and also unfair to those employees who had shaved their beards in order to wear respirators. Therefore the company issued a memo dated October 12, 1979, that announced the following rule regarding beards:

BEARD POLICY

The Syracuse Works is now in a position to comply with OSHA regulations, in particular related to respirator areas. Employees have been and are being properly trained in the use of respirators as well as medically certified. These efforts are all in the employees best interest and the ability of the employee to wear the same will become a plant-wide condition of employment.

Therefore, effective Monday, October 22, 1979, 8 A.M., beards will no longer be permitted to be worn by any employee.

The effect of this policy was to enforce a blanket prohibition on beards without regard to the work area or previously established needs for respirator usage. Benny Shanahan in the Power Plant (a designated respirator area) and Roscoe Harding and Grady Masters in the nondesignated Stores and CC Sections, respectively, were all ordered to shave their beards by their foremen.

Each of them failed to do so by the company's deadline of October 22, 1979. On that date, each of the grievants was suspended from work and was sent home with directions to shave their beards before reporting back to duty. Identical grievances were filed by each of the employees on October 22, 1979, protesting the beard policy of October 12, 1979, and his suspension thereunder. When the grievants continued in their refusal to shave their beards, they were terminated as of November 7, 1979.

POSITIONS OF THE PARTIES

The positions of the parties were relatively straightforward in this case. The union argued that the rule dated October 12, 1979, was too broad to be enforceable. It was held that the absolute ban on all beards without any consideration for an employee's demonstrated actual or potential need to wear a respirator was unenforceable. The union held that the October 12, 1979, rule, unlike the January 1979 rule, was divorced from any underlying rationale and justification that could give it validity. Because the rule was unreasonable, the union argued that it was improper for the company to terminate the three grievants for violation of the rule.

The company argued that beards interfere with the quality of the face mask seal available when a respirator is used. As a result, the health and safety workers using respirators on a regular basis or in an emergency situation are jeopardized if employees are allowed to wear beards. The company pointed out that it has contractual and managerial obligations, as well as legal and moral responsibilities, to provide a safe working environment for its employees. As a result, the company has the right and obligation to promulgate reasonable safety rules (such as the no-beard policy) and to enforce these rules, if necessary, through the use of the discipline system. Further, the company argued that the January 1979 policy that allowed for beards in some parts of the plant was administratively inconvenient and adversely affected employee morale. For these reasons, the company held that the no-beard rule was reasonable and enforceable and that the terminations of Roscoe Harding, Grady Masters, and Benny Shanahan were for just and proper cause.

DISCUSSION QUESTIONS

1. What are the attributes of a reasonable rule?

2. Was the no-beard policy of October 12, 1979, reasonable? Defend your position.

3. Should the terminations of the three grievants be upheld? Why?

29. Is This Case Arbitrable?

PARTIES: Associated Grocers of Colorado, Inc. and International Brotherhood of Teamsters, Chauffers, Warehousemen, and Helpers of America, Local 492.

ISSUE: Is this case arbitrable on the grounds that in late July or early August 1979 the company was informed by the union that the grievance was being withdrawn?

BACKGROUND

On June 1, 1979, Brent Hand was discharged from his position at Associated Grocers of Colorado, Inc.'s warehouse in Denver, Colorado. At about that time, a grievance was filed claiming the discharge was not for just cause. On June 8, 1979, and June 29, 1979, the union sent letters to the company advising it that the grievance would be taken to arbitration. After the June 29 letter, Donald Beavers, director of personnel relations for the company contacted Henry Weeks, secretary-treasurer of the union regarding the grievance. According to Beavers, Weeks asked for a week or two to review the case with his associates. Approximately two or three weeks later, a business agent of the union called the company's manager of Warehousing and Transportation, and advised him that the grievance was being withdrawn. Similar informa-

tion was given to the company at a grievance meeting approximately one week later.

According to company testimony, no further discussions occurred between the company and the union concerning Hand's grievance until October 17, 1979. At that time, the local union's attorney informed Beavers that the grievance was being taken to arbitration.

The union business agent who allegedly advised the company that this grievance was being withdrawn was no longer representing the union in October 1979.

RELEVANT CONTRACT PROVISIONS

The following contract language found in the agreement between the parties is relevant to this decision:

> ### ARTICLE 6.
> ### GRIEVANCES AND ARBITRATION.
>
> *Grievances.*
> All alleged disputes, differences or grievances respecting the interpretation, intent or meaning of this Agreement shall be handled in accordance with the terms of this Article.
>
> Unless the Union first contacts the Employer regarding any such alleged dispute, difference or grievance within ten (10) days following the date of its occurrence, it shall be deemed null and void. However, if the Union does contact the

Employer regarding any such alleged dispute, difference or grievance within said (10) days, representatives of the Employer and representatives of the Union shall get together and consider it at a meeting to be held within fifteen (15) days following the Union's contacting the Employer. If the matter is not settled to the satisfaction of the Union at this meeting, then, and in that event, the Union shall have the right to submit the alleged dispute, difference or grievance, in writing, to the Company and request arbitration in accord with the procedure set forth in the following subparagraph of this Article 6, entitled "Arbitration," provided it makes a written request to do so within fifteen (15) days following said meeting.

Arbitration.

In the event that an alleged dispute, difference or grievance respecting the interpretation, intent or meaning of this Agreement arises during the life of this Agreement, which cannot be satisfactorily settled through the grievance procedure set out directly above, there shall be no lockout, strike, stoppage of work, slowdown, boycott or picket; but the Union shall have the right to submit the matter for final decision to an arbitrator to be chosen as follows:

The Employer and the Union shall select an impartial arbitrator within ninety-six (96) hours after the Union's written request to arbitrate has been received by the Employer. Should the Employer and the Union be unable to agree upon an impartial arbitrator within said ninety-six (96) hours, then, and in that event, the impartial arbitrator shall be chosen from a list of arbitrators furnished by the Federal Mediation and Conciliation Service upon the written request of the Employer and the Union.

It is understood and agreed between the parties that the impartial arbitrator constituted as set forth directly above shall not have the power to add to, subtract from or modify any of the terms of this Agreement.

It is understood that if the impartial arbitrator shall order the reinstatement of any terminated employee due to lack of just cause for his ter-

mination, he shall have the authority to award said employee pay for all or any part of the time lost by him, less any earnings or unemployment compensation received by him, if the impartial arbitrator is of the opinion that such an award is warranted in the light of all the circumstances. If an employee is required to reimburse the Employment Security Commission for any period of time off for which the Employer is required to pay, the Employer will reimburse the employee.

The expenses of the impartial arbitrator shall be shared equally between the Employer and the Union.

The decision of the impartial arbitrator as constituted above shall be final and binding upon the parties hereto.

THE POSITION OF THE COMPANY

The company contended that although the union expressed an intention to take the grievance to arbitration in June 1979, in mid-July a union business agent informed the company that the grievance was being withdrawn. Later, this same information was conveyed to the company representatives in a grievance meeting. While notice of the union's decision not to arbitrate the matter was conveyed through a telephone conversation and then in a face-to-face meeting with company representatives rather than in writing, the company contended that these methods of communication are standard procedures for handling union-management business. Grievances between the company and the union were frequently settled or withdrawn as a result of telephone and/or face-to-face discussions. The company had every reason to believe that the business agent, as an official spokesperson for the union, was providing authoritative information, and that in fact, the grievance had been put to rest. Under these circumstances, the company argued that it was both technically improper and unfair to resurrect a grievance some two and one-half months after the company had been formally notified that the matter had been withdrawn from the grievance and arbitration process.

POSITION OF THE UNION

The union emphasized that in June 1979 two letters were sent to the company advising that the grievance was being taken to arbitration. Again, on October 17, 1979, the union advised the company that this matter was going to arbitration. At no point in time did the union give written notice that it did not intend to arbitrate the matter.

The business agent who allegedly gave conflicting notice was no longer employed by the union nor did the union have access to this individual. Problems with the use of the subpoena made it impractical to arrange an appearance of the union's former business representative at the arbitration hearing.

The union had no knowledge regarding any decision to withdraw this grievance. On the contrary, the union had every intention of pursuing this matter through the arbitration process. The union pointed out that where objections to arbitration are based on procedural grounds, arbitrators generally favor proceeding to arbitration and a review of the merits of the case.

DISCUSSION QUESTIONS

1. Under the nation's policy, what is the general view concerning the arbitration of issues such as those found in this case?

2. Is this case arbitrable?

3. What recourse does the employee have against the union for not pressing his case to arbitration as the union initially said it would?

30. "Shop Talk" or Insubordination?

PARTIES: Reynolds Metals Company and United Steelworkers of America, Local 330.

ISSUE: Did the company have just cause for issuing a four-day suspension to Irv Sills because of his using foul, filthy, and abusive language toward his immediate supervisor?

BACKGROUND

Irv Sills works as a potman at Reynolds Metals Company's Troutdale, Oregon plant. At the time of this incident, he was also the shop steward. While working the graveyard shift one night, a yardbird (an extra worker) delivered cryolite to one of the production lines. Rather than putting the cryolite in the pots, the yardbird dumped it on the floor by Sills's work station. In the past, the job of potman had included throwing cryolite on the pots. However, more recently, when yardbirds were available, particularly on the swing and graveyard shifts, the yardbirds had done this work. When the cryolite is dumped on the floor it makes a mess, and there is extra work involved when throwing it on the pots. Sills complained about the dumping of the cryolite on the floor to his foreman, but was told that since it had already been dumped, he should throw it on. He did so. However, other potmen complained to Sills as their shop steward about the same matter. Sills

once more talked to his foreman about correcting the situation. This time the argument became very heated with Sills using foul and abusive language. The arbitrator characterized Sills's choice of words as being among the most insulting in the English language. The supervisor was very humiliated by them. On the next day that Sills reported to work, he was issued a four-day disciplinary layoff because of his failure to conduct himself as a responsible employee and because of his use of foul, filthy, and abusive language toward his immediate supervisor.

POSITION OF THE UNION

The union made it clear that it did not condone the use of foul or abusive language. However, it believed that Sills was provoked into using such language and that disciplinary action was not justified. The union claimed that there was a history of bad feelings between Sills and his supervisor. Also the union claimed that the supervisor, in the past, had threatened "to get" Sills's job and to do him physical harm. The union produced witnesses who testified on these points. Additionally, the union claimed that for some time foul, abusive, and threatening language had been used by both supervisory and hourly employees in the plant to the extent that such language had become normal "shop talk." Furthermore, the company had no posted rules regarding the use of abusive language. The union did not believe that Sills should be held accountable for his words when he had been threatened with the loss of his job as well as physical harm by his supervisor. The union thought that the unacceptable language could be excused in view of the fact that the most objectionable part occurred after the argument had continued for some time. The union proposed that both sides start with a "clean slate" by implementing rules to prevent the reoccurrence of such events.

THE POSITION OF THE COMPANY

The company pointed out that the work assignment that precipitated the argument was not improper. The supervisor testified that he preferred to have the yardbirds throw the cryolite. However, he had forgotten to tell the yardbird on this occasion to do so. But, it is not unusual for a potman to do this job. For example, on the day shift it is normal procedure. Therefore the supervisor's instructions to Sills to throw the cryolite on the pots was not unreasonable. The company claimed that when Sills approached the supervisor about the problem, the supervisor tried to be cooperative and suggested that Sills talk to higher management about the problem. Despite the supervisor's efforts, Sills became very abusive and used language far more objectionable than that which could be classified as "shop talk." The company considered the language used by Sills as calculated to offend and humiliate the supervisor in front of the other employees. The company claimed that such a situation cannot be condoned if any semblance of order is to be maintained at the plant. It was pointed out that the collective bargaining agreement specifically affirms the company's right to discipline for cause. Article 4 states, "The right to promote and the right to discipline and discharge for cause are rightfully the sole responsibility of the company provided that claims of discriminatory promotion or of wrong and unjust discipline shall be subject to grievance procedure."

The company denied that the supervisor had used objectionable language and that he had threatened Sills in the past. Further, it emphasized that even if those events had occurred, they were unrelated to the incident on the night in question.

DISCUSSION QUESTIONS

1. At what point does "shop talk" become grounds for discipline?

2. Did the supervisor react unreasonably when he directed the grievant to throw the cryolite on the pots?

3. What weight should be given to the allegation that the supervisor had used abusive language in the past?

4. What weight should be given to the fact that the company did not have posted rules regarding abusive language?

5. What is insubordination? Was the grievant insubordinate? Was the discipline appropriate?

31. Demotions as Discipline

PARTIES: Republic Steel Corporation and the United Steelworkers of America, Local 4412.

ISSUE: Did the company act properly when it demoted Maxfield and Royce for poor job performance? If not, what is the appropriate remedy?

BACKGROUND

Monte Royce and John Maxfield were employed as drillers at Republic Steel Corporation's Edwards Mine. Royce had been in the driller job classification for approximately five years and Maxfield had been a driller for approximately three years. Supervision regarded both employees as competent drillers, well able to perform the duties of their job. Neither employee had ever been disciplined or disqualified for any job that they had held. A few weeks before the grievance in this case arose, it was discovered that Royce and Maxfield as well as other pinning drillers were not performing their work satisfactorily. Therefore the company undertook a program to instruct the drillers in the proper way to do their work. As part of this effort, the employees were talked to individually and in groups. Through these conversations, the drillers were instructed in the proper methods of pin drilling and

pin setting and were cautioned about the hazards of performing these operations improperly. They were also warned that they would be removed from their jobs if they were not able to do their work satisfactorily.

Shortly after the initiation of this campaign to improve the quality of drillers' work, Royce was demoted from driller to a driller's helper with a decrease in pay. The next day, Maxfield was also demoted to a helper position. He too experienced a decrease in pay as a result of this demotion. The reason stated by the company for demoting them was that they had not performed their jobs satisfactorily. Royce set seven out of nine pins improperly and Maxfield failed to abide by company procedures for determining the proper depth for drilling pin holes. Both employees were told that they would not be permanently barred from being drillers. When driller positions became available, Royce and Maxfield could bid on them. The company stated that they knew these men and their ability to do the work. They had been doing the work satisfactorily in the past. While management tried its best to help the drillers perform satisfactorily, these employees did not respond. Because of the inability of Maxfield and Royce to work in accordance with established standards, the company declared that it was appropriate for them to take some disciplinary measures. Both Royce and

Maxfield grieved their demotions and requested pay for lost earnings. The company denied these grievances.

POSITION OF THE PARTIES

The company claimed that Royce and Maxfield were properly disciplined because Royce was careless in his work and Maxfield failed to do his job as he had been instructed. The company insisted that demotion was a proper form of discipline under the circumstances in these cases. This method of disciplining employees had been in vogue at the Edwards Mine for many years and it had never been challenged by the employees or their former bargaining representative. Further, the company argued that its use of demotions as a disciplinary mechanism had been sustained in two prior arbitration awards. The company emphasized that the demotion of Maxfield and Royce did not mean that they could never become drillers again. They were told that they had the right to bid on the job when there was an opening. For these reasons, the company urged the arbitrator to deny the grievance.

The union contended that demotion is not a permissible penalty under the contract where an employee has the requisite ability to satisfactorily perform the duties of his job classification. The union argued that such a penalty results in an employee's disqualification from his job for an indefinite period of time, and therefore, it is an unjust punishment. The union also pointed out that the use of demotions as a form of discipline under-

cuts seniority. The arbitrator was urged not to give any weight to the claim that the former bargaining representative did not challenge this form of discipline and to the previous arbitration awards related to this case. The union argued that the history of this issue does not give the company the right to perpetuate past errors. The union also urged the arbitrator not to weigh the fact that Royce and Maxfield were told they could reapply for their jobs when vacancies would occur. It was argued that the grievances were sufficient notice to the company that Royce and Maxfield deemed their demotions improper and that the burden was on the company to correct its error without requiring the employees to bid for their former jobs. Therefore the union claimed that the grievances should be granted.

DISCUSSION QUESTIONS

1. Does the company have the right to demote employees for reasons other than discipline?

2. Did Maxfield and Royce commit acts warranting discipline?

3. What is the purpose of industrial discipline? Does a demotion further this purpose?

4. Should progressive or corrective discipline been used in this case? Why?

5. How would you have decided this case? If you sustained the grievance, how would you remedy the situation?

32. Fighting on the Job as Grounds for Discharge

PARTIES: Abex Corporation and International Association of Machinists, District Lodge 86.

ISSUE: Does fighting on the job provide the company just cause for terminating Bruce Hood? If not, what is the appropriate remedy?

BACKGROUND

The incident leading to the discharge under review in this case took place at approximately 12:30 P.M. on July 1, 1980. At that time, the grievant, Bruce Hood, was in the lunchroom of the Apex Corporation, located in Denver, Colorado, talking with two other employees. Ray Martin entered the lunchroom. Hood said something like "It's about time you got here." At the arbitration hearing, Hood testified that he was joking since they were all a little late returning to work from their lunch break. However, Martin took offense at Hood's comment. Martin responded by saying "What business do you have telling me I'm late when you are standing here." From this point things degenerated quickly.

Hood and Martin moved into a hallway between the lunchroom and a storage area referred to as the lean-to. Words were exchanged between the two. Names were called. At about this point, Martin pulled out a wrench. More words were ex-

changed. Martin put the wrench away. Hood and Martin were standing toe-to-toe engaged in a heated verbal exchange. At about this point, Hood claimed that Martin spit in his face. However, Martin claimed in a written statement taken the day after the altercation that as he called Hood a "pussy," some spittle escaped from his lips.

At this point, there are further discrepancies between the company's and union's accounts of the fight. Hood testified that Martin came at him and that in response, he grabbed Martin. The company's account indicated that Hood grabbed Martin, with no mention of Martin's movement toward the grievant.

Regardless of who initiated the physical aggression, both Martin and Hood, while in each other's grasp, left the hallway and entered the lean-to. It is not known for sure what happened in the lean-to. There were no witnesses to the event. However, at some later point in time (the time expired was not established), Ben Spahr, a company employee, and Jack Roe, an employee and union steward, broke up the fight. Again, the sequence of events leading up to the end of the fight is unclear. Jack Roe claimed that when he happened on the scene, someone was holding Martin (who happened to be his cousin), so he grabbed Hood. Spahr testified that when he got there, someone was restraining Hood, so he grabbed

Martin. With the intervention of Spahr, Roe, and another employee named "Red," things cooled down.

At about this time, Ron Krebel, the company's personnel director, arrived on the scene. He directed the combatants to receive medical attention. Both Hood and Martin had visible signs that they had been in a fight. Then Krebel initiated his investigation. Later on in the afternoon of July 1, 1980, Krebel talked with Hood and Martin and suspended both pending further investigation.

The next day Joseph Murdock, the company's works manager, talked to Martin and Hood, taking statements from each. After doing so, Murdock decided to terminate both employees for fighting. Murdock testified at the arbitration hearing that the company had a policy of terminating employees for fighting on company premises unless there were mitigating circumstances, such as self-defense. In this case, both employees were equally involved and both struck blows. Murdock concluded that there was no reason for unequal discipline. On July 2, 1980, both were discharged for fighting on the previous day.

Hood grieved his termination, contending that the company did not have just cause for discharging him. He requested reinstatement and that he be made whole financially.

It must be noted that Martin did not participate in this arbitration. Subsequent to his termination, he was arrested and incarcerated. Later, he was paroled to another state and the company was unable to locate him.

POSITION OF THE COMPANY

The company viewed this matter as being twofold. First, it had to be established that Bruce Hood took part in a fight. Once that was established, the appropriateness of the penalty must be reviewed.

After its investigation, the company concluded that Hood was fighting and that he was responsible for the fight. Hood made the initial remark to which Martin took offense. Later, Hood shoved Martin. The company argued that this was of special significance because it is the first time in the chain of events that physical contact was made and a blow was struck. It was also argued that Hood perpetuated the fight by dragging Martin into the lean-to. Further, Hood continued to struggle while attempts were made to break up the altercation. The company held that at no point did Hood behave either like an unwilling participant or someone who was acting strictly in self-defense, but rather as an active participant in the fight. Both Spahr and Roe testified that they saw the grievant throwing punches.

The company urged the arbitrator to closely examine Mr. Hood's credibility for two reasons. First, Martin was unavailable to provide his account of the fight. This allowed Hood to shade details in his favor. Secondly, Hood took some "liberties" in his testimony. At one point, he denied ever swinging at Martin. Later, after Roe and Spahr testified that they saw the grievant throw punches, Hood admitted that he swung at Martin. Also, Hood misrepresented his past discipline record. He initially claimed receiving one three-day suspension and one written reprimand. Later, he acknowledged at least two additional written warnings and some oral warnings.

The company concluded by stating that on balance, there was no doubt that Hood was an active participant in the fight and was equally guilty of its creation. Hood initiated the conversation with a "smart aleck" remark, continued to argue with Martin, made the first shove, and grabbed Martin around the neck, all before Martin even swung a punch. In light of these events, the company held that Hood's termination was proper.

Given the conclusion that Hood did participate in a fight, the company addressed the issue of the propriety of discharge as a penalty. The company held that the labor agreement states that management has the right to discipline or discharge for just cause and to make reasonable shop rules and regulations. The company held that it has a definite rule on fighting, which states that employees involved in a fight will be discharged unless there are mitigating circumstances such as self-defense and the individual's work record. Murdock claimed that employees are made aware of this rule as part of the hiring procedure. Although Roe, the union steward, could not recall a rule against fighting, he acknowledged that he would expect to be disciplined if he was caught fighting. Spahr testified that the plant had a rule against fighting and that immediate discharge was the penalty for violating that rule.

The company maintained that a rule banning fighting is a reasonable one since it is reasonably related to a legitimate objective of management. It was argued that a rule against fighting is a legitimate interest of management since it helps guarantee a safe workplace. The fight between Hood and Martin jeopardized their well-being, the well-being of Spahr, Roe, and "Red" who broke the fight up, and had potentially negative consequences for other workers.

The company urged the arbitrator to reject the union's contention that the rule against fighting is unenforceable since it was not posted at the plant. It was argued that employees were aware of the rule even though it was not posted. Also, fighting at the workplace is such an inappropriate activity that employees should know it is improper even if a specific rule was not communicated to the workers.

The company also urged the arbitrator to reject the union's contention that the rule against fighting had not been consistently enforced. The company noted that all fights of which management was aware led to the discharge of the participants unless there were mitigating circumstances. Examples cited by the union in which fight participants were not penalized should not be weighed since management was not notified that a fight had occurred.

The company also cited two ancillary issues that were argued to have a bearing on this matter. First, the arbitrator does not have the authority to substitute his or her judgment concerning what is an appropriate penalty for that of management's.

It was held that the company should be free to administer the type and quantity of discipline it feels is necessary, so long as that discipline is reasonable. Secondly, if the arbitrator sets the company's penalty aside, management would have little power to handle future situations. Rather than having a uniform rule specifying that fight participants will be terminated unless there are mitigating circumstances, the company would have to try to anticipate how an arbitrator would decide the issue.

POSITION OF THE UNION

The union held that Hood was not discharged for just cause. It was acknowledged that the company has the right to discipline for just cause. However, it has a responsibility to exercise this right in a fair and consistent manner. The union argued that the company failed to consistently apply the "discharge for fighting" rule. Testimony was presented describing at least four fights at or near the company's plant for which the participants were not punished. It was not established, however, that company officials were aware of any of these fights. Another fight involving two company employees, a supervisor and an employee, was described. The employee was terminated, while the supervisor only received a disciplinary layoff. In this case, the supervisor tried to reprimand the employee. Then, the employee struck the supervisor. The supervisor did not punch the employee back. The company disciplined the supervisor for the poor manner in which he reprimanded the employee. Additionally, very vague testimony was presented concerning a fight involving an employee named Howard. Those testifying were not even sure of the decade (the 1950s or 1960s) in which the incident took place.

The union noted that the company's rule concerning fighting was not written and posted. It was maintained that company rules should be written, posted in a common area, and administered in a fair and consistent manner.

The union contended that the company

failed to demonstrate that Hood provoked the fight between himself and Martin, or that the grievant was the aggressor. The company failed to show that Hood did anything but act in self-defense. It was maintained that the company failed to carry its burden to "clearly and convincingly" establish Hood's wrongdoing. The union also held that while Hood's work record was not spotless, it was good, as evidenced by his promotion to leadman. This work record should be viewed as a mitigating factor.

The union requested the arbitrator to decide in favor of the grievant, reinstate him, and make him whole for all lost wages and benefits.

DISCUSSION QUESTIONS

1. Does fighting on the job provide grounds for termination? Why?

2. To be enforceable, must the rule concerning fighting on the job be written and posted in the plant?

3. Did Hood participate in a fight in violation of a legitimate company rule? What weight should be given to Hood's claim that he was only joking when he said "It's about time you got here"? What weight should be given to Mr. Hood's claim that he only acted in self-defense?

4. The union raised the affirmative defense that the company had not consistently enforced the fighting rule. Is the burden on the union to prove that the company had been inconsistent or on the company to prove that it had been consistent?

5. How would you decide this case?

33. When can an Employee be Terminated for Absenteeism?

PARTIES: Acme Delivery Services, Inc. and International Brotherhood of Teamsters, Chauffers, Warehousemen, and Helpers of America, Local 17.

ISSUE: Did Jim Dafney's absenteeism record provide the company just cause for terminating him? If not, what is the appropriate remedy?

BACKGROUND

Acme Delivery Services, Inc. operates a transfer and storage business in Denver, Colorado. Jim Dafney had been employed by the company since the latter part of 1978. He was terminated on January 25, 1982, for excessive absenteeism. On that day, Dafney called in to report that an eye ailment prevented him from coming to work. This illness was a continuation of a condition that had also caused him to miss work on January 12 and 13, 1982. Dafney provided medical excuses covering these days to the company.

Dafney had an attendance problem dating back to 1980. In 1981 the company started maintaining records concerning employee absenteeism and tardiness. For a summary of Dafney's attendance record, see Table 1. The decision to terminate was based on his entire absenteeism record. Table 1 indicates that during 1981 Dafney was absent for all or major parts of his

shifts on 21 occasions. On six other occasions, he was allowed to use vacation days or holidays in lieu of being considered absent due to illness. On several other occasions, Dafney left work due to illness before the end of his shift. As will be discussed in more detail later, Dafney was made aware of the company's concern about his attendance problem and the need to improve by the company's use of progressive discipline. The company held that Dafney's absenteeism during January 1982 marked a continuation of the attendance problem exhibited during 1981. Because he failed to improve his attendance and because there was little hope for improvement, the decision to terminate him was made. Dafney grieved his discharge on January 27, 1983, claiming that the company did not have just cause to terminate him.

POSITION OF THE COMPANY

The company argued that it had just cause to terminate Dafney because he had been absent an excessive amount of time during his employment with the company. It was pointed out that his record would have been even worse if his supervisor, Glen Mooney, had not allowed Dafney to use vacation time and a holiday rather than sick days.

The company maintained that Dafney's absenteeism was attributable to a number of dif-

TABLE 1
Jim Dafney's attendance record for 1981
and January 1982

DATE OF ABSENCE	REASON
1–5–81	Sick
1–21–81	Sick
1–22–81	Sick
1–23–81	Sick
3–2–81	Sick
3–10–81	Sick
3–11–81	Arrived 3 hr late
3–23–81	Sick
4–20–81	Sick
4–21–81	Sick
4–27–81	Sick
5–7–81	Sick
6–15–81	Sick
6–17–81	Called in sick but took birth-day holiday
6–19–81	Went home sick after 2 hr of work
6–23–81	Sick
7–7–81	Sick but took vacation day
7–8–81	Sick but took vacation day
7–13–81	Sick but took vacation day
7–14–81	Sick but took vacation day
7–15–81	Sick but took vacation day
7–22–81	Sick
7–28–81	Car broke down
8–13–81	Sick
8–14–81	Worked 1½ hr, went home sick
9–14–81	Worked 1¼ hr, went home sick
9–25–81	Sick
10–7–81	Excused absence—vacation
10–8–81	Excused absence—vacation
11–3–81	Worked ½ hr, went home sick
11–4–81	Suspended
11–5–81	Suspended
11–6–81	Suspended
1–11–82	Worked 6 hr, went home sick
1–12–82	Sick
1–13–82	Excused absence
1–25–82	Sick

ferent ailments. Because of this, the company held that his absenteeism would probably continue if he was returned to his job. It was noted that Dafney tended to miss work a day or two at a time. The company did not challenge Dafney's claim that each absence was due to illness. Also, it was acknowledged that he followed the company's reporting procedure and secured permission from his supervisor when leaving work due to illness.

It was argued that the short-duration absences were very disruptive to the company because it was frequently difficult to secure a replacement for Dafney. This made it difficult for his job to be completed and also was an inconvenience to his co-workers who had to carry Dafney's workload.

The company emphasized that arbitral precedent supported the termination of workers for excessive absenteeism even when the absenteeism is due to sickness. The essence of this argument is that employees may become unemployable because they are unable to report to work on a regular basis. Even when there are valid grounds for the absences, termination may be warranted when the employee is no longer valuable to the employer because of unpredictable attendance.

The arbitrator was reminded that he was not free to substitute his judgment of what is excessive absenteeism for that of the company's. The arbitrator should only substitute his judgment if it is shown that the company abused its discretion. The company argued that there was no abuse of discretion in this case. Dafney had a severe absenteeism problem—the worse record in the company. Progressive discipline had been used. He had been counseled. His union steward talked to him about the problem. He was suspended for excessive absenteeism on November 4, 5, and 6, 1981. It was only when the problem continued that the company decided to terminate Dafney. It was maintained that the company's no-fault absenteeism program and the application of the program in this case were reasonable and proper.

Finally, the company argued that Dafney was also guilty of intentional conduct. At the arbitration hearing, Dafney argued that he had "cleaned up his act" and therefore, deserved leniency. He claimed that he started going to work even though he was not feeling well. The company argued that this indicated that Dafney's absenteeism was controllable, i.e., he had chosen not to go to work rather than been forced to stay home by illness. It was maintained that this indicated a lack of concern for his job. Such an employee did not deserve to keep his job.

In conclusion, the company held that Dafney's excessive absenteeism rendered him unfit for employment. Therefore the arbitrator was requested to deny the grievance.

POSITION OF THE UNION

The union argued that the termination of Dafney was not for cause as required by the labor agreement. This position was taken for several reasons. First, Dafney was legitimately ill on most of the days he was absent. He testified that his absences had been covered by doctors' statements. After Mooney told him he did not need a doctor's slip unless injured on the job, he stopped the practice. Secondly, Dafney abided by the company's notification program whenever he was absent. Simi-

larly, whenever he left work early due to illness, he notified his supervisor. Finally, the union acknowledged that Dafney had a problem with absenteeism. However, after his suspension in November 1981, he improved his attendance. He missed no full days of work from early November until his eye problem in mid-January 1982. The union emphasized that it was unfair and inconsistent with the tenets of just cause to discharge an employee who was legitimately sick. Since the termination was not for just cause, the union requested the arbitrator to reinstate Dafney to his former position with back pay and benefits.

DISCUSSION QUESTIONS

1. Does the company have the right to establish attendance guidelines and enforce those guidelines? Why?

2. Does the company's right to regulate attendance include the right to discipline employees who are legitimately ill? Defend your position.

3. Did Dafney's attendance record warrant his termination?

34. What Constitutes Just Cause for Discipline?

PARTIES: AMAX Coal Company, Eagle Butte Mine and the AMAX Employees' Committee.

ISSUE: Did the company have just cause for issuing Sam Kelley a one-day, paid disciplinary suspension (DML) when he reported to work in an intoxicated condition? If not, what is the appropriate remedy?

BACKGROUND

AMAX Coal Company operates the Eagle Butte Mine near Gillette, Wyoming. Eagle Butte is a large open pit coal mine that operates on a non-union basis. The company, however, arbitrates disputes that cannot be resolved through its internal dispute resolution procedure. Employees with problems (analogous to grievances in unionized firms) are represented in the dispute resolution procedure by members of the employees' committee. The employees' committee is elected by mine employees. The committee meets quarterly with the company to discuss proposed changes in the company's personnel policies as summarized in the company handbook. The employees' committee can also represent employees during disciplinary hearings and in arbitration. Committee members have been trained on how to prepare a case for arbitration and on how to present the case to an arbitrator.

Before reviewing the facts of this case, a discussion of the discipline system under which the action leading to arbitration took place is warranted. Since June 1, 1982, the company operated under a program entitled Positive Discipline. This system was devised and implemented with the aid of a management consulting firm. Before the program was put into effect, supervisors were trained on its use and workers were instructed concerning the program's intent, design, and procedures.

The Positive Discipline program utilizes progressive discipline to help correct deficient employee behavior. This approach relies initially on the counseling of employees with performance problems. This brings the problem to the employee's attention and, with the supervisor's assistance, if needed, helps the employee develop appropriate behavior patterns. Failure to respond to counseling can bring about the utilization of formal discipline.

The discipline phase of Positive Discipline has three basic steps. The first level of discipline is an oral reminder. If the problem persists, the employee will be given a written reminder. The third level of discipline is a decision making leave (DML). This involves a formal discussion between the employee and his or her supervisor. Then the employee is given a one-day *paid* leave designed to give the worker time to think about the problem and his or her ability to abide by company rules once back on the job. While most infractions involving a first offense will result in an oral reminder, more serious violations could result in either a written reminder or a DML could be issued. Another similar offense occurring within 12 months after the DML results in termination. With this background in mind, attention can now turn to an examination of the facts of this case.

Sam Kelly was issued a DML on October 11, 1982, for an incident occurring on October 8, 1982. Kelly reported to work as a welder on the third shift, which begins at midnight, as scheduled. Ray Biggs, Kelly's supervisor, had been advised by another employee that Kelly had liquor on his breath. Biggs decided to observe Kelly's condition. He noticed that Kelly had red, puffy eyes and exuded an odor of alcohol. Kelly had been assigned to work on top of a silo used to store coal prior to shipment. Coal silos are approximately a 100 feet high. Biggs followed him to the work location. After observing him, Biggs decided that Kelly was unfit to work.

After coming down from the silo, Kelly, Biggs, and Joe Reed, the third shift's general supervisor, met in Biggs's office to discuss Kelly's condition. Biggs claimed that he was familiar with Kelly's normal behavior as a result of being his supervisor for three and one-half years. He stated that Kelly was not acting normally on October 8, 1982. Biggs noted that during the meeting, Kelly had red, puffy eyes, slurred speech, and exhibited a high level of nervousness. Similar observations were made by Reed.

Kelly reported that he had several beers during the day but that he had stopped drinking at approximately 5:00 P.M. (about seven hours before his scheduled starting time). However, he acknowledged that he was tired as a result of having only four and one-half hours of sleep during the preceding 48 hours. He denied that he was unfit to continue working his normally scheduled hours. While he acknowledged that he may have been unsteady on top of the silo, he said it was be-

cause he was afraid of heights, not because he had been drinking.

After this meeting, Biggs and Reed decided to send Kelly home for the remainder of the shift because he was in an unfit condition to work. The next morning an investigation meeting was held to review the matter. Subsequently, the company decided to give Kelly a DML for October 11, 1982. Kelly complained that the company did not have just cause for this action.

POSITION OF THE COMPANY

The company held that the issuance of a DML to Kelly was warranted in light of the facts of this case. It has a rule, contained in the company's guidelines for the Positive Discipline program, specifying that reporting to work in an unfit condition is an offense warranting discipline. The company also established that Kelly was aware of this rule as a result of his attendance at a meeting on May 18, 1982, at which the rules were discussed.

The company argued that such a rule is a reasonable exercise of its authority. This is because it is important for employees to report to work in a condition in which they are able to fully and completely perform their jobs. The coal mining industry is a hazardous one. Therefore it is extremely important that employees are in control of all their faculties, so that there are no undue safety risks or hazards for themselves or other employees.

The company urged the arbitrator to not give any weight to Kelly's claim that he was allowed to work with a cast on his arm, and as a result, was not in full control. It was argued that such a situation is completely different than reporting unfit, at which time the employee is not likely to have complete control of his or her coordination or thinking processes. Working with a cast did not inhibit Kelly's ability to work, and more important, did not constitute a hazardous situation for himself or his fellow workers.

The company pointed out that an investigation was conducted prior to taking any action. Initially, Biggs observed Kelly's performance for approximately 45 minutes before requesting that he come down from the silo. It was argued that Biggs had supervised Kelly for about three and one-half years. As a result, he was very familiar with Kelly's normal behavior, and therefore, was able to determine that Kelly was not acting normally on October 8, 1982.

After Biggs determined that Kelly was in an unfit condition to work, Reed was brought into the situation. While in Biggs's office, Reed noticed that Kelly looked disheveled, had reddened eyes, was leaning on a desk, was noticeably nervous, and broke a cigarette in half while trying to knock off an ash. At this time, Reed agreed with Biggs's determination that Kelly was in an unfit condition to work and that he should be sent home.

The next morning, a review of the incident took place before deciding on the issuance of discipline. At this meeting, Kelly and his representative from the employees' committee, John Roberts, were given the opportunity to explain what had happened the previous night. At no time did Kelly raise the defense that his problem was attributable to his fear of heights. After this meeting, it was decided that a DML was the appropriate action.

The company maintained that it conducted a fair and objective investigation during which Kelly had the opportunity to present his side of the issue. The investigation revealed that Kelly had only two and one-half hours of sleep the night before he reported to work and four and one-half in the preceding 48 hours. As a result, he was unable to perform his job functions. The company pointed out that Kelly did not notify his supervisor that a condition existed that impaired his effectiveness. He also failed to request the day off if he could not do his work. Because Kelly was in an unfit condition, the company argued the DML was justly issued to him on October 11, 1982.

The company also argued that it has consistently applied its rules and penalties since the im-

plementation of the Positive Discipline program on June 1, 1982. Anyone reporting to work in an unfit condition had been suspended from the shift. If the investigation supported the contention that the worker was unfit, then a DML was issued. The company provided written documentation indicating that two DMLs had been issued shortly before Kelly's to workers reporting to work in unfit condition.

The company pointed out that supervisors have been instructed not to try to diagnose the cause of the unfit condition, e.g., emotional or physical illness, alcohol, drugs, etc. The focus is on identifying gross changes in behavioral patterns that might indicate that an unfit condition exists.

The company emphasized that Kelly's own testimony substantiated its claim that he was unfit to work. Kelly acknowledged that he only had two and one-half hours sleep in the preceding 24 hours and four and one-half hours sleep in the preceding 48 hours. Kelly also testified that he had been drinking earlier in the day. After being sent home from work, at approximately 2:45 A.M. to 3:00 A.M., Kelly took a blood alcohol test at a local hospital indicating an alcohol level of 0.044 percent. Assuming that the alcohol level decreases at a rate of 0.015 percent per hour, Kelly's blood alcohol level would have been approximately 0.089 percent at midnight when he reported to work. It was pointed out that a person is legally too drunk to drive in Wyoming with a blood alcohol level of 0.1 percent. The company argued that it is difficult to believe that Kelly was fit to work at 12:01 A.M. with a blood alcohol level of 0.089 percent. It was maintained that, by not getting the proper amount of sleep and exacerbating the problem with alcohol, Kelly put himself into a situation in which the supervisor had no choice but to send him home.

In summary, the company argued that Biggs and Reed properly determined that Kelly was unfit to work. In light of the seriousness of the offense, serious discipline was warranted. The arbitrator was urged to conclude that the company had just cause for issuing a DML to Kelly for reporting to work in an unfit condition on October 8, 1982.

POSITION OF THE EMPLOYEES' COMMITTEE

The employees' committee raised a number of points supporting its contention that the company did not have just cause for issuing a DML to Kelly. It was argued that Kelly was not in an unfit condition to work on October 8, 1982. He was admittedly tired but not to the degree that would interfere with his work efficiency. The blood alcohol test indicated that he was not intoxicated. Kelly was very concerned about safety issues and had been outspoken about them at meetings held at the work place. He had never been disciplined for safety reasons during his years of service with the company. In fact, he had received a five-year safety award. It was pointed out that as a single parent solely responsible for two children, he would do nothing to jeopardize his safety.

The employees' committee argued that Kelly's allegedly "abnormal" behavior was attributable to two factors. One was his extreme fear of high places. The other factor causing his nervousness was his concern about being "called on the carpet" by Reed, a new supervisor. These factors, which did not make him unfit for work, caused his apparent nervousness when Kelly met with Biggs and Reed on October 8, 1982. The company could cite no rules forbidding an employee from reporting to work with red eyes or with alcohol on his or her breath.

The employees' committee also argued that the company's rule concerning reporting to work in an unfit condition is ill-defined and provides the employees with little guidance. The only basis for deciding that Kelly was unfit for work were observations made by Biggs and Reed. The arbitrator was urged to discount Reed's observations since he had only met Kelly the night before the incident. As a result, Reed had no grounds to

conclude that Kelly's behavior was out of the ordinary. It was also noted that this case involved Reed's first DML after being promoted to his new position.

It was pointed out that no objective test was made to determine Kelly's fitness to work. While tests such as the finger-nose, heel-toe, and counting backwards were available, none were used. The employees' committee held that more concrete standards for determining fitness to work are needed. Without such standards, workers will not know what is expected of them. Employees have the right to know how the company determines that a person is not 100 percent fit for duty. This is especially so in light of the severe discipline attached to violating the unfit-for-work rule.

The need for well defined rules measured in objective terms was particularly pressing in cases involving an issue as subjective as being unfit to work. Company management acknowledged that the word "unfit" was all-encompassing. It was pointed out that Kelly was allowed to work with a cast on his arm. The employees' committee argued that a welder with his arm in a cast is not 100 percent fit. The point being made was that there are no published guidelines available for workers or supervisors to be used when deciding whether a person is unfit for work.

In summary, it was argued that the company failed to establish that Kelly was unfit. This was because the company had no set standards or rules for establishing the fitness of employees for work. Given that the company failed to establish that Kelly was unfit for work, the arbitrator was requested to reinstate Kelly with full back pay, benefits, and seniority to which he was entitled.

DISCUSSION QUESTIONS

1. What is progressive discipline? Why is it used? Is the issuing of a decision making leave (DML), for which an employee is paid, a better idea

than a disciplinary suspension as found in most systems of progressive discipline?

2. Why would Kelly complain about a DML since he did not lose any pay as a result of the company's actions?

3. What must the company demonstrate in order for the arbitrator to decide that it had just cause to issue Kelly a DML?

4. Did the company have just cause to issue Kelly a DML?

35. What Is a Workweek?

PARTIES: King Soopers, Inc. and United Food and Commercial Workers, Local 7.

ISSUE: Did the company violate the collective bargaining agreement by the way it calculated holiday pay for Brenda O'Neil? If so, how much holiday pay is O'Neil entitled to receive?

BACKGROUND

Brenda O'Neil was employed by King Soopers, Inc. in Denver, Colorado as a part-time general-merchandise clerk. During the week ending June 20, 1981, she was scheduled to work 20 hours. On Sunday, June 14, 1981, she worked 8.2 hours. After working that day, she was notified that her father had died. O'Neil took three-days funeral leave. Then she requested a leave-of-absence. The leave started June 22, 1981, and ended when O'Neil returned to work on July 19, 1981.

O'Neil had been scheduled to go on vacation on August 7, 1981. Because she had recently returned from a leave-of-absence, she requested that she be paid for the vacation time to which she was entitled and instead work during her scheduled vacation. This request was approved. She received three checks to cover the three weeks of vacation she had accrued.

O'Neil's birthday (July 22) fell during her first week back to work after the leave-of-absence.

Under the contract, an employee's birthday is a paid holiday. Therefore O'Neil expected to be paid for that day. The company acknowledged that she was eligible for holiday pay, but no payment was made. Since no hours were worked during the week immediately preceding the week with the holiday (because O'Neil was on a leave-of-absence), no holiday pay was warranted (zero divided by five equals zero). The union challenged this interpretation of the contract since it deprived O'Neil of a benefit to which she was entitled.

RELEVANT CONTRACT LANGUAGE

The following contract provision is relevant to this case:

ARTICLE 12

Holidays
Section 25 — All employees who have completed their probationary period shall be paid for the following holidays whether or not they fall on what would be a workday for the employee involved:

New Year's Day, Decoration Day, Fourth of July, Labor Day, Thanksgiving Day, Christmas Day, the employee's birthday and the employee's anniversary date of employment. . . .

Holiday pay for part-time employees who have completed their probationary period will be based on the number of hours worked in the workweek immediately prior to the week in which the holiday occurs, divided by five. . . .

POSITION OF THE UNION

The union argued that it was the intent of the parties to provide both full-time and part-time employees with holiday pay. The first paragraph of Article 12, Section 25, states that "All employees who have completed their probationary period shall be paid for . . . the employee's birthday . . ." The union emphasized that this provision uses the terms "all employees" and "*shall* be paid." However, the contract is not clear in establishing how part-time employees will be paid for holidays.

The union urged the arbitrator to reject the company's interpretation of Article 12, Section 25. It was held that the company's position was inappropriate since, to accept it, two purposes of the contract would be defeated. First, as previously mentioned, the contract specifies that all employees will be paid for holidays. Secondly, another provision of the agreement specifies that leaves-of-absence will be allowed without penalizing employees. The union maintained that the company's interpretation of Article 12, Section 25, is clearly inconsistent with the parties' intentions as reflected in the collective bargaining agreement.

The union put forth its interpretation of Article 12, Section 25. It was argued that the phrase "in the workweek immediately prior to the week in which the holiday occurs" means the last workweek in which the employee worked hours, that is, the last workweek the employee was not on vacation, on sick leave, on an approved leave-of-absence, or off work due to a workmen's compensation injury.

At the arbitration hearing, Janice Feller, the company's employment manager, testified that an employee on vacation the week before a holiday would not receive holiday pay. However, John Coe, a business agent with the union,

testified that Feller's position was different at a Step 2 grievance meeting. At that time, when asked if an employee on vacation the week before a holiday would get holiday pay, Feller responded that there would be no problem. She went on to say that the vacation hours would be used to calculate holiday pay. The union held that Feller's earlier position was quite consistent with its interpretation of the contract. Also, Feller's statement represented an admission that the parties intended for both full-time and part-time employees to receive holiday pay and that the company needed a measure of hours from which holiday pay could be calculated.

The union argued that the company was discriminating against part-time employees through its interpretation. The union urged the arbitrator to reject the company's position that the denial of holiday pay is one of the factors differentiating full-time and part-time employees. The union argued that the contract does not discriminate against part-time employees. Rather, the contract establishes that many benefits are based on the number of hours worked. It cannot be concluded that the contract provides fewer benefits to part-time employees except where benefits are linked to the number of hours worked. The union held that the contract cannot be interpreted to allow some part-time employees to receive zero compensation for holidays when that would not happen to full-time employees regardless of the circumstances.

The union proposed two possible ways to calculate the amount of holiday pay due O'Neil. One approach based holiday pay calculations on the last workweek prior to O'Neil's leave of absence. During the week ending June 20, 1981, O'Neil worked 8.2 hours and received 24 hours of funeral leave pay for a total of 32.2 hours. Dividing 32.2 hours by 5 yields 6.44 hours of holiday pay. An alternative method would use vacation pay as the basis for holiday pay. With this approach, O'Neil would be entitled to 5.6 hours of holiday pay, 28.02 hours of vacation pay divided by 5.

POSITION OF THE COMPANY

The company's position in this matter rests on the language found in Article 12, Section 25. Both methods for calculating holiday pay proposed by the union were challenged because they are inconsistent with the contract's language. The company argued it was not feasible to use vacation pay as the basis for the holiday pay calculation because O'Neil's request and the company's payment of holiday pay were subsequent to her return to work from the leave-of-absence. Therefore vacation hours cannot be used as a proxy for the number of hours worked the week prior to the holiday. Also, the holiday pay calculation is based on hours worked. Vacation hours are not counted as hours worked except for health and welfare and pension contributions.

The second method proposed by the union was to use the hours worked in the employee's last workweek prior to the holiday. The company argued that this position is inconsistent with the contract language found in Article 12, Section 25, which specifies that the holiday pay calculation be based on the number of hours worked in the week immediately prior to the week with the holiday in it. It was emphasized that the intent of the parties was to establish a uniform method for calculating holiday pay, given the diversity of schedules worked by part-time employees. The purpose of the language was to provide the part-time employee with holiday pay in an amount proportional to that employee's scheduled and worked hours. In the case at hand, O'Neil worked no hours during the week before the holiday. Therefore she was entitled to no holiday pay.

The company acknowledged that this is a harsh result. It was pointed out, however, that the opposite result could occur when an employee works extra hours in the week before a holiday. Regardless of the outcome, the company reminded the arbitrator that this case must be decided in line with the clear intent of the parties and that the arbitrator cannot give another meaning to the language.

The company also argued that, if the arbitrator accepted the union's position, a different interpretation of the term "workweek" would be created. It was maintained that the union's view would give the term "workweek" different meaning depending on the individual employee's situation. The company argued that the contract must have a uniform meaning for all employees.

For the reasons outlined above, the company maintained that O'Neil was not entitled to any holiday pay since she did not work the week immediately prior to the holiday. Because of the clear, unequivocal, and unambiguous language of Article 12, Section 25, the company urged the arbitrator to dismiss the grievance.

DISCUSSION QUESTIONS

1. What is ambiguous contract language? Is Article 12, Section 25 ambiguous? Why?

2. How do ambiguities find their way into collective bargaining agreements?

3. Evaluate the company's position in this case.

4. Evaluate the position of the union.

5. Should O'Neil receive holiday pay? If yes, to how much pay is she entitled?

36. Who can Use the New Machine?

PARTIES: FMC Corporation, Industrial Chemical Division (Form Coke Plant) and United Mine Workers of America, District 22, Local 1316.

ISSUE: Did the company violate the labor agreement by having a shipping clerk, a salaried employee, operate a forklift in the performance of his duties? If so, what is the appropriate remedy?

BACKGROUND

The FMC Corporation, Industrial Chemical Division operates a coke manufacturing facility near Kemmerer, Wyoming. The plant began operations in 1960 to test and develop a new technology for the production of coke. The facility became fully operational in 1977. Approximately 98,000 tons of coke are produced each year and shipped to FMC's elemental phosphorous plant in Pocatello, Idaho. The coke plant employs 80 people and operates 24 hours a day, seven days a week.

In 1982 the company reviewed its procedures for the handling and storing of materials at the plant. The review identified a number of material-handling problems. The safety of workers who had to physically handle heavy objects and use equipment not designed for material-handling purposes was of primary con-cern. The efficient use of the company's work force was another major consideration of the materials-handling and storage review.

The methods for unloading incoming materials was one of the problems identified. Whenever Jack Jordon, the shipping clerk (a nonbargaining unit position), could not unload items by himself, he had to call employees from maintenance or operations to help. Typically, it would be necessary for the maintenance or operations employees to use a frontend loader or crane to unload the materials. This procedure was time consuming, inefficient and, to a degree, dangerous since the equipment used to help unload materials was not specifically designed for that purpose.

As a result of the 1982 review, plant management proposed to higher company officials a plan to construct a materials-storage area and to purchase a 5000-pound capacity forklift. This plan was subsequently approved.

Once the forklift was received during the fall of 1982, the company began training workers on the safe use of the machine pursuant to OSHA regulations. Over the next several months, 16 employees were trained. Initially, maintenance and operations employees were instructed in the machine's use. It was believed that they would be able to make good use of the forklift during a scheduled plant shutdown and major overhaul. Also, operations employees were responsible on a

461

regular basis for unloading 100-pound bags of soda ash. It was believed that they would be able to use the forklift safely and efficiently during that operation.

Between November 1982 and February 1983, maintenance or operations employees used the forklift to help Jordon unload heavy and bulky objects being delivered to the plant. After concluding his training in February 1983, Jordon was able to use the forklift himself to perform most unloading operations. Therefore it was not necessary for him to request help from the maintenance or operations units except when he had to unload especially unwieldy objects or items weighing more than 5000 pounds. When goods that could not be handled by the forklift were received, Jordon still had to get help from the maintenance or operations units who continued to use a frontend loader or crane to do the job.

On April 27, 1983, bargaining unit personnel observed Jordon using a forklift to unload a truck. A grievance was filed charging that Jordon's use of the forklift constituted a violation of Article XIX(F) of the labor agreement because he is a salaried employee.

RELEVANT CONTRACT LANGUAGE

The following provisions in the labor agreement are relevant to this matter:

ARTICLE V

Rights of Management
Except as specifically surrendered or abridged by express provisions of this Agreement, the company reserves all the rights, powers, and authority customarily exercised by management and has the sole and exclusive responsibility to hire; promote; demote; discipline and discharge for just cause; maintain efficiency; choose products to be manufactured; the location of plants and facilities; scheduling of production; the methods, processes, and means of manufacturing; and the assignment of work.

ARTICLE XIX(F)

General
Supervisory employees and other employees on the salaried payroll shall not do work which will deprive members of the bargaining unit of work regularly performed by them. This does not prevent supervisory employees from performing the necessary functions of instruction, or from operating equipment or processes in emergencies when no one in the bargaining unit is available to perform the work required. This also does not prevent engineers or other salaried personnel from performing experimental work.

Any supervisor or salaried employee who is believed to have violated this clause will be reported to his supervisor within seventy-two (72) hours and a meeting of the appropriate union and company personnel will be held to investigate the incident. If the matter is not settled at this meeting, it may be submitted to the grievance procedure.

POSITION OF THE UNION

The union presented three major arguments in support of its position. First, the union maintained that the use of the forklift to unload materials should be performed by bargaining unit personnel because of the plant's past practice. The union emphasized that it was not seeking the warehouse position as part of the bargaining unit. However, past practice at the plant clearly indicated that whenever heavy items had to be unloaded, bargaining unit personnel performed that work. In other words, the union was only asking for the job of operating the forklift in situations in which bargaining unit personnel had historically been involved in the loading and unloading of materials.

The union's second argument was based on a reading of Article XIX(F) of the labor agreement. It was held that this provision unambiguously stated that salaried employees cannot perform bargaining unit work. At the arbitration hearing, two employees testified that bargaining unit employees were available to run the forklift but were not requested to do so because Jordon was using the forklift.

Finally, the union pointed out that the way the company handled the training of employees on the use of the forklift supported its position in this matter. Of the 16 employees trained on the forklift's use, 15 belonged to the bargaining unit. It was also pointed out that the company had the forklift four months before Jordon's training was completed. The union argued that both factors supported its position that the forklift was intended for use by bargaining unit personnel.

As a remedy, the union requested the arbitrator to direct the company to have only bargaining unit personnel use the forklift. The arbitrator was also requested to direct the company to pay a bargaining unit employee able to use the forklift for two and one-half hours work he could not perform because Jordon was using the forklift.

POSITION OF THE COMPANY

The company argued that the management's rights clause of the labor agreement, Article V, gave it the right to maintain plant efficiency; schedule production; choose the methods, processes, and means of production; and assign work. It was pointed out that none of these rights were surrendered or abridged by Article XIX(F). This was because bargaining unit employees were not deprived of regularly performed work because of Jordon's use of the forklift.

It was further argued that the union did not support its claim that bargaining unit personnel were deprived of work because of Jordon's use of the forklift in the performance of his shipping clerk duties. Prior to the plant's acquisition of the forklift, bargaining unit employees were called upon to use a crane or frontend loader to help Jordon unload bulky or heavy objects he could not handle alone. The use of operations or maintenance employees was necessary because cranes and frontend loaders are intended for and operated by bargaining unit personnel in the performance of their regular duties.

It was claimed that since acquiring the forklift, bargaining unit employees have still operated the frontend loader and crane when helping the shipping clerk unload items too big or too heavy for the forklift. The company maintained that the number of hours the crane and frontend loader have been used did not decrease after acquiring the forklift. Furthermore, no members of the bargaining unit were deprived of the opportunity to operate the crane or frontend loader. The company concluded that this meant that the crane and frontend loader must have been used for tasks more germane to the operations and maintenance functions. It was pointed out that since operations and maintenance personnel have not had to unload trucks, there has been more time to perform the jobs for which they were trained. As a result, the company had to subcontract fewer maintenance and construction jobs to outside vendors.

The company noted that prior to getting the forklift, bargaining unit employees were paid on an overtime basis to unload materials on rare occasions such as when freight arrived after business hours and the goods were needed immediately. This was still true after the company acquired the forklift. Therefore bargaining unit employees were not denied regular overtime pay. To further its argument that the shipping clerk's use of the forklift did not deny bargaining unit employees work, the company noted that soda ash was still being unloaded by bargaining unit personnel. The unloading of soda ash was traditionally performed by bargaining unit employees, and therefore, was still being handled by them despite the fact that, technically, soda ash is incoming freight that could be handled by the shipping clerk.

The third argument posited by the company was that Article XV of the labor agreement requires the company to make reasonable provisions for the safety of employees while at work. The company held that the forklift enhanced the job safety of all employees involved in handling materials. The purchase of separate forklifts for operations, maintenance, and shipping did not seem to be a reasonable approach for the company to take.

Like the union, the company claimed that the past practice at the plant supported its position. It was argued that past practice supported the joint use of some equipment by both bargaining unit and salaried employees in the regular performance of their job duties. The company pointed out that the forklift is no different than a pickup truck, handtruck, shovel, or broom; all are tools used by the shipping clerk as well as bargaining unit employees.

Finally, it was argued that the shipping clerk operated the forklift in the performance of his duties. It was also noted that Jordon used the forklift for almost three months before the union filed a grievance.

In conclusion, the company argued that the union, through this grievance, was attempting to deprive the shipping clerk of his regular work, gain exclusive rights to operate a piece of equip-

ment intended for joint use, and infringe upon the rights of management. By so doing, the union was trying to achieve through arbitration what it could not gain through bargaining. For these reasons, the company requested the arbitrator to deny the grievance.

DISCUSSION QUESTIONS

1. Was there a binding past practice in this case that supported the union's claim that bargaining unit personnel should use the forklift to unload trucks at the plant?

2. Assume that a binding past practice existed. Did anything occur in this case that would terminate the practice?

3. Evaluate the company's claim that the past practice supported its position that certain tools have been used by both bargaining unit and salaried personnel at the plant?

4. Does Article XIX(F) obligate the company to use bargaining unit personnel to unload trucks with the forklift?

5. How would you decide this case?

37. Should an Employee be Paid the Wage Rate of a Higher Classification When Performing that Job?

PARTIES: Indiana Reformatory and the American Federation of State, County and Municipal Employees, Indiana Council 62.

ISSUE: The issue before the arbitrator is whether Rule No. 4 permits the employer to temporarily transfer an employee to a high job classification and continue to pay the employee his regular wage rate?

BACKGROUND

John Cooper was hired at the Indiana Reformatory on December 13, 1976. He was classified as a Steam Plant Maintenance Repairman IV. Later, he became a Steam Plant Firetender. In June 1978, Cooper was classified as a Steam Plant Maintenance Mechanic II (Mechanic), the classification he held when the current grievance arose. As a Mechanic, Cooper was responsible for the repair and maintenance of the boiler and related equipment in the steam plant. The steam plant generates heat and hot water for the facility. It operates 24 hours a day, staffed on a three shift basis.

By attending Ivy Tech, a vocational school, and through experience gained in the steam plant, Cooper became qualified to perform the duties of Steam Plant Shift Operator I (Operator I). Cooper also obtained a Certificate of Competency from the Indiana Association of the National Association of Power Engineers.

Within the steam plant, the Operator I operates the boiler and other equipment. He is in charge of the shift and supervises the inmates (three in the winter and two in the summer) assigned to that shift to perform clean up work.

The Reformatory is authorized two Operators I for each of the three shifts. It is also authorized two Mechanics for the day shift and one Steam Plant Firetender for each shift. As the result of a personnel shortage, however, the steam plant did not reach its full complement of six Operators I until May 1980. Before that time only three to five Operators I were available for duty in the steam plant.

Because of the shortage, Ray Miller, Steam Plant Supervisor, requested that Cooper serve as an Operator I. Miller testified that Cooper was fully qualified to carry out the Operator I duties. Chester Martin, assistant to Miller, also said that Cooper "can do the job very well. He is an excellent Operator." In addition to performing the Operator I duties, both Miller and Martin testified that Cooper trained other employees for the Operator I classification.

During 1978 Cooper served as Operator I each Tuesday because of the shortage of persons in that classification. He also performed the duties of the classification when Operator I persons went to lunch, were absent because of illness, and during their vacations. According to employment records, during the shortage period, Cooper spent about 25 to 30 percent of his total time as an Operator I. Of that amount, he served about 5 percent on his regular day shift and the balance on overtime.

When Cooper worked as an Operator I either on his regular shift or on overtime, he was paid at the rate of his regular classification, Mechanic, and not at the higher rate of Operator I. When these circumstances arose, Cooper's salary as a Mechanic amounted to $946 per month. At that time the salary of the Operator I amounted to about $1028 per month.

On October 17, 1977, Cooper filed a complaint requesting that he be paid the Operator I rate when he served in that classification. Subsequently, that grievance was denied by the Director, State Personnel Division, and by the State Employees' Appeals Commission. Denial of the grievance was based upon Rule No. 4, Section 4-2(F)3 adopted by the State Personnel Board. It states:

> Employees requested to assume duties of positions unrelated to their own, in addition to their regular duties, may be compensated for the additional time worked at the normal rate of pay for such additional duties. Employees whose substitution on unrelated positions does not involve working more than the normal number of hours shall not be paid additional compensation for the additional duties. No such substitution shall exceed four (4) consecutive calendar weeks.

Despite the denial of Cooper's complaint of October 17, 1977, the Reformatory requested authorization to pay him the Operator I rate when he served in that classification. On March 22, 1978, R. Penn, Chief Engineer, wrote the following to N. G. Olson, Reformatory Superintendent:

> It is recommended that Mr. Cooper be raised in salary to Step E at $372.00 biweekly effective

Marth 22, 1978. Mr. Cooper must be assigned duties of a Steam Plant Shift Operator. Mr. Cooper has completed the required certification course and is certified as a Steam Plant Shift Operator. This action is being taken based upon the resignation of Mr. Stam on this date.

> Any assistance your office may be able to give in this matter is appreciated.

On the same day, March 22, 1978, Olson wrote to Cloid L. Smith, Executive Director, Department of Corrections, and said:

> Your assistance is requested in obtaining approval of the attached PD 125 to adjust the salary of Mr. John Cooper. I have discussed the powerhouse's manning situation with Mr. Penn. Effective immediately Mr. Cooper will be required to perform the duties of a Steam Plant Shift Operator. Mr. Cooper has attended the required course at IVY TECH and holds certification as required by the state personnel division. It is felt that an adjustment to the salary will compensate Mr. Cooper in accordance with duties performed, rather than requesting a waiver to the minimum qualifications for Steam Plant Shift Operator and establishing an unacceptable precedence that we would have to live with.

> Mr. Cooper has been advised that with the resignation of Mr. Stam this action must be taken. Mr. Stam's resignation leaves this agency with three (3) operators. Mr. Cooper also understands that this will change his eligible date for a merit raise.

On December 18, 1978, the Reformatory notified Cooper that its attempt was not successful. Consequently, on the same day, Cooper filed the complaint that generated this arbitration. After he filed the grievance, Cooper continued to serve when required as Operator I, and trained other persons for the classification.

Cooper's grievance states:

> On 12-17, 1978, I had to assume the duties of a Steam Plant Operator I due to the other

operators (sic) going home ill. This means that I had to operate the plant as well as supervise the inmates. I am classified as a Steam Plant Maint. Mech. II. By the State's own rules, I am not qualified to do this. I feel that this is working me out of my job classification. Not only am I being worked out of my classification, in the above mentioned matter, I am doing this higher skilled job at a lower rate of pay than an Operator I receives. I should either be paid the same rate as a Steam Plant Operator I or I should not have to do the same job that an Operator I does. I feel that this practice is wrong and I want a decision made one way or the other. I feel this problem can be solved promptly as I am not the only Powerhouse employee that has this complaint. Thank you.

In answer to the complaint, dated December 20, 1978, Ray Miller, Steam Plant Supervisor, agreed that Cooper should receive the pay rate for the Steam Plant Shift Operator I classification when he performs the duties of that classification. Miller said:

I feel the Maintenance Mechanic has to perform the same duties as the Shift Operator plus the maintenance which the Operator does not have to perform. So in my opinion the Maintenance Mechanic should be getting the same pay.

Subsequently, Cooper's complaint was denied by N. G. Olson, Superintendent of the Reformatory, and by Robert Redford, Director, State Personnel Division. On February 14, 1979, the State Employees' Appeals Commission denied the complaint without granting the petitioner a hearing, on the grounds that he failed to state a claim upon which relief can be granted.

Exercising his rights under the State Personnel Act, Cooper appealed to arbitration for the determination of his complaint.

POSITION OF THE EMPLOYEE/UNION

The testimony and evidence clearly demonstrated that Cooper is qualified to perform Operator I duties. Periodically, 25 to 30 percent of his work-

day was spent as a Steam Plant Operator I. In addition he trained other persons for this position. Both Miller and Martin, his supervisors, praised his work as an Operator I.

Consequently, it was argued that Cooper should be promoted to Operator I. If he was not promoted, it was argued that Cooper should be paid the same rate as received by an Operator I, when he performed the duties of an Operator I.

There are several reasons why Cooper should be paid the higher rate. Miller, his supervisor, recommended that Cooper be paid the Operator I rate. Also, the Superintendent and the Chief Engineer both recommended that he be paid the higher rate. It was also pointed out that Cooper faced possible discipline should he have refused assignment to the Operator I duties. It would seem that if an employee must work in a higher classification or face discipline, he should be paid at the higher rate.

In addition, it should be noted that it is common under collective bargaining contracts to compensate employees at the higher rate when temporarily transferred out of their classification. Such provisions state that should the employee be transferred temporarily to a lower paid classification, his higher rate would apply, and when transferred temporarily to a higher rated classification, the employee will be paid at the higher rate.

POSITION OF THE EMPLOYER

The state took the position that the grievance should be denied. In support of this position, two arguments were made. First, under Indiana State Personnel Rules, the minimum requirements for permanent promotion to the Operator I classification were:

Four years of full-time experience in a large institutional or industrial steam plant and obtaining within 12 months a "Certificate of Competency" from the Indiana Association of the National Association of Power Engineers; or

Possession of the "Certificate of Competency" at the time of application may substitute for six months of the required experience.

It was noted by the State that at the time of the arbitration hearing, Cooper lacked by eight months the necessary experience to qualify for promotion to Operator I.

With respect to the request to be paid the Operator I rate of pay, when performing Operator I duties, the State argued that Rule No. 4 prohibited such a practice. It was argued that under this provision the Reformatory has the legal authority to temporarily transfer an employee to work outside his regular classification. It was also pointed out that Rule No. 4 provides that "the employee transferred temporarily out of classification shall be paid at his normal rate of pay."

The only restriction on assignment of employees outside their regular classification under Rule No. 4 is that, "No such substitution shall exceed four consecutive calendar weeks." Employment records demonstrated that Cooper was never assigned to the Operator I classification for four consecutive weeks.

The State argued that in view of these Indiana State Personnel Rules, which have been adopted by the State Personnel Board, and the facts pointed out above, the grievance must be denied.

DISCUSSION QUESTIONS

1. Discuss the similarities and differences between determination of the terms of employment and grievance arbitration as represented in this case and determination of the terms of employment and grievance arbitration as it typically occurs in a unionized firm in the private sector.

2. Discuss why Cooper is entitled or is not entitled to be promoted to Operator I or compensated at that rate when he is directed to perform the duties of an Operator I?

3. Should the grievance be sustained or denied? Why?

38. Were Workers Entitled to a Cost-of-Living Increase?

PARTIES: Owens-Corning Fiberglass Corporation and the International Association of Machinists and Aerospace Workers, Local 1280.

ISSUE: Did the company violate the collective bargaining agreement when it did not pay a cost-of-living adjustment in the quarter beginning March 1, 1979? If so, what is the proper remedy?

BACKGROUND

The Owens-Corning Fiberglass Corporation is operated from Toledo, Ohio, and has a plant in Newark, Ohio. Approximately 2600 workers are employed at this plant. The International Association of Machinists and Aerospace Workers represents 450 maintenance employees. Their contract was from June 1, 1978, to June 1, 1981. Previous to the final agreement to the contract, a 75-day strike occurred. Of major concern to the employees during the strike was a cost-of-living provision. Although a cost-of-living adjustment had been in the previous contract, a different provision that removed the earlier 10-cent cap was in the contract under discussion.

Paragraphs 266, 267, and 268 of Section 5, Article X relate to the first, second, and third years, respectively, of the cost-of-living provisions. Section 5, Article X of the contract is reproduced below:

ARTICLE X—SHIFT PREMIUM AND WAGE RATES

Section 5, Cost-of-Living

266.A. In the first year of the Agreement, if the cost-of-living increases more than seven percent (7%), (204.8 on the Index), the Company will pay 1.0 cent for each 0.5 point rise over the Index base of 204.8. The Company will review at the beginning of the quarter after the Index base of 204.8 is reached, and necessary adjustments will be made effective on the Monday nearest September 1, December 1, March 1, or June 1.

267.B. In the second year of the Agreement, if the cost-of-living goes up more than seven percent (7%) over the B.L.S. Index published and in effect on June 1, 1979, the Company will pay 1.0 cent for each 0.5 point rise over the seven percent (7%) Index point. The Company will review at the beginning of the quarter after the Index goes up seven percent (7%), and necessary adjustments will be made effective on the Monday nearest September 1, December 1, March 1, or June 1.

268.C. In the third year of the Agreement, if the cost-of-living goes up more than seven percent (7%) over the B.L.S. Index published and in effect on June 1, 1980, the Company will pay 1.0 cent for each 0.5 point rise over the seven percent (7%) Index point. The Company will review at the beginning of the quarter after the Index goes up seven percent (7%) and necessary adjustments will be made effective on the Monday nearest September 1, December 1, or March 1. No review or adjustment will be made for the last quarter of the Agreement term.

269.D. The Index used to compute cost-of-living adjustments is the official B.L.S. Revised C.P.I. for the Urban Wage Earners and Clerical Workers.

270.E. The formula used to compute cost-of-living adjustments is 1.0 cent increase for each 0.5 rise in the Index.

POSITION OF THE UNION

On May 31, 1979, a grievance was filed by the members of the IAMAW, Local 1280. The union maintained that the company was in violation of Article X, Section 5, paragraph 266 by refusing to pay a 4-cent per hour cost-of-living increase for the period of March 1 through May 31, 1979. There is an established 204.8 index calculation in paragraph 266. When this figure is reached the negotiated adjustment was to become effective. The index for the month of February was 207.1. Consequently a cost-of-living payment of 4 cents per hour should have begun on March 1, 1979. Instead of making the payment at this time, no adjustment was given until June 1.

In addition, paragraph 266 does not read the same as paragraph 267 and 268. The latter paragraphs specifically state that any adjustment will be made on the basis of "the B.L.S. Index published and in effect on June 1." Paragraph 266 differs in that it reads "the Company will pay 1.0 cents for each 0.5 point rise over the Index base of 204.8."

Wes Bradley, union treasurer, maintained that the index was available in the newspaper each month prior to actual publication by the Bureau of Labor Statistics. He contended that he had read the figure in the *Newark Advocate* by March 1 and that the grieved amount should have been paid at that time. The data published by the Bureau on March 23, 1979, was not appropriate for the first year. Paragraph 266 is not am-

biguous. Clearly, paragraphs 267 and 268 do state the word "published," but it is not to be found in paragraph 266.

There was no reason for the company not to use as datum what the newspaper stated the Index would be. Its failure to do so was a clear violation of the contract. Employees should be immediately reimbursed 4 cents per hour, effective March 1, 1979.

POSITION OF THE COMPANY

Both parties recognized that during the strike and the long period of negotiation, discussions on cost-of-living were of primary concern. The reason an Index of 204.8 was inserted in paragraph 266 was the result of the available figure for June 1 being known at the time the agreement was reached. The BLS figure for Urban Wage Earners and Clerical Workers of 191.4 was published May 31, 1978, and pertained to the month of April. Seven percent of this figure gave the parties the level of 204.8. This is the only reason for the difference in the paragraphs. The 7 percent is present in all three, and each paragraph is based on the BLS Index despite the fact that a direct reference to BLS is not made in paragraph 266.

During the meeting with the Machinists on July 31, 1978, Bradley recognized that there was a lengthy discussion on how the provisions would operate. The review would continue to be made on the basis of each quarter. Using a blackboard, estimates were given to show how the 7 percent would work based on the known figure of 191.4. In the previous contract the Consumers Price Index was used, but when the Urban Wage Earners and Clerical Workers Index became available in 1978, it was decided to use this index.

This was not an estimated index and there is no way that an estimate could be used for a wage adjustment. Necessarily a lag must occur in the compilation of an index. A Special Service Company receives the index on the day of release. This company immediately mails a notation to Corning, which is received the following day. At the end of each month, tabulation requires up to three or four weeks before the index for the month can be released. On May 31, 1978, an index of 191.4 for April was received, on June 30, 1978, the index for May became available. It was 193.3. It is inconceivable that the union could have known that the index for February of 1979 was 207.1 until March 23, 1979. Because the contract calls for quarterly review, the index did not rise above 204.8 until June 1, 1979. On May 25 management learned that the index for April was 211.8, and the appropriate cost-of-living adjustment was put into effect on the Monday closest to June 1. The appropriate wage adjustment was made.

DISCUSSION QUESTIONS

1. Does the contract specify which index will be used in making cost-of-living wage adjustments?

2. Should the grievance be upheld or denied? Explain.

3. Compare the cost-of-living provisions of this contract to the typical cost-of-living contract provision.

SECTION 8
Simulations

Contract Negotiations Simulation

ACE TOY COMPANY AND SPACE-AGE WORKERS OF AMERICA

Objective: To obtain an initial understanding of what it feels like to participate in a collective bargaining session. *Time:* Allow between 45 minutes and 1 hour and one-half.

Procedures:

1. Divide into groups of three to five people. Half of the groups will be on a union negotiation team and half will be on a company negotiating team.

2. Read the background below.

3. Study the section, "Remaining Bargaining Issues," and the table on union contracts.

4. Take between 20 to 45 minutes to negotiate an agreement with the other side. If there is no agreement at that time, both sides will pay dearly in the form of a strike. Record your agreement.

BACKGROUND

Ace Toy Company of Memphis, Tennessee, produces space-age toys for distribution and sale nationally. It has 250 employees, of whom 130 are engaged in the nonunion sales force, and administrative and managerial jobs. The remaining 120 employees are engaged in the actual production of the toys and were organized in 1970 by the

Space-Age Workers of America (SWA). As the market for space-age toys boomed in the 1970s and 1980s, Ace was able to share its profits to some degree with its workers through increased wages, and thus maintained good relations with the union. There has never been a strike. Both Ace and the employees are proud of the reputation for quality products that Ace Toys has in the industry and the marketplace. As a result of the large number of space-age movies released in the early 1980s, demand for space-age toys started to increase, with orders for Ace toys alone up 50 percent in the last three months. Management is hoping to increase its market share and reduce its backlog of orders. It plans to rapidly increase its production as soon as bargaining with the union is completed. However, the union is concerned that its members may be already overworked, while the company claims that its production lines are not operating as efficiently as possible and that it needs more lines with fewer people per line.

The current union contract expires in three days. Negotiations have been going on for several weeks, and all the noneconomic items have been settled on. Bargaining is moving into marathon sessions now and the parties disagree about only five items. Ace wants to save money to finance its expansion and thus is keeping its offers low. The union, on the other hand, feels its members should share in what it sees as increased profits in the future.

REMAINING BARGAINING ISSUES

1. Pension

Current contract: Pays $8 per month per year of service to retirees.

Ace position: No Change

Union position: $12 per month per year of service.

Dollars Per Month Per Year of Service				
8	9	10	11	12
0	$5,500	11,000	16,500	22,000

Increased Annual Dollar Costs to Ace

2. Wages

Current contract: $6.00 per hour

Ace position: No Change

Union position: 80 cents per hour more

Per Hour Increases				
0	0.20	0.40	0.60	0.80
0	$49,920	99,840	149,760	199,680

Increased Annual Dollar Costs to Ace

3. Crew Size

Current contract: 12 persons per crew (ten crews)

Ace position: 11 persons per crew

Union position: One additional person per crew at a cost of $12,480 each.

Crew Size		
11	12	13
$(124,800)	0	124,800

Increased (Decreased) Annual Dollar Costs to Ace

4. Holidays

Current contract: Seven holidays

Ace position: No increase

Union position: Four more holidays

Number of Holidays				
7	8	9	10	11
0	$5,760	11,520	17,280	23,040

Increased Annual Dollar Costs to Ace

5. Medical Benefits

Current contract: Fully paid individual insurance coverage. No company-paid dependent coverage. One-half of current employees have dependents.

Ace position: Employees should pay for full dependent coverage.

Union position: Company should pay for full dependent coverage.

Ace Contribution				
0	1/4	1/2	3/4	All
0	$12,590	25,180	37,770	50,360

Increased Annual Dollar Cost To Ace

TABLE 1
Union contracts among competitors in the Memphis area

	COMPETITOR A	COMPETITOR B	COMPETITOR C	COMPETITOR D	MEMPHIS AREA
Pension payment in $ per month of service	$9.00	$12.00	$7.00	$8.00	$8.00
Hourly wage rate	6.20	7.00	5.80	6.00	6.20
Crew size	9	8	12	10	11
Holidays	10	10	5	5	8
Company contribution paid dependent medical coverage	1/4	3/4	1/2	1/4	1/4

Bargaining Simulation

HOYT N. WHEELER
University of South Carolina

JAMES E. MARTIN
Wayne State University

SWEETWATER BOTTLING COMPANY OF SAN FRANCISCO AND ALLIED WORKERS OF AMERICA, LOCAL 123

LEARNING OBJECTIVES OF THE SIMULATION

1. To recognize and understand the importance of the process of preparation in bargaining.

2. To understand intraorganizational bargaining and the problems of teamwork associated with bargaining.

3. To gain an understanding about the process of collective bargaining and the issues that are the subject of negotiations.

4. To practice the mechanics of actual bargaining to obtain a contract: trading issues, compromising, caucusing, give-and-take, and dropping issues to obtain a contract.

5. To understand the difficulty involved in agreeing upon and writing actual contract language.

6. To apply theory to actual bargaining.

GROUND RULES AND PROCEDURES

1. You will be assigned a position (union or management) and a team, and perhaps a role by your instructor.

2. Do not consult with any other member of any other team, union or management, including students who have done this simulation before.

3. Any demands, proposals, or offers must take place within the framework of the simulation facts that follow.

4. Research should be done prior to establishing positions. While originality is allowed, arguments concerning one side's position should not be falsified, but in so far as possible, be based on research and/or the facts of the case.

5. Your team may organize itself in any way *or* may receive instructions from your instructor concerning its organization.

6. Your team will need to meet to prepare for bargaining. You need to prepare your team's own demands and proposals as well as predicting the other side's demands and proposals. The exact number of issues you may bargain over will be determined by your instructor.

7. Working with your team, complete Form 1. Management teams should place their desired wage settlement on Form 1 even if they plan to make no offer or demand in the wage area. This form will be given only to your instructor.

8. In exchanging demands with the other side, make sure you make sufficient copies for all members of both teams and the instructor.

9. Your team should be prepared to present your contract, or final position, if there is no agreement, and your strategy to the class as a whole after you have settled.

10. Your instructor will have additional instructions and information about the simulation.

RESOURCES FOR PREPARATION

The Bureau of Labor Statistics of the U.S. Department of Labor has several publications presenting data on both economic and noneconomic issues including *Employment and Earnings, Area Wage Surveys* (containing information on San Francisco wage rates), *Characteristics of Major Collective Bargaining Agreements,* and the periodical *Monthly Labor Review.*

Other information is available from the Bureau of National Affairs publication *Collective Bargaining Negotiations and Contracts,* the AFL-CIO magazine *American Federationalist,* the binder service of Prentice-Hall, the binder service of the Commerce Clearing House, and the *Clause Reference Manual* of the Labor-Management Relations Service.

Standard and Poors, Moody's, and Value Line also publish industry surveys providing helpful background trends for particular industries.

BACKGROUND OF COMPANY

History

In 1938, Donald K. Horn purchased from the trustee in bankruptcy a business franchise that had failed and commenced the business of bottling and distributing Sweetwater Soda in Alameda, San Francisco, San Mateo, and Contra Costa Counties, California. The business was incorporated as Sweetwater Bottling Company of San Francisco, Inc. Sweetwater San Francisco subsequently added new soft drinks to its product line under licenses from the Sweetwater Company, Memphis, Tennessee ("The Sweetwater Company"), and presently markets Sweetwater Soda, Rock Springs Cola, and Green River Soda.

In April 1968 Sweetwater San Francisco, through a subsidiary, acquired all of the stock of Sweetwater Bottling Company of Sacramento, Inc., for a price of approximately $2,000,000 in cash, promissory notes, and assumption of promissory notes. It also obtained the franchise for Sacramento County California.

Products and Market

The principal products of Sweetwater San Francisco and its subsidiaries consist of regular and diet lemon-lime flavored soft drinks and regular and diet caffeine-free cola-like soft drinks.

Concentrated drink extract is mixed under controlled conditions with citric acid, water, and carbon dioxide to form the finished product, Sweetwater Soda, which may be placed in bottles, cans, or pre-mix containers. The other products are mixed in a similar fashion. A pre-mix container is a pressurized container that is utilized in cup vending machines and other special dispensing equipment. The products are distributed through the franchise territory in a variety of bottles and cans. Sweetwater San Francisco also sells post-mix (fountain) syrup, which is marketed to high-volume users, who mix the syrup with carbonated water and dispense it through special post-mix vending and dispensing equipment.

Products and production in the soft drink industry are subject to rules and regulations of the United States Food and Drug Administration and other federal, state, and local agencies.

Raw Materials

Sweetwater San Francisco purchases all of its concentrated extract for its products from the Sweetwater Company. The formulas for the extract and flavoring compounds are owned by the Sweetwater Company. In addition, Sweetwater San Francisco purchases citric acid, sugar, carbon dioxide gas, bottles, cans, metal crowns, cartons,

FORM 1
Bargaining agenda

HIGHLY CONFIDENTIAL
to be seen only by your team and the instructor

BARGAINING ISSUES*	A. LIMIT, RESISTANCE POINT (What you must get)	B. ASPIRATION, TARGET POINT (What you would like to get)	C. REALISTIC OBJECTIVE (What you might realistically get)	D. INITIAL OPENING BARGAINING POSITION

* List bargaining issues on the agenda in order of importance, i.e., the most important issue is listed first and the least important issue is listed last. A thru D may be the same for some issues.

bottle cases, pre-mix and post-mix containers, coolers, and vending equipment.

Retail distribution is principally through food stores, vending machines, drive-in and other restaurants, soda fountains, bars, and other retail establishments in its franchise territory.

Competition

The soft drink market is highly competitive. The products of Sweetwater San Francisco compete with other extensively advertised soft drinks produced by subsidiaries of national companies and with lesser known soft drinks produced by local bottlers and canners, and they also receive competition from substitute drinks. The market for the diet and caffeine-free soft drinks is less established than that of the older products, but is very competitive and expanding fast.

In the "take-home" market, consisting of bottled and canned soft drinks usually distributed by food stores, convenience packaging (cans and nonreturnable bottles) have been growing in importance. This development is particularly noticeable in the increasing sale of private-label canned soft drinks by major food chains. In the so-called "cold drink" market, consisting of cup and bottled vending machines, fountains, and other on-premises dispensers, Sweetwater Soda's two major competitors have accounted for a large proportion of vending machine installations. This is an important competitive factor since soft drinks imitative of Sweetwater have been more extensively marketed through vending machines than other distribution channels.

Substantial changes have taken place in the soft drink industry in recent years. Dietary soft drinks now constitute an important segment of the soft drink market. Sweetwater San Francisco competes in this market with several products. In general, its sales volume has been increasing moderately over the past few years, and that increase is reflected in its financial statements (Tables 1 and 2).

The number of cases of soft drinks sold per year and empty cases returned per year are shown below.

CASES OF SOFT DRINKS SOLD PER YEAR	
Four years ago	3,200,000
Three years ago	3,400,000
Two years ago	3,600,000
Last year	3,650,000

EMPTY CASES RETURNED PER YEAR	
Four years ago	2,870,000
Three years ago	3,180,000
Two years ago	3,290,000
Last year	3,200,000

Sweetwater San Francisco is unable to predict the extent to which sales of its products will be affected by future competition, unseasonable weather conditions, labor conditions, availability of supplies or other factors beyond its control.

Franchises

Franchises of Sweetwater San Francisco and its subsidiaries from The Sweetwater Company give the right to manufacture, sell, and distribute all products in the markets described above, and require intensive sale of the products. The Sweetwater Company agrees to sell to no other bottler in the territories granted so long as Sweetwater San Francisco maintains a dealer distribution of not less than 50 percent of the active dealer outlets in the territories. The franchise agreements grant to Sweetwater San Francisco and its subsidiaries the right to use the trademarks associated with the products. The Sweetwater Company agrees to sell to Sweetwater San Francisco and its subsidiaries Sweetwater Soda re-agents and flavoring ingredients for the products under the same terms and conditions as they are currently being furnished to other Sweetwater bottlers in the United States.

TABLE 1
Balance Sheet (Does not include Sweetwater Sacramento subsidiary)

ASSETS	December 31, Last Year
Current Assets:	
Cash	$ 799,057
Marketable securities, at cost (approximate market)	197,083
Accounts receivable, less allowance for doubtful accounts, $70,000 last year	1,849,667
Inventories, at lower cost or market	2,242,030
Prepaid expenses	234,066
Total current assets	5,321,903
Plant and Equipment, at cost:	
Land	381,000
Buildings and improvements	3,367,097
Machinery and equipment	2,567,005
Motor vehicles	1,618,416
Containers	1,601,102
Office furniture and equipment	203,935
Subtotal	9,738,555
Less accumulated depreciation	4,069,713
Net plant and equipment	5,668,842
Franchise, at Cost Less Accumulated Amortization, $1,195,231	804,769
Deferred Federal Income Tax Charges	209,779
Other Assets	17,993
Total assets	$12,023,286

LIABILITIES AND STOCKHOLDERS' EQUITY	
Current Liabilities:	
Notes payable	$ 89,508
Current installments of long-term debt	85,194
Accounts payable	1,621,731
Accrued expenses	798,531
Taxes on income	765,311
Total current liabilities	3,360,275
Customer Deposits on Containers	621,326
Accrued Longevity Pay	138,851
Long-Term Debt, Excluding Current Installments	1,403,503
Total liabilities	5,523,955
Stockholders' Equity:	
Common stock without par value. Authorized 2,000,000 shares; issued 1,000,000 shares at stated value	1,372,450
Retained earnings	5,152,566
	6,525,016
Less cost of 2000 common shares in treasury	25,685
Total stockholders' equity	6,499,331
Total liabilities and equity	$12,023,286

TABLE 2
Income Statements (Does not include Sweetwater Sacramento subsidiary)

	YEAR ENDED DECEMBER 31			
	Four years ago	Three years ago	Two years ago	Last year
Net Sales	$25,534,400	$27,424,688	$29,638,742	$30,451,322
Cost and expense:				
Cost of sales	8,278,194	8,583,624	8,949,384	9,676,005
Selling, administration and general expenses	14,074,818	15,048,921	15,994,699	16,905,731
Depreciation	567,161	581,710	626,665	500,000
Interest expense	99,652	105,554	123,079	125,175
Total	23,019,825	24,319,809	25,693,827	27,206,911
Income before taxes on income	2,514,575	3,104,879	3,944,915	3,244,411
Taxes on income:				
Federal	1,085,000	1,345,000	1,582,000	1,413,000
California Franchise Tax	125,000	163,000	207,000	170,000
Total	1,210,000	1,508,000	1,789,000	1,583,000
Net income	$1,304,575	$1,596,879	$2,155,915	$1,661,411
Per Share Data:				
Net income	$1.30	$1.60	$2.16	$1.66
Cash dividends	0.70	0.88	1.20	0.90

WORK FORCE AND EMPLOYEE RELATIONS CHARACTERISTICS

As of the end of the last calendar year, Sweetwater San Francisco employed approximately 511 persons, including about 15 management and supervisory personnel, 81 salaried sales and technical personnel, 193 production and warehouse workers and mechanics, and 222 driver-salesmen. All production and warehouse workers and driver-salesmen employed at the company's San Francisco facility are members of a bargaining unit covered by agreement with the Allied Workers of America, Local 123.

Number of plant and warehouse employees in each job classification

JOB CLASSIFICATION	NUMBERS OF WORKERS IN CLASSIFICATION	NUMBER OF WORKERS WHO ARE PROBATIONARY
Operator	90	2
Mechanic	50	3
Forklift Operator	15	1
Laborer	20	2
Janitor	8	1
Truck Driver	10	1

Number of employees in different classifications with different years of service

YEARS OF SERVICE	DRIVER-SALESMAN	OPERATOR	MECHANIC	FORKLIFT OPERATOR	LABORER	JANITOR	TRUCK DRIVER	TOTAL
30 +	10	2	2	1	0	0	0	15
20–29	50	3	2	1	2	1	1	60
15–19	60	7	4	3	2	1	3	80
10–14	45	12	7	2	2	1	1	70
5–9	35	21	10	3	5	3	1	78
2–4	16	30	14	2	2	0	2	66
1	4	13	8	2	5	1	1	34
Less than 1	2	2	3	1	2	1	1	12
Total	222	90	50	15	20	8	10	415

Age-seniority breakdown

AGE IN YEARS	SENIORITY IN YEARS								
	1	1	2–4	5–9	10–14	15–19	20–29	30 +	Total
Under 20	2	2							4
20–24	5	7	11	1					24
25–29	5	15	30	5	1				56
30–34		10	15	5	5	1			36
35–39			10	10	5	3			28
40–44				15	15	10	5		45
45–49				25	25	30	5		85
50–54				15	10	20	20		65
55–59				2	9	15	20	5	51
60–64						1	10	5	16
65–70								5	5
TOTAL	12	34	66	78	70	80	60	15	415

Driver-salesman pay — Typical (Modal) Class
Return of Empties
15,000 cases at .15 = $ 2,250.00

Commission
18,000 cases at .40 = $ 7,200.00

Salary
$425 per week   = $22,100.00

Total   = $31,500.00 per year
   Top $37,500.00 per year
   Bottom $25,500.00 per year

Wages and Benefits of Major Competitors

Competitor A: The same wages and benefits as Sweetwater San Francisco. This company is not under union contract.

Competitor B: About the same size as Sweetwater San Francisco. 15 percent higher wages in all plant and warehouse classifications. Driver-salesmen *salary* = $450.00 per week; *commission* = $.50 per case; *commission on empties* = $.16 per case. Competitor B is under union contract.

Holidays: Christmas, Easter Monday, Thanksgiving, Fourth of July, Labor Day, Good Friday, Christmas Eve Day, Employee's birthday, Memorial Day, President's Holiday, day after Thanksgiving.

Vacations: 2 weeks for 1 year
3 weeks for 5 years
4 weeks for 10 years
5 weeks for 20 years

Health Coverage: Covers both employee and dependents at company's cost.

Background of Union Representation

The company's San Francisco facility was organized by the union, the Allied Workers of America (AWA) as a result of a long and bitter organizational campaign. The leaders of the union organization drive capitalized on the unwillingness of the company to share its increasing profits with the work force. This particularly affected the production and maintenance employees, as the driver-salesmen were receiving commissions. The union pledged that it would get the company to increase the wages of the employees. The company argued that it needed the increased profits to finance the introduction of new soft drinks in order to meet the competition.

The union won the NLRB representation election by a vote of 155 to 150. The employer contested the election and appealed adverse determinations at the lower levels of the NLRB. The Board upheld the election results and certified the union as the bargaining agent for the company's production, maintenance, and sales force in San Francisco. This certification took place 18 months ago. The Sacramento operations remained non-union. After negotiating for approximately five months and experiencing a four-week strike, a one-year collective bargaining agreement resulted. That agreement is reproduced in full beginning on p. 485. The major issues in the negotiations were wages and union security.

Management believed that it lost quite a few sales because of the strike. It did not attempt to operate the San Francisco plant during the strike, but instead used its nonunion personnel to double the capacity of its much smaller Sacramento plant, and maintain some distribution of products, mostly in the eastern part of its territory. Fifty driver-salesmen, who worked out of the San Francisco plant, did not honor the picket lines the Union set up at the Sacramento and San Francisco plants. They helped with deliveries, some of which were made from the inventory at San Francisco. However, management estimated that the company still sold about 150,000 to 250,000 cases less than it would have sold that year had there not been a strike.

After the settlement, Sweetwater San Francisco quickly recovered its market share by offering expensive promotions and using overtime. The strike, including the high cost involved in attempting to service its market from Sacramento, as well as the increased labor costs resulting from the settlement, lowered the company's profits somewhat in the prior year.

Internal Union Situation

The local union members are split into several factions. The most militant employees are a group of about 40 plant operators and forklift drivers. The driver-salesmen earn good money, and are relatively satisfied with the company's treatment of them. They are less enthusiastic about the union than are the plant workers, a high percentage of whom are union members. A much lower percentage of the driver-salesmen have joined the union. The membership as a whole is deeply divided over whether the union should try to increase the wages of the driver-salesmen during the next negotiations. Many are still angry because some driver-salesmen made deliveries during the strike. However, it is recognized that the strong support of the driver-salesmen would be important if an effective strike were to be carried out in the future. Workers in the plant would also like to be able to move into the driver-salesman position more easily as openings occur.

The union negotiating committee is composed of the local union president and several workers elected by the members. The AWA local covers more employers than just this plant. There are fewer driver-salesmen on the bargaining team than plant workers.

The union is also trying to organize the salaried sales and technical personnel at Sweetwater San Francisco. There is some interest in the union by those employees, but they are awaiting the results of the next contract negotiations before making any decision. Those employees were not happy that a strike took place during the last negotiations.

Contract Administration

There have been several major areas in which grievances were filed during the term of the first contract. Some of these areas were not explicitly covered in the contract. Twenty grievances were filed under Article VII, Job Bidding. All of these grievances claimed that even though the more senior employees had the ability to do the job, the company chose an employee with less seniority to fill the position. In ten of these, the employees selected were not union members but were in the bargaining unit. Thus the union has also threatened to file unfair labor practice charges against the company if they continued to promote less senior nonmembers. The company denied any discrimination, arguing that in every disputed promotion, the less senior employee not only had more ability, but also had a better work record, and thus was more qualified to fill the new position. The company has denied these grievances at each step. However, while the union requested arbitration for all 20 cases, the company and the union agreed to delay going to arbitration on any case in the hope that the forthcoming contract negotiations would clear up all pending grievances.

Also in relation to promotions, three driver-salesmen positions became vacant during the term of the contract, only one of which was filled by a current employee. In the other two cases, employees filed grievances but the company claimed that neither had the ability to do the job. They also claimed that the contract gave them the right to hire from outside the bargaining unit when no current employee was qualified. This is a very important issue to both sides because of the large number of driver-salesmen near retirement age.

Because the current contract does not define the workweek, anytime a holiday falls during the week and the company operates the plant on a Saturday, no overtime rates are paid. While the employees are very upset about this practice, the company claims that it is necessary because many beverages are sold on holidays. Further, if an employee misses a day because of illness, and subsequently works a Saturday, the company will not pay that employee overtime pay. Forty grievances have been filed by the union on these matters and all were denied by the company. The employees feel this practice is unfair and want to rectify it in the next contract.

A further area of dispute between the union and the company is in the area of transfers. The company claims that under Article II, Company Rights and Obligations, it not only has the right to transfer employees, but also does not have to pay the employees the higher rate as long as the transfer is temporary. During one two-week pay period, half of the janitors and laborers were working on the line while 14 operators were on vacation. When the transferred employees received their paychecks at the lower pay-rate, the line immediately slowed down. The company attempted to charge the union with a violation of Article IV, No Interruption of Service, and threatened to suspend the employees involved. However, the union president convinced the company not to discipline any employees because the slowdown was caused by low morale. He assured the company that a slowdown would not happen again as long as the company paid the employees involved one week's pay at the higher rate and one at the lower rate. The company was not pleased with this solution and received a letter of agreement from the union president limiting this settlement to this case only. As a result, there were still 20 pending grievances over other "temporary" transfers, in three cases for as long as two months, for which employees were paid the lower rate. The union claims that any transfer longer than a day should be treated as a promotion. However, management claims that it can pay a lower rate for as long as it wants as long as the transfer is "temporary."

There is also some dissatisfaction within the plant about perceived wage inequities. However, no grievances have been filed on this issue.

AGREEMENT

This Agreement is entered into by the Sweetwater Bottling Company of San Francisco (herein after referred to as the Company) and the Allied Workers of America, Local 123 (herein after referred to as the Union).

ARTICLE I. UNION RIGHTS AND OBLIGATIONS

The Company recognizes the Union as the sole and exclusive collective bargaining representative of all full-time and regular part-time production and maintenance employees, including warehouse, shipping and receiving employees, transport drivers, and driver-salesmen employed by the Company at its facilities located in San Francisco, California excluding professional employees, office clerical employees, guards, and supervisors as defined in the Act, and all other employees. The Agreement shall not apply to employees covered by any other agreement with this or another union, nor to any employees who have not designated any union as their representative, nor to any other employee or nonemployee.

The Union recognizes, in consideration of the commitments undertaken by the Company, that an obligation rests upon every employee to

perform honest, efficient, and economical service in performance of his or her duties. The Union will actively support the legitimate and reasonable efforts of the Company to maintain and improve the skill, ability, and production of the working force, and to reduce waste, spoilage of materials, or production of inferior products. Furthermore, the Union and the Company agree that all dealings between them should have as a prime objective the maintenance of a productive, cooperative atmosphere that will make it possible to offer consumers a growing volume of high quality products, which will, in turn, provide employees with secure jobs and a pleasant atmosphere in which to work.

ARTICLE II. COMPANY RIGHTS AND OBLIGATIONS

The Union recognizes that the Company retains the sole and exclusive right to manage its business and to direct the work force. This shall include, but not be limited to, the right to hire, assign work and schedules, suspend, discharge for proper cause, transfer, relieve employees from duty because of lack of work or other business reasons. Prior to negotiations, management should review their present system of record keeping on plant discipline, especially as it relates to supervisors' written records of talks with employees concerning productivity, attitudes, and adherence to plant rules, the system of written notice or warnings to employees when they have fallen short of expectations, disciplinary layoff procedures and the manner in which employees are handled when discharged, review of forms used for disciplinary warnings, and the like. Examples of first-time offenses that will result in dismissal include stealing private or company property, possession of live weapons, personal conduct at work dangerous to others. Examples of second-time offenses that will result in dismissal include sleeping during working hours, leaving premises during work hours without permission, and willfully punching another employee's time card. Third-time offenses that will result in dismissal include personal work on company time and violation of common sense health and sanitation rules. These examples simply indicate the degree of offense that will result in dismissal.

The Company recognizes that an obligation rests upon it to provide adequate management and supervision that will provide for continued growth and success of the Company. It recognizes its obligation to provide fair and equal treatment to all employees along with the opportunity to help each employee develop his interests, abilities, and skills to the fullest extent practicable within the limits of the individual and the jobs available to this Company.

ARTICLE III. UNION SECURITY

All present employees with less than five (5) years service covered by the bargaining unit are required to join the Union within sixty (60) days from the signing of this contract. All employees hired on or after the date of signing shall be required to join the Union sixty (60) days after their first day of employment. Failure or refusal to join the Union shall be grounds for immediate termination for future employees. All employees who are members of the Union upon the signing of the agreement shall retain their membership in good standing in accordance with the Constitution and By-Laws of the Union as a condition of continued employment with the Company. All employees who become members of the Union after the signing of the Agreement shall be subject to the same provisions as those above.

The Company agrees for said employees to deduct from the first pay of each month, the Union dues for the preceding month, and promptly remit the same to the appropriate official of the Union. The initiation fee of the Union shall be deducted by the Company and remitted to the appropriate official of the Union in the same manner as dues collections.

The Company shall agree to refrain from interfering in the internal workings of the Union. The Company shall also agree to allow official Union representatives adequate time during the working day to perform their assigned tasks, subject to approval by management.

ARTICLE IV. NO INTERRUPTION OF SERVICE

There shall be no strikes by the Union, or by an employee(s), or lockout by the Employer during the length of the contract. A strike is defined as an intentional slowdown in or interference with the Employer's operations, interruption of production or suspension or refusal of work, any work stoppage, or any other intentional or sympathetic act designed to impede production or service of one or more employees. Any employee who participates in, advances, leads, or promotes any strike shall be subject to disciplinary action up to and including discharge.

ARTICLE V. PAID VACATIONS

A regular, full-time employee who has completed one (1) year of active employment since his latest date of employment or re-employment shall be eligible for one (1) week of paid vacation. After two (2) years of continuous employment, each employee shall be given two (2) weeks off with pay. After ten (10) years of service, each employee shall be given three (3) weeks off with pay. After twenty (20) years of service, each employee shall be given four (4) weeks off with pay.

ARTICLE VI. PAID HOLIDAYS

Regular employees shall be paid for and shall not be required to work on the following days: New Year's Day, Independence Day, Thanksgiving Day, Christmas Day, Memorial Day, Good Friday, and the day before Christmas.

ARTICLE VII. JOB BIDDING

The Company will fill vacant positions with employees who have shown an interest in the position by signing their name on a bulletin posted for no less than one working week. In choosing between two or more possible applicants, seniority, ability, and merit shall be the basis for a decision.

ARTICLE VIII. HEALTH INSURANCE

The Company shall provide health insurance for each employee, at the present benefit mix, with no coverage for dependents.

ARTICLE IX. LIFE INSURANCE

The Company shall pay for the first $10,000 of each employee's life insurance at a cost not to exceed $4 per employee per month. The employee shall pay for each additional $10,000 unit of insurance. The Company will administer all employees' life insurance matters.

ARTICLE X. DISCOUNTS

The Company shall grant all employees a 25 percent discount on all of the Company's products.

ARTICLE XI. AUTHORIZED ABSENCES

The Company shall recognize absences with full pay for funerals of close relatives (father, mother, brother, sister, spouse, or such a family tie who may have assumed the duties of one of the above toward the employee). The Contract-writing Committee agrees on two (2) days authorized absence.

ARTICLE XII. UNIFORMS

The Company shall pay for and maintain two uniforms per week consisting of shirts and slacks for all employees and including jackets for the driver-salesmen.

ARTICLE XIII. LAYOFF AND RECALL

In the event that a layoff is absolutely necessary, seniority, ability, and past performance after one year shall be the basis for determining who is laid off and who is retained. Seniority, ability, and past performance after one year shall also be the basis for recall.

ARTICLE XIV. GRIEVANCES

1. A grievance is a claim that the employer has violated an express provision of this agreement. Any employee may discuss any matter with his supervisor without invoking the formal grievance procedure.

2. The grievance must be reduced to writing, must state all of the sections of this agreement that the grievant feels have been violated by the employer, and must be signed and dated by the grievant. The grievance must be filed in duplicate, with the employer within two (2) working days (48 hours), holidays excepted, after the aggrieved employee or any shop steward knew, or should have known, the facts that gave rise to the grievance. The written grievance must be presented to the aggrieved employee's immediate supervisor, or, if he is not available, to the employer's personnel department.

3. Within the same two working days after the filing of the grievance, the grievance shall be discussed between the aggrieved employee, the shop steward, if the aggrieved employee desires his presence, and the aggrieved employee's immediate supervisor. The supervisor must give his answer, in writing, to the grievant and the shop steward within two working days after the holding of such meeting.

4. If the Union is not satisfied with the supervisor's reply, it may, within two working days after receipt by the grievant and the shop steward of the supervisor's answer, request the employer's Vice-President for Industrial Relations or his representative, in writing, for a meeting to discuss the grievance. Within two working days after

receipt of such request by the V.P. for Industrial Relations or his representative, the grievance shall be discussed in a meeting between the aggrieved employee, the Local Union President or his representative, the V.P. for Industrial Relations or his representative, and the immediate supervisor. The Employer must give a written answer to the Local Union President within two working days after the holding of such a meeting.

5. If the Union is not satisfied with this answer, it may, within two working days after receipt of the answer, request the V.P. for Industrial Relations, in writing, to take the grievance to arbitration.

6. Any fact not represented by the Union, the Employer, or the grievant during the grievance process may not be presented or relied upon by any one of these parties in the arbitration hearing.

7. Failure of either party to comply with the time limits set forth above will serve to declare the grievance as settled in favor of the other party, and no further action may be taken. Any grievance that is not filed within the time limit provided for in this section or that is not filed in accordance with the provisions of this section shall not be subject to the grievance or arbitration procedures of this agreement. However, the time limits set forth above may be extended by written mutual agreement.

8. As used in this section the term "working day" includes a scheduled working day of 24 hours.

9. No employee will be discriminated against, or in any manner disciplined, because of his filing a grievance pursuant to the provisions of this agreement.

Arbitration

1. The selection of the arbitrator will be as follows. The Federal Mediation and Conciliation Service will be requested to submit a panel of seven arbitrators from which an arbitrator will be selected. Each of the parties shall be entitled to strike three names alternately from the list. The party who is to strike the first name from the list shall be selected by lot.

2. The decision reached by the arbitrator shall be binding on all parties concerned.

3. If the arbitrator finds that one of the parties has been unreasonable in forcing the grievance to arbitration, he shall assess the expenses of the impartial arbitrator against that unreasonable party. The expenses of the impartial arbitrator shall be shared equally between the Employer and the Union.

Discipline

1. No regular employee shall be disciplined or discharged without just cause.

2. Any employee who believes that he has been discharged or otherwise disciplined in violation of this agreement may file a grievance in accordance with the provisions of the grievance procedure.

ARTICLE XV. PENSIONS

The Company will contribute $0.50 per hour per employee to the regional Allied Workers of America pension plan. For each full week worked by a driver-salesman, the Company will contribute $20 to the plan regardless of the number of hours worked. The Company will transfer the assets from the company pension plan, which formerly covered the bargaining unit employees, to the regional union plan. The Company will allocate the funds so that each employee account receives the equivalent of $0.30 per hour for all past hours worked.

ARTICLE XVI. LENGTH OF CONTRACT

The term of this contract shall be from _____ _____ to the date of termination one (1) year later, _____.

ARTICLE XVII. WAGES

The wages of employees shall be as set out in Appendix A.

ARTICLE XVIII. SEPARABILITY

Should any article of this Agreement be declared invalid by any court of last resort, the balance of the Agreement shall remain in full force and effect.

NOTE ON PENSIONS

The regional union pension plan provides for benefits that are not guaranteed, but estimated, and vary with the amount of the contribution for the particular employee and the age of his or her retirement. Either or both the employer or the employee may contribute. The following schedule is contained in the plan.

NOTE ON HEALTH INSURANCE

Health insurance covering only the employee costs $110.00 per month. This is entirely paid by the company. Coverage of dependents costs an additional $200.00 per month per employee, all of which is paid by the employee. Only half the employees currently purchase dependent coverage. This coverage is the equivalent of Blue Cross/Blue Shield insurance with broad major medical insurance. Health insurance costs have been increasing at more than twice the rate of inflation. Thus both sides are very concerned about this issue.

Schedule for estimating pensions

HOURLY CONTRIBUTION ASSUMING 2080 HOURS PER YEAR	YEARS OF CREDITED SERVICE	ESTIMATED PENSION PER MONTH ASSUMING RETIREMENT AT AGE 65
$0.30	20	$ 200
0.50	20	333
0.75	20	500
1.00	20	667
0.30	30	400
0.50	30	667
0.75	30	1000
1.00	30	1333

APPENDIX A
Wages

		HOURLY RATE OF PAY	
PLANT AND WAREHOUSE		*First 6 months*	*After 6 months*
Job classification	*Job description*		
Operator	Performs duties in relation to the operation of the bottling line	$10.00	$12.42
Mechanic	Performs repair work on equipment, machinery, and trucks	$14.00	$15.00
Forklift Operator	Operates forklift	$10.22	$12.78
Laborer	General labor	$ 8.75	$10.96
Janitor	Custodial work	$ 9.64	$12.05
Truck Driver	Drives trucks other than those making wholesale sales	$11.13	$13.91
DRIVER–SALESMAN		*SALARY*	*COMMISSION*
Driver-salesman	Drives soft-drink truck and makes sales to retailers	$425.00 per week	$0.40 per case on sale $0.15 per case on empties